Professional Real Estate Development

The ULI Guide to the Business

Richard B. Peiser with Dean Schwanke

Dearborn Financial Publishing, Inc.

the Urban Land Institute

While a great deal of care has been taken to provide accurate and current information, the ideas, suggestions, general principles, and conclusions presented in this book are subject to local, state, and federal laws and regulations, court cases, and any revisions of same. The reader is thus urged to consult legal counsel regarding any points of law—this publication should not be used as a substitute for competent legal advice.

Dearborn Financial Publishing, Inc.
Publisher: Kathleen A. Welton
Acquisitions Editor: Patrick J. Hogan
Associate Editor: Karen A. Christensen
Senior Project Editor: Jack L. Kiburz
Cover Design: The Publishing Services Group

Published by Dearborn Financial Publishing, Inc., and ULI–the Urban Land Institute

Printed in the United States of America

ULI Catalog Number P37

10 9 8 7 6 5 4 3

ISBN 0-79310-392-4

LC Catalog Number 92–4662

About ULI–the Urban Land Institute

ULI–the Urban Land Institute is a nonprofit education and research institute that is supported and directed by its members. Its mission is to provide responsible leadership in the use of land to enhance the total environment.

ULI sponsors educational programs and forums to encourage an open international exchange of ideas and sharing of experience; initiates research that anticipates emerging land use trends and issues and proposes creative solutions based on this research; provides advisory services; and publishes a wide variety of materials to disseminate information on land use and development.

Established in 1936, the Institute today has 16,000 members and associates from 40 countries representing the entire spectrum of the land use and development disciplines. They comprise developers, builders, property owners, investors, architects, public officials, planners, real estate brokers, appraisers, attorneys, engineers, financiers, academics, students, and librarians. ULI members contribute to higher standards of land use by sharing their knowledge and experience. The Institute has long been recognized as one of America's most respected and widely quoted sources of objective information on urban planning, growth, and development.

ULI–the Urban Land Institute
625 Indiana Avenue, N.W.
Washington, D.C. 20004

ULI Project Staff

J. Thomas Black
Staff Vice President, Research

Frank H. Spink, Jr.
Staff Vice President, Publications

Dean Schwanke
Project Director

Nancy H. Stewart
Managing Editor

Jill Shepherd Quinney
Nigel Quinney
Manuscript Editors

Helene Y. Redmond
Manager, Computer-Assisted Publishing

Betsy VanBuskirk
Art Director

Kim Rusch
Artist

Laurie Nicholson
Word Processor

About the Authors

Richard B. Peiser

Richard Peiser is director of the Lusk Center for Real Estate Development and academic director of the graduate real estate development program in the School of Urban and Regional Planning at the University of Southern California in Los Angeles. Through his company, Peiser Corporation, he also is engaged in apartment and affordable housing development as well as large-scale land development and management. Dr. Peiser's previous activities include faculty appointments in real estate at Southern Methodist University and Stanford University, homebuilding in partnership with Doyle Stuckey in Houston, land development with Gerald D. Hines Interests in Houston, and work on the planning staff of the New York City Planning Commission. He has published numerous articles in academic and professional journals on subjects that include new town development, urban growth, development regulation, infrastructure financing, and real estate finance. Dr. Peiser is a Fellow of ULI–the Urban Land Institute. He holds a BA from Yale University (1970), an MBA from Harvard University (1973), and a PhD from Cambridge University (1980).

Dean Schwanke

Dean Schwanke is director of the Development Information Service at ULI–the Urban Land Institute. During more than nine years with ULI, he has authored numerous articles and studies as well as two books—the *Mixed-Use Development Handbook*, published in 1987, and *Smart Buildings and Technology-Enhanced Real Estate*, published in 1985. He has also served as editor and contributing author of ULI's annual *Development Trends* report and is currently researching and writing a book on the renovation and expansion of shopping centers. He holds a BA degree from the University of Wisconsin—Madison (1977) and a master of planning degree from the University of Virginia (1982).

ULI Steering Committee

The following members of ULI served on the ULI Steering Committee for this book and have given generously of their time to guide its overall direction and to assist with a variety of necessary tasks.

Donald L. Williams
Steering Committee Chairman
Principal
Lestin Dwyer Williams
Houston, Texas

Joan S. Betts
Vice President
The Fidelity Mutual Group
Atlanta, Georgia

G. Niles Bolton
President
Niles Bolton Associates, Inc.
Atlanta, Georgia

Patricia E. Doyle
President
Patty Doyle Public Relations, Inc.
Fort Lauderdale, Florida

Fritz L. Duda
President
Fritz Duda Company
Dallas, Texas

Judith L. Hopkinson
President
Berkeley Development Corporation
Los Angeles, California

Phillip R. Hughes
Hughes Real Estate, Inc.
Greenville, South Carolina

Richard Kateley
President and CEO
Real Estate Research Corporation
Chicago, Illinois

Walter A. Koelbel, Jr.
President
Koelbel and Company
Denver, Colorado

Donald J. Mackie
Partner
Mill Creek Properties
Salado, Texas

David R. Nelson
President
The Nelson Companies
Franklin, Michigan

Ronald D. Schwab
Principal
Schwab, Twitty & Hanser Architectural Group, Inc.
West Palm Beach, Florida

Jack Willome
President
RAYCO, Inc.
San Antonio, Texas

Acknowledgments

This book owes its inception to Tom Black, staff vice president for research at ULI, who conceived of the idea of developing a basic real estate development handbook. With the endorsement of the Small-Scale Development Councils, he and then research committee chairman Don Riehl garnered the support within ULI to fund and sponsor such a book. Black and Riehl also organized the steering committee for the book, the members of which provided invaluable guidance and assistance. I am especially grateful to the steering committee not only for providing material for the book but also for introducing me to people with special expertise, locating appropriate exhibits and photographs, and reviewing various drafts. The responsibility for any errors in the final manuscript is, of course, entirely mine.

No author could have asked for a better project manager, editor, and coauthor than Dean Schwanke. He kept the project moving forward, suggested where to condense and where to expand, reorganized sections where necessary, and kept enthusiasm high within ULI as the book evolved over more years than was originally planned. In addition to managing the project, assembling photographs and graphics, and working with the rough draft, Dean wrote the chapter on retail development.

Many other individuals within ULI have also contributed to this book. It never would have happened without the efforts of Frank Spink, staff vice president for publications, who oversaw the production process and negotiated the agreement between ULI and Dearborn Financial, the publisher. Nancy Stewart coordinated production and provided invaluable editing expertise. Betsy VanBuskirk designed the book and, together with Kim Rusch, coordinated the art and graphics. Helene Redmond managed the publication through the desktop publishing and layout process. Outside ULI, Nigel Quinney and Jill Shepherd Quinney substantively edited and then proofread the entire manuscript throughout its production.

Rachelle Levitt and Mike Anikeeff of ULI's education program enabled early drafts of the material to be presented at ULI's biannual Basic Development Workshops. These workshops not only improved the presentation of material in the book, but also gave the opportunity for developers on the workshop panels to provide much of the content for the "mistakes made and lessons learned" element of the book.

Doug Porter, Bob Dunphy, Diane Suchman, and Gayle Berens contributed in numerous ways to the book through their thoughtful publications and suggestions on issues ranging from infrastructure to housing and transportation. Chris Mueller transcribed and summarized tapes of several developer presentations and profiles at ULI meetings, Dana Heiberg tracked down many of the photographs and other graphics used in the book, and Elizabeth Lawson formatted and edited several of the spreadsheets for readability.

I am forever indebted to the faculty and students in USC's Master of Real Estate Development (MRED) program. Dean Alan Kreditor, professors Dana Cuff, Dowell Myers, Eric Heikkila, Martin Krieger, Allan Kotin, Tridib Banerjee, Greg Spiess, and Richard Smith all contributed in ways too numerous to list. The influence of Yale professor Alexander Garvin also appears throughout the book, especially his unique perspective on how real estate interacts with its physical, social, and historical context.

More than 200 developers and real estate professionals have contributed to the book through their interviews and speeches to members of the Lusk Center and students. I am grateful to Sonya Savoulian, who is as responsible as any faculty member for the success of USC's MRED program, and to Shari DeLisle, Cindy Somer, and Susan Kamei for their organizational efforts with the Lusk Center and abilities to persuade the most evasive developers to come to campus. My secretary, Anna Sai, contributed in too many ways to count, helping with typing, faxes, interviews, tables, and everything else.

I have been privileged to work with six research assistants over the years who were students in the MRED program. They freely contributed the professional expertise in real estate that they brought to the program and are responsible for collecting much of the practical information in the book. Chuck Welch conducted the initial series of interviews with developers and laid much of the early groundwork. John Loper conducted further interviews and assisted in writing the initial drafts of the chapters on office and industrial development. Dante Archangeli and Tom Tillisch generated financial tables and helped to track down exhibits and tie up loose ends. Kenneth Beck applied his architectural experience to help write the office design and tenant improvement sections, and Bill Dodds brought his CPA training to bear in reviewing the financial tables. The interviews and materials compiled by these six individuals form much of the content of the book. Their assistance, together with the constant input of students in the MRED program, is pervasive.

PhD student Steve Webber wrote the case study on the Toronto office building as well as the description of responsibilities of the various real estate specialists who contribute to the development process. He also compiled the survey of the two ULI Small-Scale Development Councils that describes how members originally entered the development field.

I owe a special debt to several close friends in the development industry who have been on call day and night; Terry Lewis, Jerry Frank, Jr. and Sr., Bob Moss, Jim Goodell, and Don Mackie have answered numerous queries on the many obscure aspects of development that require an insider's interpretation.

Finally, my wife Beverly has been a frequent sounding board, proving that even physicians can have useful opinions about urban development. My children, Allison and Michael, have suffered my absences and preoccupation with the computer. It is for them that this book is written, in hopes that the urban landscape we leave them will be better than the one we started with and as good as we are capable of producing.

Richard Peiser
Los Angeles
September 1991

Foreword

Real estate developers face an awesome responsibility. The communities and buildings they create become the fabric of our civilization. They influence people's lives in a multitude of ways. What they build affects how near or how far people come to realizing the lifestyle of their dreams. Developers play a key role in determining the financial health of cities and the everyday experiences of their inhabitants. Where people play, work, and shop, how long it takes them to get there, and the quality of the environment that they find all depend to a greater or lesser extent upon the work of developers.

Developers face a much more complex world than they did even 10 years ago. Everyone has a stake in their activities. The days are past when a developer could unilaterally decide what he/she wanted to build and then build it without consulting community leaders, neighbors, and others affected by the development. The political, environmental, and financial context is changing just as rapidly as the market itself. Moreover, the development industry is going through the most wrenching adjustment since the Depression as a result of overbuilding in virtually all segments of the industry combined with the collapse of the S&L industry and the general withdrawal of many traditional sources of development financing.

At a time when the development industry as we know it seems to be collapsing, why do we need a book on how to develop real estate? Firstly, if sound development principles had been practiced by all the developers of real estate over the last decade, much of what was built never would have been conceived, let alone financed. Secondly, for those unencumbered by real estate workouts and tarnished reputations, now is perhaps the best time since the 1960s to be entering the development field. The industry is near the bottom of the long-term, 50-year real estate cycle.

Thirdly, there will always be a need for qualified developers, and they should have the best possible training. Development is not for amateurs. When projects go bankrupt or are poorly designed, the whole community loses, not just the developer and his/her financiers. Why should tenants have to put up with poorly designed spaces? Why should communities have to suffer the tax losses of ill-conceived projects and unoccupied buildings?

Successful development requires understanding not only how to develop good real estate projects but also how to determine their impacts on neighborhoods and cities. Long-term real estate values are directly tied to the quality of the urban areas in which they are situated. Developers must take an active role in protecting and enhancing the long-term economic health of the cities in which they build.

Although this book was conceived as a practical guidebook for developing five major real estate types—residential, commercial, office, industrial, and land—it is intended to do much more. Successful developers must have a thorough understanding of urban dynamics, of how and why cities grow. They must be informed critics of architecture, be knowledgeable in construction, law, public approvals, and public finance, in addition to having the normal real estate skills in financing, marketing, and property management.

Real estate development is the art—perhaps someday it will be the science—of building real estate value by managing development risk. Development expertise can be applied to much more than building new buildings and subdivisions. Development talents can be useful in such activities as buying empty office buildings and leasing them, renovating older warehouses, repositioning shopping centers by changing the tenant mix, securing development entitlements for raw land, and buying workout properties from the Resolution Trust Corporation and banks and turning them around.

Development is exciting because it is dynamic. The conditions that enabled developers to be successful in the 1970s and 1980s are different from the ones that will govern in the 1990s. As the conditions change, so will the skills that developers require to be successful. This book presents the collective wisdom of successful and unsuccessful developers acquired throughout their careers. It is organized by property type to emphasize the different risks and concerns of particular products. The overall steps are, however, the same; hence, the sequence of steps is presented in the same order for each property type.

The challenge of building more livable cities can only be met by qualified developers working together with other real estate professionals, public officials, and neighborhood representatives. Perhaps the greatest challenge is to evolve a more fair and efficient development process—one that reflects the needs and aspirations of all groups while eliminating the many hurdles that raise the costs of development without providing commensurate benefits. Of one thing we can be certain: the process will be different tomorrow from what it is today. Let us hope that tomorrow's developers are equipped to meet the challenge.

Richard Peiser
Los Angeles
September 1991

■ Contents

Chapter 1

Introduction

What Is a Developer?

Real estate development is a multifaceted business, encompassing activities that range from the renovation and re-lease of existing buildings to the purchase of raw land and the sale of improved parcels to others. Developers are the coordinators of those activities, converting ideas on paper into real property. Developers take the greatest risks in the creation or renovation of real estate—and receive the greatest rewards. Typically, developers purchase a tract of land, determine the target market, develop the building program, obtain the necessary approvals and financing, build the structure, and lease, manage, and ultimately sell it.

Development is a detail business. Successful developers know that the clause overlooked in a title policy or the soils test skipped can come back to haunt them. They also know that they are ultimately responsible for any omissions and mistakes. Even if someone else is negligent, developers must deal with the consequences. Developers know that it is best to double-check everything.

A developer must always be responsive to events as they occur—a good developer is ready for the unexpected, flexible, and prepared to shift strategy quickly. During the approval process, for example, a developer often must negotiate with neighborhood groups that seek major changes in a proposed project. If the developer is not willing to compromise, the group could have the power to kill the project altogether. A developer must be able to address citizens' concerns without compromising the project's economic viability.

Managing the development process requires special talents—not the least of which is common sense. Developers must have a clear vision of what they want to do; they must also provide strong leadership along with that clear vision. Developers by nature have strong egos and opinions, but they must be good listeners; developers cannot possibly be authorities on all the many different fields of expertise involved in a project.

Developers work with a variety of people: building professionals including architects, planners, contractors, and consultants; people in the construction trades; tenants and customers; attorneys, bankers, and investors; city officials, city staff members, inspectors, and citizens' groups; homeowners' associations; and community organizers. They must know at least something about dozens of subjects, from managing people to managing buildings. No developer is an expert in all areas. Success comes from knowing the questions to ask and of whom to ask them, what the common practices and rules of thumb are, and how to identify worthwhile advice and information.

The spark of creativity—in design, financing, and marketing—often separates successful developers from the

Russ Otto

©Peter Mauss/Esto

Real estate development is a diverse and multifaceted business, ranging from land development to restoration of existing buildings. Pictured above are The Village in Beachwood, Ohio, and the Police Building in New York City.

rest of the field. Like any creative or artistic endeavor, managing the creative process and people can be extremely difficult. Too much guidance may stifle creativity; too little may lead to unmanageable results. Obtaining creative, exciting work from the team without exceeding the budget is one of the fundamental challenges of management.

Real estate development is an organic, evolutionary process. No two developments are exactly alike, and circumstances within a development change constantly. For beginners, development often appears easier than it is. Most beginning developers have to work twice as hard as seasoned professionals to keep events moving in the right direction. At some point in almost every deal, developers wish they had not become involved; at this point developers discover how badly they want the deal.

Solving problems as they occur is the essence of day-to-day development, but learning to expect the unexpected and never leaving anything to chance may allow for fewer problems, less stress, and more satisfaction in one's career. Laying the necessary groundwork before an important meeting, arranging an introduction to the best prospective lender, creating the best possible setting for negotiations, and knowing as much as possible about the prospective tenant's or lender's needs and concerns before meeting with them helps to ensure success for a developer.

The Book's Approach and Objectives

This book describes five major types of development that beginning developers can undertake: land subdivision, multifamily residential, office, industrial, and retail. It does not discuss single-family homebuilding except insofar as land developers sell subdivided lots to homebuilders. Nor does it address specialty uses such as miniwarehouses, hotels, or recreation properties. The book focuses on developing each of the five product types from start to finish: selecting sites, performing feasibility studies, making contacts, considering alternative designs, identifying the market and designing a product specifically for it, financing the project, working with contractors, marketing the building or subdivision, and managing the completed project.

The book is organized by product type because the development process, although basically the same, is different in detail and emphasis for each product. For example, preleasing is not necessary for apartment development and has no meaning for land development, yet it is critical for office and retail development. And the way a developer subdivides the market for industrial space is irrelevant for apartment development.

This book is written for real estate professionals who want to know more about real estate development and how to perform their jobs better. Readers are assumed to be already familiar with the real estate industry, either through their daily activities in some segment of it or through personal investment. Also, by reading this book, employees of companies that serve the development industry can gain a better understanding of the role that their companies play in development: What are the rules of thumb concerning the way developers do business with them? What are the critical elements affecting the success of the development? Why does the developer care about the concrete contractor's slump test? What type of certification enables a developer to close a permanent mortgage?

The book contains three main parts: an introduction to the development process, discussion of individual product types, and a look at trends in the industry. Chapters 1 and 2 give an overview of the development process, entry into the business, and ways to select and manage the development team. Chapters 3 through 7 describe development of the five main product types: land development (chapter 3), multifamily residential development (chapter 4), office development (chapter 5), industrial development (chapter 6), and retail development (chapter 7). Because many steps are the same for all product types, chapter 4 (multifamily projects) describes in detail certain common steps, such as how to calculate returns for the overall project and for individual joint venture partners. Chapter 4 is a detailed introduction to the development process, and, after reading it, readers then should turn to the sections of the book that concern the type of development in which they have an interest. A final chapter discusses industry trends and the developer's social responsibility.

Readers should keep in mind that no two communities, and no two projects, are alike and that everything is subject to change. Although this book is intended to be a primer covering all aspects of development, it is no substitute for expert local advice from developers, attorneys, consultants, brokers, lenders, and others involved in the process.

Information is as specific as possible, with costs, rents, and financing information included for each product type. The figures indicate the magnitude of individual items and the approximate relationship of one item to another, but they are not appropriate for actual use. Costs may be two or three times higher in cities like New York and Los Angeles than they are in small towns. In some cases, figures presented here may be useful for initial crude estimates, but local sources should be consulted for information specific to particular projects.

Requirements for Success

Developers take risks. At the low extreme, developers may work for a fee, simply managing the development process as agents for other investors. They might incur a small degree of risk from investing some of their own money in the venture. At the other extreme, developers

Photo courtesy Rockefeller Center

People are attracted to the development field for many reasons, including the wealth and glamour associated with the most successful developers. But one of the most important reasons is that a developer has the opportunity to build something of lasting value; an outstanding example of a project that has endured and contributed greatly to its urban environment is Rockefeller Center in New York City.

might be fully at risk, investing the first money in the project, taking the last money out, and accepting full personal liability. Failure could mean bankruptcy.

Beginning developers usually must accept greater risk than experienced developers do because beginners lack a strong bargaining position to transfer risk to others. They often must begin with projects that, for whatever reason, more experienced developers have passed over.

Many people are attracted to development because they see or hear about the wealth and glamour of the most successful developers. They read about black-tie openings and visit high-rise office buildings and regional shopping centers that mark the major leagues of real estate. To be sure, development offers enormous rewards, tangible and intangible, and the feeling of accomplishment that comes from seeing the result of several years' effort is worth the trouble and sleepless nights along the way.

Development's tremendous risks, however, require a certain kind of personality. Individuals must be able to wait a very long time for rewards. Three or more years often pass before the developer sees the initial risk money again, not to mention profit. As a rule rather than the exception, two or three times during the course of development developers risk losing everything. Developers live with uncertainty. Events almost never go as planned, especially for beginning developers, and projects almost always seem to take twice as long and cost twice as much as initially expected.

Development also can be extremely frustrating. Developers depend on many other people to get things done, and many events, such as public approvals, are not under the developer's control. One developer recalls that when he started developing single-family houses, he often became frustrated when work crews failed to show up as promised. Only after he learned to expect them not to show up and was pleasantly surprised when they did, did building become fun.

Development requires considerable self-confidence. Until beginners develop self-confidence, they probably should work for another developer and learn about the process without incurring the risk. After they have gained confidence, beginning developers often start out with a financial partner who bears the financial risk.

Perhaps the most effective way to limit risk is to work on projects that can fail completely without causing undue stress. Even the smallest projects today typically require $50,000 to $100,000 cash upfront just to determine whether or not the developer can obtain a construction or development loan. A developer never should begin a project without at least twice as much cash available as seems necessary to get the project to the point where other funding is available. The upfront cash is only part of the total cash equity that a developer will need to complete a project. Most lenders today require a developer to invest cash equity to cover 20 to 30 percent of the total project cost. The total cash equity need not be in hand or even sufficient to purchase the land, but it should carry the project through to a point at which the developer can raise other funds from investors or lenders.

Another way to reduce risk is through the terms of the land purchase. (Chapter 3 discusses this method in detail.) Developers can limit risk substantially by having the right kind of contract to purchase land. For example, closing on land should take place as late in the process as possible. If 60-day or 90-day closings are typical in a community, beginning developers should look for a land seller who is willing to allow 180 days. If public approvals such as zoning changes are necessary, developers can make the necessary approvals a condition of purchasing the land; the land might cost more, but the extra time is worth the difference. This will allow developers to shift the risk of approval to the seller. If needed approvals or financing fall through, developers will avoid spending their own capital on now-useless land.

Expecting the unexpected is one lesson every person must learn en route to becoming a developer. Fortunately, the development process becomes easier as developers gain experience and undertake successive projects. Instead of waiting for a bank to provide a loan, developers may discover that lenders are calling them to offer to do business.

Nevertheless, the most difficult project is the first one. If it is not successful, a beginning developer may not get another chance. Thus, selecting a project that will not cause bankruptcy if it fails is imperative. Because of increasing difficulty in obtaining public approvals and financing, a developer should not be surprised if five or more projects are attempted before one gets underway. John Dawson, a real estate representative with McDonald's Corporation, says that out of 100 sites that he looked at recently, he signed earnest money contracts and paid for feasibility studies on five. None of the sites proved to be developable.

Paths for Entering the Development Field

No single path leads automatically to success in real estate development. Developers come from a variety of disciplines—real estate brokerage, mortgage banking, consulting, construction, or lending, for example. Recent specialized academic programs that award master's degrees in real estate development look for students who are already experienced real estate professionals but who want to become developers.[1]

Most people want to learn the business by working for another developer. Jobs with developers, however, are the most competitive in the real estate industry, with many people looking for relatively few jobs. Furthermore, many of the jobs that are available with developers do not provide the broad range of experience needed. Although larger developers usually hire people for a specialized area, like leasing or construction, the ideal job is to work as a project manager with full responsibility for one project, or to work for a small firm that provides the opportunity to see and do everything. Such jobs are the most difficult to find, but perseverance and the appropriate background will usually help beginning developers to obtain the ideal job.

Some positions within the real estate industry make it easier to move into development. Many developers start as homebuilders, beginning with small apartments and gradually changing to nonresidential development, or by constructing projects for other developers and then for their own clients. Developers might start as commercial brokers, putting together a deal with a major tenant as

■ 1-1 Results of a Survey: Who Becomes Developers? How Do They Start?

Members of ULI–the Urban Land Institute's Small-Scale Development Council were surveyed about their experiences as beginning developers at ULI's fall meeting in Los Angeles in 1987. The following summary, based on 36 completed surveys, gives an idea of the background of people in the development industry. (Survey results were prepared by Steve Webber, a Ph.D. candidate at the University of Southern California.)

A Profile of Developers

All respondents were actively engaged in real estate development: 56 percent owned their companies as individuals or in a partnership, and 25 percent were presidents of development companies (table A). Over the previous 10 years, most respondents developed office, residential, land development, and industrial projects (table B). Respondents represented a broad range of experience (table C). One-sixth had completed fewer than four projects over the previous 10 years, whereas another one-sixth had completed at least 20 projects during the same time. Most (81 percent) had undergraduate college degrees, and 47 percent also had earned a higher degree (table D).

Table A Respondents' Current Position

	Number
Owner of a Development Company	20
President of a Development Company	9
Vice President in a Development Company	5
Finance Officer	2

Table B Types of Projects Completed by Respondents over Previous 10 Years

	Number	Average Size
Office	128	150,000 square feet
Residential	120	170 units
Land Development	108	248 acres
Industrial	97	107,000 square feet
Retail	41	182,000 square feet
Hotel	10	200,000 square feet
Parking	2	60,000 square feet
Total	506	

Table C Number of Projects Completed by Respondents over Previous 10 Years

Number of Projects	Number of Developers
1–3	6
4–6	6
7–9	8
10–19	10
20–29	2
30+	4

Initial Experiences as Developers

Only 14 percent of the respondents began as independent developers, either as small-scale homebuilders or in existing, family-owned businesses. A majority of the respondents gained their initial real estate experience as employees in development-related organizations, including developers, consultants, brokers, and investors and other financing sources. Several respondents worked for the public sector in a planning or city manager's office.

The most popular product for these respondents' initial projects was residential development, with almost an even split between single-family houses and multifamily projects (table E). The second and third projects tended to be more evenly distributed among types, as developers experimented with several types of products (table F).

As beginning developers, most of these individuals lacked the financial and/or practical resources to carry out projects on their own. First projects involved, for most respondents, a partnership or joint venture (table G). In partnerships, the developers tended to be managing or general partners or to be involved in a deal with two or three equal partners.

Lessons Learned

If they had the opportunity to repeat a first project, these respondents would have done some things differently. During planning and construction, they would have:

- selected a better location;
- purchased (or not purchased) adjacent land for additional development;
- paid greater attention to the design of the project and its amenities;
- programmed the project to create a better mix of uses, denser development, or more profitable phasing;
- dealt with local politicians more effectively; and
- selected more experienced contractors and subcontractors instead of trying to save money with the lowest bid.

During marketing and leasing, they would have:

- emphasized marketing more;
- been more selective about commercial tenants; and
- started giving rental concessions earlier.

■ 1-1 (Continued)

With regard to financial arrangements, these respondents would have:

- structured the deal to earn greater profit than passive partners;
- negotiated better financial terms with the lender;
- worked with more compatible partners; and
- not sold the completed project.

And in general, they would have:

- made better allowances for delays;
- paid closer attention and made quicker decisions when problems arose; and
- let the market, not individual egos, dictate the size of the development.

Table D Respondents' Beginning Experience in Real Estate

	Education (Highest Schooling Attained)						
First Job Related to Real Estate	**MBA**[a]	**Law**	**MCP**[b]	**BS/BA**[c]	**BArch**[d]	**N/A**	**Total**
Worked for a Developer	5			2			7
Consultant	1	2		1	2		6
Developer	1			2		2	5
Finance Officer	1			1	1	2	5
Broker	2			1		1	4
Employed in Public Sector	1		1	1		1	4
Investment	1			1		1	3
Construction	1						1
Management	1						1
Total	14	2	1	9	3	7	36

[a]In two cases, the respondents held master's degrees in subjects other than business administration.
[b]Master of City Planning.
[c]BS/BA degrees include accounting, business, economics, finance, engineering, hotel/motel management, and political science.
[d]Bachelor of Architecture.

Table E Type of First Project

	Number	Average Size
Residential		
Single-Family	7	275 units
Multifamily	6	97 units
Industrial/Warehouse	7	150,500 square feet
Office	7	126,000 square feet
Retail	6	432,000 square feet
Land Development	2	92 acres
Hotel	1	695 rooms

Table F Type of Second and Third Projects

	Number of Second Projects	Average Size	Number of Third Projects	Average Size
Residential				
Single-Family	2	200 units	4	215 units
Multifamily	4	121 units	7	156 units
Industrial/Warehouse	6	108,700 square feet	5	124,000 square feet
Office	8	152,250 square feet	3	58,700 square feet
Retail	2	40,000 square feet	6	280,000 square feet
Land Development	4	74 acres	2	35 acres
Hotel/Motel	2	860 rooms	1	148 rooms
Mixed Use	1	1 acre	0	–

Table G Structure of Deals with Other Parties

	Number of Projects		
	First	**Second**	**Third**
Partnership	14	8	9
Joint Venture	6	9	9
Developer (Sole Owner)	5	8	7
Syndication	2	1	0

Note: Numbers may not total the same in all tables because of missing responses.

anchor in a new office building or finding a site to develop for a build-to-suit tenant. Developers also might start as mortgage brokers; by controlling a source of funding, a mortgage broker could make the transition to development by overseeing the financial side of a joint venture with an experienced developer. Many developers are willing to undertake joint ventures with a new partner if the partner proposes a deal that the developer would not otherwise be able to do.

Finding the First Deal

To start, beginning developers must control at least one of four assets—land, knowledge, tenants, or capital. If they control more than one, the task becomes easier. If developers control land, then the task is driven by supply—a site looking for a use. If developers control knowledge or tenants, then the task is driven by demand—a use looking for a site. If they have capital, they have a choice.

A Use Looking for a Site

In a sense, all development should be driven by demand. Determining who needs space—the potential buyer or tenant—and what type of space they need are the starting points for all development. The initial market analysis should define the gaps in the market and the product or products that will fill them.

Knowledge can take several forms. Many developers capitalize on their familiarity with a particular local market gained from their previous experience in the field. Knowledge of the marketplace can give beginning developers the competitive edge they need. The ability to convince potential lenders and investors that the market exists, with supporting evidence in the form of market research data or letters of intent from prospective tenants, is an invaluable asset for beginning developers, as they do not have a long track record to demonstrate their ability.

Knowledge about sources of financing is another way to break into the business. Finding money is typically a beginning developer's hardest task, but presenting a deal to a lender or investor who is looking for that particular opportunity to invest could ensure the developer's success.

Many developers enter the business by knowing about potential tenants, perhaps by developing a new building for a family business or for the company for which they work. Knowing a particular tenant's needs and controlling its decision about location might enable the developer's participation as a principal.

All of these cases start with a use looking for a site, and the use defines the requirements for the site. The developer's task is to find the site that best fits the demand.

■ 1-2 You Must Control One of These to Get Started

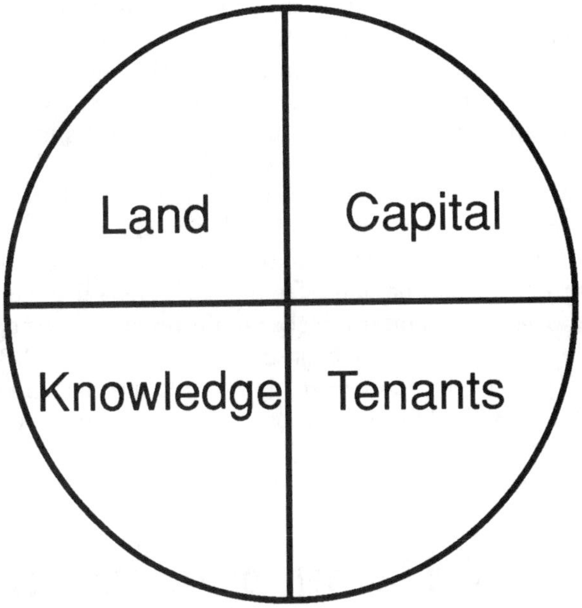

Source: ULI–the Urban Land Institute, "Basic Development Workshop Handbook" (Washington, D.C.: unpublished, 1989).

A Site Looking for a Use

Another popular starting point is controlling a well-located piece of property. Many developers start by developing family-owned or company-owned land. Others begin by convincing a landowner to contribute the land to a joint venture in which the developer manages the development. In both cases, development is driven by supply.

The first question developers must answer is, "What is the highest and best use of the land?" Beginning developers commonly decide to develop a type of product that appears to offer the highest return (office buildings, for example) without diagnosing a demand for office buildings. Unless demand is sufficient, the site will not produce an economic return. Thus, the beginner's first step is to perform a market analysis to determine the best use and to estimate absorption (units sold or square feet leased per month) for the site.

Every site at any point in time has a highest and best use that will maximize the property's value. Buyers do their own analyses of a property's highest return and best use when presenting an offer for a property that is for sale, hoping to turn a profit. In fact, a property's selling price is determined by many buyers deciding what the highest and best use is and bidding accordingly. Knowing when to drop out and let someone else win the bid for property is an important part of being a successful developer. Buying low and selling high is equally as essential to real estate as it is to the stock market. Experienced developers assert that they make their profit in large part from how well they buy the land.

Another strategy to be considered is holding a piece of land and waiting for its value to increase, rather than developing the property in its present highest and best use. A tract at the corner of two highways on the edge of town, for example, might eventually make a good site for a shopping center, but if current demand for retail space does not yet justify a shopping center, the most profitable current use may be single-family lots. Waiting five years, however, would offer a higher profit because the shopping center could then be justified (see feature box 1-3).

When the developer already owns the site, the market study serves a different purpose, indicating what to build, how much to build, the sale price or rental rate, and the amount of time that sales or leasing will require. While the market study is under way, the developer should investigate site conditions (how much of the land is buildable, what percentage contains slopes, if environmentally sensitive areas are present, if areas are prone to flooding, and so forth) and what public approvals are necessary.

Once the developer has acquired information about the market, engineering, and environmental and public approvals needed, the developer is ready to decide the development strategy. One point to keep in mind is that a large site does not necessarily need to be developed all at once. Typically, the developer's financing capacity is limited by the developer's and the partners' combined net worth, including the unencumbered value of the land (land value net of loans). One advantage of developing a small part of a larger tract of land is that the rest of the

1-3 The Concept of Present Value

An understanding of present value is essential for developers. (Any introductory textbook on principles of real estate finance describes present value. See, for example, William Brueggeman, Jeffrey Fisher, and Leo Stone, *Real Estate Finance* (Homewood, Illinois: Richard Irwin, 1989).) Present value analysis equalizes the "time value" of money. Because one can earn interest on money, $100 today will be worth $110 in one year at 10 percent interest, and $121 in two years with annual compounding. Ten percent interest represents the "opportunity cost" if one receives the money in, say, two years rather than now.

The present value of $121, received in two years, is $100. That is, the "discounted value at a 10 percent discount rate" of $121, received in two years, is $100 today. If the discount rate (opportunity cost rate) is 10 percent, then it makes no difference whether one receives $100 today or $121 in two years.

The formula for calculating present value is as follows:

$$PV = \frac{FV \times 1}{(1 + r)^n}$$

where *PV* is present value, *FV* is future value, *r* is discount rate, and *n* is number of years. Thus, the present value of $121 received in two years is:

$$PV = \frac{\$121 \times 1}{(1 + .10)^2} = 100$$

The landowner's dilemma about developing the land immediately into single-family lots or waiting for five years to develop a shopping center is solved by applying present value analysis. Suppose, for example, that land for single-family development today is worth $100,000 per acre, whereas land for a shopping center would be worth $200,000 per acre in five years. If the personal discount rate is 10 percent, then $200,000 to be received in five years is worth $124,184 today—clearly more than the value of the land if it is developed for single-family houses. The best option is to wait.

Because of the high rates of return and high risk associated with development, most developers have personal discount rates of at least 20 percent. That is, they expect to earn at least 20 percent per year on their investment during times when expected inflation is 5 percent. Inflation is a component of the discount rate:

Real return rate + *Inflation* + *Risk* = *Discount rate premium*
3% + 5% + 12% = 20%

If inflation increases to 10 percent, then a developer's required return increases to 25 percent. The risk premium depends on the particular property and might range from as low as 4 percent for a completed office building to 15 to 20 percent for a recreational land development.

In this example, the present value of $200,000, discounted at 20 percent, is only $80,375. Therefore, at the higher discount rate, the best decision is to develop the land for single-family lots today.

Which discount rate—10 percent or 20 percent—is appropriate? The answer depends on risk. In the early 1990s, land development (except for single-family homes) is considered the riskiest form of development because of uncertainties about entitlements and market absorption. Building development risk depends on local market conditions. Office development is considered more risky than industrial or apartment development.

land can be used as collateral for financing the first project. Defaulting on the loan, however, might entail the loss of the entire site: once the land is pledged as collateral, the bank may foreclose on it after default to collect any balance owed.

Development projects that begin with a site looking for a use provide an attractive way for beginning developers to start because they will not be required to locate and tie up land until a deal can be put together. Although such projects are perhaps the easiest way to get into development, the major problem is that land already owned may not be the best site to develop at a given time. Nevertheless, many properties can be developed profitably. Skillful developers can identify the most marketable use, determine a development strategy, and then implement it.

Improving the Chances of Successful Development

Selecting the first development project should not be left to accident, nor should beginners necessarily grab the first opportunity they see. The first deal is the most difficult and the most important one that the developer will ever undertake; failure means that another chance may never be offered. The first deal establishes the developer's track record, sets the tone for the quality of future developments and establishes an image in the marketplace, creates a network of business relationships for future deals, and builds relationships with bankers and investors.

A maxim of development is that it takes just as long and is just as difficult to undertake a small deal as it is to undertake a large one; therefore, developers should look for large deals. The maxim is true to a degree for experienced developers, but it is not true for beginning developers.

A principal objective of the developer's first deal is to establish a track record. The absence of a track record is perhaps the beginning developer's greatest handicap; thus, selecting the right size project is critical. The major guidelines are to look for a project that can be put together in, say, six months and to look for one that is within the developer's financial capabilities—personal resources plus those that can be raised through family, friends, or other partners. A general rule of thumb is that the combined financial net worths of the partners must be at least as large as the project's total cost. In times of tight money, the net worth requirements may be even greater. For example, suppose the developer has $50,000 cash and a personal net worth of $100,000. To undertake a $1 million project requires bringing in a partner with at least $900,000 in net worth. Finding partners with that much net worth may be difficult, but it is much easier to find partners with $1 million financial statements than those with $50 million financial statements. Furthermore, most projects today require substantial cash equity. If lenders require 20 percent equity, for example, raising $200,000 equity for a $1 million project is easier than raising $1 million equity for a $5 million project.

Smaller buildings can be developed in less time, incurring less risk and involving fewer steps. They also can be leased more quickly.[2] Although small buildings can be just as complex as larger ones, the criteria for selection should emphasize projects that do not require a lengthy and uncertain process of public approvals and complicated financing.

One exception to arguments in favor of simple deals is smaller "problem" deals that may offer an opportunity that experienced developers have passed over. For example, larger developers might decide that a site requiring special attention to problems with easements, boundaries, or flooding is not worth the necessary time and effort. A beginner, however, might be able to tie up the property at little cost while working out the problems. Another opportunity could be found with sites owned by local and state governments and redevelopment agencies, because large developers may prefer to avoid government red tape. Unless the site is simply put up for auction, however, the beginner might need to demonstrate a track record to convince government officials to work with him/her. Nonetheless, keeping officials aware of continuing interest in a project as the government works through various procedures and public hearings can give the beginner an edge when the agency finally issues a Request for Proposal.

In the final analysis, a developer's strongest assets are strength of reputation and ability to deal in good faith with a multitude of players. A large developer may be able to outlast the opposition in a contentious deal, but the best advice for a beginning developer is to avoid such situations altogether.

Managing the Development Process

Development is distinct from investment in real estate. Many firms and individuals invest in property—buying existing properties and managing them for investment purposes. Investors often incur some risk in leasing and may make minor renovations, but developers usually engage in both the development and the operating phase of the business.

Developers may take on different degrees of ownership and risk. In the following discussion, developers who operate alone and invest only their own money are said to be 100 percent owners/developers. They furnish all the cash equity, accept all the risk and liability, and receive

1-4 How Four Developers Got Started

At a session of ULI's 1989 fall meeting in New York, four developers described how they started in the development business. Their stories are summarized below. The summaries omit many details and tend to make things look easier and simpler than they actually were. They are, however, instructive about getting into the business.

Frederick Kober

Kober is president of the Christopher Company, based in Vienna, Virginia. A graduate of Stanford University and the Harvard Business School, he held several senior management positions and was president of Wildwind Development's East Coast office before he started his own firm.

When he chose to start his own development business, the climate was not good for development, but, Kober notes, "I don't think there's a good time or a bad time. The most important thing for any individual is that it's right for them."

One of the most critical issues for getting started is financing. Kober says he lived on tax refunds for a few years and borrowed against some properties that he had. "It was a very low-budget operation, but it worked."

His first project, which he identified while working for a national developer, was in Virginia Beach. The property was a sizable, unattractive tract surrounding a huge hole. He was able, however, to visualize the hole as a 40-acre lake, an easy transformation because of the high water table in the area. His concept was to develop approximately 360 contemporary housing units around the lake, creating a water-oriented project that was relatively distinctive for the area. Kober insisted on first-rate work on the project to create the proper image for the project and for his firm.

One key to tackling such an ambitious project was the strong connections Kober had developed over many years of working for another development firm. "One factor that enabled me to get the necessary financing," he notes, "is that I had some credibility from what I had been doing in the Washington market for national developers for five or six years." A developer really builds on a reputation: "The credibility you show just before you start a project and just after is very critical."

One other key he finds important for a beginning developer is the choice of consultants; the first civil engineer he chose was very important to the project's success, not only because of his engineering skills but also because he knew his way around the territory and could help greatly with public approvals.

William C. Martin

Martin started in development while he was still working on his MBA at the University of Michigan in the late 1960s. He used $500 to option a small corner property because he thought it would make a good site for a gasoline station. He then contacted the oil companies and within 60 days had sold one company an option on the property for $750. That company eventually used its option, and Martin made $20,000 while still in the MBA program. He went on to develop five other sites for gasoline stations in five years, built up equity of $50,000, and then moved on to larger development projects.

The first larger project was a 15,000-square-foot building near the University of Michigan that included a lower-level book store, a second-level restaurant, and upper-level office space. He followed with two additional similar projects, both of them very successful.

As of late 1989, the firm had completed 32 projects, using this simple philosophy: design it, build it, manage it, and own it. The firm still owns all 32 projects and has no intention of selling any of them.

Roger N. Torriero

Torriero started his own development firm, now called Griffin and Related Properties, in 1984. His educational background includes a degree in architecture from Syracuse University, a master's degree from the Academy of Fine Arts in Florence, Italy, and studies in a realty and development program at Harvard. His work experience before starting his own firm included working for a construction company in Pittsburgh and then as director of development with Pacific Mutual in Southern California, overseeing $300 million worth of development.

When he left Pacific Mutual, Torriero had a very modest short-term consulting contract—six months and $60,000—to complete his responsibility with the company. That contract represented his total capitalization, but with it he was able to open a 900-square-foot office, hire secretaries, and print letterheads and business cards.

Torriero saw an opportunity with a newly formed realty development company founded by Home Savings of America,

all the benefits. The concept of a 100 percent owner/developer is useful for analyzing development, because if a project does not make economic sense in its entirety (as viewed by someone who has all the risks and rewards), it will not make sense as a joint venture or other form of partnership.

If two or more people are involved in a development project, one or more of them might be considered devel-

Arlington Commercial Development Company, which was established to undertake joint venture projects and to develop projects for its own account. Torriero believed that if he could identify an appropriate piece of land for development, he could become a partner with Arlington Commercial. Finding such a site was no easy task, because much of the undeveloped land in Orange County was controlled by a few very large owners.

He found a property, however, at the intersection of two freeways. His research of the title found it was held in trust, with the sole beneficiary an elderly woman. Torriero believed he might have an opportunity if he could demonstrate to the woman his capability of delivering a deal and generating liquidity on behalf of her trust account. He then received a modest letter of support (with no real commitment) from Home Savings that gave him credibility with the landowner. His proposal to the landowner emphasized how the scheme could enhance surrounding parcels (which the trust owned as well). The landowner liked the development concept, and within a week the landowner, developer, and financial backer had signed a contract.

The resulting project—Griffin Towers—includes two office buildings with an atrium pavilion and 500,000 square feet of space. The first building was opened in April 1987; it was effectively 90 percent preleased (300,000 square feet) to the newly formed Unisys Corporation. To sign the lease, Unisys required partial ownership interest in the project. The project's value is $125 million—the developer's equity was $9,000. "One important lesson," Torriero notes, "is that, especially in your first project, it is better to have a small part of a real deal than 100 percent of nothing."

Elinor R. Bacon

Bacon formed The Bacon Company in 1985. The company specializes in small- to medium-size urban developments that involve adaptive use of historic structures and new construction of low- to moderate-income housing. Her background includes a master's degree in Chinese studies and temporary residence in Hong Kong, where she developed an appreciation for cities. She then went to work in Baltimore, first as housing administrator for a regional planning council and then as an estimator. One of Bacon's functions as an estimator was to inspect houses undergoing rehabilitation for the city's housing department.

After a stint with the U.S. Department of Housing and Urban Development in Washington, she returned to Baltimore to work for the Johns Hopkins Hospital as director of community development, engaging in an effort to revitalize the area east of the hospital with the development of townhouses for moderate-income residents. That job was on a contract basis, and, as the contract neared its end, she sought an opportunity to develop a city-owned parcel of land with several partners. Although the partnership was unsuccessful in its bid to develop the property, focusing on and organizing for such an opportunity was the beginning of Bacon's development career.

Bacon started on her own as a single mother with no savings, working part time as a realtor and intending to spend the rest of her time putting together a project for development. A friend from the fledgling Johns Hopkins Health Plan, the health maintenance organization (HMO) for the hospital, suggested a working relationship to set up sites for HMOs around the city. To this day, Bacon is the development consultant and develops properties as the owner's representative.

Her first project as an entrepreneur came about through a conversation over lunch with a friend who was leaving a development company to start his own firm. Bacon mentioned an opportunity to redevelop a school that the city was ready to sell. They developed a 50/50 partnership and submitted a proposal to the city to redevelop the school—against five other proposals. Bacon and her partner were offered the property, not so much because of the amount of the bid, but because the city liked the proposed use of the property.

Their scheme involved converting the school into two-story, two-bedroom, two-bathroom townhouse condominiums with basements. Every other window became a door to the individual townhouses. They reused existing slates and blackboards around the fireplaces and restored wooden floors.

Bacon's partner was able to supply the builder and architect and knew about financing as well. The deal required first buying the property for $59,000 (the appraised value) from the city; the city then took back a mortgage for all but about 10 percent. The developers obtained a construction loan from a bank for about $500,000. The completed units were sold for between $86,500 and $103,000, usually before the drywall was up.

Bacon has continued to undertake similar projects since then with a variety of partners and has found a niche for this size project—generally too small for large developers and too large for house-by-house renovators. She credits much of her success to a willingness to work hard and the persistence of a pit bull. She is now trying to determine how to undertake Bacon Company's growth and to delegate more responsibility.

opers, depending on their positions. No generally accepted definition exists to determine who is a developer and who is not, but a developer can be defined as the person or firm that is actively involved in the development process and takes the risks and receives the rewards of development. An individual firm that receives a commission for performing a service, such as finding tenants or money, is a broker rather than a developer.

■ 1-5 Timeline for Development of an Apartment or Small Office Building

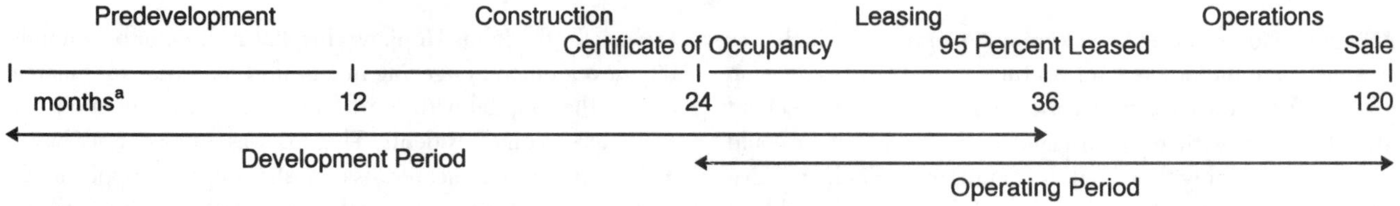

[a]Time varies widely according to a project's size, complexity, and location. Predevelopment may take two to four years or more in California, whereas it might require only 90 days in some other parts of the country.

Many people involved in a development project may incur risk. An individual who designs, builds, and leases a building for a landowner for a fee is an agent of the owner but incurs no risk in development. If, however, the fee depends on the project's success, the individual accepts development risk.

Experienced developers are able to transfer risk to others by using other people's money or finding a lender who will give them nonrecourse financing. They still carry the burden of delivering a successful project, however. In most cases, they will have something at risk somewhere along the line, such as front money for feasibility studies, investment in preliminary designs, earnest money, or personal liability on construction financing.

Development companies increasingly serve as development managers for major institutions. In this role, they perform all the normal functions of developers except that they bear no risk. The institution—a bank, an insurance company, a foreign corporation, or a major landowner—bears the risk. The developer works for a fee and usually a percentage of the profits (10 to 20 percent) if the project is successful. Historically, developers have preferred to own real estate rather than to manage it for others, because ownership has enabled them to amass wealth. Nevertheless, major developers increasingly have accepted roles as managers, either to keep their staffs busy during slow periods or to enter new markets with minimal risk.

Real Estate Cycles

"Timing is everything" is an adage especially applicable to real estate development. The importance of real estate cycles cannot be overemphasized. Like other large, capital-intensive purchases, real estate is very sensitive to changes in interest rates. Income properties (office, industrial, and retail space and apartments) provide insufficient cash flow to be financed when interest rates move above certain levels. "For-sale" developments, such as housing subdivisions, office buildings, or residential condominiums, suffer from higher financing costs and from the effect of rising interest rates on the amount of money that potential purchasers can borrow. When rates are high, buyers tend to wait for them to come back down before buying a property. The development industry is further affected by high interest rates because developers' firms typically are smaller than most corporate bank customers. When money is scarce, lenders tend to prefer their non-real-estate customers. Even very sound projects can be difficult to finance because lenders fear the unknown development risks.

The supply as well as the demand side moves up and down. Lenders exhibit a herd mentality, it seems, all preferring the same type of product or geographic area. In Dallas, for example, during the boom of the early 1980s when money was plentiful for office buildings, some lenders began to fear that the market was being overbuilt, and money was shifted from office buildings to retail centers. From 1983 to 1986, almost every shopping center in North Dallas that was older than 15 years was renovated. As suddenly as the money was turned on, it was turned off, as lenders across the country shared their concerns about the Dallas retail market.

Selecting the right time to enter development is crucial. Most beginning developers plunge ahead, regardless of the general economic climate, and often their success in financing the first project depends on their good (or bad) timing with respect to the cycle. Ironically, financing a project toward the end of a customer's preference for it (when many lenders are enthusiastic about a particular geographic area and product type) is often easier. Toward the end of the positive cycle, however, risk increases as the competition for tenants or buyers intensifies. If supply becomes really excessive, as did office space in Houston and many other cities in the late 1980s, those who were the last to enter the market are usually the first to go bankrupt, because their costs are higher and competition is fierce for tenants.

A project launched early in the positive cycle means less competition for its developer. Long lead times required for finding the right site, designing the project, and receiving zoning and other public approvals mean

■ 1-6 The Go Decision

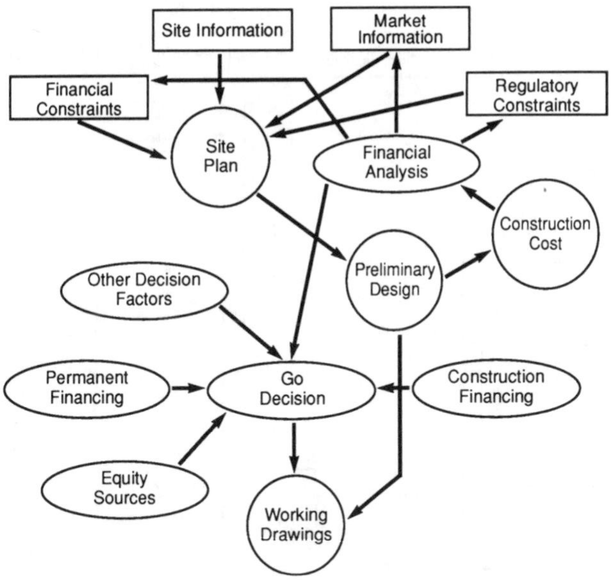

that developers must be able to perceive new market opportunities before others do—often before they have become popular among lenders.

How does a developer determine the economic trend? General economic indicators, such as unemployment rates and business failures, provide information on general economic conditions. Local conditions are much more relevant than are national conditions, although national conditions determine fluctuations in interest rates and credit availability. Commercial bankers and mortgage bankers can describe what is currently in and out of favor with the lending community, and brokers can indicate the types of properties that are selling the fastest. A developer must remember, however, that every other developer is looking at the same data at the same time.

Real estate cycles create windows of opportunity for financing and strong market demand in advance of a large supply. If beginning developers can synchronize their development efforts with the cycle, they can greatly improve their chances for success. The odds against beginners can only increase if they try to develop against the cycle.

Getting Started

The first step in the development process for beginning developers who do not already own the land is to select the target market, with respect to both geographic area and type of product. Staying close to the area in which a developer has done business for a number of years is a major advantage, for success often depends as much on personal relationships as on skills. Except for major projects (high-rise office buildings, shopping malls, major industrial parks) for which nationally recognized developers compete, local players have major advantages over outsiders. They understand the dynamics of location in the local area. They know in which direction the area is growing and how buyers, tenants, and lenders feel about various neighborhoods. They know a good price and where prices have been changing rapidly. They know whom to call when they need information or they need something done. It takes at least a year, and often longer, for a newcomer to begin to understand an area's dynamics.

Newcomers can become insiders, however, even if they are recent arrivals. The best way is to bring in a local partner who is well connected in the community—an especially important move if public approvals are required. Another way is to use banking connections from home to open doors in the new community. Whatever the approach, newcomers have to work hard to overcome the natural suspicion of outsiders and the competitive advantage of local developers who have better information and more contacts.[3]

After deciding *where* to do business, the next question is *what* to develop. For beginning developers, the answer is simple: develop a product with which you are familiar—provided that lenders will make the money available. Even developers with no previous development experience can sell potential investors and lenders on their experience with the product type if they study the local market to determine rents, competition, the regulatory environment, local tastes, local construction methods, and the types of units or buildings in greatest demand. Although beginners can successfully branch out into a new product type, they lack the background to fine-tune information about design and construction costs or to predict potential pitfalls. Beginners who do branch out cannot develop solo, however; they will probably have to bring in an experienced partner to get financing.

Identifying a product that the market lacks can make a project successful—finding that niche is the developer's challenge. Market niches are defined geographically and by product type. They can be as narrowly defined as, say, an apartment complex that has more two- and three-bedroom units than do other projects in the area or a multitenant warehouse building with front-loaded garages. The phrase "designing for a specific market" is used often in this book, because that is how developers create a competitive advantage. Finding that special market, however, usually requires more than a good market study. It requires a perception of the market that other developers do not have, because if a market opportunity is obvious, another developer is probably already building to satisfy

■ 1-7 The Development Process

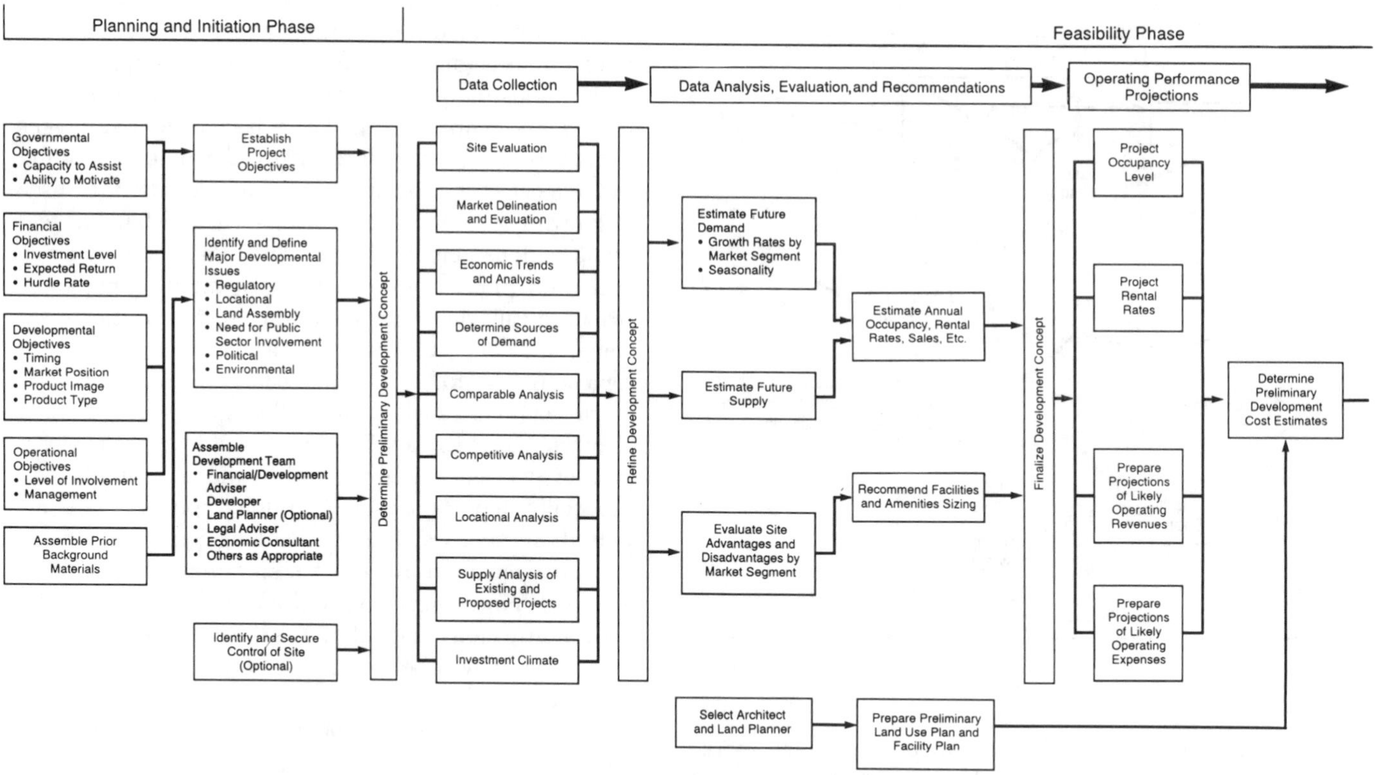

Source: Laventhol & Horwath.

the demand. Thus, the beginner must understand the market well enough to act before other developers see the opportunity.

Understanding the Stages of Development

Chapters 3 through 7, which discuss development of real estate products, are organized according to the steps required to develop that product. Figure 1-6 summarizes one view of the steps common to developing most types of property—determining a project's feasibility, design, financing, construction, marketing, operation, and management. As figure 1-7 shows, certain steps can be taken simultaneously, whereas others must be taken sequentially. For example, active preleasing for an office building begins as soon as preliminary design drawings are ready to show to prospective tenants. Preleasing occurs throughout the development period, from financing through construction. With an apartment project, leasing begins later but is also done simultaneously with other steps. Similarly, the architect can prepare construction drawings at the same time that the developer is searching for a loan.

At each stage, however, certain items must be completed before moving to the next stage. For example, before lenders consider a mortgage application, the developer usually must provide conceptual drawings, a boundary survey, title information, information about the site's feasibility, market surveys, personal financial information, and an appraisal. (Because different lenders have different requirements for appraisals, however, it may be wise not to order an appraisal until a promising lender has been identified. Otherwise, another appraisal—by someone the lender approves—might be necessary.)

The sequence of steps to be taken, and even the steps themselves, changes frequently in development. The rate of change in the development world is one of its major sources of excitement. It also gives beginning developers

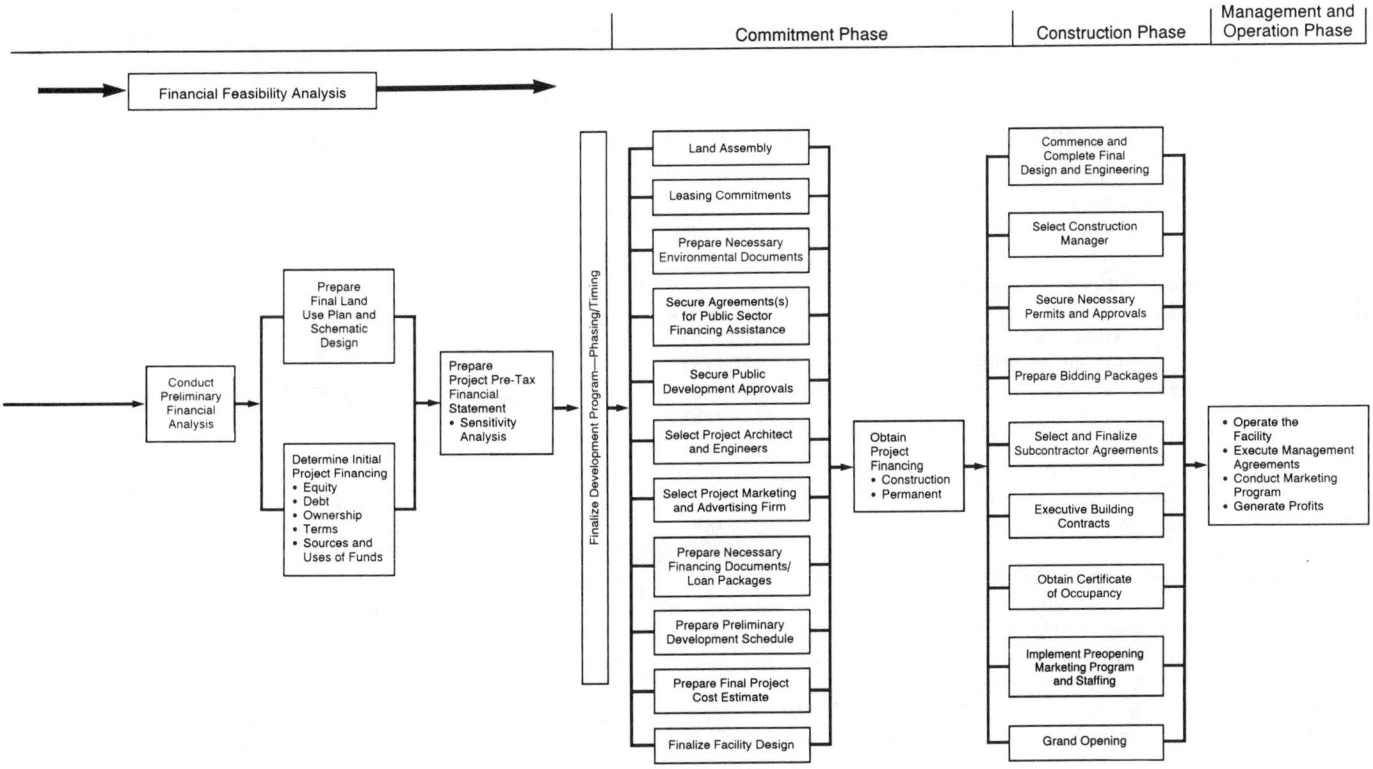

an even chance with experienced developers, because all developers must adapt to, and keep up with, changing conditions or they will fail.

Financing methods and the sequence of financing steps also change regularly. One major change, for example, occurred in the aftermath of skyrocketing inflation in the early 1980s. Developers traditionally first obtained a commitment for a permanent loan and then used that commitment (the "takeout commitment") to obtain a commitment for a construction loan. When inflation reached double digits, developers suddenly could not obtain takeout commitments. Instead, they went directly to construction lenders, who started giving "miniperm loans"—five-year loans that covered both the construction period and the operating period. By doing so, lenders and developers gambled that interest rates would change (which they did) within five years. They were also prepared to extend the loans (roll them over into new loans) if they did not. With the credit crunch of the early 1990s, developers have seen a return to traditional permanent takeout commitments, which must be secured before the developers can obtain construction financing.

The development process resembles the construction of a building. The foundation must be level if the walls are to be straight. The frame must be square if the finish is to be attractive. Each step in the process depends on the quality of previous steps. Badly negotiated or written agreements with lenders, contractors, tenants, or professionals will come back to haunt the developer. At best, they will be costly to correct. At worst, they might halt completion or occupancy of the project.

Because each stage depends on the preceding one and because the developer must depend on other people to do much of the work, an adequate monitoring system is essential. A critical path chart can be assembled for each development, showing not only the events that must occur before others can be accomplished but also how much time each step should take. It also shows which events are on the critical path (those requiring the shortest time) and which events have some slack time. Critical

■ 1-8 Developer Exposure over Time

The money that a developer can lose if a project fails is illustrated here for a 160-unit, bond-financed apartment project. Exposure is greatest just before bond closing when the developer has invested $270,000 in a project that could still fall apart if the bonds fail to close.

Time	Activity	Cost	Total Investment to Date	Current Value to Date	Exposure
7/84	Land optioned	$15,000	$15,000	$0	$15,000
	Extensions	21,000			
	Architecture	10,000			
	Inducement	10,000			
1/85	Inducement received		56,000	0[a]	56,000
3/85	Land closing	388,000	444,000	403,000[b]	41,000[c]
	Architecture	10,000			
	Appraisal and market study	10,000			
4/85	Fannie Mae commitment	24,000	488,000[d]	403,000	85,000
	Architecture	15,000			
	Equity syndication	50,000			
	Bond costs	100,000			
9/85	Bond rate secured		673,000[e]	403,000	270,000
10/85	Bonds closed	338,000	1,001,000[f]	0	

[a]The inducement is transferable but has a one-year limitation.
[b]The land value had increased by an amount sufficient to cover sales commission costs if it had to be resold.
[c]At the time of closing on the land, the earnest money ($15,000) is recovered.
[d]The Fannie Mae commitment adds value only if bonds can be sold.
[e]Most legal costs have no value if the bonds are not closed.
[f]At bond closing, the risks are substantially eliminated, since all financing parameters are fixed.
Source: Stages of investment for August Park Apartments, Dallas, Texas, developed by Peiser Corporation and Jerome Frank Investments.

■ 1-9 Typical Months Elapsed for a Small Office or Apartment Building

Stage of Development	Area with Few Regulations	Area with Many Regulations
1. Earnest Money Contract Signed	0	0
2. Earnest Money Committed	1	1
3. Market Study	2	2
4. Preliminary Design	3	3
5. Engineering Studies	6	6
6. Approvals[a]	6	24[b]
7. Financing Commitment	6	26
8. Working Drawings and Building Permits	9	36[c]
9. Land Purchase and Construction Loan Closed[d]	9	36

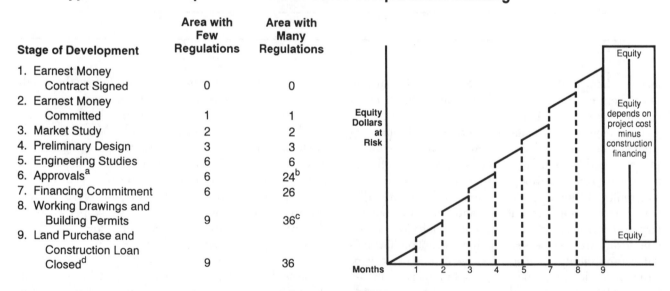

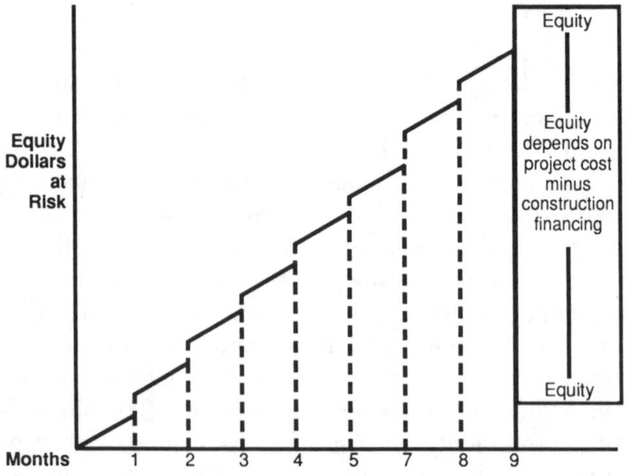

[a]Assuming no zoning changes are necessary.
[b]Environmental, political, design review, and other approvals can take two to five years.
[c]Building permits can take six to nine months after working drawings are finalized.
[d]Most sellers require closing on the land sooner than nine months, but the deal should not be finalized without tentative financing commitments and approvals in place.
Source: ULI–the Urban Land Institute, "Basic Development Workshop Handbook" (Washington, D.C.: unpublished, 1989).

path analysis makes it possible to calculate how much extra it will cost to shorten the path by paying workers overtime or paying extra freight charges to receive materials more quickly.

The early stages of development are especially important, involving many iterations of planning and analysis before the architectural plans and other arrangements are finalized. A common mistake at each phase of analysis is to go into too much detail too soon. For example, obtaining detailed working drawings before a market feasibility study is completed is a waste of money. First, the market study should influence the design. Second, if the market is not as healthy as it appeared, the developer may want to abandon the project.

Projects go through several stages of risk (see figures 1-8 and 1-9). Risk is defined as the total amount of money that can be lost. During the period in which the developer is making preliminary assessments of the market and the

1-10 Advice for Beginning Developers

Three themes emerge from the advice given by members of ULI's Small-Scale Development Council: be well prepared at all times; work with experienced people, even if they are more expensive; and anticipate delays throughout the development process.

Site Acquisition

- Correctly analyze the purchase price of a site to include usable, not total, square footage.
- Anticipate problems with sellers who are not familiar with real estate, and delays while a disputed estate is being settled.
- Analyze the site's physical constraints, including the availability of utilities.
- Conduct a soils test and check for hazardous waste.
- Identify the site's legal and political constraints, such as the availability of the required zoning or the existence of a moratorium on building.
- Research the market before purchasing the site.
- Build on the success of other developers.

Regulatory Process, Obtaining Approvals

- Be prepared to work with the community to resolve concerns and challenges to the project.
- Take time to understand the local political climate.
- Prepare for the local regulatory process and public hearings.
- Use qualified and experienced consultants, lawyers, and architects to give your project added credibility.
- Anticipate and do not underestimate delays in the approval process.

Product Selection, Market, and Economic Feasibility

- Remember that when an opportunity is obvious, it is obvious to everyone—resulting in a great deal of competition.
- Develop toward the higher end of the market for your product type, where there is more margin for error. Low-end projects typically have slimmer profit margins.
- Choose a respected market consultant with a strong reputation in the city in which your project is located.
- Decide how much time to allocate for the feasibility study. Some developers consider this step to be vital and maintain that the study should be thorough; others feel it should not be belabored.
- Make sure that extensive primary research accurately identifies all competition, whether under construction or still on the drawing boards.

Design, Site Planning, Engineering, and Construction

- Do not complete the design without paying attention to the market study.
- Work closely with the architect and the contractor.
- Be careful not to ignore important information, even if it requires redesign or additional approvals.
- Use a flexible design that can be easily adapted to different tenants' needs.
- Accept the design and recognize that it will never be perfect.
- Spend sufficient time and money to check all references before retaining contractors and subcontractors.

Construction and Development Financing

- Establish relationships with several lenders to eliminate lengthy delays.
- Deal with experienced lenders.
- Make adequate allowances for contingencies.
- Remember that it could take three to four months to process a $10 million loan—even if the lender says that it will take only six weeks.
- If the market softens, be able to cover interest out of your own pocket until the market comes back.

1-10 (Continued)

Permanent Financing

- Establish good communications with the lender.
- Prepare a detailed, professional presentation package for the lender.
- Secure the permanent loan before beginning construction. (Beginning developers might be forced to do so, even if they would prefer to wait until after the project is built and leased.)
- Be aware of trends in interest rates.

Equity Financing

- Investigate the financial records of sources of equity.
- Find two or three compatible partners who can provide or raise equity for the project.
- Do not give away too much equity position to secure funds, because nothing may be left to give if you come up short.

Joint Ventures and Partnerships

- Structure a fair deal so that no partner is burdened with excessive risk and meager profits.
- Make clear who is in charge of the project.
- Avoid establishing goals that conflict with those pursued by other partners.
- Have agreements ready to cover dissolution of the partnership.
- Monitor changes in tax legislation that could affect returns.
- Establish a record of regular, honest communications with partners.

Marketing and Leasing

- Be prepared for unanticipated changes or a weakening market.
- Find a broker you trust and can work with.
- Understand the importance of marketing the project yourself.
- Create a suitable tenant mix for commercial projects.
- Be specific about tenant improvements and tenants' responsibilities in the lease, and include escape clauses for your own protection.
- Be creative about concessions. Consider buying stock in a tenant's start-up company, paying moving expenses, or providing furnishings.
- Understand the implications of leasing versus sale on tenants' earnings and balance sheets.
- Advertise that you have made a deal or signed a lease.
- Recognize brokers with incentives such as dinners and awards.

Operations, Management, Maintenance

- Pay close attention to building management and operations. Find a first-rate building manager.
- Budget properly for postconstruction maintenance.

In General

- Stick to geographic areas and product types with which you are familiar.
- Think small. Find a first project that is within your financial capabilities and can be developed in a reasonable amount of time.
- Never begin a project just because you have financing available.
- During the feasibility stage, keep investment in the project low to maximize your flexibility.
- Do your homework. Know what the holes in the market are and how to plug them—quickly.
- Never enter a negotiation that you are not prepared to leave.
- Attend to details. Whether you are designing a building or negotiating a lease, you must be personally on top of every detail. You must rely on your professional consultants, but if you do not understand the details, you should arrange for someone else to help you.
- Do not be afraid to make a nuisance of yourself. The people you are dealing with are usually very busy and hard to reach. You may have to make several telephone calls or personal visits before you talk to them. Learn to be tenacious—nicely.
- Do not deceive yourself by ignoring facts and warning signs as they are presented to you. Be aware that self-deception occurs most often with evaluation of the market.
- Increase the time you think you need to develop a project—perhaps by twice as much. Do not promise cash payments to investors by a certain date. Be neither overly optimistic nor overly conservative in your assumptions.
- Be able to turn on a dime and switch your strategy instantly.
- Follow up *everything*. Never assume that something has been done just because you ordered it.
- If you promise something to a lender, a professional consultant, a tenant, or a purchaser, deliver.
- Communicate honestly and often with your lenders and investors. Avoid deals that show early signs of being contentious.
- Recognize that the buck stops with you. A million excuses can be found for things that go wrong in a development project, but you have the ultimate responsibility for ensuring that they go right.

site, the risk money typically is limited to what is spent on feasibility studies—analyses of soils, the floodplain, and the market and conceptual design. As soon as the earnest money on the land is committed to the project, then the unrefundable earnest money is also at risk; the money at risk escalates dramatically when the developer closes on the land, pays for financing commitments, or authorizes working drawings. These events should be delayed as long as possible, until the developer can answer as many questions as possible or obtain the best information on which to decide whether or not to proceed with the project.

Analysis of the numbers becomes more detailed and more sophisticated at each iteration. The initial contract for earnest money may require only a simple capitalization analysis to see whether or not land cost yields the desired overall return (net operation income divided by total project cost). Before the earnest money contract becomes final, however, an annual cash-flow pro forma is necessary, at least for the operating period. It should reflect the actual square footage planned, projected rents (based on the market analysis), and estimated construction costs. For the next iteration, a monthly cash flow during the construction period is necessary to convince the lender that enough cash will be available to complete the project. It will be based on still more accurate information about costs (from detailed design drawings) and revenues (including rent concessions and tenant improvement allowances). Finally, for a joint venture or equity syndication, a cash-flow statement is necessary that combines both construction and operating periods and illustrates the timing of equity requirements, distributions of cash, tax benefits, and proceeds of sales (see chapter 4).

The level of detail should correspond to the quality of information available at each stage. Preparing a monthly spread sheet for 60 months before reasonably accurate construction costs and market data have been assembled is a waste of time and money, yet developers need enough information to make a good decision at each stage. The information should be comparable in quality for all of the different parameters, and it should be as comprehensive as possible for a given level of risk money.[4]

Because each deal has its own distinctive characteristics, limiting risk as much as the developer would like is not always possible. In very hot markets, for example, a "free look" may not be possible and earnest money may be forfeitable from the first day, or the developer might have to close on the land in 60 days, before securing a firm commitment for financing. Two general principles apply: one, recognize that development is an iterative process in which each iteration brings more accurate information and puts a greater amount of money at risk; and two, spend enough money to get the quality of information needed, but do not risk more than is necessary for each level of commitment.

Summary

Real estate development requires many different talents and skills with respect to managing people and managing risk. Development is fundamentally a creative process, and managing creative people and motivating them to do their best work is one of the elements necessary for success. Development involves solving numerous problems. No matter how well planned a project is, unexpected events arise that the developer must overcome.

Notes

1. Richard Peiser, "Can Development Be Taught in the Classroom?," *Urban Land*, July 1987, pp. 2–5.

2. Operating risk may be higher for smaller projects than for larger projects, however, because the loss of one tenant can jeopardize the project's cash flow. Furthermore, a small apartment or a small office project costs more to operate per dwelling unit or per square foot. Nevertheless, total development risk is lower for a smaller project.

3. Larger developers commonly choose to diversify into a new area; they have a major advantage that beginning developers do not—staying power. Out-of-state developers might bring to a community a new concept or design that sometimes succeeds and sometimes fails. When developers from the Northeast entered the Dallas market, for example, they introduced a split-level house that had been extremely successful in the Northeast. The plan failed because local homebuyers had different tastes. To the developer's credit, the product was redesigned to meet local preferences and, in the end, did very well. If the developers had done more market research initially, however, before entering the market, they may have avoided a costly mistake.

4. Accuracy is measured by how narrow the range is around an estimate. Statistically, it is defined by the standard deviation of the estimate. For example, a construction cost estimate of $100,000 with a standard deviation of $10,000 means that actual costs should range between $90,000 and $110,000, 68 percent of the time. A standard deviation of $20,000 means that the costs should range between $80,000 and $120,000, 68 percent of the time.

Chapter 2

Organizing For Development

The Firm's Organization and Management

No matter how talented the individual, development is a team effort. A development team can be put together in one of several ways. At one extreme, a large company might include many services—from architecture to engineering—on its payroll. At the other end of the spectrum, a development company might consist of one person who hires or contracts with other companies and professionals for each service needed.

Indeed, from the perspective of organization, development is a low-cost business that is easy to enter. A development company can be started by just one person and with little or no investment in equipment or supplies beyond, perhaps, an office. Furthermore, small developers are usually able to compete effectively against larger developers. Although larger developers might obtain better prices in some areas and have easier access to money, they also tend to have higher overheads.

The key to success for small developers is the quality of their development team. Small developers can often use the same professional consultants as do larger developers and beginning developers can acquire considerable credibility in the marketplace simply by selecting their development team members judiciously.

One way to maintain a small, lean organization is to use consultants rather than in-house staff. To select a consultant who will enhance the team:

- find the best person or company available, even if they cost a little more;
- make certain that person or company has direct experience with the particular type of product under consideration;
- select people who are familiar with local conditions; and
- consult with other developers to see how well the consultant under consideration has performed on other jobs.

Finding the best team for the job takes an enormous amount of time. From the day they start in business, beginners should start obtaining names of prospects and interviewing them. Assembling a team from scratch is difficult; more experienced developers have already established a network of consultants, contractors, and professionals, and building a permanent team takes more than one project. Nonetheless, the time and effort spent in finding the best possible team is a good investment.

Forming Partnerships

The safest partnerships are those in which the partners have a long history of working together, or in which all partners have faith in the honesty and integrity of their fellow partners. Partnerships are frequently formed around specific projects. Developers, especially beginning developers, might have different sets of partners for each of several projects. Partnership arrangements usually evolve over time. Initial deals might involve several partners, each filling a major function—financing, leasing, or construction, for example. In subsequent deals, the number of partners might diminish as the developer becomes better able to obtain the needed expertise without giving a piece of the equity.

Landowners are often partners in a beginner's early projects because they not only supply equity for the deal but also make it possible to tie up the land for sufficient time to obtain the necessary approvals and financing. Key tenants might also be offered partnerships to induce them to lease space in the project—this policy is especially effective if the project can be designed around the tenant's specific needs. Both landowners and tenants, however, generally prefer to limit their risk, which can be accomplished by making them limited partners.

A common mistake in forming partnerships is to choose partners with similar rather than complementary skills.[1] Partnerships that work the best are those in which everyone shares equally in the risks and returns and is equally able to cover potential losses. In most partnerships, however, one person is wealthier than the others and will understandably be concerned about ending up with greater risk, even if the partnership allocates this burden equally. One way to address this concern is to specify that a partner who is unable to advance the necessary share of capital loses his/her interest. Another way is to give the wealthier partner more of the return, or less of the workload, to compensate for his/her greater potential liability.

A major source of problems in partnerships, especially general partnerships in which everyone has equal interests, is uneven distribution of the workload. The partners doing more work resent those doing less work, and the situation can lead to difficulties. One way to address this problem is to determine responsibilities in advance. When they are unequal, the partners doing more work might be given specific compensation. For example, one partner might receive a greater share of the construction fee, with another receiving more of the leasing fee. (To save cash, it might be preferable to accrue the fees rather than to pay them as earned.)

Because partnerships can last for years, the choice of partners is a critical decision. Large developers who bring in less-experienced partners for specific deals generally enjoy a rather one-sided partnership, ensuring them management control; beginning developers, however, do not have the negotiating power of large developers.

Working out the partnership arrangement on paper in advance, preferably with an attorney, is especially important. A written agreement from the outset that defines each partner's role, responsibilities, cash contributions, and share of liabilities and that sets out criteria for the dissolution of the partnership is an essential document. Many partners of general partnerships formed casually and on the basis of verbal assurances have been shocked to discover that they are liable for their partners' debts for events that had nothing to do with the partnership's purposes.

The ideal partnership combines someone with extensive development experience and someone whose credit is sufficient to obtain financing—that is, someone with a net worth at least equal to the total cost of the project under consideration. When money or economic conditions are soft, banks might require a net worth two or three times that of the project in question. If the partnership does not include someone with sufficient credit, then the partners will have to find someone to play that role before they can proceed. In the past, many savings and loan associations (S&Ls) and some life insurance companies had subsidiaries that engaged in joint ventures with developers. Few, however, worked with beginning developers. Today, individual investors or other developers with the necessary net worth and liquidity are more promising candidates for partnerships with beginners.

Bringing in any financial partner before the full requirements for cash equity and the amount of net worth are known is a mistake. If, for example, the financial partner is to provide the necessary financial statement, and, say, $400,000 cash equity for 50 percent of the deal, the developer may be required to give up an unnecessarily high amount of ownership if he/she later finds that an additional $100,000 cash equity is needed. On the other hand, with no financial partner waiting in the wings, a prospective lender could lose interest while the developer is locating one. The ideal situation is to line up one or more prospects in advance.

Organizational Life Cycles

The life cycle of development firms resembles the "product life cycle" of modern marketing theory. Development firms pass through three stages—startup, growth, and maturity—and each stage is characterized by different risks and opportunities. "These risks and opportunities, combined with the firm's organizational strengths and weaknesses and the personal values of the developer-entrepreneur leading the firm, are the elements that must be evaluated in formulating a strategic plan."[2]

Startup

Startup is characterized by the establishment and attainment of short-term goals—successfully completing the first few projects and making enough money to cover overhead. During this stage, firms are more likely to be "merchant builders," selling their projects after they are completed and leased, rather than "investment builders," holding them for long-term investment. "During the startup period, the developer's entrepreneurial skills are the critical ingredient. The developer has to develop contacts—with financial lenders, political leaders, investment bankers, major tenants, architects, engineers, and other consultants. Eternal optimism and the ability to withstand rejection are essential."[3]

A common pitfall during startup is to become overextended before the company has developed the staff and procedures to handle greater activity. When tenants or buyers begin to sense that a developer is not responding to their needs quickly enough, that developer's reputation is likely to suffer. The developer must build staff to handle not only increased volume but also procedures for dealing with accounting, processing, leasing, tenant complaints, lender reports, construction, property management, and project control.

Another common mistake that beginning developers make is hiring too many people too quickly. A startup business never has enough cash, and those who watch the overhead closely during startup tend to fare better than those whose first priority is projecting a high-profile image. Some of the most successful developers have built thousands of apartment units and millions of square feet of industrial and office space with a professional staff of only three or four people, contracting with consultants for virtually everything.

Growth

A firm in the growth stage has achieved a measure of success. It has instituted procedures for running the business and has assembled a team of players to cover all the major development tasks. It is beyond the point at which a single mistake on a project can lead to bankruptcy and is in a position to shape its own future through the selection of projects and their location.

Maintaining the spirit of entrepreneurship is one of the hardest challenges for growing firms. As a firm grows, its success depends on its ability to avoid the bureaucratic trappings of large organizations. The need for quick decisions entails the direct involvement of the firm's principals, no matter how large the firm becomes. When the distance between the principals and the junior staff members becomes too large, the firm either loses its ability to compete at the opportune time or blunders into situations it could have avoided had the principals exercised better oversight.

Employees who are used to the freewheeling atmosphere of a startup organization sometimes resist the increased control and the management systems that are needed to ensure proper oversight by senior management. The firm must maintain an entrepreneurial environment, one that motivates and retains qualified, aggressive people. A one-person firm succeeds because that one person accepts risk, plans the tasks, organizes the approach, and controls everything. But when the firm succeeds and the company grows, a staff is necessary to handle the workload. One of the most difficult hurdles for an entrepreneurial developer to overcome is the transition from one-person leadership to a larger organization. Not only must the right staff be in place, the founder or founders must also be able to relinquish control.[4]

Many development firms are family firms. The difficult transition in this case is from one generation to another. Often, the normal conflicts between parents and children make it difficult for the founding parent to surrender management control to the next generation, and, even after the transfer, the parent remains in the background, giving directions. Many firms never make it through this transition.

Conflict also arises in family firms because the second generation is often eager to take risks and try new projects at a time when the founding generation is becoming more averse to risks. The founding generation is inclined to keep developing the same tried-and-true projects, concentrating on managing assets, while the younger generation wants to try new projects. If the founding generation cannot find the way to let the second generation pursue its goals or have a chance to fail, the children often leave the firm. Some developer-parents insist that their children work for another firm for a period before they join the family firm. Not uncommonly, family development companies skip a generation; the second generation leaves the business to work elsewhere while the third generation enters the business. Thus, a successful transition keeps the firm alive.

Wise managers foresee the problems and plan ahead for them, recognizing their children's needs to achieve success on their own.

Maturity

Firms reach maturity after they have established a track record of successful projects and have built an organization to handle them. Mature development companies have built a network of relations with financial, political, and professional players and have financial holding power, or "deep pockets." These firms tend to focus on larger, sophisticated projects that tend to be more profitable and require fewer managers than do smaller projects. They also tend to involve less competition.

Mature firms are more averse to risk, and they fully comprehend the risks that they do take. They have built up large net worths that the owners want to protect. They do not need to assume as much risk as they did previously, as lenders and equity investors are eager to participate with them. Developers can often avoid personal liability on notes, and financial partners are willing to assume most or all financial risk in return for an equity position in the project.

Several characteristics are common to all mature firms, regardless of their size, organization, and style of management:[5]

- they know how to manage market risk, particularly in overbuilt markets;
- they know how to distribute authority and responsibility within the firm as it grows;
- they know how to evaluate the firm's effectiveness and efficiency; and, most importantly,
- they know how to find, challenge, compensate, and retain good people.

Organizational Structure

During startup, organizational structure is less of an issue than it is during growth and maturity. In the early years, most developers resist formalized organizations. Everyone reports directly to the owner, who makes all of the major decisions. As firms grow, the delegation of authority, especially in financially sensitive areas, becomes essential, because the owner's time and availability are limited. In many firms, "effecting organizational change within the firm [is] a wrenching rather than an evolutionary process. A common solution [is] to hire someone from the outside—a consultant or a new CEO—to assist in establishing clear goals and to instigate the organizational changes necessary to achieve them."[6]

In most firms, the principals control the same few decisions: the sites to purchase, financing arrangements and major leases, and sale of a project. A common practice among even very large firms is that the principals retain the responsibility for making deals, "the activities that rely on the personal contacts and [the] entrepreneurial . . . mentality. The remaining development responsibilities (site acquisition, political processing, financing, design, construction management, and marketing) are typically delegated to the development staff."[7]

Development firms are usually organized by function, by project, or by some combination of function and project. Smaller firms are more likely to be organized by project, larger ones by function. That is, owners of small firms tend to appoint one individual (the project manager, who is often a partner) to be in charge of each project, with the group working on that project responsible for all aspects of it—financing, construction, marketing, leasing, and management. In large firms, on the other hand, one group is responsible for each of those functions in all projects.[8] In some organizations, employees report to two different managers, one responsible for function, and the other for geographic area or product line. A firm's organizational structure often reflects how it has grown and evolved over time. Some of the largest firms have a project-manager structure because they have grown by giving partners responsibility for specific geographic areas and/or product types.

Compensation

How to compensate senior managers is one of the major issues facing the owners of a development firm. One answer is to give key individuals equity in the firm. According to John O'Donnell, managing general partner of O'Donnell, Armstrong & Partners, Southern California: "The reason you give employees equity is you can't pay them what they would command on the open market. Instead, you give them a stake in the future." With middle managers: "We're not basing our future on these people, so we compensate them with cash [instead]."[9] Orange County, California, developer Baron Birtcher adds: "Regional partners receive real equity because they are 'at risk.' Project managers receive phantom equity."

Phantom equity becomes an important incentive for project managers and is computed from profits like a bonus. Unlike real equity, however, the individual does not legally own an interest in the project and incurs no risk. If the individual leaves the company, tracking him/her down for a signature every time a legal event occurs is not necessary, and, if a partnership includes more than one property, phantom equity avoids the problem of having to create a new class of project-specific interest.

O'Donnell's firm measures the performance of each property each year and contributes the appropriate share of the manager's profit to a phantom equity account. If, for example, the property makes $100,000 and the manager has a 5 percent interest in it, the account is credited $5,000. If the property loses $100,000, the employee does not have to cover his/her share of the loss out of pocket, but any advances from the company to cover losses are repaid before profits are distributed. In this way, the employee does not have to worry about raising cash to cover potential liabilities.

Many firms provide for a period of five to 10 years before an employee's phantom equity in projects becomes vested. O'Donnell's firm, for example, might give an employee 2.5 percent of a project after three to five years of employment. Each year after the employee becomes vested, he/she receives an additional 0.5 percent, up to a limit of 5 percent. Employees who become vested with 2.5 percent interest beginning in the fifth year, for example, will own 4 percent of the projects with

2-1 York Companies Organization Chart Raleigh, North Carolina

The York Companies is a family firm—with three generations active in the firm—made up of four operations outlined below. The construction and real estate companies offer a full line of services in construction, real estate development, sales, and management for both commercial and residential real estate in the Raleigh, North Carolina, area. The York Companies provides an example of a mature firm that focuses primarily on one market area.

J.W. York, Chairman
Board of Directors

G. Smedes York, President

York Construction Company of Raleigh, Inc.
Philip York, Vice President

Accounting
Field
Job Administration
Planning and Development

York Inns
Arthur Palmer, General Manager

Quality Inn
Mission Valley
Accounting
Food and Beverage
Guest Service
Sales and Catering

Hospitality Inn
Accounting
Food and Beverage
Guest Service
Sales and Catering

York Retail
Sam Bass, General Manager

Sam Bass
Camera & Video, Inc.
Commercial
Consumer
Video

York Properties, Inc.
Hal V. Worth III, Vice President

Marketing and Sales Division
Commercial Real Estate
- Brokerage
- Leasing
- Appraisals

Residential Real Estate
- Sales
  - Cameron Village Office
  - Cary Office
  - Creedmoor Office
  - Falls of Neuse Office
- Administration
- Relocation

Property Management and Leasing
Shopping Centers
Office Buildings
Apartments
Industrial Buildings

Advertising and Promotions

Accounting

Maintenance and Tenant Services
Grounds Maintenance
Landscaping
Maintenance
Security
Support

Office Services

Studies and Appraisals

■ 2-2 Real Estate Executives' Salary and Bonus Compensation: 1990–1991[a]

Position	Commercial Real Estate Firms: Average Base Salary[b]	Commercial: Bonus Range as a Percent of Salary[c]	Commercial: Percent of Firms with Bonus for This Position	Residential Real Estate Firms: Average Base Salary[b]	Residential: Bonus Range as a Percent of Salary[c]	Residential: Percent of Firms with Bonus for This Position
Chief Financial Officer	$140,160	16–33%	91%	$133,250	38–61%	80%
Division Senior VP/President	110,665	18–35	89	120,585	31–54	82
VP Acquisitions	91,590	6–28	76	88,220	27–45	94
VP Marketing	91,310	23–43	81	97,833	30–40	86
VP Sales	83,875	18–31	75	69,135	23–43	82
VP Leasing	95,570	11–29	86	96,895	25–45	95
VP Asset Management	90,970	11–28	69	65,770	11–21	91
VP Administration	82,660	11–20	84	63,760	11–23	83
Project Manager	73,750	13–36	80	66,440	19–27	96
Construction Manager	75,500	13–31	76	67,800	11–33	88
Property (Asset) Manager	51,000	7–17	75	41,540	4–9	92
Controller	79,990	10–22	83	74,485	20–40	84
Financial Analyst	45,045	7–15	54	44,100	7–10	80

[a]Results from a national survey with over 150 participating firms. Data as of fall 1990.
[b]Mean of distribution.
[c]Mean low to mean high.
Source: Kibel, Green Inc., Santa Monica, California; as reported in *Urban Land*, p. 30, January 30, 1991.

which they are associated after eight years. If someone leaves the company, O'Donnell retains the right to buy out that person's interest at any time based on a current appraisal of the property. He also has the sole right to select the appraiser. If someone leaves the company without notice, he might buy out that employee's interest immediately. On the other hand, a long-time secretary who leaves to start a family or a manager who gives advanced notice (say, three months') before leaving to start his own company might receive profit distributions for years, thus enjoying the project's full potential.

No magic formula exists for determining how much equity a developer should give away to attract top managers. Beginning developers may have to pay experienced project managers 25 percent of a project's profits, whereas established developers may need to pay only 1 to 5 percent. Employees' risks are lower with a more established developer, so their shares of the profit are lower. One major developer, for example, has three levels of participation, which are given not as rewards but as career paths. The lowest level is "principal." Project managers who are star performers are eligible. They receive up to 10 percent (5 to 7.5 percent is typical) of a project in the form of phantom equity. The next level is "Profit and Loss (P&L) manager," someone in charge of a city or county area. P&L managers are responsible for several projects and principals and receive 15 to 20 percent of the profits from their areas. Their interest is also in the form of phantom equity. The top level is "general partner," reserved for managers of a region, state, or several states. General partners receive real equity, are authorized to sign documents on the firm's behalf, and incur full risk.

Strategic Planning

Most beginning developers—and even many large ones—do not have a business strategy. They respond to opportunities as they present themselves rather than deciding in advance the types of projects to pursue. Their strategy is "by default" rather than "by design." After identifying a highly specific market, these developers look for sites that best meet the market's criteria. Such an approach helps developers build expertise that will give them a competitive advantage, and, as developers become known, brokers and landowners begin to bring suitable opportunities to their attention.

Regardless of size, however, every developer should have a strategic plan. Strategic planning helps to inculcate entrepreneurship as the firm grows. In small companies, the owner embodies the entrepreneurial spirit, but maintaining that spirit can be difficult as the firm grows. Entrepreneurship usually flourishes in a decentralized system composed of small groups that have considerable autonomy. To set up a decentralized management system, a strategic plan generated by the decentralized entrepreneurial group is necessary. The plan should include budgets, a master schedule tied to the budget, and systems for approving and tracking projects. Feature box 2-3 summarizes the major issues that strategic planning should address.[10]

The strategic plan helps the company to achieve its objectives faster, because everyone understands the firm's immediate goals and longer-term objectives, and plans are the most effective when everyone has participated in preparing them. (Note that the business plan is strategic, but the budget is tactical; that is, the budget lays out the specific tactics that will be used to follow the broad strategies laid out in the business plan.) The strategic plan culminates in an "action plan," which should establish specific protocols for managers to follow—for example, policies for evaluating the competition and an area's long-term economic outlook.

Choosing Consultants and Contractors

Assembling a team of professionals to address the economic, physical, and political issues inherent in a complex development project is critical. A developer's success depends on his/her ability to coordinate the completion of a series of interrelated activities efficiently and at the appropriate time.

The development process requires the skills of many professionals: architects, landscape architects, and site planners to address project design; market consultants to determine demand and a project's economics; attorneys to handle agreements and government approvals; environmental consultants and soils engineers to analyze a site's physical limitations; surveyors and title companies

2-3 Strategic Planning: The Business Plan

I. Evaluate the present situation.

- Where has the company been?
- Where is it headed?
- How should it get there?
- What are the owner's interests and expectations?
- What is the situation regarding employees?
- What is the external environment?
  - Trends
  - Changes
  - Opportunities
  - Risks
  - Politics

II. Analyze the company's strengths and weaknesses.

- Which properties has it marketed?
- How successful have they been?
- How has the firm done in the past?
  - Capabilities
  - Threats
  - Opportunities
  - Track records

III. Specify goals for the strategic plan.

- What is the financial strategy?
- What is the firm's strategy regarding products?
  - Quality
  - Investment or merchant builder
- Does the firm need to diversify its product?
- Does the firm need to diversify its location?
- What is the firm's strategy regarding land?
  - Land banking versus carrying land in slow times
  - Developed land versus raw land
- What is the marketing strategy?
- What is the strategy regarding production and construction?
- How does the firm get the job done? What is its management and organizational strategy?

IV. Specify an action plan—programs, steps, or tasks to be carried out—concerning risk, reward, and reality.

- What is the firm doing right now?
- Where does the capital come from?
- What will be its financial needs in the next 24 months, the next 36 months?
- What are the firm's objectives? What *measurable* results is it committed to achieve?
- What action plans can be based on these results and objectives?
  - Financial results
  - Acquisition and development
  - Operations: property management, leasing, tenant improvements, customer relations
  - External financing
  - Controls and measurement
  - Responsibilities and budgets

Source: Sanford Goodkin, national executive director, Peat Marwick/Goodkin Real Estate Consulting Group, San Diego, California; and Peter Inman, senior vice president, The Wolff Company, Irvine, California. Lectures for USC Graduate Real Estate Development Program, 1988.

Assembling a team of professionals to address all of the many issues inherent in a complex development project is critical. Pictured above is Crocker Center in Boca Raton, Florida, a mixed-use complex including office, retail, and hotel uses. Mixed-use projects offer design and marketing advantages, but the development process becomes much more complicated as the number of design and other consultants increases and the level of expertise required from each of the players grows.

to provide legal descriptions of a property; contractors to supervise construction; and lenders to provide financing. Even the most seasoned developer finds that staying on top of all of a project's technical details is difficult. Beginners, especially, must rely on the skillful support of an assembled team of professionals with the practical experience and technical knowledge required to deal with important issues.

Locating a Consultant

To begin the search for a consultant with particular expertise, developers should first seek the advice of successful local developers who have completed projects similar to the one under consideration. They should ask experienced developers about the consultants they use and their level of satisfaction with the consultants' work. However, beginners also should remember that established developers consider newcomers the competition, and it may take some time to build up the trust necessary for a frank exchange of opinions. Ralph Lewis of Lewis Homes, Upland, California, suggests that beginning developers join associations of local developers or their national organizations geared toward the real estate product of interest, be it residential, shopping centers, or industrial parks. The key is to become an active member in such organizations by serving on committees and making oneself known.

Developers should obtain a list of the consultants whose work has impressed public officials and their planning staffs. Certain approvals might hinge upon the reputations of specific team members; indeed, part of a consultant's value could lie in the connections he/she maintains with the public sector.

Associations of architects, planners, and other professionals are another source of potential consultants. Such organizations usually maintain rosters of members, which are useful as a screening tool because most professional and technical organizations have defined certain standards for their members. These standards might include a certain level of education and practical experience as well as a proficiency examination. Most associations publish trade magazines that provide a wealth of information about the field and are available in local public or college libraries. Such publications are likely to contain both advertisements placed by, and articles written by, consultants.

Selecting a Consultant

Strategies for selecting consultants vary according to the type of consultant being sought. The most common approach is a series of personal interviews. Beginners should not hesitate to reveal their inexperience with the issues being addressed or to ask potential consultants to explain clearly their duties. According to Sandy Albrecht, Jr., assistant vice president of Corroon and Black, Pasadena, California, consultants will profit by dealing with a developer, so they should be expected to take the time to explain the fundamentals.

A proper interview should address the developer's concerns regarding experience and attitudes. The developer should look for a consultant with extensive experience in developing similar projects. An architect or market consultant who has concentrated on single-family residential development would be inappropriate for a developer interested in an office or retail project.

The developer must be sure to ask for references and then must contact those references and inquire about the consultant's quality of work and business conduct, ability to deliver on time and within budget, receptivity to new ideas, and professional integrity.

The developer may also inspect some of the consultant's work—marketing or environmental reports, plans and drawings, and finished projects. The developer should be comfortable with the design philosophy of a prospective member of the creative team and satisfied with the technological competence of a potential analytical consultant. The technological explosion has resulted in an array of specialized computer applications tailored to solve specific problems. Software is available for everyone, from parking consultants to property managers, and can lead to more efficient use of time and to reduced costs.

The developer must be certain that the chosen firm has the personnel and facilities available to take on the assignment. If a consultant appears to be struggling to keep up with current responsibilities, the project is likely to suffer from neglect.

Next, the developer should establish who will be the project's manager and request a meeting with that person. Several projects for which that project manager had responsibility should be examined. Also, the developer is well advised to find out what subconsultants the firm would be likely to hire.

Hiring a firm is a two-way street. While the developer is sizing up the consultant, a similar process is going on across the table. Displaying a positive attitude about the project and the consultant's potential contributions is especially important. A beginning developer should not be offended when the consultant asks about his/her experience and competence to complete a development project, the existence of adequate financial resources to pay the bills, the feasibility of the proposal, and his/her ability to make timely decisions. Consultants need to be confident about a developer's ability to meet obligations.

Finally, the developer should judge if he/she has established a rapport with the people being considered during the preliminary interview. The ability to get along with these people is essential for the project's completion, so if problems arise at this point, the developer should consider if dealing with them on a daily basis will be possible. Compatibility is a key to the project's success—and to preserving the developer's sanity.

If the developer feels uncomfortable with any aspect of the consulting firm after checking references, eliminating the firm from further consideration may be the most sensible move. If the developer's responses are favorable about the firm as a whole but not about the particular person being assigned to the project, these concerns should be raised with the firm. A larger firm should have another staff person available, but a smaller firm may not. The developer must be assured that the most qualified people will be assigned to the project.

Rates

Consultants should willingly quote a fee for their services, presenting it as a written proposal reflecting the costs for delivery of the desired product. Developers should be careful not to choose simply the lowest price; although the cost is an important factor, it must be balanced by experience and the quality of the consultant's past work. Developers should compare the proposed budgets to see how the money is allocated and identify the differences in proposals to judge if the numbers are reasonable. They also should ensure that the prices include the same types of services. For example, a lower fee could possibly exclude services that later will be required, necessitating future additional charges. A lower quotation might also exclude the amount needed to cover unforeseen incidents.

■ 2-4 Who Is Involved, and When, in the Development Process?

Site Selection: Brokers, title company, market consultants.
Feasibility Study: Market analysts, economic consultants, mortgage brokers and bankers, engineers.
Design: Architects, general contractors, surveyors, soils engineers, structural engineers, environmental consultants, land planners, landscape architects, parking consultants.
Financing: Mortgage brokers and bankers, construction lenders, permanent lenders, surety companies, appraisers.
Construction: Architects, general contractors, engineers, landscape architects.
Marketing: Brokers, public relations firms, advertising agencies, graphic artists.
Operations: Property managers.
Sale: Brokers, appraisers.
Throughout the Process: Lawyers.

Once a firm has been selected, most developers prefer to employ a fixed-price contract, using the figures quoted in the proposal. Payment can be made in several ways, depending on the nature of the product to be delivered. A schedule could be used to establish milestones, such as the delivery of a specified product that triggers an agreed-upon payment, or developers might find that allowing projections of cash flow to establish a monthly schedule is more advantageous. Smaller jobs might require a lump sum payment upfront.

Like lawyers, consultants often work according to a time and materials (T&M) agreement—developers are billed according to staff members' hourly rates and the cost of materials used to complete the task. The cost of materials includes reimbursable expenses, such as telephone calls and photocopying. T&M agreements are complicated, however, and require constant monitoring to verify the amounts that are being billed.

Retainer agreements that pay the consultant a flat monthly fee should be avoided because such arrangements can be very costly in the long run. A retainer requires a monthly payment, regardless of whether or not work is completed.

Regardless of the chosen method of compensation, both the developer and the consultant must negotiate a mutually agreeable performance contract. The contract must explicitly list each duty that the consultant is expected to complete. Services not included in the agreement probably will require future negotiations that will most likely lead to additional costs for the developer. The contract should clearly spell out a schedule for the delivery of services, including a definitive date for delivery of the final product.

Working with Consultants

After signing the agreement, the working relationship with the consultant begins. The developer must work closely with the consultant to ensure that things proceed according to schedule. The development team is made up of a group of players whose tasks are interrelated, and the tardiness or shoddy work of a single firm could set off a chain reaction and cause costly delays.

As the team leader, the developer must ensure that each consultant is provided with accurate information and that information produced by one consultant is relayed to the others. Any changes in the project's concept should be communicated immediately. The developer must be sensitive to the impact that changes in the project will have on the consultants' collective analysis; sudden change could alter requirements for the design, environmental analyses, and parking, for example. Any alterations could be costly, as consultants might demand extra compensation to address the changing elements of the project.

A healthy working relationship with consultants is vital. Developers should seek to contribute information and to ask questions throughout the process but should also show a willingness to accept consultants' ideas. Good consultants can decrease development costs and improve a project's marketability.

A developer must have the management skill necessary to coordinate consultants' efforts while ensuring that all parties respect the developer's ultimate authority to make decisions. Problems can also occur, however, when a developer's ego gets in the way of good advice. A good developer knows when to listen to and accept the advice of others.

The Design/Construction Team

The design/construction team includes an array of consultants and contractors that perform tasks ranging from site analysis and planning to building design and construction management. The work that they perform and/or manage represents the bulk of the project's total costs, and effectively managing their contributions is critical to the success of the development project.

Architects

Both beginning and experienced developers depend upon architects for advice and guidance. Some developers appoint the architect to head the design portion of a project, although most developers prefer to be their own team leaders. Beyond experience with design, architects have extensive experience with the regulatory and physical constraints placed on development and are a valuable asset in communicating with other consultants and coordinating design.

The search for an architect must be very thorough. Only those firms and individuals whose experience is compatible with the proposed project should be considered. The developer always should check a firm's credentials and make sure that it is licensed in the state in which the project will be built; government planning and building departments will not approve projects unless the architect is state approved.

The developer and the architect must share a common philosophy of design, and the developer must feel comfortable with the architect selected. A good architect respects the developer's opinions. At the same time, the developer must question every decision but respect the architect's knowledge and experience. Mutual respect is essential. Some developers prefer to hire an architect whose work has withstood the test of time; others look for an architect known for innovative designs that make a distinctive statement and may give the developer a competitive advantage.

Architects not only are responsible for creating distinctive designs, as at Fifth Avenue Place in Pittsburgh, Pennsylvania, but may also be responsible for selecting and supervising other team members—land planners, engineers, landscape architects, and parking consultants.

When the developer has found an architect whose work could enhance the project, the next step is to reach a written agreement. A standard contract provided by the American Institute of Architects (AIA) provides the basis for defining the relationship between developer and architect. AIA Document B151, *The Agreement between Owner and Architect*, clearly outlines the architect's duties in the development process. This document is widely used in real estate development. Developers should remember, however, that this agreement was written from the architects' perspective and seeks to protect their interests.[11] Developers should not accept the contract verbatim if they are uncomfortable with its language.

Architects are often responsible for selecting and supervising land planners, engineers (except soils engineers), landscape architects, and parking consultants, as well all facets of the project's design. The design phase lasts from the creation of the initial concept to the completion of the final drawings. The design is based on a program provided by the developer that outlines the project's general concept, most notably its identified uses and amenities. Initially, the architect prepares schematic drawings that include general floor and site plans and that propose basic materials and physical systems. A construction cost estimator or contractor should review the design to assess its economic implications. These schematic drawings are an important component in presentations to lenders. Most of the major design decisions are made at the stage of schematic drawings. The design team should include not only the contractor but also leasing and property management representatives. If those team members are not yet named, then the developer should ask potential contractors, brokers, and property managers to review and criticize the preliminary drawings. Changes are much cheaper to make at this stage than later.

After the developer approves the preliminary design, the architect produces specification drawings, also called "working drawings." Specifications include detailed drawings of the materials to be incorporated with the mechanical, electrical, plumbing, and heating, ventilating, and air-conditioning (HVAC) systems. Generally, drawings pass through several iterations before the final plans and specifications are finished. The developer should review these interim drawings, referred to as 25 percent, 50 percent, 75 percent, or 95 percent complete. After addressing all of the developer's concerns, the architect completes final drawings.

In reviewing partially completed designs, the developer should pay particular attention to the implications

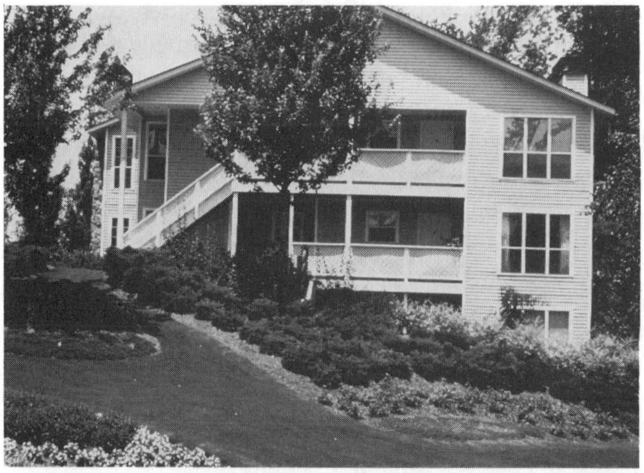

Architects should be selected carefully, based on their experience with the product to be built: top-rated office architects may know little or nothing about effectively designing apartment projects. Architects also should be familiar with local market preferences. They can be especially helpful with the nuances of targeting apartment designs to the local market. Pictured above is Post Knoll Apartments in Cobb County, Georgia.

for the potential users by visualizing how commercial tenants or residents will react to the design, asking brokers, tenants, and other developers to identify the needs of the target groups, and soliciting real estate professionals' comments on the design drawings as they progress.

The next phase of the architect's duties involves compiling the construction documents, including the package used to solicit bids from contractors. This package includes the rules for bidding, standard forms detailing the components of the bid, conditions for securing surety bonds, detailed specifications identifying all of the components of the bid, and detailed working drawings. The developer also relies on the architect's experience to analyze the bids and to help select the best contractor for the job.

Once construction begins, the architect is responsible for monitoring—but not supervising—the work site. The architect is expected to inspect the site periodically to determine if the contract documents are being adequately followed. Constant monitoring is beyond the scope of the architect's responsibility and will require additional compensation.

The developer also relies on the architect to confirm that predetermined phases during construction have been satisfactorily completed. The approval involves a "certificate of completion" necessary for disbursement of the contractor's fee. The AIA provides another preprinted certificate that addresses the architect's liability resulting from confirmation, noting that the architect's inspections are infrequent, that defects could be covered between visits, and that the architect can never be entirely sure that construction has been completed according to the plan.

The relationship between architect and developer follows one of two models. The "design-award-build" contract breaks the project into two distinct phases, with the architect completing the design phase before the developer submits the project for contractor bid. The other alternative, the "fast-track" approach, involves the contractor during the early stages of design, because the contractor's input at this stage could suggest ways to save on costs, making the project more economical and efficient to construct.

The fast-track method is primarily a cost-saving device, as it uses time efficiently to reduce the holding costs incurred during design. The developer is able to demolish existing structures, begin excavation and site preparation, and complete the foundation before the architect completes the final drawings. One of the risks involved with the fast-track approach, however, is that the project is underway before the costs have been determined.

Several methods are available for compensating architects for their services, including T&M agreements and fixed-price contracts. The latter specifies the amount that the architect will receive for completing the basic services outlined in the performance contract; any duties not listed in the contract are considered supplementary and will require additional compensation. Another method calculates architectural fees as a fixed percentage (usually 3 to 5 percent) of a project's hard costs. Architects contend that this method fairly accounts for a project's complexity, thus equating cost with an elaborate development. The disadvantage of this method is that it provides little incentive to the architect to economize, as higher costs guarantee higher fees.

Regardless of the mode of calculating compensation, the architect is always entitled to additional reimbursable expenses—travel, telephone calls, photocopying, and other out-of-pocket expenses.

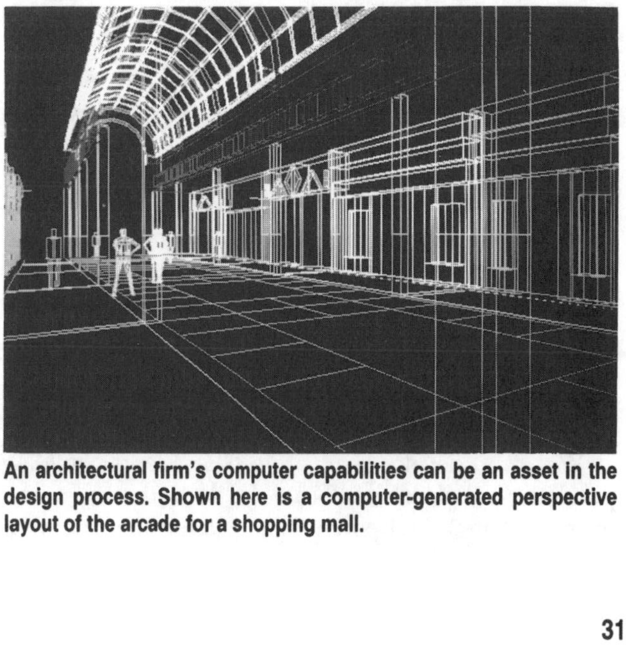

An architectural firm's computer capabilities can be an asset in the design process. Shown here is a computer-generated perspective layout of the arcade for a shopping mall.

Landscape architects are responsible for working with the architect to produce an external environment that enhances the development. Pictured is an entrance drive to Heritage Place Apartments in Orlando, Florida, illustrating how site planning, landscaping, and architectural elements can create a sense of arrival and community for a residential project.

Landscape Architects

Landscape architects do much more than plant trees and flowers. Landscape architects work with existing conditions—the topography, soil composition, and vegetation on a site—to create a distinctive site that will provide a sense of place for the project. They are responsible for working with the architect to produce an external environment that enhances the development, for devising a planting and landscape plan, and for incorporating components like plants, trees, furnishings (benches, for instance), artwork, and signs into the project. Landscape architects can also can save energy costs by selecting plants that provide shade and solve drainage problems.

Landscape architects first develop preliminary plans and then manage the completion of those plans. They obtain bids, complete working drawings and final specifications, draw up a schedule, and inspect the site to verify that the contractor implements the plan correctly.

Hiring the landscape architect is often the architect's responsibility, but developers should inspect the chosen landscape architect's work to determine if they are comfortable with the design philosophy. The American Society of Landscape Architects maintains rosters and certifies its members. Landscape architects work on a lump-sum basis to complete working drawings and specifications and, generally, on an hourly basis to supervise the completion of the plans.

Land Planners

With land development projects and larger building projects, land planners allocate the desired uses to maximize the site's total potential and determine the most efficient layout for adjacent uses, densities, and infrastructure. Individual building projects usually rely on the judgment of the architect and market consultants. The land planner's goal is to produce a plan with good internal circulation, well-placed uses and amenities, and adequate open space. Land planners should work up several schemes that expand on the developer's proposal and discuss the pros and cons of each with the developer. The developer coordinates the land planner's activities with input from marketing, engineering, economic, and political consultants to ensure that the plan is marketable, efficient, and financially and politically feasible. On land development projects, the land planner is the principal professional consultant. Reputation and past projects are the best indicators of a land planner's ability.

Engineers

Architects rely on the technical expertise of a group of engineers to ensure that the design can accommodate the required physical systems—structural, mechanical, electrical, and civil. The most prudent strategy is to allow the architect to select all the project engineers. Larger architectural firms usually have in-house engineers; smaller firms prefer to hire individual engineers as needed. Because architects work very closely with engineers, the success of the design phase depends upon a good working relationship between them. Even though the architect makes the initial selections, however, the developer should inspect the engineers' qualifications and feel comfortable with the architect's choice.

Engineers should be licensed by the state and should be members of a professional engineering society—for example, the National Society of Professional Engineers; American Society of Mechanical Engineers; or American Society of Heating, Refrigeration, and Air Conditioning Engineers (ASHRAE). The architect usually hires the engineers as subcontractors and is responsible for managing them. Design-related engineers, who work as subcontractors and are included in the architect's budget, are a prerequisite for almost all projects. During the initial design phase, the architect works with the engineers to modify drawings to accommodate the project's systems. Each engineer produces a detailed set of drawings showing the physical design of the systems for which the engineer is responsible.

Structural engineers assist the architect in designing the building's structural integrity. They work closely with soils engineers to determine the most appropriate foundation system and produce a set of drawings for the contractor explaining that system in detail, especially the structural members' sizing and connections. Mechanical engineers design plumbing and HVAC systems; electrical engineers design the electrical power and distribution systems; and civil engineers design the on-site utility systems, streets, and site grading.

Soils Engineers

Experienced developers recommend completing a soils test on a site before purchasing the property. Soils engineers conduct an array of tests to determine a site's soil stability, the level of its water table, the presence of any toxic materials, and any other conditions that will affect construction. Geotechnical engineering is not an exact science, but hiring skilled, registered professionals reduces uncertainty.

A soils engineer first removes a cross-section of the soil by boring the surface of the site to a specified depth. That sample is then taken for analysis. Laboratory tests disclose the characteristics of the soil at various levels, the firmness of each of those levels, and the presence of toxic materials. On smaller sites with no water or other potential problems, one boring test in the middle may be sufficient. On other sites, boring tests are usually completed in the middle and near the anticipated building corners. If the presence of toxic materials is suspected across the site, six or more borings may be necessary.

The soils engineer prepares a detailed report on the composition of the underlying soil, complete with an analysis of the characteristics of each layer. Soil composition is classified according to color, grain size, and firmness. Subsurface soils range from loose composition, such as gravel and sand, to solid clay and peat. The soils engineer also recommends the type of foundation system most appropriate for the site, based on the laboratory findings and tests to determine the soil's strength.

A bearing test determines the soil's ability to support, at the anticipated depth of the foundation, the planned structure. The soils engineer digs out a portion of the site to the designated level to complete the test. The soils engineer also determines the stability of the site's slope. During excavation, for example, digging straight down may be difficult because the remaining soil might cave in. The engineer is expected to use the results of the test to calculate the excavation angle that will leave the remaining soil intact.

Soils engineers participate with the architect and the structural engineer to design the most effective type of foundation system to support the proposed structure. They generally work on a lump-sum basis. A soils analysis can cost anywhere from $1,000 to $100,000, depending on the site's size and the number of test borings and types of tests necessary to study the soil.

Environmental Consultants

Environmental consultants analyze the project's impact on the surrounding community and may also perform environmental reviews to determine whether or not the site contains hazardous materials. Environmental reviews are often extremely sensitive political actions encompassing economic, social, and cultural issues. The environmental approval process, which demands great diplomacy from the developer, varies from state to state and from community to community according to local regulations, citizens' attitudes toward development, and the environmental sensitivity of the area in question.

Environmental issues are becoming increasingly important in development. Wood Forest Apartments (above) in Daytona Beach, Florida, was developed in an environmentally sensitive area and required the coordination of the Department of Environmental Regulations with the Corps of Engineers in Florida.

A developer should select an environmental consulting firm that is respected for its technical expertise and independence. Impartiality is a growing concern, not least because the results of an environmental report can become a political issue. To ensure impartiality, some cities provide a list of acceptable engineers from which a developer may choose; in California, for example, the public sector randomly assigns an environmental consulting firm to a developer.

A developer creates difficulties for the environmental consultant by changing the development plan. Each change requires simultaneous modifications to the consultant's analysis—this does not mean, however, that the developer should wait until the last minute to hire an environmental consultant.

The appropriate level of government first determines whether or not a developer is obligated to complete a formal environmental analysis. If the proposed project has the potential to affect the surrounding community adversely, an analysis is required, and an environmental consultant must perform it. The kind of analysis that must be performed is dictated by local, state, and federal laws. The least stringent type of analysis is an environmental impact statement (EIS). Established by the National Environmental Policy Act (NEPA, 1969), an EIS is simply a checklist that identifies the potential impacts that a project is expected to create. A full environmental impact report (EIR), based on local and state legislation, may be ordered when a project is expected to pose substantial dangers to the environment. EIRs are also required as a normal course of action in environmentally sensitive communities.

The environmental analysis determines what effects a project could have on the surrounding environment, particularly in terms of air quality, soils, noise, sunlight and shade, and traffic.

An EIR not only describes the proposed development, the site, and the project's effect on the community, but also proposes appropriate mitigation measures. For example, a report might find that a project will add significant amounts of traffic to surrounding city streets. In response, the consultants might propose widening certain streets, adding left-turn lanes, or converting some streets to one-way traffic.

Once a draft of the environmental report has been prepared, it is circulated for a given period in the community and public comments are invited. Thereafter, the developer's environmental consultant must produce a final report that responds to all comments. Any mitigation measures recommended by the consultant must be feasible for the developer to implement. Public bodies, usually the planning commission and/or the city council, generally include the mitigation measures in their conditions of approval for the project.

Hazardous materials have become a major concern for developers, and their presence on the site of a project can cause major delays. Consequently, environmental analysis, including soils analysis, should incorporate tests to determine the presence of toxic materials. Ascertaining a property's previous uses is important to determine the likelihood of toxic contamination. If, for example, the site was a gas station, underground storage tanks must be removed, and, if the tanks have leaked, any contaminated soils must be removed before construction begins.

The cost of hiring an environmental consultant varies according to the size and complexity of the project analysis. An EIR is more expensive than an EIS because the amount of work involved is greater. Most consultants work on a lump-sum basis, with a payment schedule worked out according to performance milestones. The consultant's contractual obligations usually end with the production of the final report, but the developer might subsequently require the consultant to make presentations and answer questions at public hearings. After the contract expires, consultant compensation is based on a T&M agreement.

Surveyors

Surveyors determine a property's physical and legal characteristics—existing easements, rights-of-way, and dedications on the site—and prepare a site map plotting these characteristics. This critical information reveals how much of the site can be built on and the allowable square footage.

Developers commonly use two types of surveys: a boundary survey that determines the boundaries of the site, with easements and other legal requirements affecting ownership of the property being plotted on a map; and a construction survey that plots the location of relevant infrastructure—water, sewers, electricity, gas lines, and roads—to assist in planning connections to utility services.

Surveyors also augment the work completed by soils engineers, analyzing a site's topography, likely runoff, slope, and the implications of the proposed location of the building.

Costs for surveyors vary according to the type of work they perform, the detail required, and the number of surveys requested. Surveyors work either on a lump-sum basis or on a T&M agreement. A survey crew of two people should be able to complete a boundary analysis for a typical 10-acre parcel in a single eight-hour day.

Parking Consultants

Parking is one of the major limiting factors for real estate development. High land values and restrictive local parking ordinances require a well-devised parking plan. A qualified parking consultant (usually not the architect) takes into account all of the significant factors involved in designing the optimum parking for the site. The parking consultant should be included early in the design process so that the architect can incorporate parking recommendations into the overall design.

Parking consultants are responsible for many aspects of a project: evaluating the economics of a surface lot versus those of a parking structure; designing an efficient configuration that maximizes the available parking area; discovering if local municipal codes can accommodate the estimated parking demand; determining whether parking should be provided free or at a competitive rate; and deciding where the points of ingress and egress will be.

Parking is an expensive undertaking, costing $1,000 to $1,200 per space for a surface lot, not including land, and $6,000 to $8,000 or more per space for a structure; underground parking may cost twice as much. Consequently, the services of a well-qualified consultant are essential. Referrals from the architect and other developers will provide a list of potential consultants whose work should be inspected by the developers before any decision is made to hire someone. Parking consultants usually work either under a lump-sum contract or at an hourly rate.

Asbestos-Abatement Professionals

The Environmental Protection Agency (EPA) has estimated that about 733,000 buildings—or 20 percent of all private and public commercial buildings in the United States—contain some form of asbestos. Renovation or adaptive use of a building constructed between 1930 and 1976 is very likely to run the risk of asbestos contamination.

Asbestos was used for fireproofing and insulation until 1973, when federal legislation prohibited its future use for those purposes. Asbestos was sprayed on underlying columns, beams, pipes, and ducts of buildings, above ceilings and behind walls. It was also used in building materials, such as tiles.

Asbestos is hazardous when friable (that is, flaky or powdery); if disturbed, its fibers become airborne and are likely to be inhaled. EPA regulates activities like renovation and demolition that could release asbestos into the air and outlines appropriate methods of disposal. Plans to rehabilitate or demolish an existing building must include the removal of any asbestos. Even the installation of sprinkler systems, electrical and plumbing repairs, and any interior reconfiguration might require some form of asbestos abatement.

Removing asbestos requires the services of qualified, well-trained professionals with extensive experience in assessing and removing asbestos; the hazards inherent in the process could lead to legal repercussions if inexperienced firms are hired to carry out the tasks. The firm selected should be bonded by a certifiable surety company. Both the consultant hired to determine the extent of the asbestos contamination and the contractor responsible for removing it should be licensed by the state. Developers may contact the regional office of EPA and the National Asbestos Council for lists of qualified asbestos-abatement professionals.

Consultants charge either by the hour or by the square foot. Charges for a typical 3,000-square-foot building, for example, might be $0.10 per square foot for the physical inspection plus approximately $70 for the laboratory tests. Estimates for removing asbestos range from $10 to $30 per square foot, based on the complexity of the job. Contractors require special clothes and tools that must be disposed of regularly.

Construction Contractors

Construction contractors are responsible for a project's physical construction. They are required to complete an array of services (both before and during construction) on time and, ideally, under budget.

Developers can select a contractor either through negotiations with a particular firm or through open bidding. To find a good contractor, developers should solicit a number of contracting firms, asking them to submit proposals or general statements of qualifications. The contractors' responses should include descriptions of past projects, client and lender references, resumes outlining the experience of their major employees, and, possibly, verification that the company is bondable. These submissions can be used to select a company for direct negotiation.

To find a good construction contractor, developers should solicit proposals or general statements of qualifications from a number of contracting firms.

In open bidding, developers send out a notice requesting bids and statements of qualifications. The problem with this approach is that contractors are reluctant to spend time bidding on a project unless they think that they have a good chance of being selected. As a result, the developer may not attract an adequate number of responses from which to choose. Two to four weeks are necessary to allow contractors to return satisfactory responses.

The most effective way to limit the number of bidders but still ensure that the targeted firms will respond involves a combination of a request for qualifications and competitive bidding. After reviewing several contractors' qualifications, developers may ask the best three, four, or five contractors to prepare a bid for the project. A preference for one contractor could result in direct negotiations with a particular firm. Developers should not feel obligated to conduct protracted bidding if they have already found the best contractor for the job.

During the design stage, a contractor or a construction-price estimator (also called a "quantity surveyor") should check the architect's drawings and formulate an estimated budget for completing the project. A permanent contractor, once hired, is responsible for completing a construction-cost estimate based on the construction drawings completed by the architect. If the developer chooses to put the project on a fast track, the contractor should be a helpful source of creative and cost-effective suggestions during the preliminary design process.

One of the contractor's tasks is to set up a projected schedule for disbursing loans from the construction lender.

The contractor's major responsibility, however, is the project's physical construction, including soliciting bids from, and then hiring, all the subcontractors—construction workers, plumbers, painters, and electrical and mechanical contractors. The contractor is legally responsible for building a safe structure and must hire the best-qualified parties.

During construction, the developer or the contractor may alter the architect's plans, using change orders. The proposed change might result from a market-based design change or from practical problems, such as the unavailability of specified materials; alternatively, the contractor may suggest cost-saving alternatives. All change orders are subject to the architect's verification and approval. If the developer does not monitor them carefully, costs can escalate dramatically.

Two basic methods are used to determine the contractor's compensation: bids or contracts. Bids are requested to be in the form of a lump sum or some derivative of a cost-plus-fee contract. A lump-sum bid is used when the design is already established and all of the construction drawings are complete before selecting the contractor. This option is rarely feasible for beginning developers, however, because they are probably not willing or able to underwrite the cost of complete drawings until the decision to construct is finalized.

Contractors' fees are based upon the size of the project, the number and amount of anticipated change orders, and so on. On a $10 million project, a contractor should be expected to charge a fee equivalent to 5 percent of total hard costs. This is on top of project overhead and on-site supervision.

A cost-plus-fee contract is a preferable means of compensating experienced contractors with excellent reputations. Under this option, all costs should be explicitly set forth in the contract—labor, salaries of accountants and other such employees, travel expenses, construction materials, supplies, equipment and tools, and fees for all subcontractors. The costs should not include overhead and administrative expenses for the contractor's main or branch offices.

The contractor must calculate the time required to complete the project as a basis for a fixed or percentage fee. Most developers avoid a percentage fee because it fails to provide the contractor with incentives to minimize construction costs.

Often, the construction lender requires that the contractor guarantee a maximum cost when the cost-plus-fee method is used. In such cases, the architect is responsible for providing drawings with sufficient detail to allow the contractor to solicit quotes from subcontractors to calculate the maximum cost.

Guaranteed maximum cost contracts can include an incentive to save costs—say, 25 to 50 percent of the developer's savings could be guaranteed to the contractor if total project costs are less than the guaranteed maximum. The developer must make sure, however, that the contractor does not sacrifice quality to receive the bonus. Other types of incentive bonuses can also save costs. A bonus for early completion pays the contractor a defined amount for completing the work on or before a specific date; some contracts pay a fixed amount for each day that work is completed before the deadline. By the same token, bonus clauses can be used to penalize the contractor for being late. Some contracts include a liquidated damage clause or a penalty clause to cover late completion. Not surprisingly, contractors dislike these clauses, which they argue destroy teamwork.

Using bonus and incentive clauses is an excellent tool for guaranteeing the contractor's performance. The developer incurs costs, however, most notably in the necessary monitoring of the contractor's performance.

A good construction job hinges upon selection of an experienced and reputable contractor. Beginners especially should select a contractor with a long track record.

Real Estate Service Firms

A variety of service firm types provide a wide range of real estate services that are critical in the development process. These firms are usually brought into a project to perform specific, short-term tasks.

Market Consultants

Successful real estate decisions hinge upon the availability of reliable and accurate information. A market consultant is retained to provide the professional assessment of a proposed project. The resulting market study analyzes the feasibility of the proposed project based on current and projected market conditions. Possessing such information reduces the risks involved with the project. Lenders, investors, and architects all use the market study.

Some developers complete their own market studies, and lenders normally accept a well-documented study by a developer for a small project. Larger projects, however, require a professional market study. Developers must have confidence in the market consultant's ability to determine the project's feasibility. A market research firm with a good reputation adds credibility to developers and their projects.

Which market consultant to hire is likely to be one of the most important decisions made during the predevelopment period. Although developers may ask other developers for recommendations, they should certainly ask

Market consultants should be chosen based on their familiarity with both the local market and the product type. Market analysis for retail projects, such as Crossroads of Lake Buena Vista in Lake Buena Vista, Florida, is very different from that for residential projects.

lenders which consultants they respect. Lenders' opinions are particularly important because their decisions depend upon the market data that prove the project's feasibility.

The unique requirements for different kinds of development reinforce the importance of retaining a consultant well versed in the type of development under consideration. A local firm that knows the market of the area in which the project will be located is usually the best choice. The type of databases that the market consultant maintains will be a useful indication of the consultant's approach. Aside from being technically proficient, the consultant must be able to understand the subtle nuances of the market that are not readily apparent to the average observer. A good market consultant can identify the proposed competition and thoughtfully analyze the political situation.

Developers should ask to see several market studies that the consultant has produced and make sure that they are comfortable with the assumptions and techniques used to appraise a market. The style of writing and presentation of the report should be carefully examined, as it will be circulated among various members of the development team as well as potential lenders and investors.

The market consultant is responsible for producing a final study that should address all of the factors affecting the feasibility of the proposed project. As a client, the smart developer looks for a comprehensive study that will give independent evidence about the marketability of the development proposal. (The specific features of the process for various property types are discussed in the appropriate sections of chapters 3 through 7.)

The final report should incorporate all of the data into a marketing strategy to help merchandise the project. The market research firm should provide a profile of tenants or buyers to be targeted and the amenities and lease terms to be offered. The architect should receive a copy of the report so that the project's design will offer uses and sizes appropriate for the market. The market study should also provide insights into the amenities and space configurations in which tenants and buyers are interested.

A market consultant's fee is based on the level of detail that the developer requests. For a preliminary analysis or a quick inventory of the market, the consultant might work on an hourly basis, but larger, more-complex studies are executed as a fixed contract.

Appraisers

Appraisers produce an estimate of a property's value based on standard methodologies. A professional appraisal will be required by investors, potential buyers, and lenders, who rely on appraisal reports to arrive at a market value that will set the amount of the loan for the proposed project.

Lending institutions usually employ in-house appraisers or select an independent outside firm. If the lender leaves selection up to the developer, he/she should ask for a list of people that the lender prefers to use. A reputable appraiser will add credibility to the loan application. Professional appraiser organizations can supply references. Appraisers must demonstrate certain minimum standards to gain admission to any of these organizations.

The appraisal report should state the market value of the property and offer supporting evidence. Three methodologies can be used to complete an appraisal: the income approach, the market approach, and the cost approach.

The income approach is preferred for all income-producing property including commercial, industrial, office, and rental apartments. Value is determined by dividing the project's net operating income by an appropriate capitalization rate. The market approach uses recent information about the sales of properties similar to the subject property to determine a market value. This approach is used most often with single-family residential, condominium properties, and land sales. The cost approach estimates the actual cost to construct a project similar to the project under consideration. It is used to determine the value of recently completed buildings. The developer must ensure that the appraiser uses the standard techniques and professionally accepted forms to produce a credible report. Appraisal costs range from $500 for a single-family house to $10,000 for a large office building.

Attorneys

Many facets of real estate development—for example, taxes, land use, leases, and joint venture partnerships—require separate legal specialists. No single attorney can be familiar with all of these topics. For zoning and other activities involving public hearings, an attorney with a proven success rate in cases involving a particular public body might be the proper choice. The ability to work behind the scenes with the local planning staff and politicians may be more important than appearing at public hearings. In any case, a law firm should be chosen that has attorneys with specific experience in the real estate issues likely to arise. Other developers of the type of project under consideration can recommend good attorneys.

Attorneys are essential for producing partnership or syndication agreements and contracts for consultants, making property deals for the development site, and negotiating the public approval process. The process of obtaining public approvals can be an intimidating maze for a beginning developer without an attorney and may lead to costly delays.

Most developers request that a partner of the law firm or a well-established attorney works on their cases, preferring to pay a little more for the top person to guarantee the best job. For technical work like syndications and contracts, highly recommended junior associates with three or four years of experience may provide the most cost-effective work from a large law firm. Attorneys generally bill clients on an hourly basis. The developer should obtain an estimate of the total cost for a given job before authorizing it.

Title Companies

Title companies certify who holds title to property and guarantee the purchaser and lender that the property is free and clear of unexpected mortgage, tax, easement, and other liens that may cloud the title of property. Title companies will defend any future claims against properties that they insure. The type of title policy determines the extent of the protection. Developers must read the policy carefully before signing it. Most policies follow a standard format, but many real estate investors fail to understand what protection their title policy provides, a misunderstanding that can lead to problems.

When selecting a title company, developers should make sure that the company has the financial strength to back any potential claims and should research its record of service to find out how long a company takes to obtain a clean title. Most title representatives work for a commission, and they are very accommodating because they want repeat business.

Title companies provide a number of other services in addition to title insurance. They provide, free of charge, both current and potential customers with a profile of a property in which the customer is interested. That profile details who owns it, property taxes paid, liens, easements, size of improvements and the lot, grant and trust deeds, notes, and most recent sale price. Local data, such as comparable sales information and plat maps, are also provided.

A preliminary title report can be prepared for a fee, specifying current liens against the property. The preliminary title is not an insurance policy but a reading of the existing title. It highlights any potential problems that a future owner may need to clear from a property before title is transferred.

Title fees, obtained from any representative of the company, are usually applicable statewide and are quoted on a scale that slides according to the sale price of the property being insured. More often than not, the seller pays for title insurance.

Surety Companies

Developers need insurance to guard against a consultant's or contractor's failure to perform an agreed-upon task. Such a failure may have serious economic and legal consequences. For instance, a contractor's failure to meet obligations could result in a lien on the developer's property. All public works projects must, by law, be bonded for performance, because liens cannot be placed on public property. Private projects do not have to be bonded, but in most instances some form of bond is recommended. Contractors are generally required to be "bondable," meaning that they qualify for surety coverage.

General contractors deal directly with a surety company to obtain performance and payment bonds. The developer is required to inform all contractors that bonds will be required before bids are submitted, and contractors consequently adjust their bids to pass on the cost of bonds to the developer. Bondable contractors generally establish a relationship with one surety company and fix an upper bonding limit of credit, which restricts the amount of bondable work that the contractor can perform.

Construction bonds are a specialized product, offered by few insurance companies. Other developers can identify respectable carriers for a beginner, if necessary.

A surety bond involves a three-party contract in which a surety company (or, simply, a "surety") joins with a principal, usually the contractor, in guaranteeing the specific performance of an act to the developer or municipality, also referred to as the beneficiary.

Bonding should not be interpreted as a negative comment upon the contractor. It is, rather, a validation of the contractor's ability to deliver a finished product. Before issuing a bond, the surety thoroughly analyzes the contractor's firm, including the qualifications of its staff, its financial stability, its management structure and previous experience, and inventories its equipment.

Based on these facts, the surety makes an appraisal of the contractor's ability to complete the project. If the firm is deemed stable, the surety issues the appropriate bonds, and work can proceed. Even if the developer chooses not to require any construction bonds, the surety's seal of approval is an affirmation of the contractor's quality.

There are three main types of bonds: performance, payment, and completion. Performance bonds guarantee the developer that if the contractor fails to complete the agreed-upon contract, the surety is responsible for seeing that the work is finished. The agreement allows the surety to compensate the developer equal to the amount of money needed to complete the project or to hire a contractor to finish the job. Lenders occasionally insist on bond coverage for their own protection. The general contractor, either at the developer's request or on its own, requires subcontractors to purchase performance bonds.

Payment bonds guarantee that the surety will meet obligations if the contractor defaults on payments to laborers, subcontractors, or suppliers, protecting the property against liens that might be imposed in response to nonpayment. Developers and/or lenders often require the general contractor to purchase these bonds to protect them against any future claims of nonpayment made by subcontractors or suppliers. Payment bonds usually are issued concurrently with performance bonds; both bonds often appear on the same form.

Completion bonds, often referred to as "developer off-site" or "subdivision bonds," insure local municipalities that specified off-site improvements will be completed. Many states require local municipalities to secure the bonds as assurance that the developer will complete the improvements.

The developer may require bid bonds during the solicitation of contractors' bids. A bid bond, issued by a surety, guarantees the developer that the winning contractors will honor their accepted bids. If, for example, a winning contractor finds out that its bid was significantly lower than the others submitted, it may be tempted to withdraw the offer. In such instances, the surety pays damages to the developer, in theory to compensate for time and money lost.

In most states, surety companies must charge uniform rates. Each surety establishes its rates and underwriting standards and then files them with the state insurance department or its equivalent. For performance and payment bonds, the rate charged is the same whether 50 or 100 percent of the contract price is guaranteed; therefore, developers should ask for 100 percent coverage. Rates are based on the contract price and are calculated on a graduated payment scale. The rates for completion bonds are generally higher because they involve additional underwriting.

Opinion is divided about the need to secure the various forms of surety bonds. Performance and payment bonds cost roughly 1 percent of the construction costs, so it is up to the developer to decide whether or not bonding is worth the abated risk.

Real Estate Brokers/Leasing Agents

Real estate brokers and leasing agents are hired to lease or sell a project to prospective tenants and buyers. Developers benefit greatly from the services of a skilled salesperson who is able quickly to lease or sell a project completely.

Developers must decide whether to sign an agreement with an outside real estate broker or to place an agent on the payroll. The decision is usually based on the type and magnitude of the project.

The use of in-house agents is most appropriate for large projects and large development firms that can carry the cost. The benefit of an in-house staff is that the developer hires the staff during initial planning, and the agent becomes very familiar with the project, providing input during design and merchandising.

Small development firms may find it useful to retain outside brokers who are knowledgeable about the local market and who have lower carrying costs. Brokers are usually aware of potential tenants that have existing leases that are about to expire; brokers from large brokerage houses may have information about regional or national tenants.

It is essential to interview representatives from a number of firms in order to select a firm with experience with the type of project under consideration. During an interview, the project should be presented carefully. If the broker does not respond positively to the project, another broker should be found. If developers find that prospective brokers currently represent competitive developments, they should decline to hire them because of potential conflicts of interest. Retaining a broker who has faith in the project and who can commit the energy necessary to ensure its success will be a major benefit to the development process.

The working relationship between developer and broker is defined in a contract referred to as a "listing agreement." Under an open listing agreement, the developer may recruit several brokers and is responsible for paying a commission only to the one who sells or leases the property. In addition, if the developer completes a transaction without the broker's assistance, no commission is necessary. An exclusive listing agreement involves, as its name suggests, a single broker.

The most common form of agreement for developers is an "exclusive right-to-sell listing." In this instance, the developer selects one broker, who automatically receives the commission no matter who sells the property, including the developer.

The broker is responsible for attracting prospective tenants or buyers and persuading them to lease or buy the project. An active broker will be well informed about the market, able to identify and recruit interested parties, and prepared to comment upon the project's design during its early stages, informing the developer and architect what amenities are currently popular in the market.

The marketing of a project ensures its success; but who should control the marketing process is debatable. Allowing brokers to plan, implement, and pay for the promotional campaign involves them and gives them a sense of responsibility. Developers who prefer to pay for the promotion themselves prefer the control they enjoy in deciding on the timing and intensity of marketing.

The broker's responsibility is to negotiate leases with prospects while keeping in mind the developer's personal goals with respect to rates of return and preferred type of tenant. The developer should establish lease guidelines for the broker to follow. He/she should readily accept leases presented by the broker within those guidelines so as to maintain his/her credibility with the brokerage community. Developers who lose that credibility quickly lose activity on their property. Once the project is leased, the developer may either retain the broker to lease space as it becomes available or rely on the property manager to do so.

The developer should negotiate a schedule for commissions that will provide incentive to lease or sell the building as quickly as possible—for example, by providing higher commission rates early in the project to gain momentum.

Real estate brokers work almost exclusively for commission. The broker and the developer negotiate the rate of compensation, which varies according to the type, size, and geographic location of the project. In general, commissions for property sales are based on a percentage of the total price (see figure 2-5).

Lease commissions payable to the broker are calculated as an annual percentage of the value of the signed lease for each year of the lease. Over the term of the lease, the percentages paid to the broker are scaled down (see figure 2-6). Half of the aggregate commission typically is paid at execution of the lease and half at move-in.

■ 2-5 Typical Real Estate Sales Commissions

Property Type	Percent of Total Price
Raw Land	5–10%
Single-Family Houses	6–7
Housing Tract	2–4
Apartment Building	3–5
Office Building	3–5
Industrial Building	4–5
Shopping Center	4–5
Hotels	3–5

■ 2-6 Typical Lease Commissions

	Percent of Total Lease Years						
Property Type	1	2	3	4	5	6–10	10+
Shopping Center	6%	5%	4%	4%	3%	3%	3%
Office Building	6	5	4	4	3	3	3
Industrial	5	4	3	2	1	1	1

Source: John McMahon, *Property Development*, 2nd ed. (New York: McGraw-Hill, 1989), p. 400.

■ 2-7 Developing a Marketing Strategy

Public Relations/Advertising Agencies

Project promotion spreads the word about the project to the community and differentiates it from the competition in the minds of potential users. Developers often tend to neglect promotion, hoping instead that the project will sell itself; this is almost invariably a mistake.

Part of the process of selecting a public relations or advertising agency involves attending presentations at which the agencies under consideration offer examples of their previous work, samples relevant to the proposed project, and promotional ideas for the project.

Public relations firms not only produce news releases, press kits, newsletters, and mailings conveying information about the project, but also create situations that will give the project positive exposure in the community. Different projects and product types require different approaches to attract interest from potential consumers, and the agency chooses which tool is most appropriate for a given project. The agency should also be a source of creative ideas to market the project effectively.

Good promotional plans draw attention to the project at strategic moments—groundbreaking and topping-off ceremonies, for example. A good public relations firm can be an invaluable asset when a project is proposed in a contentious political environment. A well-conceived campaign can gain favorable publicity for the project and sell it to the community. Organized community events, complete with well-designed presentations, introduce the company and the project to the neighborhood and local politicians and will leave a favorable impression.

A public relations firm can handle advertising, and an advertising agency can handle public relations. Advertising involves placing advertisements strategically to promote the project and maximize its exposure. Many different media and promotional techniques are available, including newspapers, radio and television, and outdoor signs. The advertising firm designs the advertisements and presents them to the developer for approval. Advertising firms generally work on monthly retainers plus expenses to cover radio, television, newspaper, billboard, or magazine advertising.

Property Managers

Once the project is complete and occupancy begins, the developer becomes a landlord intent on maximizing the project's value. Professional property managers are skilled at maintaining high occupancy rates and low maintenance costs. Addressing the needs of the project's tenants and maintaining the property deserves full-time attention.

The decision whether or not to use an outside property manager is based on a developer's assessment of how much time he/she wishes to invest in the project. Property management is extremely time consuming, and most developers prefer to delegate responsibility to a qualified property manager. The time that a developer spends on

Ineffective property management and maintenance—including even the smallest details—can lead to a shoddy or unkempt image for a project.

management could probably be put to better use pursuing new opportunities for investment, but being one's own property manager creates constant contact with tenants, providing a developer with an opportunity to learn firsthand the aspects of the project that are most effective and what should be changed in future developments. Most larger developers manage their own properties through an in-house staff or subsidiary. Nevertheless, beginning developers should be circumspect about the time that property management consumes if they are inadequately staffed or inexperienced.

Experience with the type of project under consideration is probably the most important aspect to look for when selecting a property management firm. The Institute of Real Estate Management (IREM), part of the National Association of Realtors, is a good source for potential property managers. Individuals with the appropriate qualifications can earn the designation Certified Property Manager from IREM, and firms can earn the designation Accredited Management Organization, which must be renewed, based on performance, every three years.

Smaller and inexperienced developers should retain a private property management firm. Developers should obtain a list of properties that prospective management firms currently service and should interview selected tenants and landlords.

A property manager looks after the building as soon as tenants start to move in. Day-to-day management operations include collecting rent, paying expenses, maintaining the common area, and ensuring that necessary repairs are carried out.

The manager should provide a comprehensive physical plan specifying regular inspections, scheduled maintenance, and replacements. Budgeting and planning for the year ahead will reduce operating costs and diminish the likelihood of costly emergency repairs. The ability to reduce operating costs substantially increases the value of the investment.

Managers address all aspects of the developer's relationship with tenants. Initially, managers should supervise moving in, making sure that everything proceeds smoothly for the new tenants. Effective managers maintain constant communication with the tenants so that any problems that might arise can be quickly resolved and so that the developer is not bothered by tenant complaints. If the developer does receive complaints directly from the tenants, the property manager is ineffective and should be replaced.

Operations run more smoothly when the management company is given authority to sign contracts, release funds for scheduled maintenance, and so on. The agreement between the developer and manager can specify dollar limits that the manager can spend before the property owner's approval is required, with the owner's approval necessary in the instance of anticipated expenditures.

IREM urges that funds belonging to the property owner and to the management firm be maintained in separate accounts.[12] The management firm should set up a trust account to protect the owner's funds and prevent any commingling between the funds required to operate the building. Audit reports should be prepared regularly (preferably, at least twice a year) so that the developer can verify rental collections, deposits, occupancies, vacancies, and expenses.

The manager is responsible for filling vacancies as they arise. High turnover rates mean require the manager to assume an active role in leasing.

Property managers receive 3 to 5 percent of the gross rent for all types of projects. Compensation does not include maintenance costs for the project, which the owner reimburses to the management firm.

Brokerage firms often offer to manage a project, and are sometimes as willing simply to break even or take a loss in their managerial role in return for the right to receive all the potential fees from leasing or sales generated by the project. Developers should be wary of these propositions. In general, brokers' skills do not match those of firms specializing in property management.

Lenders

Lenders have two major concerns: the developer and the project. Lenders first evaluate the developer's experience and credibility, seeking answers to questions such as: Has the developer defaulted on a note before? How much is the company worth? Will the developer guarantee the note?

Lenders then analyze the developer's project, assessing such issues as: Does the project make good economic sense? Is its location advantageous? Is the cost estimate accurate? If the improvements are already constructed, is the project sufficiently preleased?

Even experienced developers need to convince lenders about the economic viability of their projects. Beginning developers must sell themselves and their firm as well.

Working with Lenders

Construction lenders lend money to build and lease a project. Permanent lenders finance the project once it is built through long-term mortgages. To both sets of lenders, the developer's potential gain is much less important than their own potential loss. Lenders tend to be averse to risks and will examine the developer's ability to weather the risks that he/she is incurring—for instance, can the developer withstand national fluctuations in the interest rate during the development period. Lenders will be concerned about the developer's ability to get the necessary equity if rates go from 10 to 12 percent, causing the mortgage amount to be reduced.

Relying on their knowledge of the area, lenders weigh the developer's potential for success in a project against their own fees and exposure. With construction loans for over $15 million and often smaller amounts, lenders usually require the developer to hire a market feasibility consultant. Permanent lenders are concerned with a project's long-term success.

The amount of preleasing that lenders prefer depends, in general, on the type of project and whether the developer is seeking construction or permanent financing. Apartment buildings require little preleasing for either type of financing. Office projects usually must be at least one-third leased before a construction lender will fund the construction note and two-thirds leased to get a forward commitment from a permanent lender. Preleasing commitments for retail and industrial projects fluctuate dramatically with the market. Some developers and lenders believe that, in a strong market, preleasing space at bargain rates in the hope of receiving higher rents later is not wise.

Lenders study a project's tenant mix carefully. Strong anchor tenants with high credit ratings and a diversity of other tenants are desirable in both retail and office projects. Construction lenders are concerned about tenant mix because they depend on the permanent lender to take out the construction note. Thus, determining the criteria for tenant mix before leasing begins is a critical step. Special projects such as miniwarehouses and automarts are harder to finance because they incur above-average risk. Some lenders will finance them, although at a higher loan rate.

Lenders are also concerned about the developer's financial capability, managerial capability, and character:

- *Financial backing/equity.* Both permanent and construction lenders are interested in the sources of excess capital. Does the developer have enough resources to carry the project, or will the lender be expected to do so? Many developers have failed because they have not planned cash flow.
- *Managerial capability.* Does the developer understand real estate? In particular, does he/she know how to work with the city, with subcontractors, and so on? The developer must assemble a development team that satisfies these concerns.
- *Character.* Does the developer usually repay debts? Does the developer keep promises? Is he/she litigious? Lenders shy away from people who go to court every time a problem occurs.

To find a lender, developers can begin by making a list of prospects. They may want to start at the bottom of the list and practice their presentations before introducing the project to a lender with which they really want to work.

Developers should answer all of the lenders' concerns, realizing that the lenders' greatest fear is that they will be left with an uneconomic project. Developers must demonstrate their commitment, resolution, and professionalism. The more problems to which developers respond before lenders point them out, the better. Some lenders are very offended to be told that a developer is shopping for a loan—discretion is thus advisable.

Construction Lenders

Several different types of lenders finance construction loans, and the specific institution funding a project depends on the development team's level of experience and the type and size of the project. Most construction loans today have interest rates that float with prime.

Beginning developers should start their search for construction financing with a banker they know. They should ask for referrals and choose half a dozen potential lenders. They also may solicit the advice of other developers in the field.

Most of all, developers need to be aware of the lenders' concerns and try to address them before they become problems. They must stay in close touch with their lenders during construction. If a project is falling behind schedule or going over budget, its developer should inform his/her lender quickly and not allow the lender to hear the news from someone else.

Types of Institutions

The following types of financial institutions are potential sources of real estate loans.

Commercial banks. Commercial banks are a principal source of both construction and miniperm loans. They usually prefer to lend money for a short term—one to three years—through construction and leasing, at which time the construction lender is paid off by the permanent lender. For larger developers, commercial banks will grant miniperm loans up to five years. These loans were especially attractive during periods of high inflation when developers expected permanent mortgage rates to fall. One hundred percent financing is sometimes available on a superior project, although 70 to 80 percent financing is more common. In the tight money markets of the early 1990s, 60 to 65 percent loans are often the only financing available. Beginning developers are more likely to find a local bank than a larger national bank to fund their first few projects. After three or four successful projects, larger national banks, which tend to lend greater amounts of money, will show more interest. Banks are reluctant to participate in joint ventures but will take part in participating mortgages, which allow them to foreclose on a bad loan if they need to.

Savings and loan institutions. Similar to banks, S&Ls lend on smaller projects for the short term. Traditionally, they have been willing to participate in joint ventures with developers and to work with beginning developers. However, the S&L crisis of the late 1980s has made them much less of a factor in real estate lending.

In joint ventures, S&Ls often use development/management agreements and maintain title to the property in their name, so that removing a troubled developer is easy. Unlike banks, they are willing to take the risk of ownership liability to avoid the problems of removing an unsuccessful developer through foreclosure. S&Ls charge between 1.5 and 3 percent over the prime rate for financing, depending on the developer's experience. Beyond the note, they split the profits with the developer at some percentage, often 50/50. S&Ls have acted as both general and limited partners in the past. Smaller S&Ls more commonly act as limited partners on projects that cost between $1 million and $2 million. Because S&Ls prefer short-term commitments of three to five years, the parties should sign a written understanding before commitment and construction that explains how and when the project will be sold. Although S&Ls were a prime source—perhaps the major source—of financing for beginning developers in the 1980s, their role in joint ventures in the 1990s will be greatly diminished.

Insurance companies. These institutions fund large projects with long-term loans, typically 10 years, and provide both construction and permanent financing. Loans typically have fixed rates, unlike those from most construction lenders. Beginning developers with no track record probably will have difficulty attracting an insurance company to a project.

Pension funds. Recently, pension funds have made a great impact on real estate because of their sudden infusion of large amounts of money. Originally, they limited themselves to mortgages; more recently, they have begun financing construction loans. Generally, pension funds finance large projects undertaken by experienced developers. They usually supply funds for a long term at a fixed rate.

Foreign investors. Japanese financial and construction companies are new players in the U.S. financial market. They concentrate in larger cities and usually form joint ventures with their development partners. Japanese firms seek a developer to push the project through the approval stage while they fund and construct the project. Foreign investors from a number of other Pacific Rim and European countries are also active players—notably, Canada, The Netherlands, Britain, Germany, Hong Kong, Taiwan, and Korea. Although they prefer to buy developed properties, they also have been important sources of development capital, primarily for larger firms.

Syndications and real estate investment trusts (REITs). Syndications and REITs provide a way of carving up real estate ownership into small pieces that many people can afford. They have been used for raising both equity capital and mortgage financing for development projects. Both vehicles limit investor liability and provide pass-through tax benefits that flow directly to the investor, thus avoiding the additional layers of taxation associated with corporate ownership.

Prior to the 1986 Tax Reform Act, syndications were a primary source of equity capital for development. The Tax Reform Act eliminated many of the tax benefits that make syndications so attractive, and they have been in decline ever since. Similarly, REITs were important sources of capital in the early 1970s but have never fully recovered from the bankruptcies and poor performance that plagued many of them during and after the 1974 recession.

Neither syndications nor REITs are currently significant sources of capital for development. However, they are still active in certain markets and are likely to become more so as tax laws change and other sources of financing, such as S&Ls, decline.

Private investors and joint ventures. Probably the most common type of financial partner for a beginning developer is a private investor, who can be almost anyone. Usually, a private party puts up the necessary equity and is willing to sign for the construction note. Occasionally, a private investor will fund a project's total cost. The split for either deal is typically 50/50 of any profit or cash flow from the project. Because the investor is risking 100 percent of the cost for only 50 percent of the profit, he/she must have complete confidence in both the project and the developer's reputation before pursuing a deal. Beginning developers may have to give away more than 50 percent of the profit to raise capital, especially if the investor has personal liability on the construction note.

Working with Construction Lenders

Developers must recognize and address the varied concerns of construction lenders.

- *Design.* Design is of growing concern to lenders. The general trend is toward better-quality projects.
- *Permits.* Developers must make sure that all permits are in place so that the project is prey neither to delays nor to moratoriums. Even if the building permits are obtained, the entitlements (the rights to proceed) must be secured.[13]
- *Toxic waste.* Most lenders require a borrower to indemnify and hold them free and harmless of any liability resulting from toxic or hazardous waste located on the site.
- *Insurance.* The builder's risk and general liability insurance must be in place, and, usually, lenders are named as additional beneficiaries.
- *Capacity of developer.* If the developer is suddenly injured, lenders evaluate whether associates or partners can complete the project, or whether the lender must bring in another individual.
- *Credibility/integrity/cash.* Lenders analyze everything that may prevent the completion of the project.
- *Disbursements/inspections/lien releases.* Most lenders inspect the site monthly to verify requests for payments. If lenders have problems with lien releases, they write joint checks to the developer and contractor. A joint check must be endorsed by all payees and helps a lender to avoid paying twice for services or materials received under lien laws.
- *Standby commitments.* Standby commitments provide assurance to construction lenders that their loans will be paid off. Developers often secure standby commitments when permanent financing is unavailable. Normally, the standby commitment is never exercised because developers find permanent financing before their construction loans expire.

Standby commitments are available from certain banks, insurance companies, credit companies, and REITs. Fees for the standby commitment run 1 to 2 percent of the total loan amount each year that it is in force but unfunded. If the standby loan is actually funded, interest rates typically run 5 percent or more over the prime rate. Although standby commitments are expensive, they allow developers to proceed in situations where a construction lender demands some form of takeout commitment before it will fund the construction loan.

Permanent Lenders

Most of the lenders that provide construction financing also provide permanent financing. Permanent financing usually has fixed interest rates, and the term of notes tends to be limited to five or 10 years to reduce the lender's risk. At the end of that time, the note is renegotiated or another lender assumes it.

Most of the concerns listed previously for construction lenders apply equally to permanent lenders.

A developer should discover and address these concerns before the project is complete, especially if the project goes forward without a takeout commitment in place during construction. Permanent lenders look to the property more than to the borrower for assurance that they will not lose their investment. In other words, a strong and fully leased property owned by a financially weak party will obtain financing quicker than an unleased property with a strong owner.

To locate permanent lenders, a developer needs to find out which lenders in the local area fund projects of a size and type similar to the developer's project. A developer should thoroughly understand the lenders' criteria—the percentage that must be preleased, for example—and should compare annual percentage rates and look at total borrowing costs, including fees, points, and interest rates.

Once the loan agreement is operational, the developer must make prompt and punctual payments, maintain the project in good operating order, and keep all insurance and taxes up to date. If problems arise, the lender should be informed immediately. By being candid, a developer will gain respect and find it easier to obtain financing the next time.

Mortgage Bankers and Brokers

Both mortgage bankers and brokers help developers obtain financing for their projects. In some cases, the broker assists the developer in getting financing but does not have direct access to funds, whereas the banker has direct access to funds and usually services the loan as well. The relationship between the banker or broker and the client differs somewhat as well. The banker has a fiduciary relationship with the client, whereas the broker merely looks for the best loan for the client.

Some developers believe that using a mortgage broker adds an unnecessary middleman and that developers who already have a banker should start there to look for financing. Others say mortgage brokers are necessary because loans are becoming very complex in today's market and that a financial specialist, such as a broker, can help find more creative solutions to financing.

Every mortgage banker or broker is not suited for every project, however. Developers should not be afraid to ask brokers and bankers for their credentials and references and should find out which projects they have financed and how well versed they are in the real estate business. Developers must also question how a prospective lender's specific system works: How do the developer and contractor request draws? Will the lender allow a land draw upfront? How often will the lender visit the site or inspect a completed building? How and when are interest, points, and origination fees paid? At the same time, developers can indicate their readiness to use a lender's services again if they prove to be satisfactory this time. Eventually, developers may want to approach lenders with the idea of starting a long-term relationship.

Mortgage brokers' fees vary. For residential for-sale housing, the standard fee is 1 percent of the loan amount. Commercial mortgage brokers and bankers likewise usually charge about 1 percent of the loan amount. This fee is in addition to points, the application fee, the appraisal fee, and all of the other standard costs of a loan. The computation of annual percentage rates is usually a good way to compare loans if the developer does not intend to pay back the note early.

Conclusion

Development is a team effort. The lenders, contractors, professional consultants, and other specialists described in this chapter represent the major players with whom developers must be familiar, but they are not the only ones. As development becomes increasingly complex, other talents and specialties must be found. For example, environmental and political consultants were only rarely employed as recently as five years ago. Today, they are commonly part of the development team.

Successful development depends on the developer's ability to manage the many participants in the development process. He/she must be able to recognize quality work and must know when to ask questions, who to ask, and what to ask. The developer must strike a delicate balance between trust in the decisions of the players on the team and constant vigilance. If mistakes are made, no matter who made them, the developer is ultimately responsible. Even if the developer is not at fault, he/she invariably ends up paying for the mistakes—either directly or indirectly through delay and higher interest costs.

Notes

1. This point was made during a lecture at Southern Methodist University by Bill Parsons, president, Cambridge Companies, Dallas, Texas, in 1986.

2. Richard Hardy, "Strategic Planning in Development Firms," *The Journal of Real Estate Development*, vol.1, no. 4, Spring 1986.

3. Ibid., p. 29.

4. This information taken from Peter Inman, senior vice president, development and management, The Wolff Company, Irvine, California.

5. This list taken from Diane R. Suchman, *Managing a Development Company* (Washington, D.C.: ULI–the Urban Land Institute, 1987), pp. 2–3.

6. Ibid., p. 3.

7. Hardy, "Strategic Planning in Development Firms," p. 35.

8. Small homebuilding firms and industrial developers also tend to be organized by function, because the nature of their business is repetition. Repetition, especially in leasing and construction, lends itself to more functional organization, in which activities are more specialized and often require less highly trained workers.

9. USC Lusk Center for Real Estate Development, Spring Retreat, Desert Hot Springs, 1989. O'Donnell is a trustee of ULI–the Urban Land Institute.

10. See also Kenneth R. Andrews, *The Concept of Corporate Strategy* (Homewood, Illinois: Richard D. Irwin, 1980); Bruce D. Henderson, *Henderson on Corporate Strategy* (Cambridge, Massachusetts: Abt Books, 1979); and Kenichi Ohmae, *The Mind of the Strategist* (New York: Penguin Books, 1982).

11. Emanuel Harper, "Negotiating Architectural Contracts," *Real Estate Review*, Summer 1987, pp. 65–74; and Fall 1987, pp. 50–56.

12. Institute of Real Estate Management, *Managing the Office Building*, rev. ed. (Chicago: author, 1986).

13. In some states, such as California and Hawaii, construction has been halted under building moratoriums after building permits have been obtained but before significant construction (in particular, structural framing) has been completed.

Chapter 3

Land Development

Introduction

The subdivision process is the principal mechanism by which cities are developed. Technically, "subdivision" describes the legal and physical steps that a developer must take in order to convert raw land into developed land. These steps, which may apply to tracts of any size intended for any use, are examined in this chapter in the context of the development of small residential subdivisions.[1]

Subdivision is a vital part of a city's growth. It determines a city's appearance, the segregation or mixture of its land uses, and, most importantly, its urban infrastructure—namely, its roads and systems for drainage, water, sewer, roads, electricity, telephone, and gas.

Many current subdivision regulations have evolved because earlier regulations did not provide adequate streets, utilities, setbacks, and development densities to create a suitable living environment. Developers have often led the way toward better regulation, their projects demonstrating how improved standards lead to superior development patterns.

Each decade has brought new problems and concerns that have changed the land development regulatory process. Developers today must be more mindful than ever of the impact that their projects may have on local communities. Even when their projects conform to existing zoning requirements, developers are finding that they must justify their projects to local communities in terms of beneficial (or at least not adverse) impacts on the environment, traffic, tax base, and schools, parks, and other public facilities. Thus, in the broader sphere of urban development, developers must understand the complex relationships that tie the private and the public sectors together.

Subdividing Land

The subdivision process by which land is transformed from a raw to a developed state has three stages: first, raw land; second, semideveloped land, usually divided into 20- to 100-acre tracts, with roads and utilities extended to the edge of the property; and, third, developed or "subdivided" land, platted into individual homesites and five- to 10-acre commercial parcels ready for building. Figure 3-1 shows the structure of the land conversion industry and the roles of the various players.

The process of converting raw land to semideveloped land differs from region to region, depending on the pattern of landownership, the capacity of local developers and financial institutions, and the institutional mechanisms for providing roads and utilities. To ease the

3-1 The Structure of the Land Conversion Industry and the Role of the Predeveloper

	Types of Land Investors				
	Buyer of Raw Land	Land Speculator	Predeveloper	Land Developer	Builder/End User
Major Function	Begins conversion	Holds the property waiting for growth to approach	Analyzes market and plans development; clears all regulatory hurdles	Installs utilities; completes subdividing program	Builds structures for sale, rent, or own use; may employ general contractor
Typical Financing	Noninstitutional		May attract institution Investment on selective basis	May be able to obtain construction loans and long-term real estate investors	
Typically Sells To	Land speculator	Other speculators. Last in line sell to some type of developer	Land developer or end user	Other (smaller) builders or end users	
Typical Length of Tenure	10+ years	8–10 years	2–5 years	1+ years	Indeterminate

Source: Alan Rabinowitz, *Land Investment and the Predevelopment Process* (New York: Quorum Books, 1988), p. 26.

conversion process, states such as California and Texas rely heavily on special districts created to finance utility services. Where such vehicles do not exist, developers either must wait for the community or utility company to furnish utility service or must pay for the extension of roads and utility lines themselves.

The conversion of raw land to semideveloped land tends to be undertaken by larger developers. Such developers typically work with 500- to 1,000-acre tracts of land, which they subdivide into smaller 20- to 100-acre parcels. They provide the major infrastructure, including arterial roads, utilities, and drainage systems for the smaller parcels so that they can subsequently be subdivided into lots that are ready for building.

Where small farms exist at the urban fringe, the developer may skip the second stage and convert the raw land directly into subdivided lots. Normally, however, the conversion process from raw to semideveloped land occurs beyond the existing urban fringe.

Land does not become available for development in a smooth pattern. Farmers, estate owners, and other landholders often sell for reasons such as a death or retirement and not because a buyer has made an attractive offer.[2] Consequently, land rarely becomes developable in large, continuous tracts. Leapfrog development, or "sprawl," is the inevitable result.

Although planners and others have criticized urban sprawl as the costly and unsightly result of unplanned development, recent researchers have found that sprawl is a natural result of the growth process.[3] A major criticism of sprawl is that it leads to uniformly lower densities and causes a city to spread out. In fact, however, the land parcels that are passed over during the first wave of development tend to be developed later, at higher densities. Attempts to prevent leapfrog development by withholding zoning permits or prohibiting utility installation may lead to lower densities overall.

Because developers are the central players in the conversion of raw land to developed land, they must understand the dynamics of the urban land market—that is, how the forces of urban growth and housing demand will be affected by various forms of regulation.

Historically, developers assumed that they had the right to develop land as long as they met the restrictions imposed by zoning and other land use regulations. This presumption of "development rights" is rapidly dissolving. Even where developers' projects conform to existing zoning, development rights may be subject to reduction, depending on the attitudes of neighboring homeowners and the political environment. The likelihood of obtaining necessary approvals in a timely fashion is one of the major risks that developers must evaluate before committing themselves to a project. Developers must be well versed in local politics and have an abundance of personal alliances, since even relatively problem-free tracts will require a significant amount of government processing.

The land available for development is constrained by many factors, including ownership patterns, government regulations, site conditions, and the availability of infrastructure.

Many current trends, such as the control of growth through caps on building permits, are often contrary to the best interests of a community. These trends are politically popular with voters who associate the problems of growth with overly rapid development. However, the rationing of building permits and other approaches that artificially constrain supply are not the best solutions to such problems because they adversely affect virtually everyone who does not already own his/her "dream home" in the community. Developers must become more involved in the regulatory decision-making process and must be prepared to help educate their communities. They must work with community leaders to develop constructive approaches that deal with the problems of growth without causing unintended side effects such as skyrocketing housing prices.

Land Development versus Building Development

This chapter focuses on small-scale land development, typically involving 20 to 50 acres. Although the techniques described here apply to any form of land development, beginning developers are most likely to become involved with one of three product types: single-family residential subdivisions; planned unit subdivisions; and small mixed-use subdivisions. Industrial/office park development, which is also a popular form of land development, is discussed in chapter 6.

Many developers engage in both land development and building development (houses, apartments, warehouses, and so forth). When they perform both activities on the same tract, they often view the two activities as a single project. Except where very small tracts are involved, this is a mistake. Land development and building development are distinct businesses and each should be analyzed on its own merits.

Many considerations arise when a developer is in charge of both land and building development on the same property. For instance, other builders will be reluctant to buy any excess land because of the competition from the developer's own building activities, especially in light of the developer's cost advantage. Selling land to other builders may be more difficult if lots are available in other subdivisions in the area. The problem of building on some lots and selling others can be alleviated by bringing in builders that will target their product to a different segment of the market.

Project Feasibility

Although development opportunities exist for many different types of land, beginning land developers are well advised to search for comparatively problem-free tracts of land—land that is already served by utilities and is, or is likely to be, appropriately zoned. Although raw land may be available, the resources and the time required to bring utilities to a tract and to obtain the necessary public approvals generally go beyond the capabilities of beginning developers. The beginners' time and money are better spent building a track record of completed, successful smaller projects.

Market Analysis before Site Selection

Market analysis occurs at two separate times—before site selection and after site selection. The objective of market analysis before site selection is to identify the holes in the marketplace. Large developers have the luxury of investigating a number of markets to select the most competitive product type and location. Beginning developers have neither the time nor the resources required to embark upon such an exploration. In addition, they usually want to remain close to home. If possible, their projects should be near enough for them to keep a close watch over on-site progress. Also, local planning bodies and regulatory agencies tend to view local developers more favorably than out-of-towners, thereby giving these developers the "home-town advantage."

This it not to say that more distant opportunities should be overlooked automatically. Unique opportunities can arise anywhere. Nevertheless, beginning developers have enough difficulties to overcome without the additional handicaps of distance and unfamiliarity with local officials and building practices.

A developer's primary market decisions concern the project's use, location, and size. If a developer has no preference for a specific use, then he/she must analyze each segment of the market—residential, industrial, commercial, or mixed-use. Real estate markets are highly segmented, and a developer cannot infer from the fact that because, say, residential, is in demand, retail is also in demand.

If the developer has already identified the land use for which excess demand exists, the purpose of the market analysis is to identify the particular market segment (for instance, mid-priced, custom-built, single-family houses) and the location where the demand is greatest. The developer can pay a market research firm to do the analysis, but many developers prefer to do their own research at this stage.

The major sources of information are lenders, brokers, and, especially, builders to which the land developer will sell the developed sites. Developers can obtain a wealth of information at little cost, although the effort will take time and energy. Major local lenders, market research firms, and brokers often publish quarterly or annual reports for apartments, office space, single-family houses, and industrial space. Developers should identify those firms that specialize in building their proposed product types and then should discuss their intentions with them. Since developers and homebuilders are prospective clients, those firms will usually be eager to provide assistance.

The most important questions to which developers want answers concern the market for the proposed product type:

- Where are the hot areas or parts of town?
- What are the hot segments of the market?
- If a builder owned land in that area, what would he/she build?
- For what types of building are lenders giving loans?
- For what types of building are lenders not giving loans?
- What physical features and amenities are especially popular?
- Who else is developing in a particular area? What are they building? How many units (or square feet) are planned for the future?
- How many units are they selling per month?
- Who are the main builders?
- What are the standard terms that builders are using to buy lots?

Some major homebuilders project the annual number of units needed by price category throughout their metropolitan area.[4] They break down the number of houses sold in each quadrant of the city, grouped by $10,000 intervals. For example, suppose they project that 56 percent of all new houses will be sold in the western part of town and that 75 percent of the houses will be priced under $100,000. If the total projected demand for the city is, say, 5,000 houses in 1988, the demand for houses costing under $100,000 in the western section of town would be 2,100 units (560 times 75 percent times 5,000).

After estimating demand, developers should next ask themselves how much of that demand they can capture? The answer depends on the number of competitors that are building in the quadrant and the number of subdivisions in which they are building. Suppose a given area contains 3,000 lots in 20 subdivisions. If each of four developers has five of the subdivisions, each developer's pro-rata share of the market capture would be 25 percent, or 525 lots (25 percent times 2,100). Many developers use a weighting scheme to allocate more lots to subdivisions that possess better amenities, terrain, or management. They also look at historical absorption rates by different subdivisions and developers. Depending on the weights, the analysis will indicate that the developers should capture more or less than their pro-rata share. If they anticipate selling twice their pro-rata share, however, then the other developers must, theoretically, lose market share by the same amount. This, though, is unrealistic since the developers who lose sales will cut prices until they regain their share.

The demand for finished lots depends on the demand for houses—not just for any houses, but for houses in the price range that justifies the lot price. If demand for those houses declines, so will the demand for lots. Similarly, if the demand for industrial space declines, so will the demand for industrial building sites. Land developers make two common mistakes. The first mistake is to forget that their product is an intermediate good—a good that is used in producing an end product. The second mistake is to allocate too much land to office and retail use because those uses command higher sales prices. Developers tend to forget that higher-priced uses generally have slower absorption rates. Also, land absorption for higher-density projects takes longer, by definition, than does land absorption for lower-density projects, since more units must be sold to absorb each acre of land.

The ratio of lot price to house price has risen steadily over the last 30 years. Thirty years ago, lot cost rarely accounted for more than 15 percent of total house price. Today, it may vary from 15 to 50 percent. Higher ratios, from 30 to 50 percent, are found in areas in which land costs are high, such as infill sites in high-income suburbs. A general rule of thumb is that builders should pay approximately 20 percent of the finished house price for the lot. Thus, if they build houses that sell for $100,000, they can afford to pay $20,000 for the lot. The developer, however, should not rely on rules of thumb, but, rather, should carefully investigate local market conditions.

Suppose the absorption rate is 10 units per month for $100,000 houses, as compared to 15 units per month for $80,000 houses. Builders of the $100,000 houses will pay

$20,000 per lot rather than $16,000 per lot for the smaller houses. If developers proceed with their projects under the assumption that they can sell $20,000 lots, they may be in trouble if the market turns out to favor the smaller houses. Even if they are willing to accept the lower sales price of $16,000 per lot, their lenders may set loan covenants that prevent the sale.[5]

Thus, developers' assessments of the market determine where they should look for land and how much they can afford to pay for it. Market research is a critical first step, not only for selecting a site but also for determining the types of builders that should be approached. Even while still looking for sites, developers can be generating interest among builders.

Site Selection and Acquisition

After defining the target market, developers must look for a site. Beginning developers face a number of limitations that can be overcome only by extra work. Some tips:

- choose a manageable area for the search,
- set an appropriate time frame for investigating conditions, and
- do not depend exclusively on brokers to find sites.

Because they lack the reputation and contacts of experienced developers, beginning developers are less likely to hear about deals firsthand. Deals that have been "on the street" are not necessarily bad deals, however. Landowners may take time to realize the true value of their property. Or, developers may pass on deals for other reasons—for instance, the site may be too small or otherwise inappropriate for the use that the developers had in mind.

In addition to working with a network of brokers, developers should also talk to landowners whose land is not currently for sale. Direct contact may generate a deal. It can also lead to a possible joint venture or favorable terms of purchase.

Site Evaluation

The relative importance of various factors of subdivision development depends on the end user of the subdivided lots. The major site evaluation factors are summarized in feature box 3-2, and greater detail regarding site evaluation for residential development can be found in chapter 4.

3-2 Site Evaluation Factors

Market Area and Competition

Location and Neighborhood:

- proximity to key locations in metropolitan area,
- quality of surrounding environment,
- existing housing/other structures,
- schools and churches,
- parks and recreational facilities,
- amenities,
- shopping,
- public improvements.

Size and Shape

Accessibility and Visibility

Site Conditions:

- slopes,
- vegetation,
- grading or fill required to build,
- existing structures,
- hydrology and drainage patterns,
- toxic wastes,
- soil properties,
- wildlife/endangered species,
- sensitive land.

Legal Constraints:

- utility easements,
- private easements,
- deed restrictions,
- covenants that run with the land.

Utilities:

- water,
- sewer,
- electricity,
- gas,
- telephone,
- cable television.

Zoning and Regulatory Environment:

- development climate,
- exactions,
- impact fees,
- future takings,
- future road widenings,
- approvals needed,
- citizen participation/opposition,
- approval process.

More than 1,000 items should be checked before buying a site.[6] Among the more important items, the developer should:

- Make sure that all easements are plotted on a map. Any easement problems should be cleared up, and any purchase arrangements for easements should be made, before closing.
- Check Federal Housing Authority (FHA) requirements concerning width of roads, culs-de-sac, and other design requirements.
- Make sure that no one is likely to delay or stop the sale.
- Make sure that utilities such as water, sewer, gas, electricity, telephone, and cable television are available.
- Find out if all necessary development approvals will be granted.
- Make sure that the builders will be able to obtain building permits.
- Check for drainage problems, and ascertain the level of the water table, which will affect sewer lines, septic tanks, and foundations.
- Check for environmental problems, especially if a lake, pond, or swamp lies on the land. Avoid wetlands—they usually involve too much time-consuming red tape.
- Beware of sulfates in the soil that eat away concrete and masonry.
- Check for radon, a harmful derivative of uranium that is present in many areas.
- Check earthquake maps to make sure that faults do not cross the land.
- Check flood insurance/floodplain maps.
- Check historical aerial photos that may show evidence of toxic-waste problems such as storage tanks on the site.
- Check for landfill sites close by—methane gas could cause explosions.
- Check to see that power lines are not hazardous.
- Look for smoke, fumes, or odors. Check land at all times of the day.
- Always walk the land.

Site Acquisition

In land development, as in other forms of development, purchasing a site with a three-stage contract is customary. The three stages are: first, a free-look period; second, a period during which earnest money is forfeitable; and third, closing. Most purchasers try to get as much time as they can to close with as little money at risk as possible. For sellers, the reverse is true. Sellers want the closing to occur as quickly as possible with as much forfeitable earnest money at stake as possible. The terms depend very much on the state of the market.

In slow markets, one can usually obtain favorable terms of purchase. With fewer buyers than sellers, the sellers are more willing to give a potential purchaser more time to investigate their property without requiring hard earnest money. In a hot market, sellers are less afraid of losing a deal and are more concerned about tying up their property when another buyer may be just around the

While an attractive setting and good highway access are obvious advantages, hundreds of additional factors and details must be evaluated before acquiring a site.

■ 3-3 Summary of Home Builder Press's *Land Buying Checklist* by Ralph M. Lewis

Purchasing Agreement Data: Ownership information, environmental statements, improvements, buildable area, price, real estate agent, seller financing, escrow agent and fees, and deposits needed.

Condition of Title: Title report, lawsuits, existing loans, taxes, judgments or mechanic's liens, building restrictions, assessments, easements, crops, and other agreements.

Physical Aspects: Topography, drainage, survey, special zones, environmental conditions (including soils, flood areas, wetlands, toxic or hazardous waste, vegetation, seismic faults, adjoining land), views, access, and any other adverse conditions.

Utility Availability: Gas, electric, water, wells, sewer, telephone, cable television, street lights, joint trenching, storm drainage, police, fire, trash collection, utility costs.

Entitlements: Governing body, moratoriums, ordinances, zoning, redevelopment area, condemnations, special assessments, requirements, and reports, subdivision approval timetable.

Development Costs: All on-site and off-site costs, all building and subdivision fees, overhead, refundable costs, and cost per lot.

Market Area and Proposed Product: Product type, target markets, competition, resale market, neighborhood, commercial and industrial developments, military and government installations, employment, schools, shopping, transportation, day care, advice of experts.

Financial Projections, Resale Market, and Postclosing Checklist.

Source: Ralph M. Lewis, *Land Buying Checklist* (Washington, D.C.: Home Builder Press, National Association of Home Builders, 1990).

corner. Developers, of course, must respond to the market conditions accordingly.

In addition, if the site is held by numerous owners, the progression of the project is further complicated because all of the necessary parcels must first be acquired. Land assembly can be a tricky business and usually requires sophisticated negotiation and acquisition techniques to ensure that the owner of the last or other key parcels does not insist on an exorbitantly high sales price.

The terms of acquisition set the stage for everything else. When buying land, developers are chiefly concerned about whether or not they can build what they want to build and if they have time to check out title, physical conditions, utilities, market, financing, economics, and design feasibility.

To overcome the difficulties and potential setbacks of inexperience, a beginning developer must look harder—do more firsthand research and dig deeper; narrow the search to a particular area and establish strong brokerage contacts there; and find out about sites that are not yet on the market or that require too much extra work to interest larger developers. The extra work should be discounted in the price.

Because of the complications associated with land development, developers should always use an attorney during land acquisition, no matter how straightforward a transaction might appear to be.

Contingencies. Contingencies in the land purchase contract refer to events that must occur before the earnest money "goes hard" and before the closing takes place. Beginning developers often make the mistake of including many unnecessary contingency clauses that only complicate the negotiations. One or two blanket clauses will suffice. The most all-encompassing clause is one that makes the sale "subject to obtaining financing."

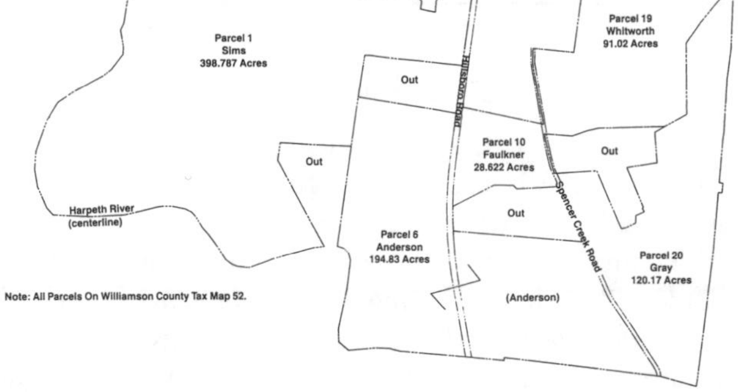

At the 836-acre Fieldstone Farms in Franklin, Tennessee, four outparcels still exist within the overall site made up of six acquired parcels.

3-4 Steps for Site Acquisition

Prior to Offer

1. Verify that a market for the property type exists.
2. Determine the price you can pay by running preliminary financial pro formas.
3. Determine whether or not the seller can sell the property for the price you want to pay. (Determine what the seller paid for the property and outstanding mortgages on the property.)
4. Find out why the seller is selling the property. (Is the sale necessary, or can the seller wait for a better price?)
5. Check the market for comparable properties in the area and their prices.

Offer

1. Ask for at least 60 days' due diligence. If a broker brought the developer the deal, the developer might expect that four or five other developers were also contacted by the broker, and, therefore, a 60-day due diligence may not be acceptable to the seller.
2. Place a refundable deposit, or "earnest money."
3. Request specific due diligence that must be provided by the seller, such as existing soils reports, hazardous-waste clearances, preliminary design and engineering studies, preapproved plans, and agency approvals.

Due Diligence

1. If a zoning change must be made for the project, ask for closing to be contingent on zoning approvals—if it is not approved, the earnest money is refunded. Be sure to state in the offer exactly what constitutes approval, such as:
   - general plan approval;
   - zoning approval;
   - conditional use permits, or variances;
   - development agreements;
   - tentative tract or parcel map;
   - final tract or parcel map;
   - grading plan approval;
   - site plan approval;
   - design approval; and
   - building permits.
2. Other questions to answer include the following:
   - Can good title be secured?
   - How much of the site is buildable? What are the easements, slopes, soils, floodplain, drainage, and geological conditions?
   - Can you build what you want to? How many units, of what size and at what density, can be built? Can parking and amenities be built?
   - Can financing be obtained?
3. Items to accomplish before closing on the land are:
   - preliminary design drawings;
   - mortgage package preparation;
   - commitment from permanent lenders;
   - commitment from construction lenders;
   - receipt of regulatory approvals, or assurances that they can be obtained; and
   - selection of contractor and property manager (who should assist in designing the project).
4. If more time is needed, ask the seller for it. If the seller refuses, ask for the deposit money back, and pull out of the deal.

Closing

1. This typically occurs 60 days after due diligence is complete, although longer periods can often be negotiated.
2. Closing can be made dependent on a variety of factors, including the availability of financing and the removal of toxic wastes.

If, for whatever reason, financing is not available, then earnest money is returned. Another encompassing clause is "subject to buyer's acceptance of feasibility studies." The contract may spell out the feasibility studies to include soils, title, marketing, site planning, and economic feasibility. As long as the clause gives the buyer discretion to approve the reports, it effectively gives the buyer a way out of the contract.

Most sellers will not give a blanket contingency for more than 30 to 60 days. Sophisticated sellers understand that such clauses amount to a free-look period. Local market conditions determine whether or not sellers will give buyers a free look; in hot markets they will not.

In areas where extensive public approvals make the allowable building density uncertain, some developers purchase sites on the basis of price per residential unit and/or buildable square foot. An important contingency in the purchase agreement is that the seller must support the developer in obtaining zoning and other necessary approvals. The seller's incentive to give this support is that the price will depend on the size of the building that is approved. For example, if the price is $30 per buildable square foot and permission is given to build 100,000 square feet on the site, then the purchase price would be $3 million. If approval for only 75,000 square feet is given, the price would be $2.25 million.

No standard amount of earnest money is required, but, as a general rule of thumb, 3 to 5 percent of the purchase price is required for a 90- to 120-day closing. Since the earnest money theoretically compensates the seller for holding his/her property off the market, the earnest money usually bears some relation to the seller's holding cost. Land financing is expensive—usually at least two points (2 percent) over prime. Suppose the prime rate is 10 percent. If land financing is 12 percent per annum, then a four-month closing would suggest holding costs of 4 percent (4/12 times 12 percent). Thus, a 4 percent earnest money deposit would compensate the seller for holding the property off the market. In most land purchase contracts, the earnest money "goes hard" (is forfeitable) after the free-look period.

Every developer has at least one horror story to tell concerning a land purchase. Most stories relate to easements, toxic wastes, title, or other problems that showed up after closing. In hot markets, sellers may sometimes try to get out of a sale because they have received a higher offer. Although each state has its own property law, buyers generally control a purchase contract as long as they strictly observe its terms. Most contracts state that a clause is waived if the buyer does not raise concerns in writing before the expiration date of the clause or contingency. However, if the clause (such as buyer's approval of title reports) is not automatically waived according to the contract, the seller may argue that the buyer failed to perform in a timely fashion and, therefore, that the contract is null and void. If the seller tries to get out of the contract before the expiration date, the threat of *lis pendens*, or pending litigation, usually is sufficient to bring the seller back to the table. Pending litigation makes it very difficult to sell the property to anyone else and can tie up a property for as long as five years.

Release provisions. One of the most important areas of negotiation for land development concerns the release provisions of seller financing (also called "land note" or "purchase-money note"). Release provisions refer to the process by which developers remove individual parcels within larger tracts from the sellers' land notes. Release provisions also are a major part of the negotiation with the developers' lenders (discussed in the financing section of this chapter).

Lenders require a first lien on developers' property. Lien priorities are determined strictly by the date that a mortgage is created. Thus, land notes automatically have first lien position, unless sellers specifically subordinate land notes to land development loans. Developers must "release" land from the land note before they can obtain financing from lenders. Even if developers finance development costs out of their own pockets, land must be released from the land note in order to deliver clear title to builders or other buyers of the lots. Buyers will need clear title before they can obtain construction financing. However, buyers may view land note financing as a plus during the predevelopment period before they take down the construction loan, as long as they have the option of paying it off at any time.

The land sellers' main concern is that they will be left holding a note with inadequate underlying security. They want strict release provisions that require the developer to pay down much more on the land note than the actual value of the land to be released. This would leave more land as security for the unpaid portion of the note. The developer's objective, on the other hand, is to achieve maximum flexibility in the acreage and location of land that he/she wants to release. Ideally, the developer wants to be able to release the maximum amount of land for the minimum amount of money.

Jack Willome, president of RAYCO, Inc., in San Antonio, Texas, uses the following clause in purchase contracts whenever possible: "The note is prepayable from time to time without penalty; all prepayments are credited toward the next principal installments coming due."[7] Suppose a developer purchases 100 acres for $1 million, with an eight-year land note for $800,000, or $8,000 per acre. The note is amortized at the rate of $100,000 per year. Suppose he/she also negotiates a partial release provision (the clause that allows a developer to release part of the property from the note) that calls for a payment of $12,000 per acre. If the developer wants to sell 25 acres to a builder, then he/she must pay the seller $300,000 (25 times $12,000) to release the land. Without the above language, the developer's $300,000 payment reduces the seller's note from $800,000 to $500,000. Instead of reducing the note principal balance immediately, the special language permits the developer to pay interest only on the note for the next three years. The clause "all prepayments are credited toward the next principal installments coming due" means that the next three principal installments are paid by the $300,000 payment but that repayment of the note is not accelerated. The developer will not have to make another principal payment for three years. Without the language in the clause, the seller would probably construe that the $300,000 payment simply shortens the remaining life of the note from eight to five years. The developer, of course, wants the note to run as long as possible so that he/she will not be required to sell the land prematurely or to find other financing sources to pay off the land note.

Developers never want to release more land from the note than is necessary at any one time. Thus, they should try to avoid release provisions that call for releasing land in strips or contiguous properties.[8] The release requirements should not start at one point on the property and then move in strips across the property to the other end. If releases must occur on contiguous properties, developers would be forced to release the entire property in order to develop or sell a tract at the other end. Sellers will rightfully be concerned if developers can release the most valuable frontage land and then abandon the rest of the project. To get around this problem, the release provision can assign values to parcels or strips within the property that reflect the market values. Thus, frontage land may have a release price that is significantly higher than that for nonfrontage land. Alternatively, the provision may call for the developers to release two acres of nonfrontage land for every acre released from the frontage—defined as a band within, say, 300 feet of the main road.

Key Points of a Purchase Contract

Don Mackie, managing partner of Mill Creek Properties, Salado, Texas, has summarized some of the key elements of a land purchase to which he was a party.[9] These clauses and provisions should be included as part of the initial purchase contract so that no later renegotiation with the seller will be necessary.

- *Supplementary note procedure.* This will allow the sale of subparcels (parcels within the original tract) to builders and other developers on terms without paying off the underlying first lien. This provision, which must be specifically negotiated, allows the developer to pass the seller financing on to the builders through a "supplementary note." This note gives the builders more time before they need to pay the full lot cost. Nevertheless, unless the seller is willing to subordinate the seller financing, the supplementary note has first lien position. This means that the builders who purchase the subparcels must pay off the note before they can obtain construction financing, because construction lenders also require a first lien position. In fact, builders usually pay off the supplementary note with the first draw under the construction note.
- *Out-of sequence releases.* This clause satisfies the developer's need to release certain parcels out of sequence for major utility or amenity facilities.
- *Joinder and subordination.* This clause provides for the seller to join in any applications for government approvals made by the developer within 30 days. It also provides for the seller's subordination agreements, required by any government authority for the filing of subdivision maps or street dedications.
- *Subordination of subparcels.* Most sellers are unlikely to allow subordination of their note to development lenders. However, they may be willing to allow subordination on one or two subparcels. This can help the developer obtain the development loan without paying off the land note.
- *Seller's "comfort language."* The seller is not required to execute any documents until he/she has approved the purchaser's general land use plan.
- *Ability to extend closing.* This clause permits the purchaser to extend the closing by 30 or 60 days by paying additional earnest money.
- *Letters of credit as earnest money.* The developer can greatly reduce upfront cash requirements if the seller will accept letters of credit as earnest money. Letters of credit (LCs) can be cashed by the seller on a certain date or should certain events occur, such as a purchaser's failure to close. An example of this type of clause might be: "Purchaser may extend the closing for 60 days by depositing an additional $50,000 letter of credit as additional escrow deposit."
- *Property taxes.* Many municipalities and counties have "open space" or "agricultural land" holding categories that give the owner a reduction in taxes. When the land is developed, the owner must repay the tax savings for the previous three or five years, which can amount to a major unexpected cost to the developer if he/she does not provide for it in the purchase agreement. An example of such a provision is: "Seller agrees to pay all *ad valorem* tax assessments or penalties assessed for any period prior to the closing, due to any change in ownership or usage of the property."
- *Title insurance.* The seller usually (though not always) pays the title insurance policy. However, many title insurance policies have standard exception clauses, such as a survey exception.[10] The party responsible for paying the insurance premium for deleting these exceptions is subject to negotiation.
- *Seller's remedy.* If the purchaser defaults, the seller's sole remedy is to receive the escrow deposit as liquidated damages. This clause prevents the seller from pursuing the purchaser for more money if the sale falls through.

The above clauses constitute only a small fraction of all of those included in a standard purchase contract. They are highlighted here because they represent items that the purchaser should try to negotiate with the seller. Many sophisticated developers use a specially prepared "standard form" that includes such clauses. However, sophisticated sellers will insist on using their own standard forms. In that case, these clauses will probably have to be added. The assistance of an experienced real estate attorney should always be sought in the preparation of the purchase contract.

3-5 Tips for Land Acquisition

Conversations with a variety of successful developers (Richard Gleitman, Jona Goldrich, Ralph Lewis, and David Ball)[a] have produced a number of useful tips regarding land acquisition.

- Make sure that the owner is really willing to sell the land. One developer found that his bid for a site condemned by a local school district was being used only for the owner's negotiations with the school district over condemnation price.
- Do not let the seller dictate the use of the property after the sale.
- Beware of fabricated appraisals of sites that have not been physically analyzed for hazardous or other undesirable conditions.
- Where rezoning is necessary, attempt to buy the land on a per-unit basis if possible so that the landowner has an incentive to help you obtain increased densities.
- If you will need a conditional use permit or variance, ask the current owner to sign a waiver to allow you to act as his/her agent in dealing with the city during the escrow period.
- If you obtain seller financing, make sure that the seller frees up some of the land so that you can build on it. You need to be able to give the construction lender a first lien on the land.
- In some states, such as California, you should use a deed of trust for purchase money mortgages so that the seller cannot claim a deficiency judgment against you if you default.
- Concerning "no-waste" clauses, be sure to read the fine print on the trust deed form because you may not be able to remove trees or buildings on the property until the note is paid off.
- Make sure you select a title company that is strong enough to back you up if you need to defend a lawsuit involving title. Some nationwide title companies enfranchise their local offices separately so that you do not have the backing of the national company.
- Make sure that the seller's warranties survive the close of escrow.
- Beware of broker commissions. A broker who casually mentions a property as you drive by it may try to collect a commission if you later buy it.

[a]Richard Gleitman is president of R.J. Investments Associates, Sherman Oaks, California. Jona Goldrich is president of Goldrich and Kest Industries, Culver City, California. Ralph Lewis is chairman of Lewis Homes, Upland, California. David Ball is vice president of Arnel Development, Costa Mesa, California.

Market Analysis after Site Selection

After tying up a site, the developer should reanalyze the target market. Special features of the specific site may indicate a different market from the one identified during the market analysis undertaken before the site selection.

The reanalysis should concentrate on location, neighborhood, and amenities. For example, suppose a developer's initial target market is buyers of semicustom houses—individually designed houses that are built on a speculative basis and are usually sold during, or shortly after, construction—selling from $130,000 to $150,000. If the neighboring subdivision contains tract-homes selling for less than $100,000, the developer may have trouble marketing a more upscale product, even if other factors are favorable. Alternatively, if a developer finds a site adjacent to a new subdivision where homebuilders are targeting the same market, he/she may decide to compete with them directly. In fact, the builders may wish to extend construction to the developer's subdivision when they run out of lots next door. On the other hand, if the builders already are committed to a two- or three-year building program next door, the developer may prefer to alter his/her target market.

The market analysis at this stage serves three purposes. It helps the developer to plan by determining the specific target market and, therefore, the size and shape of lots, amenities, and other fundamental aspects; obtain a loan and supply the appropriate documentation; and attract builders and subdevelopers.

Unless a subdivision is very small, or the developer has preselected the builders, a local market research firm that specializes in subdivision development should be hired. The market research firm should already have a database covering all of the competing subdivisions. From its analysis of the market potential of the developer's site, the market research firm should be able to assist the developer in determining the best market for the lots. From a land development perspective, the market report should provide the total number of lots that the developer can sell per month, grouped by lot size and price range. The report should document total housing demand for the metropolitan area and, from that number, make projections of demand for the specific product type that the developer's project will serve.

An important fact to keep in mind is that developed lots are an intermediate factor in the production of housing. Although a shortage of housing may exist, a surplus

3-6 What to Look for In a Good Market Study

Proper Delineation of the Market Area. The geographic area in which competing subdivisions are sampled should be large enough to include the entire quadrant of the city in which your project is located.

Proper Delineation of the Competing Market Product types. Do not define a market so narrowly that you omit certain competition. This leads to an underestimate of supply. For example, low-cost single-family houses compete with condominiums for buyers.

The Capture Rate. The capture rate of lots for the subdivision should take into account both the total demand in the marketplace and the number of other subdivisions. In metropolitan areas with populations over 1 million, capture rates in excess of 5 percent for *any* project, even new towns, are suspect.

Employment and Absorption Rates. Projections of demand should be based both on employment projections and historic absorption rates in the area. Large increases relative to historic absorption rates are always suspect.

---

of lots may also exist. Therefore, the market study should highlight demand and supply for both the final housing product and developed lots.

Regulatory Process

Zoning and Platting

The process of subdividing a land tract is called "platting." Platting also usually involves a zoning change. In urban fringes, land will often be zoned "agriculture" or some other nonurban designation.

Every city has a different procedure for zoning.[11] The process can take anywhere from three months to six years, depending on how sensitive the site is environmentally and politically. Many sites are also subject to the approval of special agencies or commissions; these approvals add further costs and time. For example, land in California that is located generally within 1,000 yards of the ocean is subject to the California Coastal Commission's jurisdiction. Fulfilling the Commission's requirements may add years to the time necessary to secure approval for a subdivision. The Commission's requirements and limitations, such as anticipated density, may be extremely strict. Since even many experienced developers lack the staying power to pilot a site through the Commission's process, beginning developers are well advised to avoid situations that involve lengthy and expensive approval processes.

Platting process. Platting is the official procedure by which land is subdivided into smaller legal entities. It is the means by which cities and counties enforce standards for streets and lots and record new lot descriptions in subdivisions. The legal description of a house lot typically follows this form: "Lot 10 of Block 7143 of Fondren Southwest III Subdivision, Harris County, Texas." The legal description parallels the platting procedure. The developer submits a plat of the property showing individual blocks and lots. In this example, the subdivision number III indicates that two previous subdivisions have been platted under the name Fondren Southwest.

In some areas, platting requires a public hearing, even if the intended use conforms to the zoning. In other areas, no public hearing is required as long as the platted lots are consistent with the zoning and with all other subdivision regulations such as the following:

- street width;
- turning radius (designed for fire trucks);
- maximum cul-de-sac street length;
- lot size—total area, minimum width and depth;
- alley requirements, if any;
- frontyard, backyard, and sideyard setbacks;
- number of units per acre; and
- minimum size of units.

Figure 3-7 shows a sample subdivision regulation table.

The number of units permitted to be built on a given parcel usually depends on a combination of several factors including minimum lot width and depth, alley requirements, and street rights-of-way. The target market will determine whether a developer will want to plat the greatest possible number of lots or create larger lots for more expensive houses. A developer should never seek to attain the highest allowable density unless he/she has previously determined that the resulting lot sizes are consistent with the target market.

Replatting a previously platted area can present unexpected difficulties, especially if the developer must "abandon" (that is, remove from official maps) old streets or alleys. In Dallas, Peiser Corporation was investigating a site when it found unexpectedly that *all* of the abutting property owners had to agree to the abandonment of a mapped, but never built, alley. With 50 homeowners involved, the likelihood of unanimous agreement was almost nil. Peiser Corporation passed on the site, despite having invested considerable time and money.

In addition to platting requirements, the subdivision may be subject to restrictive covenants imposed by the seller or a previous owner. Restrictive covenants should show up in the initial title search and may have a profound influence on the type of development allowable on a particular site.

■ 3-7 City of Pasadena: Summary of Zoning Regulations for Residential Uses

Zone	Land Use	Maximum Height (Feet)	Required Yards (Feet) Front	Side	Rear	Minimum Lot Area (Square Feet) Per Lot	Per Dwelling Unit	Minimum Lot Width (Feet)	Maximum Building Area (%)	Parking Spaces per Dwelling Unit
RS 1	One-family residence 1 unit/acre	32	25[a]	5 minimum or 10% of lot width, 10 maximum[b]	25	40,000	40,000	100	35%	2 covered
RS 2	One-family residence 2 units/acre Any RS-1 use	32	25	5 Same as RS-1	25	20,000	20,000	100	35	2 covered
RS 4	One-family residence 4 units/acre Any RS-1 use	32	25	5 Same as RS-1	25	12,000	12,000	75	35	2 covered
RS 6	One-family residence 6 units/acre Any RS-1 use	32	25	5 Same as RS-1	25	7,200	7,200	55	35	2 covered
RM 16	Multifamily residence 16 units/acre Any RS use	36	20	10[f,h] Corner lots require 15	10	7,200	2,750	55	40	2 covered per unit 550 square feet or larger[c,d]
RM 16-1	Multifamily residence 14 units/acre Any RS use	36	40	10 Corner lots require 30	20	12,000	3,000	75	35	Same as RM-16[c,d]
RM 32	Multifamily residence 32 units/acre Any RS use Group residential	36	20	10 Corner lots require 15[g]	10[g]	10,000	1,360[e]	60	60	Same as RM-16[c,d]
RM 48	Multifamily residence 48 units/acre Any RM-32 use	60	20	10 Corner lots require 15[g]	10[g]	10,000	910[e]	60	60	Same as RM-16[c,d]

[a]Building line conformity, maximum frontyards in R districts: Section 17.64.180.
[b]Sideyards of corner lots: 10 percent of lot width or 10 feet minimum, 25 feet maximum. See Development Standards, Section 17.20.020.
[c]Parking requirements for RM zones: 1.5 covered spaces per unit less than 550 square feet. Developments with 20 units or more shall provide one guest parking space for each 10 units. See Section 17.68.030.
[d]Compact car parking spaces in RM zones: Section 17.68.100.
[e]Low- to moderate-income and/or design density bonuses are available in RM-32 and RM-48 zones. See Additional Development Standards, RM-32 and RM-48 Districts, Section 17.24(D).
[f]Building Modulation: RM-16, RM-16-1: Additional Development Standards, Section 17.24.050(G)
RM-32, RM-48: Additional Development Standards, Section 17.24.050 (M) (N).
[g]Interior side- and rearyards in RM-32 and RM-48 zones require an additional five feet of setback for every 10 feet of building height, or portion thereof, above 25 feet. See additional Development Standards, RM-36, RM-48, Section 17.24.050(J).
[h]Five-foot for structures not exceeding nine feet in height measured to the top plate.
Source: City of Pasadena, California, Planning Department, July 1, 1985.

3-8 Subdivision Filing Procedure for Los Angeles County

The procedure for Los Angeles County involves filing first a tentative tract map and then a final tract map. The tentative map goes to a subdivision committee composed of key department personnel and to all advisory agencies, such as those for streets, utilities, fire, and environment. The subdivision committee recommends changes and conditions and sets a public hearing date at the planning commission. If the tentative tract map is approved, the developer must wait 30 days for approval of the final tract map, during which time interested parties may file an appeal. The developer has up to two years, plus a possible two-year extension, to apply for approval of the final map.

The final tract map must incorporate all of the changes and conditions introduced during the tentative map stage. Minor changes in lot configuration are allowed; however, for any changes in density or total number of units, the developer must file a revised map that goes through the same steps as does a tentative map. The final tract map is not subject to a public hearing, just to a review to ensure that it complies with the conditions.

The major issues for subdivision approval include:

1. Consistency with the county's General Plan.
2. Zoning, subdivisions, and other county and state standards.
3. Topography and site suitability.
4. Design and layout.
5. Availability of public services and facilities.
6. Accessibility.
7. Compatibility with existing and proposed uses.
8. Environmental impact. (An environmental questionnaire must be completed and submitted in conjunction with the application for subdivision.)

Filing a subdivision application. Every jurisdiction has a different procedure to follow for obtaining subdivision approval. Most jurisdictions have at least a two-stage process that requires planning commission approval and then city council or county supervisor approval. A typical subdivision process, the platting procedure for Los Angeles County, is described in feature box 3-8.

Regulatory Concerns

Land development regulation has become so complicated in so many areas that it would take an entire book to describe the many different forms of regulation that a developer will encounter. Staying on top of new local ordinances is not enough. A developer must know which regulations are about to come into force, which are still under discussion, and which are only vague proposals. The lead times required to get a development off the ground are not only often long, but also increasing. In Houston in the mid-1970s, developers complained that six to nine months were often required to obtain the necessary approvals to develop a subdivision. In San Diego in the late 1980s, developers were grateful if they could clear all of the approval hurdles in less than three years. The more agencies involved, the longer it takes. Projects in California's coastal zone and in environmentally sensitive mountain areas have been known to take eight years or longer to secure approvals.

Four major regulatory issues will affect most land developers in the 1990s: vesting of development rights, growth controls, environmental issues, and traffic.

Vesting of development rights. Historically, if developers had, or could obtain, zoning, they had the right to build what the zoning allowed. If they bought a property that was already zoned, they were entitled, without public hearings, to develop the property within the limits established by the zoning. The presumption that zoning confers the right to develop a property has been changing in many parts of the country. As in other regulatory areas, California has led the way. In the 1976 *Avco* decision,[12] the developer was not allowed to proceed with land development, even though he had installed streets and utilities. In other words, the developer's right to develop was not "vested," despite the fact that he had spent considerable money on improving the land. More recently, the standard for vesting has become even more stringent. The developer not only must have received a building permit but also must have completed a substantial part of the foundation in order to obtain the "vested right" to proceed. A land developer who cannot deliver building permits will soon be out of business.

In California, Florida, and Hawaii, development agreements have become a popular solution to the problem of securing vested development rights. Development agreements, which are negotiated between the developer and the municipality, ensure that the ground rules under which a developer builds are the same as those that were in effect at the time the agreement was signed. Development agreements protect the developer's right to build a specified number of residential units or square feet of nonresidential space in exchange for providing certain facilities to the community. Although development agreements have never been tested in court, both developers and municipalities believe that they provide protection against changes in zoning, density, moratoriums, and other regulations.

Growth controls. Growth management programs attempt to control an entire community's rate of development rather than to respond to each private developer as applications are submitted. Growth management provisions are often incorporated into local zoning ordinances. Typical provisions include:

- zoning and subdivision approval linked to capital budgeting investments in infrastructure;
- establishment of growth boundaries to limit the supply of developable land—growth boundaries usually provide for a holding area where future development is anticipated;
- ceilings on the amount of space that can be constructed in the jurisdiction;
- linkages between development and availability of water supply or sewage-treatment capacity;
- linkages between projects and specific public facilities, such as transit or road improvements; and
- ceilings on the number of building permits that can be issued each year.

Growth management is not a new issue. Communities have been able to limit the number of building permits that they issue annually, ever since the *Ramapo*[13] and *Petaluma*[14] decisions in the 1970s. The difference today is that growth management has become so widespread. For instance, between 1971 and 1988, 179 different growth-control programs were instituted in California. The number has increased each year; approximately 60 programs were passed in 1986 and 1987.[15] Growth-control measures have been passed or are now being considered in several parts of the country, including Boston, New York City, and Washington, D.C.

Communities adopt antigrowth attitudes for two main reasons: first, as a reaction to changing community character—as rural or low-density areas are developed, the visual environment begins to change; and, second, in response to an overburdening of infrastructure—schools, sewers, parks and open space, and, most importantly, the impact of traffic on local roads. Traffic concerns are often used as a factor in determining when and how much development will be allowed in areas affected by growth-control legislation.

Environmental issues. Since the late 1970s, developers of larger projects have been required to submit environmental impact reports (EIRs) in order to receive project approval in certain areas. Throughout the 1980s, the size of projects that required an EIR steadily decreased. This trend promises to continue so that, in time, almost all development projects will be required to produce some form of environmental impact analysis.

The effects of a project are summarized in an EIR. Frequently, such statements deal only with impact beyond the site boundaries, but in large projects such as a new community, the most consequential impacts may be within the site. EIRs are circulated to interested parties, and comments are invited. The responses of reviewers are then appended to the statement, which may be modified as a result of the comments received. Federal legislation allows litigation over the adequacy of coverage in an EIR, a step which can cause great delays.[16]

One of the most sensitive aspects of EIRs concerns hazardous waste. On a project outside of Houston, for example, the EIR reported some open pools of oil adjacent to a new subdivision, but no further research was done. More than 300 houses had been built in the subdivision when it was discovered that the oil pools were toxic. The homebuyers sued the builder, the developer, the

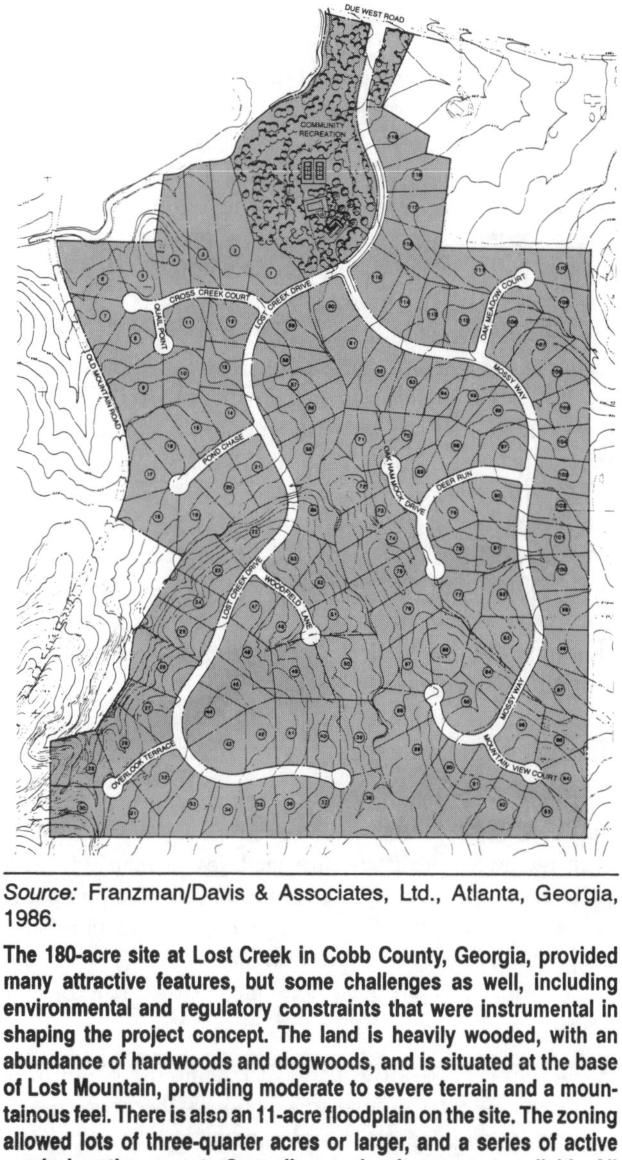

Source: Franzman/Davis & Associates, Ltd., Atlanta, Georgia, 1986.

The 180-acre site at Lost Creek in Cobb County, Georgia, provided many attractive features, but some challenges as well, including environmental and regulatory constraints that were instrumental in shaping the project concept. The land is heavily wooded, with an abundance of hardwoods and dogwoods, and is situated at the base of Lost Mountain, providing moderate to severe terrain and a mountainous feel. There is also an 11-acre floodplain on the site. The zoning allowed lots of three-quarter acres or larger, and a series of active creeks lace the property. Sewer lines to the site were not available. All of these features led the developer toward a large-lot community concept of large homes.

engineers, the lenders, and almost everyone else remotely connected with the subdivision. The eventual settlement was for millions of dollars.

For land developers, toxic waste has become one of the foremost concerns of the 1990s. Environmental quality standards in many areas are now very strict, and many sites will have some sort of problem with toxic waste. Virtually every parcel that has ever been farmed, used industrially, or drilled for oil is likely to have some form of toxic-waste problem, from pesticide dump to groundwater contamination. The cost of cleaning up a site may be minor, or it may run into millions of dollars. Developers must, therefore, investigate possible toxic-waste deposits on a site before buying it. Lenders will require a clean site before they will loan on it. If developers already own a site where toxic waste is discovered, they are responsible for the clean-up.

Traffic. The development of single-family housing in the suburbs has been a national trend since World War II. Many people moved to the suburbs to escape congestion, crime, and other urban problems. Houses were followed by shopping centers, which were followed by jobs. Recently, even corporate headquarters, which previously could be found only in downtowns, have moved to suburban office centers.

Traffic congestion in the suburbs is becoming at least as bad as congestion in the cities. The low-density, semirural lifestyle that attracted many people to the suburbs has been lost. As a result, concerns about traffic lie at the root of growth moratoriums and the slow-growth movement. Many areas require developers to furnish traffic studies as part of the review process. Cites are requiring developers to pay for major off-site road improvements, and, sometimes, for freeway interchanges, in order to receive planning approval. Even small developers must demonstrate that their projects will not overburden existing roads.

Financing Infrastructure

Regulatory uncertainty is integrally tied to the time and cost of providing or obtaining necessary infrastructure facilities. Infrastructure facilities primarily include utilities, roads, and drainage, but may also include parks, schools, treatment plants, fire and police stations, and major transportation improvements.

A variety of methods for financing infrastructure are used:[17]

- General taxes—historically, street and utility improvements have been financed by bonds that were repaid by general property tax revenues.
- Government grants—historically, federal grants have assisted local communities in building water- and sewage-treatment plants and other infrastructure.
- Impact fees and developer fees—these fees are imposed on the developer at the time of platting or building permit and are usually computed on a per-unit or per-square-foot basis.
- User fees and charges—these are a traditional means of obtaining revenues. Monthly fees (water and sewer fees, for example) are pledged to repay bonds issued to finance the facilities and to pay operating and maintenance expenses.
- Assessment districts—these districts can issue bonds and impose a special tax levy on property owners who benefit from specific public improvements within the district.
- Special districts—these are similar to assessment districts, except that their governing bodies are separate from the local government. They can issue bonds and levy taxes on property owners within their jurisdiction.
- Road clubs—developers join together to pay for, or reimburse the county for, installing roads or other needed infrastructure. Road club charges are placed on homeowners' tax bills and are amortized over five to 10 years.
- Tax increment financing—increases in tax revenues that result from new development in a specified area are earmarked for public improvements or services in that area.
- Developer exactions—the developer is required to install or pay for community facilities such as roads, parks, police and fire stations, libraries, and school sites, in return for platting or building approval.

Developers must have a thorough understanding of infrastructure financing, because a major portion of the cost of land development is associated with on- and off-site roads, utilities, and other infrastructure. Developers must understand how their development will affect the revenues and costs of the local jurisdiction in which they want to build. Developers and municipalities are engaged in a constant tug-of-war about the division of the cost of infrastructure.

Much of the slow-growth movement is motivated by the belief among existing homeowners that they are required to pay an unfair portion of the cost of facilities that will be used by future homeowners in the same subdivisions. Every new generation of homeowners benefits from the previous generations' investment in infrastructure.[18] Major infrastructure investment—typically, streets and utilities—is characterized by debt payments over 20- to 30-year periods, slow deterioration, and periodic replacement. When the financing life is shorter than the economic life of a facility, and when a community's growth rate is more than 3 percent per year, the residents of that community pay for benefits faster than they receive them. When taxes to pay for growth rise, dissension between current residents and future residents (represented by the developer) soon follows.

The main justification for impact fees and other development charges is that they will alleviate the burden that growth imposes on existing homeowners. Developers can expect more and more communities to impose impact fees, and those fees can reach prohibitive levels—several Southern California communities levied impact fees exceeding $25,000 per unit in 1991.

The appropriate level of impact fees is subject to debate. Theoretically, impact fees may be imposed on developers for their share of any facilities from which they benefit, including those that have been installed and paid for earlier. The facilities may be off site and may not even benefit the developer's project directly.

The legal test for impact fees is that a "rational nexus," or rational relationship, between the fees charged and the benefits received by the future residents of the development can be proved to exist. The developer should not be expected to pay the entire cost of facilities that benefit other residents of the community.

Ironically, growth moratoriums and building permit caps are motivated, in part, by the lack of adequate impact fees. Residents who vote for moratoriums claim that developers are not paying their full share of the cost that they impose on a community. Developers may find that it is in their own best interest to support a sound system of impact fees, although a community should not expect development to pay more than its fair share. See figure 3-9 for a sample fee structure.

Unfortunately, developers are caught in the middle of a tax revolt in many parts of the country. As development fees have become popular, and developers have accepted them, communities have looked to developers to provide an ever-increasing share of the costs of urban services—so much so that, in many communities, new residents are subsidizing existing residents.

Many cities now require developers to pay for half of the cost of major arterials that abut their property.[19] Also, developers often must pay for some or all of the new utility lines required to serve their property. These off-site requirements have a major impact on the location of subdivisions. Even for very large developments, the cost of bringing in water and sewer services from more than a mile away is prohibitive. Unless the municipality is able to underwrite the cost either directly or through some form of special district, the amount that developers can afford to pay for off-site facilities is limited.

Although many jurisdictions require that the developer pays for the infrastructure on the front end, they also require that other property owners who benefit from that infrastructure reimburse the developer later, when those owners subdivide their own property. This procedure allows the developer to recoup the cost, albeit over the course of years. However, most communities do not give the developer any interest on his/her front-end investment; thus, effectively, the developer's current project alone must support the off-site infrastructure.

Avoiding Pitfalls

From a public policy point of view, many regulations serve vital functions—protecting the environment, reducing flooding, controlling traffic, and ensuring that adequate infrastructure is built. From the developer's point of view, however, increasing government regulation adds considerably to the time, expense, and risk of land development—arguably, the type of development hardest hit by regulation.

The larger the land development project, the more likely it is to become the community's target of special regulatory concern. One way to minimize the impact of regulation is to choose infill areas located in older jurisdictions that have more established regulations. These may present other problems, however, since infill tracts are surrounded by existing development, and developers may have to deal with vocal homeowners' groups.

In general, developers can reduce the regulatory risk by following these suggestions:

- stay closely in touch with city or county planning staff;
- monitor pending ordinances and referendums;
- join the local building industry association, which should be in touch with everything in progress;
- once a concern has been identified that may affect the project, consult the regulatory agency's staff and, if necessary, an attorney to find out how to protect or exempt the project;
- consider working with redevelopment agencies that often have the powers to cut red tape and expedite approvals;
- consider using a development agreement to protect development rights; and
- select local architects, engineers, and zoning and other consultants that have worked extensively in the community.

In addition, two key guidelines should be adhered to: maintain flexibility, and work with the community and homeowners.

Maintaining flexibility. Regulatory uncertainty is changing the way in which developers buy land. Increasingly, the price of land is tied to the number of units or square footage that can be built on a site. This shifts the approval risk, in part, from developers to sellers, because the purchase price is lower if developers cannot get permission to build a prenegotiated number of units or square feet. In general, most land sellers are unwilling to accept regulatory risk after closing. At best, developers may have a nonrecourse note that allows them to give the property

■ 3-9 Development Fees in Los Alamitos California: 1989

Assumes: A 10-acre, 50-unit subdivision, valued at $195,000 per acre; 1,500-square-foot house with a 400-square-foot garage, three bedrooms, two bathrooms, valued at $100,000; typical street improvements.

Fee Category	Fee per Unit	Notes
Environmental		
Initial Determination	$1	
EIR Processing		$50 deposit against actual expense
Planning		
General Plan Amendment	9	$450
Zone Change	9	$450
Tentative Tract Map	19	$500 processing fee + $20 per first five parcels + $10 each remaining + cost of any private consulting firm
Site Plan Review		$10 minor; $500 major
Building—Edition		
Building	646	
Plan Check %	420	
Electrical	65	Schedule + 65% plan check + $20 issuance
Mechanical	61	Schedule + 65% plan check + $20 issuance
Plumbing	183	$4.50 per fixture + 65% plan check + $20 issuance
Engineering and Subdivision		
Final Tract Map	100	Plus plan check fee deposit of $500 + $20 per parcel
Sewer		$25,000 to $100,000, $1,250 + 4% of estimate
Water		$100,001 to $1,000,000, $4,000 + 3.5% of estimate
Storm Drain		Plan check fee deposit required on estimated hours of work
Street		Same as above
Grading		
Capital Facilities and Connections		
Water	1,163	For city-installed 1" meter service
Sewer	85	Per dwelling unit inspection fee
Sanitation District Annex	1,500	Per acre District 3
Drainage	0	None
Transportation Corridor	0	None
Other Traffic	0	None
Park Facilities	327	Per dwelling unit park and recreation tax
School Fees		
Los Alamitos Unified	2,340	$1.56 per square foot
Other Fees		
Excise Tax	75	$65 duplex; $45 apartment
Environmental Reserve Tax	225	$.15 per square foot of construction

Source: Building Industry Association of Southern California, Orange County Region, "Land Development Fee Survey for Orange County 1989–1990," Santa Ana, California, October 1989.

back without penalty (other than loss of equity) if new regulations are passed by the municipality that severely restrict or stop development.

At the same time that government approvals are becoming harder to obtain, planning commissions and city councils are requiring developers to meet specific timetables. Developers are often required to build roads and community facilities by a specific time, often in advance of selling lots. In some cases, developers must commit to building a specified number of units per year. However, the cyclical nature of the real estate industry makes periods of boom and bust inevitable. Developers must retain the flexibility to build more units when times are good and to reduce production (and public commitments) when times are bad.

Developers should also retain the flexibility to program the mix of units for each development phase. Because of the almost inevitable delay between approvals and construction, developers must be able to let market conditions at the time of construction determine the final mix. Otherwise, developers may be forced to sell lots to homebuilders to meet a market that is no longer in demand and may be precluded from selling lots for houses that are currently hot. For larger projects, developers should work in increments that are small enough for them to vary the product mix as the market indicates.

Working with the community. The relationship between a developer and homeowners' groups is often critical to a project's success. The most common objection raised by homeowners' groups to a proposed subdivision is that it will reduce the quality of the neighborhood—bringing in people who have smaller incomes and live in smaller houses, or exacerbating traffic problems. The developer's best counter argument is to emphasize the quality of the planned development.

Most experienced developers claim that, instead of hiring someone to represent them, they prefer to talk to homeowners' groups themselves. Developers need to convince the community that they will keep their promises, a trust which is more likely to be gained in person.

Although doing nothing and hoping that no one will notice a project is a temptation for developers, this obviously is not the best approach. Homeowners' groups in most parts of the country are too aware of, and involved with, development for the developer to rely solely on the quiet approval of the planning commission and the city council. Such groups become particularly intransigent when they feel that they are being ignored—especially if they do not learn about proposed projects until the public hearing. If opposition coalesces at the end of the approval process, often the developer will be required first to come to terms with the homeowners' groups and then to start the process again.

A better approach is to identify in advance the groups that may have an interest in, or concern about, the project and then to seek them out. A developer should be careful also to identify the most influential leaders in a local community. Peiser Corporation, for example, lost a zoning case on a land development because it met with the president of the local homeowners' association but not with the leader of opinion in the community, a minister, who turned against the project in part because he was not consulted initially.

In urban fringe development, opposition tends to focus on two subjects: spillover costs and inadequate infrastructure.

Concerns regarding the imposition of costs on property owners and the overburdening of existing roads, schools, or other public facilities usually have to be addressed by developers in meetings with other property owners and neighborhood groups.

The developer of a small-scale project does not need to talk to homeowners' groups if the project is consistent with local zoning and land use; however, for larger projects and for those projects that require a zoning change or increase in density, the following approach is recommended:[20]

- educate the public affected by the project;
- talk to planning departments early in the course of the project to explore options;
- be aware that the public hearing process is not adequate for addressing homeowners' opposition;
- be proactive with residents—talk to the city council or legislators to get in touch with citizens' groups, develop contacts with them, and, possibly, form a citizens' advisory committee;
- use graphics to communicate plans to those who are not at the public hearing;
- know that fear of the unknown motivates citizens' groups—be certain that all plans are clearly explained;
- allocate time for the development staff to communicate with the public;
- seek out or form homeowners' groups to maintain communication within the community; and
- if problems arise, use mediators instead of lawyers.

Financial Feasibility Analysis

Financial feasibility analysis for land development is performed in two stages. The first stage is a one-column summary pro forma called a "quick-and-dirty" analysis; the second stage is a multiperiod cash-flow analysis. Developers should perform both stages of analysis before they commit earnest money to a project. They should then update the cash-flow analysis on a regular basis as they establish sales, price, and cost information with greater accuracy. The multiperiod cash-flow analysis becomes the major tool for determining the project's economic feasibility and for convincing lenders and investors to support the project.

Gross versus Net Developable Acreage

One of the most confusing concepts in the feasibility analysis for beginning developers to grasp is the distinction between gross acres, net developable acres, and net-net acres.[21] Gross acres refers to the total acreage, all-inclusive, at the time of purchase. Net developable acreage, or net acreage, omits major streets, open spaces that are significant to the entire project, floodplains, and easements. Net-net acres takes net developable acres and omits interior street rights-of-way, alleys, and any other areas that are not actually for sale. The total net-net acres should equal the total area actually sold—the aggregate total area of building lots plus multifamily and nonresidential reserve sites.

Most rough calculations are performed on the basis of net developable acres, which includes interior streets. When a developer investigates a new piece of property, one of the most important pieces of information, therefore, is the amount of land not developable because of floodplains, easements, major road rights-of-way, or dedications for schools, parks, or other community facilities. The remaining acreage is used for calculating the number of lots and the number of acres of apartments or commercial reserves to be sold separately.

A reasonably good estimate can be made of the number of lots that can be fitted on a specified property by using yield formulas. For example, 7,500-square-foot lots produce a typical yield of four lots per acre:

4 lots x 7,500 square feet per lot =	30,000 square feet
Estimated street right-of-way =	12,000 square feet
Total =	42,000 square feet (or about 1 acre)

The yield differs from city to city, depending on the standard street rights-of-way and whether or not the city requires alleys. Also, most planners allow for some wastage because, for example, corner lots are larger, and irregularly shaped sites are difficult to develop efficiently.

The developer should check with a local planner for lot yield, but the following rules of thumb may serve as starters. Deduct 25 percent of the acreage for streets (30 percent if alleys are required), and then divide the remainder by the lot size. (See figure 3-10. Representative densities for residential development are presented in figure 3-11.)

Land Use Budget

The land use budget is used to allocate the total net developable acreage to different land uses and product types. It is determined by the market, based on the product type that is being absorbed the fastest and at the highest price. An example of the land use budget for a 100-acre site is shown in figure 3-12.

The land use budget should be established before meeting with the land planner. A common mistake that developers make is to let the land planner, not the market, determine the land use budget. The land use budget becomes the major initial input into the financial feasibility analysis. In the example in figure 3-12, only the residential and retail land totaling 85 acres is salable (revenue producing). The community facilities, parks, and arterial highway dedication are not.

■ 3-10 Approximate Residential Lot Yield Per Acre for Different Lot Sizes

Lot Size (Square Feet)	Lot Yield per Acre[a] With Alleys	Lot Yield per Acre[a] Without Alleys
10,000	3.0	3.3
8,500	3.6	3.8
7,500	4.1	4.4
6,500	4.7	5.0
6,000	5.1	5.4
5,000	6.1	6.5
4,000	7.0–8.0	7.5–8.5

[a]The number of lots yielded per acre is only a crude estimate for initial calculation purposes.

■ 3-11 Densities by Residential Type

	FAR	Net Density (Units per Acre)	Gross Density
Single-Family	0.2	8	5
Zero-Lot-Line Detached	0.3	8–10	6
Two-Family Detached	0.3	10–12	7
Row Houses	0.5	16–24	12
Stacked Townhouses	0.8	25–40	18
Three-Story Walkup Apartments	1.0	40–45	30
Three-Story Walkup Over Parking	1.0	50–60	40
Six-Story Elevator Apartments	1.4	65–75	60
13-Story Elevator Apartments	1.8	85–100	75

Source: Kevin Lynch and Gary Hack, *Site Planning*, 3rd ed. (Cambridge, Massachusetts: MIT Press, 1985), p. 253. Upward adjustments have been made to density ranges for apartments.

■ 3-12 Example of a Land Use Budget

	Land Use Budget (Acres)	Absorption (Acres per Year)
Residential		
Single-Family—7,500-square-foot lots	40	10
Single-Family—5,000-square-foot lots	20	6
Apartments (30 units per acre)	10	5
Retail	15	5
Community Facilities	2	–
Parks and Open Space	8	–
Subtotal	95	
Arterial Highway Dedication	5	
Total	100	

■ 3-13 The Effect of Present Value Factors On Land Allocation for Different Uses

Year	Present Value Factor at 15 Percent[a]	Profit on One Acre of Retail Land[b]	Profit on One Acre of Single-Family Land[b]
0	1.000	$200,000 (1)	$80,000 (8)
1	.869	173,800[c] (2)	69,520 (10)
2	.756	151,200 (3)	60,480 (12)
3	.657	131,400 (4)	
4	.571	114,200 (5)	
5	.497	99,400 (6)	
6	.432	86,400 (7)	
7	.375	75,000 (9)	
8	.327	65,400 (11)	

[a]Opportunity cost is 15 percent annually.
[b]Parenthetical numbers indicate the order of allocation.
[c]Values are computed by multiplying value in year 0 by the factor for the year (for instance, $200,000 times .869 equals $173,800).

The absorption rate of the land is based on the amount of acres that can be sold each year. The above rates indicate that it should take four years to sell out the 7,500-square-foot single-family lots, over three years for the 5,000-square-foot lots, two years for the apartment land, and three years for the retail land.

The ideal land use budget maximizes the value of the property by allocating as much land as possible to high-value uses. However, developers often allocate too much land to high-value uses such as office or retail, which have very slow absorption rates.

Another difficulty is distinguishing between end-user absorption and land sales to builders and other developers. If enough land for 20 or 30 years of absorption has been reserved for office and retail use, it is tempting simply to assume that the unsold inventory will be sold to "land investors" at the end of the development life—say, three or five years later. The developer must, however, assume a significant discount (25 to 50 percent or more) in the sales price relative to end-user "retail" sales. The developer must remember that buyers will have to wait until end-user demand warrants building out the site, and so will not pay retail prices for the land.

For example, suppose that retail land can be sold for a net profit of $200,000 per acre versus 7,500-square-foot single-family lots for $20,000 each ($80,000 per acre). Suppose also that demand for retail land is one acre per year versus 40 lots (10 acres) per year for single-family lots. If the opportunity cost is 15 percent, then in present value terms—as figure 3-13 shows—one acre of residential land sold today is worth more ($80,000) than one acre of retail land sold in seven years ($75,000).

Suppose that the site has 35 acres. The developer must determine the amount of land to set aside for retail depending on the present value of the land and the absorption rate. The developer should allocate land to the highest-value use as long as the present value of that year's absorption rate is greater than the next-highest-value use. In the example in figure 3-14, the developer would allocate the first seven acres of land to retail use because the present value is greater than that for single-family land sold today, even though it will not be consumed by the marketplace for up to six years. However, the next 10 acres would go to single-family land because the present value ($80,000) is higher than the value of the retail land sold in seven years ($75,000). Ten acres is allocated to single-family use because that is the amount of single-family land that can be sold in one year. The next acre would go to retail. The next 10 acres would go to single-family lots. If 35 acres were allocated, the final budget would be 26 acres of single-family and nine acres of retail. The lowest-value land (single-family, present value equals $60,480) would be the last to be allocated. Through the eleventh allocation, nine acres of retail and 20 acres of single-family land are used. Six acres for the twelfth allocation brings the total up to 35 acres.

This procedure for allocating land is an application of linear programming to real estate.[22] It works for any number of uses and can be done by hand. The only information needed is net developable acreage, sales price, development cost, and absorption rate for each land use or product type. The suggested discount rate is 5 percent above the current development-loan interest rate. The resulting land use allocation is only a guideline for the land use budget and will probably be modified by zoning, political, or environmental constraints. Nevertheless, a market-based land use allocation is the only

3-14 Allocation of Land for 35-Acre Tract Using Present Value Approach[a]

Year	Retail Use (Acres)[b]	Single-Family Use (Acres)[b]
0	1 (1)	10 (8)
1	1 (2)	10 (10)
2	1 (3)	6 (12)
3	1 (4)	
4	1 (5)	
5	1 (6)	
6	1 (7)	
7	1 (9)	
8	1 (11)	
Total	9	26

[a]Given annual absorption rates of one acre of retail and 10 acres of single-family land.
[b]Parenthetical numbers indicate order of allocation.

accurate and reliable method for determining the land use budget, and it should determine the land use plan, not vice versa.

Quick-and-Dirty Analysis

The developer performs financial feasibility several times during the course of a project. The first analysis is performed before the developer ties up the property with an earnest money contract. The analysis becomes successively more thorough and complex as the deal progresses. A good financial feasibility analysis becomes the basis for managing the project once it goes into construction. The categories in the analysis should coincide with the chart of accounts.

Quick-and-dirty analysis, which is a summary statement of the sales revenues, costs, and interest, provides a rough estimate of expected profit. Suppose a developer is considering a 45-acre site that can be developed at an average density of four single-family lots per acre. Figure 3-15 shows the information necessary to evaluate the site. Note that for the initial analysis a site plan is not necessary. Even for the first analysis, however, the developer should obtain a rough idea of the total amounts of developable and nondevelopable acreage. The land purchase price may be quoted on the basis of either gross or net developable acreage, depending on the purchase contract. As discussed above, the initial analysis should be based on the number of *net developable acres*.

Suppose that the site has two acres that must be dedicated for a widening of the major frontage road plus three acres in the floodplain. The net developable acreage would be 40 acres. After examining the market, suppose that the developer wants to build 7,500-square-foot lots with a yield of four lots per acre (the balance of the land goes toward streets, wider corner lots, and allowance for irregularly shaped parcels). The market study should provide a reliable estimate of the value of the finished lots before the developer does the initial pro forma. Keep in mind that the sales price depends on the marketing of the lots—a bulk sale to one builder will produce a lower price than a piecemeal sale to 20 builders.

A rough estimate of cost may be obtained from other developers, civil engineers, and grading and utility contractors. With this information, sales prices, and sales commissions, a developer can produce the quick-and-dirty analysis shown in figure 3-15.

One of the questions quick-and-dirty analysis raises concerns the appropriate amount of return. Some bankers recommend at least a 30 percent ratio of profit to total costs. In figure 3-15, that ratio is only 18.8 percent ($885,000 divided by $4,715,000). However, such ratios are not very meaningful because they do not provide any indication of return on equity, nor do they take into account the holding period. For example, a 30 percent return on equity in one year would be good, whereas a 30 percent return over three years would be only 10 percent per year uncompounded, and 9.14 percent per year compounded.[23] Because time value of money is not indicated in the quick-and-dirty calculation, comparison to alternative investments is not possible.

3-15 Quick-and-Dirty Analysis for Land Development

Revenues	
40 acres x 4 lots per acre x $35,000 per lot =	$5,600,000
Costs	
Land	$2,563,000
Development Excluding Financing (40 acres x $30,000 per acre)	1,200,000
Marketing (6% of sales)	387,000
Administration (5% of hard costs)	60,000
Subtotal	$4,210,000
Financing	$505,000
Average balance of $2,105,000 for 2 years at 12% interest[a]	
Total Costs	$4,715,000
Profit (Revenues minus Costs)	$885,000

[a]The loan amount covers 100 percent of the development costs. The average balance shown is simply half of the subtotal ($4,210,000), although a more accurate estimate would start with land cost, peak at the end of construction, say one year, and decline to zero over the sales period.

Other shortcomings of quick-and-dirty analysis include:

- no indication of how quickly lots are sold;
- no means of introducing inflation;
- haphazard computation of interest on the development loan;
- no information regarding when funds are needed or the amount needed; and
- no means of computing present values or internal rates of return.

The loan calculation is the weakest part of the quick-and-dirty analysis. In the example above, the loan amount is chosen so that it covers all of the costs, including loan interest, which usually can be borrowed. However, the size of the loan depends on how quickly the lots are sold—one of the factors that the quick-and-dirty analysis does not take into account. Whether or not the loan amount will cover 100 percent of the costs depends on the raw land appraisal, the development cost, and the borrower's credit. In 1991, most land development projects required some form of equity.

The main advantage of the quick-and-dirty analysis is that it forces the developer to make explicit assumptions concerning land uses, site planning, sales rates, prices, costs, and financing. This information is the foundation for all subsequent investigation. It is a rough indication of whether or not the deal makes economic sense.

Multiperiod Cash-Flow Analysis

Multiperiod cash-flow analysis, also called discounted cash-flow (DCF) analysis, is an application of the capital asset pricing model to real estate.[24] The cash-flow analysis assigns revenues and expenditures from the summary quick-and-dirty analysis to specific periods of time.

Feature box 3-16 shows a DCF analysis for Rustic Woods, a project in Bedford, Texas. Several items should be noted:

- *Time periods.* Select intervals that give between five and 10 time periods of analysis. For example, for a sale of 120 lots at the rate of 30 lots per quarter, plus 12 months for development, the total time required is about two years. Quarterly time periods (three months per period) would provide eight periods in total, a good starting point for analysis. For larger projects that require, say, 10 years to develop, annual periods would be appropriate for the first DCF analysis. In very large projects, such as new communities with 20- to 30-year lives, two-year intervals are preferable.
- *Level of detail.* The developer must remember that the purpose of the early runs of the DCF analysis is to obtain a picture of the total project. Beginners often go into too much detail at first, forgetting that every item in the spreadsheet is subject to change. Since the developer has not yet done a detailed site plan, and sales and cost estimates are, at best, rough approximations, a monthly cash-flow analysis would be meaningless. The spreadsheet can always be elaborated by adding more periods and more line items as more information becomes available. Usually, the developer should wait to prepare a monthly cash-flow forecast until the site plan has been adopted, the market study has been completed, contract bids are available, and a monthly forecast for loan approval is needed.
- *Time period zero.* Time period 0 should always be included in cash-flow analysis. Period 0 represents the starting period of analysis and can be set for any time. For existing projects, period 0 is recommended to be set three to six months earlier than the present date—at some point at which the exact amount of money spent to date is known. In projects where money has already been spent, a line item on the spread sheet, "costs to date," should be added that aggregates the total money spent, as of time 0. For new projects, time 0 is normally selected as the closing date. Any costs incurred prior to closing are simply included under the land cost or cost-to-date category.
- *Timing of sales.* The developer should allow enough time to develop the property and investigate the effects of slower-than-anticipated sales rates. One of the computer runs should assume half of the expected sales pace (twice the amount of time anticipated to sell out the project) and compute the maximum loan amount needed for this downside case.
- *Inflation.* DCF models typically include three different inflation rates—price inflation, cost inflation, and the inflation rate implicit in the interest rate. These rates are correlated. If the inflation rate in sales prices is 10 percent, a 10 percent interest rate is not appropriate because interest rates are a function of inflation in the economy. A 10 percent inflation rate would instead suggest a 15 to 18 percent interest rate (10 percent inflation plus 3 percent real rate of return plus 2 to 5 percent risk). Higher inflation assumptions make a project look better than it probably is. Lenders are rightfully cautious of overly optimistic inflation assumptions and may insist on a DCF analysis run with zero inflation in sales prices.
- *Releases.* Releases represent the amount by which the land note and the development loan must be reduced as sales are made. The cash-flow analysis shows the release amounts as a "cash out" item (lines 126 and 127). Loan repayments should be handled explicitly as a "cash out" line item, just as loan draws should be included separately as a "cash in" item.
- *Before-tax computation.* Before-tax rates of return may be used for evaluating the economic feasibility of a land development project as long as they are com-

pared to before-tax returns from other investment opportunities. Unlike income-property development, in which tax benefits are an important part of the return, land development offers no special tax benefits. The Internal Revenue Service (IRS) treats the land developer as a "dealer in land" and, as such, the developer must pay ordinary tax on reported profits. For example, if the developer's tax rate is 33 percent, then the developer would pay $333 in tax on each $1,000 of profit.

- *Return measures.* The economic internal rate of return (IRR) (line 159) is the unleveraged IRR for the project. It assumes that all cash requirements are financed from cash equity and is computed on "profit before financing," which is the same as "sales minus costs" (lines 98 and 114), exclusive of all financing. The economic return should be at least 15 to 20 percent.[25] It should exceed the cost of borrowing money so that the developer can obtain "positive leverage." If, for example, the economic IRR is 15 percent, and the development-loan interest rate is 12 percent, then the developer's return on equity will be higher than 15 percent. "Negative leverage" exists when the return is less than the loan rate. Positive leverage means that as the developer borrows more, the return on equity increases. The economic return in the exhibit is 22 percent.
- *Return on equity.* The return on equity (line 160) is also an IRR calculation. In contrast to the economic IRR, the return on equity does take financing into account. The developer's cash investment, plus any "in-kind" equity such as land contribution, is represented as cash outflows. The "cash flows after financing" (line 128 and "Results") are the cash inflows to the developer. Often, no cash inflows will occur until the development loan is fully retired. The return on equity should be higher than the economic IRR because the amount of equity is usually only a fraction, say 20 percent, of total project cost. The return on equity should always be higher than the loan interest rate because equity investors have lower priority to cash flows than mortgage holders and thus incur more risk. Note that if the project is financed by 100 percent equity (no debt), then the return on equity will be the same as the economic IRR. In the exhibit, the IRR on $300,000 equity is a healthy 63.8 percent.

The rate of return that constitutes an acceptable return on equity varies. Most developers require a return on equity that is 12 to 15 percent higher than that which they could obtain on risk-free government bonds. If, for example, one-year Treasury bills (T-bills) are paying 8 percent, most developers want a return on equity of 20 to 25 percent.

If no equity is invested (that is, the project is 100 percent financed), then the return on equity is infinite. An infinite return does not necessarily mean that the project is economically feasible. Even if the project equity is zero, the *economic* IRR should be at least 5 percent above the T-bill rates and preferably in the 15 to 20 percent range.

According to standard finance theory, net present value (NPV) criteria offer a better method for rank ordering projects than do IRR criteria because they provide the value in today's dollars of the wealth that will be generated in the future by a project. The appropriate discount rate is the developer's opportunity-cost rate—what he/she can earn in alternative investments of similar risk. The project with the highest NPV is preferred. If only one project is being considered, then the NPV should be sufficient to justify the time and risk of development, even if the developer has no equity invested in the project. For example, suppose the NPV on a four-year project with $1 million equity, discounted at 15 percent, is $200,000. This means that the developer would have earned the equivalent of $200,000 in today's dollars over and above a 15 percent return on his/her initial investment. The developer should determine if the project is worth the time and risk involved. If he/she must work full time on the project for four years or sign personally on a $5 million loan, it probably is not.

An important fact to remember is that all returns move with inflation. When inflation is running at 4 percent annually,[26] an investor can earn 7 to 8 percent by investing in T-bills. Because of the greater risk, comparable real estate returns on equity (for 4 percent inflation) should average 12 to 15 percent for income properties and 15 to 20 percent for development projects. When inflation is 8 percent, T-bills produce returns of 10 to 12 percent and real estate returns should be 16 to 20 percent for income properties and at least 20 to 25 percent for development projects.

Developers often must extend personal guarantees on loans, even when they have no equity invested in a project. Some developers treat their guarantee as equity and compute an IRR on that basis. Since the guarantee is a contingent liability rather than a cash investment, the appropriate return on the guarantee is not comparable to normal rates of return on equity in the form of hard cash.

Design and Site Planning

Land planning begins with a marketing concept for the houses, apartments, or other buildings that will ultimately be built on the finished lots. The end product—the size, style, and quality of house, apartment, or nonresidential use—dictates how the land should be subdivided.

Good subdivision design involves much more than an engineer's efficient layout for streets and utilities. The most cost-efficient plan often is the rectangular grid layout that became popular in tract-home subdivisions in the 1940s and 1950s. However, the most profitable plan is one that takes advantage of the natural features on a site or provides other interesting features or focal points.

■ 3-16 Detailed Land Development Analysis For Rustic Woods, Bedford, Texas

The land development financial analysis is a multiperiod discounted cash-flow analysis schedule for the life of the project. Its principal purpose is threefold: first, to compute returns to the overall project (100 percent owner/developer); second, to compute loan requirements; and third, to compute returns to joint venture participants. It is a before-tax computation. In most cases, land developers are considered dealers in land, and their earnings are taxed as they would be in any other business. Since land development does not offer the same tax benefits (such as depreciation) as does income-property ownership, before-tax analysis may be used for making decisions.

Land development financing is similar to construction financing during the development period of income property. No permanent mortgage exists since the purpose of land development is to sell developed lots to end users—homebuilders and income-property developers. Land development analysis resembles Stage 4 of the income-property analysis outlined in chapter 4 (development period cash flows), except that it is usually performed on a quarterly or annual basis rather than a monthly basis. The type of analysis presented here determines the building program, phasing, and expense budget that the project can support. Like Stage 2 analysis for income properties, the analysis is performed several times during the feasibility period. Changes are made in the cost and sales assumptions as more accurate information becomes available. Thus, the land development analysis is the land developer's equivalent of the architect's sketch pad, just as Stage 2 analysis is the income-property developer's sketch pad. The cash-flow analysis for land development may be used both for planning the project and for obtaining financing.

Results (in $000s)

Profit before Interest	$1,799	Cash Flow after Financing	$1,529
Less Interest	570	Less Repayment of Equity	300
		Less Unpaid Loan Balance	0
Profit	$1,229	Profit	$1,229

Unleveraged Economic Return[a] (Cash Flows before Interest and Financing)

Net Present Value @ 15%	$452
IRR	22.0%

Quarter	Net Profit
0	($2,580)
1	(410)
2	(282)
3	(179)
4	186
5	452
6	611
7	692
8	671
9	728
10	745
11	764
12	401
Total	$1,799

Leveraged Return on Equity[b] (Net Cash Flows after Financing)

Net Present Value @ 15%	$692
IRR	63.8%

Quarter	Equity	Cash Inflow
0	$300	$ 0
1	0	0
2	0	0
3	0	0
4	0	0
5	0	0
6	0	0
7	0	0
8	0	0
9	0	0
10	0	362
11	0	764
12	0	401
Total	$300	$1,529

■ 3-16 (Continued)

QUARTERLY REVENUES						
Sales (Lots)[d]		**Total**	**0**[c]	**1**	**2**	**3**
Goodman Homes		50				
Ryland Homes		68				
David Weekly Homes		45				
Total		163	0	0	0	0
	Price Escalation per Period[f]	**Price per Lot**				
Sales Prices (in $000s)[e]				**1**	**2**	**3**
Goodman Homes	2.5%	$28		$28	$29	$29
Ryland Homes	2.5%	28.50		29	29	30
David Weekly Homes	2.5%	29.00		29	30	30
Sales Revenues (in $000s)[g]		**Total**	**0**	**1**	**2**	**3**
Residential		$1,654	$0	$0	$0	$0
Apartments		2,343	0	0	0	0
Office		1,544	0	0	0	0
Total		$5,541	$0	$0	$0	$0
DETAILED DEVELOPMENT COSTS (in $000s)		**Total**				
Land		$2,563				
General and Administrative		48				
Engineering Design		65				
Field Surveying		70				
Contingency		56				
Other Development Costs						
Inspection Fees	$ 6					
Filing Fees	2					
Advertising	0					
Soils Report	2					
Legal Fees	8					
Accounting Fees	3					
Loan Fees and Expenses	11					
Appraisal Costs	5					
Total Other Development Costs		$37				
Construction Costs						
Underground Electric	$ 33					
Gas	44					
On-Site Utilities	235					
Off-Site Utilities	45					
Total Utilities		$357				
Site Excavation		93				
Street Paving		296				
Other Construction Costs						
Street Lights	$ 6					
Entry and Landscape	25					
FHA Lot Grading	21					
City Sidewalks	0					
Lab Testing	0					
Total Other Construction Costs		$ 52				
Real Estate Taxes		76				
Subdivision Maintenance		18				
Total Development Costs		$3,731				
QUARTERLY DEVELOPMENT COSTS (in $000s)[h]	**Inflation**	**Total**	**0**[i]	**1**	**2**	**3**
Land		$2,563	2,563			
General and Administrative	1.5%	48		12	12	12
Engineering Design		65		65		
Field Surveying		70		70		
Contingency	1.5%	56		10	10	10
Other Development Costs	1.5%	37	17	10	10	
Utilities		357		150	150	57
Site Excavation		93		93		
Street Paving		296			100	100
Other Construction Costs	1.5%	52				
Taxes	1.5%	76				
Subdivision Maintenance	1.5%	18				
Interest Rate per Quarter				2.5%	2.5%	2.5%
Total		$3,731				

4	**5**	**6**	**7**	**8**	**9**	**10**	**11**	**12**
6	6	6	6	6	6	6	6	2
4	3	7	9	9	9	9	9	9
3	6	6	6	6	6	6	6	
13	15	19	21	21	21	21	21	11

4	**5**	**6**	**7**	**8**	**9**	**10**	**11**	**12**
$30	$31	$32	$32	$33	$34	$35	$36	$37
31	31	32	33	34	35	36	36	37
31	32	33	34	34	35	36	37	38

4	**5**	**6**	**7**	**8**	**9**	**10**	**11**	**12**
$181	$185	$190	$195	$200	$205	$210	$215	$ 73
123	94	226	297	305	313	320	328	337
94	192	197	202	207	212	217	223	0
$398	$471	$613	$694	$712	$730	$747	$766	$410

4	**5**	**6**	**7**	**8**	**9**	**10**	**11**	**12**
12								
10	16							
96								
52								
35				35				6
2	2	2	2	2	2	2	2	2
2.5%	2.5%	2.5%	2.5%	2.5%	2.5%	2.5%	2.5%	2.5%

3-16 (Continued)

		Data Input	Total	0	1	2	3
72							
73	**LAND NOTE (in $000s)**[j]		Total	0	1	2	3
74	Total Land Cost			$2,563			
75	Lots Sold	$15.72	163	0	0	0	0
76	Downpayment	1.10	$1,000	1,000			
77	Beginning Lots Released	$18.1		55	55	55	55
78	Lots Released from Note Repayment			0	0	0	0
79	Released Lot Inventory (lines 77+78–75)			55	55	55	55
80	Lots To Be Released		22	0	0	0	0
81	Land Note		$1,563	1,563			
82	Repayment Terms					0%	0%
83	Minimum Land Payments			0	0	0	0
84	Maximum Land Note Balance			$1,563	1,563	1,563	1,563
85							
86	Starting Balance			1,563	1,563	1,563	1,563
87	Land Note Releases	18	0	0	0	0	0
88	Remaining Balance			1,563	1,563	1,563	1,563
89	Additional Note Payments			0	0	0	0
90	Ending Balance			1,563	1,563	1,563	1,563
91							
92	Interest for Quarter	2.5%	273		39	39	39
93	Land Note Total		273	(1,563)	39	39	39
94							
95	**CASH FLOW SUMMARY**[k] **(in $000s)**		Total	0	1	2	3
96	**Income**						
97	Sales Revenue[l]		$5,541	0	0	0	0
98	Total Income		5,541	0	0	0	0
99							
100	**Expenses**[m]						
101	Land[n]		2,563	2,563	0	0	0
102	General and Administrative		49	0	12	12	12
103	Engineering Design		65	0	65	0	0
104	Field Surveying		70	0	70	0	0
105	Contingency		57	0	10	10	10
106	Other Development Costs		37	17	10	10	0
107	Utilities		357	0	150	150	57
108	Site Excavation		93	0	93	0	0
109	Street Paving		296	0	0	100	100
110	Other Construction Costs		54	0	0	0	0
111	Taxes		83	0	0	0	0
112	Subdivision Maintenance		18	0	0	0	0
113	Marketing[o]	0.0%	0	0	0	0	0
114	Total Expenses		3,742	2,580	410	282	179
115							
116	Profit before Interest[p]		1,799	(2,580)	(410)	(282)	(179)
117							
118	Less Development Loan Interest[q]		297	0	24	34	42
119	Less Land Note Interest[r]		273	0	39	39	39
120	Net Profit		$1,229	(2,580)	(473)	(355)	(260)
121							
122	**Financing**						
123	+ Equity		300	300			
124	+ Development Loan Borrowings[s]		1,997	717	473	355	260
125	+ Land Note Borrowings[t]		1,563	1,563	0	0	0
126	– Development Loan Repayments[u]		(1,997)	0	0	0	0
127	– Land Note Repayments[v]		(1,563)	0	0	0	0
128	Cash Flow after Financing[w]		1,529	0	0	0	0
129	Cumulative Cash Position		$1,529	0	0	0	0
130							

4	**5**	**6**	**7**	**8**	**9**	**10**	**11**	**12**
13	15	19	21	21	21	21	21	11
55	42	44	43	39	35	31	10	0
0	17	17	17	17	17	0	0	0
42	44	43	39	35	31	10	0	0
0	0	0	0	0	0	0	11	11
0%	20%	20%	20%	20%	20%			
0	313	313	313	312	312	0	0	0
1,563	1,250	938	625	312	0	0	0	0
1,563	1,563	1,250	937	624	312	0	0	0
0	0	0	0	0	0	0	0	0
1,563	1,563	1,250	937	624	312	0	0	0
0	313	313	313	312	312	0	0	0
1,563	1,250	937	624	312	0	0	0	0
39	39	31	23	16	8	0	0	0
39	352	344	336	328	320	0	0	0
4	**5**	**6**	**7**	**8**	**9**	**10**	**11**	**12**
398	471	613	694	712	730	747	766	410
398	471	613	694	712	730	747	766	410
0	0	0	0	0	0	0	0	0
13	0	0	0	0	0	0	0	0
0	0	0	0	0	0	0	0	0
0	0	0	0	0	0	0	0	0
10	17	0	0	0	0	0	0	0
0	0	0	0	0	0	0	0	0
0	0	0	0	0	0	0	0	0
0	0	0	0	0	0	0	0	0
96	0	0	0	0	0	0	0	0
54	0	0	0	0	0	0	0	0
37	0	0	0	39	0	0	0	7
2	2	2	2	2	2	2	2	2
0	0	0	0	0	0	0	0	0
212	19	2	2	41	2	2	2	9
186	452	611	692	671	728	745	764	401
44	42	38	31	23	14	5	0	0
39	39	31	23	16	8	0	0	0
103	371	542	638	632	706	740	764	401
44	42	38	31	23	14	0	0	0
0	0	0	0	0	0	0	0	0
(147)	(100)	(267)	(356)	(343)	(408)	(376)	0	0
0	(313)	(313)	(313)	(312)	(312)	0	0	0
0	0	0	0	0	0	364	764	401
0	0	0	0	0	0	364	1,128	1,529

■ 3-16 (Continued)

131	**CASH ACCOUNT AND LOAN CALCULATION[x] ($000s)**						
132	**Cash Account**		**Total**	**0**	**1**	**2**	**3**
133	Starting Cash Balance			0	0	0	0
134	Additions to Equity		300	300	0	0	0
135	Profit before Interest		1,799	(2,580)	(410)	(282)	(179)
136	Land Note		(273)	1,563	(39)	(39)	(39)
137	Subtotal		1,826	(717)	(449)	(321)	(218)
138							
139	Amount to be Financed before Interest		1,705	717	449	321	218
140	Cash Available for Loan and Interest			0	0	0	0
141							
142	Loan Repayments		1,997	0	0	0	0
143	Interest		5	0	0	0	0
144	Ending Cash Balance		1,529	0	0	0	0
145							
146	**Loan Account ($000s)**						
147	Beginning Balance			0	717	1,190	1,545
148	Loan Draws[y]			717	449	321	218
149	Loan Repayments[z]			0	0	0	0
150	Trial Ending Balance			717	1,166	1,511	1,763
151	Average Balance			0	942	1,351	1,654
152	Interest Rate			0.0%	2.5%	2.5%	2.5%
153	Interest[aa]			0	24	34	42
154	Interest Paid from Cash			0	0	0	0
155	Ending Balance			717	1,190	1,545	1,805
156	Borrowings after Interest			717	473	355	260
157							
158	NPV and IRR Calculations:[bb]	**IRR**					
159	(1) Economic Return (Line 116)	22.0%	1,799	(2,580)	(410)	(282)	(179)
160	(2) Return on Equity (Lines 128–123)	63.8%	1,229	(300)	0	0	0
161	Cumulative Return on Equity			(300)	(300)	(300)	(300)
162							
163	**INVESTOR RETURN ANALYSIS FOR A JOINT VENTURE[cc] (in $000s)**	**Data**					
164	**Cash Flows to Investors**	**Input**	**Total**	**0**	**1**	**2**	**3**
165	Cash in/Cash out		$1,529	0	0	0	0
166	Starting Equity Balance				300	318	337
167	Equity Investment[dd]		300	300	0	0	0
168	Subtotal			300	300	318	337
169	Cumulative Preferred Return[ee]	6.00%		0	18	19	20
170	Noncumulative Preferred Return[ff]	0		0	0	0	0
171	Preferred Return Paid		40	0	0	0	0
172	Preferred Return Accrued		207	0	18	19	20
173	Subtotal			300	318	337	357
174	Reduction of Equity		507	0	0	0	0
175	Ending Equity Balance			300	318	337	357
176							
177	Cash for Distribution		979	0	0	0	0
178	Equity Partner[gg]	50%	490	0	0	0	0
179	Developer[gg]	50%	490	0	0	0	0
180							
181	**Rate of Return Calculation**						
182	Equity Partner Investment		(300)	(300)	0	0	0
183	Preferred Return		40	0	0	0	0
184	Reduction of Equity		507	0	0	0	0
185	Cash Distribution		492	0	0	0	0
186	Total Cash Flows to Investors		$739	(300)	0	0	0
187							
188	Net Present Value	12.00%	1.0%				
189	IRR[hh]		48.69%				

4	5	6	7	8	9	10	11	12
0	0	0	0	0	0	0	362	1,126
0	0	0	0	0	0	0	0	0
186	452	611	692	671	728	745	764	401
(39)	(352)	(344)	(336)	(328)	(320)	0	0	0
147	100	267	356	343	408	745	1,128	1,529
0	0	0	0	0	0	0	0	0
147	100	267	356	342	407	745	1,126	1,527
147	100	267	356	343	408	376	0	0
0	0	0	0	0	0	5	0	0
0	0	0	0	0	0	364	1,128	1,529
1,805	1,702	1,644	1,415	1,090	771	378	0	0
0	0	0	0	0	0	0	0	0
147	100	267	356	342	407	378	0	0
1,658	1,602	1,377	1,059	747	362	0	0	0
1,732	1,652	1,511	1,237	919	566	188	0	0
2.5%	2.5%	2.5%	2.5%	2.5%	2.5%	2.5%	2.5%	2.5%
44	42	38	31	23	14	5	0	0
0	0	0	0	0	0	5	0	0
1,702	1,644	1,415	1,090	770	376	0	0	0
44	42	38	31	23	14	0	0	0
186	452	611	692	671	728	745	764	401
0	0	0	0	0	0	364	764	401
(300)	(300)	(300)	(300)	(300)	(300)	64	828	1,229

4	5	6	7	8	9	10	11	12
0	0	0	0	0	0	364	764	401
357	378	401	425	451	478	507	173	0
0	0	0	0	0	0	0	0	0
357	378	401	425	451	478	507	173	0
21	23	24	26	27	29	30	10	0
0	0	0	0	0	0	0	0	0
0	0	0	0	0	0	30	10	0
21	23	24	26	27	29	0	0	0
378	401	425	451	478	507	507	173	0
0	0	0	0	0	0	334	173	0
378	401	425	451	478	507	175	0	0
0	0	0	0	0	0	0	581	401
0	0	0	0	0	0	0	291	201
0	0	0	0	0	0	0	291	201
0	0	0	0	0	0	0	0	0
0	0	0	0	0	0	30	10	0
0	0	0	0	0	0	334	173	0
0	0	0	0	0	0	0	291	201
0	0	0	0	0	0	362	474	201

[a]The economic return is computed on the cash flows before financing (line 116). Thus, it is an all-equity rate of return. The economic return should be significantly greater than the interest rate on financing. Otherwise, no profit will be left over after financing costs are paid.
[b]The return on equity is computed on cash flows after financing (line 160). A leveraged rate of return gives the IRR on equity for the entire project (the owner/developer provides all necessary equity).
[c]Each period is a quarter. The number of periods per year should be chosen to produce five to 15 periods overall. A 10-year project is best analyzed with annual periods (10 periods), a 20-year project with two-year periods (10 periods), and a three-year project with quarterly periods (12 periods).
[d]Sales by product type are entered for each period. Units of measurement do not have to be the same. Thus, residential sales may be expressed as number of lots sold per period; office space is expressed in acres sold per period.
[e]Sales prices are expressed in the same units as are sales. Thus, if residential sales are expressed in lots, sales prices should be expressed in price per lot.
[f]Lot prices may be escalated at a given rate per period.
[g]Sales revenue is computed from the number of acres or units sold per period times the price per period.
[h]Costs are entered by category and period. Detailed cost breakdowns for individual categories, such as utilities, are best handled in supporting spreadsheets (see lines 22 through 55), since an overabundance of detail makes the analysis more difficult to follow.
[i]Time 0 should be treated as a separate period. Typically, Time 0 is the time of closing. Costs incurred prior to Time 0 should be lumped together as "start-up costs."
[j]The land note defines the terms, if any, of the land purchase from the land seller. It specifies the initial acres released by the downpayment (55 acres, in line 77), the release price for the remaining acres ($18,100), and the repayment terms of the land note (line 82). If releases from sales are slower than those required under the amortization terms of the land note, then the shortfall is covered by the development loan or additional equity.
[k]The cash-flow summary presents the net cash flows from the land development.
[l]From line 20.
[m]Expenses summarizes the cost entries in lines 57 through 70. Figures in the summary are higher in most categories because they include inflation.
[n]From line 58. Even if land is contributed to the deal, its cost should be included as an expense.
[o]Some cost categories, such as marketing, are typically calculated as percentages of sales revenues (line 97). Because lots were presold in Rustic Woods, no entry is made for marketing.
[p]Profit before interest is derived from line 97 minus line 114. This line gives the "economic" cash flows, before financing, found in the results summary on page 1 of the analysis.
[q]From line 153.
[r]From line 92.
[s]From line 156.
[t]From line 81.
[u]From line 149.
[v]From line 89.
[w]Cash flow after financing is the primary output of the analysis. This line, combined with equity (line 123), is summarized in the results on page 1 of the analysis (see note b).
[x]A primary purpose of the analysis is to determine the amount and timing of development-loan requirements. Cash equity (or land equity that is considered "cash" if it is contributed to the deal) is infused into the project initially. As money becomes available from sales it is used to retire the development loan.
[y]Land development loans are not revolving lines of credit. Once a partial repayment is made, the amount repaid cannot be reborrowed at a later date, unless the developer makes special arrangements with the lender.
[z]Development-loan repayments, called "releases," are typically a negotiated ratio, usually 1.1 to 1.3 times the loan amount per lot. Release prices are usually assigned to each lot, depending on its relative value. In this analysis, all positive cash flows are assumed to go towards paying down the development loan until it is fully retired.
[aa]Interest on the development loan typically is borrowed as part of the development loan. It may, however, be funded by cash payments rather than additional borrowing.
[bb]IRRs are calculated on the profit before interest (line 116) and cash flows after financing and interest (line 128 minus line 123). These IRRs are included in the results on page 71.
[cc]The investor-return analysis is a before-tax computation of cash flows to the developer and investors in a joint venture. If the landowner contributes the land to the deal, the land value is treated as cash equity for purposes of this calculation.
[dd]From line 123.
[ee]Preferred returns are priority returns of cash flow to the investors. Cumulative preferred returns are accumulated into succeeding periods whenever the amount of cash available is insufficient to pay the preferred return in the current period.
[ff]Noncumulative preferred returns are not accumulated into future periods. If the amount of cash from the current period is insufficient to pay the noncumulative preferred return, it is forgotten.
[gg]The cash distribution percentages are negotiated between the developer and the equity investors.
[hh]The investors' IRR is computed on line 189. The IRR is that discount rate for which the present value of future cash flows (362, 475, and 201 in Periods 10, 11, and 12) equals the initial investment ($300 in Period 0). Since the periods are quarters, the IRR is multiplied by 4 to give an annualized rate of return.
Note: Due to rounding, some totals may not add exactly.

Radburn, New Jersey, pioneered numerous planning concepts, including the separation of pedestrians from automobiles.

Evolution of Subdivision Design

In this century, the evolution of subdivision design has been shaped primarily by three forces: the automobile, increasing housing costs, and the environment.

The Automobile

Automobiles have long been the most dominant influence on subdivision design. Indeed, private automobiles helped to create suburban growth by allowing workers to live at some distance from public transportation lines. Without the automobile, low-density single-family housing would not have been possible.

Suburban streets have always been designed to accommodate automobile circulation and parking; suburban houses have always been designed with garages—first for one car, then for two or three cars. Over the years, innovative methods of dealing with cars have been tried and perfected. A three-level hierarchy of streets and separation of pedestrians from cars was pioneered in Radburn, New Jersey, in 1929.[27] Culs-de-sac were also first introduced in Radburn to reduce traffic on residential streets. Since Radburn, the problem of off-street parking has become a chief concern in development of all kinds. Developers are now required to provide traffic plans and mitigation measures to obtain development approval in many communities.

Increasing Housing Costs

Housing costs have risen faster than personal incomes—and national inflation rates—throughout the postwar period. This escalation in costs has been driven principally by increasing land prices spurred by a limited supply of well-located land and by labor-intensive construction methods.

One of the few tools left to developers to help hold down housing costs is a more-intensive use of land. Developers have responded to rising costs by building at ever-higher densities, thereby reducing unit land costs. In the 1950s, a typical single-family suburban house occupied a one-acre lot; today, a similar house is unlikely

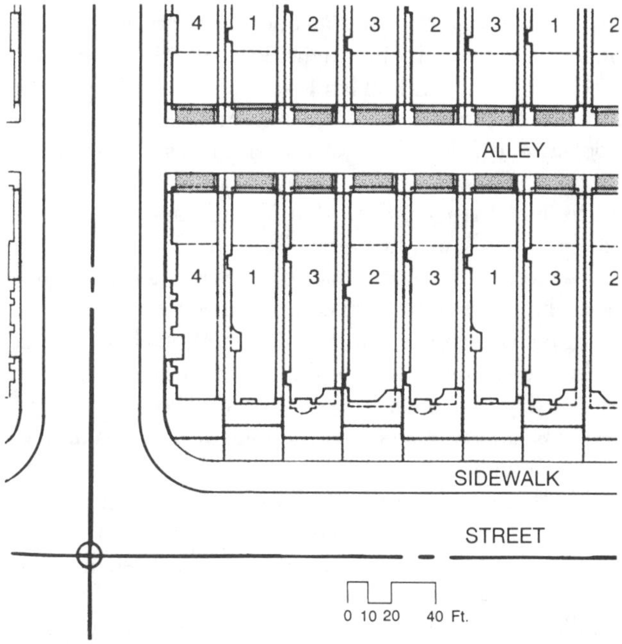

Ocean Pointe Site Plan—Typical Dimensions:

Lot Width: 25 feet	Street Right-of-Way Width: 25 feet
Lot Depth: 115 feet	Sidewalk Width: 12.5 feet
Front Setback: 24 feet	Alley Width: 20 feet
Rear Setback: 7.5 feet	Driveway Width: 16 feet
Sideyard Width: 3 feet	

©Marshal Safron

Developers have been fighting high land costs by building at higher densities. At Ocean Pointe in Huntington Beach, California, single-family lots are 25 feet wide and densities are 9.3 dwelling units per acre, very high for single-family detached housing.

to be built on a lot larger than one-quarter of an acre. The need to achieve higher densities has stimulated new methods of subdividing land—cluster houses in planned unit developments (PUDs), patio houses, zero-lot-line houses, and Z-lots. This evolution in design has had to follow the same slow pace as major institutional and attitudinal changes. City platting ordinances had to be changed to allow new types of lots; banks needed to be convinced of the economic viability of new configurations; homebuyers had to accept the new designs.

In many respects, construction methods have altered little since Roman times. Although an increasing number of housing components (roof trusses, floor joists, wall sections, and cabinets, for example) are now "manufactured," much is still done by hand. The promise of the 1960s that manufactured housing would greatly reduce housing costs never materialized. Cost savings of 10 to 20 percent have been achieved in manufactured housing, chiefly in the areas of time and interest, but both the public and municipalities have been slow to accept it. Also, lenders and government agencies have been reluctant to treat manufactured housing the same way they treat conventional housing.

Developers have responded to rising labor costs by building smaller, more-efficient houses. Construction quality has improved in many ways—better insulation, energy-efficient windows and mechanical systems, improved methods of waterproofing, and new materials that need little maintenance. However, what has been gained by such cost-saving efficiencies has been lost to increasing environmental, safety, and growth regulations. Housing costs have increased faster than incomes. Rising costs will place further pressures on developers to build at higher densities in order to reduce per-unit land costs.

The Environment

The third major force that has influenced subdivision design is the environment. As the environmental movement has gained momentum, its influence has touched all aspects of the development industry, including subdivision design. Environmental concerns in many communities have led to stricter open-space requirements, reduced overall densities, and avoidance of environmentally sensitive wetlands and canyons. The effect of these concerns has been to restrict the amount of developable land and its permissible uses.

All development puts stress on land. One of the first considerations of developers should be how to develop a particular parcel of land at a reasonable profit without violating that parcel's natural features. Or, if the natural features are attractive, developers should determine which development practices, if any, will enhance the environment. Developers do not just react to regulatory policy; they help create it, for better or worse, by their actions.

Environmentally sensitive areas can become major assets for a project if properly handled. At Eastover in New Orleans, wetlands are effectively used to provide attractive home settings.

Developers can incorporate environmental and conservation factors into their projects in many ways. For example, they can:

- reserve open spaces that enhance natural characteristics, such as stands of trees or bodies of water;
- devise methods of protecting areas of natural beauty, and reserve areas for recreation;
- integrate storm-drainage features and water-retention areas into the site plan—properly designed, they can become major assets;
- locate open space upwind from residential areas to help reduce noise and to take advantage of lower temperatures;
- create rich landscaping and planting areas that enhance a project's appearance, control temperature and sound, and promote clean air;
- establish homeowners' associations to provide for constant care of planting areas;
- prevent erosion of steeply sloping areas; and
- avoid water and air contamination, land damage, erosion, and excessive noise during construction.

Sensitivity to Design Issues

Good developers contribute almost as much to the design of subdivisions as do their planners. Their awareness and sensitivity to marketing issues complement the planners' skills and knowledge about layout and infrastructure design.

Considerable time and effort are required to develop a critical eye and an accurate intuition about site design. Following are some steps that beginning developers can take to educate themselves about subdivision design:

- become familiar with the classic subdivisions and with new communities;
- visit new and old development projects both locally and further afield;
- talk to other developers and architects about the types of designs that do and do not work in their projects;
- talk to brokers and sales agents at several subdivisions—they usually hear customers' "uncensored" reactions; and
- attend plan review sessions at meetings held by professional organizations.

A developer also should be familiar with classic examples of each major building type. This is best accomplished through travel and courses in architectural history. Understanding architecture and urban design history is vital because it allows a developer not only to examine structures that have survived both social and technological change but also to develop a sense of style. Many architectural motifs on modern buildings echo those from earlier eras. For example, postmodern buildings of the 1980s echo art deco buildings of the 1930s, which, in turn, have their roots in art nouveau buildings of the early 1900s.

Good developers supplement their knowledge of design with the opinions and tastes of homebuyers in the area. Developers can interview homebuyers to discover what aspects people like about the design of a certain subdivision, what aspects they did not like about other subdivisions, and how well a subdivision meets the needs of different age groups.

Cluster Development, Neotraditional Plans, and PUDs

Among the key planning concepts with which the developer should be familiar are cluster development, neotraditional planning, and PUDs. In cluster development, houses are built at higher densities in certain areas so that other areas can be preserved as open space. Gross density remains the same for cluster developments as for traditional tract housing, in which housing is spread uniformly over the entire tract.

Each cluster tends to contain houses of a similar style. Styles usually vary slightly from cluster to cluster. Cluster planning requires more design skills than does conventional subdivision planning; unskilled planning or exploitation of the cluster concept can easily generate an ugly bunching of dwellings.

In recent years, a school of thought has challenged the cluster development approach, emphasizing neotraditional planning concepts that incorporate uniform lotting patterns as with tract housing, but also grid street patterns, small blocks, town centers, and other planning elements to create a land use pattern similar to that found in traditional small New England or Midwestern towns. Seaside in Walton County, Florida, is a small resort community that is among the earliest examples of the neotraditional approach.

Whereas cluster and neotraditional development are design concepts, PUD is a legal concept. PUDs are zoning classifications now allowed by most cities. Some cities use other names, such as "residential unit development" and "planned development," but the purpose remains the same. In PUDs, traditional zoning classifications are discarded. The PUD is approved as an entity. It may combine commercial and residential uses, include several types of residential product, and provide open space and common areas with recreational and community facilities.

In a PUD, the site of the residential areas may be outlined and a certain number of units may be designated, but no detail regarding the specific site plan is required. Some cities require later public review of the

specific site plan, others do not. Developers have the right to build a certain number of units or a certain number of square feet of commercial or office space, as long as they conform to the stipulations of the PUD ordinance.

PUDs usually involve negotiations between the developer, the reviewing agencies, and the public. The negotiations give the community an opportunity to tailor development proposals to meet community objectives. Often, the developer will be required to place more land in open space or commit more land to community facilities than originally planned. In return, the developer may receive permission to build more units than the regular zoning would allow.

A PUD can be an important tool if a mixture of land uses on a particular project is desired. Planning theory has been leaning toward mixed-use development over the last 20 years and away from the separation of land uses that began in the 1910s. Both planners and the public have discovered that commercial, office, and residential uses can be combined on the same site to create an exciting environment as long as residential areas are screened from irritants such as truck loading, parking, and noise.

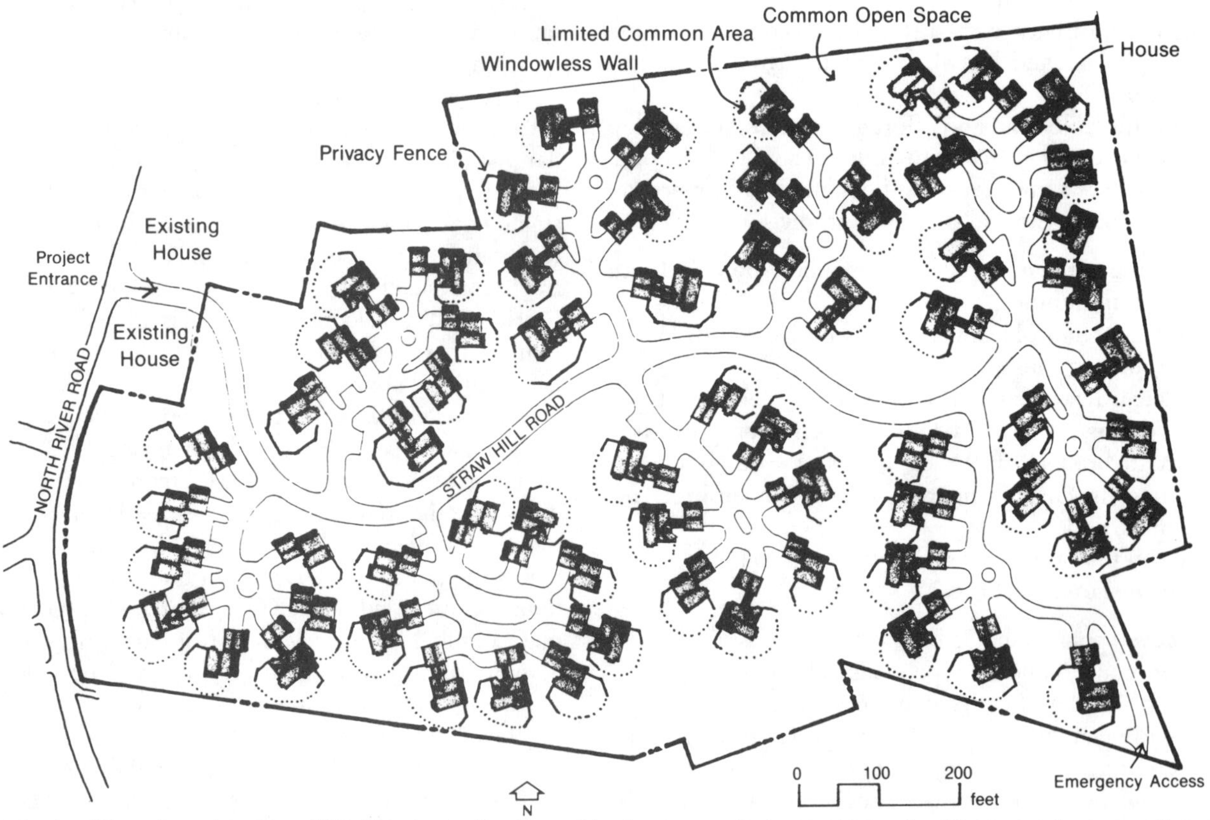

In cluster developments such as Straw Hill in Manchester, New Hampshire, houses are clustered at higher densities in certain areas so that other areas can be preserved as open space.

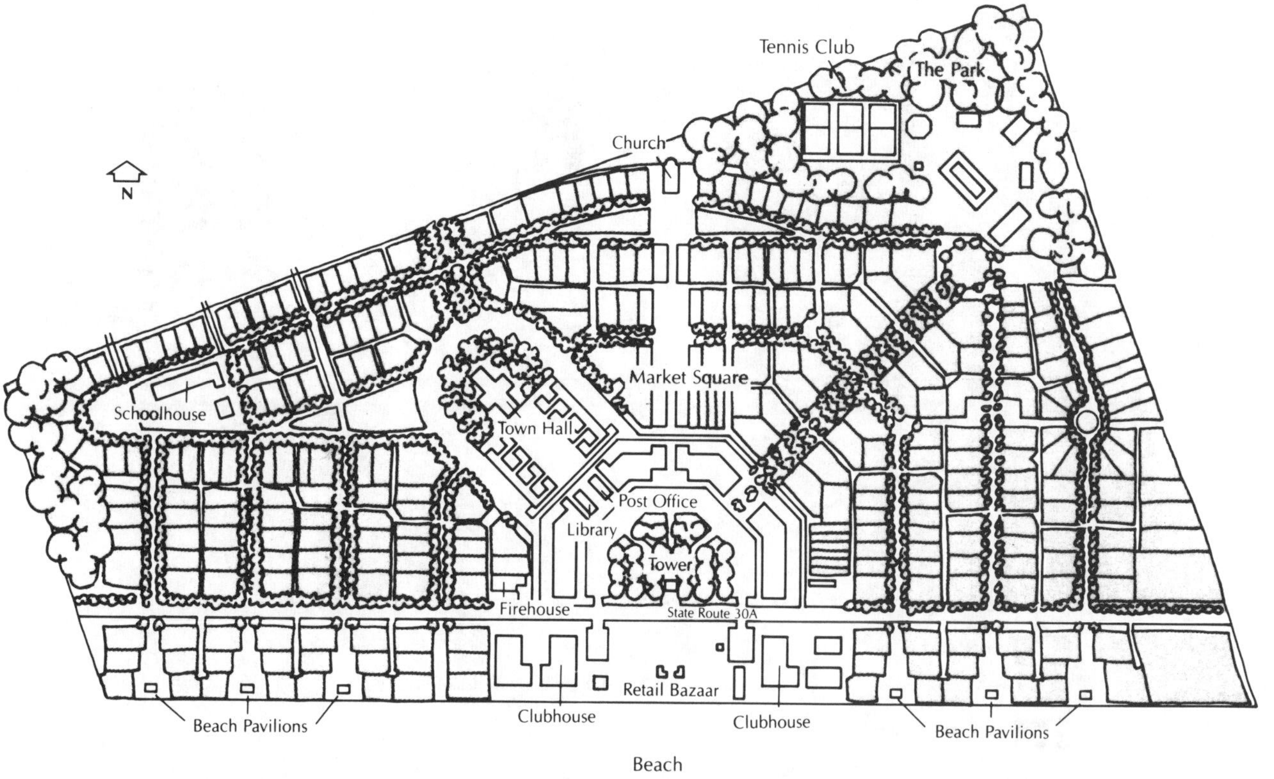

Seaside in Walton County, Florida, is a small (80-acre) second-home community that exemplifies the pedestrian orientation of neotraditional planning concepts, including grid streets, uniform lotting, and a town center.

Site Planning Processes

After the site investigation has been completed and base maps have been prepared, the land planner should present the developer with a site plan that describes a number of different approaches toward developing the site.

The site plan, which combines information regarding the target market with the base map, must consider many different items:

- topography;
- geology;
- utilities;
- natural vegetation;
- drainage;
- vistas;
- neighboring uses;
- easements and restrictions;
- patterns of pedestrian and bicycle and other vehicular circulation—ingress and egress, sidewalks, and alleys;
- vehicular and other storage;
- private and public open space;
- market information;
- sales office location;
- visitor parking;
- sight lines;
- buffers for noise and privacy; and
- building types.[28]

The design process involves much trial and error. It requires developers to consider the future users and their relationship to every aspect of the site. The site planner first produces a schematic site plan that shows road layouts and tentative lot layouts, circulation patterns, open space, amenities, and recreation areas. Throughout the schematic planning phase, developers must ensure that the plan will meet their marketing and financial objectives. Developers should mentally drive down every street, examining traffic patterns, and walk around every house, imagining the views from each window. They should consider such aspects as attractive vistas, landscaping, and the homeowners' privacy. They should also envision the entrance to the subdivision, the playgrounds, and the street crossings.

Developers should not wait for finished drawings before reviewing the schematic plans and should always

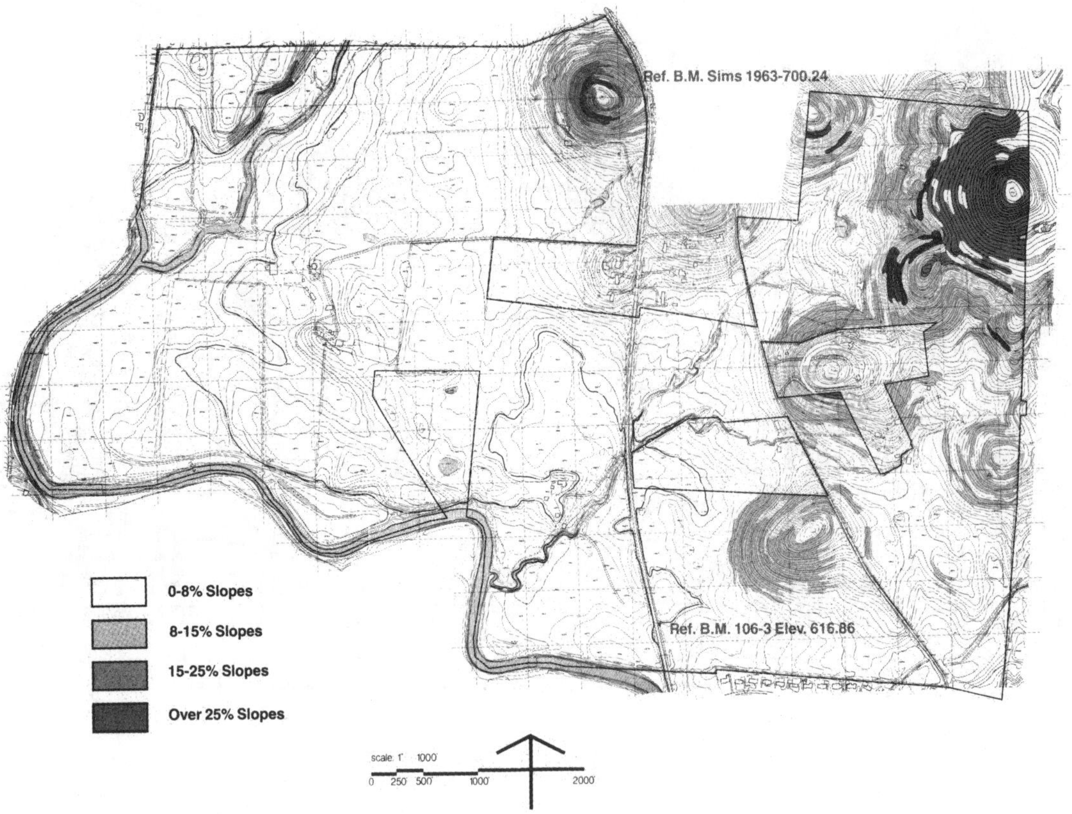

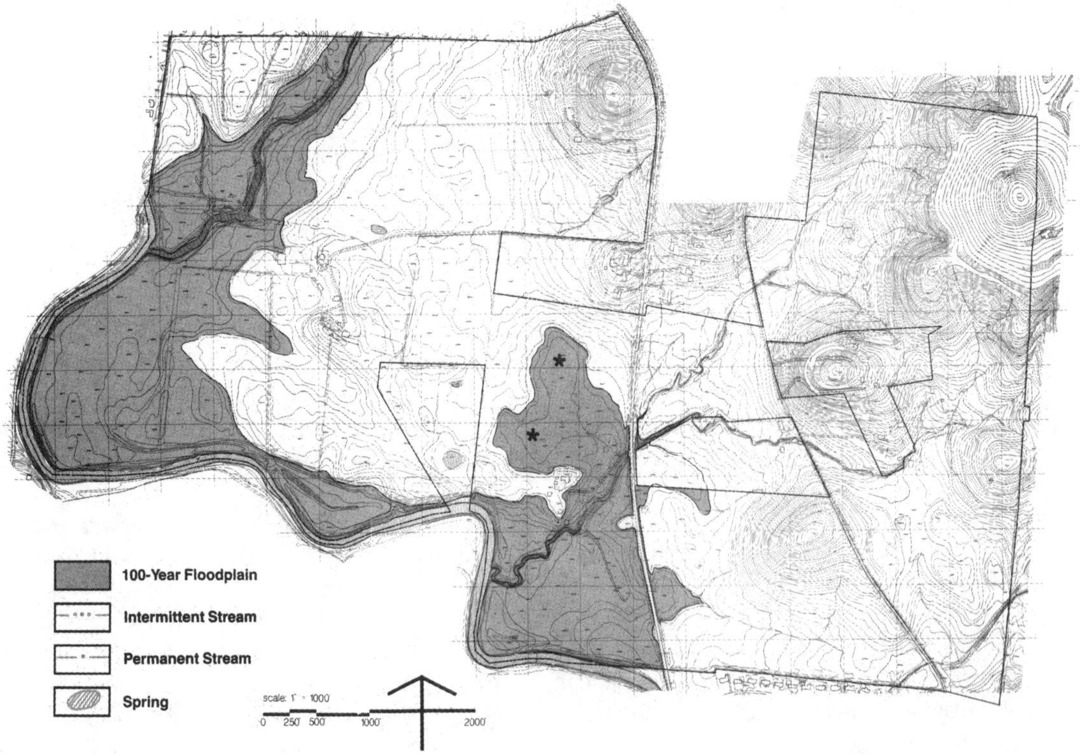

In planning the 836-acre Fieldstone Farms project in Franklin, Tennessee, numerous site maps were prepared to analyze factors such as soils, slopes, floodplains, and vegetation.

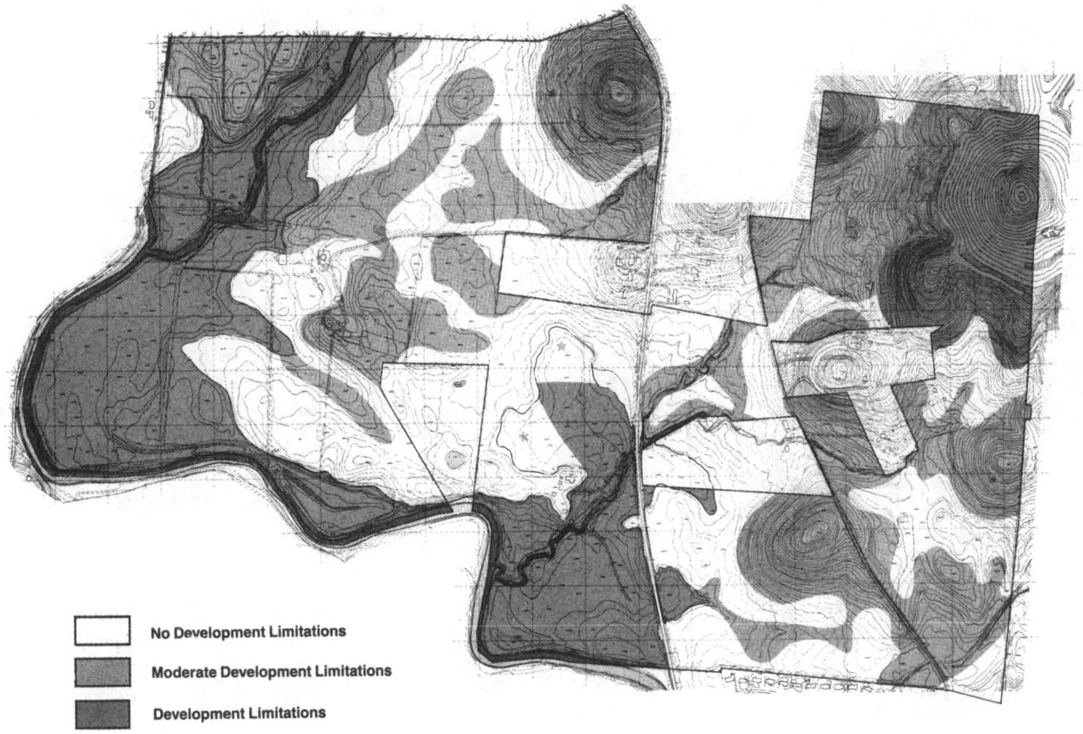

The site analysis at Fieldstone Farms resulted in a map dividing the site into three primary areas based on their suitability for development.

work closely with the planner. A team approach usually works best. The contractor, civil engineer, political consultant (if needed), and sales staff should be involved as early as possible. Review sessions of rough drawings of alternative schemes should be held at regular intervals.

When the developer is satisfied with the schematic plan, the planner produces the final version. The final plan will also go through several iterations. Because it ultimately will be submitted to the city for plat approval, the final plan must show the boundary lines, dimensions, and curvatures of every lot and street. For presentation purposes, planners will usually draw a rooftop plan, showing the positioning of prototype houses on each lot. Models of the subdivision can also be a useful tool both for winning public approvals and attracting buyers.

Site Information

The design process begins with the production of a base map. All subsequent design drawings are based on the graphic information contained in the base map. That information is in turn obtained from a variety of federal sources—including the U.S. Geological Survey and U.S. Department of Agriculture—as well as from local sources. Zoning maps can be purchased either from city zoning departments or from private companies, which usually also sell aerial photographs. City halls, local libraries, utility agencies, state highway departments, and local engineering firms are good sources for topographic maps, soil surveys, soil borings, percolation tests, and previous environmental assessments. Title companies are the source for existing easements, rights-of-way, and subdivision restriction information.

Topographic Survey

Site planning begins with the topographic map that shows the contours of the property, rock outcroppings, springs, marshes, wetlands, soil types, and vegetation. Although topographic maps are available for many counties, on-site surveys are often needed to obtain more accurate information.

The topographic map should show the following:

- contours with intervals of one foot where slopes average 3 percent or less, two feet where slopes are between 3 and 10 percent, and five feet where slopes exceed 10 percent;
- all existing buildings, walls, fence lines, culverts, bridges, and roadways;

Jess Smith/Photosmith

On-site streams and water features can become major amenities and design features for a development, as is the case with this waterfall at Wynstone in North Barrington, Illinois.

- location and spot elevation of rock outcroppings, high points, water courses, depressions, ponds, marsh areas, and previous flood elevations;
- floodplain boundaries;
- outline of wooded areas—including location, size, variety, and caliper of all specimen trees;
- boundary lines of the property; and
- location of test pits or borings to determine subsoil conditions.

Site Map

Developers should prepare a site map at a scale of one inch to 500 feet that shows the surrounding neighborhood and the major roads leading to the site. The map can be later used for advertising, brochures in support of loan applications, and government approvals. In addition to location information, the map should show:

- major land uses around the project;
- transportation routes;
- comprehensive plan designations;
- existing easements;
- existing zoning of surrounding areas;
- location of airport noise zones, if any;
- jurisdiction boundaries for cities and for special districts such as schools, police, fire, and sanitation; and
- lot sizes and dimensions of surrounding property.

Boundary Survey

The boundary survey shows bearings, distances, curves, and angles for all outside boundaries. In addition to boundary measurements, it should show the location of all streets and utilities and any encroachments, easements, and official county benchmarks from which boundary surveys are measured or triangulation locations near the property.

The boundary survey should include a precise calculation of the total area of the site as well as flood areas, easements, and subparcels. The area calculations are used for four purposes:

- to determine the number of allowable units based on zoning information;
- to determine net developable area (the size of this area serves as the basis for both site planning and analyzing the economics of the project);
- to determine sales price—often, the sales price is calculated on a per-square-foot basis (for instance, $2 per net developable or per gross square foot) rather than on a fixed total price; and
- to give a legal description of the site.

Utilities Map

The utilities map is prepared at the same scale as the boundary survey. It shows the location of:

- all utility easements and rights-of-way;
- existing underground and overhead utility lines for telephone, electricity, and street lighting, including pole locations;
- existing sanitary sewers, storm drains, manholes, open drainage channels, and catch basins, and the size of each;
- rail lines and rail rights-of-way;
- existing water, gas, electric, and steam mains, underground conduits, and the size of each; and
- police and fire-alarm call boxes.

Concept Development

Once the base maps have been prepared and accurate gross and net developable acreage calculations have been made, the true design process begins. Before the planner begins drawing, the *developer* should define the target market, the end-user product (including specific lot sizes), and the approximate number of units needed to make the project economically feasible.

The base maps outline the developable areas as well as important features such as lakes, trees, and hills on the site. The developer should determine on the basis of the site's physical condition and specific market which features will become focal points for the design. For example, a creek is often excluded from the developable area because of floodplain problems; however, it may be the site's best amenity. The developer would have the option of either including the creek as part of a few large private lots that back up to it or designating the creek as public open space and designing the plan around it.

Because lots that adjoin open space sell at a premium, developers must maximize the value of the developed property subject to market absorption and zoning constraints. Developers usually achieve high returns by placing higher-density products, such as zero-lot-line lots, next to focal features. Access to focal features for those units that do not have frontage will increase their value.

If the development's use is incompatible with uses on adjacent property, the project almost certainly will arouse the hostility of local homeowners and will be rejected at the public hearing for zoning or site plan approval. For example, if single-family houses face a developer's property, any non-single-family use is likely to draw objections from the neighbors. Although different uses on adjoining properties are actually appropriate in many situations, the burden falls on the developer to demonstrate the reason for not maintaining consistency in use or density.

Many residential tracts border major streets along which commercial and apartment uses may be developed. The developer should reserve as much land as possible for commercial and apartment uses because such frontage usually sells for three to four times the value of single-family land. The amount of land to reserve varies from city to city. However, if a shopping center or office use is contemplated, then a strip 200 to 300 feet deep along the frontage road is appropriate.

The downside risk in reserving a large amount of commercial or apartment frontage is that, in the event that the market for commercial or apartment land is slow, the vacant lot will serve as an unattractive front entrance to the project. If commercial or apartment frontage is retained, the entrance into the residential part of the tract should be very carefully designed and landscaped. A divided parkway entrance with a permanent sign and attractive landscaping has become a common feature of many subdivisions. In smaller subdivisions, the parkway usually narrows down to a standard two-way collector street (36 feet of pavement) after 100 or 200 feet from the entrance.

Streets and Street Hierarchy

In order to reduce costs, developers should create a hierarchy of streets. The subdivision of Radburn, New Jersey, pioneered a street hierarchy in the 1920s that is embodied in plans today. This three-tiered hierarchy should be provided in plans for communities that involve more than 50 acres. The hierarchy is as follows:

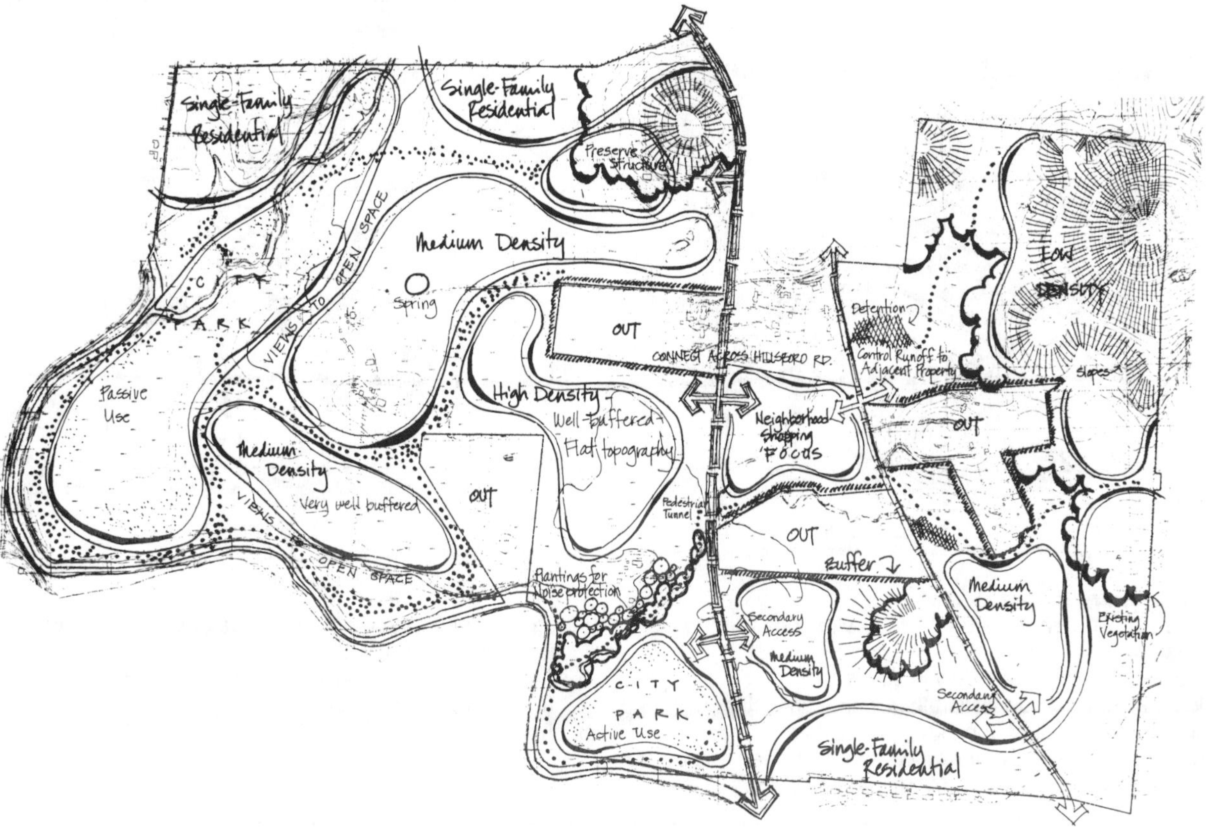

A rough sketch of the conceptual land use plan for Fieldstone Farms in Franklin, Tennessee, emphasizes land uses, densities, and site features.

■ 3-17 Hierarchy of Streets

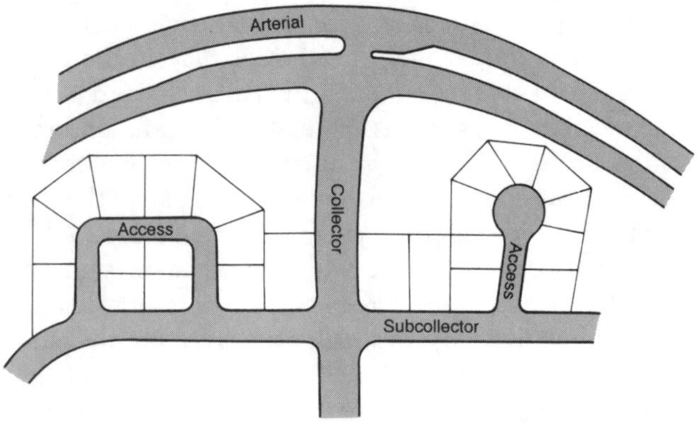

Source: American Society of Civil Engineers, National Association of Home Builders, and ULI–the Urban Land Institute, ***Residential Streets***, 2nd ed. (Washington, D.C.: authors, 1990), p.26.

- arterial streets (48 to 72 feet of pavement, 100-foot rights-of-way) that connect the subdivision to other subdivisions;
- collector streets (36 to 44 feet curb-to-curb, 60- to 70-foot rights-of-way) that preferably have no direct access to homes along their frontages and carry vehicles from arterials to minor streets; and
- minor streets (28 to 30 feet of pavement, 50- to 60-foot rights-of-way) laid out as loops or culs-de-sac fronted by low-intensity uses;

Figure 3-17 provides a slight variation on this hierachy, dividing minor streets into subcollector and access. Roads are the most expensive item in site development. By minimizing the amount of road needed for each unit, costs can be significantly reduced. Long, continuous streets with narrow deep lots are the most cost-effective but are often less visually interesting. A road hierarchy lowers cost by reducing the amount of pavement needed for interior streets.

Streets traditionally serve many functions besides that of passage. They serve as play areas, meeting areas, marketplaces, and workspaces. Planners must provide safe streets that are wide enough for passage and yet maintain enough street space for pedestrian activity.

Superblocks of 50 acres help reduce through-traffic. Penetrated by minor loops and culs-de-sac for internal traffic use, they move through-traffic to the perimeter arterials. The superblock concept also allows for interior open spaces and pathways that minimize the number of necessary street crossings. Early subdivisions, such as Radburn, that incorporated superblocks sought to separate pedestrian and automobile access completely. However, developers have found that culs-de-sac inevitably

■ 3-18 Local Street Guidelines at Westpark

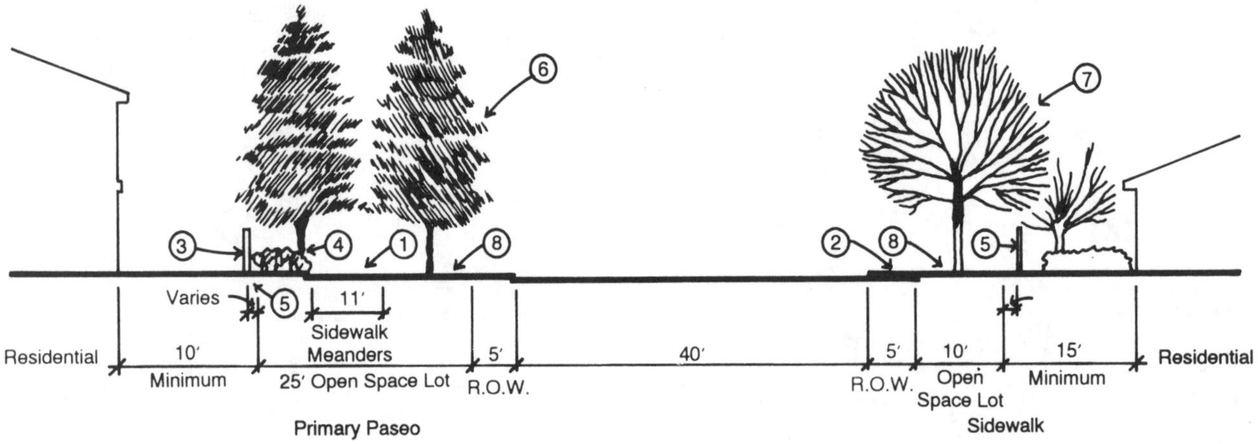

Typical Section of Local Street

1. Sidewalk: Primary paseo—11-foot-wide meandering sidewalk.
2. Sidewalk: 5-foot-wide sidewalk at curb.
3. Wall: Patio or garden walls blend with architecture and should vary in height, location, and design.
4. Shrubs: Rich variety of flowering and evergreen shrubs in casual massings to compliment architecture.
5. Vines: Encouraged on walls. Adequate planting pockets required between walls and walks.
6. Trees: Pinus canariensis with accent clusters.
7. Trees: Cupaniopsis anarcardiodes.
8. Turf.

Source: Westpark Design Guidelines, The Irvine Company, Newport Beach, California, 1985.

are used as play areas by children and for other social activities, thereby promoting the need to build pathways that link culs-de-sac to internal parks. Recently, however, neotraditionalist planners have moved away from superblocks and toward smaller parcels and traditional grids.

Site Engineering

Adequate grading and the optimal provision of water, gas, electricity, telephone, sewage, and stormwater utility services are critical elements of site design. Developers should never leave the decision about these elements to their civil engineers, but they should ensure that engineering considerations play a vital role. Engineering and land development costs also play a key role in land use planning. For example, developers must consider the cost of providing utilities to each lot in a subdivision when deciding the number of lots to develop; they must determine whether or not the value of adding two more lots will be less than the resulting utility costs.[29]

Grading

The grading plan, perhaps the most delicate part of the development, must contain precise details and take into consideration factors such as the amount of dirt that will be excavated from the streets, the finished heights of lots, steep areas that may require retaining walls, and graded areas that may be subject to future erosion (developers are liable for erosion even after they have sold all the lots on a site).

Grading is used as an engineering tool to correct unfavorable subsoil conditions and in the creation of:

- drainage swales;
- berms and noise barriers;
- proper topsoil depth for planting areas;
- circulation routes for paths and roads; and
- suitable subsoil conditions for facilities.

Grading is also used for aesthetic purposes to provide privacy, create sight lines, emphasize site topography or provide interest to a flat site, and connect structures to the streetscape and planting areas.

Modern excavating contractors use laser technology for the rough and fine grading of a site. By setting a rotating laser beam at a predetermined elevation, the amount of dirt to be removed from an area can be determined simply by reading the elevation of the bottom of the blade relative to that of the laser beam.

Homebuilders usually do their own fine grading of lots in addition to that done by the land developer. However, if the grading is unusually extensive, or if homebuilders must haul dirt away from the site, they may ask the developer for a rebate. The land developer is contractually obligated to deliver lots that meet a reasonable standard of grading. In some cases, the developer may contract to deliver lots that are ready to build on and that require no further grading (apart from the removal of loose topsoil before setting foundations).

James Oesch Photography

Grading underway at Southlake Landing at Montclair in Prince William County, Virginia.

Storm Drainage and Floodplains

Storm drainage carries away runoff surface water. In low-density developments with lots of at least one-half acre, natural drainage may suffice. However, in denser developments some form of storm drainage is always needed.

Gently rolling sites are the easiest and cheapest to drain; flat sites and steep sites are the most difficult and expensive. As with grading, drainage problems can come back to haunt a developer long after the lots have been sold.

One of the first feasibility studies that developers perform before buying a site is a floodplain study. Land that is within the 100-year floodplain—that is, the area that is expected to flood once every 100 years—is usually not developable. Hydrology engineers or civil engineers can easily determine from floodplain maps[30] the amount of land that lies within the 100-year floodplain.

In some localities, land within the 100-year floodplain *is* developable, albeit with restrictions. New and existing structures within the 100-year floodplain can be mortgaged by federally insured institutions, but only if the structure carries flood insurance. To qualify for flood insurance, the finished floor elevations must be at least one foot above the 100-year floodplain.

To alter floodplain areas, developers must apply for a permit from the Environmental Protection Agency (EPA), U.S. Army Corps of Engineers (Corps), or any other body that has authority over the local wetlands or creek system. However, any changes that developers make must reduce neither the total amount of on-site water-storage capacity nor the flow of water through the property. For example, suppose the floodplain currently holds three acre-feet of water[31] based on the volume of water that could be accommodated inside the floodplain area without flooding other areas. If developers want to channelize the flood area to enlarge the buildable area of a site, they still must provide for three acre-feet of on-site storage. This may mean dredging the channel to make it deeper or digging other storage ponds. (See Addison Business Center case study, at the end of chapter 6.)

The Corps designates not only 100-year floodplains but also floodways. The floodway is that portion of a channel and floodplain of a stream designated to provide passage of the 100-year flood, as defined by the Corps, without increasing elevation of the flood by more than one foot. Developers may place building piers and other structures within the floodplain but not within floodways. Floodways must retain the same or better water-flow rate after development as before it; otherwise floodplain lines are likely to rise upstream from the development. Developers can alter the floodway, but any changes must be engineered properly to preserve water flow and must be permitted by the appropriate authorities, including the Corps.

Wetlands Mitigation

Irrespective of the frequency with which they flood, areas within a property may be defined as wetlands and thus come under the jurisdiction of the EPA. Although at present the EPA, the Corps, the U.S. Fish and Wildlife Service, and other federal and state agencies have different definitions of wetlands, the various agencies are working together to arrive at a consensus.

Wetlands come in many forms, including ephemerally wet swales, intermittent streams, hardpan vernal pools, and volcanic mud-flow vernal pools. Generally speaking, if by any standards an area can be classified as a wetland, one or more government agencies will probably do so.

In evaluating a site that contains wetlands, developers should hire a qualified biologist to conduct a preliminary wetlands evaluation report, map potential wetland sites on the property, and suggest mitigation measures and alternative approaches to the design of the property.[32]

Sanitary Sewers

The layout of the sanitary system is determined by the topography of the site and the location of the outfall point—that is, the point of connection—to the sewer main. If the sewer main that connects the subdivision to the treatment plant is not located at the low point of the

■ 3-19 Westpark Design Guidelines: San Diego Creek Flood Control Channel

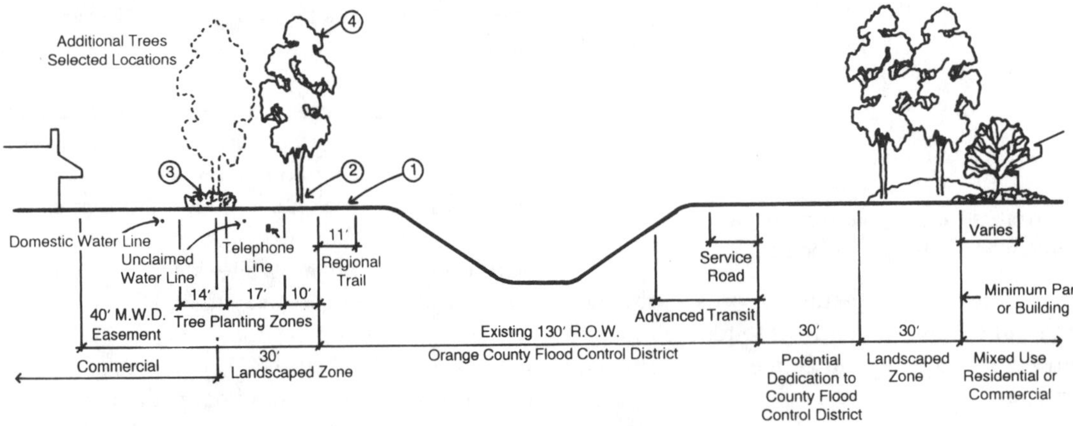

Typical Section

1. Walks: An 11-foot-wide regional trail runs along north side of creek.
2. Ground Plane: Groundcover to transition to San Diego Creek Channel.
3. Shrubs: Informal shrub planting.
4. Trees: Rows of Eucalyptus Rudis, formal planting.

Within the East/West Activity Corridor, 30-foot-wide landscaped areas featuring rows of tall vertical eucalyptus trees will be provided along both sides of the San Diego Creek Channel as visual buffers.

Source: Westpark Design Guidelines, The Irvine Company, Newport Beach, California, 1985.

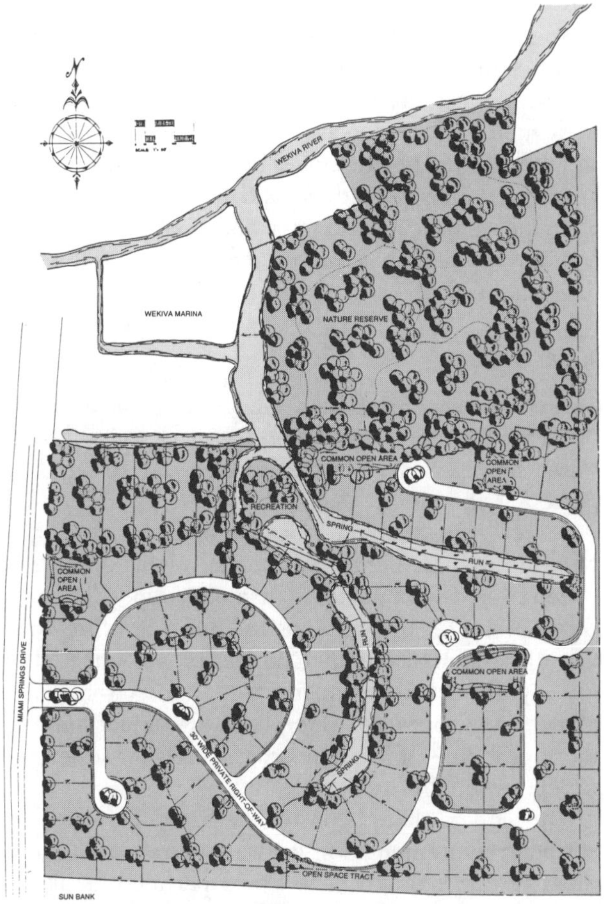

Sweetwater Springs in Seminole County, Florida, is located on a very sensitive 52-acre site—along the Wekiva River—that includes a wooded area surrounding a system of spring pools and wetlands. The 79-unit, single-family project plan includes a 600-foot buffer along the river and a 70-foot building setback to the springs. A program for wetlands mitigation was also developed, and a special sewage system was created that uses two lift stations rather than the normal one and cuts no deeper than 14 feet rather than the normal 25 feet. This was done to prevent contamination of the site's surface waters and shallow aquifers.

site, the developer may have to provide a pumping station, since sewage cannot, of course, flow uphill.

Beginning developers should avoid tracts of land for which nearby sewage and water services are not available, because the cost of bringing these services in from off-site locations can be prohibitive. Where major off-site utility improvements are necessary, developers usually require sites of 300 to 500 acres to support the investment. Creating a utility district to provide service, or building a plant where none exists, could take two or more years.

One option available to developers whose sites do not have sanitary service is to buy or lease a package-treatment plant, a small self-contained sewage treatment facility, to serve the subdivision and design the system to tie eventually into the community's system. This option works in rural areas and in communities that are accustomed to working with package-treatment technology.

Septic tank systems are discouraged, except in rural areas. Their use depends on soil conditions. In most areas, septic tanks are allowed only on lots at least one-half of an acre in size. Minimum requirements of three-quarters of an acre or one acre are not uncommon. If a well is included on the same site as a septic tank, even larger lots are sometimes necessary to prevent contamination of the well water.

In planning a sewer system, the developer should investigate the following:

- sewage capacity requirements—these vary from city to city, but 100 gallons per person, per day (gpd), is common;
- the available capacity of the treatment plant and connector lines;
- the number of hookups that are contracted and not yet installed;
- the municipality's method of charging for sewer installation; and
- the persons responsible for issuing permits and establishing requirements for discharging treated sewage into natural watercourses.

Sanitary sewer lines normally are located within the street rights-of-way but not under the road pavement. House connections to sewers should be at least six inches in diameter in order to avoid clogging; all lateral sewers should be at least eight inches in diameter. Sanitary lines and water lines should be laid in different trenches, although some cities allow a double-shelf trench that contains the sanitary sewer on the bottom and the water lines on the shelf.

Water System

A central water system is standard in urban communities. Like the requirements for sewage capacity, those for water supply vary from city to city, but 100 gpd, per person, is common.

Water mains should be located in street rights-of-way or in utility easements. Residential mains average between six and eight inches in diameter, depending on the water pressure. Branch lines to houses are three-quarters-of-an-inch or one-inch copper pipe connected to a five-eighths or a three-quarters-of-an-inch water meter, respectively. Because water lines are under pressure, their location is of less concern than it is for sewer lines, which rely on gravity flow.

Developers should consult the fire department concerning requirements for water pressure and the placement of fire hydrants. The fire department is likely to restrict cul-de-sac depth and the maximum distance between fire hydrants and structures.

Water, sewer, and drainage lines should, of course, be installed before streets are paved. If this is not possible, developers should lay underground culverts where the lines cross the streets so that the utility contractor can pull the lines through at a later time; if this is not done, the streets will have to be torn up in order to lay the lines.

Electricity, Gas, Telephone, and Cable Television

Electricity, gas, telephone, and cable television services are typically installed and operated by private companies. Designating the location of utility easements is an essential step in the process of land planning. If the land planner does not specify a location, the electric company will do so with little regard for aesthetic considerations. Usually, easements run along the back five or 10 feet of each lot.

Most planners prefer to place all electrical power transformers underground, but local custom usually dictates whether lines are above or below ground. The installation of transformers underground can be done at a reasonable cost and prevents vandalism and the need for frequent maintenance. If transformers are located above ground, they can be hidden and protected from vandals by wooden lattices with thorny shrubs or similar landscaping devices.

Although electricity, gas, telephone, and cable tend to play a smaller role in site design than do public utilities such as water, sewer, and drainage, they still determine where structures can be built on each lot. The developer should talk to each utility provider as early as possible. Delays in obtaining services—which is the rule rather than the exception—can easily throw off the developer's schedule and hold up final sales.

Lotting

Lot size and shape determines the density and the type of structure that can be built. The marketplace has defined a hierarchy of single-family housing types, determined primarily by the placement of the garage on the lot. From highest to lowest value, this hierarchy is as follows:

- The garage entrance faces the back of the house (*rear-loaded*) or is located in a separate structure behind the house, preferably connected by a breezeway. The garage doors either are not visible from the street or are set back so that they do not affect the main facade of the house as seen from the street. The minimum lot width required is 50 feet.
- The garage is attached to the house in front. The garage doors are perpendicular to the street (*side-loaded*) with a turn-in driveway. The wall of the garage facing the street often has windows or relief to disguise the garage, which preferably covers less than half of the house frontage. The minimum lot width required is 40 feet.
- The garage doors face the street (*front-loaded*). The narrower the house and lot are, the more the garage doors dominate the front facade.

Houses with front-loaded garages are not necessarily inexpensive. In costly urban locations, very expensive houses may be built on lots that are only 30 to 40 feet wide—$5 million townhouses in New York City can be found on 15-foot-wide lots. The designer's challenge is to make front-loaded houses look higher-end. Careful site planning and landscaping increase in importance as lots become smaller. The adroit use of paving tiles, tile roofs, masonry materials, garage doors, planters, courtyards, iron fences, and architecturally coordinated facades can give houses in a dense project a higher-end look.

The appearance of a subdivision from the street plays an important role in marketing the houses—both when houses are new and when they are resold. Subtle differences in design can create substantial differences in value. For example, two-story facades generally look more imposing than do single-story facades. Likewise, houses on 60-foot lots look noticeably more impressive than houses on

© Jess Smith/Photosmith

Lot size and shape determine density and the type of structure that can be built, affecting such design elements as the orientation of the garages. Narrower lots usually require garages to face the street; wider lots allow a perpendicular arrangement.

50-foot lots. The extra 10 feet allows an extra set of windows on the front of the house, which makes the house look significantly larger from the street. Houses that are set back 30 feet from the street with a front lawn look more expensive than houses set back 25 feet. Buyers may not be able to describe immediately why they prefer one house over another; nevertheless, the differences in size have the same effect on buyers as do nine-foot ceilings instead of standard eight-foot ceilings. Subconsciously or otherwise, people appreciate greater space.

Experienced developers, like good architects, understand which items of design create value. However, even developers who have a good intuitive feel for specific measurements, who understand the difference that one or two feet can make, spend time in the field investigating why people react more favorably to one design element than to another. Buyers also react differently in different markets. They may like certain features such as deeper front yards but not be able to afford the additional cost. Developers often make models or even construct full-scale mock-ups of a new design so that they can see how it will work and can make changes during the design stage.

Larger lots (one-half of an acre, or more) do not require necessarily the same infrastructure as smaller lots. Sidewalks, curbing, grass strips, and catchment basins can all be adjusted to the density of the development. A single-family subdivision of 40,000-square-foot lots on minor streets need not be developed with the same street improvements required for higher-density, multifamily development.

The lot layout should seek to achieve a variety of goals, including:

- a favorable site that does not require excessive grading or unusually deep foundation footings;
- the presence of sufficient usable area for outdoor activity—one or two larger areas are preferable to four small areas;
- adequate surface drainage away from the house, with slopes running toward the front or rear of the house—land developers should grade the lots so that they all drain toward the storm drainage system;
- a minimum degree of on-lot grading and a maximum retention of specimen trees; and
- a minimum number of adjoining lots—preferably, no more than three (one on each side and one along the back).

Corner lots should be 10 feet wider than interior lots in order to permit adequate sideyard space on the side street. Square corner lots permit diagonal placement of the house. If the streets are not too busy, corner lots usually sell at a premium because the garage can be reached from the side street, thereby creating more usable lawn area. Acute angles at street intersections

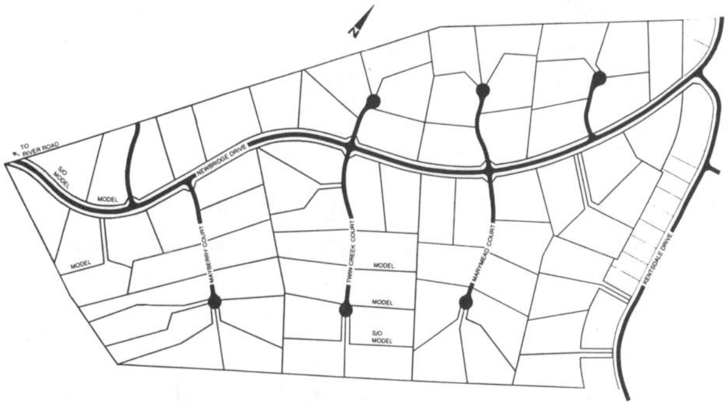

Teversall in Potomac, Maryland, is a large-lot subdivision of 71 homes on two-acre lots.

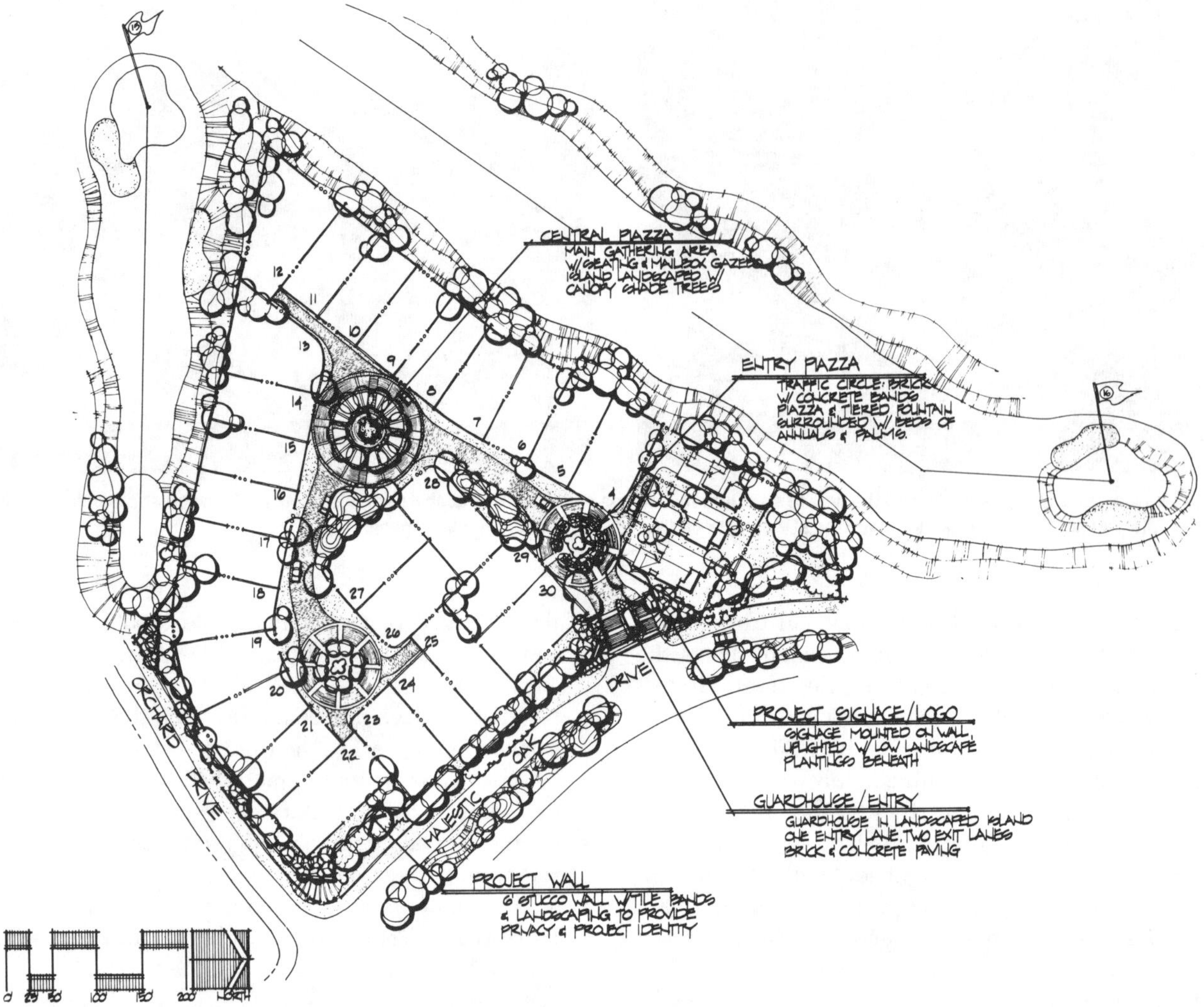

At Villa D'Este at Sweetwater in Longwood, Florida, a private enclave of 30 houses on a 6.8-acre site, privacy and security are ensured by orienting the lots around an interior, gate-controlled court and by using walls along roadways.

should be avoided whenever possible because they make house placement difficult.

Curvilinear streets often create irregularly shaped lots that enjoy much drive-by appeal. A potential problem for the developer, however, is that such lots may have to be resurveyed when the builder is ready to start construction—often because the iron pins that mark the lot corners tend to get moved or lost during construction of other houses.

If the development adjoins a busy street, the developer can lay out houses on deep lots that back up to the street. In order to market these "back-up lots" successfully, the developer should build a permanent wall along the street, preferably out of brick or concrete, and install plants. Alternatively, the developer could build a service street that adjoins the highway and front the houses on the service street. If room permits, small culs-de-sac are the best solution.

Higher Densities

Land costs as a percentage of house value have risen steadily over the last three decades, from 15 to 25 percent on average. In certain parts of major cities, land costs may now exceed 50 percent of house value.

Nevertheless, estate houses in an exclusive multiacre compound that offer extreme privacy remain an American icon. For the wealthy commuter, estate houses are now being rescaled to fit on one-quarter-acre lots. These houses (called "small-lot villas") typically have two-story facades that face the street, giving an impression of height, volume, and value. "Consumers," note the authors of a recent book on high-density housing, "favor symmetrical plans and the use of high-quality materials on the curb side of the house."[33]

Other traditional housing types are also being rescaled and redesigned for modern use. Resort bungalows, ranging from 900 to 2,000 square feet, are becoming year-round patio houses. Middle-income "cottages" are re-emerging as small-lot, single-family houses on 4,000- to 7,000-square-foot lots. Duplexes, while still popular in some areas, are being replaced by zero-lot-line and Z-lot houses. Townhouses with flat row-house facades are re-appearing as attached single-family houses and "cluster houses" with varied facades and private yards.

These changes are often the result of innovations in land development. Escalating land costs have fueled a search for better-designed, higher-density development. In some cases, new housing designs, such as Z-lots, have led the way to new forms of land development.

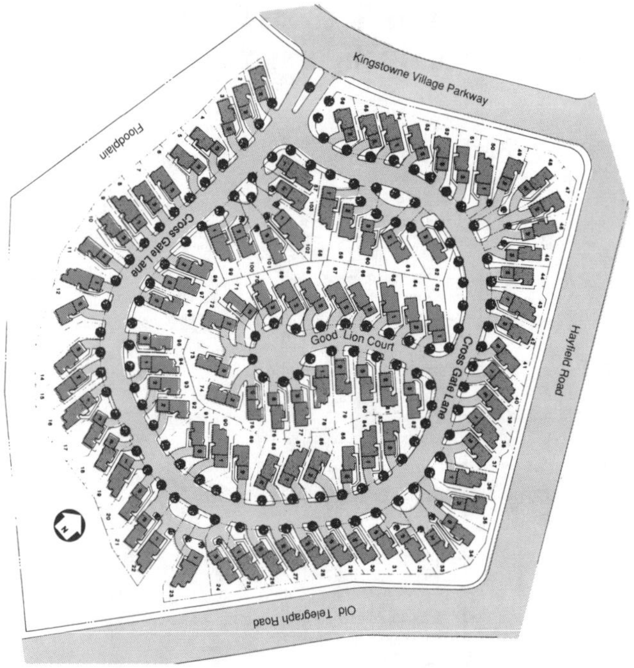

A gross density of 4.9 units per acre was achieved at Nottingham in Fairfax County, Virginia, by using Z-lots.

Zero-Lot-Line or Patio Houses

Traditionally, city zoning codes have established minimum sideyard setbacks ranging from three feet to 10 percent of the lot width. Houses that are built with three- or five-foot sideyards have unusable spaces along their sides. Windows from one house often look into windows of the next house, only six feet away.

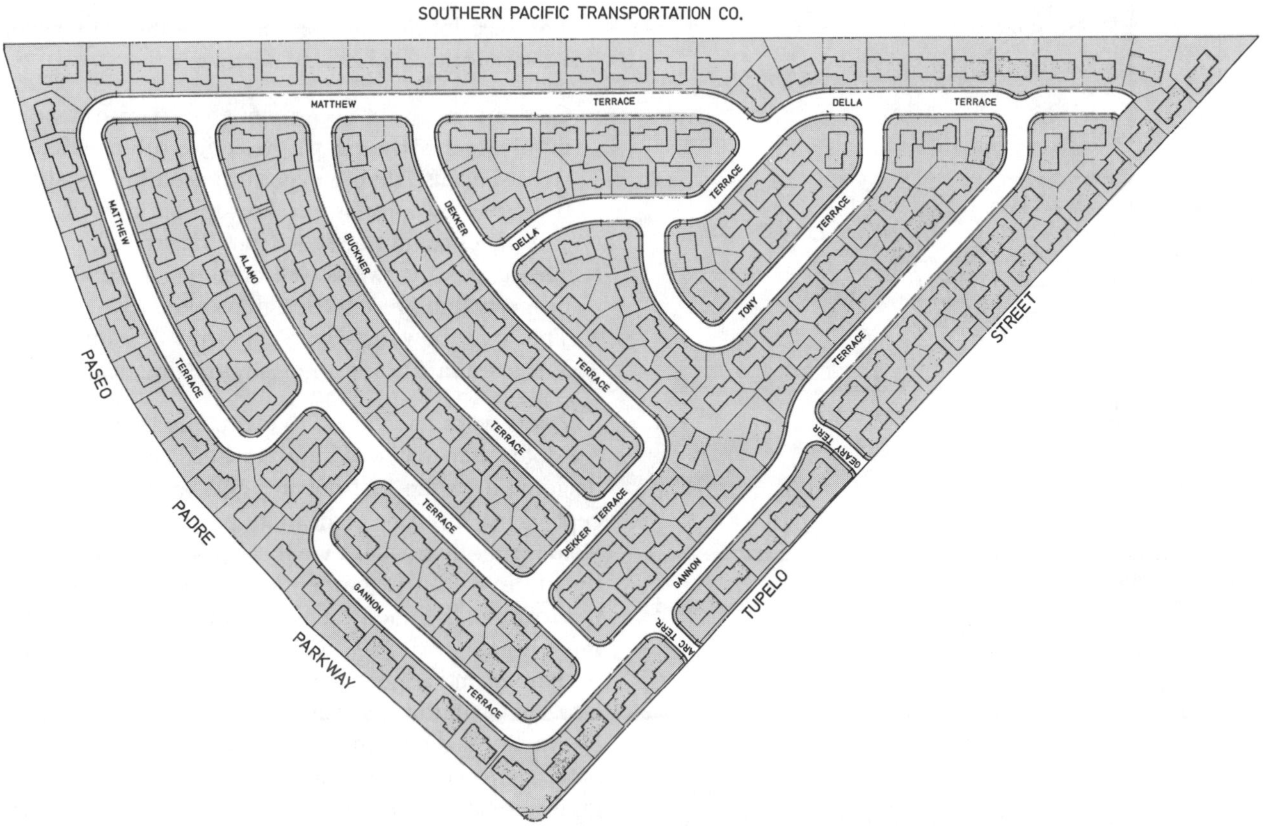

Using a copyrighted interlocking lot design plan and zero-lot-line approach, California Meadows in Fremont, California, achieves a gross density of 8.7 units per acre.

■ 3-20 Lot Yield Analysis for Different Zero-Lot-Line Configurations

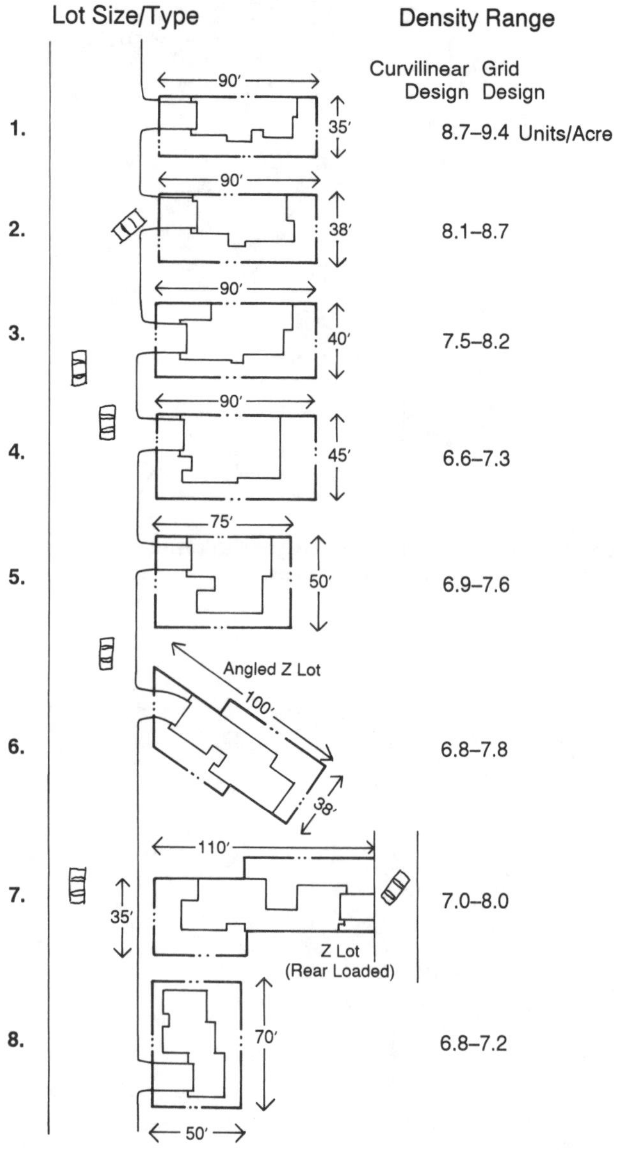

Density ranges based on:

- Representative 10-acre irregular site with both curvilinear and grid layouts and relatively flat.
- Comfortable, achievable densities.
- No recreation centers or common open space.
- 50-foot dedicated street right-of-way.
- 32-foot private street system—can increase density by ± 1/2 unit per acre.
- The individual characteristics and constraints of each site. Actual densities obtained will vary both up and down from these generalized guidelines.

Source: Richardson-Nagy-Martin, Newport Beach, California.

Zero-lot-line lots, which allow densities of up to nine units per acre, were created to make sideyards more usable. Today, most major cities and high-growth counties have modified their zoning codes to allow for them.

Zero-lot-line means that the houses are "left- or right-justified," that is, one side of the house is built on the lot line so that the sideyard can be twice the normal width on the other side (10 feet is considered the minimum width for usable space). The side of the house on the lot line usually is a solid wall. Also, each lot must take care of its own drainage. If builders want to design a roof that drains water onto the next property, they must obtain a drainage easement from the owner of that property. In addition, a maintenance agreement, which can be made before construction while the builder or developer owns all of the lots, must be recorded if using the neighbor's lot to maintain the wall on the lot-line side of the house is necessary. Good architects have mastered the challenge of designing zero-lot-line houses (also called patio houses) by creating patio space to provide light to rooms on the zero-lot-line side of the houses. Figure 3-20 shows various zero-lot-line configurations and associated densities.

Z-Lots

The zero-lot-line concept has a number of problems that intensify as lots become narrower:[34]

- Cars are not well accommodated. Two-car garages dominate the streetscape. Residents often park on the street because their garages are used for storage and the driveway apron is too short for parking.
- Entrances cannot be seen from the street.
- The long, windowless wall on the side adjoining the property line presents design problems.
- The long, bowling-alley shape of the patio and the L-shaped yard are aesthetically and practically limited.

Z-lots were introduced to overcome these problems. A Z-lot is shaped like a Z, and the house is laid out on the diagonal between its frontyard and backyard. The concept yields seven or eight units per acre. Although the yield is slightly smaller than that for zero-lot-line houses, the loss in density is compensated for by the possibility of improvements in house design and streetscape, such as more usable yard space, a more varied streetscape, more entrances, and a more flexible floor plan, unconstrained by a long, windowless wall.

Small-lot, high-density housing does not work well with scattered-lot or multiple-builder land sales programs because house design must be carefully coordinated. The land plan, in fact, should be drawn up concurrently with the house plan. Other considerations in the planning of successful Z-lots include:[35]

- Narrow lots or Z-lots do not work well on hillsides with slopes greater than 3 or 4 percent.
- Window sight lines must be carefully worked out—second-floor windows should not compromise yard privacy.
- Drainage requirements must be carefully studied.

- Major rooms should be oriented towards patios to create a greater feeling of spaciousness.
- The streetscape is especially important. Walls and fences that are visible from the street should be coordinated in terms of their color and materials. Side or front entrances should be used. The developer should fully landscape the frontyards and streetscape.
- The appeal of the diagonal Z-lot and similar concepts involving the use of easements may be limited to buyers that understand the implications of the easement and access agreements.
- Enabling statutes may be required in new jurisdictions where Z-lots have not been tried previously.

Other Small-Lot Variations

Other variations on the Z-lot concept include angled Z-lots, wide-shallow lots, and zipper-lots. Angled Z-lots not only make houses appear wider than they actually are, but also permit side-loaded garages. However, on very narrow lots (35 to 40 feet wide), they may create the impression that the houses are attached rather than detached.

In wide-shallow developments, lots are 55 to 70 feet wide but only 55 to 70 feet deep, allowing the developer to achieve densities of seven units per acre. Wider lots

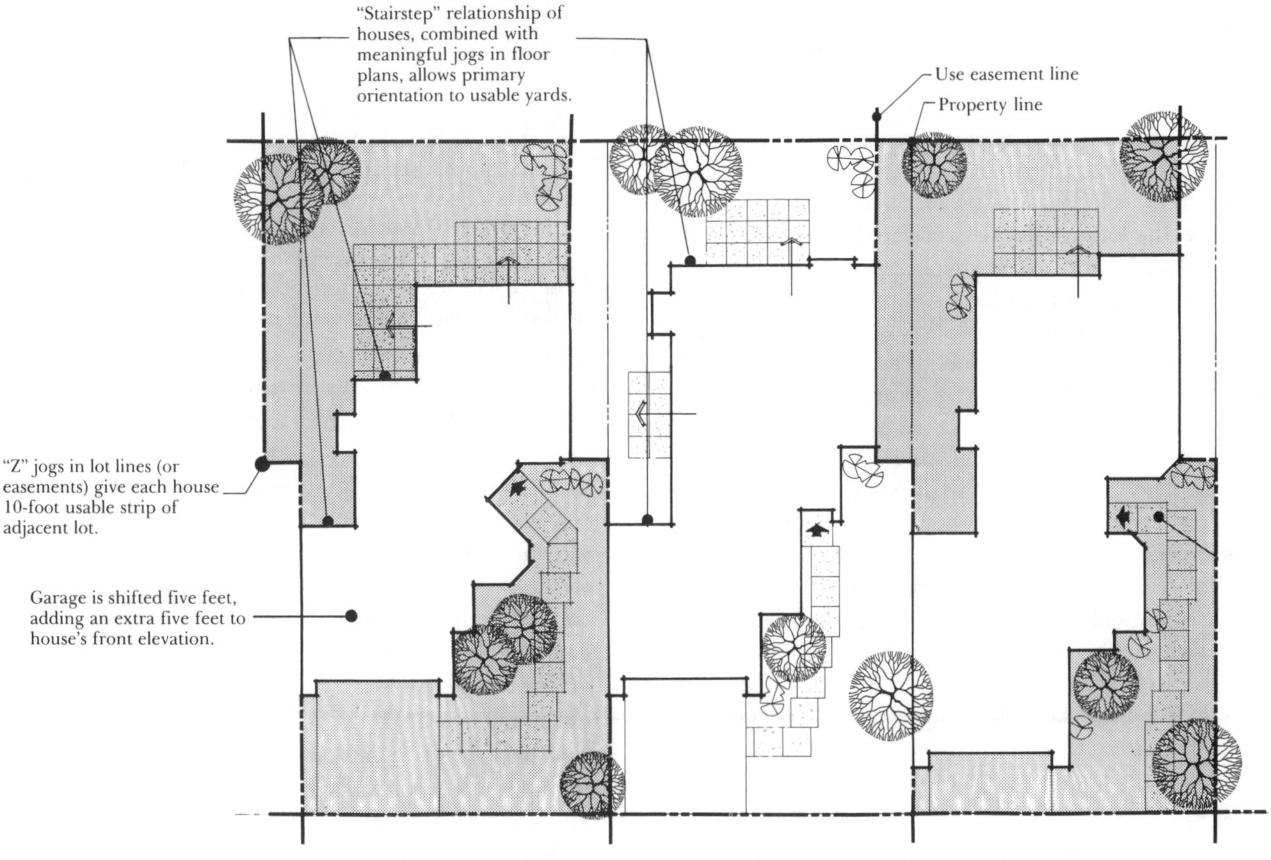
"Stairstep" relationship of houses, combined with meaningful jogs in floor plans, allows primary orientation to usable yards.
Use easement line
Property line
"Z" jogs in lot lines (or easements) give each house 10-foot usable strip of adjacent lot.
Garage is shifted five feet, adding an extra five feet to house's front elevation.

Westpark Promenade's Z-lot plan creates more usable yard space and privacy than does a typical zero-lot-line development.

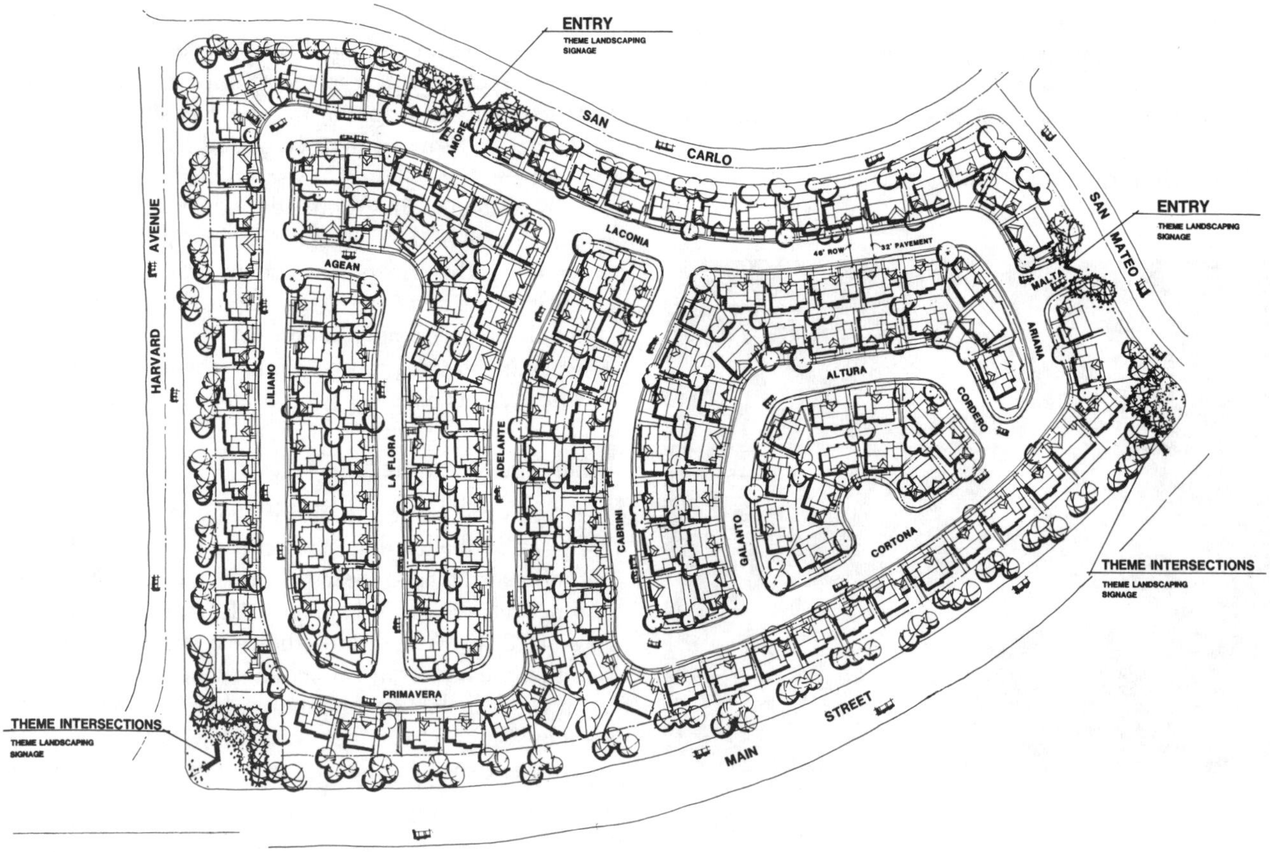

A wide-lot concept was used to achieve 7.8 units per acre at Barcelona in Westpark in Irvine, California.

add proportionately to street and utility costs, but buyers are usually prepared to pay more for the greater curb appeal. Wide-shallow lots usually necessitate two-story houses. If the lots are less than 65 feet deep, the back-to-back rearyards may be too small for privacy. Lot depths of 70 feet are recommended.

Zipper-lots are like wide-shallow lots except that space is borrowed from adjacent lots to avoid the problem of narrow, rectangular rearyards. Easements are used to make the rearyards of back-to-back houses abut on an angled, rather than a parallel, property line. The main disadvantages of zipper-lots are the complexity of the plot plan, loss of privacy from second-story windows that overlook the neighbor's backyard, and possible resistance from buyers and government jurisdictions. Nevertheless, they offer a creative solution to high-density housing in selected markets.

With careful design, densities of seven to eight units per acre are achievable in a single-family detached setting. Even higher densities of 10 to 12 units per acre are possible for small senior-housing units or projects without garages.

Refinements in site planning and unit design are making it possible to achieve greater densities without sacrificing privacy and livability. The fact that properly designed small-lot detached housing can make, and fit into, high-quality neighborhoods needs to be made known to local planning and zoning officials and to typically cynical community residents. Without their acceptance of high-density single-family concepts, the affordability crisis in areas with high land costs clearly will remain unsolved.[36]

That acceptance will be easier to secure if developers avoid a number of pitfalls in designing small-lot, high-density housing. These errors include:[37]

- designing floor plans that overbuild the lot or do not maximize the use of outdoor spaces;
- placing two-story houses on lots so that they block sunlight;
- designing atriums that are expensive, are too small, cause water problems, and are unattractive when adjacent to high roofs;
- designing streetscapes that make the units appear attached rather than detached;
- failing to consider walls, easements, and overhanging gutters when designing lot drainage; and
- failing to provide driveway aprons large enough to permit off-street parking.

Financing

The major difference between land development and income-property development is that land is usually subdivided and sold rapidly, whereas income-property usually is held and operated over a period of years. The holding period is the key to deciding the appropriate type of financing. Land development is financed by a short-term development or construction loan. Income-property development is financed by both a construction loan and a permanent mortgage, the latter of which is known as a "takeout loan." For income-property development, the construction lender must rely on the permanent lender to ensure that the construction loan will be retired. For land development, the construction lender must rely on the developer's ability to sell the finished lots within the agreed time frame and at the scheduled prices.

Success in land development—and the developer's ability to repay the development loan—thus depends on the successful marketing of the lots. Because no takeout exists for construction lenders, they must be satisfied that the developer will be able to sell enough lots fast enough to pay off the loan. Often, construction lenders will require other collateral, such as letters of credit, in addition to a mortgage on the property. Also, the loan amount is limited to 60 to 80 percent of the projected sales proceeds, to provide a cushion in the event that sales occur more slowly than projected. Slower sales translate into greater interest costs because the development-loan balance is reduced more slowly than the developer initially projected.

Obtaining Financing

The most difficult task for beginning developers is to obtain financing. Unless developers have enough personal wealth to finance a project themselves, they will need to convince lenders to provide them with financing. In the past, developers could obtain almost 100 percent financing without accepting personal liability. Now, however, developers must contribute equity and sign loans personally in most situations.

A developer's equity can be furnished either in cash or in land. Suppose, for instance, that a developer purchased land for a project at the cost of $100,000. The market value of that land subsequently rose to $300,000. If the total cost of the developer's proposed project is $1 million ($700,000 for development costs plus the market value of the land), the developer could probably find lenders willing to loan 80 percent of that amount. In other words, the lenders require $200,000 equity. Because the market value of the land is $200,000 greater than the original land cost, the developer should be able to use the land equity to satisfy the lenders' $200,000 requirement. In fact, the loan would cover the developer's original $100,000 land cost because the $800,000 commitment exceeds the development cost of $700,000 by $100,000.

The development loan is a short-term demand note, a form of construction financing rather than permanent financing. The development lender must hold a first lien position on the land. If the developer has a purchase-money note (PMN) from the seller, he/she will need either to pay it off or to ask the seller to subordinate it to the development loan.

The terms of the PMN play a vital role in financing the project. The developer would prefer, of course, that the PMN survive as long as possible, since it takes the place of equity that would otherwise have to be raised or money that would have to be borrowed. The development lender, on the other hand, would prefer the land to be free and clear for additional security.

On larger tracts, the downpayment for the land should provide for the releasing of the first parcel that the developer plans to develop from the PMN. The land that is to be released first must be designated specifically in the purchase contract and the PMN mortgage in order to avoid any conflict or confusion. The unencumbered parcel can provide the initial security (first lien) for the development loan, although the developer may have to provide additional collateral. The development loan covers other tracts as they are released from the PMN.

The contractor will be able to build improvements only on those parcels for which the development lender has a first lien. If the contractor begins work on any part of the land before the lender has perfected the lien, the lender may halt construction until possible lien conflicts are cleared. Clearing lien conflicts can take several months because every supplier that has delivered material to the property and every subcontractor that has worked on the property must sign a lien waiver indicating that they have received full payment.

Builder Precommitments

As part of the market feasibility stage, the developer obtains from area builders indications of interest in purchasing the lots.[38]

Next, the developer must secure builders' commitment letters, which are part of the documentation that the developer will have to submit to the lender to obtain a loan commitment. The commitment letter specifies the number of lots each builder will buy in the project.

Ideally, the developer will have commitments for most of the lots on a site before approaching potential lenders. However, although the commitments help to reduce the market risk, they do not guarantee that the lots will be sold, unless they are backed by letters of credit (LCs).

■ 3-21 Example of a Builder Commitment Letter

ABC Homes

March 13, 1991

XYZ Development

Gentlemen:

ABC Homes, Inc., is prepared to enter into a contract mutually agreed upon to purchase 60 to 68 single-family lots in the ________ Subdivision of the City of __________________. This contract shall include the following terms and conditions:

1. Purchaser: ABC Homes, Inc., or assigns.
2. Purchaser shall have the right to approve the subdivision plat prior to filing such plat for approval by the City of ______________.
3. Purchase Price: $28,000 per lot.
4. Takedown Schedule: Purchaser shall close 10 lots 30 days from completion of development of the subdivision and shall close 10 lots per quarter, calculated from the date of the first closing, until Purchaser has closed 60 to 68 lots. Completion of development is generally defined to mean final unconditional acceptance of the Subdivision by the City of ____________, completion of installation of underground electric distribution system to service each lot, and completion of installation of the gas distribution system to service each lot.
5. The purchase price for each lot purchased, after the initial purchase, shall bear interest, payable to the seller at the final closing, from the date of the initial closing, at a rate equal to ______________ prime interest rate, plus 1 percent.
6. Seller shall pay a commission equal to 5 percent of the base price of each lot to ____________ at each closing.
7. Earnest money shall be in the form of a letter of credit in the amount of $84,000.00.

This letter expresses our desire and intent to enter into a contract with Seller to purchase the lots upon the general terms and conditions contained herein. This letter is not binding upon either Purchaser or Seller.

Sincerely,

[signature]

Executive Vice President
ABC Homes, Inc.

AGREED AND ACCEPTED THIS ________ DAY OF ______________, 19__.

____

XYZ Development Executives

Don Mackie, partner of Mill Creek Properties, Salado, Texas, states that "most banks know that an unsecured builder commitment letter has no collateral value." He points out: "In 1985, if you had good appraisals (paper equity), a little real equity in the form of earnest money, and commitment letters from reputable builders, you could get your subdivision financed. Now, it takes major equity and a bankable builder." To be bankable, a builder's commitments must be backed by LCs. This requirement makes the developer's job substantially more difficult. Builders, who are often underfinanced, are reluctant to guarantee that they will purchase the lots. The developer either must convince his/her lender that the builders' commitments are solid or must provide proof with the LCs. The developer should know the type of documentation that lenders will require before talking to builders.

If the lender requires firm commitments backed by LCs, then the developer must address that requirement as part of the deal with the builders.

Builders' Purchase Terms

The purchase terms that builders require for lots vary according to local market conditions. Downpayments range from $100 earnest money to 10 percent, or even 20 percent, of the purchase price. Builders pay the earnest money when they reserve the lots. The balance is covered by a note that sets the interest rate beginning the day that the developer delivers finished lots. The lot-purchase contract usually defines "lot delivery" as the date on which the city accepts the street dedications or the engineer certifies that the project is substantially complete.

In slow markets and in workout situations (situations in which the developer has defaulted on the loan), builders will hold a stronger position than will the developer. For example, in the aftermath of the oil recession of the mid-1980s, builders in Austin, Texas, could tie up a large number of lots for very little money. To generate builder interest, developers sometimes subordinated to the construction lender the land note on builders' model houses.[39] This allowed builders to reduce upfront cost. Builders constructed, say, three model houses and six "spec" houses (houses that are built on the speculative assumption that they will be sold while under construction). Developers gave builders a rolling option so that builders were able to take down more land as the spec houses were sold.[40]

Another approach that developers use to generate builder interest in slow markets or workout situations is to discount the initial lots. For example, if the lots normally sell for $20,000, developers may sell the first two lots to builders for $10,000 and the next two for $15,000.

Tips for Dealing with Lenders

Beginning developers must remember that each deal with a land development lender is unique. However, although terms are subject to local market and economic conditions, several factors always should be considered for a three- to five-year project:

- Borrow enough money at the beginning of the project—do not think that a loan can be renegotiated later or that lots can be sold faster.
- Allow enough time on the loan to complete the project or provide for automatic rollover provisions, even though the lender will charge for the rollover option.
- Typical loan points for the land development loan are two points upfront and one point per year, starting in the third year. Points are calculated on the total loan request, not on the amount drawn to date. For example, two points on a $1.5 million loan request would be $30,000.
- The loan can be structured as a two-year construction loan with three automatic renewals.
- Development loans are a form of construction loan. The amounts by which developers pay down the loan cannot later be borrowed again. If possible, developers should structure the development loan as a revolving line of credit that allows borrowing up to the limit of the credit line, regardless of repayments already made. (This may require the provision of additional collateral as the lots are sold.)
- One of the major items for negotiation is the release price of lots. The development lender holds a first mortgage on the entire property. The lender must release its lien on the property so that the purchaser can obtain construction financing. The release price is subject to negotiation between the developer and the lender. Ideally, the release price simply would be a pro-rata share of the development loan. For example, if the development loan is $1 million for 100 lots, then the sale of one lot would retire the loan by 1 divided by 100 times $1 million, or $10,000 per lot. Most lenders will set the release price at 1.2 to 1.5 times the pro-rata share (called the "multiple"). For a 1.2 multiple, the release price would be 1.2 times $10,000, or $12,000 per lot. Thus, every time a lot is sold, the developer pays down the loan by $12,000.

  The lender often wants a high multiple, 1.3 or greater, for releasing lots. The developer wants a multiple as low as possible, 1.2 or lower, since cash flow is needed. In return for a low multiple, the lender may require some form of credit enhancement, such as an LC or second lien on other property.

Joint Ventures

In the earlier cash-flow analyses in this chapter, the developer was assumed to own 100 percent of the deal, investing 100 percent of the equity and receiving 100 percent of the cash flows. The developer also would have 100 percent of the downside risk and liability. However, all or any part of a land development project may be packaged in a variety of different joint venture formats.

Joint ventures may be structured in a variety of legal forms, including general partnerships, limited partnerships (usually used for syndications), and corporations in which the venturing parties hold stock. Joint ventures also may be created de facto by loan agreements that give the land seller or development lender a share in the profits. In this chapter, the business side of joint venture structuring is the focus. The various legal forms are described in chapter 2.

Developer and Landowner

One of the most common forms of joint ventures is that between a developer and a landowner. The land is entered into the deal at a negotiated price, which usually covers in full the equity that the developer may need to obtain development financing. The landowner may hold either a purchase-money mortgage that is subordinated to the development loan or a first priority for receipt of positive cash flows. The order in which cash flows are distributed (the order of "cash-distribution priorities") might be as follows:

- *Priority 1:* The landowner is returned the land value.
- *Priority 2:* The landowner receives a preferred return (either cumulative or noncumulative)[41] on the equity.
- *Priority 3:* The developer receives a development fee.
- *Priority 4:* The developer and the landowner split the remaining profits.

If the landowner has a subordinated PMN on the land, the loan agreement will provide for releases similar to those in the development-loan agreement. Both liens must be released before the homebuilder or other buyer of the lots can free and clear title. The homebuilder needs free and clear title in order to obtain construction financing. For example, suppose a subdivision has both bank financing and a subordinated PMN from the seller. Suppose also that the PMN calls for repayment of $10,000 in order to release a lot from the note, and that the development loan calls for $20,000 repayment. If the developer sells 10 lots for $35,000 each, the cash flows would be:

Sales revenue:	
10 x $35,000 =	$350,000
Repayment of development loan:	
10 x $20,000 =	(200,000)
Repayment of PMN:	
10 x $10,000 =	(100,000)
Cash available for distribution:	$ 50,000

Most joint venture agreements provide for the venture to retain "cash available for distribution" as working capital, until the development loan is retired. Alternatively, such cash could be given to the landowner until land equity has been recovered, or it could be considered profit and be divided between the joint venturers. Of course, the landowner would prefer to receive first priority on all cash flows until recovering the value of the land equity.

Sometimes, the land sales revenue will not cover the required loan-release payments for a given parcel or series of lots. In that case, the joint venturers would be required to invest new equity into the venture to cover the cash deficit. The development-loan agreement may require the lender's approval for sales below a certain price, although the developer would prefer to have full control over pricing decisions.

Developer and Investor

Joint ventures between the developer and third-party investors are a common alternative to joint ventures with the landowner. The third-party investors (called third-party because they are not involved in the original transaction) furnish the cash equity needed to complete the deal. For example, in the deal shown between developer and landowner, the developer would purchase the land outright from the land seller.[42] The investors would put up the cash needed to purchase the land, which was the landowner's equity in the first deal. The developer's arrangement with the investors might closely resemble the deal with the landowner, with respect to cash-distribution priorities:

- *Priority 1:* All cash available goes to investors until they have received their total cash investment.
- *Priority 2:* The next cash available also goes to the investors until they have received, say, an 8 percent cumulative (or noncumulative) return on their investment.
- *Priority 3:* The next cash available goes to the developer until he/she has received the agreed fee.
- *Priority 4:* All remaining cash available is divided 50/50 between the developer and the investors.

As before, every term of the deal is negotiable, including the order of priorities and the amount of personal liability on the development loan.

A common joint venture format in the 1960s and 1970s called for a straightforward 50/50 split between the developer and the investors, without any priorities. This format is still used by some of the largest developers, but beginning developers will find that they must give a larger share to investors to attract their interest. Under a 50/50 split, developers are able to take out profit as each acre is sold. The risk to investors is that developers may sell off the prime tracts, take all of the profit, and then fail to sell off the balance of the project, leaving the investors with a loss. Today, most investors prefer to receive back all of their equity before developers participate in any profit.

Developer and Lender

The lender may provide 100 percent financing for a deal, in exchange for some percentage of the profits. From the developer's point of view, this is perhaps the easiest form of joint venture because it involves only one other party.

The lender can structure involvement in a variety of ways. The financing can be considered a 100 percent loan, or some portion can be considered equity. The difference between a 100 percent loan and, say, an 80 percent loan minus 20 percent equity is that the equity portion of a 100 percent loan usually receives a "preferred return" rather than "interest." The preferred return is paid when cash is available, whereas interest must be paid immediately. Some development loans have accrual provisions that allow interest to be accrued in a fashion similar to that for preferred returns. They allow the project to accrue unpaid interest into future periods until cash is available to pay it. Prior to the S&L crisis in the late 1980s, S&Ls served as the most common joint venture lending partner for developers. The percentage split of profits varied with the experience and net worth of the developer. With stronger developers, the profit split could be 50/50. The split with less-experienced developers could be 65/35 or 70/30, with the lender receiving the larger share. Joint ventures with lenders usually allow developers to receive a fee for administrative expenses. A fee in the range of 5 to 10 percent of hard construction costs is common. Although few S&Ls are in the market for joint ventures now, private investors and some pension funds are cautiously taking their place.

Construction

The construction phase of land development consists primarily of grading, drainage, streets, and utilities. Although land development involves fewer subcontractors than does building construction, the process can be just as complicated, not least because of the role played by the public sector. The facilities built by land developers usually are dedicated to the city to become part of the city's urban infrastructure. The city maintains the streets, and the utility company, which may also be a city agency, maintains water and sewer lines. Consequently, all facilities must be built in strict accordance with city and utility company standards.

If possible, the contractor should be a part of the development team from the beginning. Even if developers choose to select a contractor after plans and specs are completed, they should go over preliminary plans with a contractor that can offer money-saving advice concerning various aspects of the design layout.

Don Mackie of Mill Creek Properties offers a number of tips for dealing with general contractors in land development situations:

- Negotiated-price contracts are better than competitive-bid contracts. On smaller jobs, developers should negotiate with two or three contractors simultaneously and take the best deal.
- A fixed contractor fee of, say, $5,000 to $10,000 for $100,000 to $200,000 jobs (costs based on actual dollars spent, verifiable by audit) is recommended. For change orders, developers should pay the contractor the additional cost but no additional fee. Equipment is charged to the job based on direct time in operation.
- Developers should hire a member of an engineering company for which business currently is slow to be on site to check that everything is installed properly. Developers should not rely solely on the engineer's certification and should ensure that the engineer will spend enough time on site. The engineer of record (responsible for the original drawings) should certify the work (check progress three to four times per week), but the on-site engineer should check that everything is installed properly.
- The standard 10 percent retention of payment for subcontractors is recommended. Subcontractors should sign lien releases and "bills-paid" affidavits with every draw request. The general contractor must obtain these affidavits and releases from the subcontractors and suppliers before paying them.
- If the contractor is not performing satisfactorily, developers should notify the contractor in writing (by registered mail), citing the specific paragraphs of the contract that are being violated and stating the possible consequences if performance does not improve by a certain date.
- When hiring a general contractor to construct for-sale housing, developers should include a clause that states that any deceptive trade practice suits that are not warranty items belong to the general contractor, not the developer.

Terry Lewis, president of Devon Development in Dallas,[43] explains how he serves as his own general contractor, hiring various subcontractors to do the work. He employs four subcontractors: the excavation subcontractor for dirt moving; the utility subcontractor for water, storm, and sanitary sewer installation; the paving subcontractor for concrete curb and gutter or asphalt paving; and the underground utility contractor for the installation of electricity, gas, telephone, and cable. Lewis states that the most difficult coordination problem is controlling the condition of the site during the transition from one subcontractor to the next.

The only deterrent to subcontracting in this manner is the difficulty that sometimes arises in coordinating the work of the separate subcontractors. For example, the paving contractor may complain that the utility contractor left the manholes too high or that more dirt is needed. The developer/general contractor must then choose between paying a late charge to the paving contractor that must wait until the utility contractor comes back to correct the problem or paying the paving contractor an exorbitant fee to fix it. If the project is coordinated correctly, the utility contractor is still on the site when the paving contractor arrives, allowing any apparent problems to be solved immediately. The general contractor is encouraged to withhold 10 percent of the contract price until the city accepts the utilities.

Another major problem that developers encounter is deliberate bidding mistakes. Most contracts are bid not on a fixed-price basis, but on a price-per-unit calculated basis from the engineer's estimate of quantities. If subcontractors see an area in which the quantity of an item was underestimated, they may bid lower on other items so that they get the job. They will deliberately bid high on the item for which the quantity was underestimated so that the developer ends up paying more on the total contract after the correct quantity has been determined. Lewis claims that engineers should not be allowed both to bid and to supervise the site, otherwise developers will never know if money was lost. Lewis prefers to negotiate a price-per-unit contract and then convert the bid to a fixed-price contract. He may pay a little more to allow for a margin of error in the quantity takeoff, but he avoids major overcharges.

Lewis cites a number of important points to remember during construction:

- Supervise subcontractors closely. A subcontractor that needs a piece of equipment for another job is likely to remove it unless the developer is watching closely.
- Plan drainage correctly for each lot. The usual five to 10 feet of fall from one side of the property to the other is a sufficient slope. Storm sewers are normally located in the streets, so lots should slope toward the street where possible. As many lots as possible should be higher than curb height. Excavating shallow streets may save money at the front end but may cost money in the long run.
- Work closely with the electric utility contractor to determine the location and price of transformers.
- Design and execute grading carefully. Dirt slopes of up to one-in-three[44] are much cheaper to construct than concrete or timber retaining walls, but a poorly executed grading job can lead to costly repairs, backcharges by builders, and even homeowner lawsuits.
- If FHA financing is planned for houses in the subdivision, pay especially close attention to grading requirements. FHA requires that the grade between the garage and the street must exceed 14 percent, as measured from the back of the sidewalk to the garage. If the pad for the lot is too high, the house will not qualify for an FHA loan. One solution is for the builder to drop the level of the garage to meet FHA's requirement. This requires the builder to spend more money; however, the developer usually pays the extra cost one way or another if he/she agrees to deliver an FHA-approved subdivision.
- If possible, obtain all rights for off-site easements and drainage before buying the property. The seller should assist the developer in this effort, according to specific terms that should be negotiated in the earnest money contract.

Marketing

Subdivision marketing begins before the developer closes on the land and continues until the last lot is sold. Various aspects of marketing, including public relations, advertising, staffing, and merchandising, are described in detail in chapter 4. Certain items, however, are unique to land development.

Marketing for the land developer focuses both on the sale of lots to builders and the sale of houses to homebuyers. The primary marketing objective, of course, is selling lots to builders. Except for large-volume builders, which may purchase large blocks of lots outright, most builders take down a few lots at a time. Thus, the developer's lot sales depend on the builders' success in selling houses.

In most subdivisions, builders either handle the sale of their houses themselves or use outside brokers. The developer is not involved directly with house sales; nevertheless, the developer can assist the builders' efforts by undertaking advertising and public relations for the subdivision as a whole and by ensuring that the subdivision has as much marketing appeal as is possible.

Virtually the entire development process can be viewed as a marketing exercise. Even before selecting a site, the developer should have identified the target market, and every step of the process, from lot design to selection of builders, should be consistent with the needs of that market.

The market determines:

- the demand and price range for the houses;
- the product type or mix of product types;
- the appropriate builders for a subdivision;
- the design of the lots;
- the types of permanent financing for builders;
- the variety and quality of amenities;
- the type of public relations to be conducted;
- the design of brochures and advertising material; and
- the means by which the homebuilders will market their houses to the end buyer.

Flowers, stone walls, and attractive street signs create a pleasant entrance, first impression, and marketing appeal at Brentwood Country Club, a small upscale golf course community in Brentwood, Tennessee, a suburb of Nashville.

Marketing to Homebuilders

Many different methods can be used to market a subdivision. Apartment, retail, or office sites will be marketed directly to building developers. Exclusive custom house subdivisions may be sold directly to homebuyers. In most cases, however, the developer sells lots to builders, that, in turn, sell to homebuyers. Builders typically market their product in one of three ways:

- They may build model houses from which homebuyers may select their preference. Builders typically offer varying degrees of options in interior finish and location within the subdivision. This approach is used primarily for tract-homes. Depending on the market, tract homebuilders typically build 25 to 200 houses per year in a given subdivision.
- They may build houses on spec to be sold during or after construction. The buyer contracts for the house during or after construction. The builder passes title when the house is complete. This approach is used for "semicustom" houses. Semicustom homebuilders typically build five to 25 houses per year in a given subdivision.
- They may sell lots to homebuyers on which the builder builds a custom-designed house. The transfer of ownership of the lot from the builder to the homebuyer usually occurs at the time of completion of the house. Custom homebuilders typically build one to 10 houses per year in a given subdivision.

Developers' market studies should indicate the types of builders to approach. Don Mackie recommends that developers begin with a "bell-cow builder"—a builder that has enough identity in the market to attract the public. He categorizes builders in Austin, Texas, into three groups:

- first-tier builders that have widely recognized names and build at least 500 houses per year throughout the city;
- second-tier builders that have less recognized names and that build between 100 and 500 houses per year; and
- third-tier builders that are little known and that build less than 100 houses per year.

Mackie advises that developers should not let first-tier builders control their subdivisions.

> They will want 10 to 15 lots at the beginning and a rolling option on the rest. They will build four models and construct six to 10 specs at a time. You need to give them enough lots for models and specs, with a one-for-one rolling option as they sell the specs.
>
> In pioneering areas, you convince builders by telling them how much you will spend on promotion: "Here's what we will spend. If we don't do what we promise, we will take the lots back." You get better absorption if you can keep traffic moving around in the subdivision. On small, 200-lot subdivisions, you must choose between selling all the lots to one bell-cow or working with small builders that take one or two lots each.

Mackie adds that developers need 300 to 500 lots to run a cost-effective on-site marketing program. In a 300-lot subdivision, he would sell half of the lots to the "market maker" and the rest to three other builders. The market maker will attract many potential buyers. The smaller builders will use one of their spec houses as a model and an office.

To obtain commitments from builders, developers should make contacts with potential builders as soon as the land is tied up. A local builder will often be more familiar with an area than will the most careful market researchers, and developers should solicit its advice on the target market and its preferred products.

In order to broaden their markets, larger subdivisions (200 houses or more) often will include two to 10 homebuilders that will build two or three different product types at different price ranges. A 300-house subdivision may, for example, be divided into two sections with one production (tract-home) builder taking down 150 lots and two to 10 custom builders taking down the other 150 lots—the mix, of course, depending on the market. The developer should retain some flexibility for allocating more lots to one builder than to another as sales progress. A rolling option that allows builders to take down blocks of five, 10, or 20 lots at a time helps the developer avoid the problem of losing lot sales if one product type is not moving as quickly as another.

Some developers prefer to contact prospective builders directly; others prefer to work through one or several brokers that know an area very well. Robert Moss, executive vice president of Cityplace Development Corporation, Dallas, Texas,[45] suggests that developers should examine the different homebuilders that build the type and price of product that the market studies recommend. Beginning developers should be able to compete effectively against well-established developers by offering builders three things: a continuing lot inventory, minimum cash upfront, and seller financing. Although Moss recommends that builders put up 10 percent downpayment, he advises beginning developers to settle for any amount that is sufficient to hold the builders' interest.

After preliminary contact has been made with prospective builders, and as soon as a preliminary plat is available, the developer should prepare a marketing package. This package should include: site location information; neighborhood information, such as shopping, schools, daycare facilities, churches, and recreation; and data about the site, including the subdivision plan, restrictive covenants, amenities, and the marketing program.

Terms for buying subdivision lots vary, depending on the market. In softer markets, builders may put down only $1,000 cash per lot, or less, as evidence of a commitment. When the commitments are made before site development, builders are not obligated to "take down" or "close" on the stipulated number of lots until the engineer has certified that the lots are ready for building. Before then, builders only have the option to buy the lots at the specified price. The option (or purchase contract) is not a specific performance contract. In other words, if builders fail to close, they only lose their earnest money.

Once the lots are ready for building, builders are usually liable for interest on the lots that are committed but not yet closed. If a rolling option exists, builders are committed to taking down a certain number of lots at a time. Either the builders may pay cash for the lots, with funds provided by the construction lender, or the developer may finance the lots for builders during the period between closing and start of construction. For example, builders may commit to take down five lots immediately for model houses and have an option to purchase 30 lots every six months, beginning January 1. If the builders exercise the option, the interest meter starts running on January 1 for the portion of the 30 lots not closed on January 1. Six months later, if the builders do not exercise the option on the next 30 lots, they are released for sale to other builders.

Marketing Larger Parcels

In addition to single-family lots, developers often sell commercial reserve sites, outparcels, and apartment and office sites. Reaching potential buyers for these sites requires an approach similar to that for marketing office park and industrial park sites.

Two main sources of business are outside brokers and "drive-bys." Mackie claims that outside brokers are the best investment and urges that developers pay them a generous commission. Although advertising is not an especially effective technique, newsletters and broker parties do help to generate and maintain broker interest. On-site representation—a place provided for brokers to come in and talk to prospects—is desirable.

Typically, the buyer of a $1 million site puts up $25,000 to $50,000 of earnest money, in cash or by way of a letter of credit (LC). Standard closing times range from 60 to 120 days, depending on the market. In Austin, Mackie comments, buyers usually close directly into a construction loan: "Buyers almost always want the option to buy or the right of first refusal on adjoining sites." Although he recommends that developers try to avoid giving these options, Mackie notes that developers often must grant them as a component of a larger deal. "This is especially important during the initial project stages when the developer is trying to encourage building construction to enhance absorption."[46]

Direct Marketing to the Public

For most land development projects, developers are not directly involved in retail sales to the general public. In townhouse, condominium, and recreational developments, however, they may be.

Marketing budgets are based on a percentage of gross sales; 5 to 7 percent is common for nonrecreational projects and 10 to 12 percent for recreational projects. The budget includes 1 to 2 percent for advertising and the balance for sales staff and cooperating broker compensation.

In larger metropolitan areas, most developers prefer to use their own in-house sales staff to handle direct marketing. Even if they use an outside brokerage firm, developers need their own marketing director and sufficient in-house staff to represent their interests in day-to-day negotiations. In smaller market areas with populations of less than 100,000, serious consideration should be given to using one or more local realtor firms as sales staff or as a source of sales referrals.

The sooner a marketing director is hired, the better. Before construction begins, the marketing director can help by getting to know the market area. Because the director will be directly responsible for sales results, he/she should possess an intimate knowledge of sales techniques, ability to motivate sales personnel, and first-hand experience with the types of products being sold. A minimum of two sales people should be hired, with one or two more available to help out during peak periods.

Some developers argue that sales people should be paid on commission, others advocate a combination of salary and unlimited commission. Prizes, bonuses, and competitions are proven good practices. Higher commission rates may be paid for selling certain "problem" lots or houses, and bonuses should be awarded if sales personnel exceed monthly or yearly quotas.

Marketing low-priced tract-homes requires a different approach to that for marketing high-priced custom houses. If sales are routine, the best method of compensation may be salary. In higher-priced housing, however, sales are seldom routine. Marketing for these houses may include offering special financing and a wide variety of building modifications. Furthermore, because a buyer with a substantial amount of money usually has a greater selection of houses from which to choose, salesmanship is at a premium. A cooperative broker arrangement also is more important for higher-priced houses.

An effective sales program requires thorough training and constant motivation. Money is a good motivator, but sales people also need to be kept enthusiastic. Good sales programs usually include:

- well-paid, well-trained, and motivated sales staff;
- regular sales meetings to discuss prospects and sales policies;
- a system for communicating with, and following up on, prospective buyers;
- a system for obtaining leads and referrals;
- a reporting system to inform management of buyer objections, preferences, and attitudes; and
- a customer-service system for handling the selection of decorative items such as paint color and wallpaper, and for taking care of closing details, occupancy procedures, and postconstruction warranty and service details.

Merchandising and Advertising

Whereas advertising is intended to reach people and to persuade them to visit a subdivision, merchandising is designed to stimulate the desire of potential buyers once they come to the site. The developer's advertising should focus on the quality of life enjoyed by the residents by emphasizing recreational opportunities, schools, and other services available both inside the subdivision and within the surrounding community.

Large-scale subdivisions of 500 houses or more will support a visitors' center in which all builders in the subdivision can merchandise their houses. The center should be equipped so that prospective purchasers can get an initial impression of all products available in the subdivision. Smaller subdivisions generally will support only a very modest visitors' center.

The developer should encourage all of the builders to place their models in the same area. In this way, the builders receive the same economies of scale as those enjoyed by car dealerships that locate together along a freeway. Each builder builds two to four houses in separate, but interconnected, areas. The model house park should be large enough to show the land plan—including common spaces and pedestrian paths. The developer is responsible for the landscaping and the common-area maintenance. Dirty streets and unkempt construction areas generate ill will among current residents of the area and deter potential buyers.[47]

The design of the sales office and arrangement of model units is central to the merchandising plan. Signs should lead visitors directly to the sales office, the model houses, and the major amenities. They also should direct visitors clearly to the exits. Signs restricting smoking and eating should be low-key, pleasant, and inoffensive.

Development Maintenance

Among the developer's most important tasks is the creation of a proper set of mechanisms to handle long-term maintenance after the project is complete. The developer must ensure the future of the project, not just to protect his/her own investment, but to protect the investment and living environment of the future residents of the subdivision.

A developer's stewardship of the land may take many forms. First, a developer may make express guarantees or warranties concerning the care of streets, landscaping, and amenities when selling lots to builders. Second, a developer normally will create and record a set of deed restrictions and protective covenants. The covenants enable residents to enforce maintenance and building standards when other residents violate the restrictions. Third, a developer normally will create a homeowners' association that bears the responsibility for long-term maintenance and helps to build a sense of community. Fourth, in most cases, a developer will dedicate the streets to the city or county. The city or county then takes responsibility for various public services, such as street cleaning, parkway mowing, and trash removal. Since the types of public services available differ from city to city, a developer must make sure that all public services are provided.

Protective Covenants

Protective covenants, which embody the agreements between the seller and purchaser covering the use of land, are private-party contracts between the land subdivider and the lot or unit purchasers. The developer uses covenants to create and ensure a specific living environment in the subdivision. Purchasers of lots and houses in the subdivision perceive the covenants as assurance that the developer will proceed to develop the property as planned and that other purchasers will maintain the property as planned. Strict enforcement of suitable covenants gives each lot owner the best possible assurance that no other lot owner within the protected area can use his/her property in a way that will depress values, change the character of the neighborhood, or create a nuisance. Lenders and government agencies, such as FHA and VA, often require covenants as a means of protecting the quality of the neighborhood and the condition of the houses.

Deed restrictions and covenants serve a variety of purposes:

- They can augment zoning and other public land use controls by applying additional restrictions to size of lots, size and location of structures, setbacks, yard requirements, architectural design, and permitted uses. If both public and private restrictions apply, the more restrictive condition is operative. For example, Greenway Parks, in Dallas, abides by subdivision restrictions that were recorded in the late 1920s. The covenants stipulate a minimum sideyard width of five feet. The zoning, however, stipulates a minimum sideyard that is 10 percent of the front lot width. Thus, for lots with 80 feet of frontage, the operative restriction is the zoning, which requires sideyards of at least eight feet in width.
- Covenants provide a workable method of conserving the environmental characteristics of a neighborhood by stipulating building envelopes for additions to houses and regulating the types of landscaping, fencing, walls, garages and outbuildings, and even the exterior paint color that may be used.
- Affirmative covenants may be used to ensure that certain land remains as open space and that the developer will preserve certain natural features within that space.
- Covenants may restrict certain uses or activities such as car repairs, boat storage, or on-street overnight parking.
- Covenants may create a mechanism for assessing homeowners on the upkeep and maintenance of common facilities.

Covenants and deed restrictions are recorded in the public land records for the jurisdiction at the same time that the subdivision plat is recorded. They should be made superior to any mortgage liens that may be on record prior to the recording of the covenant. This ensures that everyone is bound by the restrictions, even someone buying a house through foreclosure.

Although the covenants are automatically superior to any future lien, many covenants and restrictions also provide for an automatic lien for payment of homeowners' association fees and assessments. The documents must provide that the lien for assessments be automatically subordinated to purchase-money liens.[48] Covenants should take the form of blanket provisions that apply to the whole subdivision, and they should be specifically referenced in each deed. These covenants, together with the recorded plat, legally establish a general scheme for the development. Not all covenants are legally enforceable, however. Covenants that seek to exclude any buyer by race, religion, or ethnic background are both unconstitutional and unenforceable.

Usually, developers do not want to be the enforcers of covenants, unless a long-term building involvement requires them to keep control over an area. Subdividers may retain control over enforcement as long as they are active in the subdivision. Thereafter, however, the covenants should grant enforcement powers to the homeowners' association as well as to individual owners. Some cities also require a provision that lets the city take over enforcement under certain circumstances.[49]

The covenants should not be recorded until developers have received preliminary subdivision approvals. Furthermore, if developers intend to use FHA, VA, or other sources of federal financing (such as the Government National Mortgage Association (GNMA) or the Federal National Mortgage Association (FNMA)), they should ensure that the proposed covenants meet with the approval of those agencies. The FHA and VA have jointly developed acceptable model legal documents, although the same coordination has not taken place with FNMA and GNMA.

Design Controls

The design control provisions should reflect the tastes and attitudes of the target market. The types of design controls and degrees of constraint will differ, depending on whether the target market is builders of tract-homes or of custom houses. For the developer who is selling finished sites, the best mechanism for design control is to include an "approval of plans" clause in the purchase agreements for building sites.

Even though individual designs may be attractive, incongruous styles may detract from the overall appearance of a subdivision. A design review committee should, therefore, be established to approve proposed designs. Such a committee will also shield the developer from accusations of arbitrariness.

Encouraging a good design is easier than discouraging a bad one. The developer's primary tool is to specify dimensional limitations on features such as yard setbacks, building heights, bulk, and signs. Too many restrictions, though, may lead to boring uniformity. For example, the city of Highland Park, a wealthy inner suburb of Dallas, passed severe yard coverage limitations. Builders of houses that averaged 6,000 to 7,000 square feet responded by building two-story boxes that completely filled the allowable building envelope. Similar boxes have appeared on small lots in Beverly Hills, California, where soaring lot prices virtually guarantee that buyers will build houses as large as possible on their lots.

One of the most difficult areas to control is future alterations and additions. Materials are difficult to match. Costs change over time. New fire codes may prohibit the use of certain materials. The covenants, therefore, should provide for a variance procedure to accommodate changes over time. The design review committee must consider precedents when it approves variances from the specified restrictions.

Other Covenants

Cost covenants are unsuccessful. A $30,000 minimum cost requirement, for example, may build a mansion in the 1920s but a cottage in 1990. The simplest method for establishing quality is to set minimum square footage standards for living area, exclusive of garages, basements, and accessory buildings.

In cluster house, patio, and townhouse subdivisions, where houses are attached, the long-term value of a development requires a covenant that protects other owners when one house is damaged or destroyed by fire or other causes. Such a covenant should make owners of damaged property responsible for rebuilding or restoring the property promptly. The restoration should be substantially in accordance with the architecture and engineering plans and with the specs for the original buildings.

If a subdivision includes common open space, a covenant should be included that provides for the use, preservation, and limitation on future development of the space. Open-space easements may be used to ensure long-term protection of common open space. In some cases, the granting of open-space easements to the community may be a basis for obtaining planning approval of the development.

Boats, mobile houses, campers, and trucks all require special storage areas. The developer may want to include a covenant that either prohibits on-site parking of these vehicles or requires visual screening. Alternatively, the covenant may limit parking to specified areas, such as backyards. Other restrictive covenants may prohibit keeping certain types of pets or livestock on site, cutting mature trees, repairing automobiles, and parking inoperable vehicles.

■ 3-22 Westpark Design Guidelines

Building Massing and Scale

The architectural image of Westpark will be perceived primarily from public spaces such as streets, parks, and greenbelts. Therefore, building massing, scale, and roof forms constitute the primary design components and require careful articulation. Emphasis should be on horizontal forms south of Alton Parkway and on vertical elements within the activity corridor.

Appropriate:

Articulation of wall planes (required).

Projections and recesses to provide shadow and depth (required).

Simple, bold forms (encouraged).

Combinations of one- and two-story forms conveying sense of human scale (encouraged).

Inappropriate:

Large expanses of flat wall planes vertically or horizontally (prohibited).

Roof Pitches and Materials

Principal roof forms should be gable or hip with pitches from 4:12 to 6:12. All pitched roof materials should be clay or concrete tile from the approved color and material board to ensure a continuity of textures and colors. Minimal flat roof areas should have gravel surface with color to match roof tile. Short roof overhangs are encouraged with simple plaster fascias. Exposed rafter tails are not permitted.

Appropriate:

Gable and hip roof forms (required).

Combining one- and two-story elements (encouraged).

Varying plate heights and ridge heights (encouraged).

Discretionary:

Small areas of flat and shed roofs (limited).

Inappropriate:

Gambrel, mansard, and "period" style roofs (prohibited).

Source: Westpark Design Guidelines, The Irvine Company, Newport Beach, California, 1985.

Developers walk a fine line between introducing too little and too much restriction. Developers want to maintain the value of the subdivision without overly limiting their market. A potential homebuyer who cannot keep his/her boat or motorhome on the property will probably look elsewhere for a house. To the extent that developers want to limit on-site parking for certain vehicles and activities such as car repair, they should attempt to provide alternative locations.

Effective Term and Revision

Although some covenants may be drawn up with a definite termination date, covenants should generally be designed to renew themselves automatically and run with the land indefinitely. Property owners also should be able to revise the covenants with the approval of a stipulated percentage of other property owners. The developer may decide to allow some covenants to be revisable with a simple majority vote, whereas other covenants may require approval by 75 percent or even 90 percent of the property owners. The developer may also want to allow homeowners to revise some covenants, such as changes in fencing, after three to five years while others, such as "single-family use only," may be revised only after 25 to 40 years. Proposed revisions in covenants should be submitted sufficiently ahead of time to allow property owners to review them—three years for major covenants and one year for minor covenants.

Residential developers disagree about whether or not the developer should retain the power to make minor amendments to covenants. Some feel that to be able to adjust building lines and make modifications in design character from one phase to another is essential for the developer. Others feel that such modifications should be handled through the design review committee. Developers who frequently amend covenants risk hurting their credibility with property owners who may doubt the developers' intentions to fulfill promises and carry out future development plans.

Enforcement

Legally, anyone who is bound by covenants may enforce them against anyone else who is bound by them. Since this may set neighbor against neighbor, providing a homeowners' association with the power of enforcement is the best solution. Failure to enforce a covenant in a timely fashion may render the covenant void. For example, in a Dallas subdivision, the homeowners did not enforce a covenant that restricted fencing of an open-space easement running along the back of the owners' lots. Several years later, the homeowners' association attempted to enforce the covenant against several homeowners who had fenced the open space. The homeowners successfully challenged the association on the grounds that the covenant was void for lack of previous enforcement.

Community and Condominium Associations

Types

Four main types of homeowners' associations exist.

Community association with automatic membership. In most subdivisions in which fee-simple interest in the lots is conveyed to buyers, membership in a community association occurs automatically when a buyer purchases a dwelling or improved lot. The association may hold title to real property such as open space and recreation facilities within the subdivision. It is responsible for preserving and maintaining the property. Members have perpetual access to the common property. They must pay assessments to finance the association's activities and must uphold the covenants.

Condominium association. This resembles the community association, except for the form of ownership. When someone purchases a condominium, he/she obtains title only to the interior space of their particular unit. The structure, lobbies, elevators, and surrounding land belong to all of the owners as "tenants in common." Owners are automatically members of the condominium association and have voting privileges and responsibilities for operating and maintaining the common facilities.

Funded community trust. This is an alternative to the automatic membership association. The funded community trust holds and maintains the common areas within a development. The funded trust differs from a community association in that a fiduciary organization, such as a bank, is the trustee responsible for the costs of overseeing maintenance of the property.

Community associations often hold title to community facilities—such as playgrounds—and open space, and are responsible for preserving and maintaining the property.

The funded community trust limits the ability of owners to act directly on their own behalf. The advantage of the trust is that it eliminates much of the day-to-day governance and participatory requirements of members. This form has not been used widely, primarily because banks and other institutions have been reluctant to become trustees.

Nonautomatic association. This provides for the voluntary support of homeowners. This form of association, however, does not work if the development owns common properties because, if owners are not automatically members, assessments cannot be mandated. A nonautomatic association cannot participate in the enforcement of covenants and, therefore, can only serve as a focus of interest and social pressure for conformance.

Legal Framework

An automatic community association includes five major legal elements: a subdivision plat, an enabling declaration, articles of incorporation, bylaws, and individual deeds for each parcel.

The subdivision plat is the recorded map showing individual lots, legal descriptions, common spaces, and easements. The plat should indicate areas that will be dedicated to the association as well as those that will not be dedicated for use by the general public (often called reserve parcels). It also should reference and be recorded with the enabling declaration, which sets forth the management and ownership of common areas, the lien rights of the association against all lots, the amendment procedures, the enforcement procedures, and the rights of voting members.

The articles of incorporation and bylaws are the formal documents for creating a corporation with the state. The articles of incorporation set forth the initial board of directors, procedures for appointing new directors, membership and voting rights, amendment procedures, dissolution procedures, and the severability of provisions.[50] The bylaws of the association describe the rules by which the association will conduct business. They set forth the composition and duties of the board and the indemnification of officers of the association and describe the role and composition of subboards, such as the design review board.

Each individual deed conveyed by the developer should reference the declaration of the association. The developer should summarize the formation, responsibilities, and activities of the association in a brochure that homebuilders in the subdivision can give to their buyers.

The developer must create the association and file the articles of incorporation and bylaws before selling any lots to homebuilders or individual buyers. Any sales that predate the establishment of the association are exempted from the association. Consequently, forming the community association is a critical part of the developer's activities.

The Developer's Role

Homeowners' associations, protective covenants, and the common facilities managed by homeowners' associations are as important to the overall success of a subdivision as are the engineering and design of the subdivision. If handled properly, they can serve as a major component of the developer's marketing strategy.

Commonly owned land and facilities are usually donated by the developer to the homeowners' association. The costs are covered by lot sales to builders. For property-tax purposes, permanently dedicated open space should not be assessed at the same rate as residential lots, since the value of the open space is already reflected in the price of the lots.

During the course of development, the developer usually maintains the open space and common facilities. These responsibilities are turned over to the association when the development is completed. Control of the association passes from the developer to the residents when the residents elect the officers of the association. The developer should design the accounts and recordkeeping so that the transition to the association will be smooth.

The developer establishes the initial property assessments, which must reflect realistically the number of residents of the community at any one time. Since buyers evaluate monthly association assessments the same way they do monthly mortgage payments, the assessments cannot be too high. Although the developer would like to place as much of the burden as possible on the association, he/she should keep the assessment competitive with that of other subdivisions.

James Oesch Photography

Land development offers developers the opportunity to build on a relatively large scale and to shape the growth of cities, thus requiring a conscientious and civic-minded approach. Pictured is Avenel in Potomac, Maryland.

Residents appear to be somewhat more tolerant of association dues than they are of general taxes because the results of dues are more directly apparent. The upper limit to place on dues rates depends on local conditions. In Orange County, for example, before Proposition 13 limited property taxes to 1 percent of the house purchase price, homeowners tolerated a combined tax bill (property taxes plus special district assessments) of up to 2 percent of the house value. Homeowners may tolerate as much as an additional half percentage point per year in association dues in areas in which the association owns and operates substantial common open space and recreation facilities.

Conclusion

Beginning developers will find many opportunities in land development. In some cases, land development may be combined with building development, but, in general, it should be considered a separate business to be evaluated on its own merits. Even though a developer may intend to build houses on the land after it is developed, the finished lots should provide a reasonable profit on the land development portion of the business at lot prices that are competitive with prices of finished lots in other subdivisions.

Land development is considered one of the riskier forms of development because it is so dependent on the public sector for approvals and infrastructure support.

■ Rustic Woods
Bedford, Texas

Rustic Woods is a 35-acre subdivision, with 163 single-family lots, in Bedford, Texas. A suburb of Fort Worth, Bedford lies just west of the Dallas/Fort Worth Airport, off Highway 121 (the major highway connecting Fort Worth to the airport), between a triangle of three major highways. The Rustic Woods project is a well-executed land development that was launched at a time when the Dallas economy fell precipitously, following the oil recession of the mid-1980s. The lots were targeted at higher-end volume homebuilders that produce houses averaging 1,800 to 2,200 square feet. Prices for homes were slated to cost between $105,000 and $135,000.

The developer of the Rustic Woods project, Terry Lewis, began working in 1968 as manager for the construction division of the Zale Corporation. His division was in charge of building new stores and, later, the firm's headquarters building. In 1980, Lewis joined Capcon, a Texas-based apartment syndication firm, as a development partner. He built four apartment communities in partnership with three other Capcon principals. He left Capcon in 1985 to form the Devon Companies and has concentrated since on land development and apartment building construction. Because of his construction background, Lewis took on his own general contracting in addition to development.

The project features 163 lots on a 35-acre site served by two curvilinear loop roads and several culs-de-sac.

Background and Site Selection

When Lewis began scouting out a suitable development site in 1985, single-family housing in Dallas was booming. He found the Bedford property through a broker. Bedford was a middle-income suburb with a recently burgeoning development community. Indeed, the site was virtually the last piece of land available in Bedford that was suitable for single-family dwellings. Lewis bought his tract out of a larger, 100-acre area then under development.

When Lewis started to work on his development early in 1986, economic conditions in Dallas were still healthy, and loans could still be obtained from S&L associations. But cracks would soon become visible, conditions would soon tighten, and, in fact, by the time Lewis began looking for money, he was forced to presell the subdivision to ensure financing.

Lewis reached an oral agreement with the sellers of the land in February 1986. Hammering out the contract, however, engaged their lawyers for a full six weeks. The purchase price amounted to $2,563,000, of which, on March 27, Lewis put up $20,000 in nonrefundable earnest money. Within the next 60 days he was required to put up an additional $80,000, amounting to $100,000 in earnest money.

Because of the earlier subdivision, the property involved a reassemblage of land from some 30 owners. Reassembling these lots posed a number of possible title difficulties for the new owners. Not surprisingly, the number of title exceptions—those conditions not covered by title insurance—was overwhelming.

Consequently, Lewis insisted on a general warranty deed and offered nonrefundable earnest money to entice the sellers. Apart from a 30-day feasibility period, during which 80 percent of all earnest money was refundable, the deal was contingent upon replatting of the lots—seller and buyer jointly appealed to the city to abandon a street map that existed from an older, undeveloped subdivision. The originally mapped and platted streets were vacated and the new streets replatted. Initially, April 27 was the designated closing date, though Lewis could extend it by paying $660 per day in interest until May 25. To rezone the property, the seller had to make strong representations to the city council concerning the kinds of homebuyers that would be living in the new subdivisions. Lewis set forth deed restrictions that included 80 percent all-brick chimneys, timberline roofs, and the right to approve potential homebuilders. These restrictions made the search for builders for the subdivision even more difficult.

Feasibility and Financing

Most of the feasibility work was accomplished during the six weeks of negotiations between Lewis's attorneys and those of the sellers. After discussions with brokers and builders, Lewis's staff had predetermined the target market and the lot sizes he would have to apportion. In a very short time, Lewis had to complete contracts with the builders, expedite plans for a preliminary plat so that he could calculate unit and lot prices,

Rustic Woods (Continued)

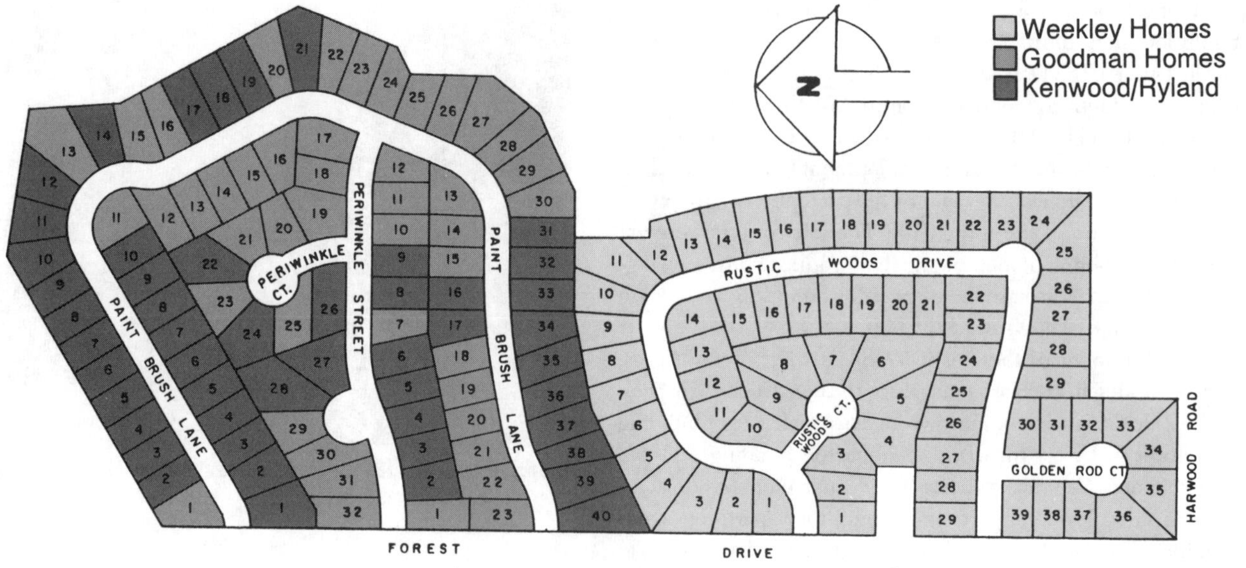

Rustic Woods site plan.

and arrange for an MAI appraisal. Feasibility costs included $7,000 for engineering, $5,000 for appraisal, $12,000 for "leg work," and $20,000 in nonrefundable earnest money—amounting to a total of $44,000 of funds at risk.

While Lewis was looking for financing, lenders' concerns about the Fort Worth economy had begun to mount. Lewis experienced grave difficulties in finding a lender. His previous subdivision had been funded by a bank that did not insist on presales. This time, however, even with presales in hand, he experienced considerable difficulty. Ultimately, he found a willing S&L through a loan broker who received one point.

To put together a sufficiently large financial statement, Lewis formed a 50/50 joint venture with a financial partner. Their combined net worth was about $6 million, of which 10 to 15 percent was liquid. The joint venture received a $4.2 million loan, for which $508,000 had to be posted in letters of credit. The builders' letters of credit totaled $200,000. The sellers of the land put up a $150,000 letter of credit out of eagerness to make the sale. Lewis posted a letter of credit for the remaining $158,000.

Design and Construction

The plan for Rustic Woods divides the site into two principal sections served by the two primary loop roads. Five entrances are provided onto the adjacent Forest Drive, an unusually large number for such a small site. Lots are relatively uniform in size, typically 60 by 110 feet, and range from approximately 6,500 to 8,500 square feet.

Several of the outstanding design and construction problems that Lewis had to overcome were the following:

- Off-site sewer: The sewer line was brought in from 400 feet off site.
- Off-site paving: Half of an adjacent street (some 1,400 feet) needed improvement. Although not required to, Lewis put a two-inch topping on the remaining half of the street to improve its appearance.
- Off-site water: A 12-inch water line was extended 2,000 feet to the property.
- Special engineering requirements: Lewis had to determine whether or not the city would require concrete bottoms in the creek bed. The city ultimately allowed him to leave the creek in its natural state.
- Escrows: For the city to widen another street, $22,000 had to be put in escrow.
- Off-site gas: Gas was brought in from 3,000 feet off site. Lewis eventually received a rebate from the gas company as new connections were made.

Lewis's company, Devon, was the general subcontractor for the subdivision. For this, it received a cost-plus-5-percent fee (the joint venture received a 5 percent management fee for the development). Subcontractors were hired to perform the work—a grading contractor, a utility contractor, a street contractor, and a conduit contractor, who installed sleeves for the utility companies.

The construction for the subdivision was generally straightforward, but among the problems encountered was a delay in paving caused by the inability of the utility company to provide services in a timely manner. Another problem was that contractors were always breaking each other's lines and blaming each other for the breakage. To avoid conflicts during the construction phase, Lewis insisted on coordination meetings with all subcontractors.

Marketing and Operations

To market the lots, Lewis worked closely with three brokers that took the preliminary plats around to builders in the mid-cities area near Dallas–Ft. Worth airport. The overall strategy was to presell all the lots with a two-year takedown schedule. The brokers each received in commission $500 per lot. The target market was higher-end, volume homebuilders who built for second-time, move-up homebuyers. As a result of the brokers' efforts, three builders committed to buy the subdivision lots: David Weekly of Houston, which built 250 homes a year; Steve Goodman Homes, which built 200 homes per year; and Kenwood Homes, which built 100 homes per year.

The overall strategy was to sell out 163 lots within 24 months. The three builders each took down between three and six lots, priced at $28,000 each. The lots were "substantially completed" when the city issued a letter stating its intent to send out building permits.

The project is attractively landscaped, including a traditional sidewalk pedestrian system, and has a mature neighborhood feel.

Lots were sold to three separate homebuilders; the target market was higher-end, volume homebuilders who built for second-time, move-up homebuyers.

After determining the number of lots they wanted, the builders negotiated the takedown rate. Lewis said he was selling his lots at a price that was $3,000 under market value in order to presell them quickly. The builders furnished transferable assignable letters of credit for 5 percent of the total lot price in nonrefundable earnest money. Kenwood later resold some lots to Ryland Homes for $31,000.

As with most developments, after the homebuilders began building, they found problems in the location of the sewer and water taps and pins. Water had eroded some of the building pads around where the houses would be built. Lewis's contract with the builders required him to grade the land so that the builders' necessity for regrading was minimal. When Lewis received calls from the builders concerning missing lot pins, he instructed his subs to bill the builders if they found the lot pins—otherwise they were told to bill him.

Lewis filed deed restrictions at the same time that he filed the plats. He did not set up a homeowners' association because there were not common areas to be maintained. Moreover, Lewis had previously found that it is harder to deal with the Veterans' Administration (VA) on loans if subdivisions have homeowners' associations, especially since the VA insisted on giving special approval in such instances.

The Dallas recession proved to be more severe than people had anticipated. The homebuilders in Rustic Woods experienced slower home sales than they had originally projected, slowing the takedown of lots. Despite the slower sales, however, Rustic Woods turned out to be a profitable development for

■ Rustic Woods (Continued)

Lewis. He is one of only a few developers who can make such a claim for a Dallas subdivision built in the late 1980s.

Experienced Gained

- It is important to hire an experienced superintendent who can be counted on to remain on site every day to coordinate the work, therefore minimizing the number of construction problems that occur.
- Off-site easements should be obtained from adjoining property owners before committing to the project. On an earlier subdivision, an engineer had told Lewis not to worry about securing a particular easement. A neighbor later declared that he wanted $100,000 for the easement. Lewis was forced to go through the city to condemn the easement. This necessitated costly appraisal and a three- to four-month delay. Eventually, the neighbor was paid $30,000 and Lewis had to pay $10,000 in interest for the delay in the project. With foresight, the developer might have obtained the easement for $5,000 or $10,000.

Developer:
Devon Companies
4004 Beltline Road, Suite 210
Addison, Texas 75244
(214) 385-0508

Land Planner:
Washington and Associates
Hurst, Texas

■ Project Data

Land Use Information:
Site Area: 35 acres
Total Lots/Dwelling Units: 163
Gross Density: 3.89 dwelling units per acre
Typical Lot Size: 6,600 square feet (60 by 110 feet)

Development Costs

Land Costs	$2,563,359
Interest Allocation	567,510
Soft Costs:	
General and Administration Expenses	48,000
Engineering Design	65,000
Field Surveying	70,000
Inspection Fees	6,000
Filing Fees	1,960
Advertising	0
Soils Report	1,640
Legal Fees	7,600
Accounting Fees	3,000
Loan Fees and Expenses	10,704
Appraisal Costs	4,500
Development Contingency	12,296
Total Soft Costs	$230,700
Construction Costs:	
Texas Power and Light Underground	$33,382
Street Lights	5,565
Lone Star Gas	43,866
Entry and Landscape	25,000
Site Clearing and Excavation	93,024
On-Site Utilities	235,000
Off-Site Utilities	45,000
Street Paving	296,084
FHA Lot Grading	20,976
City Sidewalks	0
Laboratory Testing	100
Contingency	40,434
Total Construction Costs	$838,431
Total	$4,200,000

See Land Development Analysis in figure 3-16 for further financial information.

Home Price Range: $100,000 to $120,000
Typical Lot Price: $28,000

Beginning developers should concentrate on smaller deals that involve fewer complexities. Problem sites, such as those containing environmentally sensitive areas, can offer attractive opportunities, but developers should be wary of spending several years on a site that may not be worth the effort when completed.

Beginning land developers will find that obtaining financing without significant cash equity and strong financial statements is a difficult process. Nevertheless, land development offers the opportunity to use commitments from builders as collateral for securing financing. Beginning developers will find that seller financing and joint ventures with landowners and financial institutions will enable them to take part in a variety of opportunities and successfully launch a development career.

Although opportunities are always present for beginning developers, so are pitfalls. Cities are holding land developers responsible for an ever-higher share of the cost of providing public facilities and solving environmental problems. In many cases, developers are becoming the de facto agents of cities in building arterial streets, libraries, fire stations, and sewer and drainage facilities and in cleaning up toxic waste and restoring environmentally sensitive land. The liability of developers for construction standards, especially streets, utilities, and drainage, extends for many years after developers have sold out of the subdivision.

Cities and land developers have always formed a kind of partnership because land development has been the primary vehicle by which cities grew in population and employment. As the burdens of responsibility shift more and more toward developers, so developers must come to understand not only how to build financially successful subdivisions but also how to ensure the fiscal health of their cities.

Notes

1. The author is particularly grateful for the review comments made on this chapter by ULI Steering Committee member Don Mackie.

2. H. James Brown, R.S. Phillips, and N.A. Roberts, "Land Markets at the Urban Fringe," *Journal of the American Planning Association*, April 1981, pp. 131–44.

3. See J.C. Ohls and David Pines, "Discontinuous Urban Development and Economic Efficiency," *Land Economics*, August 1975, pp. 224–34; J.R. Ottensmann, "Urban Sprawl, Land Values, and Density of Development," *Land Economics*, November 1977, pp. 389–400; Richard B. Peiser, "Does it Pay to Plan Suburban Growth?" *Journal of the American Planning Association*, Autumn 1984, pp. 419–33; and Richard B. Peiser, "Density and Urban Sprawl," *Land Economics*, August 1989, pp. 193–204.

4. This information taken from an interview with Jack Willome, president, RAYCO, Inc., San Antonio, Texas, 1987.

5. The lenders' release price from the loan may be higher than $16,000; thus, the developers would have to make up the difference.

6. See Ralph Lewis, *Land Buying Checklist* (Washington, D.C.: National Association of Home Builders, 1987).

7. From an interview with Jack Willome in 1987.

8. Ibid.

9. From an interview with Don Mackie in July 1987.

10. Title insurance companies do not survey property and, therefore, do not insure against encroachments and boundary disputes that would be disclosed by a proper survey. However, a correct survey is one that corresponds to the description in the deed, and if the description in the deed is wrong, the title insurance company is liable. The company is insuring the accuracy of the documents.

11. For a glossary of zoning terms and a general description of the process, see Michael J. Meshenberg, *The Language of Zoning: A Glossary of Words and Phrases*, Report No. 322 (Chicago: American Society of Planning Officials, 1976).

12. *Avco Community Developers, Inc.* v. *South Coast Regional Commission*, 553 P.2d 546 (Cal. Sup. Ct., 1976).

13. *Golden* v. *Planning Board of the Town of Ramapo*, 285 N.E.2d 291 (N.Y. Ct. App., 1972).

14. *Construction Industry Association* v. *City of Petaluma*, 522 F.2d 897 (9th Cir. 1975).

15. See USC Planning Institute and Peat Marwick/Goodkin Real Estate, *Riverside County Growth Management Study* (Los Angeles: University of Southern California, 1988).

16. Kevin Lynch and Gary Hack, *Site Planning*, 3rd ed. (Cambridge, Massachusetts: MIT Press, 1985), p. 124.

17. See Douglas R. Porter and Richard B. Peiser, *Financing Infrastructure to Support Community Growth* (Washington, D.C.: ULI–the Urban Land Institute, 1984).

18. See Thomas P. Snyder and Michael A. Stegman, *Paying for Growth: Using Development Fees to Finance Infrastructure* (Washington, D.C.: ULI–the Urban Land Institute, 1986).

19. The city might require the developer to pay for, say, the first one or two lanes of paving, with the city paying the rest. Alternatively, it might require the developer to pay for or install the entire arterial, with subsequent reimbursement by other developers whose subdivisions front the arterial.

20. From an interview in 1988 with Jim Fawcett, associate director, Seabrant Program, USC, Los Angeles.

21. Ralph Martin, president of Richardson, Nagy, Martin, Newport Beach, California, in an interview in 1988, observed that although the terms gross and net acres are commonly used and understood, net-net acres is far less popular.

22. Richard B. Peiser, "Optimizing Profits from Land Use Planning," *Urban Land*, September 1982, pp. 6–10.

23. The compound return is $(1 + 0.3)^{1/3} - 1 = .09139$ or 9.139 percent. The general formula is $(1 + r)^{1/n} - 1$, where r equals the total rate of return and n equals holding period.

24. See Richard Brealy and S. Myers, *Principles of Corporate Finance* (New York: McGraw-Hill, 1984), pp. 164–92.

25. All return figures presented here are IRRs. They give the annual return on equity per year that should be made on an alternative investment (with annual compounding) to accumulate the same total amount of money by the end of the life of the project.

26. Technically, interest rates reflect "inflation expectations" rather than past or current inflation. Inflation expectations are collective attitudes about future inflation rates over specific periods of time. When current inflation rates are high, say 10 percent, short-term yields tend to exceed longer-term yields, reflecting the expectations of buyers and sellers of bond instruments that long-term inflation will decrease.

27. Radburn was established by the City Housing Corporation, led by Henry Wright and Clarence Stein. See Eugenie Ladner Birch, "Radburn and the American Planning Movement," *APA Journal*, October 1980, pp. 424–39.

28. See Robert D. Katz, *Design of the Housing Site: A Critique of American Practice* (Urbana, Illinois: Building Research Council, 1967), pp. 20–40.

29. This information was provided by Carl L. Darling, partner of Crossroads West Development, Sacramento, California, October 1989.

30. Floodplain maps are generated from historic storm information and personal recollections of an area's residents. Since records in most areas do not extend back as far as 100 years, the floodplain line is an educated guess, not a fact.

31. An acre-foot of water is the amount of water one-foot deep that would cover one acre of land.

32. A comprehensive analysis of wetlands mitigation and regulation is provided in David Salvesen's *Wetlands: Mitigating and Regulating Development Impacts* (Washington, D.C.: ULI–the Urban Land Institute, 1990).

33. Lloyd W. Bookout and James W. Wentling, *Density by Design* (Washington, D.C.: ULI–the Urban Land Institute, 1988), pp. 10–15.

34. See Walter J. Richardson, "Designing High-Density, Single-Family Housing," *Urban Land*, February 1988, pp. 15–20.

35. Ibid., p. 17.

36. Ibid., p. 17.

37. Ibid, pp. 15–20.

38. If the developer intends to build on all of the lots him/herself rather than selling to other builders, then the financing may be more complicated. The bank would look at equity and financing needs for the entire project, including not only land but also houses.

39. Developers often provide seller financing to builders until the builders are ready to take down (close) and build on the lots. The seller financing automatically has a senior (first lien) position to any other financing such as the builder's construction loan, which the builder's construction lender will not allow. The developer, however, may *subordinate* the seller's loan to the builder's construction lender. The seller's loan, in this case, does *not* have to be retired before building occurs, thus lowering the builder's cash requirements.

40. This information taken from an interview with Don Mackie in 1987.

41. The difference between cumulative and noncumulative preferred returns is discussed in chapter 4.

42. The purchase could take place with or without a PMN. Land sellers tend to be less willing to subordinate a PMN to the development loan if they do not have an ongoing interest in the joint venture.

43. This is taken from an interview with Terry Lewis in September 1988.

44. This means one foot of vertical drop per three feet of horizontal distance.

45. This is taken from an interview with Robert W. Moss in September 1988.

46. The information for this section was taken from an interview with Don Mackie in September, 1988.

47. This information was taken from an interview with Robert W. Moss in September 1988.

48. This information was taken from an interview with Don Mackie in September 1988.

49. Houston, for example, has an administrative procedure for enforcing deed restrictions and covenants. This simplifies the process by eliminating the need for homeowners to file lawsuits to enforce covenants against their neighbors. (Interview with Kerry Lowe, vice president and general counsel, Coussoulis Development Company, San Benardino, California, 1987.)

50. Severability provisions allow for the continued enforcement of covenants and restrictions, even if certain covenants are deemed illegal (such as race restrictions) and are thus unenforceable.

Chapter 4

Multifamily Residential Development

Introduction

This chapter begins the discussion of income-property development. Although it focuses on multifamily residential development—and primarily on rental-income property—it also covers topics common to all forms of development. Rather than presenting separate generic discussions of the development process throughout this book, this chapter incorporates a detailed discussion of each step of the development process into its treatment of rental and condominium apartment development. (Several generic subject areas, such as site acquisition, the regulatory process, and site engineering are covered in detail in chapter 3.) Chapters 5, 6, and 7 discuss the particular applications of each step in the process to the other major forms of income-property development—office, industrial, and retail development. (This book does not deal specifically with the development of single-family houses; readers interested in that subject can obtain more information from the National Association of Home Builders.[1])

Like other aspects of the housing industry, and like real estate in general, multifamily residential development is highly cyclical. Construction activity depends on both national and local economic conditions, the latter including local attitudes toward multifamily housing and local market conditions. Typically, in times of low interest rates, multifamily units are built by the thousands. Conversely, when interest rates are high (12 percent or above), multifamily construction slows considerably.

In the early 1980s, syndicators brought huge inflows of equity to finance apartment development in tax-driven deals offering little or no cash flow. Sales prices of apartment projects rose to uneconomic levels, often with zero and even negative cash-on-cash returns. The Tax Reform Act of 1986 effectively eliminated the market for these types of investments by limiting the ability of investors to write off tax losses against other income, and project values have accordingly adjusted downward. However, if the future follows past patterns, further changes in the tax treatment of rental housing can be expected.

Major demographic trends also exert substantial influence on multifamily construction. As local growth rates influence the overall demand for units, so the composition of the population influences the demand for particular types of multifamily housing. The aging of the baby boom generation will continue to play a leading role in the demand for housing. In the 1970s and early 1980s, the high proportion of the population aged between 20 and 35 created enormous demand for adult multifamily complexes. In the 1990s, however, many babyboomers will be in their 40s and early 50s, and the market for these complexes will inevitably and significantly decrease while the demand for senior housing will increase.

A number of obstacles confront today's multifamily residential developers:

- Well-located, suitable, and affordable sites for multifamily development are in short supply.
- Rent levels are very competitive. Rent controls exist in many areas and rents have not kept pace with inflation while operating costs have risen faster than the consumer price index (CPI).
- High construction and operating costs make it difficult to develop affordable multifamily housing—the market that is the largest and most underserved.
- Neighborhood opposition to multifamily housing has intensified. Community organizations are becoming major power brokers in determining what gets built and where.
- Tenants are becoming more sophisticated with respect to building design and amenities. Projects with small rooms, small kitchens, minimal fittings, inadequate parking, or site overcrowding are difficult to rent.

However, after the Reagan and Bush administrations, during which construction of low- and moderate-income housing has received little encouragement from the federal government, the problem of a declining stock of lower-rent apartments is likely to raise housing issues high on the national agenda again. Multifamily developers will be the major agents for delivering new products at both ends of the income spectrum. Increased federal support is likely to provide new opportunities for those developers who are aware of the different initiatives and who are willing to endure the bureaucratic complexities that participation in federal programs involves.

Product Types

Residential building development includes everything from single-family houses to high-rise apartment buildings and condominiums. The market can be segmented in a variety of ways:

- for-sale versus rental products—single-family houses and condominium apartments versus rental apartments and rental houses;
- design—number of stories and parking arrangement; and
- type of construction—wood frame versus concrete or steel.

Within each general product category, further distinctions can be made based on the segmentation of the target market—segmented by income, family composition, and age. Each segment demands different room arrangements, room sizes, finish details, and amenities. Figure 4-1 summarizes the basic design categories for single-family and multifamily products.

Product types are often confused with forms of ownership. "Apartment," for example, is often used as a generic term covering both multifamily rental and for-sale (condominium) products. Although the form of ownership greatly influences product design, marketing, and financing, it may refer to any product type. Technically, any rental property can be designed for, or converted to, "for-sale" property. Similarly, any "for-sale" product can be operated as rental property, if subdivision restrictions permit it.

This chapter focuses on multifamily residential development—rental and condominium apartments. No standard definition of multifamily or apartment types exists, but four major categories are evident:

- *Garden Apartments.* One-, two-, and sometimes three-story walk-up buildings built of wood frame on slab, with repeated floor plans. Two or four apartments share each stairway landing. Parking is at grade or tucked under part of the building. Densities range between 16 and 40 units per acre.
- *Low-Rise Apartments.* Three- or four-story walk-up or elevator buildings on top of parking. Constructed of wood frame on top of concrete deck. Fire sprinklers are usually required. Densities range between 40 and 80 units per acre.
- *Mid-Rise Apartments.* Five to 10 stories, with elevators and central halls for apartment access on each floor. Buildings are usually long and squat. Densities range between 60 and 120 units per acre.

■ 4-1 Residential Product Types

Single-Family Product (One to Two Units per Lot)

- Single-family houses (one unit per lot)
- Patio houses (or zero-lot-line)
- Duplexes (two units per lot)
- Townhouses (attached buildings on separate lots)

Multifamily Product (Multiple Units per Lot)

- Garden apartments (wood frame construction)
- Low-rise apartments
- Mid-rise apartments
- High-rise apartments

Two-story garden apartments, such as Siena at Renaissance Park in Atlanta, can offer a pleasant low-rise atmosphere for the tenant/buyer and low-cost construction for the developer.

- *High-Rise Apartments.* Above 10 stories, constructed of concrete or steel. Cost per square foot is almost double that for wood frame. Densities range between 80 and 200 units per acre.

Getting Started

Many multifamily residential developers start by building single-family houses. Methods of construction and issues regarding marketing and design are similar whether a developer is building single-family or multifamily houses. The differences are often ones of scale and whether the units are for sale or for rent.

Most homebuilders (that is, builders of single-family houses) act as their own general contractors, and much of their profit in homebuilding is derived from construction. Profit margins, which typically range between 10 and 15 percent over hard and soft costs, must cover construction risk.

Many multifamily developers also do their own construction, but others hire third-party general contractors. Unless they already own a construction company, beginning developers should probably begin with a third-party general contractor. Once they have developed a track record, then they can consider bringing construction in-house.

The general contractor absorbs the construction risk and earns the construction profit, which typically runs between 5 and 8 percent of hard construction costs. The development profit, which typically runs between 10 and 15 percent of total cost, is in addition to the contractor's profit. The development profit represents the difference between total cost and the capitalized value—the market value—of the property when leased.

In general, backgrounds, approaches, and concepts vary greatly for developers' first projects, some of which are profiled in the case studies in feature box 4-2; the key to success, however, is to execute skillfully the steps in the development process, which is outlined in the following sections.

Project Feasibility

Project feasibility encompasses a number of activities that a developer must perform before committing to a given project. As the analysis of feasibility progresses, the developer acquires more information that will tell him/her whether or not to proceed further. During the feasibility period, the project may be canceled at any time, usually limiting losses to the costs of the feasibility study plus the cost of tying up the land. Positive information, however, usually justifies making the next increment of expenditure to acquire additional information.

Project feasibility includes four major activities:

- market analysis;
- site selection/engineering feasibility;
- regulatory approvals; and
- financial feasibility.

In some cases, these activities are performed sequentially. More often, they are done simultaneously. However, developers must be satisfied that all four activities have been completed satisfactorily before making a final go/no-go decision. Moreover, developers must treat the findings of their research objectively and not become enamored with the site or concept.

Developers rarely close on a site until they are certain that the project will go ahead—in practice, that means when a financing commitment is received, or, preferably, after it is signed, sealed, and delivered. For beginning developers, most of the steps taken during the feasibility period are aimed at securing financing and ensuring that no unexpected surprises show up later during construction or lease-up.

Market Analysis

Market analysis should precede site selection because the choice of sites depends on the market that the developer wants to target. High-quality market information is essential in order to determine accurately what to build, who to build for, and how much to build.

If the developer is familiar with the local submarket, a market study may be needed only to support a loan application. If the developer does not know the market well, however, the market study should be done before decisions are made concerning where and what to build; indeed, the primary benefit of analyzing the market before selecting a site is that such an analysis will help to identify the holes in the market.

■ 4-2 How Three Residential Developers Started in Business

C.C. Mow
Century West Development
Santa Monica, California

C.C. Mow and three partners (two engineers and one builder) formed Century West Development, Inc., in the late 1970s. Mow, a researcher at the RAND Corporation, wanted a new career in which he could earn residuals from his hard work. Having previously owned some apartment buildings, which gave him familiarity with real estate, he realized that he could build apartments more cheaply than he could buy existing buildings. With money he had saved or borrowed from his relatives, Mow began developing apartments, first on a part-time basis, and then full-time.

Mow and his partners now concentrate on one of the prime areas in the Los Angeles area—the westside of Los Angeles. At present, they joint venture with large financial firms and have a pool of investors who supply equity. Mow believes that the most important advice for beginning developers to remember is to avoid being overly bullish and to prepare for downturns in the economy.

Alan Casden
Casden Properties
Beverly Hills, California

Alan Casden, chairman of Casden Properties, began his career as an accountant with Kenneth Leventhal & Company, a major accounting firm specializing in real estate. At Kenneth Leventhal, Casden was introduced to development through his clients. Bob Mayer persuaded Casden to leave accounting and become CEO of the Mayer Group, a residential construction firm. Casden's first job was to straighten out the financial affairs of the company. "We were selling apartment projects without including overhead, lease-up, and fees in our costs."

The years 1974–1975 were tough times in the apartment business. "We were buying land in San Fernando Valley where apartments had no pizzazz—no amenities, landscaping, or other special features. Casden spent every minute on weekends looking at projects. Even though he was CEO, he worked on the floor renting apartments. "I had to know how to do that." Casden advises beginning developers: "You must understand the intricacies of the marketplace. Know who you are going to rent to." Casden says that one of his biggest mistakes was not getting involved in the construction process early enough. "I thought we had good people, but the construction people kept taking out our additions. They would save two cents, which cost us $20 in sales price. They would spend extra money to strengthen walls but then would take out sound proofing and upgraded appliances that everybody hears and sees."

In 1980, First City Financial, a Canadian firm, bought out Bob Mayer's interest. Casden became CEO of the new firm, which built a chain of hotels and some 2,000 apartment units per year. In 1982, Casden bought out their interest and most of the California assets, developing several thousand units in partnership with Coast Savings and Loan Association. He bought out Coast Savings' interest in 1990 and is now concentrating on developing multifamily apartments in California.

Casden believes that his biggest mistake was not to buy more land in 1987 when the land market became very competitive. Today, land is a very scarce commodity.

Haskel Iny
Homestead Group Associates
Los Angeles, California

Haskel Iny comes from a family that has been involved in the construction industry for 30 years. After attending UCLA and Santa Monica City College, Iny began working in 1977 as an independent broker, a career that allowed him to learn more about the development process as he put together real estate packages for developer clients.

Iny's first project was four townhouses, which, he says, was not a winner. His father signed the loans, but Haskel did all of the work. He learned what not to do and what to expect from deals. In 1978, Iny became affiliated with Ronnie and Noam Schwartz with whom he formed the Homestead Group. Their first project was an 11,000-square-foot office building. "We had a miserable time getting a loan. We had to work through a loan broker because we didn't know any banks. We felt everybody was out to take advantage of us because we didn't know what we were doing. In retrospect, I know that was not the case." He advises beginning developers to level with everybody. "Don't be afraid to say, 'It's my first project; show me the way.'" In 1990, Homestead Group completed four projects and is concentrating on rehabilitating apartments and creating value through management.

■ 4-3 Time Line of Events

Ideally, the developer does not close on the land until he/she is ready to start construction. In most cases, however, the land seller will not wait that long.

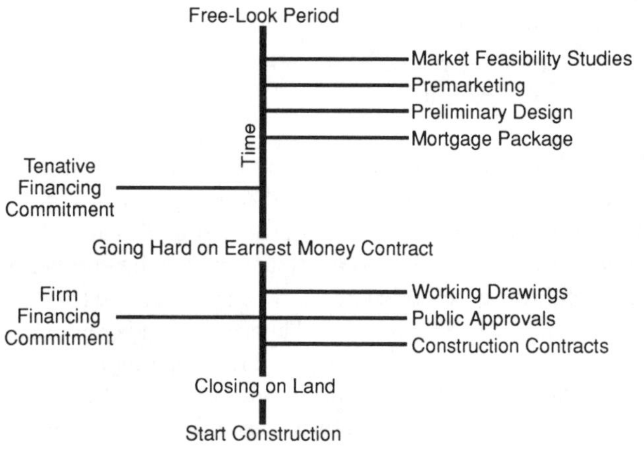

The more clearly a developer defines the market he/she wishes to serve, the more specific are the requirements for a site. For example, when a developer knows who his/her prospective homebuyers or tenants may be—their preferences, their income level, their family situation—then he/she has the facts needed to make wise decisions. Particular market needs imply particular site requirements. If a need for high-end apartments is identified, for example, a developer should be willing to pay more for a superior site with special amenities such as views, creeks, and recreational opportunities.

The market study in the early stages does not need to be as comprehensively detailed as it will have to be in the future. Market information is not only time-consuming but also expensive to obtain, and a developer should concentrate on specific issues:

- What geographic submarkets have the greatest need for apartments?
- What product type is in greatest need?
- What are the characteristics of renters who have the greatest need for more apartments, in terms of age, income, and household size and composition?
- What types of features, amenities, and services do renters expect?
- What product types attract renters and why?

Note that the focus is on "greatest need" rather than on vacancy rates or hottest areas. Need is measured by the relationship between demand (the absorption rate for new units) and supply of units (existing and anticipated) for a particular submarket. The submarket is identified not only by geographic area but also by product type and renter profile.

Developers often confuse existing supply with need. Certainly, historic absorption rates of existing supply are an important source of information for predicting future absorption, but because a particular product type is absent from an area does not necessarily mean that demand exists for that product type. "Often a product type is not there because no supply is equivalent to no demand."[2]

Once a site is selected, the submarket should be analyzed in much greater detail. By collecting submarket information on rents, unit sizes, types of renters, levels of activity, and vacancies for each unit type, a developer will be able to determine how best to target a project. A project-by-project catalog of competitive projects should be created and used to decide whether to engage in direct competition with other local buildings or to cater to a market niche that shows need and little competition.

To summarize, the goals of residential market analysis are:

- To identify holes in the market—market niches where demand exceeds supply; locations and circumstances that offer special opportunities to build a project serving a particular niche.
- To define the target market for the project as narrowly as possible—number of units needed with particular design, amenity, and cost characteristics (number of rooms, size, mix of units, features, and so forth).
- To develop a market strategy—whether to compete directly with other projects or to look for monopoly opportunities by finding market niches.

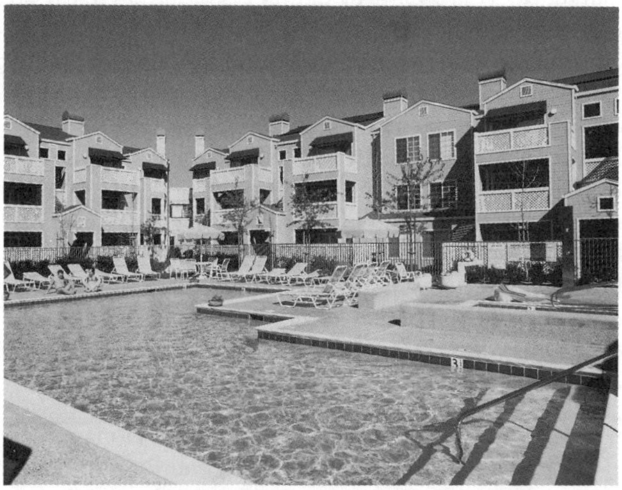

One of the many objectives of market analysis is to determine the types of features, amenities, and services that renters prefer. Swimming pools are a must in some markets, whereas in others they are less necessary. Pictured is Hacienda Gardens in Pleasanton, California.

Demand and Supply Factors in Market Analysis

A formal market analysis increases in importance as developers move further away from familiar locations and product types. Beginning developers are unlikely to have the firsthand knowledge of local market conditions required to compete successfully and therefore need to make an extra effort to collect market information before making even basic site selection decisions. The factors with which they should be concerned include the market area, supply and demand, and net market absorption.

Market area. The developer's first task is to define the geographic study area. The study usually starts with the metropolitan area (data is available for Metropolitan Statistical Areas—MSAs) or the city in which the project is to be located. Ultimately, it will focus on the narrow submarket area in which the project will be competing directly. For rental apartments and condominiums, the submarket is defined as the area of generally comparable population characteristics and is usually limited to one or two neighborhoods. Although the employment center or corridor that the project serves generally defines the broader market, the "primary market area" is usually restricted to a radius of two or three miles around the project and may even be smaller, especially if freeways, railroads, or other barriers exist between neighborhoods.

A "secondary market area" should also be defined. This area includes apartment projects that may not be directly competitive but that offer an alternative to renters who are less sensitive about location.

The importance of defining the correct market area cannot be overemphasized. All too often, beginning developers omit competing projects or include so large an area that absorption rates are overestimated. Also, many market areas are hard to define because they have no particular identity in the marketplace. This poses problems not only for market definition but also for future lease-up and sales, because projects perform better in areas that have distinctive identities. Creating a market identity where none exists can be quite a challenge.

Demand factors. On the demand side, the market study measures the number of households with particular age, size, and income characteristics. Market research firms employ many statistical techniques to refine their estimates of the number of households, but their basic approach is the same and takes into account the following factors:

- employment growth in basic industries (manufacturing and other industries that generate sales outside the city);
- employment growth in service industries (retail, local government, real estate, professionals, and others whose activities support the local community);
- percentage of growth expected to occur in the submarket;
- household size—families with children, couples without children, singles, divorcees with children, and so on;
- age distribution;
- social characteristics;
- education characteristics; and
- income distribution.

Each of these factors must be carefully analyzed so that the developer understands the characteristics of the target population groups. From these statistics and other market surveys, the market analyst estimates the number of households expected to appear over the next two to three years, and hence the number of apartment and condominium units expected to be needed. These estimates should be broken down into absorption rates for individual product types. For example, a study that indicates demand of 500 apartments per year for a given market area is incomplete. It should subdivide that number according to product type: say, 350 adult units, 100 of which are luxury units, and 150 family units, 50 of which are luxury.

Supply factors. The supply of housing includes the existing housing stock, the units currently under construction, and the units that may be under construction in the future. The vacancy rate is usually considered the most important indicator of market need. Submarket vacancy rates, however, can be very misleading. For example, vacancies may be 40 percent in older, non-air-conditioned buildings but as low as 5 percent in newer buildings. Equally, a 15 percent vacancy rate in a submarket with only 100 total units may be quickly absorbed, especially if a new company is planning to move into the area; elsewhere, however, 15 percent may indicate a very soft market. A more meaningful measure is the total number of months of existing and planned inventory (for example, 12 months' worth of absorption—300 units of vacant inventory absorbed at the rate of 25 units per month). This figure takes into account both demand factors (annual absorption) and supply factors.

Information on the existing housing stock and vacancy rates can best be determined by personal inspection and interviews with managers of surrounding apartment complexes. Even though such information may be proprietary, most managers are willing to cooperate, especially if the developer promises to reciprocate when his/her project is completed. Other sources of information include local real estate boards, local homeowners' and apartment associations, public utility companies, mortgage companies, lending institutions, and the Federal Housing Administration (FHA).

The most common mistake that developers make in estimating supply is to ignore units on the drawing board—

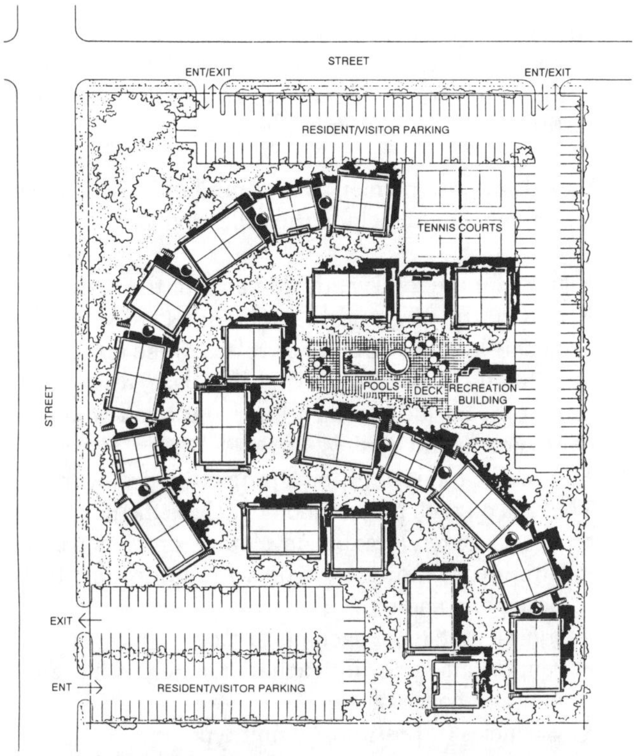

The most important objective of market analysis is to identify and describe a target market; the project is then designed to fit the parameters of that market. Pictured above is a site plan and product concept, targeted to recreation-oriented singles and young families, that could be used in numerous market situations around the country. The buildings consist of four back-to-back units per floor in two- and three-story structures, and are located on an 8.3-acre site. Landscaped recreation areas and amenities are woven between structures, and parking is located at the exterior of the site. The design is by Spiess Wheeler Partners, Ajit N. Dighe, Greg Spiess A.I.A., Los Angeles.

in other words, units that have not been announced and do not yet appear on any of the standard sources, such as city building permits. Often, local brokers, bankers, and architects will be the best-informed sources concerning planned units. Of course, many such units may never be built, but the "most-likely" estimate of the number of units that will be built should be included in the projections of supply.

Net market absorption. The end product of the market analysis is the number of units of a particular product type that a submarket can absorb over a given period. Suppose that an analysis indicates demand for middle-income adult apartments of 1,000 units per year in a quadrant of the city where a developer wishes to develop. Suppose, also, that the current inventory of existing vacant units is 500 apartments, with another 500 units under construction, and that the developer is aware of 300 units on the drawing board. Realistically, the developer probably has learned of only half of all the units planned (for a total of 600), but of the planned units perhaps only 60 percent (360) will actually be built. Thus, the total supply of units is estimated to be 1,360 (500 + 500 + 360).

If demand is 1,000 units per year, or 83 per month, then the market has approximately a 16-month inventory. If the developer's project would begin leasing in 12 months, then the current competition should only be about four months' worth of inventory.

What is a reasonable "number of months absorption" of existing inventory? Although no widely accepted guidelines exist, depending on the size of the project, the developer should attempt to scale the project so that he/she can lease it within 12 months from the date it opens for occupancy. A "soft market" is usually one that has 18 months or more of existing inventory plus units under construction. Since this excludes planned units, which will come on-stream while the project is under construction, the total anticipated inventory may be 24 months or more including planned units. If the project takes a year to build, the soft market will still have a year's supply or more of units when the project is ready for leasing. The developer may still be able to lease the project within 12 months, but he/she will have to capture more than the pro-rata share of market demand.

Market Study Guidelines

Market studies serve two purposes: they facilitate internal decision making, and they provide documentation for lenders and investors. Lenders and investors are suspicious of market analyses because developers often perform them as *post facto* justifications of decisions already made. Lenders and investors also know that developers can always find someone to write a market study showing that an area has a strong market.

In order for the market study to be most useful, both to lenders and investors and to developers, developers should observe the following guidelines.

1. Give specific directions to the market research firm concerning boundaries of both primary and secondary areas to be researched and the types of product to be researched. The larger the boundaries and the greater the number of product types, the more expensive the study will be.
2. Be aware that general statistical information is, by itself, inadequate for making market decisions. Critical differences exist between market studies that collect general statistics on the market and those that gather data on specific projects. The latter type is significantly more expensive but is essential unless developers are certain that the market is good and that the competition is weak. General statistics—housing inventory, vacancies, average rents, average unit sizes, number of housing starts the past five years,

number and dollar volume of permits, number of completions—are a useful starting point, but they must be supplemented with survey data from projects within the specific market area. Even if the market research firm has a data bank with project-by-project information, the research should be updated to reflect current conditions.

3. Although vacancy rates may be helpful indicators of market demand in areas where rates are very low, in general, developers should not base their decisions about whether or not to proceed with a project on these alone. The preferred indicator is the number of months of inventory existing, under construction, and on the drawing boards in the marketplace. The number of months of inventory correlates directly with the amount of interest reserve that developers will need.
4. Developers should be sure to hire the best firm to undertake the market study. Firms that specialize in rental apartments and condominiums for particular market areas will have information at their fingertips that other firms will charge thousands of dollars to replicate. Developers certainly do not want to pay a firm to collect raw data from scratch. Developers should evaluate firms on the basis of their information bases and track records: How accurate have they been in their projections? Which banks and other financial institutions rely on their studies?

A good study of the market for multifamily residential development should include the following:

1. Figures for the total yearly demand for the metropolitan area, the city, and the submarket in which the project is located. "Demand" refers to the number of multifamily units that the marketplace will absorb during the period in which the project will be under construction and leasing.
2. Figures for total supply on a project-by-project basis. The data on each project should include the following:
   - target market, location, developer, completion date;
   - number of units by type (one-bedroom, two-bedroom, and so on);
   - square footage of each unit type;
   - rent or sales price for each unit, along with premiums and concessions;
   - vacancies (if possible, by unit type);

4-4 Advice on Market Analysis

Interviews with experienced residential developers have generated a number of useful pointers with respect to market analysis.

- Although a developer in a small town may capture 50 percent of a market, in a large metropolitan area the same developer probably will not get more than 5 percent. Robert Engstrom, president of Robert Engstrom Companies of Minneapolis, believes that capturing more than 2.5 percent of any market that absorbs more than 15,000 housing units per year is an ambitious undertaking.
- In an unfamiliar market, a new developer will normally estimate his/her potential share of the market by studying what success other developers have enjoyed in the area with a similar type of product and sales promotion program. A developer should gather as much statistical data as possible, make extensive field investigations, identify growth patterns and areas, and check on utility and zoning moratoriums.
- Some developers maintain that most marketing errors are made by strangers in an area. James Klingbeil, president of the Klingbeil Group of Dublin, Ohio, disagrees: "The basic fact-finding chore and analysis of the demographic data are the same whether in your own backyard or a foreign market. Economic indicators are similar enough to have a common denominator—namely, the ability to buy or rent. It is extremely important, though, to identify the idiosyncrasies that exist within the foreign market." Some modification in the design of the product is usually required to meet local tastes. Klingbeil views market studies as "essential in all cases. . . . It is disastrous to impose your personal likes, philosophies, and concepts on the future residents without benefit of research."
- Although market data is critical, a developer should assess his/her ability to deliver a particular product and form his/her own judgment concerning the market share that can be captured. Robert Carey, president of Urban Centre Developments Ltd. of Oakland, California, believes that market analysis should be regarded as a definition of the needs of certain groups of people, not as a road map for development.
- In collecting market information, a developer should not just drive the area or rely on the architect to do the market research. Stanley Brent, president of Stanley M. Brent AIA, Inc., Sherman Oaks, California, observes that a developer can rely on the architect for building codes, for determining what to build, and for information about what other developers are doing in the area. However, a developer should not rely on the architect to determine unit sizes, amenities, and other features that depend on the tastes and preferences of the particular target market.

- amenities of complexes; and
- amenities of individual units (appliances, fireplaces, and so on).

3. An assessment of how many units (for-rent or for-sale) the market will absorb each month by unit type. Developers should guard against anticipating unreasonably large capture rates.

Site Selection

According to an old real estate adage, the worst reason for developing a parcel is because you already own it. Ideally, developers will first come up with an idea and then will locate a suitable site. Many sites, however, are developed by owners who want to do something with their land. Although owning a plot of land may not by itself be a good reason for developing it, land should not be eliminated from consideration just because one does own it. Almost every site is developable for something. The developer's challenge is to identify the "highest and best use"—the use that maximizes the value of the property.

In acquiring the site (site acquisition guidelines are outlined in chapter 3), the ability to buy more time during the acquisition process can be crucial for beginning developers. For example, when Peiser Corporation and Jerome Frank Investments purchased a site in Dallas for a 160-unit apartment project, they had what seemed to be a comfortable 120-day period in which to close. The project was economically attractive only if the partnership could obtain permission to issue tax-exempt housing revenue bonds, which were a popular financing tool before the Tax Reform Act of 1986. Approval from the city council was needed to issue the bonds. Because housing revenue bonds were a new program for the city of Dallas, the city council kept postponing the hearing date to allow more time to work out the details of the bond program. Fortunately, the partnership had negotiated the right to extend the closing by up to three months, at a cost of $5,000 per month, and the extra time allowed the partners to receive the necessary approvals.

Location and Neighborhood

Real estate professionals often say that the success of a real estate project depends on three factors: location, location, and location. Location has many dimensions and has been the subject of considerable debate and comment in professional and academic journals.[3] This author has argued elsewhere that location can be categorized by "macrolocation" factors and "microlocation" factors.[4] Macrolocation refers to a property's proximity to major urban nodes, whereas microlocation refers to a property's immediate environs. A property's long-term value depends not only on current macrolocation and microlocation attributes but also on how these are changing over time.

Broadmoor Pines, a luxury rental apartment project in Colorado Springs, Colorado, is located on a 15.4-acre site on the lower slope of Cheyenne Mountain, some 600 feet above the city in a neighborhood of luxury single-family detached homes. This attractive site, which provides both mountain and city views, was a key factor in the project's achieving 100 percent occupancy at aggressive rents in its first year.

Both macrolocation and microlocation influence multifamily residential development. Macrolocation factors determine what part of the city offers the best long-run potential for value preservation and enhancement—proximity to downtown and suburban employment centers, major growth corridors, medical centers, regional shopping and entertainment, regional parks, and recreation. Microlocation factors determine how well a site is situated within its immediate neighborhood. Such factors include access to freeways or arterial roads, schools, parks, and daycare and health facilities. Ideally, a site will be visible from a major arterial or even a freeway and yet will be situated to give privacy, a sense of security, and a low noise level.

The ability to foresee changes in the urban fabric before others do is one of the hallmarks of the most successful developers. Whether their predictions are based on careful research, intuition, luck, or some combination of all three, successful developers understand the dynamics of location well enough to survive over the long term.

An important component of their success is tied to the health of the cities or suburbs in which they build. If the level of public services in a city declines, real estate values decline as well. Successful developers understand how much they depend on the physical and financial health of the communities in which they build—that is why so many of them are active in public affairs.

Size and Shape

The best size and shape for a site vary according to such local market conditions as lease-up rates, acceptable unit densities, and preferred amenity packages. For example, suppose a developer wants to build a project that can be leased within 12 months from its completion. If 15 units can be leased per month (180 units per year), and the product being built has an average density of 24 units per acre, then the ideal site would be 7.5 acres. The size of a site is also influenced by property management considerations. Although the optimum number of units varies with each project, many developers consider 150 or 200 units as the minimum number necessary to support a full-time maintenance staff. They look for sites that are large enough to accommodate that many units.

Design options increase as the size of the site increases. A site that is too narrow prevents the inclusion of double-loaded parking or back-to-back units, which increase efficiency and reduce cost.[5] A site that is too deep, however, may require either a loop road or a costly turnaround for fire trucks. A developer should always draw up a preliminary site plan to see how a site lays out before going hard on an earnest money contract.

Beginning developers should look for individual tracts that are large enough to accommodate the type of product they want to build. They should avoid tracts that require assembling several parcels under different ownership. The process of tract assemblage is virtually a development business in itself, offering its own risks and rewards. Problems in assembling tracts include multiple closings, extra legal costs, multiple lenders, and the possibility that key parcels will not close. Incomplete assemblage carries costly penalties for developers who may have to pay exorbitant prices for outparcels or who may have to spend extra money on design and construction in order to squeeze as many units as possible within an inadequate site.

Accessibility and Visibility

In evaluating a residential site's accessibility, a developer should ask the following questions:

- How will prospective tenants approach the property? What will they see as they drive to the site that may make it more or less desirable? (In brochures and advertisements, developers often select the most attractive, although not necessarily the shortest, route to a project.)
- How will visitors enter the property? Will they be able to turn left across traffic? Can median strip or curb cuts be obtained if necessary?
- Will the current level of traffic support the additional traffic generated by a new development?
- What is the heaviest traffic burden that the planned project will create? Will that burden prevent residents from exiting the project easily?
- How long will it take residents to travel to work, schools, shops, and recreational facilities?
- Is the site served by public transportation?
- Is road construction planned? If so, rentals will be severely impaired during the construction period.
- Are existing roads adequate for the type of development planned? (In general, high-density development

4-5 Advice on Site Selection

Every developer maintains a mental or written checklist of what to look for when buying land for multifamily development. Several prominent developers offer the following advice.

Richard Gleitman, president, R.J. Investments Associates, Sherman Oaks, California, states that a "good address" for medium- and high-priced projects is important. Because local tradition plays the leading role in determining what is considered a "good address," Gleitman looks for sites in established locations. His development strategy is to buy land and build for a long-term hold. He looks for:

- locations for which there is high demand;
- areas where development is already well established;
- sites near to competition;
- high-quality competition;
- commercial activities within walking distance; and
- sites with as much frontage as possible, ideally with visibility from freeways and canyon arterials.

Niles Bolton, president of Niles Bolton Associates, Inc., of Atlanta, disagrees about visibility. He argues that economics and design trends have altered visibility requirements: "The project should have just enough frontage for a nice landscape and dramatic entrance." The bulk of the land without frontage is cheaper and quieter and gives tenants a feeling of seclusion. Also, the developer does not have to discount rents for units facing on a main road.

Jona Goldrich, CEO of Goldrich & Kest of Culver City, California, recommends that developers do not become overly attracted to cheap land. He does not look for bargains on land price, even though apartment land prices in Los Angeles run as high as $50 per square foot. Apartment land in the Los Angeles area is typically sold on a per-unit basis. Goldrich used to buy land in Los Angeles at $2,000 per unit for an $8,000 total cost per unit, but he now buys land at $20,000 per unit for an $80,000 total cost per unit. "If you make a mistake—for example, you buy land at $10,000 per unit but rent is $300 less than in other areas—then you're in a hole." Although a developer might save $10,000 on the cost of the land, the developer will lose $36,000 in value relative to other projects ($300 per month multiplied by 12 months, capitalized at 10 percent).

requires collector and/or arterial street access, whereas lower-density development can be undertaken on smaller interior streets.)

Visibility is critical for marketing and leasing—after all, if people cannot see the project, how will they know it is there? A developer can do several things to increase a project's visibility, including using special design elements, special landscaping features, striking colors, offsite signage, and nighttime lighting, especially of the frontage. The aim should be the creation of an appealing, distinctive project.

Site Conditions

Apartment and condominium development offers somewhat more latitude with respect to the physical characteristics of a site than do other types of development. A developer of multifamily residential projects is less constrained by slopes and by the size and shape of parcels because residential building pads tend to be smaller and more flexible than, say, pads for office or industrial buildings. Nonetheless, a developer must still carefully evaluate every potential site in terms of its slope, soil, geology, vegetation, and hydrology.

Slope and topography. Developers have always been attracted to hilltops and other places offering views. Moderately sloping sites are preferable to either steep or flat land. Slopes create opportunities for more interesting design such as split-level units and varied rooflines. They also help to reduce the amount of excavation needed to provide structured parking in denser developments (densities greater than 40 units per acre usually require some form of structured parking).

Improvement costs, on the other hand, rise sharply on slopes over 10 percent. Retaining walls, special piers, and other foundations can add to the time and cost of construction. Furthermore, some cities, such as San Diego, have adopted hillside development ordinances that restrict development of steeply sloping sites. Flat land may also create additional expense. Sewers must slope downward to create flow; thus, pumping stations may be required if a site is entirely flat or if part of the site lies below the connection point to the city sewer line.

Geology, hydrology, and soils. In earthquake-prone areas, a geologic survey is essential. If a site is crossed by fault lines, it may be unbuildable. The same is true of a site in an area with abandoned subterranean mines. Even though building around the fault line or mine may be possible, obtaining insurance may be impossible. Proximity to a fault line creates an intractable marketing problem.

If a site contains, or borders on, a creek, a floodplain study must be conducted. Some portion of the site will almost certainly be unbuildable. A developer should be able to obtain a rough approximation of how much land lies within the floodplain by hiring a civil engineer who has done previous work in the immediate area. Standing water on a site suggests the presence of an underground stream, which must be located.

Strode Eckert Photographic

At French Prairie Village Apartments in Wilsonville, Oregon, two site conditions played important roles in the project plan. First, the adjacent Willamette River was used to create an attractive waterfront greenway for the project. Second, the site is adjacent to a golf course, and its irrigation runoff is captured and reused to create a series of canals and water features throughout the project.

Like floodplains, soil conditions are problematic. Even if a site looks clean, a developer should always hire a geologist to take soil samples of a site before the developer purchases it. Geologists usually take at least one core sample near each corner of a property and one or more in the center of a property, in order to determine what type of soil is present, its viscosity, its plasticity, and how deep the underlying bedrock is.

Good soil, like sandy loam, is moderately pervious to water. Clay soils, however, expand and contract with water, which may cause foundations to crack. Impervious soils saturate quickly and cause increased water runoff. If rock is located near the surface of a site, excavation may cost 10 to 20 times as much as a site with deep soil.

Vegetation. Plant cover provides useful information concerning soil and weather conditions. Kevin Lynch notes in his book *Site Planning*: "Red maple, alder, tupelo, hemlock, and willow indicate wet ground that is poorly drained. Oak and hickory grow on warm, dry land; spruce and fir in cold, moist places. Pitch pine and scrub oak are signs of very dry land and of good drainage. Red cedars mark poor soil. This list can easily be extended in any locality. It is a list worth learning and using as a predictor of site constraints."[6]

Special efforts should be made to preserve mature trees. Large, healthy trees—although they can be saved

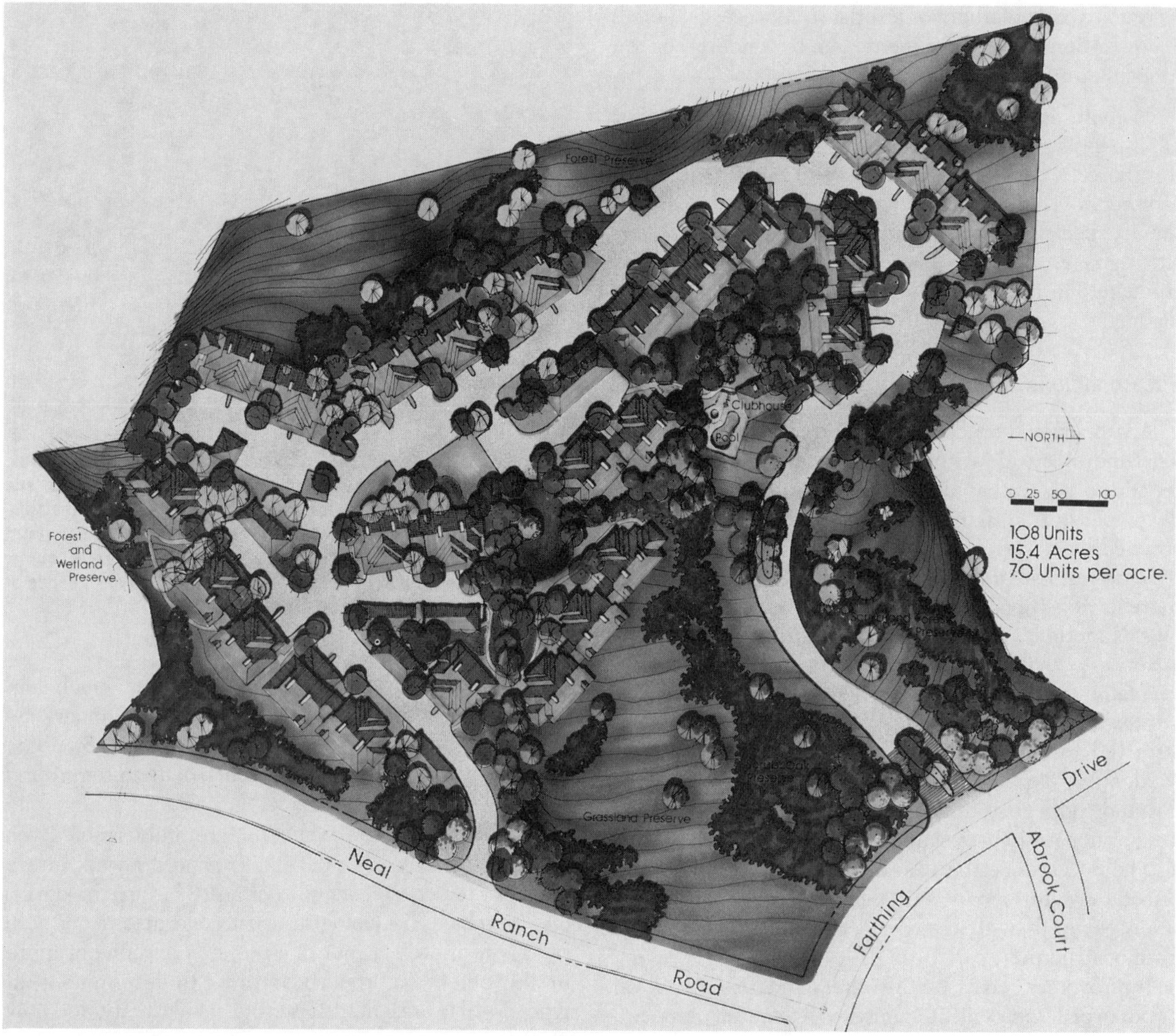

At Broadmoor Pines in Colorado Springs, existing trees and vegetation were primary site assets, and only 18 of the site's existing 137 mature pine trees had to be removed in the development process.

for no more than it costs to plant a small sapling—face several dangers. Heavy foot traffic or parking cars daily under a tree compacts the soil and may kill the tree. Workmen often do not like saving trees because it may make their work more time-consuming and costly. Trees often die during construction because of paint or chemical poisoning. Even if they survive construction, they often die later because their root systems have been disturbed or because the amount of water they receive has been changed. A developer should consult an arborist about saving trees, and should clearly mark and place a protective barrier around trees that are to be preserved.

Existing buildings. Developers should proceed with caution before demolishing existing buildings on a site. Most cities have laws that protect historic structures, and some cities have laws that restrict the eviction of tenants. Before purchasing a site for complete renovation or redevelopment, developers should make certain that they can evict the current tenants. Eviction can take a long time—often four to six months or more—and can be expensive, especially if relocation assistance is required from the developer.

Easements and Covenants

An easement is a right of one party to use the property of another. The beneficiary of the easement is called the "dominant tenant." The property owner who initially gave or sold the easement and his/her successors are "servient" tenants who must give the dominant tenant and his/her successors the rights created by the easement. Unless easements are created with a specific termination date, they survive indefinitely. Only the beneficiary of the easement—the dominant tenant—can extinguish them. Subsequent owners of property that have existing easements often may have to purchase the easement back from the current beneficiaries.

Protective covenants, also called "deed restrictions," are private restrictions that "run with the land"—that is, once created, they remain in force for all future buyers or heirs. Deed restrictions may be created by a property owner at any time. Once created, however, they remain in force unless all parties subject to the covenants agree to remove them.

Developers usually establish deed restrictions at the time that they subdivide, or "plat," a property. Some covenants expire automatically after a number of years under state statute, but others never expire. To be enforceable, covenants usually must be filed with the county recorder and thus will appear in a title search.

Developers must carefully review any and all deed restrictions, for deed restrictions can kill a project even after developers have invested many months of time and money. In Dallas, for example, one case involved a subdivision that still had single-family restrictions in place despite the presence of many nonresidential uses. A developer bought a property within that subdivision, assuming that the existing nonresidential uses effectively voided the restrictions. However, although the developer may have been able to overturn the restrictions in court, he found that no bank would loan him money on a site that had use restrictions against the intended use. The developer lost the property.

A dominant tenant who knows that the servient tenant must have a release from an easement to proceed with development enjoys a powerful bargaining position and can exact almost any price for that release. Land sellers usually have more rapport with the dominant tenant than the developer will have as a new buyer. Therefore, developers should enlist sellers' assistance to clear up any easement problems before closing on the land.

Several important points should be borne in mind regarding easements:

- Easements, especially utility easements, often do not show up on plats. Double-check with the utility companies.
- Never rely on a site plan provided by the seller. Always order a title survey before going hard on the contract. The title survey will indicate any recorded easements.
- Pipeline, utility, and other easements in gross[7] usually give the utility company the right to make repairs within the easement at any time. If, for instance, a concrete driveway has been built over the easement, a utility company may still enter the property with minimum notice to repair or maintain the utility line without liability or obligation to restore any damage done to the owner's improvements. Where possible, developers should try to locate easements in green belts, pedestrian pathways, and other open spaces.

Utilities

Water, sanitary and storm sewers, electricity, gas, cable television, and telephone service are, of course, critical factors in site selection. Before purchasing a site, a developer should always confirm that services are not only nearby but also available. It is not unusual, for instance, for a major water line to run adjacent to a property but be unavailable to that property because the line's capacity is already committed or because the city is concerned about a loss in water pressure. To verify that service is available, a developer should never simply take the word of the land seller and should instead visit the appropriate city departments or pay a civil engineer to do so.

Water and sanitary sewer services are the most costly utilities to bring in from off site. When utilities must be brought in from off site, the developer should undertake the work him/herself, if possible, in order to ensure that the work is performed speedily. Electricity, gas, and telephone services are usually provided by private utility companies. Except for remote sites, utility companies usually will provide service to the site at no cost to the developer. Each locality has its own fee structure and method of handling service.

A developer should ask the following questions concerning utilities:

- How long will it take to obtain service?
- How much will it cost?
- When is payment due?
- When does one have to apply for service?
- Are public hearings involved?—these may cause delays and increase the political risk.
- Is the provision of service subject to any potential moratoriums?
- Are easements needed from any other property owners before services can be obtained?
- Is the capacity of the service adequate?

Regulatory Issues

Securing the necessary regulatory approvals has become the developer's primary concern in many communities. Current trends indicate that the regulatory process will become increasingly difficult. As it does so, the ability to pass safely through the regulatory minefield will play an increasingly important role in determining the success of a developer.

The increasing complexity of development regulation has created a whole new field of development—namely, developers who bear the risk of obtaining necessary approvals and entitlements (as discussed in chapter 3). Even where land is appropriately zoned, no guarantee exists that developers will be able to build what they want to build. New players in the regulatory process, such as design review boards and neighborhood planning committees, must approve developers' plans before a building permit is issued. New setback, parking, environmental, air-quality, and fire code regulations affect the density that developers can achieve on a parcel, irrespective of the allowable density under the zoning.

The regulatory process is described more fully in chapter 3. The following issues focus principally on multifamily residential development.

Zoning

Zoning determines the building envelope and the density for a site. Specific issues that are usually covered in the zoning code include the number of units allowed, parking requirements, height limitations, setback restrictions, floor/area ratios, and unit size requirements. Some zoning codes give actual density constraints (for instance, up to 24 units per acre), whereas others stipulate minimum land area per unit (for instance, 1,500 square feet of land per unit). The other major zoning constraint for apartments is parking. One parking space per bedroom (up to two spaces for a three-bedroom apartment), plus visitor spaces, is a common requirement. A developer may petition to change the zoning or obtain a variance, but this is often a long and arduous process, especially if higher densities are involved.

Venice Renaissance in Venice, California, contains 66 market-rate condominiums, 23 rental units for the elderly, and 30,000 square feet of ground-level commercial space. Securing entitlements required rezoning from residential to mixed use, a height variance, a parking variance, 14 public discretionary hearings, dozens of formal and informal meetings with community groups, and about two and one-half years of full-time commitment by the developer. To win community support and approval, the developer privately subsidized and reserved 23 rental apartments for the elderly and provided much-needed parking for beach visitors.

Fire Codes

Fire codes have particular importance for residential construction because residential buildings are usually wood frame and therefore especially prone to the risk of fire. Fire codes determine the number of stairways that each unit requires as well as the maximum distance that each unit must be from a fire plug. The codes directly affect the number of units that can be placed on a site as well as the cost of building them.

Many communities are encouraging developers to install fire sprinklers in their apartment projects by imposing stringent requirements on wood frame construction without sprinkler systems. Beginning developers should consult architects who are familiar with local fire codes and the type of product under consideration in order to determine the best way to meet fire regulations.

Rent Control

Apart from the obvious economic disadvantages of rent control that restricts rent increases, developers find financing harder to obtain for projects in communities with rent control. Rent control laws differ dramatically from community to community. Most rent control laws exempt new projects. Many laws also allow the landlord to raise rents to market rates when a tenant moves out. However, some communities, such as Santa Monica, California, do not allow rents to be raised to market value, even when a unit is vacated. Not surprisingly, few new apartment buildings are built in Santa Monica.

The threat of rent control can hurt developers almost as much as its enactment. Even if existing rent control regulations exempt new buildings, the possibility of a future referendum or of a vote by the city council to place new buildings under rent control creates damaging uncertainty.

Building Codes

Specification standards stipulating which materials can be used in the construction of dwelling units are gradually being replaced by performance standards, which give developers more latitude with respect to materials. However, developers must still deal with a diverse set of codes that is inconsistently applied.

Building codes differ not only from city to city but also from suburb to suburb. And building under various government programs may impose more stringent standards than local codes specify. For example, Dallas developer Jerome J. Frank once lamented that the FHA required better bathroom fixtures in low-income apartments than he used in luxury homes.

Developers and architects can only design and build to the codes as interpreted by local governmental authorities having jurisdiction at the time. A major problem for developers is that governments will not accept any responsibility for plan review. Although one department may review and stamp a plan "approved," the local government's field inspectors, who exercise considerable control over a project, often interpret the codes differently and will not advance an opinion prior to construction. Building associations are working on this discrepancy that can cause major problems for a project's design, construction, and financing.

Condominium Conversions

Condominium conversions—the conversion of rental units to for-sale units—provide an attractive entry point for beginning developers because seller financing is often available. The development process is shorter and less risky than in other types of multifamily residential development; the amount of money that developers must raise is also usually smaller. The major risk involves carrying interest for the units during the sale period and renovation expenses for upgrading the units.

Condominium conversions are subject to special regulations in many communities. Concern over preserving their rental housing stock has caused cities such as New York City to pass laws that limit or complicate condominium conversion. Not surprisingly, restrictions on conversion often are found in communities with strict rent control laws. Rent control reduces the incentive for developers to build new units and reduces the value of existing apartment complexes, thus increasing the premium for converting them to condominiums.

Before entering the conversion business, developers should carefully investigate local procedures, which can be time-consuming and intricate. The advice of an attorney who specializes in condominium conversion is highly desirable and should be sought before developers commit to a project.

Financial Feasibility Analysis

Evaluating financial feasibility for all income-property development involves several stages of analysis, each more detailed than the last as one moves from land purchase to a final go/no-go decision on a property. How much analysis is necessary before purchasing land? Experienced developers working in their own area know from past experience what they can spend. They know the local market and, therefore, know when they see a good deal.

Beginning developers, however, must overcome several handicaps:

- lack of experience concerning what is a workable price;
- lack of visibility in the brokerage community, hence they hear about most deals only after larger players have rejected them; and
- less staying power, so they must be more careful as to which deals they pursue.

Sophisticated developers perform numerous stages of analysis for income properties, ranging from simple capitalization analysis to monthly construction period cash-flow analysis. The main difficulty that developers face in terms of feasibility studies is understanding what type of analysis is appropriate at what stage. Too much detail is a waste of time and money. Too little detail gives insufficient information on which to base informed decisions.

Financial feasibility analysis may be broken down into five stages:

- *Stage 1:* Simple capitalization approach. Cash-on-cash return.
- *Stage 2:* Discounted cash-flow (DCF) analysis of operating period.
- *Stage 3:* DCF analysis of combined development period and operating period.
- *Stage 4:* Monthly cash-flow analysis for construction and lease-up period.
- *Stage 5:* DCF analysis for investors.

Stages 1 and 2 should always be performed before a developer goes hard on a piece of land. They are discussed here as part of the feasibility analysis and are similar to the analyses described in chapter 3. Stages 3, 4, and 5 are part of the necessary documentation for obtaining construction financing and soliciting joint venture or investor partners. They are discussed under the section on financing, later in this chapter.

The following discussion assumes that the reader has some familiarity with real estate finance. Readers who have not taken a course in real estate finance may want to supplement this discussion with a good real estate finance textbook.[8] The analysis is generally applicable to other income-property types, although the costs and revenues will obviously differ and be measured in different terms.

Stage 1: Simple Capitalization

Simple capitalization techniques, useful when evaluating different sites, allow the developer to calculate what he/she can roughly afford to spend for land.

The information needed for simple capitalization analysis, and suggested sources of that information, include:

- market rents or unit sale prices—based on rents and prices of neighboring properties and on information available from leasing agents, property managers, and brokers;
- construction costs per square foot—information obtainable from neighboring builders and general contractors who specialize in the product type under consideration;
- permanent-loan interest rates—obtainable from mortgage bankers and savings and loan (S&L) associations; and
- operating costs—obtainable from property management companies.

Before undertaking even rudimentary analysis, an estimate must be made of the number of units that will fit on the property. Except for infill lot development, a developer should usually not try to develop at the maximum allowable density under the zoning. Instead, a developer should consult an architect as to the density he/she is likely to achieve with a particular configuration (such as all two-story buildings, or all three-story buildings, or some mixture). A developer's anticipated treatment of parking will significantly influence both the desired density and the construction cost. After estimating the density and average unit size, the net operating income (NOI) has to be computed (see figure 4-6).

■ 4-6 Illustrative Example of the Calculation of Net Operating Income

Income:	
Average unit size = 750 square feet	
Average monthly rent = $0.55 per square foot	
Monthly income per apartment (750 x $0.55) = $412.50	
Annual income per apartment ($412.50 x 12) = $4,950	
Number of apartments = 150	
Potential gross annual income ($4,950 x 150)	$742,500
Vacancy factor = 5%[a]	($37,125)
Adjusted gross income	$705,375
Operating expenses:	
150 units x 750 square feet per unit = 112,500 square feet	
Expenses per square foot per year = $2.00	
Annual operating expenses (112,500 x $2)	($225,000)
NOI ($705,375 – $225,000)	$480,375

[a]Five percent is only a "standard" figure. Developers should adopt a realistic vacancy factor for their particular projects.

■ 4-7 Illustrative Example of the Calculation of Project Cost

Land cost ($1.80 x 5.136 acres x 43,560 square feet per acre)	$402,700
Construction costs (150 units x 750 square feet per unit x $30 per square foot)	$3,375,000
Soft costs (30%[a] x $3,375,000)	$1,012,500
Total project cost	$4,790,200

[a]Thirty percent is only an estimate for interest, professional fees, marketing, and leasing costs. A long lease-up period would require a long interest carry and a higher estimate.

The next step is to calculate project cost. Suppose the final negotiated land price is $1.80 per square foot for 5.136 acres, or $402,703 altogether. The land cost is combined with hard and soft construction costs to obtain an estimate of total project cost. Hard and soft construction costs at this stage are projected on the basis of how many units per acre can be achieved and on the average size per unit based on the anticipated target market. Taking the example in figure 4-6 of 150 units with an average size of 750 square feet per unit, figure 4-7 assumes that hard construction costs are $30 per square foot—that figure obtained from a contractor's rough estimate for the product type.

Armed with figures for both the NOI and the total project cost, the overall capitalization rate can be calculated:

$$\frac{\text{NOI}}{\text{Total Project Cost}} = \frac{\$480{,}375}{\$4{,}790{,}200} = 10.03\%$$

What is the appropriate capitalization rate (k)? The answer depends on the project—its location, amenities, quality, appreciation potential, and so forth. But if completed apartment projects in the area are selling based on 9 percent capitalization (cap, for short) rates, then a project not yet developed should probably have at least a 10 percent cap rate. The above analysis suggests that the project is marginally attractive. The overall return is sufficient, however, to justify more extensive investigation.

In the above example, if 10 percent is the required cap rate, then the NOI of $480,375, capitalized at 10 percent, suggests a total project value of $4,803,750.

If the project can be built and leased for less than $4,803,750, the difference is what is termed "development profit." Some developers will not proceed unless development profit is at least 10 or 15 percent of total project cost.

Rules of thumb for development profit work better for office and retail development than for apartment development. Historically, tax advantages associated with apartment development have provided a significant part of the developer's return. Because of tax benefits, investors typically accepted cap rates and overall returns (NOI divided by total project cost) that were lower, around 10 percent, than those for retail and industrial projects, which ranged between 11 and 13 percent. The Tax Reform Act of 1986 greatly reduced the tax benefits associated with apartments. Acceptable overall return requirements appear to have risen as a result.[9]

One way for a developer to obtain a rough estimate of what he/she can afford to pay for the land is to calculate the total project value, as above, and then to subtract the total cost excluding land. The difference represents the highest amount that the developer can afford to pay for the land before the project loses money.

Total project value	$4,803,750
Current project cost	(4,790,200)
Margin	13,550
Land cost	402,700
Allowable land cost	$416,250

The most a developer could afford to pay for land per square foot is calculated by dividing the allowable land cost by the total square footage of land (5.136 acres times 43,560 square feet per acre):

$$\frac{\$416{,}250}{5.136 \times 43{,}560} = \$1.86 \text{ per square foot}$$

At $1.86 per square foot, the land would consume all of the development profit. If the developer wanted, say, a 10 percent profit on total cost, then the allowable land cost would be lower. Often, no land is available at the "allowable price." In that case, a developer must reexamine his/her major assumptions to see if room exists either to raise the NOI or to lower the project cost. The major variables are:

- density (number of units per acre);
- market rent per square foot;
- operating expenses;
- construction cost per square foot;
- soft costs; and
- capitalization rate.

Stage 2: Discounted Cash-Flow Analysis of Operating Period

If simple capitalization analysis provides acceptable results, the developer should proceed to the next stage, which is discounted cash-flow (DCF) analysis. Although many developers may not perform a DCF analysis until they have already secured a site with an earnest money contract, it is advisable to perform a DCF analysis even before the earnest money contract is submitted. Even if the developer has no money at risk, he/she will be investing considerable time and effort evaluating the site. The more a developer knows about the economics going in, the better position he/she will be in to bargain effectively with the seller. Indeed, DCF analysis is particularly useful for negotiating with a seller to demonstrate how large a building is required to support the asking price. Even if the seller will not drop the price, a developer may be able to tie the price to the number of units or square feet for which permission to build is obtained.

Although DCF analysis may appear lengthy, many computer programs are available that allow the analysis to be performed in less than an hour. Furthermore, the procedure is one of the principal analytical tools taught in all real estate finance courses. The ability to perform DCF analysis is a prerequisite to being a developer in the 1990s.[10]

The developer should expect to prepare between three and six different versions of DCF analysis over the course of a project as various assumptions are refined with greater accuracy. The final version is presented to potential permanent lenders (or mortgage brokers) for a financing commitment. Each version should contain better information than the previous version. The advantage of using either Lotus or a similar spreadsheet computer program is that refinements to the original analysis can be made quickly and simply. DCF analysis becomes the developer's equivalent of the architect's sketchbook.

Stage 2 DCF analysis is performed on the *operating phase* of the project. This phase commences when the buildings are placed in service. For convenience, the permanent mortgage is assumed to be funded immediately, even though in reality it probably will not be funded until the project is 80 or 90 percent leased. An annual cash-flow analysis should be performed for a seven- or 10-year holding period with an assumed sale at the end. The project cost includes all hard and soft costs up to the time that the building is placed in service.

4-8 The Development Period and the Operating Period

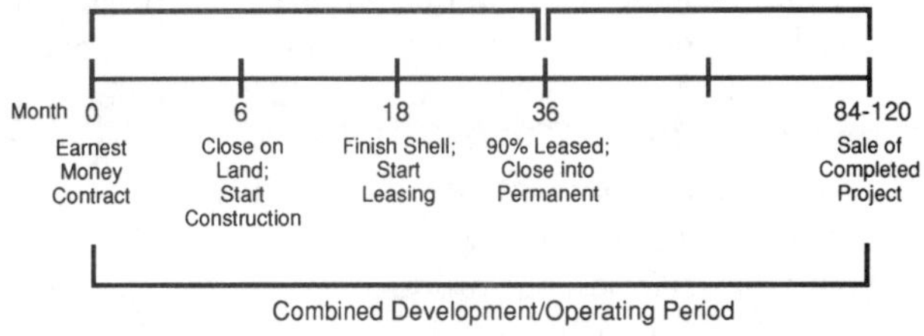

For simplicity, all depreciable assets are lumped into one category, "building depreciation." Mortgage rates are taken from current market rates. The mortgage amount is determined from the current market and either is taken to be 70 to 80 percent of the total project cost, including negative cash flows during initial lease up, or is based on the debt coverage ratio—also called the debt service coverage ratio—(DCR) For example, if the DCR is 1.2 and the NOI is $480,375, then the mortgage amount is:

$$\frac{\$480{,}375}{1.2} = \$400{,}312 \text{ per year or } \$33{,}359 \text{ per month}$$

The loan amount would be that which gives a monthly payment of $33,359 for a given interest rate and term:

$$PV\,(PMT = \$33{,}359,\ \ R = \frac{10\%}{12},\ \ N = 30 \times 12) = \$3{,}801{,}285$$

where PV = present value of the annuity, PMT = monthly payment, R = monthly interest rate, and N = term in months.

The DCF analysis of a project should be updated at each of the following three times.

1. *Before a developer submits the earnest money contract.*
   By setting up the DCF model at this stage, subsequent updates will be easy to accomplish. In order to create a DCF model, a developer will need the following information in addition to that used for the simple capitalization:
   - density assumption based either on what the developer plans to build or on densities of similar projects in the vicinity of the site;
   - more accurate figures for soft costs with financing points, interest, legal, marketing, administration, architecture, and engineering costs.

   The purpose of the analysis at this stage is to reconfirm that the project is worth the time and investment required to proceed with the feasibility studies.

   In addition to determining whether or not the project is feasible, this first DCF computation will provide an estimate of how large the negative cash flows will be during lease-up of the project. If, for example, a 16-month lease-up is anticipated for the project to reach 95 percent occupancy, then the average occupancy rate during the first year would be 35.6 percent, and during the second year 91.2 percent. Thereafter, it would be 95 percent (see figure 4-10).

   Subtracting the average occupancy rate for each year from 100 percent produces the average vacancy rate—in this case, 64.4 percent (100 minus 35.6) and 8.96 percent (100 minus 91.04) for the first and second years, respectively. The figures for average vacancy rates would be used in the DCF analysis to determine cash flows in the first two years or until the project reached stabilized occupancy. The first one or two operating years usually have negative cash flows that represent additional equity that must be infused into the project. They become part of the cash-flow stream for purposes of computing the IRR. Most developers add the negative cash flows into project cost under a heading (not shown in feature box 4-9), "operating reserve during lease-up."
2. *After a developer signs the earnest money contract but before he/she goes hard on the contract.*
   By this time, the developer should have formed a firm idea of what he/she plans to build. With the architect, the developer should lay out the site and develop a site plan and building program that defines the number of units obtainable, the mix of units, and average unit sizes. From the developer's own market study and with the input of a professional marketing consultant, the developer should focus clearly on a target market for his/her project. Equipped with this information, the developer can arrive at more detailed rental-income projections based on a breakdown of unit types and more accurate rents per unit.

   The decision to go hard on the earnest money contract usually hinges on the findings of feasibility studies, especially those regarding soils, floodplains, utilities, easements, and zoning. The main purpose of the studies is to uncover any factors that may affect what can be built and how much it will cost. This information is critical before the developer's at-risk investment is increased through nonrefundable earnest money. Any information that affects costs or densities should be fed into the DCF model to determine if the project is still feasible.
3. *After a developer goes hard on the land purchase contract but before he/she closes on the land.*
   Obviously, the developer wants to accomplish as much as possible before having to close on the land. At the very least, the developer will want to have a tentative financing commitment. To obtain the financing commitment, most beginning developers will want to use a mortgage broker, unless they have already established good, personal contacts with institutions that offer permanent financing. (The contents of the mortgage package and the procedure for finding financing are explained in the financing section of this chapter.)

   The following information is needed to produce both the mortgage brochure and the next iteration of the DCF:
   - market studies that define unit mix, unit size, style, amenities, and rent per unit;

■ 4-9 Stage 2 Analysis: Discounted Cash-Flow (DCF) Analysis for the Operating Period

DCF analysis for operations—the second stage of financial feasibility analysis—covers the operating period, sometimes known as the investment period, of a project. The analysis converts the simple one-year pro forma numbers derived from simple capitalization analysis into a multiyear analysis, beginning with the opening of the building for occupancy. The resulting returns on equity are similar to those that an investor who bought a completely developed but unoccupied building would receive.

Real estate appraisers use a form of Stage 2 DCF analysis. Appraisers and some lenders focus on the *unleveraged before-tax analysis* because those numbers give the "pure real estate value" of the property (without financing or income-tax considerations). Both forms of analysis may be done from the same spreadsheet simply by changing the mortgage and income-tax assumptions. The unleveraged rate of return is computed on the NOI for each year of ownership, starting from the time that the building is fully occupied° and ending with the sale of the project. Appraisers calculate the present value of the future cash-flow stream at a discount rate determined by the market (usually 12 to 15 percent). The resulting present value represents the full value of the building once it is fully leased.

Developers use Stage 2 DCF analysis to determine if the proposed building offers an attractive rate of return. They will perform the analysis many times as more information becomes available concerning the design of the building, development costs, and anticipated rents. Like appraisers, developers may focus during the initial runs of DCF analysis on the "overall return" of the project—the internal rate of return (IRR) on total project cost without financing. This return should range between 13 and 15 percent or higher, depending on the type of property, location, interest, and inflation rates. (The higher the inflation rate, the higher the overall return.)

Although the overall return is important, developers are primarily interested in the return on equity. This is expressed as an IRR and takes into account the financing (leverage) and personal income taxes of the owner/developer. At this second stage of financial feasibility analysis, developers are interested in the returns on the project as a single, undivided investment where one individual puts up all the equity and receives all the returns. Later, in Stage 5, developers will look at the returns to individual participants in a joint venture or syndication to raise the required equity.

The example presented here shows the leveraged analysis of a project with mortgage financing. Developers focus on the leveraged after-tax returns on equity because investment in the project must compete with returns available from other investments, such as stocks and bonds.

°Full occupancy means that 90 or 95 percent of the total units are occupied. The percentage depends on the average vacancy rate in the area.

Summary of Results*

Total Project Cost	$6,658,761
Mortgage	5,224,388
Equity	$1,434,373
Net Cash Flows	
Equity	($1,434,373)
Cumulative Annual Cash Flows	1,504,143
Cash from Sale	5,093,625
Net Cash before Tax	$5,163,395
Total Annual Taxes Saved	0
Tax from Sale	(1,445,753)
Net Cash after Tax	$3,717,642
Internal Rate of Return	24%

Year	Equity	Total Before-Tax Cash Flow	Total After-Tax Cash Flow
0	($1,108,335)	$ 0	$ 0
1	(326,038)	0	0
2		172,041	172,041
3		201,861	201,861
4		232,876	232,876
5		265,130	265,130
6		298,675	298,675
7		333,560	333,560
Sale		5,093,625	3,647,874

■ 4-9 (Continued)

Operating Income and Expense Summary

	Income Units[b]	Number of Units	Rent per SF[c]	SF per Unit	Total SF	Rent per Month	Total Rent per Year
1	A-1 1 Bedroom, 1 Bath	36	$0.72	590	21,240	$ 425	$ 183,514
2	A-2 1 Bedroom, Den, 1 Bath	20	0.70	741	14,820	519	124,488
3	B-1 2 Bedroom, 2 Bath	24	0.69	832	19,968	574	165,335
4	B-2 2 Bedroom, 2 Bath	46	0.68	952	43,792	647	357,343
5	C-1 3 Bedroom, 2 Bath	32	0.67	1,050	33,600	704	270,144
6							
7	Total	158	$0.69		133,420	$2,868	$1,100,823

8			
9			
10	Gross Rent (from above)		$1,100,823
11	Vacancy	5%	(55,041)
12			
13	Adjusted Gross Rent		$1,045,782
14	Miscellaneous Income		25,000
15			
16	Revenues	$8.03 per SF	$1,070,782
17			
18	**Expenses**		
19		**Per Month**	**Per Year**
20	Payroll[d]		
21	Manager	$1,700	$20,400
22	Assistant Manager/Bookkeeper	1,100	13,200
23	Maintenance	1,600	19,200
24	Porter for Grounds	1,000	12,000
25			
26	Subtotal	$5,400	$64,800
27		**Per SF**	**Per Year**
28	Payroll Taxes and Insurance	$0.20	$ 12,960
29	Advertising and Promotion	$0.15	20,013
30	Maintenance Supplies	0.40	53,368
31	Administration, Management, Telephone	0.40	53,368
32	Utilities for Common Area	0.40	53,368
33	Real Estate Taxes	0.48	64,042
34	Insurance	0.24	32,021
35			
36	Total Expenses[e]	$2.65	$353,940
37			
38	**Net Operating Income**	$5.37	$716,843

Development Costs Summary

		Assumptions	Cost per SF	Amount	Cost per Building SF	Cost per Unit
39	**Land**	5.13 acres	$2.25	$502,791	$3.77	$3,182
40	Land Carry (Rate = 12%, 3 Months)[f]	(223,463 SF)		15,084	0.11	95
41	Approval Fees and Startup Costs			35,000	0.26	222
42				$552,875	$4.14	$3,499
43						
44	**Building**		**Cost per SF**			
45	Construction[g]		$35.00	$4,669,700	$35.00	$29,555
46	Architecture			20,000	0.15	127
47	Engineering and Appraisal			35,000	0.26	222
48	Furnishings			10,000	0.07	63
49	Marketing			45,000	0.34	285
50	Professional Fees			5,000	0.04	32
51	Subtotal–Construction Costs			$4,784,700	$35.86	$30,284

■ 4-9 (Continued)

		Rate (%)	Months	Amount	Cost per Building SF	Cost per Unit
52						
53	**Construction Financing**[h]	**Rate (%)**	**Months**	**Amount**	**Cost per Building SF**	**Cost per Unit**
54	Interest on $5,224,388	10.50%	12	$365,707	$2.74	$2,315
55	Miscellaneous			5,000	0.04	32
56	Subtotal—Construction Financing			$370,707	$2.78	$2,347
57						
58	**Financing Transaction Costs**					
59	Mortgage Broker	1.00		$ 52,244	$0.39	$331
60	Construction Loan Points[i]	1.00		52,244	0.39	331
61	Permanent Loan Points	1.00		52,244	0.39	331
62	Attorney Fees	0.50		26,122	0.20	165
63	Subtotal—Transaction Costs	3.50		$182,854	$1.37	$1,158
64			**Cost**			
65	**Insurance, Taxes, and Other**		**per SF**			
66	Title Insurance		$0.22	$29,352	$0.22	$186
67	Liability Insurance			10,000	0.07	63
68	Property Taxes during Construction			10,000	0.07	63
69	Audit Cost			3,000	0.02	19
70	Subtotal—Insurance, Taxes, and Other			$52,352	$0.38	$331
71						
72	Subtotal—Land, Construction, Financing			$5,943,488	$44.53	$37,619
73						
74	Operating Reserve During Lease-Up[j]			$ 326,038	$ 2.44	$ 2,064
75	Development Fee (5% of Hard Costs)			239,235	1.79	1,514
76	Contingency[k]			150,000	1.12	949
77						
78	**Total Project Cost**			$6,658,761	$49.88	$42,146
79						
80	Overall Capitalization Rate (NOI/Cost)[l]	10.77%				

Other Assumptions

81	Total Project Cost	$6,658,761	
82	Total Capital Cost	$6,332,723	(calculated: Project Cost less Operating Reserve)
83	Operating Reserve	$326,038	(from line 146)
84	NPV Discount Rate	20.00%	
85	Years for Analysis	7	
86			
87	Mortgage Input Data		
88	Equity[m]	$1,434,373	
89	Principal Amount[n]	$5,224,388	(calculated from Monthly Payment below)
90	Interest Rate	10.50%	
91	Term (Years)	30	
92	Monthly Payment	$47,790	(calculated using DCR of 1.25)
93	Annual Payment	$573,474	
94			
95	Depreciation		
96	Building Basis[o]	$5,829,932	(calculated: Project Cost less Land less Operating Reserve)
97	Life (in Years)	27.5	
98	Factor[p]	1.00	
99	Depreciation—Straight Line	$211,998	
100			
101	Annual Cash Flows		
102	Gross Rent (Overrides Other Income)	$1,100,823	
103	Rentable SF	133,420	
104	Rent per SF	$8.25	
105	Rent Appreciation Rate	4.00%	
106	Vacancy Rate[q]	5.00%	

■ 4-9 (Continued)

		Year	1	2	3	4	5	6	7
107		Year	1	2	3	4	5	6	7
108	Expenses per SF[r,s]		2.65	2.76	2.87	2.98	3.10	3.23	3.36
109	(or Operating Expenses in $)								
110	(or Operating Expenses as Percentage of Gross Income)								
111									
112	Tax Rate[t]				28%				
113									
114	Sale Price Data								
115	Capitalization Rate at Sale[u]				9.00%				
116	(or Price Appreciation Rate)								
117	(or Sales Price in $)								
118	Sales Commissions and Expenses				4.00%				

Annual Mortgage and Depreciation Calculation

		0	1	2	3	4	5	6	7
	Mortgage Calculation								
119	Beginning Balance	$5,224,388	$5,224,388	$5,198,240	$5,169,210	$5,136,981	$5,101,200	$5,061,476	$5,017,374
120	Ending Balance	5,224,388	5,198,240	5,169,210	5,136,981	5,101,200	5,061,476	5,017,374	4,968,412
121	Amortization of Principal		26,148	29,030	32,229	35,781	39,724	44,102	48,962
122	Interest		547,326	544,444	541,245	537,693	533,750	529,372	524,512
123									
124	**Depreciation Calculation**								
125	Beginning Balance	$5,829,932	$5,829,932	$5,617,934	$5,405,936	$5,193,939	$4,981,941	$4,769,944	$4,557,946
126	Less Annual Depreciation		211,998	211,998	211,997	211,998	211,997	211,998	211,997
127	Ending Balance	5,829,932	5,617,934	5,405,936	5,193,939	4,981,941	4,769,944	4,557,946	4,345,949
128	Cumulative Depreciation Taken		211,998	423,996	635,993	847,991	1,059,988	1,271,986	1,483,983
129	Cumulative Staight Line		211,998	423,996	635,993	847,991	1,059,988	1,271,986	1,483,983
130	Recapture		0	0	0	0	0	0	0
131	Remaining Book Value[v]		6,120,725	5,908,727	5,696,730	5,484,732	5,272,735	5,060,737	4,848,740

Annual Cash Flows

		Assumptions	1	2	3	4	5	6	7
	Before-Tax Cash Flow								
132	Gross Rent		$1,100,823	$1,144,856	$1,190,650	$1,238,276	$1,287,807	$1,339,320	$1,392,892
133	Vacancy Rate[w]		46.69%	5.00%	5.00%	5.00%	5.00%	5.00%	5.00%
134	Vacancy		514,023	57,243	59,533	61,914	64,390	66,966	69,645
135	Adjusted Gross Income		586,800	1,087,613	1,131,117	1,176,362	1,223,417	1,272,354	1,323,247
136	Other Income	4.00%	14,576	26,000	27,040	28,122	29,247	30,417	31,634
137	Total Revenue		601,376	1,113,613	1,158,157	1,204,484	1,252,664	1,302,771	1,354,881
138									
139	Operating Expenses	4.00%	353,940	368,098	382,822	398,134	414,060	430,622	447,847
140	Other Expenses ($)		0	0	0	0	0	0	0
141	Total Expenses		353,940	368,098	382,822	398,134	414,060	430,622	447,847
142									
143	Net Operating Income		247,436	745,515	775,335	806,350	838,604	872,149	907,034
144									
145	Annual Debt Service		(573,474)	(573,474)	(573,474)	(573,474)	(573,474)	(573,474)	(573,474)
146	Operating Reserve during Lease-Up[x]		326,038						
147	Total Before-Tax Cash Flow		0	172,041	201,861	232,876	265,130	298,675	333,560
148									
149	**Tax Calculation**								
150	Net Operating Income		247,436	745,515	775,335	806,350	838,604	872,149	907,034
151	Interest		(547,326)	(544,444)	(541,245)	(537,693)	(533,750)	(529,372)	(524,512)
152	Depreciation		(211,998)	(211,998)	(211,997)	(211,998)	(211,997)	(211,998)	(211,997)
153	Taxable Income (Loss)		(511,888)	(10,927)	22,093	56,659	92,857	130,779	170,525
154	Passive Loss Offset[y]		0	0	22,093	56,659	92,857	130,779	170,525
155	Taxable Income		0	0	0	0	0	0	0

■ 4-9 (Continued)

		Assumptions	1	2	3	4	5	6	7
156	Passive Loss Carryforward[z]		$(511,888)	$(522,815)	$(500,722)	$(444,063)	$(351,206)	$(220,427)	$(49,902)
157	Taxes	28.00%	0	0	0	0	0	0	0
158									
159	**After-Tax Cash Flow**								
160	Before-Tax Cash Flow		0	172,041	201,861	232,876	265,130	298,675	333,560
161	Less Taxes		0	0	0	0	0	0	0
162	Total Cash Flow after Tax		0	172,041	201,861	232,876	265,130	298,675	333,560

Sale Calculation for Seven Annual Holding Periods[aa]

		Assumptions	1	2	3	4	5	6	7
	Cash from Sale before Tax								
163	Sales Price		$8,283,499	$8,614,835	$8,959,446	$9,317,825	$9,690,539	$10,078,159	$10,481,289
164	Less Commission	4.00%	331,340	344,593	358,378	372,713	387,622	403,126	419,252
165	Adjusted Sales Price		7,952,159	8,270,242	8,601,068	8,945,112	9,302,917	9,675,033	10,062,037
166	Less Mortgage Balance		5,198,240	5,169,210	5,136,981	5,101,200	5,061,476	5,017,374	4,968,412
167	Total Cash from Sale before Tax		2,753,919	3,101,032	3,464,087	3,843,912	4,241,441	4,657,659	5,093,625
168									
169	**Taxes**								
170	Adjusted Sales Price		7,952,159	8,270,242	8,601,068	8,945,112	9,302,917	9,675,033	10,062,037
171	Less Remaining Book Value		6,120,725	5,908,727	5,696,730	5,484,732	5,272,735	5,060,737	4,848,740
172	Total Taxable Gain		1,831,434	2,361,515	2,904,338	3,460,380	4,030,182	4,614,296	5,213,297
173	Passive Loss Carryforward		(511,888)	(522,815)	(500,722)	(444,063)	(351,206)	(220,427)	(49,902)
174	Capital Gain		1,319,546	1,838,700	2,403,616	3,016,317	3,678,976	4,393,869	5,163,395
175									
176	Tax on Capital Gain	28.00%	369,473	514,836	673,013	844,569	1,030,113	1,230,283	1,445,751
177	Total Tax from Sale		369,473	514,836	673,013	844,569	1,030,113	1,230,283	1,445,751
178									
179	**Cash from Sale after Tax**								
180	Cash from Sale before Tax		2,753,919	3,101,032	3,464,087	3,843,912	4,241,441	4,657,659	5,093,625
181	Less Tax		369,473	514,836	673,013	844,569	1,030,113	1,230,283	1,445,751
182	Total Cash from Sale after Tax		2,384,446	2,586,196	2,791,074	2,999,343	3,211,328	3,427,376	3,647,874

Return Measures

		0	1	2	3	4	5	6	7
183	**Internal Rates of Return for 7-Year Holding Period**								
184	Equity (—)[bb]	$(1,108,335)	$(326,038)	$ 0	$ 0	$ 0	$ 0	$ 0	$ 0
185	Annual Cash Flows		0	172,041	201,861	232,876	265,130	298,675	333,560
186	Cash from Sale before Tax								5,093,625
187	Total Before-Tax Cash Flow	(1,108,335)	(326,038)	172,041	201,861	232,876	265,130	298,675	5,427,185
188									
189	Before-Tax IRR[cc]	28.55%							
190	After-Tax Cash Flows	0	0	172,041	201,861	232,876	265,130	298,675	333,560
191	Cash from Sale after Tax								3,647,874
192	Total After-Tax Cash Flow	(1,108,335)	(326,038)	172,041	201,861	232,876	265,130	298,675	3,981,434
193									
194	After-Tax IRR	24.01%							
195									
196	**Simple Return Measures**[dd]								
197	NOI/Purchase Price		3.72%	11.20%	11.64%	12.11%	12.59%	13.10%	13.62%
198	Before-Tax Cash Flow/Equity		0.00%	11.99%	14.07%	16.24%	18.48%	20.82%	23.25%
199	Tax Shelter/Equity		0.00%	0.00%	1.54%	3.95%	6.47%	9.12%	11.89%
200									
201	**Multiple Holding Period Returns**								
202	After-Tax IRR[ee]		85.72%	43.73%	33.57%	29.09%	26.61%	25.06%	24.01%
203	Net Present Value @ 20%		505,838	446,174	392,885	345,837	304,728	269,133	238,569

■ 4-9 (Continued)

[a]The project offers before-tax cash flows of $6,597,768 including cash from sale, after-tax cash flows of $5,152,017, and net cash after tax of $3,717,642 on equity of $1,434,373 with an after-tax IRR of 24 percent. Before-tax and after-tax cash flows are taken from lines 187 and 192.
[b]Apartment units are broken down by unit type. Unit types and their square footages are refined as the design is refined.
[c]Rents per square foot decrease as units increase in size.
[d]Monthly salaries are enumerated for each employee.
[e]Operating costs are estimated in dollars per square foot per year as estimated by an experienced property manager.
[f]Land carry refers to interest paid to the land seller as part of the land purchase contract.
[g]Construction cost is computed from the total square footage of the project (line 7, 133,420) multiplied by $35 per square foot. In initial runs of this analysis, construction cost may be based on information obtained in a telephone call to a contractor, whereas later runs will use actual bids.
[h]The construction loan equals the permanent loan (see line 89). Construction interest assumes that the average balance is two-thirds of the outstanding loan. See note n for discussion of mortgage calculation.
[i]Construction-loan points should be amortized over the life of the construction loan. In this exhibit, for simplicity purposes, such points have been grouped and amortized with the costs associated with the permanent-loan origination.
[j]Operating reserve during lease-up is the sum of the cash subsidies in line 146 required to cover negative cash flows during lease-up.
[k]Contingency is the estimated reserve for unanticipated costs (approximately 3 percent of hard costs).
[l]The 10.77 percent cap rate based on NOI/capital cost compares favorably with the cap rate estimated at year of sale of 9 percent. The difference between the two cap rates indicates the "value added" in the development process.
[m]Equity is the difference between total project costs and the amount of permanent financing that the project can support, and is calculated as follows:

Total project cost	$6,658,761
Mortgage	(5,224,388)
Equity	$1,434,373

[n]Principal amount of the 30-year mortgage is calculated from NOI (line 38):
PV (monthly NOI/DCR, monthly interest rate, term in months)
where DCR = 1.25
PV ($716,843/12/1.25, 10.5/12%, 30 x 12) = $5,224,387
[o]For simplicity, all depreciable and amortizable costs are lumped together as one asset:

Total project cost	$6,658,760
Land	(502,791)
Operating reserve	(326,037)
Building basis	$5,829,932

- architectural and engineering conceptual design drawings, developed from the market study information, that have sufficient detail to be used to obtain construction-cost estimates within 5 percent of the final bid;
- construction-cost estimates from two or three general contractors (unless, of course, the developer has either in-house construction capabilities or a contractor as part of the team). For purposes of comparison, the contractors' bids should follow the 16 categories laid out on the standard form issued by the American Institute of Architects. The developer should be especially careful to specify what the bid will include and what it will not include.

The Go/No-Go Decision

Each stage in the project feasibility process requires a go/no-go decision. A decision to go does not commit the developer to construction; it does, however, cause the developer to ascend to the next level of investment and risk. Each level may involve either substantial commitment or very little. For example, some projects may have all necessary regulatory approvals already in place, there-

■ 4-10 Calculating the Average Occupancy Rate

If lease-up is expected to take 16 months to reach 95 percent occupancy, then the average occupancy rate for each year is computed thus:

Year 1:

$$\frac{12 \text{ months}}{16 \text{ months}} \times 95\% = \frac{71.25\%}{2} = 35.6\%$$

Year 2:

$$\frac{(71.25\% + 95\%)}{2} = 83.215\% \times \frac{4 \text{ months}}{12 \text{ months}} = 27.71$$

$$95.000\% \times \frac{8 \text{ months}}{12 \text{ months}} = 63.33$$

Average Occupancy = 91.04%

4-9 (Continued)

[p]The depreciation factor provides the option of accelerating the annual depreciation expense. The exhibit uses the following formula to compute the annual depreciation expense: Building basis x (1/the building's life) x acceleration factor, or 5,829,932 x .036363 x 1.
[q]Vacancy may be higher than 5 percent, depending on supply and demand factors.
[r]Operating expenses can be expressed based on estimated cost per square foot, a set annual payment, or as a percentage of gross income.
[s]Expenses per square foot (from line 36) are inflated at 4 percent per year. Apartments usually encounter a steeper rise in expenses after three or four years.
[t]Estimated marginal income-tax rate for owner/developer.
[u]The sales price can be estimated using a cap rate or a price appreciation factor.
[v]The remaining book value is equal to the cost of the building, including the development fee, and the land (line 42) minus the cumulative depreciation taken (line 128).
[w]Average vacancy for the first year is computed from the expected leasing rate. Based on early marketing studies, the project is expected to lease 15 units per month. Average leasing for the year is: 158 units/15 units per month = 10.53 months to reach 100 percent occupancy. Average occupancy for Year 1 is calculated as follows: 10.53/12 months x 0.95/2 + (12 – 10.53)/12 months x 0.95 = 0.5331 for the year. 1 – 0.5331 average occupancy = 0.4669 average vacancy for the year.
[x]Operating reserve during lease-up is the additional investment required of the owner/developer to cover all negative cash flows.
[y]Under the Tax Reform Act of 1986, negative taxable income is considered a "passive loss" that may only be offset against passive income. Passive losses for the project are carried forward as an offset to passive income in Years 2 through 7, giving zero tax in Years 1 through 7 (line 161).
[z]Remaining passive losses may be written off against taxable gains at the time of sale.
[aa]Sale calculation shows cash flows for all seven holding periods—what the cash flows would be if the property were sold at the end of each year.
[bb]For purposes of this analysis, equity is assumed to be injected into the project when needed. However, the developer will probably have to put up all of the required equity before the construction lender will fund the construction loan.
[cc]The before-tax IRR and after-tax IRR are the two key return measures that the developer focuses on. At this stage, IRRs measure returns for "the whole pie." After-tax leveraged IRRs should be in the 25 percent range (some developers require 30 percent or more).
[dd]The simple return measures are rules of thumb. NOI/purchase price indicates the overall cap rate. Before-tax cash flow/equity indicates the cash-on-cash return on equity investment. Tax shelter/equity indicates the return on investment provided by tax shelter.
[ee]IRRs given for each year assume that the project was sold at the end of that year. For example, the IRR for a three-year holding period would be 33.57 percent.

by allowing the developer to apply directly for a building permit as soon as construction drawings and financing have been obtained. Other projects may require little investment in feasibility studies: the physical aspects of the site may already be known; the lender may do its own appraisal; the market may be proven through past experience; preliminary engineering may be unnecessary; or the architect may provide preliminary design drawings "on spec."

The importance of holding down front-end costs cannot be overemphasized. This is pure risk money since the odds are still heavily against a project going ahead, even after a developer has decided to go hard on the land. The key to success is knowing what information is required and how to obtain it at the lowest cost. A developer must walk that fine line between spending money unnecessarily and doing insufficient investigation to evaluate the property properly.

The two most important decisions—especially for small developers with limited resources—involve purchase of the land and commencement of construction, both of which usually require the largest financial commitments. Other major decision points are illustrated in feature box 4-11.

The DCF analysis provides various data that influence the go/no-go decision to purchase the site:

- expected dollar profit;
- the IRR;
- the amount of money needed;
- the amount of equity needed; and
- the length of the commitment.

However, the decision to purchase is not made solely on the basis of the DCF analysis. The developer must also weigh other available investments, the amount of risk involved in the project, and a host of other considerations including:

- Does the developer have the personnel and capital resources to carry through the project?
- Is this really the project that the developer wants to spend the next three years or so working on?
- Is the project worth the developer's time, effort, and risk?
- Is the project of such a scale that the developer can survive major delays and unforeseen difficulties? If not, is this project worth risking the loss of all the developer's assets?

4-11 Developer Exposure over Time

The following tables show the sequence of equity investment for August Park, a 158-unit apartment project developed by Peiser Corporation and Jerome Frank Investments. The project was financed by Federal National Mortgage Association (Fannie Mae) bonds. The land maintained its value after closing in March 1985, but all other expenses on the project were at risk until the bonds for financing the project were sold in October 1985.

Time Line of Preconstruction Risk for August Park

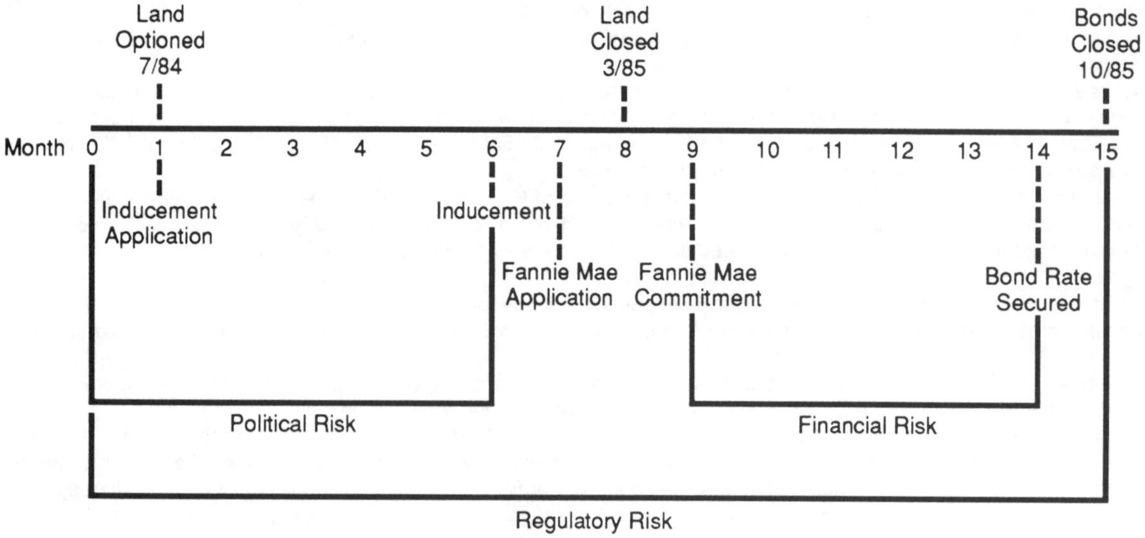

Breakdown of Preconstruction Risk at August Park

Time	Activity	Cost	Total Investment to Date	Current Value to Date	Exposure
7/84	Land optioned	$ 15,000	$ 15,000	$ 0	$ 15,000
	Extensions	21,000			
	Architecture	10,000			
	Bond inducement fee	10,000			
1/85	Inducement received		56,000	0[a]	56,000
3/85	Land closing	388,000	444,000	403,000[b]	41,000[c]
	Architecture	10,000			
	Appraisal and market study	10,000			
4/85	Fannie Mae commitment	24,000	488,000[d]	403,000	85,000
	Architecture	15,000			
	Engineering	20,000			
	Equity syndication	50,000			
	Bond costs	100,000			
9/85	Bond rate secured		673,000[e]	403,000	270,000
10/85	Bonds closed	338,000	1,011,000[f]	1,011,000	0

[a]The inducement is transferable but has a one-year limitation.
[b]The land value had increased by sufficient amount to cover sales commission costs if it had to be resold.
[c]At the time of closing on the land, the earnest money ($15,000) is recovered.
[d]The FNMA commitment adds value only if bonds can be sold.
[e]Most legal costs have no value if the bonds are not closed.
[f]At bond closing, the risks are substantially eliminated, since all financing parameters are fixed.
Source: Richard B. Peiser, "The Decline of Housing Revenue Bond–Financed Development," *The Real Estate Finance Journal*, Spring 1988, p. 61.

Design

The developer's approach to design depends entirely on his/her target market. The rental apartment and condominium market is segmented into many submarkets, and each submarket calls for many design features specific to that market. No matter how good the numbers on a project might look on paper, if the product does not satisfy the market's needs at a price the market can afford, the project will not succeed.

Each building type offers a different set of problems and opportunities for design. Luxury garden apartments, for example, typically include some or all of the following design features:

- generously sized bedrooms and kitchens;
- tile bathrooms;
- tile or wood entries;
- vaulted ceilings;
- nine-foot-high ceilings;
- fireplaces;
- balconies;
- microwave ovens, trash compactors, and washer-dryers;
- club facilities with exercise rooms and tennis courts;
- double-glazed windows with energy-efficient air cavities or plastic separators for sound proofing;
- security systems;
- elevators; and
- covered parking.

Each of these features increases development costs. But in the highest-end apartments, renters will pay for all of them, and the increased rent more than justifies the additional cost. In fact, competition may make it difficult to rent the project if it does not have these features.

By comparison, renters of lower-end apartments will be unwilling to pay for many such features. Even so, in Texas, for example, even the lowest-end garden apartments will have the following features:

- club rooms and swimming pools;
- private balconies;
- outside storage;
- cable television; and
- central heat and air conditioning.

The developer is responsible for establishing the guidelines within which the architect will work. The developer should choose an architect experienced with the particular product that the developer wants to build, but he/she should not let the architect define the product to be built. The architect should not be allowed to dictate the unit sizes, amenities, and unit mix; these decisions should be made jointly and on the basis of the results of the market analysis for the subarea in which the developer is building. Although the architect's mission is to design the project, the developer must also have certain design skills in order to give the architect the required guidance. The ability to visualize what is portrayed by an architect's floor plan is vital to success as a developer.

Time spent scrutinizing the plans during the design stage is among the most important time that the developer will spend on the entire project. The developer should mentally walk through every unit, look out every window, and envisage every view inside the apartment. What does a guest first see when opening the front door? Remember, that view is the same first impression that renters or buyers will receive when they open the door to see model units. It is much cheaper and easier to fix something with the architect at the design stage than it is out in the field, or worse, after the building is built.

Multifamily residential buildings are among the most complex buildings to design. They need to accommodate all the functional needs of a large number of people at a relatively high density while protecting the privacy of individuals and families. At the same time, they must also provide a sense of ownership and community among an often transitory population. Multifamily residential design is often the result of a series of compromises between notions of ideal living conditions (derived from single-family house concepts) and the economic realities of higher-density dwelling.

Site Design

According to architect Jack Craycroft, senior partner, Jack Craycroft Architects, Dallas,[11] a "good sound apartment design starts with the site plan." He likens the design process to carving away at a block of stone, so that exterior spaces are shaped by the remaining forms of the buildings themselves.

The primary determinants of the site plan are the desired and permitted density, parking layout, and fire access requirements. The density of the project is, in turn, determined by zoning and the market. Generally speaking, one-story apartments or townhouses will yield between 10 and 15 units per acre, two-story garden apartments with surface parking will comfortably yield densities of 20 to 30 units to the acre, and three-story garden apartments with surface parking will yield densities of up to 40 units per acre. (Some kind of structured parking, usually accommodated in one or two levels under the apartments or in a separate structure, is required to achieve densities greater than 40 units per acre.)

Fire codes typically permit a maximum distance of 150 feet between a fire road or hydrant and a building. Local fire officials should be consulted early in the design process to determine requirements.

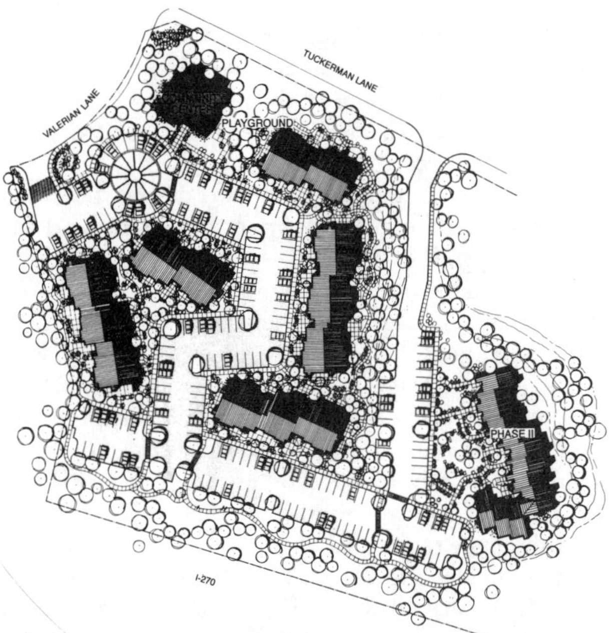

At Timberlawn Crescent in Rockville, Maryland, the site plan features 107 one-, two-, and three-bedroom units, stacked to resemble townhouses, on 9.8 acres. The gross density is 11 units per acre (20 units per acre net), and the plan includes a pathway system, a community center, and 219 parking spaces.

As a reasonable guideline, approximately one-third of the site plan for a garden apartment project should contain building area, one-third should be allotted to parking areas, and the remaining third should be open space. Any plan that provides less than that amount of open space may seem overly crowded. In garden apartments, the open space often takes the form of courtyards, which work well as interior focal points of activity if they are large enough to provide separation between units. The size of a courtyard should increase with the height of the buildings that enclose it; as a rule of thumb, the narrowest dimension of a courtyard should be at least equal to the height of the buildings surrounding it.

Parking

In designing a project, parking—its dimensions, arrangement, and location—is more important than building coverage. 1.75 parking spaces per unit is a recommended standard, and two spaces per unit is mandatory in condominium or for-sale housing in most areas. Parking occupies between one-and-one-half to two times the space that dwelling units take up. Each car needs 300 to 350 square feet, including driveways. Thus, for example, consider a three-story apartment building with two-bedroom units averaging 900 square feet. The building footprint for the unit is 300 square feet (900 divided by three stories). If, as is often the case, two-bedroom units require two parking places, then for each unit footprint of 300 square feet, 600 to 700 square feet of parking is necessary. In addition to parking for units, guest parking is advisable, as are dedicated spaces for the project's leasing office.

Parking placement is a critical design element. When a project is oriented to the periphery to take advantage of views or to allow direct access from units to parks, parking clusters should be located in the center of the project. When the surroundings are not to be featured, a project should be turned inward to face the common greens and site amenities, and the parking should be placed on the periphery.

Parking should not invade interior open space. Interior open spaces are any project's best feature. If possible, pedestrian circulation should be kept separate from vehicular access, although walking distances between parking and units should be as short as possible. For access to interior courtyards, breezeways should be located between every two or three units.

The common preference for hiding cars may run counter to market preferences in working-class communities where cars are often a tenant's most important possession. According to Dallas developer Jerome J. Frank, Sr., of Jerome Frank Investments, the ability to look out one's window to keep an eye on the car can be an important plus in renting.[12]

Concrete parking areas and driveways are cost-effective in the long run. Although they cost more initially, they look better and are cheaper to maintain than asphalt parking.

In most parts of the country, garages are no longer considered essential, which is fortunate because collecting an economic rent for covered spaces is almost impossible. For example, if underground parking space for two cars costs $15,000 to construct, then the developer needs approximately $150 (or 1 percent of the construction cost) additional rent per month to cover interest, amortization, and minor maintenance. In most areas, the developer is lucky to collect $40 per space. But if the market demands covered spaces, they must be provided and their cost covered out of the apartment rent.

Parking structures are feasible only in areas where land is expensive or where luxury apartments or condominiums are planned. Underground garages and hillside cut-outs for parking can be especially expensive because fireproofing, waterproofing, and drainage or sump pumps are required.

Carports are built less often today than they were in the 1960s, but they remain an attractive solution to the problem of covered parking, especially in areas with severe climates. Care should be taken to build them well, since flimsy carports have collapsed in heavy winds, rains, and snow, damaging the cars below.

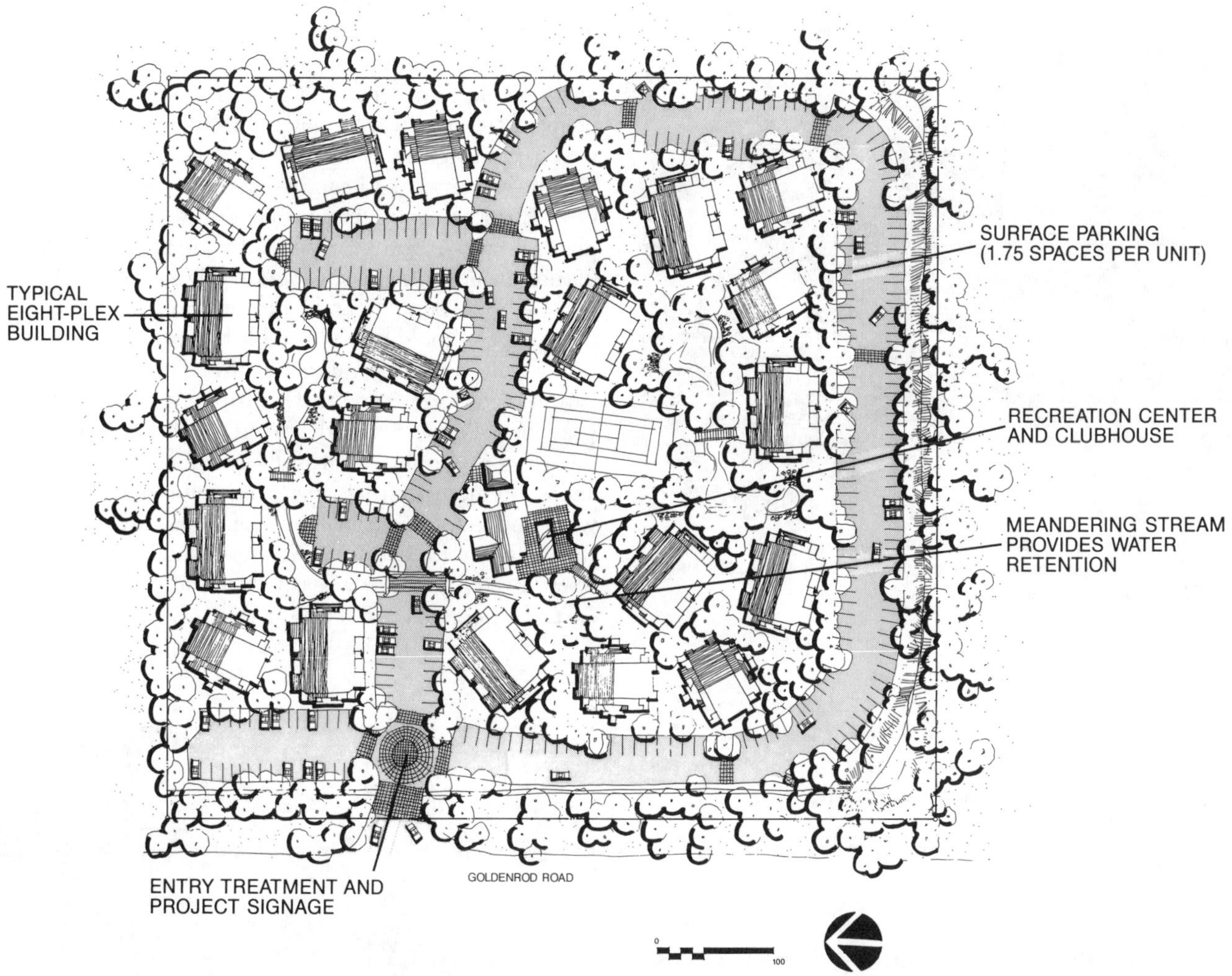

At Woodbridge Apartments in Orlando, Florida, a 168-unit project of eight-plex buildings, 294 surface parking spaces are provided (1.75 spaces per unit) on the 9.32-acre site.

Amenities and Landscaping

The selection of amenities begins with the market analysis. What some communities consider standard, other communities will adjudge luxurious. The question that must always be asked of amenities is: Will renters pay for them?

Generally, if amenities are wanted and used, residents will pay a reasonable price for them—unless, of course, the operating costs do not correspond with the residents' income levels. Therefore, the developer should design not only what the residents like, but also what they can afford.

Swimming pools and outdoor jacuzzis are standard amenities in many areas. Interesting shapes and heavily landscaped pools can add much to the appearance and marketability of a complex. Because of its prominence, the pool area deserves special attention, and its design should not be left to a pool contractor. In complexes designed for families, a wading pool for children separate from the adult pool should be provided.

Pools should be carefully landscaped so that planting areas do not catch chlorinated pool water. Other landscaping should be as maintenance-free as possible. Focal planting areas with seasonal color should be located near the project's entrance, the leasing office, the pool, and the courtyards. The landscaping plan and sprinkler system should be designed as an integral part of the site plan. Detailed plant design may be left until later, but the general plan should be completed before construction begins. Indeed, many local governments require a landscaping plan before they will issue a building permit.

Tennis courts are very land-intensive and are usually included only in larger projects. Depending on the particular market niche, a play area for children or a daycare center may be a valuable amenity to include. If the

Stan Caplan

An interior courtyard featuring a fountain, a pool, walkways, and attractive plantings provides a luxurious landscape and atmosphere at 555 Barrington in Los Angeles.

project incorporates a clubhouse, it should be centrally located, usually as one of the edges of a courtyard. The leasing office should be located near the clubhouse and should be visible to passing street traffic.

Exterior Design

Regional traditions and climate play very important roles in the exterior design of apartment buildings. Brick is a common material throughout the South and along the East Coast. Stucco is very popular in the Southwest, whereas wood siding is most common in the northern United States. The choice of exterior materials and styling is closely related to the marketing of the project and the preferences of the target population. The character of the surrounding area is always an important design consideration. For example, the appropriate design for urban infill locations differs from that for suburban and urban fringe locations.

Economies of scale can be achieved by repeating building types. The fewer the building types, the greater the potential for minimizing costs. Wall segments, foundation cables, and roof trellises can be manufactured in groups, and labor costs fall when more work can be done by semiskilled workers. At the same time, however, marketability may require considerable variety of appearance. Long, straight walls and rooflines should be avoided. Individual buildings should not extend more than 200 feet.

The building's exterior should express the individuality of the apartment units within. Useful as private outdoor space, balconies are often instrumental design elements in denoting individual apartments. Six feet is usually considered the optimum depth for a usable balcony—anything larger may cause excessive shading of windows below; anything smaller may be useful only for storage, which is unsightly. Balconies that are inset are more visually attractive, and can be useful in establishing privacy. Inset balconies, in combination with an L-shaped plan, allow two rooms to open onto one balcony. Solid or partially solid railings also increase privacy, although they may decrease sunlight and block interior views.

The roof should help to establish a residential character as well as to shed rain and snow. The silhouettes of various roof forms can create a friendly, village-like impression. Like the rest of the exterior of the building, roof design is determined partly by regional traditions and styles. Remember that apartment buildings are large, wide buildings, and a shallow roof slope (say, less than a five-inch rise for every 12-inch horizontal run—called a "5 in 12 pitch") may prove visually unsatisfying. The extra cost of a steeper slope is minimal.

Peter Burg

Exterior materials of lapped cedar siding, tile roofs, and brick detailing give Golfbrook Apartments in Longwood, Florida, the sought-after look of durability and traditionalism.

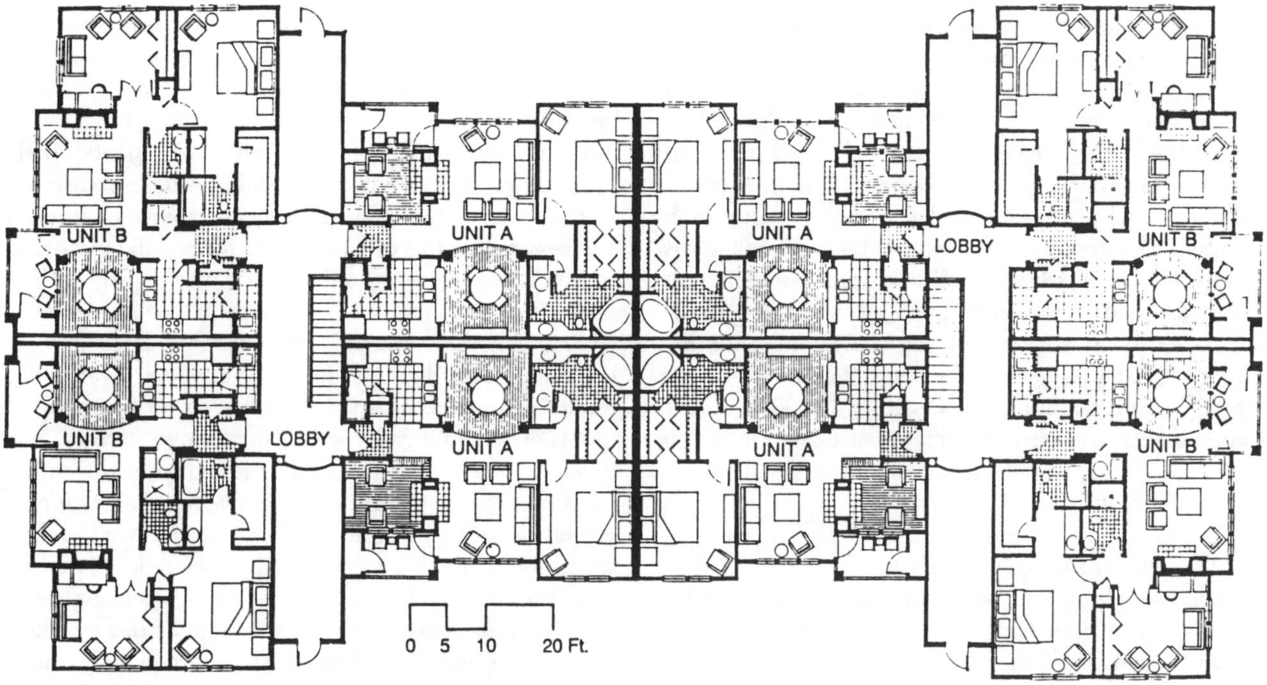

At Siena in Renaissance Park, the design calls for eight units per floor (including four different unit types), most of which are either 852 (unit A) or 1,022 (unit B) square feet. All units are designed with fireplaces, nine-foot-high ceilings, ceramic-tiled foyers, oversized windows, and an outdoor deck or patio.

Interior Design

One of the chief objectives in designing an apartment interior is to make a relatively small space seem larger than it is. Large windows and angled walls that lead the eye around corners can help in this regard. L-shaped units offer greater design opportunities than do square or rectangular units. Providing taller volumes of space in top-floor units can be an especially effective means of increasing the impression of space for only a marginal increase in cost.

Windows are important not only for the views they offer but also for the light and ventilation they permit. Natural ventilation of an apartment requires that windows be placed on at least two exposures, not necessarily in the same room but preferably on opposite walls. In any room, natural lighting is improved when light comes from more than one direction.

Adequate kitchen and storage areas make apartments more livable. The kitchen should provide a minimum of 16 feet of counter space, including room for appliances. Each bedroom should offer a minimum of 12 feet of linear closet space, and guest and linen closets should provide another four linear feet of storage. These standards can be met in a floor plan of 600 square feet in a one-bedroom apartment and 850 square feet in a two-bedroom apartment. In smaller units, some compromises may be necessary.

Generally, bedrooms should not open directly off the living room—except in the case of a second bedroom used as a den. At least one bathroom should be accessible from the hall, without walking through a bedroom. Every room should have a ceiling light, and every wall should have at least one wall plug.

All details should be carefully considered. In small apartments, for example, circulation is critical, and the developer should pay careful attention to how the doors will open, so as to minimize conflicts and obstructions. In larger projects, full-scale mock-ups of prototypical units are often built. Such mock-ups serve two main purposes: first, they allow discovery of problems in the design; and second, subcontractors can use the mock-ups to familiarize themselves with the plan, to make decisions about the placement of wiring, plumbing, and ductwork, and to correct potential conflicts between subcontractors. For example, a plumbing pipe may interfere with the best route for an air-conditioning duct. Such conflicts often do not become apparent until the construction stage. The cost of building mock-ups is more than repaid in terms of time saved and aggravation avoided during the course of construction.

The finish materials in an apartment should be chosen not only for ease of maintenance but also to reflect the tastes of the market. Linoleum or vinyl tile is commonly used in kitchens, baths, and entries, although ceramic tile or stone may be used in higher-end apartments. Other rooms are almost always carpeted, the quality of the carpet varying with the market.

Bookcases, paneling, ceiling fans, and mirrors all can increase a unit's sense of quality but are desirable only if supportable by the market. Fireplaces, for instance, take up space, and many tenants of smaller apartments are reluctant to pay the increased rent charged for such amenities. The appropriateness of unit amenities such as washer/dryers, or washer/dryer hookups, also depends on the market. In order to recover amenity costs, the developer should be able to increase an apartment's monthly rent by at least 1 percent of the construction cost of any amenities. For example, units with a $1,000 fireplace should be able to command rents at least $10 per month higher than those without fireplaces. Otherwise, the amenity is not cost-effective.

Separate heating, ventilation, and air-conditioning (HVAC) systems for each unit should be provided. The mechanical systems can be contained within the walls, ceilings, or roof spaces of the unit but will require an outside compressor. The compressor can be located either on the roof, where it must be screened and integrated with the roof design, or on the ground outside the unit, where its noise is more noticeable and where it may create an obstruction. Also, all units should be prewired for cable television, telephones, and security systems.

Utility meters and trash bins, always potentially unsightly, should not be overlooked in the design phase. A bank of meters, for example, can create a powerful, albeit not necessarily desirable, design element. Bear in mind that utility companies want to group meters together and can usually place their meters where they choose.

Design Issues

Privacy and Security

The layout of apartment buildings needs to provide privacy for each apartment, regardless of the project's density. Fortunately, many of the techniques employed in the design of the site, the units, and building exteriors are devices for creating visual separations between units. Sometimes, building codes provide useful criteria: for example, a code might stipulate that a wall with windows should be separated from a facing wall with windows by at least 30 feet, that a wall with windows should be separated from a facing wall without windows by at least 20 feet, and that two outside walls without windows should be separated by a minimum of 10 feet. Vertical and horizontal projections such as walls and balconies should be used to ensure that units cannot be seen either from other apartments or from common spaces.

Security is becoming an increasingly important issue in site design. A plan that minimizes the number of entries to a project will provide greater control of traffic and, therefore, better security. Unit entries should not be hidden from view, and walkways and breezeways should be visible from several points. Exterior lighting can do much to create a feeling of security for tenants. At the same time, exterior lighting should be designed so that light sources do not shine directly into apartment units or adjacent properties or cause glare for passing motorists.

Studies of successful subsidized housing projects have shown that tenants take better care of their apartments when a transition area of "semiprivate" space is provided between the outdoor public space and their private apartment. This concept can also work well for luxury apartments. The semiprivate space may range from an inset doorway to a fenced-in front patio. Inside the unit, a transition space should also be provided. Units that open directly into the living room do not rent as well as those with a foyer or at least some kind of separation—perhaps simply a different floor material—from the living room.

Privacy for individual apartments is increased by fences, walls, and plantings used as screens between patios, buildings, and the street. With duplex or two-story arrangements, garden apartments take on characteristics of townhouses. High-end apartments in Irvine, California, for example, are being designed so that the second-floor unit has a ground-level entry with an interior staircase. The second-floor living room opens onto a high-ceiling foyer to create a sense of space. The private ground-floor entries have special appeal if the unit is to be converted to condominium use.

Rental Apartments versus Condominiums

Rental housing and for-sale (condominium) housing differ in their design in a number of respects. Security and privacy are even more important issues in condominiums. If rental and for-sale units are combined in the same complex, they should be physically separated because their close proximity hurts the sale of condominiums. Renters are not confronted with the long-term investment of a mortgage and are less likely to be critical of a less-desirable location within the complex as a whole. Many condominium complexes forbid investor-owned units because owner-occupants do not want to live next to renters.

Some condominium developers recommend higher bedroom counts in the unit mix. In general, there should be a smaller number but a greater variety of dwelling units per building in a condominium as compared to a rental project. In the condominium, room sizes should be larger, by at least 10 to 15 percent. Kitchens need additional equipment. Baths must have better appointments and color variety. Closets and general storage areas must be larger.

■ 4-12 Hints for Successful Multifamily Residential Design

Interviews with members of ULI's Residential Development Council generated a wealth of advice regarding the design of multifamily residential projects.

- Be flexible when targeting a market. In the event that the market for a project turns out to be very different from the developer's initial expectation, the presence within the project of basic features with a broad market appeal will help sales or rentals.
- Common areas for stairs, elevators, corridors, lobbies, laundries, and so forth should occupy no more than 18 to 20 percent of the total heated rentable areas.
- Property managers can make many useful contributions to the design process and should be included in all design review meetings.
- Do not put family units on the third floor.
- Renters look primarily at total rent, not rent per square foot. Design units to meet the affordability requirements of the target market.
- Condominiums often end up as rental units because of changing market conditions. Make sure a project will not bring financial ruin if units must be rented rather than sold.
- Where possible, buildings should enclose a project's open space, creating courtyards free from cars. Views of cars detract from the courtyard environment and may reduce attainable rents.
- Avoid creating canyon-like areas and barracks-like buildings.
- Avoid placing air-conditioner condensing units in areas where children will play.
- Plan ahead for trash disposal. Make containers easy to reach, easy to clean around, and screened, where possible.
- The U.S. Post Office requires that mail boxes be grouped together. Place mail boxes near the manager's office so that the manager can see tenants as they come and go.
- Provide storage facilities near the pool for outdoor furniture during the winter.
- The leasing office should be visible from the street, easy to find, and have reserved parking close by.

One-quarter to one-half more parking spaces per condominium unit are often required as compared to rental units. Also, the condominium spaces should be identified and separated from the rental unit spaces. Assigned spaces can, however, create management problems as a result of the misuse of those spaces.

In general, condominium units are hard to sell before they are completed because buyers have trouble visualizing the final result. Furnished model units are thus worth the time and expense they require because they help buyers to picture how their individual units will function.

Designing to Save Costs

Trade-offs between construction costs and operating costs are common. For example, the use of exterior wood siding may save construction costs but, because such siding tends to leak, may increase maintenance costs. High-maintenance materials will also depress the sales value of a rental project because a proper statement of operating expenses will indicate the extent to which replacement reserves and maintenance expenses reduce NOI.

Good design can help to reduce costs by diminishing the amount of labor needed to maintain a project. For instance, in projects built before and during the 1960s, most complexes had enclosed entry areas for each group of apartments. However, each entry required janitors to maintain the area, wax floors, and clean windows. Open entries, which save on maintenance costs, have now become standard throughout the industry in garden apartments.

Some elements of design are, however, more costly than they were 20 years ago. Separate water, electricity, and gas meters were rare until soaring utility bills in the 1970s virtually mandated separate metering and separate heating and air-conditioning units. The additional cost was justified not only by tenants paying for their own utilities but also by renters' preferences for separate HVAC controls and by the advantage of separate meters for future conversion to condominiums.

Design Process

Preliminary Plans

Some developers feel that the safest way to deal with local government officials is to tell them very little until documents are submitted for project approval. This is not, however, a wise policy. If any public review is required, the developer should meet with an official of the reviewing agency before drawing up preliminary plans. A preapplication conference is a useful means of meeting the planning staff and learning their likes and dislikes. In turn, the planning staff can inform the developer of the requirements that must be met and the factors to consider during the planning stage. The conference also gives the developer the chance to "involve" the staff in the project, thereby encouraging a sense of cooperation that is likely to make the entire project proceed more smoothly.

Even in cases where the developer can apply directly for a building permit, he/she can obtain valuable information from members of the planning department before starting to draw up design plans. For example, the fire inspector at one building department informed Peiser Corporation and Jerome Frank Investments of proposed changes that their architect had not heard of regarding the regulations governing fire walls. The changes made it more economical to use sprinklers than floor-to-rafter fire-rated partitions. Six months later, when they returned for plan approval, the proposed changes had taken effect. Thus, the fire inspector's forewarning saved Peiser and Frank the time and money that would otherwise have been necessary to redraw the plans.

A developer should not spend too much money on preliminary plans in case, as often happens, the project does not proceed. At the same time, however, sufficient care should be taken so that the plans satisfy government agencies and financial backers. Furthermore, the most creative part of the design process often occurs in drawing preliminary plans. The preliminary plan phase sometimes is divided into a rough-concept planning phase and a refined schematic phase. Rough concept plans consist of floor plan and elevation drawings that may be prepared for testing the market for financing and for tenants, whereas refined schematic drawings represent the last opportunity for major design decisions. Refined schematic drawings also are used for lender and tenant solicitations, but architects view this stage as the primary one for designing a project. Once the plans are approved, most major features of a project cannot be changed.

Final Plans

Final plans and specifications (specs) become part of the official contract package used by the contractor and submitted to the lender and the city building department. They include the construction drawings and material specs that are required to build the project.

Unless a developer is certain that his/her project will go ahead, final plans and specs should not be ordered until all feasibility studies are completed, all predevelopment approvals—such as zoning changes—are in place, and a tentative financing commitment is received. Final plans and specs, which typically cost three or four times as much as the preliminary plans, represent a major increase in at-risk investment. They must be completed in their entirety before they can be submitted to the city for a building permit.[13] And in cities such as Los Angeles, the building permit process is so lengthy (six months or more) that a developer cannot afford to make any major changes to the plans once they have been submitted.

Because the drawings and specs become contract documents, the more precise they are, the better. At the same time, items such as air-conditioning equipment should not be specified too exactly in case the contractor can make a cost-saving substitution.

Change orders during construction are the single largest source of construction-cost overruns. Unfortunately, they are unavoidable. Nonetheless, the fewer changes that are made, the fewer opportunities the contractor or subcontractor has to raise the contract price. If the developer has done his/her homework properly during the preliminary plan phase, the process of obtaining final drawings should be routine. The time for intensive review and refinement is during the preliminary plan stage, and both the architect and engineer should be able to produce final plans and specs with little interruption from the developer. The contractor should be involved in reviewing the drawings so as to minimize problems in the field.

Financing

Rental apartment projects, like other income-property developments, have traditionally relied primarily on three types of financing: construction loans, permanent loans, and equity.

For-sale condominium projects, like land development, usually involve only equity and a construction loan, the latter covering the construction period and the lease-up period. The buyers of the condominiums obtain their own permanent loans. By contrast, in apartment projects, a permanent loan also comes into play, "taking out" the construction loan when the apartment reaches a specified level of income or occupancy. The amount of the construction loan usually equals that of the permanent loan because the construction lender will lend up to, but no more than, the amount that the permanent lender will fund. The construction lender looks to the permanent lender's funds to retire the construction loan.

Equity makes up the difference between the total project cost and the amount of the construction and permanent loans. In the and 1970s and early 1980s, construction and permanent loans often covered 100 percent of project costs, and developers were not required to contribute additional equity. However, today stiffer loan coverage requirements usually demand that equity covers between 15 and 25 percent of the total project costs.

Equity is the most expensive funding source because equity investors receive returns only after other lenders have been repaid. Construction lenders usually require developers to invest some or all of the needed equity in a project before they will begin to fund the construction loan. During the operating period, after the permanent mortgage has been obtained, equity investors receive cash flow only to the extent that money is available after the mortgage debt service has been paid. If there is a shortfall, developers (or their investors) are responsible for providing additional equity to cover the shortfall so that the bank always receives its full debt service. Otherwise, the permanent mortgage goes into default, and lenders can foreclose on the project.

To calculate the allowable mortgage amount, the permanent lender takes the lower amount given by two measures: the loan-to-value (L/V) ratio and the debt/coverage ratio (DCR). This calculation is illustrated in figure 4-13.

From figure 4-13, Test 1 (L/V) gives a mortgage amount of $800,000, whereas Test 2 (DCR) gives a mortgage amount of $791,324. The lender would typically give the developer the lower amount, rounded off to, say, $791,000. And if total project costs were $950,000, then the developer would need equity of $169,000—the difference between total project costs and allowable mortgage.

For beginning developers, the task of finding lenders is perhaps their hardest job. Lenders look chiefly at three things—track record, credit, and the project itself. By definition, beginning developers lack a track record, and they rarely have the financial net worth of more experienced developers. Thus, the project must be well above average in terms of its market feasibility, design, and economic appeal to capture a lender's interest. Beginning developers can improve their chances of securing loans by joint venturing with experienced developers and/or wealthy individuals. Beginning developers should also bear in mind that smaller, localized lenders are more likely than large banks to consider requests from inexperienced developers. Many developers begin as homebuilders, which allows them to build relationships with lenders that carry over to subsequent larger projects. Lenders are just as concerned about the way developers handle their business (meet deadlines, handle draw requests, build within budget, and so forth) as they are about the size of developers' previous projects. For a review of the various financial institutions that provide either construction or permanent financing for real estate, see chapter 2.

■ 4-13 Calculating the Allowable Mortgage Amount

The amount of the mortgage loan is based on the lower amount of two ratio calculations:

1. Loan-to-value ratio (L/V)—the ratio of mortgage amount to the appraised value must be less than some specified ratio, say, 80 percent.
2. Debt coverage ratio (DCR)—the ratio of NOI to the debt service (NOI divided by debt service) must be greater than some specified ratio, usually 1.15 to 1.30.

For example, suppose that the NOI on a property is $100,000 per year and that the appraised value is $1 million. Suppose also that the L/V ratio must be less than or equal to 80 percent and that the DCR must be at least 1.2.

TEST 1: $L/V \leq 80\%$

80% x $1,000,000 = **$800,000**

TEST 2: $DCR \nless 1.2$

Given mortgage interest rate = 10%

Term = 30 years

$$\frac{NOI}{1.2} = \frac{\$100{,}000}{1.2} = \$83{,}000 \text{ per year,}$$

or $6,944.44 per month (maximum allowable debt service)

$$\text{Present value } (PMT = \$6{,}944.44,\ \%i = \frac{10}{12},\ n = 30 \times 12) = \mathbf{\$791{,}324}$$

PMT = the annuity payment; *%i* = the percent interest; *n* = the term.

Construction Loans

Traditionally, developers obtained a permanent-loan commitment before they obtained a construction-loan commitment, even though construction financing occurs before permanent financing does. The construction lender made the loan with the promise that the loan would be retired by the permanent loan at some specified date. In the early 1980s, however, when interest rates soared, open-ended construction loans without permanent takeouts became common. Floating-rate "miniperms"—three- to five-year construction loans that carried over into the operating period—were loaned on the (correct) expectation that permanent rates would come down. The provision of open-ended loans, though, generally depends on the track records and financial statements of developers. Beginning developers usually must still have a permanent takeout commitment, unless they possess a very strong financial statement and an excellent credit history.

The construction loan is characterized by its short-term, installment-draw pattern, variable interest rate, and single repayment when the project is completed. Interest payments are added to the loan balance so that developers do not have to pay them until the loan reaches its limit. Construction loans are almost invariably made by institutional lenders, namely, banks, S&Ls, and sometimes insurance companies.

Construction loans suffer from a high degree of uncertainty: delays caused by weather conditions, labor troubles, and material shortages; cost overruns; contractor and subcontractor bankruptcies; and leasing risk (lease-up rates and rents that fall below expectations). Consequently, lenders providing construction funding take special precautions to ensure their protection.

Furthermore, construction lenders have become increasingly suspicious of the viability of the permanent commitment. Permanent loans sometimes contain such stringent covenants that developers must meet before funding is provided that the takeout loans are unlikely to materialize. In negotiating permanent takeouts, developers must take care that they have "bankable" commitments—commitments that construction lenders will lend against.

The lender's security comes from two sources: the project and the developer's credit. The developer is usually required to sign personally on the construction loan and must show a net worth at least equal to the loan. During economic downturns, the credit requirements may become very strong, and the developer may have to prove a *liquid* net worth (in cash, stocks, and bonds) equal to the amount of the loan.

For apartments, the construction loan usually runs for one to two years. Interest rates depend on the developer's credit and typically range between 1 and 3 percent over prime, with 1 or 2 points upfront.[14]

If the total project cost exceeds the amount of the construction loan, construction lenders will usually require a beginning developer to put the necessary equity into the project on the front end, before he/she can draw down on the construction loan. Any necessary equity must therefore be raised before construction can begin.

Interest is calculated each month on the average daily balance. Developers may make precise calculations of their interest requirements (as illustrated in figure 4-14), but banks will have their own method for computing interest. For example, if a total loan amount is $1 million with a one-year term at 10 percent interest, a bank may apply a standard factor as high as 0.75 to determine the average loan balance, even though a developer may show the average loan balance to be 0.50 of the final amount.

Lenders almost always require a first lien on the property. Thus, any prior loans such as seller financing must be paid off, releasing the senior liens, at the time of the first construction draw.

Construction-loan draws are tied to stages in the construction process, called "percent completion," based on an appraisal of the work completed to date. The appraisal is done either by the developer, his architect, or an inspector hired by the lender. If the value as measured by percent completion is lower, additional draws will not be permitted, irrespective of the dollar amount expended by the developer, The developer makes a detailed line item budget of off-site expenses such as street improvements and traffic signals, on-site expenses such as asphalt and landscaping, and direct construction expenses for the whole project. "For example," observes David Ball, vice president of Arnel Development of Costa Mesa, California, "he may tell the lender he is 50 percent done with concrete and want 50 percent funding of the line item for concrete. The lender's inspector may check and say that

■ 4-14 Calculating Interest for a Construction Loan

Suppose a developer has a $1 million construction loan with 2 points ($20,000) paid upfront (out of loan proceeds). Assuming 10 percent annual interest, interest on the construction loan and the draw schedule are as follows:

The bank will accrue interest monthly. The loan must be repaid at the end of the twelfth month.

Month	Beginning Balance	Interest Charges	Current Draws	Ending Balance
0			$ 20,000	$ 20,000
1	$ 20,000	$ 167	40,000	60,167
2	60,167	501	80,000	140,668
3	140,668	1,172	80,000	221,840
4	221,840	1,849	100,000	323,689
5	323,689	2,697	100,000	426,386
6	426,386	3,553	100,000	529,940
7	529,940	4,416	100,000	634,356
8	634,356	5,286	100,000	739,642
9	739,642	6,164	100,000	845,806
10	845,806	7,048	100,000	952,854
11	952,854	7,940	80,000	1,040,795
12	1,040,795	8,673	0	1,049,468
Total		49,468	1,000,000	

Total Amount to be Repaid to the Bank: $1,049,468
Effective Yield to the Bank: 14.49%

■ 4-15 Advice on Construction Loans

Several points to keep in mind regarding construction loans include the following:

- Never start construction until the construction lender has perfected the construction lien. A prominent Houston developer once told his contractor that he could start foundation work on a condominium project. The lender came out to do a site inspection. When he saw that material was already at the site, he knew that some supplier or laborer had established a prior lien on the property. The supplier could file a mechanics lien claim against the developer that would be superior to the lender's lien. The lender refused to fund the construction loan until all contractors, subcontractors, and their suppliers had signed releases that they had been paid everything that was owed them. Jumping the gun cost the developer three months before the construction lender was willing to go ahead.
- Construction lenders sometimes try to arrange a "Dutch International" loan—where the developer pays interest on the full loan amount despite having drawn only upon a small part of it. Do not agree to such loans.
- A construction loan should provide for individual disbursements rather than for one or two draws per month.
- One traditional advantage of going to S&Ls for financing was their willingness to take out their own construction loans. Some commercial banks use miniperm loans to accomplish the same objective, although typically only for larger developers.
- Check the documentation and procedures that the lender requires for draws. Construction lenders sometimes will allow the developer to post letters of credit in lieu of front-end equity. If so, the developer can reduce his/her front-end cash requirements, but he/she must have sufficient resources or investor backing to secure the letter of credit.

only 40 percent of the work has been done. Then the developer negotiates or explains why 50 percent is done, and the two parties come to terms."

Permanent Financing

Permanent financing is a critical ingredient in the development process, especially for projects undertaken by beginning developers who are unlikely to receive construction financing without a permanent-loan take-out. Permanent loans take many forms. In addition to bullet loans and the standard fixed-rate, adjustable-rate, and variable-rate mortgages,[15] lenders will consider participating loans and convertible loans. Participating loans give lenders a participation in cash flows after debt service and sometimes a participation in residual cash flows from sale. These participations, called "kickers," raise lenders' IRRs above the loan rate by 2 or 3 percent—a sufficient amount for lenders to consider funding 80 to 100 percent of project costs. A comparison of a standard bullet loan with two lender participation loans is presented in feature box 4-16, illustrating how these different approaches change the loan terms, cash flows, and

■ 4-16 Comparison of Bullet and Participating Loans for a Prototypical Income-Producing Development

Bullet loans are standard fixed-rate mortgages, amortizable over 30 years but with a five-, seven-, or 10-year call (repayment) provision. Participating loans, commonly made by pension funds, give the lender a participation in annual cash flows and proceeds from sale. The developer or the lender may receive a priority cash flow before the participation is calculated.

A. Assumptions

Project Cost	$11,000,000
Net Rentable Square Feet	93,000
Depreciable Basis of Building	$9,500,000
Depreciation Method	31 1/2 years SL
Initial Gross Potential Income	$1,674,000
Income Appreciation Rate	4%
Vacancy Rate	5%
Initial Operating Expenses	$419,000
Expense Inflation Rate	4%
Ordinary Tax Rate	28%
Costs of Sale	4%
Holding Period	5 years

■ 4-16 (Continued)

B. Loan Terms ($000s)

	Bullet Loan	Participating Loan with Developer Priorities	Participating Loan with Lender Priorities
Required Debt Coverage Ratios (DCRs)	1.20	1.15	1.15
Maximum Loan-to-Value (L/V) Ratio	75%	90%	90%
Loan Amount	$8,788	$10,546	$10,546
Note Rate	9.60%	8.75%	8.75%
Loan Fee	0%	0%	0%
Loan Amortization (Years)	30	30	30
Cash-Flow Kicker to Lender	–	50%	50%
Owner's Threshold Cash Flow	–	$20	–
Lender's Threshold	–	–	$20
Reversion Kicker to Lender	–	50%	50%
Owner's Threshold Reversion	–	$200	–
Lender's Threshold Reversion	–	–	$200
Land Sale Price	–	–	–
Land Lease Payment Rate	–	–	–
Land Repurchase Price	–	–	–

C. After-Tax Cash Flows from First Year of Operations ($000s)

	Bullet Loan	Participating Loan with Developer Priorities	Participating Loan with Lender Priorities
Annual Tax Liabilities			
Net Operating Income (NOI)	$1,172	$1,172	$1,172
Less: Interest	844	920	920
Depreciation	302	302	302
Land Lease	–	–	–
Lender Participation	–	78[a]	98
Taxable Income	$ 26	$ (128)	$ (148)
Taxes Paid (Saved)	$ 7	$ (36)	$ (41)
Annual After-Tax Cash Flow			
Net Operating Income (NOI)	$1,172	$1,172	$1,172
Less: Land Lease	–	–	–
Mortgage Payment	896	996	996
Threshold Amount Paid to Developer	–	20	–
Threshold Amount Paid to Lender	–	–	20
Cash Flow Subject to Participation	$ 275	$ 156	$ 156
Less: Lender Participation	–	78	78
Before-Tax Cash Flow	$ 275	$ 98[b]	$ 78[c]
Less: Taxes Paid (Saved)	7	(36)	(41)
After-Tax Cash Flow	$ 268	$ 134	$ 119

yields. The best approach depends on the developer's situation and preferences. The summary statistics indicate that the participating loan with owner priorities gives the highest return to the developer as measured by the net present value—$427,000. The participating loan with lender priorities gives the highest return to the lender—12.52 percent.

Figure 4-17 provides typical permanent-loan terms (for the year 1989) from five different types of financial institutions.

Another popular variation on standard mortgages provides a *note* rate, which is higher than the *pay* rate. The note rate is the nominal interest rate on the mortgage, say, 12 percent. The pay rate (used to determine the monthly debt service) may be set lower, at, say, 10 percent, because the cash flow on a property will not cover mortgage costs at the note rate. The difference is accrued until the property is sold. The advantage of a lower pay rate is that the borrower can obtain a larger loan than if the mortgage payment were calculated from the note rate, because the

■ 4-16 (Continued)

D. After-Tax Cash Flows from Sale ($000s)

	Bullet Loan	Participating Loan with Developer Priorities	Participating Loan with Lender Priorities
Tax Liability upon Sale			
Net Sales Price	$13,160	$13,160	$13,160
Less: Adjusted Tax Basis	9,492	9,492	9,492
Taxable Capital Gain	$ 3,668	$ 3,668	$ 3,668
Tax on Capital Gain	1,027	1,027	1,027
Tax Savings from Lender Payments	–	402	458
Total Tax Liability	$ 1,027	$ 625	$ 569
After-Tax Cash Flows upon Sale			
Net Sales Price	$13,160	$13,160	$13,160
Less: Land Purchase Price	–	–	–
Mortgage Balance	$ 8,466	$10,092	$10,092
Threshold Amount Paid to Owner	–	200	–
Threshold Amount Paid to Lender	–	–	200
Cash Flow Subject to Participation	$ 4,694	$ 2,868	$ 2,868
Less: Lender Participation	–	1,434	1,434
Threshold Amount Paid to Owner	–	200	–
Before-Tax Cash Flow	$ 4,694	$ 1,634	$ 1,434
Less: Tax Liability	1,027	625	569
After-Tax Cash Flow from Sale	$ 3,667	$ 1,009	$ 865

E. Summary Statistics for Developer and Lender ($000s)

	Bullet Loan	Participating Loan with Owner Priorities	Participating Loan with Lender Priorities
Developer:			
Sale at End of Year	5	5	5
Owner's Equity Contribution	$2,211	$ 454	$ 454
Undiscounted Before-Tax Net Cash Flows	$4,348	$ 1,915	$ 1,615
Net Present Value of Cash Flows Discounted at 20%	$ 227	$ 427	$ 327
Lender:			
Loan Amount	$8,788	$10,546	$10,546
L/V Ratio	75%	90%	90%
Effective DCR	1.31	1.18	1.18
Lender Yield	9.59%	12.05%	12.52%

[a]Calculated below.
[b]Includes threshold amount paid to owner.
[c]Includes threshold amount paid to lender.
Source: David Ling and Richard Peiser, "Choosing among Alternative Financing Structures: The Developer's Dilemma," *Real Estate Review*, vol. 17, no. 2, Summer 1987, pp. 39–46.

lower interest rate reduces the mortgage payment. (See figure 4-18 for an illustration of the calculation.)

Financing Issues

Personal Guarantees and Loan Funding

Although standard practices differ from area to area and from time to time, most developers must personally guarantee their construction loans. Often, they must also guarantee some part of their permanent loans, at least until their projects reach some threshold level of debt coverage or occupancy.

Lenders' requirements with respect to personal liability depend on the lending environment. In the 1970s and early 1980s, developers rarely had to guarantee development loans personally. Lenders could look only to the

■ 4-17 Comparison of Typical Permanent Loan Terms from Different Types of Lenders

	Savings and Loans	Banks	Life Company	Pension Fund	Credit Company
Net Operating Income (NOI)	$1,000,000	$1,000,000	$1,000,000	$1,000,000	$1,000,000
Term (Years)	15	5	5	10	5
Type	Variable	Fixed	Fixed	Fixed with 50% participation	Variable
Note Rate Spread (%)	11 DCOF + 250[a]	T-Bill + 175[b]	T-Bill + 125	T-Bill +100	P + 1½[c]
Note Rate (%)	11.25	10.25	9.75	9	12
Amortization (Years)	30	30	30	0	0
Constant (%)	11.66	10.75	10.31	9	12
Pay Rate (%)	Same	Same	Same	Same	9½
Debt Coverage Ratio (DCR)	1.05	1.10	1.15	1.15	1.10
Maximum Loan Amount Test 1	$8,168,000	$8,457,000	$8,434,000	$9,662,000	$9,569,000
Net Operating Income (NOI)	$1,000,000	$1,000,000	$1,000,000	$1,000,000	$1,000,000
Cap Rate (%)	8.0	8.25	8.25	8.25	8.0
Value	$12,500,000	$12,121,000	$12,121,000	$12,121,000	$12,500,000
Loan-to-Value (L/V) Ratio (%)	80	75	75	85	90
Maximum Loan Amount Test 2	$10,000,000	$9,091,000	$9,091,000	$10,303,000	$10,000,000
Maximum Loan	$8,168,000	$8,457,000	$8,434,000	$9,662,000	$9,569,000

[a]Monthly weighted average cost of funds for all S&Ls in the 11th District of the Federal Reserve plus 250 basis points (2.5 percent over the S&L industry's average cost of funds).
[b]Treasury bills of the same term (five or 10 years).
[c]Prime interest rate—rate to prime customers.
Source: Steve Bram, George Smith/Grubb & Ellis Financial, Los Angeles, October 1989.

property for repayment of the development loan. Aggressive lending practices in the mid-1980s led many lenders, especially savings institutions, to make bad loans for projects on which developers defaulted. Since then, lenders have become much more conservative in their lending practices and now generally require that developers personally guarantee development loans. The current trend may reverse direction in the future, but, for the early 1990s, beginning developers should be prepared to sign personally on their development loans.

How do developers trade out personal liability? No developer wants to be a perpetual guarantor of the loan, and many developers refuse to agree to unconditional liability and will negotiate for some performance criteria that release them from personal liability. Some alternative compromises include the following:

- Lenders cannot call on the guarantor directly in the event of default. They must instead foreclose on the defaulting property and obtain a legal decision against the guarantor. Because judicial foreclosures can be time-consuming and expensive, lenders may prefer to take over the property immediately in return for releasing the developer from some or all of his/her liability under the guarantee.
- The note limits the amount of any deficiency over time. For example, if the loan is current for three years, then the guarantor's liability reduces to, say, 50 percent of any deficiency.
- The note states that if all the land improvements have been installed within budget, and if the project has been completed, the developer's (guarantor's) liability reduces to zero after three years.
- The developer places money in escrow to cover potential losses. Suppose a developer undertakes a project appraised at $12 million but requiring only $10 million in costs. The developer may borrow the full $12 million, leaving $2 million in escrow to eliminate any personal liability. This solution, of course, involves added interest cost, which, in turn, adds to the risk of the project.
- Personal liability may be defined to mean either the "top half" or "bottom half" of the loan. Suppose the developer guarantees the top half of a loan. If a project with a $10 million loan sells for $7 million, the guar-

■ 4-18 Mortgage Calculation: Pay Rate Versus Note Rate

Suppose a mortgage has the following terms:

Mortgage Amount	$1,000,000
Term	30 years
Note Rate	12%
Pay Rate	10%

The monthly payment under the note rate would be:

PMT (*PV* = $1,000,000, %*i* = 12/12, *n* = 30 x 12)[a] =	$10,286.13 per month

The monthly payment under the pay rate would be:

PMT (*PV* = $1,000,000, %*i* = 10/12, *n* = 30 x 12) =	$8,775.71 per month
Difference in Payments (Accrued)	$1,510.42 per month

The borrower would pay the lower amount, $8,775.71, and would accrue the difference of $1,510.42 per month. Suppose the borrower wanted to retire the mortgage after five years (60 months). The borrower would calculate the mortgage balance under the note rate:

PV (*PMT* = $10,286.13, %*i* = 12/12, *n* = 300)[b] =	$976,632.18

Next, the borrower would calculate the accrued interest:

FV (*PMT* = $1,510.42, %*i* = 12/12, *n* = 60) =	$ 123,354.71
Total Payment to Retire Mortgage	$1,099,986.89

To retire the mortgage, the borrower would pay the combined amount, or $1,099,986.89.

To check the calculation, the present value of the monthly payments plus the present value of the combined payment at retirement, discounted at the note rate, should equal the initial mortgage of $1,000,000:

PV (*PMT* = $8,775.71, %*i* = 12/12, *n* = 60) =	$ 394,512.64
PV (*FV* = $1,099,986.89, %*i* = 12/12, *n* = 60) =	$ 605,487.36
Total	$1,000,000.00

[a]*PMT* = the mortgage payment; *PV* = the mortgage amount; %*i* = the interest rate; *n* = the term; all represented as monthly figures.
[b]The ending balance on a mortgage is calculated on the *remaining* number of payments: 30 – 5 years = 25 years x 12 months = 300 months remaining on the mortgage.

antee of the top half means that the developer owes the deficient $3 million. If the developer guarantees the bottom half, then nothing is owed unless the project sells for less than $5 million. In some cases, ambiguously worded loan documents that fail to specify whether the developer is guaranteeing the top or bottom half of a loan have caused the developer and lender to end up in court. The prospect of a long court battle to satisfy the deficiency has motivated some lenders to settle with developers.

Beginning developers will find it difficult to eliminate personal liability altogether, but they can negotiate to limit it. If they can limit their liability to a specified amount, they may sell pieces of that liability to their investors along with pieces of the transaction.

Closings

Obtaining the funding (closing) for a permanent loan may involve almost as much work as originally securing the lenders' commitment to provide that funding. The loan commitment document specifies the requirements for permanent-loan funding. Typical requirements include a certified rent roll showing what the property is generating in cash flow and the terms of signed leases. Loan closing can be an exasperating process, and any points not clearly spelled out in the original commitment can come back to haunt the developer at closing. For example, to qualify for loan funding, loan documents may be ambiguous concerning whether a project must be 90 percent leased, 90 percent occupied, or 90 percent occupied and paying rent. Lenders will usually take the most restrictive interpretation, so developers are well advised to ensure that qualifying standards are described precisely.

Some loan commitments require that a project have attained certain rental objectives—say, 80 percent occupancy for a specified period—one month, six months, or 12 months. Obviously, the shorter the period for qualification, the better for the developer.

Lenders may also require that releases, credit reports, or other paperwork be conducted for all tenants. Such procedures should be confirmed at the outset, thereby allowing the property manager to obtain the necessary documentation as tenants lease the units.

Closing on condominium loans can pose a different set of problems than closing on apartment loans. When markets are soft, sales may not reach targets set by permanent lenders, and developers may find themselves obliged to give investors unsold units in lieu of a cash return. If a developer subsequently decides to consolidate ownership and to convert a project to a rental project, the price of, or interest rates on, those units may be very high.

How difficult loan closings are depends on the local real estate market at the time of closing. When conditions become soft, lenders naturally become more concerned about the safety of their investments and thus more rigorous in the enforcement of the various requirements for closing.

Government Programs

Government programs are no longer as fruitful a source of financing for beginning developers as they used to be. Over the years, numerous government programs have been created to generate low- and moderate-income housing. Many of those programs have been curtailed in recent years, but new federal legislation passed in 1990 may provide new sources.

In the 1980s, the dominant program was tax-exempt housing revenue bonds (HRBs). HRBs grew out of industrial revenue bonds (IRBs), which were originally introduced to foster new industrial development in depressed areas. Interest rates on both IRBs and HRBs were typically 2.5 percent below conventional interest rates; such favorable interest rates were possible because the bonds were rated AAA and guaranteed by the federal government.

To qualify for tax-exempt status, developers originally had to set aside 20 percent of the units in a project for low- or moderate-income tenants (that is, tenants whose incomes were no higher than 80 percent of the median income for the area) and had to meet the U.S. Department of Housing and Urban Development's (HUD's) income requirements under Section 8 of the Housing and Community Development Acts of 1937. A state or local housing agency had to be created to issue the bonds. Especially in areas where median incomes were very high, many developers found that they could make good profits on projects with HRB funding.

The 1986 Tax Reform Act changed the law, however. Although tax-exempt status was still available, tenant-income requirements became stricter; 20 percent of the units in a project henceforth had to be dedicated to

■ 4-19 The Contents of a Mortgage Application Package

Applications for both construction and permanent financing should be accompanied by a mortgage package—usually a notebook or a bound document—that includes as many of the following items as are appropriate:[a]

Introduction

- letter of transmittal;
- loan application (supplied by lending institution and filled out by ownership group);
- documentation of good-faith deposits; and
- mortgage loan submission summary sheet that summarizes the major aspects of the project and terms of the loan request.

Property Description and Rationale

- community profile;
- description of the physical aspects of the property;
- acquisition, title, and zoning; and
- attachments, including location maps, aerial photographs, surveys, floodplain maps, and so forth.

Economics

- survey of competitive developments;
- financial forecasts for the project; and
- analysis of the economic base of the local community.

Development Plan

- land comparables showing sales prices of similar tracts of land in the area;
- overall development plan;
- complete engineering data covering soil tests, bearing strength, grading, road specifications, drainage, floodplain surveys, and so forth; and
- copy of purchase option.

Buildings

- plans and specs of proposed buildings with architectural drawings.

Credit Information

- Dun and Bradstreet reports on individuals in the ownership group or partners in the joint venture;
- copy of the purchase-money mortgage from the seller (if any) and a financial statement of the landowner; and
- financial statements of the applicants.

[a]Much of this information is adapted from Michael Beyard, *Business and Industrial Park Development Handbook* (Washington, D.C.: ULI–the Urban Land Institute, 1987), p. 79.

renters with incomes below 50 percent of the median income, or, alternatively, 40 percent of the units had to be rented to persons with incomes below 60 percent of the median income. In California, the value of bonds issued dropped from $900 million in 1984 and $3.5 billion in 1985 to less than $100 million in 1986 and 1987.

Building under government programs was, and still is, very time-consuming and frustrating. Government programs require considerable paperwork and often contain vague guidelines that encourage differences in interpretation. Associated legal costs can also be onerous. Bond deals, for example, involve as many as nine different parties, each represented by its own attorney. The developer pays everyone's fees, and since the attorneys do not work directly for the developer, monitoring their time and fees is difficult.

Yet, despite the added costs, bond programs generated many thousands of housing units throughout the United States. The sale of tax credits for low-income housing remains an important source of funds for apartments, although it must be supplemented by other forms of subsidy (which redevelopment agencies and HUD may provide) to make low- and moderate-income apartments financially feasible. Whether or not the federal government will again provide attractive and substantial funding for residential development remains to be seen. Beginning developers should certainly monitor any moves in that direction.

Financial Analysis

The first two of the five stages of financial feasibility analysis have been described earlier in this chapter. It is now time to consider the final three stages, which provide the information and documentation necessary to obtain the permanent loan, the construction loan, and the equity. In brief, the stages are:

Stage 3. Combined Analysis: DCF analysis of the combined development period and operating period. This should be performed after all feasibility studies are completed and before the land is closed or a final commitment to the project has been made. Its primary purpose is to give the developer an overall view of cash flows, funding requirements, and returns.

Stage 4. Monthly Cash Flows: monthly cash-flow analysis for the construction and lease-up period. This usually follows Stage 3 analysis. It serves as the primary documentation for the construction lender and allows the developer to see monthly cash-flow sources and uses during the development period.

Stage 5. Joint Venture Analysis: DCF analysis for equity investors. The purpose of this analysis is to determine the best deal from the developer's perspective for raising equity from investors or joint venture partners. The results of the analysis are used for raising money from potential equity partners.

Although the work required to complete Stages 3, 4, and 5 is wasted if a developer decides not to close on the land for a project, that decision may hinge on the developer's ability to obtain financing or equity. In practice, therefore, Stages 3, 4, and 5 are usually undertaken before a final commitment has been made to go ahead with a project and close on the land. Nevertheless, a developer should expend a large amount of time and energy on a detailed analysis only when such detail is warranted.

Stage 3: Combined Development and Operating Periods

Of the five stages, Stage 3 is the only one that gives a developer an overall picture of a project, including both the development and the operating periods. At the same time, however, it is the one stage that may be omitted, the DCF analysis of the operating period (Stage 2 analysis) having already provided sufficient information for a developer to make an informed decision about a project. The major purpose of the combined analysis is to give a developer a more accurate picture of cash-flow needs during construction and lease-up and to determine the IRR for the entire project, from land purchase through sale of the completed building.

Even though some analysts may wait until they have done a monthly analysis (Stage 4) to perform the combined analysis, it is preferable to use a simpler spreadsheet that computes cash flows over the development period on a quarterly basis and then converts them to annual cash flows so that they can be combined with the annual cash flows for the operating period. A quarterly or monthly cash-flow analysis for the entire holding period merely generates a lot of numbers that lenders will not examine and that may obscure the developer's vision.

The combined analysis, which incorporates construction phasing and lease-up timing estimates, should also take into account any differences between occupancy and cash flow (such as periods when rental concessions are expected). These projections on the revenue side of the spreadsheet are not as detailed as they will be for the monthly analysis, but any major item affecting the amount or timing of revenues and expenditures should be made explicit in the analysis.

Stage 4: Monthly Cash Flows during the Development Period

This analysis, which is the most detailed projection of all, is used to determine exactly how much money is needed from all potential sources during the development

■ 4-20 Stage 3 Analysis: Combined Development and Operating Period Cash Flows

Stage 3 analysis is a refinement of Stage 2 analysis with two major modifications. First, it combines both the development and the operating periods, whereas Stage 2 covers the operating period only. Second, the development-period cash flows are programmed quarterly to give a better estimate of loan and equity requirements.

In Stage 2, all development-period cash flows, including construction interest, were summarized in a single table and entered into the spreadsheet as one aggregate number representing "total project cost." The cash flows began with the operating period—when the building received its certificate of occupancy. The resulting IRRs covered the operating period. They reflect the return that a buyer who bought the property for the total project cost and sold it seven years later would receive.

Stage 3 analysis provides a more-detailed picture of the cash flows during the development period. Line 47 shows that the maximum cash equity requirement is $1,032,604 in the eighth quarter. The quarterly cash flows for the development period are consolidated into annual cash flows for the combined analysis of the development and operating periods in lines 101–129.

Development Period Quarterly Cash Flows

				Quarter			
			Total	0	1	2	3
	Rent Calculation						
1	Apartments Leased	158					
2	SF per Unit[b]	844					
3	Cumulative SF Leased						
4	Rent from New Leases	$0.688					
5	Miscellaneous Income[c]						
6	Total Income						
7	Cumulative Income	281,629					
8	Free Rent (2 Weeks)[d]	16.67%					
9	Normal Vacancy[e]	5.00%					
10	Net Collections						
11	Expenses (SF per year)	$2.65					
12							
13	Net Operating Income						
14	Permanent Debt Service[f]	143,370					
15	Cash Flow before Construction						
16	Costs and Financing						
17							
18	**Development Costs[g]**						
19	Land		552,875	552,875			
20	Construction Hard Costs[h]		4,784,700		1,196,175	1,196,175	1,196,175
21	Financing Transaction Costs		182,854	182,854			
22	Insurance, Taxes, Audit, Miscellaneous		57,352	39,352	2,500	2,500	2,500
23	Development Fee		239,235				
24	Contingency[i]		150,000				
25	Total Costs		5,967,016	775,081	1,198,675	1,198,675	1,198,675
26							
27	Cash Flow before Financing		(5,288,051)	(775,081)	(1,198,675)	(1,198,675)	(1,198,675)
	Financing						
28	Equity[j]		1,000,000	775,081	224,919		
29	Permanent Loan Balance						
30							
31	Construction Loan	5,224,387					
32	Beginning Balance		0	0	0	999,317	2,255,689
33	Borrowings		4,716,334	0	973,756	1,198,675	1,198,675
34	Permanent Loan Repayments[k]		5,224,387		0	0	0

The after-tax IRR on equity for the entire life of the project is 22.36 percent (line 129). The IRRs for Stage 3 tend to be lower than for Stage 2 because the investment of equity is assumed to occur at the beginning of the development period rather than at the beginning of the operating period (as in Stage 2). Since the equity does not earn any return during the development period, the IRRs are lower. On the other hand, Stage 3 analysis provides a more accurate estimate of construction costs, occupancy, and rents. These, in turn, give a more accurate estimate of construction-loan draws and construction-loan interest.

Finally, although Stage 3 provides interesting information for the developer, it is the one stage that may be skipped. The developer may prefer to go directly to Stage 4 with its monthly cash-flow projections. Stage 4 does not provide a picture of the overall performance since it covers only the development period. However, the developer can either redo Stage 2 analysis using the interest estimates generated by Stage 4, or the developer can go on to Stage 5, which provides the returns to equity investors in a syndication or joint venture.

Quarter								
4	5	6	7	8	9	10	11	12
15	45	45	45	8				
12,666	37,999	37,999	37,999	6,755				
12,666	50,666	88,665	126,665	133,420	133,420	133,420	133,420	133,420
26,144	78,431	78,431	78,431	13,943	0	0	0	0
593	1,780	1,780	1,780	316	0	0	0	0
26,737	80,211	80,211	80,211	14,259	0	0	0	0
26,737	106,948	187,159	267,370	281,629	281,629	281,629	281,629	281,629
4,456	13,369	13,369	13,369	2,377	0	0	0	0
0	0	0	0	14,081	14,081	14,081	14,081	14,081
22,281	93,579	173,790	254,001	265,171	267,548	267,548	267,548	267,548
8,392	33,566	58,741	83,915	88,391	88,391	88,391	88,391	88,391
13,889	60,013	115,049	170,086	176,780	179,157	179,157	179,157	179,157
0	0	0	0	0	143,370	143,370	143,370	143,370
					35,787	35,787	35,787	35,787
1,196,175								
2,500	8,000							
	100,000							
				139,235				
				150,000				
1,198,675	108,000	0	0	289,235	0	0	0	0
(1,184,786)	(47,987)	115,049	170,086	(112,455)	35,787	35,787	35,787	35,787
					5,224,387	5,224,387	5,224,387	5,224,387
3,545,041	4,853,985	5,030,649	5,047,655	5,010,070	5,224,387	0	0	0
1,184,786	47,987	0	0	112,455	0	0	0	0
0	0	0	0	0	5,224,387	0	0	0

Development Period Quarterly Cash Flows (Continued)

				Quarter			
			Total	0	1	2	3
35	Trial Ending Balance		0	0	973,756	2,197,992	3,454,364
36	Positive Cash Flow			0	0	0	0
37	Interest (per Quarter)	2.63%	825,792		25,561	57,697	90,677
38	Ending Balance before Limit		0	0	999,317	2,255,689	3,545,041
39	Ending Balance after Limit		0	0	999,317	2,255,689	3,545,041
40							
41	Additional Requirements[l]		32,604	0	0	0	0
42	Positive Cash Flow after Limit		0	0	0	0	0
43	Equity Account						
44	Additional Requirements		32,604	0	0	0	0
45	Positive Cash Flow after Limit		0	0	0	0	0
46	Cash Flow after Permanent		143,148	0	0	0	0
47	Ending Balance[m]		889,456	775,081	1,000,000	1,000,000	1,000,000

Annual Analysis[n]: Uses and Sources of Funds

				Year		
			Total	0	1	2
48						
49						
50	**Uses of Funds**					
51	Land		552,875	552,875		
52	Construction Hard Costs		4,784,700	0	4,784,700	
53	Financing Costs		182,854	182,854	0	0
54	Insurance, Taxes, Audit, Miscellaneous		57,352	39,352	10,000	8,000
55	Development Fee		239,235	0	0	239,235
56	Contingency		150,000	0	0	150,000
57	Construction Loan Interest (Capitalized)[o]	4 Qtrs	298,093		298,093	
58	Total Capital Costs		6,265,109	775,081	5,092,793	397,235
59						
60	Net Operating Income		1,252,445		13,889	521,928
61	Construction Loan Interest (Operations)		527,699			527,699
62	Permanent Debt Service[p]		573,480			
63	Cash Flow from Operations[q]		151,266	0	13,889	(5,771)
64						
65	Total Uses[r]		6,113,843	775,081	5,078,904	403,006
66						
67	**Sources of Funds**					
68	Construction Loan Balance[s]		0	0	4,853,985	5,224,387
69	Permanent Loan Balance		5,224,387			
70	Equity Balance		889,456	775,081	1,000,000	1,032,604
71						
72	Construction Loan Sources[t]		0	0	4,853,985	370,402
73	Permanent Loan Sources		5,224,387	0	0	0
74	Equity Sources		889,456	775,081	224,919	32,604
75						
76	Total Sources[u]		6,113,843	775,081	5,078,904	403,006
77						
78	Equity for Capital Investment			775,081	238,808	26,833
79	(Equity Source minus Operating Cash Flow)[v]					
80	Equity for Capital Investment			775,081	238,808	26,833
81	(Capital Costs minus Loans)[w]					

	Quarter								
	4	5	6	7	8	9	10	11	12
	4,729,827	4,901,972	5,030,649	5,047,655	5,122,525	0	0	0	0
	0	0	115,049	170,086	0	0	0	0	0
	124,158	128,677	132,055	132,501	134,466	0	0	0	0
	4,853,985	5,030,649	5,047,655	5,010,070	5,256,991	0	0	0	0
	4,853,985	5,030,649	5,047,655	5,010,070	5,224,387	0	0	0	0
	0	0	0	0	32,604	0	0	0	0
	0	0	0	0	0	0	0	0	0
	0	0	0	0	32,604	0	0	0	0
	0	0	0	0	0	0	0	0	0
	0	0	0	0	0	35,787	35,787	35,787	35,787
	1,000,000	1,000,000	1,000,000	1,000,000	1,032,604	996,817	961,030	925,243	889,456

	Year							
	3	4	5	6	7	8	9	10
	0							
	0							
	0							
	0							
	0							
	716,628							
	0							
	573,480							
	143,148							
	(143,148)							
	0							
	5,224,387							
	889,456							
	(5,224,387)							
	5,224,387							
	(143,148)							
	(143,148)							
	0							
	0							

■ 4-20 (Continued)

Annual Analysis[n]: Financing Computations

				Total	Year 0	Year 1	Year 2
	Permanent Loan Computation						
82							
83	Mortgage Amount		$5,224,387	0			
84	Term (Years)		30	0			
85	Interest Rate		10.50%				
86	Monthly Payment		47,790				
87	Quarterly Payment		143,370				
88	Quarter of Funding		9				
89	Month of Funding		25				
90	Remaining Months (End of Year)		360				
91	Ending Balance		$5,224,387				
92	Amortization						
93	Interest—(Annual Payment = 573,480)						
94							
95	**Depreciation and Amortization Computation**						
96		**Life**	**Costs**				
97	Construction Hard Costs[x]	27.5	4,784,700				86,995
98	Financing Costs	30.0	182,854				3,048
99	Other Costs[y]	27.5	446,587				8,120
100	Capitalized Construction Loan Interest	27.5	298,093				5,420
	Total		5,712,234				103,583

Combined Annual Cash Flows

			Total	0	1	2
101	Net Operating Income	4.00%	7,138,986		13,889	521,928
102	Construction Interest during Operations[z]		527,699		0	527,699
103	Permanent Debt Service	573,480	4,587,840			
104						
105	Cash Flow before Tax		2,023,447	0	13,889	(5,771)
106						
107	Tax Calculation					
108	Net Operating Income		7,138,986		13,889	521,928
109	Less Construction Interest		527,699		0	527,699
110	Less Permanent Interest		4,277,556		0	0
111	Less Depreciation/Amortization		1,760,895		0	103,583
112	Taxable Income		572,836	0	13,889	(109,354)
113	Passive Loss Offset		153,595			
114	Taxable Income		419,241		13,889	(109,354)
115	Passive Loss Carryforward[aa]		0		0	(109,354)
116	Taxes	28.00%	160,395		3,889	0
117						
118	Cash Flow before Tax[bb]		2,023,447		13,889	(5,771)
119	Cash Flow before Taxes from Sale[cc]		5,144,905			
120	Net Equity Investment[dd]		(1,040,722)	(775,081)	(238,808)	(26,833)
121	Net Cash Flows before Tax		6,127,630	(775,081)	(224,919)	(32,604)
122	IRR before Tax	25.59%				
123						
124	Taxes[ee]		160,395		3,889	0
125	Taxes from Sale		1,497,675			
126	Total Taxes		1,658,070	0	3,889	0
127						
128	Net Cash Flow after Tax[ff]		4,469,560	(775,081)	(228,808)	(32,604)
129	IRR after Tax[gg]	22.36%				

Year							
3	4	5	6	7	8	9	10
25							
348	336	324	312	300	288	276	264
$5,198,291	$5,169,261	$5,137,031	$5,101,250	$5,061,526	$5,017,424	$4,968,461	$4,914,103
26,096	29,030	32,230	35,781	39,724	44,102	48,963	54,358
547,384	544,450	541,250	537,699	533,756	529,378	524,517	519,122
173,989	173,989	173,989	173,989	173,989	173,989	173,989	173,989
6,095	6,095	6,095	6,095	6,095	6,095	6,095	6,095
16,240	16,240	16,240	16,240	16,240	16,240	16,240	16,240
10,840	10,840	10,840	10,840	10,840	10,840	10,840	10,840
207,164	207,164	207,164	207,164	207,164	207,164	207,164	207,164
716,628	745,293	775,105	806,109	838,353	871,887	906,762	943,032
0							
573,480	573,480	573,480	573,480	573,480	573,480	573,480	573,480
143,148	171,813	201,625	232,629	264,873	298,407	333,282	369,552
716,628	745,293	775,105	806,109	838,353	871,887	906,762	943,032
0	0	0	0	0	0	0	0
547,384	544,450	541,250	537,699	533,756	529,378	524,517	519,122
207,164	207,164	207,164	207,164	207,164	207,164	207,164	207,164
(37,920)	(6,321)	26,691	61,246	97,433	135,345	175,081	216,746
0	0	26,691	61,246	65,658	0	0	0
(37,920)	(6,321)	0	0	31,775	135,345	175,081	216,746
(147,274)	(153,595)	(126,904)	(65,658)	0	0	0	0
0	0	0	0	8,897	37,897	49,023	60,689
143,148	171,813	201,625	232,629	264,873	298,407	333,282	369,552
							5,144,905
0							
143,148	171,813	201,625	232,629	264,873	298,407	333,282	5,514,457
0	0	0	0	8,897	37,897	49,023	60,689
							1,497,675
0	0	0	0	8,897	37,897	49,023	1,558,364
143,148	171,813	201,625	232,629	255,976	260,510	284,259	3,956,093

■ 4-20 (Continued)

Sale Calculation

				Year 10	Total
	Cash Flows from Sale				
130	Sales Capitalization Rate	9.00%			
131	Net Operating Income in Year 10	943,032			
132	Sales Price			10,478,133	
133	Commission/Selling Expense	4.00%		419,125	
134					
135	Net Sales Price			10,059,008	
136	Retire Mortgage Balance[hh]			4,914,103	
137					
138	Cash Flow before Tax			5,144,905	5,144,905
139					
140	**Taxes from Sale**				
141					
142	Net Sales Price	10,059,008			
143	Depreciation Basis	5,712,234			
144	Plus Land	552,875			
145	Total Basis	6,265,109			
146	Total Deduction Taken[ii]	1,760,895			
147	Remaining Basis	4,504,214			
148	Capital Gain	5,554,794			
149	Deduct Unamortized Construction Interest[jj]	(205,953)			
150	Deduct Passive Loss Carryforward[kk]	0			
151	Net Capital Gain	5,348,841	28%	1,497,675	
152	Total Tax from Sale			1,497,675	1,497,675
153					
154	Cash Flow after Tax				3,647,230

[a]To facilitate understanding of this spreadsheet, readers may want to copy the pages and assemble them into one large spreadsheet.
[b]Average unit size is taken from Stage 2. Although unit types can be computed separately, at this stage of analysis it is better to group all apartment types together and employ an average square footage per apartment.
[c]Income associated with vending, laundry, and forfeited deposits.
[d]Free rent is computed by multiplying one-sixth (one-half month divided by three months) by line 6.
[e]Normal vacancy enters the equation once the occupancy rate reaches 95 percent. Without a deduction for normal vacancy, effective gross income would rise to 100 percent of gross potential income.
[f]Permanent debt service begins when the permanent mortgage is funded in the ninth quarter. Terms for debt service are defined beginning at line 83.
[g]Construction costs are taken from Stage 2 to facilitate comparison:

Total project cost (Stage 2, line 78)	$6,658,761
Operating reserve (Stage 2, line 74)	– 326,038
Construction interest (Stage 2, line 54)	– 365,707
Total costs (Stage 3, line 25)	$5,967,016

[h]Construction is assumed to take one year (four quarters).
[i]The contingency is assumed to be spent at the end of the second year.

period. Because it is the primary documentation for the construction lender, it should cover the full term of the construction loan through its repayment by the permanent loan.

The monthly cash flow illustrated in feature box 4-21 includes not only the construction-loan cash flows but also all other sources of funds, including equity and a secondary loan. Most deals will be simpler, involving only a construction loan and equity. However, many equity syndications call for investors to spread their investment over several years. For example, suppose an investor in a $100,000 unit makes five $20,000 payments spread over five years. If the developer needs the full $100,000 within the first year, he/she will have to borrow the other $80,000

[j]The first $1 million of equity is invested in Quarters 0 and 1 before any construction-loan draws are allowed.
[k]The permanent-loan funds come in at the beginning of the third year.
[l]Borrowings in the eighth quarter exceed the maximum allowed for the construction loan; therefore, $32,604 must be funded by additional equity contribution.
[m]The total equity requirement of $1,032,604 is required in the eighth quarter.
[n]The annual analysis aggregates the quarterly cash flows for insertion into the second iteration of the DCF (Stage 2) analysis. The development-period cash flows for the first three years become the first three years of the combined cash-flow analysis in lines 101 through 129. The sale calculation for Year 10 appears in lines 130 through 154.
[o]To simplify the calculation, the entire project is assumed to receive its certificate of occupancy at the same time, after one year. Thus, the first four quarters of construction interest are capitalized. After that, construction interest is expensed (see line 61).
[p]From line 14. The permanent mortgage is assumed to fund at the beginning of the third year.
[q]Cash flow from operations is calculated as line 60 minus lines 61 and 62. The negative cash flow of –$5,771 in Year 2 represents an additional use of funds.
[r]Positive cash flow in Year 3 represents a negative use.
[s]From line 39, fourth quarter. Similarly, all numbers in lines 68 through 70 are the end-of-year balances (fourth, eighth, and twelfth quarters) for the respective accounts.
[t]Lines 72 through 74 give the annual change in the account balances of lines 68 through 70. An increase in the account balance represents an infusion of funds from that source.
[u]If there is no error, sources will equal uses.
[v]Equity for capital investment is the equity required for building the project as distinct from the equity required to cover negative cash flows from operations—a number needed for later computations (line 120). For Year 2, of the total equity sources ($32,604 in line 74), $5,771 was required for negative cash flows from operations; $26,833 was required for capital investment.
[w]Line 80 is a checkpoint for the analysis. In addition to the computation in line 78, net equity for capital investment is the difference between total capital expenditures (line 58) minus total loan sources (lines 72 plus 73): $26,833 = $397,235 – $370,402.
[x]Under the half-year convention, a half-year's depreciation is taken in Year 2, the year the project is placed in service.
[y]To simplify calculations, insurance, taxes, audit, and miscellaneous ($57,352), development fee ($239,235), and contingency ($150,000) are lumped together as "other costs" and amortized over 27.5 years. The contingency here is treated as a capital cost, whereas it is written off as an operating cost in Stages 4 and 5.
[z]After the first year, construction-loan interest is deducted currently (see note n).
[aa]The passive-loss rules are described in Stage 2. Accrued passive losses from prior years (line 115) may be used to offset taxable income. Passive losses are used up in Year 7.
[bb]Cash flow before tax is calculated at line 105.
[cc]Cash flow before tax from sale comes from line 138.
[dd]From line 78. Equity for capital investment covers equity required for project costs other than operating deficits. Operating deficits are already included in the cash-flow analysis in line 121.
[ee]Taxes is from line 116.
[ff]Net cash flow after tax in the year of sale is calculated from line 121 minus line 126.
[gg]The after-tax IRR is 22.36 percent. This compares to 24.01 percent for the Stage 2 analysis. Total capital costs are $6,256,109 in Stage 3 and $6,332,723 in Stage 2. The difference occurs because capitalized construction interest is lower in Stage 3. The lower costs in Stage 3 are counterbalanced by the fact that the equity investment receives no return for the development period. Also, the 10-year analysis tends to bring the IRR down because the profit generated by sale of the property (at a cap rate lower than the initial cap rate) occurs later.
[hh]The mortgage balance comes from line 91, Year 10.
[ii]Total deductions taken comes from line 111.
[jj]Unamortized construction interest is deductible at time of sale.
[kk]Any remaining passive loss carryforward is deductible at time of sale.
Note: Some columns may not add exactly, due to rounding.

through a secondary loan secured by the investor notes. The feature box shows what the cash flows for the secondary loan would be. This information is vital not only for negotiating with the secondary lender (called the "investor-note lender") but also for convincing the construction lender that the necessary equity funds will be available. Lenders are very reluctant to make loans against investor notes unless the investors have put up irrevocable letters of credit. They fear that investors may fail to make future installment payments, especially if the project proves economically unsuccessful. Ideally, the construction lender will also handle the secondary investor note loan; the lender may, however, require that the secondary loan come from another bank.

4-21 Stage 4 Analysis: Monthly Cash Flows During the Development Period

Stage 4 analysis provides the detailed monthly cash flows during the development period. It usually runs from the time that the developer funds the construction loan until the project reaches stabilized occupancy, after the permanent loan has taken out the construction loan. Where a long lead time exists before the construction loan is funded, the analysis may begin earlier in order to track cash outlays during predevelopment. Stage 4 analysis runs from two to three years for most apartment

Operating Income and Expenses

			Absorption	Year 1	Year 2	Month			
				Total	Total	0	1	2	3
	Absorption[a]	Total	Units per Month[b,c]		Lease-Up Month:		0	0	0
1	A-1 1 Bedroom, 1 Bath	36	4				0	0	0
2	A-2 1 Bedroom, Den, 1 Bath	20	3				0	0	0
3	B-1 2 Bedroom, 1 1/2 Bath	24	2				0	0	0
4	B-2 2 Bedroom, 2 Bath	46	4				0	0	0
5	C-1 3 Bedroom, 2 Bath	32	8				0	0	0
6	Total Units	158	21	106	158	0	0	0	0
7	Occupancy %					0.00%	0.00%	0.00%	0.00%
8									
9	Rental Income and Expenses	Base Rent[d]							
10	A-1 1 Bedroom, 1 Bath	$425	$183,515	$16,992	$166,523	$0	$0	$0	$0
11	A-2 1 Bedroom, Den, 1 Bath	519	136,418	15,560	120,858	0	0	0	0
12	B-1 2 Bedroom, 1 1/2 Bath	574	144,668	11,481	133,187	0	0	0	0
13	B-2 2 Bedroom, 2 Bath	647	319,798	25,894	293,904	0	0	0	0
14	C-1 3 Bedroom, 2 Bath	704	326,424	56,280	270,144	0	0	0	0
15									
16	Total Monthly Income	$91,735	$1,110,823	$126,207	$984,616	$0	$0	$0	$0
17									
18	New Rental Income		$91,736	$50,484	$41,252	$0	$0	$0	$0
19	Free Rent (2 Weeks)[e,f]	$0.50	45,871	25,243	20,628	0	0	0	0
20	Income after Free Rent		1,064,952	100,964	963,988	0	0	0	0
21	Normal Vacancy[g]	5.00%	25,139	0	25,139	0	0	0	0
22	Adjusted Gross Rent		$1,039,813	$100,964	$938,849	$0	$0	$0	$0
23									
24	Other Income	$25,000	$25,226	$2,867	$22,359	$0	$0	$0	$0
25									
26	Total Rental Income		$1,065,039	$103,831	$961,208	$0	$0	$0	$0
27									
28	Operating Expenses[h,i]	$2.65	414,465	88,000	326,465	0	0	0	0
29									
30	Net Operating Income		$650,574	$15,831	$634,743	$0	$0	$0	$0

Development Period Sources and Uses

			Year 1	Year 2	Month			
		Total	Total	Total	0	1	2	3
	Sources							
31	Equity[j]	($101,909)	$0	($101,909)	$0	$0	$0	$0
32	Equity from Equity Account[k]	1,000,000	1,000,000	0	798,081	201,919	0	0
33	Permanent Loan[l]	5,224,387		5,224,387	0	0	0	0
34	Construction Loan[m]	0	4,808,354	(4,808,354)	0	243,333	393,156	396,760
35	Interest Income	0	0	0		0	0	0
36	Net Operating Income	650,574	15,831	634,743		0	0	0
37	Total Sources	$6,773,052	$5,824,185	$948,867	$798,081	$445,252	$393,156	$396,760
38								
39	Uses[n,o]							
40	Land	$502,791	$502,791	$0	$502,791			

projects, depending on the length of development. It may run longer for office buildings, depending on when the permanent mortgage is funded and the building reaches stabilized occupancy and income.

The primary purpose of the monthly cash-flow analysis is to determine exactly how much equity will be required and to refine the estimates of interest reserves to cover construction and operating deficits during lease-up.

Month											
4	5	6	7	8	9	10	11	12	13	14	15
0	0	0	0	0	1	2	3	4	5	6	7
0	0	0	0	0	4	8	12	16	20	24	28
0	0	0	0	0	3	6	9	12	15	18	20
0	0	0	0	0	2	4	6	8	10	12	14
0	0	0	0	0	4	8	12	16	20	24	28
0	0	0	0	0	8	16	24	32	32	32	32
0	0	0	0	0	21	42	63	84	97	110	122
0.00%	0.00%	0.00%	0.00%	0.00%	13.29%	26.58%	39.87%	53.16%	61.39%	69.62%	77.22%
$0	$0	$0	$0	$0	$1,699	$3,398	$5,098	$6,797	$8,496	$10,195	$11,894
0	0	0	0	0	1,556	3,112	4,668	6,224	7,781	9,337	10,374
0	0	0	0	0	1,148	2,296	3,444	4,593	5,741	6,889	8,037
0	0	0	0	0	2,589	5,179	7,768	10,358	12,947	15,537	18,126
0	0	0	0	0	5,628	11,256	16,884	22,512	22,512	22,512	22,512
$0	$0	$0	$0	$0	$12,620	$25,241	$37,862	$50,484	$57,477	$64,470	$70,943
$0	$0	$0	$0	$0	$12,620	$12,621	$12,621	$12,622	$6,993	$6,993	$6,473
0	0	0	0	0	6,310	6,311	6,311	6,311	3,497	3,497	3,237
0	0	0	0	0	6,310	18,930	31,551	44,173	53,980	60,973	67,706
0	0	0	0	0	0	0	0	0	0	0	0
$0	$0	$0	$0	$0	$6,310	$18,930	$31,551	$44,173	$53,980	$60,973	$67,706
$0	$0	$0	$0	$0	$287	$573	$860	$1,147	$1,305	$1,464	$1,611
$0	$0	$0	$0	$0	$6,597	$19,503	$32,411	$45,320	$55,285	$62,437	$69,317
0	0	0	0	12,000	16,000	20,000	20,000	20,000	20,000	22,000	24,000
$0	$0	$0	$0	($12,000)	($9,403)	($497)	$12,411	$25,320	$35,285	$40,437	$45,317

Month											
4	5	6	7	8	9	10	11	12	13	14	15
$0	$0	$0	$0	$0	$0	$0	$0	$0	$0	($297,903)	$2,611
0	0	0	0	0	0	0	0	0	0	0	0
0	0	0	0	0	0	0	0	0	0	5,224,387	0
400,397	404,067	407,771	426,578	442,543	435,954	429,999	418,964	408,832	10,639	(4,818,993)	0
0	0	0	0	0	0	0	0	0	0	0	0
0	0	0	0	(12,000)	(9,403)	(497)	12,411	25,320	35,285	40,437	45,317
$400,397	$404,067	$407,771	$426,578	$430,543	$426,551	$429,502	$431,375	$434,152	$45,924	$147,928	$47,928

■ 4-21 (Continued)

Stage 4 analysis shows that a $1 million equity investment (line 79) is adequate. With this equity investment, the construction loan (line 75) does not reach its limit of $5,224,387 when it is retired by the permanent loan in month 14. At the end of month 24, the equity balance is $101,909 (line 89). Thus, the net equity investment at the end of the second year is $898,091 ($1,000,000 minus $101,909).

Operating Income and Expenses (Continued)

		Month								
		16	17	18	19	20	21	22	23	24
	Absorption[a] Lease-Up Month:	**8**	**9**	**10**	**11**	**12**	**13**	**14**	**15**	**16**
1	A-1 1 Bedroom, 1 Bath	32	36	36	36	36	36	36	36	36
2	A-2 1 Bedroom, Den, 1 Bath	20	20	20	20	20	20	20	20	20
3	B-1 2 Bedroom, 1 1/2 Bath	16	18	20	22	24	24	24	24	24
4	B-2 2 Bedroom, 2 Bath	32	36	40	44	46	46	46	46	46
5	C-1 3 Bedroom, 2 Bath	32	32	32	32	32	32	32	32	32
6	Total Units	132	142	148	154	158	158	158	158	158
7	Occupancy %	83.54%	89.87%	93.67%	97.47%	100.00%	100.00%	100.00%	100.00%	100.00%
8										
9	**Rental Income and Expenses**									
10	A-1 1 Bedroom, 1 Bath	$13,594	$15,293	$15,293	$15,293	$15,293	$15,293	$15,293	$15,293	$15,293
11	A-2 1 Bedroom, Den, 1 Bath	10,374	10,374	10,374	10,374	10,374	10,374	10,374	10,374	10,374
12	B-1 2 Bedroom, 1 1/2 Bath	9,185	10,333	11,482	12,630	13,778	13,778	13,778	13,778	13,778
13	B-2 2 Bedroom, 2 Bath	20,716	23,305	25,894	28,484	29,779	29,779	29,779	29,779	29,779
14	C-1 3 Bedroom, 2 Bath	22,512	22,512	22,512	22,512	22,512	22,512	22,512	22,512	22,512
15										
16	Total Monthly Income	$76,381	$81,817	$85,555	$89,293	$91,736	$91,736	$91,736	$91,736	$91,736
17										
18	New Rental Income	$5,438	$5,436	$3,738	$3,738	$2,443	$0	$0	$0	$0
19	Free Rent (2 Weeks)[e,f]	2,719	2,718	1,869	1,869	1,222	0	0	0	0
20	Income after Free Rent	73,662	79,099	83,686	87,424	90,514	91,736	91,736	91,736	91,736
21	Normal Vacancy[g]	0	0	0	2,204	4,587	4,587	4,587	4,587	4,587
22	Adjusted Gross Rent	$73,662	$79,099	$83,686	$85,220	$85,927	$87,149	$87,149	$87,149	$87,149
23										
24	Other Income	$1,735	$1,858	$1,943	$2,028	$2,083	$2,083	$2,083	$2,083	$2,083
25										
26	Total Rental Income	$75,397	$80,957	$85,629	$87,248	$88,010	$89,232	$89,232	$89,232	$89,232
27										
28	Operating Expenses[h,i]	26,000	28,000	29,495	29,495	29,495	29,495	29,495	29,495	29,495
29										
30	Net Operating Income	$49,397	$52,957	$56,134	$57,753	$58,515	$59,737	$59,737	$59,737	$59,737

Development Period Sources and Uses (Continued)

		Month								
		16	17	18	19	20	21	22	23	24
	Sources									
31	Equity[j]	($2,969)	($6,529)	($9,706)	($11,325)	($12,087)	($13,309)	($13,309)	($13,309)	$275,926
32	Equity from Equity Account[k]	0	0	0	0	0	0	0	0	0
33	Permanent Loan[l]	0	0	0	0	0	0	0	0	0
34	Construction Loan[m]	0	0	0	0	0	0	0	0	0
35	Interest Income	0	0	0	0	0	0	0	0	0
36	Net Operation Income	49,397	52,957	56,134	57,753	58,515	59,737	59,737	59,737	59,737
37	Total Sources	$46,428	$46,428	$46,428	$46,428	$46,428	$46,428	$46,428	$46,428	$335,663
38										
39	**Uses[n,o]**									
40	Land									

■ 4-21 (Continued)

Development Period Sources and Uses (Continued)

			Year 1	Year 2	Month			
		Total	Total	Total	0	1	2	3
41	Approval Fees	35,000	35,000	0	35,000			
42	Architectural and Engineering	55,000	55,000	0	20,000	35,000		
43	Construction	4,669,700	4,669,704	0		389,142	389,142	389,142
44	Models and Furnishings	10,000	10,000	0				
45	Marketing[p]	45,000	40,000	5,000				
46	Professional Fees	5,000	5,000	0	5,000			
47	Permanent Financing	182,854	182,854	0	182,854			
48	Land Interest	15,084	15,084	0	15,084			
49	Title Insurance	29,352	29,352	0	29,352			
50	Liability Insurance	10,000	10,000	0		10,000		
51	Property Taxes	10,000	10,000	0		10,000		
52	Audit Cost and Miscellaneous Expenses	8,000	8,000	0	8,000			
53	Development/General Partners Fee[q]	239,235	0	239,235				
54	Operating Contingency[r]	150,000	0	150,000				
55	Miscellaneous	0	0	0				
56	Miscellaneous	0	0	0		0	0	0
57	Subtotal	$5,967,020	$5,572,785	$394,235	$798,081	$444,142	$389,142	$389,142
58								
59	Construction Loan Interest[s,t]	$295,324	$251,400	$43,924	$0	$1,110	$4,014	$7,618
60	Permanent Loan Payment	510,708	0	510,708	0	0	0	0
61	Total Uses	$6,773,052	$5,824,185	$948,867	$798,081	$445,252	$393,156	$396,760
62								
63	Sources minus Uses[u]	$0	$0	$0	$0	$0	$0	$0

Loan and Equity Computations

				Year 1	Year 2	Start	Month		
			Total	Total	Total	Date	1	2	3
64	**Construction Loan**	$5,224,387							
65									
66	Beginning Balance			$0	$4,808,354	$0	$0	$243,333	$636,489
67	Draws before Interest		$4,523,669	4,556,954	(33,285)	0	242,223	389,142	389,142
68	Funding from Permanent[v]				(4,818,993)	0	0	0	0
69	Trial Ending Balance					0	242,223	632,475	1,025,631
70	Average Balance[w]					0	121,112	437,904	831,060
71	Interest	0.92%	$295,324	251,400	43,924	0	1,110	4,014	7,618
72	Draws after Interest					0	243,333	393,156	396,760
73	Trial Equity Balance after Interest					0	243,333	636,489	1,033,249
74	Interest Funded from Equity		$0	0	0	0	0	0	0
75	Ending Balance		4,818,993	4,808,354	0	0	243,333	636,489	1,033,249
76									
77	**Equity Funds**	$1,000,000							
78									
79	Additions to Equity[x]		$1,000,000	$1,000,000	$0	$1,000,000			
80	Interest Income on Investor Notes		0	0	0				
81	Infusion from Other Loans		0	0	0				$0
82	Beginning Balance		1,000,000	1,000,000	0	1,000,000	$201,919	$0	0
83	Draws		(1,278,537)	(1,000,000)	(278,537)	(798,081)	(201,919)	0	0
84	Repayments/Additions to Equity[y]		380,446	0	380,446	0	0	0	0
85	Trial Ending Balance		0	0	0	201,919	0	0	0
86	Investor Loan Funding	$0	0	0	0	0	0	0	0
87	Trial Ending Balance		101,909	0	101,909	201,919	0	0	0
88	Repayments of Investor Notes		0	0	0	0	0	0	0
89	Ending Balance[z]	$0	101,909	0	101,909	201,919	0	0	0
90	Average Balance		239,872	0	239,872	600,960	100,960	0	0
91	Interest Income[aa]	0.00%	0	0	0	0	0	0	0

■ 4-21 (Continued)

Development Period Sources and Uses (Continued)

		Month								
		4	5	6	7	8	9	10	11	12
41	Approval Fees									
42	Architectural and Engineering									
43	Construction	389,142	389,142	389,142	389,142	389,142	389,142	389,142	389,142	389,142
44	Models and Furnishings				5,000	5,000				
45	Marketing[p]				10,000	10,000	7,000	6,000	4,000	3,000
46	Professional Fees									
47	Permanent Financing									
48	Land Interest									
49	Title Insurance									
50	Liability Insurance									
51	Property Taxes									
52	Audit Cost and Miscellaneous Expenses									
53	Development/General Partners Fee[q]									
54	Operating Contingency[r]									
55	Miscellaneous									
56	Miscellaneous		0	0	0	0	0	0	0	0
57	Subtotal	$389,142	$389,142	$389,142	$404,142	$404,142	$396,142	$395,142	$393,142	$392,142
58										
59	Construction Loan Interest[s,t]	$11,255	$14,925	$18,629	$22,436	$26,401	$30,409	$34,360	$38,233	$42,010
60	Permanent Loan Payment	0	0	0	0	0	0	0	0	0
61	Total Uses	$400,397	$404,067	$407,771	$426,578	$430,543	$426,551	$429,502	$431,375	$434,152
62										
63	Sources Minus Uses[u]	$0	$0	$0	$0	$0	$0	$0	$0	$0

Loan and Equity Computations (Continued)

		Month								
		4	5	6	7	8	9	10	11	12
64	**Construction Loan**									
65										
66	Beginning Balance	$1,033,249	$1,433,646	$1,837,713	$2,245,484	$2,672,062	$3,114,605	$3,550,559	$3,980,558	$4,399,522
67	Draws before Interest	389,142	389,142	389,142	404,142	416,142	405,545	395,639	380,731	366,822
68	Funding from Permanent[v]	0	0	0	0	0	0	0	0	0
69	Trial Ending Balance	1,422,391	1,822,788	2,226,855	2,649,626	3,088,204	3,520,150	3,946,198	4,361,289	4,766,344
70	Average Balance[w]	1,227,820	1,628,217	2,032,284	2,447,555	2,880,133	3,317,378	3,748,379	4,170,924	4,582,933
71	Interest	11,255	14,925	18,629	22,436	26,401	30,409	34,360	38,233	42,010
72	Draws after Interest	400,397	404,067	407,771	426,578	442,543	435,954	429,999	418,964	408,832
73	Trial Equity Balance after Interest	1,433,646	1,837,713	2,245,484	2,672,062	3,114,605	3,550,559	3,980,558	4,399,522	4,808,354
74	Interest Funded from Equity	0	0	0	0	0	0	0	0	0
75	Ending Balance	1,433,646	1,837,713	2,245,484	2,672,062	3,114,605	3,550,559	3,980,558	4,399,522	4,808,354
76										
77	**Equity Funds**									
78										
79	Additions to Equity[x]									
80	Interest Income on Investor Notes									
81	Infusion from Other Loans					$0				
82	Beginning Balance	$0	$0	$0	$0	0	$0	$0	$0	$0
83	Draws	0	0	0	0	0	0	0	0	0
84	Repayments/Additions to Equity[y]	0	0	0	0	0	0	0	0	0
85	Trial Ending Balance	0	0	0	0	0	0	0	0	0
86	Investor Loan Funding	0	0	0	0	0	0	0	0	0
87	Trial Ending Balance	0	0	0	0	0	0	0	0	0
88	Repayments of Investor Notes	0	0	0	0	0	0	0	0	0
89	Ending Balance[z]	0	0	0	0	0	0	0	0	0
90	Average Balance	0	0	0	0	0	0	0	0	0
91	Interest Income[aa]	0	0	0	0	0	0	0	0	0

Month											
13	14	15	16	17	18	19	20	21	22	23	24
2,000	1,500	1,500									
	100,000										139,235
											150,000
0	0	0	0	0	0	0	0	0	0	0	0
$2,000	$101,500	$1,500	$0	$0	$0	$0	$0	$0	$0	$0	$289,235
$43,924	$0	$0	$0	$0	$0	$0	$0	$0	$0	$0	$0
0	46,428	46,428	46,428	46,428	46,428	46,428	46,428	46,428	46,428	46,428	46,428
$45,924	$147,928	$47,928	$46,428	$46,428	$46,428	$46,428	$46,428	$46,428	$46,428	$46,428	$335,663
$0	$0	$0	$0	$0	$0	$0	$0	$0	$0	$0	$0

Month											
13	14	15	16	17	18	19	20	21	22	23	24
$4,808,354	$4,818,993	$0	$0	$0	$0	$0	$0	$0	$0	$0	$0
(33,285)	0	0	0	0	0	0	0	0	0	0	0
0	4,818,993	0	0	0	0	0	0	0	0	0	0
4,775,069	0	0	0	0	0	0	0	0	0	0	0
4,791,712	0	0	0	0	0	0	0	0	0	0	0
43,924	0	0	0	0	0	0	0	0	0	0	0
10,639	0	0	0	0	0	0	0	0	0	0	0
4,818,993	0	0	0	0	0	0	0	0	0	0	0
0	0	0	0	0	0	0	0	0	0	0	0
4,818,993	0	0	0	0	0	0	0	0	0	0	0
							$0				
							0				
$0	$0	$297,903	$295,292	$298,261	$304,790	$314,496	$325,821	$337,908	$351,217	$364,526	$377,835
0	0	(2,611)	0	0	0	0	0	0	0	0	(275,926)
0	297,903	0	2,969	6,529	9,706	11,325	12,087	13,309	13,309	13,309	0
0	297,903	295,292	298,261	304,790	314,496	325,821	337,908	351,217	364,526	377,835	101,909
0	0	0	0	0	0	0	0	0	0	0	0
0	297,903	295,292	298,261	304,790	314,496	325,821	337,908	351,217	364,526	377,835	101,909
0	0	0	0	0	0	0	0	0	0	0	0
0	297,903	295,292	298,261	304,790	314,496	325,821	337,908	351,217	364,526	377,835	101,909
0	148,952	296,598	296,777	301,526	309,643	320,159	331,865	344,563	357,872	371,181	239,872

■ 4-21 (Continued)

Loan and Equity Computations (Continued)

			Total	Year 1 Total	Year 2 Total	Start Date	Month 1	Month 2	Month 3
92	**Permanent Loan**	$5,224,387							
93									
94	Interest Rate[bb]	10.15%							
95	Term	30							
96	Previously Funded		$5,201,146	$0	$5,201,146	$0	$0	$0	$0
97	Current Amount Funded[cc]		5,224,387	0	5,224,387	0	0	0	0
98	Total Funded		5,201,146	0	5,201,146	0	0	0	0
99	Monthly Payment		510,708	0	510,708	0	0	0	0
100	Ending Balance		5,198,711	0	5,198,711	0	0	0	0
101	Amortization		25,676	0	25,676	0	0	0	0
102	Interest		485,032	0	485,032	0	0	0	0
103									
104									
105	**Capitalized Interest Allocation**								
106									
107	Units with Certificate of Occupancy[dd]		158	100	58		0	0	0
108	Cumulative Percentage						0.00%	0.00%	0.00%
109	Adjusted Rental Income		$1,065,039	$103,831	$961,208		$0	$0	$0
110	Operating Expenses		414,465	88,000	326,465		0	0	0
111	Net Operating Income		650,574	15,831	634,743		0	0	0
112	Total Interest and Amortization		806,032	251,400	554,632		1,110	4,014	7,618
113	Construction Loan		295,324	251,400	43,924		1,110	4,014	7,618
114	Capitalized Interest[ee]		187,886	171,762	16,124		1,110	4,014	7,618
115	Operating Interest		107,438	79,638	27,800		0	0	0
116	Permanent Interest and Amortization		510,708	0	510,708		0	0	0

[a]The total inventory of space is listed by unit type.

[b]The number of units leased each month (absorbed by the market place).

[c]The first units are occupied nine months after construction. Note that certificates of occupancy must be received on the first phase of units (line 107) before they can be occupied.

[d]Base rent per unit per month.

[e]Rental concessions. Here, one-half of one month (two weeks) of free rent is assumed.

[f]Free rent ends after the last units are leased in Month 20.

[g]The normal vacancy rate (5 percent is assumed here) provides the upper limit to occupancy. Once the absorption schedule exceeds 95 percent occupancy, the difference above 95 percent is subtracted in the form of "normal vacancy."

[h]Operating expenses of $2.65 per square foot per annum are taken from the Stage 2 analysis. Normally, a more-refined figure would be available for the Stage 4 analysis.

[i]Operating expenses for the leasing office and manager's salary begin two to three months before initial occupancy.

[j]Beginning in Month 16, the project has positive cash flow from operations in every month. Month 24 is when the remaining development/general partner (G.P.) fee is paid.

[k]Here, the bank is assumed to require the developer to invest $1 million equity before the construction loan begins to fund (see note o). The amount of equity is determined from previous computer spreadsheets by assuming a zero equity account balance and computing the equity requirement in line 31. Some banks may allow the developer to invest the equity after the construction loan is fully funded if they are assured that the equity is available (the developer may post a letter of credit).

[l]The permanent-loan amount happens to exceed the construction-loan balance when it funds in Month 14. The difference is cash that goes back to the equity investors (line 84).

Equity: Joint Ventures and Syndications

Developers use a variety of joint venture formats to raise equity, provide loan guarantees, and secure financing. This section focuses on joint ventures with equity partners.

Syndications are a form of joint venture in which equity from a number of smaller investors is raised through either a private or a public offering subject to regulations of the Securities and Exchange Commission. Investors in syndications receive a security interest similar to that paid by stocks or bonds, whereas joint ventures between only a

Loan and Equity Computations (Continued)

Month										
4	5	6	7	8	9	10	11	12	13	14
$0	$0	$0	$0	$0	$0	$0	$0	$0	$0	$0
0	0	0	0	0	0	0	0	0	0	5,224,387
0	0	0	0	0	0	0	0	0	0	5,224,387
0	0	0	0	0	0	0	0	0	0	46,428
0	0	0	0	0	0	0	0	0	0	5,222,162
0	0	0	0	0	0	0	0	0	0	2,225
0	0	0	0	0	0	0	0	0	0	44,203
0	0	0	0	50	0	0	50	0	0	58
0.00%	0.00%	0.00%	0.00%	31.65%	31.65%	31.65%	63.29%	63.29%	63.29%	100.00%
$0	$0	$0	$0	$0	$6,597	$19,503	$32,411	$45,320	$55,285	$62,437
0	0	0	0	12,000	16,000	20,000	20,000	20,000	20,000	22,000
0	0	0	0	(12,000)	(9,403)	(497)	12,411	25,320	35,285	40,437
11,255	14,925	18,629	22,436	26,401	30,409	34,360	38,233	42,010	43,924	46,428
11,255	14,925	18,629	22,436	26,401	30,409	34,360	38,233	42,010	43,924	0
11,255	14,925	18,629	22,436	18,046	20,786	23,487	14,035	15,421	16,124	0
0	0	0	0	8,355	9,623	10,873	24,198	26,589	27,800	0
0	0	0	0	0	0	0	0	0	0	46,428

[m]The construction loan is used to fund cash requirements after the equity is invested.
[n]All expenditures made prior to the beginning of the spreadsheet are included under the "Start Date" column. Financing costs, for example, includes fees paid to the mortgage broker and construction and permanent lenders over several months preceding the start date of the analysis.
[o]All cash uses are entered into the spreadsheet in the month that the expenditure is expected to occur. Construction costs are divided here into 12 equal monthly installments. These estimates would later be refined as the anticipated draw schedule is determined.
[p]Marketing expenses for brochures begin at least two to three months before initial occupancy.
[q]The remaining development/G.P. fee is assumed to be paid in Month 24. The timing of this payment depends on the terms of the deal with the lender.
[r]The contingency is also assumed to be used in Month 24. Alternatively, it could be spread out over the construction or lease-up period. It should appear somewhere, however, or equity requirements will be understated.
[s]Construction-loan interest is computed in line 71.
[t]Total construction-loan interest is lower than that projected in the Stage 2 analysis even though the interest rate is higher (11 percent versus 10.5 percent) because here the construction loan begins to fund after $1 million equity is invested, whereas it is assumed to fund immediately in the Stage 2 analysis. Of course, these assumptions may be changed according to the deal. The differences between Stage 2 and Stage 4 analysis here reflect typical refinements in the developer's expectations about the deal as more information is collected over time.
[u]Sources minus uses of cash must equal zero.
[v]The construction-loan balance is paid off by the permanent loan.
[w]Assumes construction-loan draws are taken at midmonth (or equally during the month).

few parties typically, but not necessarily, involve direct real estate interests.

Every joint venture deal is unique. Nonetheless, certain formats are more common, such as those described by the following three developers during interviews held in 1987.

Harry Mow, president of Century West Development of Santa Monica, California, recommends "keeping it simple. If you cut too sharp a deal with your investors, you probably won't get them to invest in another deal." Mow, whose company does its own construction, adds a 15 percent fee to the hard and soft costs (excluding land

■ 4-21 (Continued)

Loan and Equity Computations (Continued)

Month 15	16	17	18	19	20	21	22	23	24
$5,222,162	$5,219,905	$5,217,628	$5,215,333	$5,213,018	$5,210,683	$5,208,329	$5,205,955	$5,203,561	$5,201,146
0	0	0	0	0	0	0	0	0	0
5,222,162	5,219,905	5,217,628	5,215,333	5,213,018	5,210,683	5,208,329	5,205,955	5,203,561	5,201,146
46,428	46,428	46,428	46,428	46,428	46,428	46,428	46,428	46,428	46,428
5,219,905	5,217,628	5,215,333	5,213,018	5,210,683	5,208,329	5,205,955	5,203,561	5,201,146	5,198,711
2,257	2,277	2,295	2,315	2,335	2,354	2,374	2,394	2,415	2,435
44,171	44,151	44,133	44,113	44,093	44,074	44,054	44,034	44,013	43,993
0	0	0	0	0	0	0	0	0	0
100.00%	100.00%	100.00%	100.00%	100.00%	100.00%	100.00%	100.00%	100.00%	100.00%
$69,317	$75,397	$80,957	$85,629	$87,248	$88,010	$89,232	$89,232	$89,232	$89,232
24,000	26,000	28,000	29,495	29,495	29,495	29,495	29,495	29,495	29,495
45,317	49,397	52,957	56,134	57,753	58,515	59,737	59,737	59,737	59,737
46,428	46,428	46,428	46,428	46,428	46,428	46,428	46,428	46,428	46,428
0	0	0	0	0	0	0	0	0	0
0	0	0	0	0	0	0	0	0	0
0	0	0	0	0	0	0	0	0	0
46,428	46,428	46,428	46,428	46,428	46,428	46,428	46,428	46,428	46,428

[x]The construction lender dictates when equity must be invested. Here, it is shown in Time 0.

[y]The investor's recovery of equity is equal to the difference between the permanent-loan funding ($5,224,387) and the construction-loan balance ($4,818,993) minus the difference between sources and uses:

Permanent loan	$5,224,387
Construction loan	–4,818,993
	$ 405,394
NOI—Month 14 (line 28)	40,437
Uses—Month 14 (line 61)	– 147,928
	– 107,491
Repayments/additions to equity	$ 297,903 (Month 14)

[z]The equity balance in Month 24 is the amount of equity left to return to the investors after the two-year "development period."

[aa]The developer usually earns interest (at short-term deposit rates) on the unused portion of the equity held in the equity account.

[bb]Terms of the permanent loan reflect the lower rate (10.15 percent) negotiated with the lender rather than the anticipated rate (10.5 percent) in Stage 2.

[cc]The permanent loan funds in Month 14.

[dd]The first 50 units are completed eight months into construction.

[ee]When units receive their certificates of occupancy, they are placed into operation for depreciation purposes. When this occurs, interest (whether from the construction loan or permanent loan) may be deducted currently rather than being capitalized. Capitalized construction interest must be amortized over the depreciable life of the building (27.5 years for residential buildings). Capitalized construction interest ($187,886) and construction- and permanent-loan interest and amortization related to operations ($107,438 plus $510,708 equals $618,146) are numbers required for the Stage 5 analysis.

and financing costs). The fee pays the superintendent, the project manager, corporate overheads, and the costs of raising equity. If the construction loan is sufficiently large to cover the cost, the 15 percent fee is paid in installments during construction. Otherwise, it is left in as a loan to the partnership until the property is sold.

Cash flow from operations and sale of the property is distributed in the following order of priority:

- First, the limited partners receive back their capital.
- Second, the limited partners receive a 6 percent cumulative return.

- Third, the limited partners and the general partners split the remainder equally. The developer also receives a 5 percent or 6 percent management fee and a 6 percent brokerage fee for selling the property.

Richard Gleitman, president, R.J. Investments Associates of Sherman Oaks, California, gives his equity partners—who tended initially to be friends and business associates—50 percent of the profits and an 8 percent noncumulative preferred return. He recovers all cash advances for a project from the equity partners when they make their initial investment. Gleitman creates the joint venture prior to the close of land escrow as soon as he has reliable financial projections. Gleitman's firm charges a minimal contractor's fee—2 to 3 percent of hard costs—and a larger management fee—4 to 5 percent—that helps cover the cost of using the largest, most-active outside broker in an area to sell a project.

In his first deal, Paul Schultheis, president, Real Property Investment, Inc. of Arcadia, California, raised $400,000 in cash, splitting profits 50/50 with investors after they received back their capital. Since he had no previous direct experience, Schultheis brought in a builder and a broker/marketing director as fellow general partners. He and his brother acquired the land, secured planning approvals, and performed the front-end work. The broker received 10 percent of the general partners' share of the deal; the three other partners received 30 percent each. Today, Schultheis gives neither the broker nor the builder any interest, as he is now able to pay for their services in cash.

Cumulative versus Noncumulative Preferred Returns

Equity investors in most joint ventures receive priority return of their investment, a cumulative or noncumulative preferred return, and 50 to 80 percent of the remaining profits. In the case of a *cumulative preferred return*, any unpaid preferred return in one period is accumulated until funds are available to pay it in a later period. A *noncumulative preferred return* does not accumulate in this fashion, and unpaid returns during a period of insufficient cash flow are left unpaid. Figure 4-23 shows how the cash flows and IRRs would differ for the same deal under the two different preferred-return structures. Both deals illustrate a 10 percent preferred return with a 50/50 split of the remaining profits. Note that the cumulative preferred return is accrued in Years 1 and 2 because the cash flows of $5,000 and $8,000 are insufficient to cover the 10 percent preferred return of $10,000; the outstanding sum is finally paid off in Year 5. Because of the accumulation provision, the total cash flow to the investor is $104,000, as compared to $100,500 in the noncumulative case. The investor's IRR is 17.02 percent, as compared to 16.60 percent. Note also that the developer's total cash flow is less in the cumulative case, $54,000 as

■ 4-22 Reconciliation between Stage 2 and Stage 4

The main purpose of Stage 4 analysis is to refine the interest calculations, which are crude approximations in Stage 2 analysis. Because several months usually pass between the time that Stage 2 and Stage 4 analysis is done, many of the cost assumptions are also refined during that period as actual expenditures occur and firm construction bids are received. To facilitate the comparison here, total capital costs are the same as in Stage 2 analysis:

Stage 2 Analysis:

Total project cost (line 78)	$6,658,761
Construction interest (line 54)	– 365,707
Operating reserve (line 74)	– 326,038
Total capital cost	$5,967,016

Stage 4 Analysis:

Uses subtotal (line 61)	$6,773,052
Construction-loan interest and permanent-debt service	– 806,032
Total capital cost (line 57)	$5,967,020

How to Interpret Stage 4 Results

What is the total project cost and how much equity will actually be needed?

Permanent mortgage	$5,224,387
Equity	1,000,000
Total investment	6,224,387
Equity balance (line 89, Month 24) (see note z)	– 101,909
Net investment	$6,122,478

The same figure for total cost can be reached by adding total capital cost and interest (minus NOI):

Total capital cost (from above)	$5,967,020
Construction interest (line 59)	295,324
Permanent-mortgage interest (line 60)	510,708
NOI (line 30)	– 650,574
Net investment	$6,122,478

opposed to $57,500, because the investor receives more from the same total project cash flows.

In some deals involving cumulative preferred returns, the "accrued return balance" earns interest. Many developers, however, prefer not to pay such interest because it further reduces their share of the proceeds without enhancing the marketability of their deals.

Investors' Chief Concerns

Investors are most concerned with the following five aspects of joint venture deals.

Preferred return yields. These yields have ranged from 10 to 12 percent in the highly inflationary years of the early 1980s to between 5 and 8 percent in 1991.

Share of residual profits. In deals sold privately and in joint ventures with financial institutions or large investors, profits are most commonly split 50/50 between the developer and investors. In public syndications, however, the profit split is usually 25/75 or 20/80 because those stockbrokers and financial planners who sell the deals claim that investors are reluctant to buy into projects that offer lower returns.

■ 4-23 Cumulative versus Noncumulative Preferred Returns

		Years						
		0	1	2	3	4	5	Total
	Project's Cash Flows							
1	Equity Investment	($100,000)						($100,000)
2	Cash Flows from Operations		$5,000	$8,000	$10,000	$15,000	$20,000	58,000
3	Cash Flows from Sale						200,000	200,000
4								
5	Total	($100,000)	$5,000	$8,000	$10,000	$15,000	$220,000	$158,000
6								
7	**Cumulative Preferred Return**							
8	Preferred Return Owed	10.00%	$10,000	$10,000	$10,000	$10,000	$10,000	$50,000
9	Preferred Return Paid		5,000	8,000	10,000	10,000	10,000	43,000
10	Unpaid Preferred Return		5,000	2,000	0	0	0	7,000
11								
12	Preferred Return Accrued		$5,000	$7,000	$7,000	$7,000	$2,000	
13	Accrued Return Paid		0	0	0	5,000	2,000	7,000
14	Accrued Return Balance		5,000	7,000	7,000	2,000	0	0
15								
16	Return of Equity		$0	$0	$0	$0	$100,000	$100,000
17	Equity Balance	100,000	100,000	100,000	100,000	100,000	0	0
18								
19	Cash Flow for Distribution		$0	$0	$0	$0	$108,000	$108,000
20	50% to Investor		0	0	0	0	54,000	54,000
21	50% to Developer		0	0	0	0	54,000	54,000
22								
23	Net Cash Flow to Investor	($100,000)	$5,000	$8,000	$10,000	$15,000	$166,000	$104,000
24	Investor's IRR	17.02%						
25								
26	**Noncumulative Preferred Return**							
27	Preferred Return Owed	10.00%	$10,000	$10,000	$10,000	$10,000	$10,000	$50,000
28	Preferred Return Paid		5,000	8,000	10,000	10,000	10,000	43,000
29	Unpaid Preferred Return		5,000	2,000	0	0	0	7,000
30								
31	Preferred Return Accrued		$0	$0	$0	$0	$0	
32	Accrued Return Paid		0	0	0	0	0	0
33	Accrued Return Balance		0	0	0	0	0	0
34								
35	Return of Equity		$0	$0	$0	$5,000	$95,000	$100,000
36	Equity Balance	$100,000	100,000	100,000	100,000	95,000	0	0
37								
38	Cash Flow for Distribution		$0	$0	$0	$0	$115,000	$115,000
39	50% to Investor		0	0	0	0	57,500	57,500
40	50% to Developer		0	0	0	0	57,500	57,500
41								
42	Net Cash Flow to Investor	($100,000)	$5,000	$8,000	$10,000	$15,000	$162,500	$100,500
43	Investor's IRR	16.60%						

Downside liabilities. Most syndications and joint ventures are structured as limited partnerships that restrict the downside liabilities of investors. Unless investors sign notes for more than their direct equity investment, their downside risk is limited to the loss of their equity.

Cash calls. Cash calls occur when a partnership requires additional equity from the investors to meet its obligations. More-sophisticated investors tend to be more concerned over the handling of cash calls.

Most partnership agreements have provisions that penalize partners for not making cash calls. For example, consider a partner, Smith, who has invested $50,000 out of a total equity of $100,000 for a 50 percent interest. Suppose there is a $10,000 cash call from each partner. Smith fails to come up with his $10,000, so the other partner must come up with $20,000. In a pro-rata dilution arrangement, the other partner would have invested $70,000 out of a total of $120,000, reducing Smith's interest to $50,000 out of $120,000, or 41.66 percent. A penalty clause might reduce Smith's ownership by, say, 1 percent for each $1,000 he fails to produce, giving him a 31.66 percent interest. In the extreme, although not uncommon, case, Smith could lose his entire interest.

Front-end fees. Front-end (or upfront) fees may fall into various categories such as construction management, development, leasing, syndication, organization, and fundraising fees. Because the categorization of fees has important tax consequences, developers should consult a specialist in real estate tax accounting to prepare the documents.[16]

The treatment of front-end fees differs considerably between private offerings and public syndications (including Regulation D private offerings to 35 or fewer "nonqualified" investors).[17] Stockbrokers and financial planners selling public syndications and Regulation D private offerings focus on the ratio of front-end fees to total equity raised and frequently will not offer a deal where front-end fees account for more than 25 percent of total equity. By comparison, in private joint ventures, front-end fees often exceed 25 percent of total equity. This is especially true of new apartment projects in which the developer also is the contractor. The construction fee alone may exceed 25 percent of the equity since it is based on total construction costs. For example, a 6 percent construction fee on a $1 million construction cost would be $60,000. If $200,000 equity were needed, this fee alone would be 30 percent of the equity raised.

The Advantages of Private Offerings

On the surface, public offerings and Regulation D syndications may appear to be better deals for the investor. However, for three reasons they usually tend not to be. First, developers dislike giving away more profits than necessary and so prefer to engage in private ventures. The deals sold by outside brokers are therefore commonly those for which the developer could not raise private money and may, consequently, be of dubious worth. Second, Regulation D offerings and public offerings involve much greater expense for legal work, due diligence, and broker commissions. Third, developers must make a certain level of profit or they will not stay in business. If they must take lower upfront fees and a lower share of residual profits, they usually compensate by "selling" the project to the syndication at a higher price.

For example, Harry Mow's company, Century West, packages deals in which the front-end load on a $1 million deal with 80 percent financing is 45 percent of the equity rather than the 25 percent figure preferred by syndicators. Figure 4-24 illustrates how a public or Regulation D private offering sold by a broker-dealer would differ from Mow's inhouse deal structure. The public syndication offering has a lower ratio of fees to equity but a

■ 4-24 Example of Front-End Fees for Two Types of Offerings

	In-House Private Offering	Public and Private Offerings Sold by Broker-Dealers
Land	$200,000	$200,000
Hard and Soft Costs (excluding land and financing)	600,000	670,000
Financing	110,000	110,000
Project Cost	$910,000	$980,000[a]
Front-End Fees	$ 90,000[b]	$ 50,000[c]
Total Cost	$1,000,000	$1,030,000
Less Mortgage (80%)	800,000	824,000
	$ 200,000	$ 206,000
Front-End Fees	$ 90,000	$ 50,000
Equity Raised	$200,000	$206,000
Ratio of Front-End Fees to Equity Raised	45.00%	24.27%
Profit Split		
General Partners	50.00%	20.00%
Limited Partners	50.00%	80.00%

[a]Cost is higher because the syndication purchases the project from the developer at a higher price to give the developer adequate profit.
[b]15 percent of hard and soft costs.
[c]Front-end fees are set arbitrarily to be less than 25 percent of equity raised.

4-25 Tips on Joint Ventures and Deal Packaging

- In drawing up the partnership agreement, be very clear as to the rights and duties of each partner. Use arbitration to solve disputes.
- Beware of "dilution squeeze-down" provisions that allow the investors to squeeze the developer out if a project does not generate a given level of current return.
- Some developers recommend overborrowing if possible because it allows them to withdraw money from a project without tax. However, overborrowing increases the risk of default.
- Make sure that investors have no right to tell the developer how to run the project.
- If investors commit money to be paid in the future, make sure that the money is available by persuading the investors to post letters of credit.

higher total project price to the partnership, and therefore higher risks to the investors.

In addition to the higher front-end load in private offerings, Century West receives 50 percent of the residual profits after the investor receives a 6 percent preferred return. Despite the seemingly higher fees, Century West's deals have been very well received by investors who appreciate the opportunity to buy into projects at cost rather than at a higher price that includes development profit.

Economically speaking, the ratio of front-end fees to total equity raised is much less important than the investor's expected returns. Unfortunately, brokers, financial planners, and others who sell real estate securities focus on such ratios rather than on the likelihood that investors will achieve certain levels of return. Nevertheless, as long as real estate securities are marketed incorrectly, developers must package their deals to raise the equity.

Stage 5: Joint Ventures and Syndications

The major purpose of Stage 5 analysis is to determine how developers can best structure deals for raising equity. Developers must give investors sufficient return to attract them (and perhaps more to encourage their reinvestment in other deals) and still retain the largest possible share of the profits.

Stage 5 analysis comes in two different types. The simpler form, an extension of the Stage 2 DCF analysis, should always be performed because it provides developers with most of the information that they need. The before-tax cash flows to the investors are computed (using a format similar to that presented in figure 4-23) from the overall cash flows to the property. The before-tax cash flows from operations and sale are allocated according to the priorities of the proposed deal structure, and a before-tax IRR is computed for the investors. This return should probably be at least 15 percent, unless unusual tax benefits, such as those for historic structures or low-income housing, are involved.

The complex form of Stage 5 analysis adds the following information to the simple form:

- after-tax cash flows and IRRs;
- exact timing of investment;
- installment payments, if made;
- interest on installment notes, if made;
- record of capital accounts; and
- accurate taxable-income allocations.

The resulting information gives an accurate representation of the after-tax benefits to an investor and can be used for private-placement memorandums or brochures presenting public offerings. Customarily, such memorandums and brochures include a disclaimer from the accountant who has helped prepare the material that the sources for the numbers have not been verified. Despite this disclaimer, the involvement of an accountant lends credibility to the offering package and is mandatory if the package is to be sold through a broker-dealer[18] or other outside agent. (See pages 184 through 194 for an example of Stage 5 analysis.)

Construction

General contracting is a distinct business from development (see chapter 2 for a general discussion of construction contractors). Many general contractors engage in development, and many developers, especially of residential products, engage in construction; nonetheless, they are two different businesses, each with its own set of risks and rewards. In general, if a project makes economic sense only if the developer can earn a contractor's profit, then it is not worth pursuing. Many projects that developers undertook to keep their contracting organizations busy have led those developers into bankruptcy.

Most of the major difficulties faced by developers who perform their own construction arise from the fact that they must run another business—a labor- and detail-intensive business—that leaves them insufficient time to pay adequate attention to their development activities.[19] Most of the major benefits stem from developers' ability to take care of construction problems rapidly and to exercise control over change-order costs. It may also be noted that construction offers a relatively easy entry into development; many homebuilders draw effectively on their construction background to make the transition into apartment development.

For example, Terry Lewis, a Dallas apartment developer, began his development career as the construction partner with three other partners in a development complex. Later, after starting his own development company, he was invited to joint venture with money partners in several other projects because he had a construction arm. Lewis admits that construction helped pay the bills when funds for development dried up in Dallas in 1986. However, he also looks forward to getting out of construction as soon as development opportunities improve because construction takes so much time away from his pursuit of more-profitable development deals.

Residential construction differs from nonresidential construction in many ways. Typically, residential construction involves smaller subcontractors, a smaller scale of construction, and a less-skilled, nonunion workforce. The architect's role is also more limited in residential than in nonresidential development. Usually, the architect is not involved in the residential bidding process, nor does the architect manage the subcontractors' work for compliance with plans and specs. Any time that the architect does spend is usually priced on a time basis instead of a fixed-fee basis, thus raising costs for developers who keep changing their minds.

Managing and Scheduling the Job

Delays are the norm rather than the exception in construction. Most problems occur around scheduling different subcontractors or material deliveries, hence the importance of employing a good construction manager who can monitor the work of subcontractors as well as deal with the architects, engineers, and city inspectors. A job superintendent—ideally, one with a least two or three years' experience on comparable projects—should always be on site to prevent subcontractors from leaving during the day and to settle disputes between subcontractors regarding issues such as responsibility for cleaning up.

One benefit of developing multifamily residential projects containing several buildings rather than one large building is that, with proper scheduling, the first units can be occupied and producing income well before the last units are completed. The contractor can facilitate early completions by paying subcontractors on the basis of buildings completed rather than on percentage-of-contract completed. The subcontractors, on the other hand, may prefer to run their crews from building to building. For example, a framing contractor may prefer to frame the first story of all buildings before starting the second story. Therefore, the developer may need to negotiate a rolling completion schedule as part of the subcontractor's contract.

Niles Bolton & Associates

Effective design and construction require coordination between many players, including designers, construction managers, and subcontractors. The above is an example of poor entrance and drainage design that could have been avoided if the landscape architect had reviewed the engineering plans.

Inspections

Construction involves numerous inspections, all of which must be correctly performed if the developer/contractor is to guard against liability. In addition to city building inspectors, an outside inspector is usually required by the construction lender to verify that work is completed in conformance with plans and specs. The developer should ask the lender for recommendations for an inspector and then consult with other builders on that inspector's reputation. Most lenders will cooperate with a developer to find a mutually agreeable inspector.

Jerome Frank, Sr., head of Jerome Frank Investments in Dallas, recommends that developers hire an outside inspector on any project above $2 million, even if the bank does not require it. Inspectors not only protect developers and the bank from lawsuits by independently verifying that work is correctly performed, but also help to provide pressure to ensure that the work of subcontractors conforms to plans.

On government-funded projects, such as those funded by the U.S. Department of Housing and Urban Development, a government inspector may work on the site. When changes or additional requirements are made in the middle of a job, Frank advises: "Never do work unless you get a change order approved by the proper authorities or you will never get paid for it."

Frank asserts that developers must undertake several inspections in order to protect themselves, including an independent engineering inspection of all foundations (to check that they are level and correctly located and elevated and to test the strength of cable tendons and concrete), and a verification that soil compaction has

■ 4-26 Stage 5 Analysis: Structuring The Equity Syndication

The purpose of Stage 5 analysis is to determine the returns that individual participants will receive if they invest in a limited partnership or joint venture for a project. The analysis takes the cash flows calculated for the entire project in Stage 2 and allocates them to the developer and investors according to each party's share of the deal.

Although Stage 5 analysis may be used in formal presentations designed to attract investors, developers use it primarily to structure their deals. Initially, developers may only focus on before-tax cash flows to determine how much preferred return or the percentage of profits they must give away to attract the necessary equity. Ultimately, they will also undertake after-tax analysis like that shown here to determine the actual after-tax rates of return. Because of the complexity of Stage 5 analysis and frequent changes in the tax law, a tax accountant should check the results before developers use them to solicit investors.

Stage 5 analysis often is performed immediately after Stage 2 analysis, when developers are trying to structure the best way

Project Costs

			Years	
		Total	0	1
	Development Costs[a]			
1	Land Cost	$502,791	$502,791	
2	Land Carry	15,084	15,084	
3	Approval Fees	35,000	35,000	
4	Architectural and Engineering	55,000	55,000	
5	Building Construction[b]	4,435,700		4,435,700
6	Personal Property, Models and Furniture	244,000		244,000
7	Marketing	45,000		40,000
8	Loan Fees: Construction	52,244	52,244	
9	Loan Fees: Permanent and Attorney	130,610	130,610	
10	Professional Fees, Insurance, Audit, Miscellaneous	52,352	42,352	10,000
11	Property Taxes during Construction	10,000		10,000
12	Development/General Partner Fee	239,235		239,235
13	Operating Contingency[c]	150,000		
14	Subtotal	$5,967,016	$833,081	$4,978,935
15				
16	Capitalized Construction Interest	$187,887		$171,763
17	Cost Subtotal	$6,154,903	$833,081	$5,150,698
18				
19	**Cash Deficit from Operations**			
20	Net Operating Income	$650,577		$15,833
21	Less Contingency	(150,000)		
22	Construction-Loan Interest	(107,439)		(79,639)
23	Permanent Debt Service	(510,707)		
24	Operating Deficit	($117,569)	$0	($63,806)
25				
26	Cash for Operating Deficits	$117,569	$0	$63,806
27	Partnership Accounting and Management	20,000		10,000
28	Less Cash for Contingency	(150,000)		
29	Cash Balance[d]	81,916		
30	Total Project Cost[e]	$6,224,388	$833,081	$5,224,504
	Costs of Raising Equity[f]			
31	Underwriting	$90,000	$90,000	
32	Syndication Cost[g]	20,000	20,000	
33	Organization Cost[g]	30,000	30,000	
34	Tax Planning[g]	10,000	10,000	
35		$150,000	$150,000	$0
36				
37	Total Uses	$6,374,388	$983,081	$5,224,504
38				
39	Financing:			
40	Permanent Loan[h]	$5,224,387		
41	Equity	1,150,000		
42	Total Sources	$6,374,387		

to raise the necessary debt and equity. However, the final version of Stage 5 analysis usually is performed after Stage 4. It incorporates the more-accurate interest reserve and equity estimates generated by monthly cash-flow analysis in Stage 4.

The figures used in the accompanying spreadsheet are taken from the example of Stage 4 analysis in figure 4-21 combined with the operating-period cash flows of Stage 2 analysis.

The before-tax and after-tax returns on equity are the major decision variables computed by the Stage 5 analysis. The returns in this example show that the limited partners would receive a before-tax IRR of 24.25 percent (line 178) and an after-tax IRR of 20.23 percent (line 189). These returns are competitive with other investment opportunities of similar risk and compare favorably to after-tax Treasury-bill rates in 1989 of around 6 percent. A three-year scheduled pay-in by investors produces an after-tax IRR of 22.63 percent (line 214).

Year					
2	3	4	5	6	7
5,000					
150,000					
$155,000	$0	$0	$0	$0	$0
$16,124					
$171,124	$0	$0	$0	$0	$0
$634,744					
(150,000)					
(27,800)					
(510,707)					
($53,763)	$0	$0	$0	$0	$0
$53,763					
10,000					
(150,000)					
81,916					
$166,803	$0	$0	$0	$0	$0
$0	$0	$0	$0	$0	$0
$166,803	$0	$0	$0	$0	$0

■ 4-26 (Continued)

			Total	Years 0	Years 1

Taxable Income Calculation

			Total	0	1
	Income				
43	Scheduled Net Operating Income[i]		$4,850,054	$0	$15,833
44	Less Contingency		150,000		0
45	Net Operating Income		$4,700,054	$0	$15,833
46	Interest Income[j]		0		0
47	Total Income		$4,700,054	$0	$15,833
48					
49	**Deductions**				
50	Partnership Accounting and Management[k]		$70,000		$10,000
51	Interest on Construction Loan		107,439		79,639
52	Interest on Permanent Loan		3,079,783		
53					
54	Depreciation and Amortization[l]				
55	Building, Architectural, and Approvals	27.5	$980,568		
56	Personal Property[m]	7	191,714		
57	Marketing Expenses		45,000		$40,000
58	Loan Fees: Construction[n]	1	52,244		52,244
59	Loan Fees: Permanent[n]	30	26,122		
60	Professional Fees, Insurance, Etc.	1	52,352		52,352
61	Property Taxes—Construction	27.5	2,167		
62	Development Fee/Leasing	2	100,000		50,000
63	Development Fee/Capitalized	27.5	30,168		
64	Organization Cost	5	30,000		
65	Tax Planning	5	10,000		
66	Capitalized Construction Interest[o]	27.5	40,709		
67	Total Depreciation and Amortization		$1,561,044	$0	$194,596
68	Total Deductions		4,818,266	0	284,235
69	Taxable Income		($118,212)	$0	($268,402)
70					
71	**Taxable Income Share**				
72	Limited Partners[p]	99%	($117,030)	$0	($265,718)
73	General Partners	1%	(1,182)	0	(2,684)

Annual Cash Flows

			Total	0	1
	Before-Tax Cash Flows				
74	Total Income		$4,700,054	$0	$15,833
75	Construction Interest for Operations		107,439		79,639
76	Permanent Debt Service		3,296,380		
77	Net Cash Flow before Reserves		$1,296,235		(63,806)
78	Plus Reserves		0		0
79	Cash Throwoff		$1,296,235	0	(63,806)
80	Less Partnership Accounting and Management		70,000		10,000
81	Cash from Equity Account		137,569		73,806
82	Net Cash Throwoff		$1,363,804	0	0
83	Less Preferred Return Paid[q]		(309,927)		0
84	Less Arrearage Paid		(42,723)		0
85	Subtotal		$1,011,154		0
86	Repayment of Equity		1,011,154		0
87	Cash for Distribution		$0		$0
88	Limited Partners[r]	65%	0		0
89	General Partner	35%	0		0

Year					
2	3	4	5	6	7
$634,744	$775,337	$806,351	$838,605	$872,149	$907,035
150,000					
$484,744	$775,337	$806,351	$838,605	$872,149	$907,035
0					
$484,744	$775,337	$806,351	$838,605	$872,149	$907,035
$10,000	$10,000	$10,000	$10,000	$10,000	$10,000
27,800					
485,018	526,258	522,974	519,340	515,321	510,873
$157,714	$164,571	$164,571	$164,571	$164,571	$164,571
17,429	34,857	34,857	34,857	34,857	34,857
5,000					
4,354	4,354	4,354	4,354	4,354	4,354
348	364	364	364	364	364
50,000					
4,852	5,063	5,063	5,063	5,063	5,063
6,000	6,000	6,000	6,000	6,000	
2,000	2,000	2,000	2,000	2,000	
6,548	6,832	6,832	6,832	6,832	6,832
$254,244	$224,041	$224,041	$224,041	$224,041	$216,041
777,062	760,298	757,014	753,381	749,361	736,914
($292,318)	$15,039	$49,337	$85,224	$122,788	$170,121
($289,395)	$14,888	$48,843	$84,372	$121,560	$168,420
(2,923)	150	493	852	1,228	1,701
$484,744	$775,337	$806,351	$838,605	$872,149	$907,035
27,800					
510,707	557,135	557,135	557,135	557,135	557,135
(53,763)	218,202	249,216	281,470	315,014	349,900
0	0	0	0	0	0
(53,764)	218,202	249,216	281,470	315,014	349,900
10,000	10,000	10,000	10,000	10,000	10,000
63,763					
0	208,202	239,216	271,470	305,014	339,900
0	(85,447)	(79,044)	(66,230)	(49,811)	(29,395)
0	(42,723)	0	0	0	0
0	80,033	160,172	205,240	255,203	310,506
0	80,033	160,172	205,240	255,203	310,506
$0	$0	$0	$0	$0	$0
0	0	0	0	0	0
0	0	0	0	0	0

■ 4-26 (Continued)

				Years	
			Total	0	1
90					
91	**Preferred Return Calculation**				
92	Partner Investment[s]			$1,150,000	$0
93	Repayment of Unused Equity		($81,916)		0
94	Beginning Partner Balance			1,150,000	1,150,000
95	Repayment of Equity				
96	Partner Balance after Equity Repayment				
97	Preferred Return Owed[t]	8%	352,650		0
98	Preferred Return Paid		309,927		0
99	Arrearage Paid		42,723		0
100	Arrearage Balance		0		0
101					
102	**Permanent Mortgage Calculations**			Interest	
103	Permanent Loan Terms:		Amount	Rate	Term
104	Loan Terms		$5,224,387	10.15%	30
105	Months since Funding				
106	Ending Balance				
107	Amortization				
108	Interest				
109	Annual Debt Service		46,428 Monthly	Payment	

Gains from Sale

	Cash Flows from Sale		
110	Sales Price[u]	9%	$10,078,167
111	Selling Expenses	6%	604,690
112	Adjusted Sales Price		$9,473,477
113	Less Mortgage Balance		(5,007,790)
114	Cash Flow From Sale		$4,465,686
115			
116	Return of Investor Equity[v]		$56,930
117	Preferred Return Arrearage		0
118	Balance for Distribution		$4,408,756
119			
120	Cash to Limited Partners	65%	$2,865,691
121	Cash to General Partners	35%	1,543,065
122			
123	Total to Limited Partners		$2,922,622
124	Total to General Partners		1,543,065
125			
126	**Taxes from Sale**		
127	Remaining Basis Calculation		**Total**
128	Cost Subtotal		$6,154,903
129	Operating Contingency[w]		(150,000)
130	Costs of Raising Equity		150,000
131	Net Basis		$6,154,903
132	Total Depreciation and Amortization Taken[x]		1,561,044
133			
134	Remaining Book Value		$4,593,859
135			
136	**Gain from Sale**		**Year 7**
137	Adjusted Sales Price[y]		$9,473,477
138	Remaining Book Value		4,593,859
139	Total Taxable Gain		$4,879,617
140	Less Capital Gain Chargeback:		
141	Limited Partners[z]		$469,680
142	General Partners		1,182
143	Unallocated Gain		$4,408,755
144	Limited Partners	65%	2,865,691
145	General Partners	35%	1,543,064

Year					
2	3	4	5	6	7
$0					
(81,916)	$0	$0	$0	$0	$0
1,068,084	1,068,084	988,051	827,879	622,639	367,436
0	80,033	160,172	205,240	255,203	310,506
1,068,084	988,051	827,879	622,639	367,436	56,930
42,723	85,447	79,044	66,230	49,811	29,395
0	85,447	79,044	66,230	49,811	29,395
0	42,723	0	0	0	0
42,723	0	0	0	0	0
11	23	35	47	59	71
$5,198,698	$5,167,821	$5,133,660	$5,095,866	$5,054,052	$5,007,790
25,689	30,877	34,161	37,794	41,814	46,261
485,018	526,258	522,974	519,340	515,321	510,873
510,707	557,135	557,135	557,135	557,135	557,135
					$10,078,167
					604,690
					9,473,477
					(5,007,790)
					4,465,686
					$56,930
					0
					4,408,756
					$2,865,691
					1,543,065
					2,922,622
					1,543,065

4-26 (Continued)

No.	Item		Total	Years 0	Years 1
	Capital Accounts[aa]				
	Limited Partners				
146	Contributions		$1,150,000	$1,150,000	
147	Less Return of Capital		81,916	0	$0
148	Less Annual Cash Distributions		1,363,804	0	0
149	Less Annual Taxable Loss		117,030	0	265,718
150	Capital Account Balance		(412,750)	1,150,000	884,282
151	Less Return of Equity		56,930		
152	Less Preferred Return Arrearage		0		
153	Capital Account Balance		($469,680)		
154					
155	Capital Gain Chargeback		$469,680		
156	Unallocated Gain	4,408,755			
157	Gain Allocation[bb]	65%	2,865,691		
158	Less Cash from Sale[cc]		(2,865,691)		
159	Capital Account Balance		$0		
160					
161	**General Partners**				
162	Contributions		$0	$0	$0
163	Less Return of Capital		0		
164	Less Annual Cash Distributions		0	0	0
165	Less Annual Taxable Loss		1,182	0	2,684
166	Capital Account Balance		($1,182)	$0	($2,684)
167					
168	Capital Gain Chargeback		$1,182		
169	Unallocated Gain	4,408,755			
170	Gain Allocation	35%	1,543,064		
171	Less Cash to General Partner[cc]		(1,543,065)		
172	Capital Account Balance		$0		
	Investor Returns				
173	Partner Investment		($1,150,000)	($1,150,000)	
174	Repayment of Unused Equity		81,916	0	$0
175	Total Annual Cash Flows to Limited Partner[dd]		1,363,804	0	0
176	Total Cash from Sale before Tax[ee]		2,922,622		
177	Net Cash Flows before Tax		$3,218,342	($1,150,000)	$0
178	IRR before Tax[ff]		24.25%		
179	Calculation of After-Tax Cash Flows and IRR				
180	Equity Investment		($1,068,084)	(1,150,000)	
181	Annual Cash Flows to Limited Partner		1,363,804		0
182	Tax[gg]	28%	$0	$0	$0
183					
184	Annual Cash Flows after Tax		$295,720	($1,150,000)	$0
185	Cash Flow before Tax from Sale[hh]		2,922,622		
186	Tax on Gain from Sale[ii]		901,136		
187					
188	After-Tax Cash Flow		$2,317,206	($1,150,000)	$0
189	IRR after Tax[jj]		20.23%		
190					
191	Tax Computation				
192	Taxable Income to Limited Partner[kk]		($117,030)		($265,718)
193	Less Carryforward Offset[ll]		438,083		0
194					
195	Net Taxable Income		($555,113)		($265,718)
196	Tax	28%	0		0

Year					
2	3	4	5	6	7
$81,916	$0	$0	$0	$0	$0
0	208,202	239,216	271,470	305,014	339,900
289,395	(14,888)	(48,843)	(84,372)	(121,560)	(168,420)
512,971	319,657	129,284	(57,815)	(241,269)	(412,750)
					56,930
					0
					(469,680)
					469,680
					4,408,755
					2,865,691
					(2,865,691)
					$0
$0	$0	$0	$0	$0	$0
0	0	0	0	0	0
2,923	(150)	(493)	(852)	(1,228)	(1,701)
($5,607)	($5,457)	($4,963)	($4,111)	($2,883)	($1,182)
					1,182
					4,408,755
					1,543,064
					(1,543,065)
					0
$81,916	$0	$0	$0	$0	$0
0	208,202	239,216	271,470	305,014	339,900
					2,922,622
$81,916	$208,202	$239,216	$271,470	$305,014	$3,262,522
81,916					
0	208,202	239,216	271,470	305,014	339,900
$0	$0	$0	$0	$0	$0
$81,916	$208,202	$239,216	$271,470	$305,014	$339,900
					2,922,622
					901,136
$81,916	$208,202	$239,216	$271,470	$305,014	$2,361,386
($289,395)	$14,888	$48,843	$84,372	$121,560	$168,420
0	14,888	48,843	84,372	121,560	168,420
($289,395)	$0	$0	$0	$0	$0
0	0	0	0	0	0

			Total	Years 0	Years 1
197	Passive Loss Carryforward		(117,030)		
198					
199	Total Gain from Sale[mm]				
200	Less Passive Loss Carryforward				
201	Net Gain from Sale				
202	Tax	28%			

Investor Financing

203	Cash Investment[nn]	3	$1,150,000	$383,333	$383,333
204	Balance			766,667	383,333
205	Interest on Balance	12%	138,000	0	92,000
206	Tax Savings	28%	38,640	0	25,760
207	Return of Unused Equity		81,916	0	0
208	Net Investment		1,167,444	383,333	449,573
209	After-Tax Cash Flows		3,385,290		0
210	Combined with Net Investment		2,217,846	(383,333)	(449,573)
211	Number of Units	25			
212	Per-Unit Cash Flows		$88,714	($15,333)	($17,983)
213					
214	After-Tax IRR[oo]		22.63%		

Investment Returns on a $46,000 Unit[pp]

219								Net
220		Per Unit	Investor	Note Tax	Before-Tax	Tax	After-Tax	After-Tax
221	Year	Investment	Note Interest	Savings	Cash Flow	On Sale	Cash Flow	Cash Flows
222								
223	0	($15,333)	$ 0	$ 0	$ 0	$ 0	$ 0	($15,333)
224	1	(15,333)	(3,680)	1,030	0	0	0	(17,983)
225	2	(15,333)	(1,840)	515	3,277	0	3,277	(13,381)
226	3	0	0	0	8,328	0	8,328	8,328
227	4	0	0	0	9,569	0	9,569	9,569
228	5	0	0	0	10,859	0	10,859	10,859
229	6	0	0	0	12,201	0	12,201	12,201
230	7	0	0	0	130,501	(36,045)	94,455	94,455
231								
232	Total	($46,000)	($5,520)	$1,546	$174,734	($36,045)	$138,688	$88,714
233				qq	rr		ss	
234				After-Tax IRR	22.63%			

[a]Project costs are entered in the year in which they occur.

[b]Construction costs of $4,669,700 in Stage 4 are divided into building construction ($4,435,700) and personal property ($234,000). Models and furnishings ($10,000) are also considered personal property, bringing the total to $244,000.

[c]The contingency is assumed to be spent in Year 2.

[d]$81,916 is returned to the partners at the end of Year 2. It is the cash balance in Month 24 ($101,916 in Stage 4) minus $20,000 for partnership accounting and management expenses not included in the Stage 4 computation.

[e]Total project cost is the sum of lines 17, 26, 27, and 29 less line 28.

[f]All costs associated with raising the equity are enumerated separately. Underwriting costs represent brokerage commissions for raising the equity ($90,000 commissions represents 7.8 percent of $1,500,000 equity raised). Commissions typically run 6 percent to 10 percent of the total equity raised, depending on the size of the broker organization that is required.

[g]Syndication costs, organization expenses, and tax planning cover legal work, printing, due diligence, and accounting expenses.

[h]See line 104 for loan terms.

[i]NOI for Years 1 and 2 is taken from Stage 4. NOI for Years 3 through 7 is taken from Stage 2 analysis.

[j]Interest income may be earned on equity held by the partnership in interest-bearing accounts until it is required by the project.

Year					
2	3	4	5	6	7
(555,113)	(540,224)	(491,381)	(407,009)	(215,449)	117,030
					$3,335,371
					(117,030)
					3,218,314
					901,136
$383,333	$0	$0	$0	$0	$0
0	0	0	0	0	0
46,000	0	0	0	0	0
12,880	0	0	0	0	0
81,916	0	0	0	0	0
334,537	0	0	0	0	0
0	208,202	239,216	271,470	305,014	2,361,386
(334,537)	208,202	239,216	271,470	305,014	2,361,386
($13,381)	$8,328	$9,569	$10,859	$12,201	$94,455

[k]The partnership has annual accounting expenses that are not included in the project-level cash flows of Stages 2 or 4.

[l]The tax code specifies the period over which various items must be amortized or depreciated. In most cases, the write-off begins when the building is "placed in service" (when the certificate of occupancy is received).

[m]Personal property is amortized over seven years as compared to the 27.5 years for a residential building.

[n]Loan fees for construction and permanent loans are listed separately because construction-loan fees may be amortized over the life of the construction loan, whereas permanent-loan fees must be amortized over the life of the permanent loan.

[o]Construction interest and property taxes must be capitalized and amortized over the building's depreciable life (27.5 years for residential buildings).

[p]Here the limited partners receive 99 percent and the general partners receive 1 percent of the taxable income during operations.

[q]An 8 percent preferred return is paid when sufficient cash is available. Preferred returns are accrued when cash is insufficient.

[r]After the limited partners recover their equity investment and the preferred return is paid, the remaining cash flow is distributed, 65 percent to the limited partners and 35 percent to the general partners.

[s]Partner investment is the sum of $1,000,000 equity required for the property plus $150,000 cost to raise the equity.

[t]The illustrated deal is structured so that partners begin to receive a preferred return after 18 months, when the property is expected to generate positive cash flows.

[u]The sales price is taken from Stage 2. The sales price is determined by capitalizing the NOI in Year 7 at 9 percent.

[v]After paying off the mortgage, the investors first receive back their remaining equity investment plus any preferred-return arrearage.

[w]The operating contingency was deducted for income-tax purposes in Year 2; therefore, it is excluded from the cost basis when computing the gain on sale.

[x]Total depreciation and amortization taken over the seven-year holding period is computed in line 67.

[y]The adjusted sales price is from line 112.

[z]Capital gain chargeback is calculated in line 155 for limited partners and line 168 for general partners.

[aa]Capital accounts represent a running total of the net dollars that partners have invested in the project at any given time. Capital accounts are increased by new equity investment, cash infusion to cover operating losses, and taxable income; they are decreased by repayment of equity and taxable losses. The Internal Revenue Service looks at capital accounts to determine whether or not a fair allocation of taxable income has been accomplished. When the project is sold, the capital accounts should equal zero after all cash has been disbursed and all taxable income has been properly allocated. In deals in which they have enjoyed the major benefits (usually 99 percent) of tax losses during operations, capital accounts have the effect of raising the share of taxable gain-at-sale that limited partners must absorb.

[bb]From line 144. If the gain allocation is properly computed, it will equal the cash from sale to the limited partners (line 120) so that the capital account equals zero.

[cc]Cash from sale is calculated at line 120 for the limited partners and at line 121 for the general partners.

[dd]Total annual cash flow is shown at line 82. In this example, all of the net cash throwoff is distributed to the limited partners.

[ee]Total cash flow from sale before tax is calculated at line 123.

[ff]The before-tax IRR to the limited partners is 24.25 percent.

[gg]The income tax related to income from operations is calculated at line 196.
[hh]Total cash from sale before tax is found at line 123.
[ii]The income tax related to income from the sale of the project is calculated at line 202.
[jj]The after-tax IRR is a competitive 20.23 percent.
[kk]The taxable income allocated to limited partners is computed at line 72.
[ll]Under the 1986 Tax Reform Act, real estate income is considered passive income. Passive losses may be offset against passive income but otherwise must be deferred until the property generates passive income or is sold. Here, it is assumed that the investors do not have other passive income. Passive losses are carried forward until Years 3 through 7, when they are used to offset current taxable income. The passive loss carryforward is calculated at line 197.
[mm]Total gain from sale is the sum of the capital gain chargeback $469,680 (line 141) and the limited partner's share of the remaining gain from sale, $2,865,691 (line 144).
[nn]This section computes the returns to the limited partners if they have a three-year pay-in of $383,333 per year instead of a one-time pay-in of $1,150,000. The amount of the unpaid limited partner investment is secured by investor notes. The investor notes accrue interest at 12 percent.
[oo]The after-tax IRR to investors under a three-year pay-in is 22.63 percent.
[pp]If the total equity is divided into 25 unit shares, each share will be $46,000.
[qq]The limited partners are charged 12 percent interest on the deferred pay-in balance (investor notes). The interest paid to the partnership is assumed to be fully deductible on the individual limited partners' income-tax returns.
[rr]The before-tax cash flows on an investment of $46,000 total $174,735.
[ss]The after-tax cash flows total $138,688.

been properly performed. "These and other inspections done by an independent firm cost a little more but save money in the long run."[20]

The developer's liability, as well as the contractor's, can extend many years after the completion of a building.

Subcontractors and Draws

Typically, apartment subcontractors are smaller than nonresidential subcontractors and are not bonded. In order to be competitive, most builders rely on such non-union subcontractors but also appreciate that they sometimes will go out of business or fail to complete a job. Developers should not automatically avoid working with a financially weak subcontractor. They should, though, check on the subcontractor's clients, suppliers, banks, and record, and make sure that the subcontractor pays social security. "Just be careful," cautions Frank. "Check his insurance coverage. If he doesn't have liability insurance, then you arrange for him to get it and charge him for it."

Every time a subcontractor makes a draw, the developer/contractor should have the subcontractor sign a lien waiver and an affidavit showing that bills, suppliers, taxes, and insurance have been paid and then should attach the lien waiver to the check stub and file it under the job.

The purpose of the lien waiver is to prevent subcontractors from subsequently claiming nonpayment or one of their suppliers from filing a lien. Liens, even completely unwarranted, can delay loan closings and sales. If a lien is filed, a developer can bond around it or leave money in escrow to cover the potential liability.

One of the most difficult problems in construction is removing a subcontractor whose work is substandard. To reduce the associated delays, some developers require subcontractors to sign a stringent subcontract that provides for their removal for slow work or nonperformance.

Insurance

A good insurance agent who specializes in construction is invaluable to a contractor. Developers/contractors must be familiar with many different types of insurance: worker's compensation insurance, subcontractor's general liability insurance, builder's risk insurance, completed operations insurance, and contractor's equipment floater. Like the general contractor, subcontractors must have their own builder's risk insurance that covers, say, the theft of material from a site. "Get a copy of their insurance," says Frank. "Do not let them bring any vehicle or piece of equipment onto the job unless they show you their insurance. And check copies of their workmen's compensation, general liability, and builder's risk insurance before you let them begin."

Frank also recommends taking out completed operations insurance, which protects builders from claims for injury or damage caused by building collapse or structure failure after its completion. It does not, however, cover faulty workmanship.

Marketing

Marketing begins while a project is still on the drawing board and does not end until a project is sold. In the residential development business, developers do not attempt to create a market. A housing product has been designed for a specific segment or segments of the population. Marketing is the process of finding those people and attracting them to the site at a time when they are in a position to buy or rent.

Marketing serves a number of objectives:

- analyzing what market to pursue and what product to build;
- persuading—through careful presentation—buyers and renters that the product meets their specific needs;
- packaging the product and offering assistance to enable those people to buy or rent it; and
- ensuring afterwards that the product meets their expectations.

Insufficient predevelopment market research can result in a product that has been built for a certain market but does not appeal to that market. In such cases, developers must determine which market the product does appeal to and then repackage it to attract that market. Although almost any product will sell or rent at a low enough price, its developer is unlikely to turn a profit if prices must be discounted.

Market analysis has been described in detail in the feasibility section of this chapter. It must be stressed, however, that market analysis is vital not only for predevelopment feasibility studies but also throughout the life of a project. Ongoing market analysis assesses the accuracy of the original analysis of the target market and identifies any important changes in market projections, rents, prices, and even the target market itself. Typically, between 12 and 24 months elapse from completion of the first market study to the leasing of a project, and, in the interim, major changes may have occurred in the market. The developer must constantly monitor the market, especially by watching neighboring projects in order to remain up-to-date on current rental activity, pricing, concessions, and preferred physical characteristics and amenities. Changing market strategy in midstream can substantially increase construction and operating costs, but failing to respond to market changes can be fatal.

Developing a Coherent Market Strategy

The cornerstone of any market strategy is its target market. Once that has been identified through market analysis, every aspect of development—from design through to management—should reinforce the appeal of the project to that market.

Market strategy begins with determining the family composition, age, and income of prospective tenants or buyers. Randall Lewis, executive vice president/director of marketing for Lewis Homes, Upland, California, illustrates how that determination can influence product design. For example:

- If the prospective market has young children, the second bedroom should be located next to the master bedroom.
- If the market has teenage children, the master and the second bedrooms should be kept apart.
- If the market is singles living together, design two master bedrooms and include a larger pantry for food storage.

Lewis emphasizes that "the little things make your product different and exciting. You should talk to suppliers, market consultants, brokers, managers, and potential customers to get ideas." Setting up "focus groups" of current and prospective tenants to discuss topics such as amenities and landscaping helps developers stay in touch with consumers.

Lewis also recommends surveying prospective and established tenants and interviewing people who opted for other projects. "All of these surveys are inexpensive ways of doing market research."

After the development program and marketing strategy are established, preparation of a project objectives document (see feature box 4-27) can help the marketing team understand the strategy as well as the basic facts about the product and the market.

Leasing/Selling

Leasing/selling should begin well before a project is completed. Haskel Iny, of Homestead Group Associates, for instance, starts marketing a project three months before it is ready for occupancy. He sends letters to neighboring apartment complexes and advertises heavily. He also hires three people to do leasing: "I don't want to miss prospects." Even developers with in-house leasing staffs need to maintain a good image with the brokerage community and realtors. Most developers feel that commissions paid to outside brokers is money well spent, especially as a guard against a project developing a bad image. For example, Doyle Stuckey, a Houston homebuilder, learned that brokers were telling clients as they drove by one of his subdivisions that it had flooding and construction problems. The false rumors were clearly hurting business. He says that he learned the hard way to work with the brokerage community.

4-27 Project Objectives Document

John Math, a Florida-based marketing consultant, recommends that developers prepare a project objectives document that summarizes their marketing strategy and provides a sourcebook for the members of the development and marketing team. The document should contain the following information:

Rental and For-Sale Products

- The architectural program to direct the designer and site planner and to inform the marketing team about the program's features.
- All staff and consultant requirements and responsibilities.
- A summary of the overall marketing program listing proposed media plans, public relations policies, and promotional campaigns.
- A detailed leasing or sales program from preleasing/presales to 100 percent occupancy/sale.
- An analysis of the competition's strong and weak points.
- A listing of property management requirements.
- An outline of the chain of command and of each person's responsibilities, including a statement of who attends which meetings.
- Preliminary budgets, schedules, and pro formas for each area of concern.

For-Sale Products

- Proposed financing and customer administration requirements.
- An explanation of how service and warranties will be handled.
- Procedures for all departments, covering both the buyer and the company from point-of-sale through contract, selections, construction, financing, closing, warranty, and turnover.
- Procedures for moving from construction to administration and for transferring control from administration to the homeowners'/condominium association.

Source: John R. Math, "Project Management: Well-Planned Program Key to Success," *Florida Home Builder*, May 1988, p. 1.

Leasing agents and sales people set the tone for a project. Their friendliness, demeanor, dress, and knowledge are all critical elements of success. Some developers use leasing companies that specialize in grand openings and initial leasing only. Other developers prefer to have the same team continue to manage the property. Some leasing companies specialize in the initial lease-up of new projects; such companies may, however, exercise little discrimination regarding the people to whom they lease units—they are rewarded according to the number of leases they sign rather than the long-term performance of the project. The developer should monitor the creditworthiness of the tenants very carefully.

Pricing

Pricing, the most important tool for influencing leasing in the short run, cannot be based on pro-forma projections. Rents must reflect current market conditions, especially the prices charged by neighboring projects. Pricing should be monitored weekly, or even daily. Conditions change quickly, and a vacant unit costs a developer much more than a slight reduction in rent. However, if a developer is obliged to charge an above-market rental rate—because, say, a permanent mortgage requires that certain rent levels are achieved before closing[21]—then that developer must find other incentives to get the *effective* rental rate in line with the market. Fortunately, a developer who is forced to maintain above-market rents can take many actions to make his/her project more competitive. For instance, the developer can:

- Reduce the amount of deposit required.
- Offer accruing deposits, where tenants make little or no initial deposit and earn deposit credits at the rate of $20 or $30 per month, which they receive at the end of six months or so. (This incentive also helps improve punctual payments of rent.)
- Provide free cable television or other services that normally carry a monthly charge.
- Install additional appliances such as microwave ovens, ceiling fans, and washer/dryers. (Such appliances represent a permanent capital improvement to the unit.)
- Offer privileges at health or other clubs.

Point-of-sale incentives are also invaluable tools for selling condominiums. The amount and type of sales incentive depends largely on local market conditions. In very soft markets, free vacations and even cars have been offered as special incentives; more commonly, prospective buyers are tempted by household appliances or additional decorating allowances for carpet, wallpaper, window coverings, or light fixtures.

Staffing

Most rental apartment developers prefer to build projects that contain at least 150 or 200 units—the minimum number necessary to support a full complement of staff: property manager, assistant manager, repair man, and porter. Because apartments experience regular turnover and must be continuously re-leased, the staff is very important to the continued marketability of the project.

In many urban areas, however, assembling a site that will support 150 units is very difficult, so developers have learned how to cope with smaller complexes. For example, Haskel Iny hires a couple to manage a 60-unit complex. "They receive a free apartment plus $10 per unit. I prefer to pay top dollar because it pays if they lease an apartment one week sooner." For an 18-unit complex, C.C. Mow employs a resident manager who receives a free apartment unit plus $20 to $30 per unit managed. Mow looks for stability in a manager—for someone who has lived in the area for several years, who is aggressive, friendly, and a good leasing or sales agent.

John Math[22] recommends that to sell between 50 and 100 condominium units a developer should hire a sales manager plus one sales person. For projects of between 100 and 200 units, two sales persons should be hired. Their total compensation should amount to 1.5 to 3 percent of the gross sales. Many successful sales people prefer to work totally on commission. If a developer expects them to be in the office during certain hours of the day, they should receive a salary plus commission or draw against commission.

Public Relations

The purpose of public relations is to create a favorable public image. The result of good public relations is free advertising.

Public relations plays an important role both off and on site. Developers who enjoy good off-site public relations are active in their communities with civic groups, the local chamber of commerce, churches, and so forth. Developers who promote on-site public relations ensure that visitors to their sites receive a positive general impression—a neat and orderly site and sales office, polite staff, and so on.

Public relations experts are particularly useful to developers by virtue of their relations with local news media. Through their contacts, they should be able to obtain coverage for announcements and news releases about a new property. Potentially newsworthy events include purchasing the land, obtaining financing, closing loans, groundbreaking, grand opening, first family move-ins, attaining certain lease hurdles, human interest stories about tenants (especially stories that highlight a special feature of the project, such as units for the handicapped), and special events. Other stories may be crafted about the product itself, featuring such elements as the design of the interior or exterior.

Public relations firms may also stage special events for a developer. Useful events include press parties, previews of a complex for community leaders and media representatives, and sponsored community events aimed at fundraising. Awards competitions are another fruitful source of favorable publicity and provide third-party endorsement for a project.

Newsletters are a particularly effective public relations tool. Their frequency depends on the size of, and the level of activity within, an individual project; apartment projects may issue only one or two newsletters per year, whereas master-planned communities may publish one per month. Newsletters, which function essentially as direct-mail pieces, should be sent to residents, area employers, brokers, prospects, and neighborhood stores and community facilities. They are helpful for attracting prospective buyers and tenants and for informing current residents about what is going on in the neighborhood and project. Most importantly, newsletters suggest to residents that the developer cares about them—an attitude that they pass on to others. Newsletters tend to combine product and sales information with human interest stories. Usually, an advertising agency does the creative design and a public relations firm writes the copy, though many public relations firms will handle everything.

Production costs vary dramatically, but a four-sided, one-color newsletter may cost (in 1990 prices) up to $2,000 for the writing, $500 for graphics, and $500 for printing 2,000 copies. If full color is used, color separation for each photograph costs approximately $100 and half-tones for each black-and-white print cost approximately $10. For example, a four-sided newsletter with full color on the back and black and white on the front costs $1,100 for printing the first 1,000 copies, $500 for five color photographs, and $200 for 20 black-and-white photographs, for a total price of $1,800. One thousand additional copies will cost $350.[23]

Randall Lewis, vice president of Lewis Homes, based in Upland, California, says that a successful public relations campaign waged by a large development firm should target different publics with different messages:[24]

- Land sellers—building faith in the developer's ability to perform.
- Lenders—building faith in the developer's capacity to deliver what he/she promises and to repay loans.
- Government—announcing that the company takes care of consumer complaints and is a good citizen in its dealings with the public sector.

■ 4-28 Public Relations Task List

A developer who hires a public relations firm to work on his/her behalf should expect that firm to undertake the following tasks (these tasks may also be undertaken by the developer or by someone on the developer's staff):

1. Develop a program.
2. Identify story lines:
   - announcements of commissions,
   - personnel appointments,
   - awards,
   - design stories, etc.
3. Compile factsheets/biographies for the developer's company and its principals.
4. Write simple, concise releases that include all pertinent facts.
5. Develop a press list.
6. Make personal contact with news media representatives on the press list.
7. Establish contacts with national trade publications and consumer magazines/newspapers.
8. Try to place interview articles for the development company's principals.
9. Obtain media kits and editorial calendars for all national trade publications.
10. Plan regular visits to national media. Invite media representatives to visit the developer's offices and projects.
11. Obtain annual awards competition calendars. Coordinate design competition entries.
12. Try to place the company's principals as speakers for local, regional, and national conferences.
13. Develop a photograph file of people and projects. Develop a graphics file of renderings, logos, and so forth.
14. Develop a mailing list of the developer's old, present, and potential clients to use for promotional mailings (in absence of marketing director).
15. Reprint articles about the developer's projects that appear in magazines and newspapers. Use them, accompanied by a letter, for direct mailings to client list.
16. Consider publishing a company newsletter.
17. Establish contact with the public relations directors of all of the developer's clients, and coordinate projects to secure mention for the developer's projects in clients' news-releases and advertisements.
18. Call or send thank-you notes to press who feature the developer's projects.
19. Develop special events.
20. Encourage the developer's participation in professional organizations and community organizations and activities.

Source: Interview with Patty Doyle, president, Patty Doyle Public Relations, Fort Lauderdale, Florida, in September 1988.

- Future employees—creating the impression that the company is a fun and profitable place to work.
- Competitors—conveying a sense of mutual respect and a shared readiness to work together in industry and civic organizations to address common problems.
- Customers—establishing the developer's preoccupation with satisfying the demands of the customer.
- Media—conveying respect and a willingness to share information.

Advertising

The primary purpose of advertising is to motivate potential tenants and buyers to visit a project. Advertising, although vital, can be very expensive. Thus, a developer needs to discover which advertising medium is the most cost-effective. Relative cost-effectiveness varies from area to area, and a developer should undertake firsthand research by talking to other local developers, property managers, and advertising agencies.

The most-famous advertising agency in a city may not necessarily be the best for a beginning developer who requires considerable personal attention. A developer should interview at least three firms, obtain recommendations from their clients, and then select a firm that is genuinely interested in his/her account.

Advertising agencies provide various services, including developing a long-range advertising strategy, planning individual programs, selecting the best media for presentation, preparing copy and design layouts, and monitoring the performance of its efforts.

Advertising for a project will typically employ a common logo, theme, and style. A well-crafted logo can be used not only in advertising but also on signage, brochures, stationery, and even as a design motif. A project's name likewise plays an important role in creating an image for a project. New developers should promote a project's name first, with the developer's name of secondary importance. Names should be descriptive, not misleading. For example, a complex should not be named "Forest Hills" if it sits on Kansas prairie land.

What advertising works best? Every area and product differs, but Jim Maddingly, president of LumaCorp, Inc., of Dallas, rates the cost-effectiveness of advertising for apartments in his area as follows:

1. Neighborhood newspapers.
2. Bootleg signs.[25]
3. Brochures left on the counters of neighborhood stores.
4. Metropolitan newspapers.
5. Radio and television.

How much should be spent on advertising? Advertising agencies recommend at least 1 percent of hard costs. That percentage can vary, though, according to factors such as market conditions and size of project—larger projects tend to enjoy economies of scale in terms of the amount spent on advertising per unit.

Brochures

Developers should ensure that advertising brochures are begun at least two months before they will be needed. The brochures should be ready to be mailed to local employers, brokers, community leaders, and apartment locators during construction as part of premarketing. Despite the need for early preparation, brochures should not tie developers to specific figures; therefore, they should contain neither prices—which change continually—nor bound floor plans—people always want the floor plan that has already been rented or sold out. The square footage of a unit should be omitted from a floor plan unless its inclusion is a very competitive advantage. Special features and amenities, however, should be emphasized.[26]

Many developers opt for a folder with a high-quality printed cover and pockets inside for inserts. The jacket is the major printing expense; inserts can be changed and updated as needed. Brochures can be of all shapes and colors. When people are shopping around for apartments, they will pick up a number of brochures and are, of course, more likely to notice distinctive brochures. Brochures that fold into the shape of, say, a door key or a house may cost extra to print but are more memorable.

Newspaper Advertising

Layout and copy for newspaper advertisement should be simple and specific and should not exaggerate the attributes of a project. The name of the developer should be included, as should clear directions to the project; in this respect, maps are helpful and allow prospective tenants to be directed along the route that creates the most favorable impression as they approach the project.

Classified advertisements, the least-expensive form of newspaper advertising, are a must for rental housing. At the same time, however, the quantity and similarity of classified advertisements makes it hard for any one project to stand out.

Radio and Television

Radio advertising is useful for drawing attention to grand openings of larger projects and groups of projects by one developer. To select a station, first check listener profiles and pick a station whose general programming is similar to the tastes of the target market. In addition to spot advertisements, live remote broadcasts work well during times when many people are out driving.

Radio advertisements may generate considerable traffic on site. If a developer is not prepared to handle a large number of people on site, the advertisements may do more harm than good.

Television is the most expensive medium. It probably is not cost-effective in large metropolitan areas, but it may be effective in smaller markets for grand openings.

Signs

Billboards help establish name identity and may be useful as directional signs near a project. Transit advertising—such as bus banners, bus benches, and commuter station posters—can also be an effective way of keeping the developer's name in the public eye.

Direction signs are probably the most effective signs of all. Removable bootleg signs are an inexpensive and efficient means of bringing people to the project from major arterials within a two-mile radius.

Merchandising

Whereas advertising is intended to tell people about a project and entice them to visit it, merchandising is concerned with on-site displays and practices.

The first impressions of visitors are critical to a project's success. Particular attention should be paid to the condition of entrances, signs, landscaping, and buildings. A pleasant environment should be created as soon as possible, even while construction is still in progress. A well-designed and carefully located entrance not only helps merchandising but also bolsters a project's future identification in the neighborhood. Entrance signs and nameplates should be modest, designed to blend with the character of the community. Generous landscaping may be expensive, but it is also cost-effective—as a visit to any successful project will demonstrate.

Restrictive signs (prohibiting, say, smoking) should be pleasant and inoffensive and should be designed, where possible, to relate to other merchandising features.

Design of the Sales Office

The sales office should be easy to find and should open up to attractive views of interior courtyards or other features of the project. Its design must harmonize with the project's architecture.

Robb Miller Photography

This combined clubhouse and leasing office at Hacienda Gardens Apartments in Pleasanton, California, provides an attractive first impression for the potential renter.

Within the sales office, brochures, models, and maps should be placed so that visitors may view them at their leisure. Drawings of the apartment site plan and unit plans make attractive and informative wall-hangings. Graphics give visitors an impression of what an uncompleted project will eventually look like. Perspective drawings are important. Remember that visualizing a project from two-dimensional plans is difficult for most people. Small models of the project, although expensive, make attractive focal points and can help renters and buyers see how their apartments are located with respect to major amenities, access, security, and views. Aerial photographs also help to show a project's locational relationship to off-site facilities such as schools, churches, libraries, daycare centers, shops, and parks.

Model Units

Model units play an important part in selling and leasing by giving customers a sense both of what the unit will look like and what they can do to personalize it. The model units should be close to the sales office, offer pleasant views of either the project or the surrounding area, and benefit from afternoon sunlight, the afternoon being the most popular time for visitors.

Although decorating a sample of every unit type is unnecessary, those units that are decorated are likely to lease or sell more quickly. Model decor should be selected to appeal to the target market. Current trends in decorating are moving away from standard furniture toward lavishly decorated units with small-size furniture that makes units look larger. Many decorators are making extensive use of wall paintings, plants, and mirrors. Nonstandard built-ins should, however, be avoided because they may mislead customers and because the model units may be moved to different locations within the complex once the project leases up. Moods may be enhanced through the use of background music, colors, and lighting.

Condominium Sales

The marketing process for condominiums is similar to that for single-family houses. Despite their desire to sell units during construction, developers have found that few buyers will commit themselves before they have seen the completed lobbies and amenities.

For smaller projects, an in-house sales staff is often uneconomical, and many developers tend to use outside brokers who are paid on commission. Developers who own other apartment houses or condominiums find that word-of-mouth advertising can be very effective. Some developers send out announcements to tenants or owners at their previous projects every time they open a new project. Paying a referral fee of, say, $50 to tenants or owners in other projects often helps to generate sales. However, in some states this practice violates real estate license laws.

The popularity of condominiums seems to swing more dramatically than that of other types of housing. In Los Angeles, in the early 1980s, for example, the market for condominiums was very strong. For several years thereafter, however, the market became very competitive as the bloated inventory of units was sold off, and lower interest rates made single-family houses relatively more attractive. In the late 1980s, the market swung the other way as single-family house prices escalated, and condominiums again became relatively inexpensive.

Many developers and lenders restrict non-owner-occupied units under the assumption that absentee own-

A model unit at Brickyard Landing in Point Richmond, California. Model decor should be selected to appeal to the target market.

ers take less care of their property and thereby depress sales to owner-occupants who will pay the highest prices. At the same time, developers need to be flexible and prepared to respond to changing market conditions. Paul Schultheis, a developer in Arcadia, California, undertook a condominium project during a downturn in the market: "We set up an intensive marketing budget with an all-out push for 90 days. Only three out of the 16 units were sold. We decided to change direction and set the building up as an apartment. Now we own a deluxe-deluxe apartment house." Similarly, Terry Lewis, president of Devon Development Company, in Dallas, recalls several projects that his firm conceived as condominium projects in Dallas/Ft. Worth.[27] Because of slow sales, the firm subsequently decided to operate the projects as rental apartments.

Operations and Management

No matter how well it is designed and built, an apartment project will be profitable only if it is well managed. Furthermore, management must be competent at many levels, such as the following, in order for a project to succeed:

- initial leasing;
- re-leasing and controlling turnover;
- rent collection;
- maintenance and repairs;
- record keeping;
- reporting to owners;
- landscaping and exterior appearance of the building;
- hiring and training new staff;
- dealing with tenant complaints about physical problems;
- dealing with tenant complaints about other tenants;
- maintaining good relations with brokers, firms, and community organizations; and
- maintaining good relations with managers of neighboring apartments in order to share information on bad tenants and work together on security and other common problems.

Although the operation and management of condominiums is the responsibility of unit owners through their condominium association, the legal framework for the condominium association must be established by the developer (see chapter 3).

Even though most developers would prefer not to be in the management business, many feel that only by managing their own projects can they get the service they need. Beginning developers usually do not have an organization in place, however, and must therefore rely on outside managers.

In selecting outside managers, beginning developers should look for companies with a good reputation for managing a particular type of property in terms of size, design, and tenant characteristics. James Maddingly, president of Luma Corporation, Dallas, Texas, advises developers to "look for someone who recognizes that property management is something that happens on site at the property, not in the district or corporate office. Select a management company by shopping their properties. What impression do on-site personnel give you? Get references from other developers. Do they get reports out on time? Are the reports understandable and informative?"

Maddingly also advocates investigating on-site procedures for collecting rents and accounting: "Look at the company's training manual for employees. How often are on-site personnel audited? Ask to see an example of an audit." An audit should be performed at least twice a year, and preferably quarterly. The auditor, who should appear unannounced, reviews collection reports, rent rolls, and individual leases and inspects vacant units to ensure that no "skimming" is occurring.

The management company should prepare monthly reports that show gross potential income, actual income, and line-by-line expenses. The reports should also detail which units are vacant and which are nonrevenue (free-rent) producing. Cash receipts should be deposited daily. Monthly cash collection reports should be reviewed and approved by off-site staff.

■ 4-29 Sources of Information on Apartment Management

The Institute of Real Estate Management, an arm of the National Association of Realtors, located in Chicago, runs a well-known training program for apartment managers. Graduates receive the designation of "Certified Property Manager" (CPM). The Institute also publishes books on apartment management, including the following:

How To Be a Successful Apartment Rental Consultant (1981)—available on cassette tapes.

Income/Expense Analysis: Federally Assisted Apartments (1988).

Edward N. Kelley, *Practical Apartment Management* (1981).

Mark Lee Levine, *Landlords'-Owners' Liability* (1979).

The On-Site Residential Manager Self-Study Program (1978)—available on cassette tapes.

Rosetta E. Parker, *Housing For The Elderly: The Handbook for Managers* (1984).

4-30 Typical Property Management Problems

A stable occupancy with low turnover and high-quality tenants who pay market-rate rents punctually is every property manager's goal. However, even the best managers encounter problems. The following advice is based upon years of experience:

- If you make promises, deliver.
- Check the credit history of new tenants through credit agencies and previous landlords.
- Collect the first month's rent plus a security deposit from new tenants to guard against their leaving without giving notice.
- In a slow market, the trick is to hold on to your current tenants. Make sure that your incentives to managers adequately reward renewals of leases.
- For lease renewals, have your manager meet with the tenant 45 days before the tenant's lease expires.
- Deal with problems quickly and efficiently. Problems that are not resolved only grow.
- Fewer callbacks by tenants on maintenance and repairs mean lower turnovers.
- Property management problems are usually about people, not property.
- When cash flow is low, try to minimize cutbacks on maintenance, repairs, and replacements. Cutbacks dispirit on-site staff and lead to a lower standard of maintenance.

Hiring Staff

Property management is a people business. Jerome Frank, Jr., who works with his father, Jerome Frank, Sr. (mentioned earlier), argues that staff motivation is as important as the physical property in maintaining high occupancy and low turnover. "People who are willing to get away from their desks are the ones you want. The property manager's abilities to motivate, to market, and to keep in touch with tenants and staff are more important than skill at paperwork."

Frank advises: "The major property companies theoretically give the best training but not the best incentive commissions. When hiring staff, you should visit the properties of the major developers. Evaluate their leasing and management programs. Hire their people. When someone gives you a resume, note who has trained them." Frank says that he attracts older experienced managers by telling them: "I know you're experienced. You want more control and responsibility. You will have control of your own property. We can make decisions quickly. We're more entrepreneurial. There are no layers of management to go through."[28]

Turnover

Every turnover entails a minimum loss of two weeks' rent plus up to $500 in cleaning and carpet shampooing costs. In garden apartments, for example, turnover rates average 55 percent per year and can reach as high as 70 percent.

Turnover occurs for many reasons, some of which—say, a tenant's change of job—lie outside the control of the developer. However, the developer can reduce turnover caused by poor construction, design, maintenance, or management. Residents become disenchanted if their refrigerator leaks, if their unit is too noisy, or if they cannot find parking.

Property management experts stress the importance of communication in the reduction of turnover. Owners should communicate often and regularly with managers and staff so that all parties understand their goals, objectives, and concerns. On-site managers should communicate regularly with the residents, thereby answering questions and reducing uncertainty among tenants. For example, if a swimming pool must be emptied to make repairs, tenants should know when they will be able to use it again.

Problem tenants can create difficulties for an entire complex. Controlling noise and other irritants among neighboring tenants is critical for maintaining low turnover. The property manager sets the stage for tenants from the beginning; he/she should go over a written list of rules and regulations for the apartment house before tenants move in and should ask tenants to sign the rules signifying that they understand them. When problems arise between tenants, the manager should first try to reach an amicable solution with both parties. Moving a tenant to a different unit sometimes solves the problem. If one party is at fault and an amicable solution does not work, then the lease should be used to enforce the rules of the property, up to and including eviction. Timely response and firm enforcement of rules is vital for maintaining good tenant relations.

Selling the Property

The lifecycle of property management has three stages: lease-up, stabilizing income, and positioning the property for sale. The third stage usually involves a different management approach from the first two.

When the time comes to sell a project, on-site staff should be informed about the developer's goals and given some financial incentive to motivate them to help put the apartment in the best possible condition, physically and financially, for sale. Experienced developers recommend, however, that residents should not be informed of a pending sale. Each tenant should receive a letter imme-

The Queen Anne Seattle, Washington

Queen Anne High School has long been one of Seattle's most noteworthy architectural landmarks. Inspired by English late Renaissance palaces, the 1909 building is considered the finest work of architect James Stephen, who designed dozens of Seattle schools. A 1929 addition, while somewhat simplified, was true to the character of the 1909 building's load-bearing masonry facade. Two 1955 additions (for a cafeteria and industrial arts classes) with facades of simple, unornamented curtain walls, stand in contrast to the older buildings. The building complex illustrates a half-century progression in construction methods and attitudes toward educational facilities.

The school was closed in 1981 because of declining enrollments, but the neighborhood wanted to save the building. Neighbors were involved early in planning, and a feasible alternative—converting the school into a housing complex—received strong support from the community. In 1984, the school district, in cooperation with the Historic Seattle Preservation and Development Authority, chose Lorig Associates and The Bumgardner Architects in a design and development competition to convert the vacant buildings to residential use. As a first step, the development/design team succeeded in placing the school on the National Register of Historic Places, making it eligible for historic renovation tax credits totaling $1.6 million.

The Site

Queen Anne Hill, approximately two miles north of downtown Seattle, overlooks downtown and Puget Sound. The site is surrounded predominantly by residential uses, including single-family dwellings on the immediate south and multifamily units on the immediate east. On the west side is a gymnasium, and a new elementary school is being built to the north. Because of its location atop the hill, the school is visible from numerous points around the city.

Development and Financing

In selecting the developer, the school district acted through the quasi-public Historic Seattle Preservation and Development Authority. A request for proposals specified that proposals be submitted by a team, including a developer, an architect, and a contractor. Six teams originally bid for the project, and Lorig Associates was chosen in 1984. The deal that was then negotiated involved a 50-year ground lease of the site, with two 20-year options to extend the lease.

The developer was not required to pay ground rent until construction was completed; thereafter, the annual ground rent of $60,000 would accrue for three years, with 12 percent interest on the rent not paid. After three years, the developer was required to pay $60,000 rent per year, or 8 percent of the net operating income, whichever was greater. Any rent exceeding $60,000 per year would be used to retire the accrued rent, which had to be paid off in 10 years. The structure of the deal allowed investors to be repaid early in the process.

The partnership that was established involved 55 units of $40,000 each, or $2.2 million in equity. The remaining funds

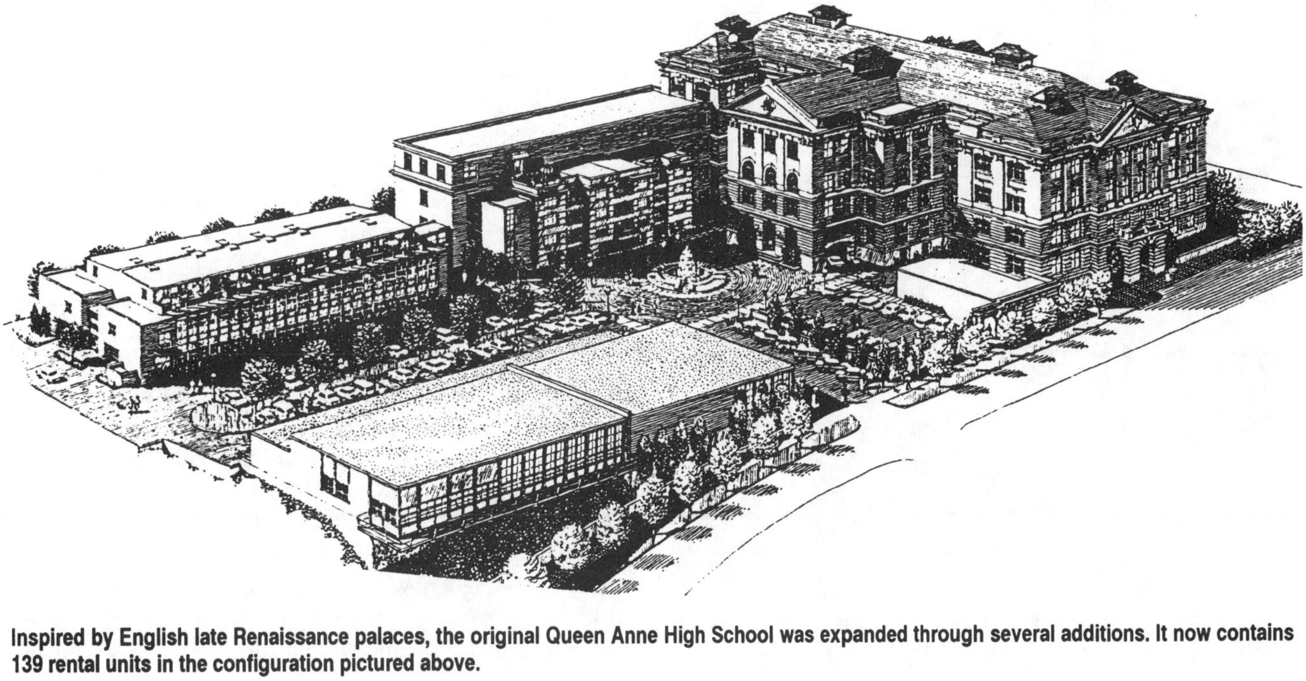

Inspired by English late Renaissance palaces, the original Queen Anne High School was expanded through several additions. It now contains 139 rental units in the configuration pictured above.

A 1929 auditorium/gym addition blocked off the attractive rear facade of the building; the developer chose to demolish this addition to open the center of the site for a new main entrance at grade, with an entrance courtyard giving access to new on-site parking and landscaping.

necessary—about $7 million—were obtained through a construction loan from Crosslands Mortgage of Brooklyn. A permanent loan was later arranged with Northwestern Mutual Life. The project was set up to allow conversion to condominiums, but no plans have been made to do so in the foreseeable future.

Construction began in March 1986, and the project was completed in March 1987.

Original blackboards have been retained in many units, and some residents have commissioned artists to create murals.

Planning and Design

The site consisted of the original 1909 building on the north side, a 1929 classroom and auditorium/gymnasium addition in the middle, and two separate 1955 additions separated by a court on the southern end. Turning a space the size of a large department store into housing—while dealing with existing windows, two-foot-thick masonry walls, and a jumble of deteriorated or poorly placed additions and breezeways—is a bit like working a big Rubik's cube, according to the architects.

In evaluating the existing site, the team first determined that the 1929 auditorium/gymnasium should be demolished to reveal the attractive south facade of the original building. Doing so would also provide a pleasant open area at the center of the site, which was subsequently designed to include a grand porte cochere, a formal courtyard paved in cobblestones, parking, and a circular drive with a large fountain at its center.

The remaining buildings were redesigned according to their structure. The 1909 building, for instance, was converted into 90 apartments, including lofts in the high-ceilinged library. The developer constructed a small, four-story addition to the 1929 classroom building, which was too narrow for a double-loaded corridor, to create 21 apartments in the addition.

The 1955 industrial arts addition was converted into 16 apartments—eight of which are two-level, two-bedroom units with rooftop terraces—through the addition of a third floor. The ground floor was converted into 38 parking spaces. Finally, the 1955 cafeteria addition was converted into 53 secured parking spaces.

A high school, where rooms are interspersed with laboratories and study halls, presents a much bigger challenge in redesign than an elementary school, where the pattern of rooms is repetitive. The redesign of the Queen Anne involved exploration, photography, and a study of old drawings, and the designers had the contractors test the strength of the masonry walls and analyze the structure. Very little bolstering was required, as the already massive 1909 building was reinforced after a 1949 earthquake. Among the problems in restoration the developer faced were the replacement or restoration of 900 windows and the removal of asbestos used to insulate steam pipes.

The Queen Anne sits atop Queen Anne Hill and is visible from numerous points around the city.

The project includes this four-story addition to the 1929 classroom building.

A variety of unit configurations accommodate such diverse prospective renters as single parents, young professionals, families, and unrelated singles. Although virtually every unit has some distinctive feature, the 139 units come in 39 basic shapes. In contrast with standard apartments in Seattle, the Queen Anne offers high-volume rooms (12-foot ceilings are typical) with many details, including classroom chalkboards in many of the units.

Marketing

The developer did extensive market research before proceeding with the project. It involved checking every building in the neighborhood for size of units, rents, and so on to eliminate guessing about what the market would tolerate. Rents at the Queen Anne range from $523 per month for a studio to $1,050 for two-bedroom, two-level units (1988 dollars). The building now has 200 residents, half men and half women, with an average age of 32; 80 singles, with the remainder couples, including nontraditional couples, live there. Average annual income is $28,000, and 63 percent of the tenants moved from within the city limits.

The press covered the project closely—so closely that the leasing team did not have to spend nearly what had been planned on marketing; people kept pouring in the front door. Seattle's two major newspapers did full-page features the week before the grand opening, and Historic Seattle organized a tour

■ The Queen Anne (Continued)

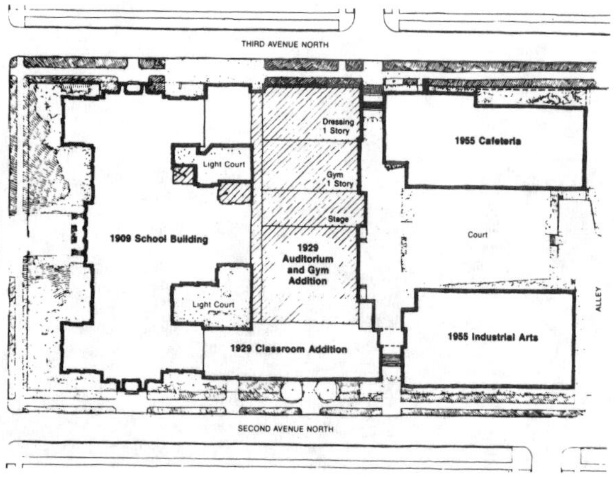

Site plan before conversion.

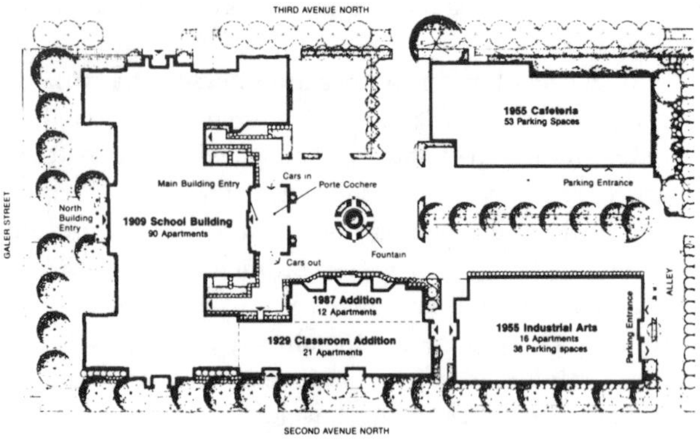

Site plan after conversion.

weekend that turned out 8,500 people. As a result, 40 percent of the units were leased with barely any advertising before the Queen Anne formally opened. The remaining units were rented within three months.

Experience Gained

- Each of the team members—the developer, the architect, and the contractor—had prior experience with both rehabilitation and residential construction. As a result, construction entailed no major pitfalls or unforeseen problems. The project was actually completed two months ahead of schedule.
- Working with a negotiated contract with a preselected contractor avoided the sort of adversarial relationship typical of projects awarded to the contractor submitting the lowest bid. The team worked together from the start with an eye always on the budget, and the contractor was involved in the design process.
- Through previous experience, the developer recognized that the success of a residential rehabilitation project largely depends on the quality and character of the building and the neighborhood. A good building and a good location afford the opportunity to charge higher rents, making the difference between a profitable and an unprofitable venture.

Developer/Manager:
Lorig Associates
2001 Western Avenue, Suite 300
Seattle, Washington 98121
(206) 728-7660

Architect:
The Bumgardner Architects
101 Stewart Street, Suite 200
Seattle, Washington 98101
(206) 223-1361

Construction:
J.M. Rafn Company
Seattle, Washington

Landscape Architect:
Robert Shinbo Associates
Seattle, Washington 98101

Source: ULI–the Urban Land Institute, "The Queen Anne," *Project Reference File*, vol. 18, no. 6, April–June 1988.

---

mediately after the sale. In some states, such as Texas, the law requires that tenants be notified within 48 hours of a sale about the status of their security deposits, which are transferred with the asset.

Cash flow is generally the most important consideration for buyers. Some steps will increase short-term cash flow at the expense of long-term profitability. For example, some developers are less selective about tenants to increase occupancy and the rent roll. However, if a sale does not go through, the owner will have to do some cleaning out of unreliable or troublesome tenants.

■ Project Data

Land Use Information:
Site Area: 2.85 acres
Gross Density: 48.8 dwelling units per acre
Total Dwelling Units: 139
Current Vacancy: 2 percent

Parking:
Total Spaces: 173
Parking Index: 1.25 spaces per unit
Visitor Spaces: 12
Handicapped Spaces: 7
Compact Car Spaces: 66

Economic Information:
Site Acquisition Cost: Option fee $7,500

Site Improvement Costs:	
Excavation and Grading	$ 47,470
Sewer/Water	23,063
Paving	25,853
Curbs/Sidewalks	10,145
Landscaping	60,575
Demolition	405,970
Other	59,418
Total	$632,494

Construction Costs:	
Structural	$ 134,227
Carpentry	648,177
Electrical	512,920
Plumbing	363,423
HVAC	62,290
Elevators	96,859
Other	3,904,610
Total	$5,722,506

Amenities Costs:	
Fountain ($25,000 + $12,500 installation)	$37,500
Roof Deck	2,500
Tanning Room	5,000
Total	$45,000

Total Hard Costs: $6,400,000[a]
Total Soft Costs: $2,860,000

Unit Information:

Unit Type	Number Built	Monthly Rent	Number of Bedrooms/ Baths
Studio	6	$ 523	0/1
Loft Studio	25	$ 558	0/1
Studio Alcove	16	$ 591	0/1
1-Bedroom	31	$ 716	1/1
1-Bedroom Platform	27	$ 720	1/1
2-Bedroom Flats	15	$1,004	2/1–2
2-Bedroom Townhouses	8	$1,050	2/2
2-Bedroom Platforms	6	$ 942	2/2
1-Bedroom Townhouses	5	$ 775	1/1–1½

Total Projected Monthly Income: $97,500

Monthly Operating Expenses:	
Taxes (historic building leased from public agency)	$ 0
Insurance	2,500
Sewer	1,500
Repairs/Maintenance	6,420
Utilities	2,700
Legal	100
Accounting/Management	3,500
Marketing	500
Miscellaneous Salaries	7,900
Total	$25,120

[a]Includes site improvement, construction, and amenities.

Conclusion

Beginning developers will find multifamily residential development one of the easier points of entry into the development industry, especially if they have some background in homebuilding. As with other types of development, multifamily housing is rapidly evolving and, in many markets, oversupplied. Generic apartment designs that may have worked in the 1970s and 1980s now require more careful planning. The process begins and ends with market analysis. If the depth, characteristics, and preferences of the target market are not correctly identified, delivering a product that best serves the market needs is impossible.

The reduction of tax benefits under the 1986 Tax Reform Act has made it more difficult to raise equity money than was the case in the early 1980s. On the other hand, few new projects are going ahead that do not provide an economic rate of return. This trend should offer long-term benefits to developers who will face less tax-motivated competition.

More-stringent fire codes, parking requirements, density restrictions, and amenity standards are raising the cost of apartment construction. At the same time, the scarcity of land, rising neighborhood opposition to development, stricter environmental regulations, and growing difficulties with public approvals are raising the price of land for apartments. Historically, rents have lagged behind inflation in the general economy. Rents will have to rise more sharply than they have in the past in order for apartment units to remain economically sound—a trend that is likely to increase pressures for rent control in many communities. Developers will have to work closely with public officials and community leaders to explain to them why rents rise and why rent control can have such an adverse impact on the supply of new units.

Notes

1. Two works recommended by the National Association of Home Builders are Adam Starchild, *Start Your Own Construction and Land Development Business* (Chicago: Nelson-Hall, 1983), and Robert A. Wolf, *How to Become a Developer* (Novato, California: Crittenden Books, 1984).

2. From an interview in 1987 with Joan Betts, vice president, Fidelity Mutual Life Insurance Company, Atlanta, Georgia.

3. Interested readers may refer to the following works: F. Adams, G. Milgram, E. Green, and C. Mansfield, "Undeveloped Land Prices during Urbanization: A Micro-Empirical Study over Time," *Review of Economic Statistics*, vol. 1, no. 2, May 1968, pp. 248–58; M. Fujita and H. Ogawa, "Multiple Equilibria and Structural Transition of Non-Monocentric Urban Configurations," *Regional Science and Urban Economics*, vol. 12, 1982, pp. 161–96; Homer Hoyt, *The Structure and Growth of Residential Neighborhoods in American Cities*, U.S. Federal Housing Administration (Washington, D.C.: U.S. Government Printing Office, 1939); D. Grether and P. Mieszkowski, "Determinants of Real Estate Values," *Journal of Urban Economics*, vol. 1, 1974, pp. 127–46; Edwin S. Mills, "Studies in the Structure of the Urban Economy," in *Resources for the Future* (Baltimore: Johns Hopkins University Press, 1972); Richard F. Muth, *Cities and Housing* (Chicago: The University of Chicago Press, 1969); and J. Yinger, "Estimating the Relationship between Location and the Price of Housing," *Journal of Regional Science*, vol. 19, no. 3, 1979, pp. 271–86.

4. See Richard B. Peiser, "The Determinants of Nonresidential Urban Land Values," *Journal of Urban Economics*, vol. 22, 1987, pp. 340–60.

5. Double-loaded parking has parking stalls on both sides of the driveway. Back-to-back apartment units are units that adjoin the back of another unit along the rear wall. This shared wall can accommodate plumbing for both units and reduces the total amount of outside wall per unit, thereby saving money.

6. Kevin Lynch, *Site Planning*, 2nd edition (Cambridge, Massachusetts: MIT Press, 1971), p. 81.

7. An easement in gross is an easement that does not benefit another specific tract of real estate but benefits a specific individual or business by permitting him/her to use land. An example is a right-of-way for a power company.

8. For example, William Brueggeman, Jeffrey Fisher, and Leo Stone, *Real Estate Finance* (Homewood, Illinois: Richard D. Irwin, 1989).

9. Overall returns must rise because, without tax benefits, other sources of benefit—namely, cash flow and NOI—become more important.

10. For further information on how to do DCF analysis, see Brueggeman, Fisher, and Stone, *Real Estate Finance*; J.B. Kau and C.F. Sirmans, *Real Estate* (New York: McGraw-Hill, 1985); and C.H. Wurtzebach and M.E. Miles, *Modern Real Estate* (New York: McGraw-Hill, 1985).

11. From an interview with Craycroft in 1989.

12. From an interview with Frank in 1987.

13. For large projects, demolition and foundation permits are sometimes obtained before the other building permits. Only the foundation drawings must be submitted.

14. A "point" represents a front-end fee equal to 1 percent of the loan amount. Points are usually paid out of the loan proceeds. On a $1 million loan with 2 points, the lender would receive $20,000 in fees, and the developer would receive the net amount of $980,000. Points are a normal part of the developer's financing costs and should be added into the soft costs.

15. See Brueggeman, Fisher, and Stone, *Real Estate Finance*, chapters 4 and 5, for instruction in the mechanics of mortgage calculation.

16. Real estate tax accounting is a highly specialized area. Although non-real estate accountants will be familiar with depreciation rules, the categorization of upfront fees requires consulting a specialist. Too often, beginners select advisers who do not have the necessary familiarity and experience in the technical aspects of real estate partnership tax and law.

17. Regulation D private offerings are not subject to the intense review by public agencies that public offerings receive. Public offerings must be offered to no more than 35 "nonqualified" investors, who are defined as investors with personal net

worths less than $1 million or incomes less than $200,000 per year. A Regulation D private offering may be offered to an unlimited number of "qualified" investors.

18. Broker-dealers are licensed by the National Association of Securities Dealers to sell syndications and other securities.

19. See, for instance, John B. Parker, "The Equidon Story: Learning from Adversity," *Urban Land*, July 1988, pp. 21–5, in which a developer cites the pitfalls of starting his own construction company. When his company cut back on its in-house development, the construction company did more outside work, which caused its fee structure to deteriorate and its risk to escalate.

20. From an interview with Frank in May 1988.

21. Permanent lenders have been stung by artificially inflated rental rates and usually require full disclosure of all rental concessions.

22. Math, a Florida-based marketing consultant, was interviewed by ULI Steering Committee member, Patty Doyle.

23. These costs are for a newsletter issued in Fort Lauderdale, Florida. Information provided by Patty Doyle.

24. These comments taken from a lecture given by Lewis at USC in 1988.

25. Bootleg signs are removable direction signs placed on major streets and expressway off-ramps in the vicinity of the project. Some firms specialize in placing and removing these signs during grand openings and heavy-traffic weekends; alternatively, the property manager may place them. If they are not removed, the owner may be cited for violating local sign ordinances.

26. Much of this advice is from Robert Engstrom, president of Robert Engstrom Companies of Minneapolis.

27. From an interview in 1988 with Lewis.

28. From an interview with Frank in 1988.

Chapter 5

Office Development

Introduction

Office development is one of the most complex and competitive segments of the development industry. Office developers come in all sizes, ranging from one-person companies to large international development firms. Office users are likewise characterized by their diversity, occupying spaces that can range from 500-square-foot executive offices to complexes that contain several million square feet.

This chapter[1] focuses on the types of office buildings most frequently built by beginning developers—buildings costing under $10 million and typically ranging in size from 5,000 to 100,000 square feet. The particular problems and perspectives in developing larger office projects are noted where they differ significantly from those encountered in smaller projects.

Office developers begin their work with either a market analysis or a tenant. Speculative—or "spec"—developers determine a target market, find a suitable site, design the building, find lead tenants, obtain necessary public approvals, obtain financing, construct the building, and lease it. Developers who begin with a tenant build the building to the tenant's specifications.

Categorizing Office Development

Office development employs an apparently bewildering array of classifications and categorizations that seeks to differentiate buildings on a wide variety of bases. Perhaps the most basic classification divides the quality of office space into three types:

- Class A space—buildings with excellent location and access, high-quality tenants and materials, and rents that are competitive with other new buildings.
- Class B space—buildings with good locations, management, and construction; little functional obsolescence or deterioration.
- Class C—buildings between 15 and 25 years old with steady occupancy.

In many cities, the amount of Class A space is typically half that of Class B and Class C space.[2]

Office buildings can be classified by product, markets, and location.

Products

A subdivision of the market by building type would include:

- High-Rise—typically over 20 stories.
- Mid-Rise—four to 15 stories high.
- Low-Rise—one to three stories high.

■ 5-1 Characteristics Determining Office Classifications

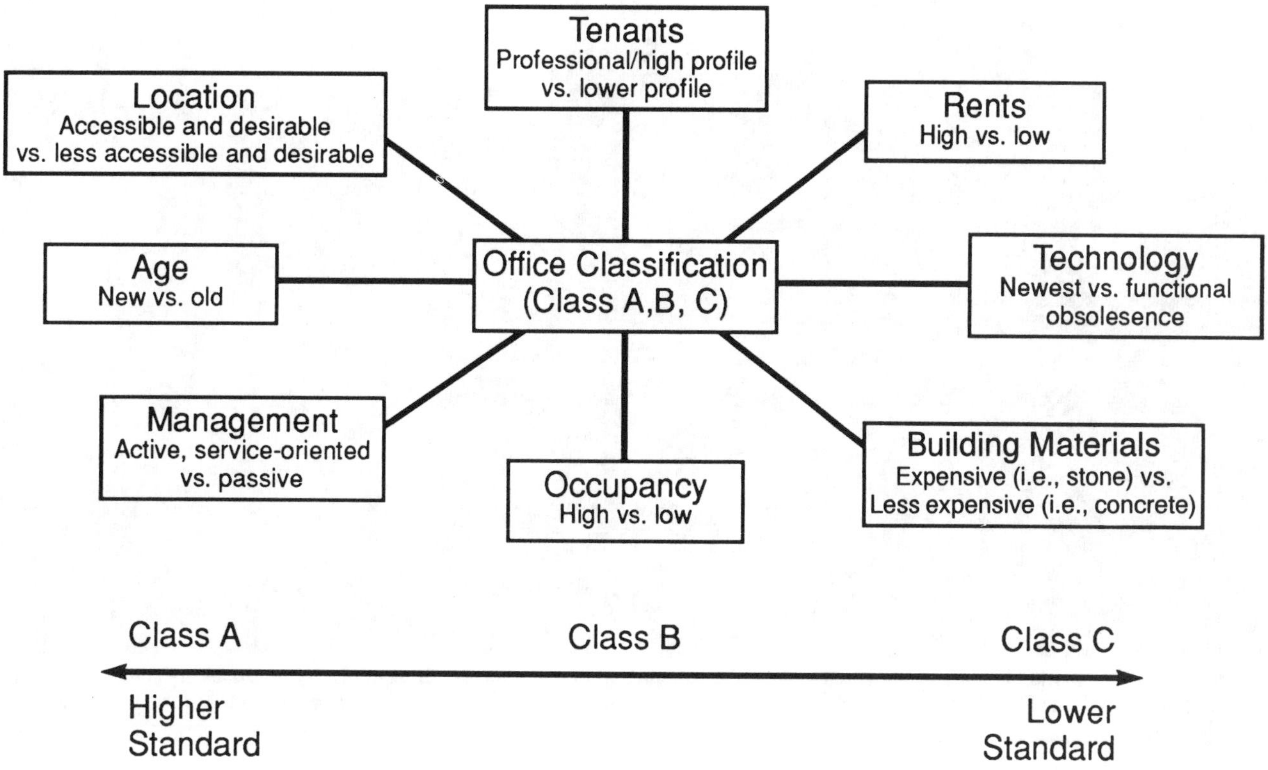

- Garden Office—one to five stories with extensive landscaping.
- Research and Development (R&D)—one to five stories with laboratory, clean-room space, and perhaps some light manufacturing space (office/industrial hybrid).
- Office/Tech—similar to R&D, except that office/tech typically does not include manufacturing space.

Markets

ULI's *Office Development Handbook*[3] divides office markets into five broad categories:

- Major Institutional/Professional—large projects occupied by banks and similar institutions. Prime locations are critical to such users.
- General Commercial—buildings that serve this market are typically smaller than those occupied by major institutions and address is less important. Tenants may have a strong sales orientation and require proximity to markets and transportation, convenient auto access, and adequate parking.
- Medical/Dental—professional office building space for sale or rent near major hospitals has become a distinct submarket. Parking and plumbing requirements are much greater than for other office categories.
- Office/Warehouse—office uses found in high-quality industrial parks that typically offer easy access and a concentration of employment-related services. Office users are attracted by the lower cost of land in such parks and by the availability of less-costly and more-flexible building alternatives.
- Pure Industrial—office space that is part of major manufacturing operations.

Locations

As these descriptions indicate, each of the five types of office users tends to prefer a particular type of location. Within most urban areas, at least four distinct locational nodes can be found:

- Central Business District (CBD)—the major concentration of large office buildings occurs in the downtown area of most large cities.

The office building market is highly segmented and can be categorized in many ways—for example, by products, by market served, and by location. Three Little Falls Centre, in Wilmington, Delaware, is a low-rise suburban building that serves as the world headquarters for HIMONT, USA.

- Suburban Office Nodes—concentrations of major and smaller office buildings are often found near freeway intersections and major suburban shopping centers. These suburban office nodes are characterized by low- to mid-rise office buildings and offer abundant parking, easy access, and lower rents than the CBD. Tenants typically include regional headquarters offices and smaller companies and service organizations that do not need to be in the CBD. Increasingly, suburban centers are attracting major law firms, accounting firms, and even corporate headquarters.
- Neighborhood Offices—small office buildings are frequently located in suburban areas, away from the major nodes, where they serve the needs of local residents by providing space for service and professional businesses. Neighborhood offices can be either integral parts of neighborhood shopping centers or free-standing buildings.
- Business Parks—office buildings are frequently an integral part of business/industrial parks. They tend to be small- to medium-size buildings of one to three stories, and they often offer bulk space to large users. R&D office buildings, with capabilities for laboratory space but limited warehousing space, are typically located in business parks.

Trends in Office Building Development

Since the 1950s and the construction of the interstate highway system, offices have steadily been relocating from the CBDs into outlying suburban areas. Such areas offer not only low land and construction costs but also shorter commutes and, therefore, lower transportation costs for employees. Throughout the country, many suburban office districts have emerged, such as Tyson's Corner in the Washington, D.C., area and Irvine–Newport Beach in Southern California.

The large amount of space available in suburban office nodes offers many advantages: ample parking, nearby housing, and the opportunity for extensive landscaping and open space. Unfortunately, the rapid development of these suburban nodes has created traffic congestion—one of the problems that originally motivated the companies to move to the suburbs. In fact, suburban traffic problems are regenerating interest in inner-city locations, and beginning developers may find attractive opportunities in inner-city redevelopment and infill, not least because the time and cost of public approvals is lower in such areas. Resolving suburban traffic congestion is rapidly becoming one of the major urban issues of the 1990s.

Aside from transportation, various demographic, technological, and market trends are helping to shape the future demand for, and location of, office space.

The migration of firms and people to the Southern and Western United States has provided many opportunities for developers. Many firms are moving their corporate headquarters and other functions into the "Sunbelt" areas, thereby promoting increased office construction in those areas. The rate of movement to Texas and other oil states slowed in the late 1980s due to the regional recession there, but the availability of low-cost housing and the promise of economic recovery are likely to fuel continued migration.

Cities in the Northeast, such as Boston, New York City, and Washington, D.C., enjoyed a boom during the late 1980s due to expansion in technology-based industries, financial services, and government services, but in the early 1990s these industries were on the decline.

In general, a shifting economy will continue to cause uneven regional office development patterns. A good understanding of what is changing in the office employment market is critical in discerning new development opportunities.

Another factor that will affect the workplace of the future is the increasing computerization of the office. The so-called "smart building" is becoming a reality as office tenants are requiring more extensive and sophisticated telephone and computer network systems, ideally integrated into the design of the building. Increased demand for telephone lines, internal wiring systems for computers, satellite transmitting facilities, and other advanced telecommunications equipment will all be important considerations in the design of office buildings. The demand for office space and the character of office work is also likely to be significantly affected by a growth in the number of workers able to work from home via personal computers, modems, fax machines, and other such technology.

Changing energy technology is altering the way that office buildings are designed and managed. Since the oil crisis of the 1970s, energy conservation and energy management have become important aspects of property management, and the oil crisis of 1990 has only heightened this issue further. Energy management systems that control heating and ventilation and can substantially reduce operating expenses are becoming critical components of an office building. Many utility companies are encouraging the use of cogeneration and off-peak cooling systems through special financial incentives and technical assistance.

In addition, state or locally mandated energy conservation requirements are affecting the design of buildings. Some local regulations restrict the amount of windows permitted in a new building (in order to limit the loss of heat), require solar water heating, specify insulation levels, or require water-conserving plumbing fixtures and landscaping. All of these rules and regulations must be considered when designing and when computing the budget for an office building.

During the 1980s, in response to increased demand and easy financing, the United States experienced a major boom in office construction. Many office buildings were built by developers who used cheap money generated by partnerships that wanted tax write-offs rather than positive cash flows. S&Ls, banks, pension funds, and insurance companies were also keen to fund office projects, even marginal projects. As a result, much more space was constructed than the market could possibly absorb within a reasonable period of time. Although some markets continue to need more office space, many cities will not return to normal occupancy rates (of 90 to 95 percent) until the mid- or late-1990s.

Project Feasibility

Market Analysis

The first task for developers contemplating office development, as with any type of development, is to conduct an initial market analysis. This task will require the assistance of a market research firm. Before selecting which firm to hire, developers should carefully evaluate the extent of survey information available in-house to each of the major market research firms. Some experts recommend that developers focus on market research firms that maintain or have access to substantial databases. Major brokerage firms maintain data on every tenant and every building in many cities. They know when tenants' leases expire, what the terms of those leases are, and who will decide whether or not to renew those leases. These firms also know what the current trends in the market are and what segments of the market have the largest unmet demand (or the smallest oversupply). Some firms will provide this information only if they receive an exclusive listing on the property. However, since leasing decisions have their own criteria separate from market research decisions, developers should refuse to accept such conditions.

Demand

Analysis of demand for office space begins with an analysis of the economic base of the local metropolitan area. Specifically, this involves studying the existing employers and industries in the market and their growth potential. Projected employment growth is the key item, and this should be broken down by industry and, ulti-

Market analysis must determine the preferences and requirements of users in the market, including issues such as floor sizes, corner offices, balconies, amenities, and location. River Forum (above), located along the Willamette River in Portland, Oregon, offers numerous corner offices, balconies, and an attractive brick exterior.

mately, should yield office-based employment growth projections for the local economy. Local governments and chambers of commerce are good sources for employment projections, although these should be carefully analyzed to ensure that they are realistic and not merely wishful thinking. Any report or analysis that forecasts that employment growth will significantly exceed past trends should be thoroughly scrutinized. The projections should take into consideration new firms moving into the area as well as the expansion of existing firms.

Market analysis must also attempt to determine the preferences and requirements of users in the market. Approximately 95 percent of tenants in a new building come from existing businesses located within a 60-mile radius of the site. Companies seek new space primarily for one of five reasons:

- to accommodate additional personnel or a new subsidiary;
- to expand an existing business into a new area;
- to improve the quality of the office environment;
- to consolidate dispersed activities into a single space; and
- to improve corporate image (thereby improving both sales and customer contacts and enhancing employee morale).

The size of potential tenants affects the overall design of a building, including its average floor area, number of entrances, and the location of any hallways. A large, single tenant may rent entire floors, whereas small tenants will need common halls to serve their individual suites.

The market analysis should also focus on whether the market contains headquarters, regional, or branch office users. The type of tenant affects the architectural design with respect to office depths, corridor widths, parking, and amenities. A large institutional tenant, for example, may be more concerned about its ability to use the space efficiently. On the other hand, in a market dominated by small, corporate headquarters users, the image of a building, its amenities (for instance, the availability of recreation facilities, security, and reserved parking), and its ability to provide its tenants individual identities will be major concerns.

The space requirements of potential users will inevitably affect the design and type of facility. For instance, large users frequently desire large bay depths (the distance between the glass line and the building core), but small users generally want smaller bay depths to increase the number of offices per suite that have windows. Space requirements will themselves be influenced by a potential tenant's employee mix. Nationally, the average space allotted each employee is 250 square feet; however, whereas secretaries generally require between 100 and 150 square feet, a typical president's office might occupy as much as 400 square feet.

Once data on potential tenants has been collected by a market researcher and the expected employment growth has been calculated for a specified time period, the following equation can be used to estimate the total square footage demanded:

$$\text{Number of projected employees} \times \text{Space per employee} = \text{Projected office space demand}$$

The demand is expressed in terms of net rentable square footage demanded per year. The time dimension—absorption per year—is the most important part of the market analysis. Without it, the analysis is meaningless.

Two rules of thumb are useful in calculating the demand for office space. First, all Class C space over 50 years old will likely be replaced within the next 20 years. Second, most firms that wish to move are looking for 10 to 20 percent more space than they currently occupy.

Supply

After establishing the market demand, the developer must focus on the supply of office space within the market. A thorough survey of existing, planned, and potential office projects should be undertaken either by the developer or by a market analyst. Such an inventory should include the following items:

- location,
- gross and net building area,
- scheduled rent per square foot,
- lease terms,
- tenant-finish allowances,
- building services,
- parking provided and parking charges,
- building amenities (restaurants, conference facilities, health clubs, and so forth), and
- list of tenants and contact person.

These data are used to determine the market niche in which the development under study will compete. It provides the basis for estimating rents, concessions, design features, and desired amenities.

Black's Guide (published annually by Black's Research Service, Inc., Redbank, New Jersey) provides a good overview of the type and amount of office space that is being offered in many cities. It is not definitive and the information is dated, but it provides an excellent starting point. Also, the local chapter of the Building Owners and Managers Association (BOMA) is a good source for information on existing inventory. *BOMA Experience Exchange Reports*, published by the association's local chapters, have useful information on occupancy and operating expenses and revenues for representative buildings.

From the study of supply, the developer can determine the total existing supply plus the future supply of office space. By subtracting the expected supply from the expected demand for office space, the deficit or surplus of office space for a particular period can be determined. This knowledge allows the developer to estimate the market conditions that will prevail when his/her building comes on line. If demand is increasing faster than supply, vacancy rates should be falling, creating a more favorable market for the developer. Alternatively, if supply is increasing faster than demand, vacancy rates should be increasing.

A natural vacancy rate due to turnover is inevitable. The total square footage of supply should be adjusted by the natural vacancy rate, which tends to increase in faster-growing cities. A very rapidly growing city may have a

A thorough survey of existing, planned, and potential office projects must be undertaken, focusing on both the broad market as well as the immediate nodal competitors. Pictured is Metro Center (center) in Stamford, Connecticut.

natural vacancy rate of over 10 percent, whereas the rate in a stagnant city may be only 3 percent. In the equation below, the market supply, natural vacancy, and total demand are expressed in square footages. Care should be taken to be consistent in terms of how space is measured; either net rental square footage or gross square footage may be used, but not both:

$$\frac{\text{Total market supply} - \text{Natural vacancy}}{\text{Total demand per year}} = \begin{array}{c}\text{Months of}\\ \text{existing inventory}\end{array}$$

For example, suppose the natural vacancy rate in a city is estimated at 5 percent, or, say, 50,000 square feet of the total inventory of 1 million square feet. If total existing market supply is 150,000 square feet, and annual absorption is 100,000 square feet per year, then the market contains one-and-one-half years' worth (18 months) of existing supply. When the natural vacancy of 50,000 square feet is taken into account, the "excess supply" drops to one year. Suppose another 200,000 square feet is on the drawing boards of local developers, according to the information collected from bankers, brokers, and city planning staff. Not all of this space will actually be built, so only some percentage of it, say 50 percent, should be added to total market supply. If another 100,000 square feet (50 percent times 200,000) is added to the existing supply of 100,000 square feet, the total existing and planned supply becomes two years:

$$\frac{150{,}000 - 50{,}000 + 100{,}000}{100{,}000} = \begin{array}{c}\text{2.0 years' worth of existing}\\ \text{and planned inventory}\end{array}$$

Should a developer build in a market that has two years' worth of existing and planned inventory? No firm guidelines exist for determining what constitutes a soft market, although a market with less than 12 months' worth of inventory is generally considered a strong market, 12 to 24 months' worth a normal market, and more than 24 months' worth (18 months in slower-growing areas) a weak market. With a building that will enter the market in 12 months, a developer will face a 12-month existing inventory in the above example. If the building adds 50,000 square feet to the inventory, then in 12 months the inventory will be 150,000 square feet. If the developer captures a pro-rata share (33 percent) of the total inventory, the building will take 18 months to lease.

Developers usually believe that they can outperform the market because they have either superior location, product design, cost advantages, or leasing personnel; however, obviously not everyone can outperform the market, and it is a grave mistake to plan on doing so. Developers should have sufficient cash available to cover situations in which leasing takes longer than indicated by the pro-rata capture rate. In the current example, the developer should expect to take 18 months to lease the building but should also be able to cover a slower lease-up of 24 to 30 months.

Effective Rental Rates

One of the most important distinctions to understand in office market analysis is the difference between quoted rents and effective rents. With the glut of office space in the early 1980s, a plethora of devices were introduced for maintaining future rent levels while effectively reducing current rents. Developers focused on what rent they had to achieve by a certain date under the terms of their permanent-mortgage commitment and would offer tenants free rent or extra allowance on their space improvements (called "tenant improvements") to induce them to lease space, as long as the rent in the lease met the lenders' requirements for funding the mortgage or releasing the developers' personal liability.

Such concessions are standard operating practice today, and lenders accept them. However, lenders have become more sophisticated in how they review lease agreements before funding a loan. Like tenants, they now focus on *effective* rents.

Rental concessions are harder for market analysts to identify than are street rents. Brokers and leasing agents have an incentive to overstate rents or understate concessions because they do not want future prospects to know what they gave

■ 5-2 Effective Office Rent Calculation

Suppose a developer has an office space of 1,000 square feet with a nominal rent of $24 per square foot for five years ($2 per month). Concessions include six months' free rent and $3 per square foot in extra tenant improvements. The tenant's discount rate (opportunity cost of money) is 12 percent or 1 percent per month.

To find the effective rent, the developer must convert the lease and the free rent to present value. This can be computed either on a per-square-foot basis or on the total lease area.

Present value (*PV*)of lease per square foot:	
PV ($2 per month, 1% per month interest, 60 months)	$89.91
Less:	
Present value of free rent per square foot:	
PV ($2 per month, 1% per month interest, 6 months)	11.59
Extra tenant improvements (already stated as present value)	3.00
Present value of effective rent	$75.32
Convert present value to equivalent monthly rent	
PMT ($75.32 *PV*, 1% per month interest, 60 months)	$ 1.67
	x 12 months
Effective annual rent per square foot	$20.04

away on earlier deals. Hence, analysts may be misled and report that rents are higher than they actually are.

The market study should provide the information necessary to compute rental rates and the estimated absorption rate during lease-up, as well as the types of concessions necessary to compete with other developers. These numbers will be used directly in the financial analysis. The percentage of the total absorption that a project will

■ 5-3 Sample Office Market Study

Class A Office Space—Los Angeles CBD, April 30, 1988

Building Name and Address	Year Completed	Floors	Rentable Space (Square Feet)	Available Direct and *Sublease* (Square Feet)	Percent Vacant Direct and *Sublease*	Total Project Leased (Square Feet)	Pending Leases (Square Feet)	Largest Contiguous Block (Square Feet)	Quoted Rental Rate (Per Square Foot)
1. Biltmore Tower 500 South Grand Avenue	1987	24	137,601	57,323 *0*	41.7% *0.0*	80,278	0	23,496	$23.50–33.50 Gross
2. Biltmore Court 520 South Grand Avenue	1987	11	231,191	174,673 *0*	75.6 *0.0*	56,518	57,000	51,996	20.00–28.00 Gross
3. 1000 Wilshire Building 1000 Wilshire Boulevard	1987	21	452,000	42,366 *63,489*	9.4 *14.0*	409,634	10,000	17,830 45,278	28.00–34.00 Gross
4. Wilshire Financial Center 1100 Wilshire Boulevard	1986	38	298,179	254,200 *0*	85.3 *0.0*	43,979	30,000	145,000	25.00–28.00 Gross
5. Chase Plaza 801 South Grand Avenue	1986	22	435,000	79,000 *21,048*	18.2 *4.8*	356,000	20,000	61,500 21,048	29.00–31.00 Gross
6. One California Plaza 300 South Grand Avenue	1985	42	936,864	131,020 *0*	14.0 *0.0*	805,844	32,967	46,066	21.50–29.50 NNN
7. Citicorp Plaza I 725 South Figueroa Street	1985	41	895,058	54,602 *0*	6.1 *0.0*	840,456	10,000	13,000 0	23.00–25.00 NNN
8. International Tower 888 South Figueroa Street	1985	20	410,000	95,826 *0*	23.4 *0.0*	314,174	10,000	55,000	25.00–31.00 Gross

Absorption of First-Class Downtown Office Space, 1980–1992

Year	Completed Projects During Year (Square Feet)	Available Supply (Including Prior Year's Surplus) (Square Feet)	Preleased (Known Future Absorption) (Square Feet)	Absorption (and Estimated Future Demand) (Square Feet)	Surplus (Deficit at Year End) (Square Feet)	Total Inventory of First-Class Office Space (Square Feet)	Year-End Vacancy
Actual Year 1980	641,000	667,714	–	640,000	27,714	8,509,946	0.3%
Actual Year 1981	1,168,027	1,195,741	–	1,066,000	129,741	9,677,973	1.3
Actual Year 1982	3,402,421	3,532,162	–	1,500,000	2,032,162	13,080,394	15.5
Actual Year 1983	1,185,424	3,217,586	–	1,000,000	2,217,586	14,265,818	15.5
Actual Year 1984	126,000	2,343,586	–	1,000,000	1,343,586	14,391,818	9.3
Actual Year 1985	2,827,416	4,171,002	–	1,440,707	2,730,295	17,219,234	15.9
Actual Year 1986	733,179	3,463,474	–	1,667,398	1,796,076	17,952,413	10.0
Actual Year 1987	820,792	2,616,868	–	886,739	1,730,129	18,773,205	9.2
Projected Year 1988	873,807	2,603,936	284,556	1,000,000	1,603,936	19,647,012	8.2
Projected Year 1989	1,300,920	2,904,856	873,062	1,250,000	1,654,856	20,947,932	7.9
Projected Year 1990	1,631,598	3,286,454	–	1,250,000	2,036,454	22,579,530	9.0
Projected Year 1991	3,150,000	5,186,454	500,000	1,250,000	3,936,454	25,729,530	15.3
Undetermined	2,347,307	6,283,761	–	1,250,000	5,033,761	28,076,837	17.9

■ 5-3 (Continued)

Vacancy Forecast: Under Construction/Planned New Completions (as of April 30, 1988)

Project Name	Size (Square Feet)	1988 (Square Feet)	1989 (Square Feet)	1990 (Square Feet)	1991 (Square Feet)	Undetermined (Square Feet)
Home Savings	247,763	247,763				
Arco Center	626,044	626,044				
Library Tower	1,300,920		1,300,920			
Fig Plaza II	307,307					307,307
865 South Figueroa	681,598			681,598		
Fig/Wilshire	950,000			950,000		
Harbor Towers	400,000					400,000
777 Tower	900,000				900,000	
Grand Place	1,000,000				1,000,000	
Pacific Atlas	635,000					635,000
California Plaza II	1,250,000				1,250,000	
Hammerson Prop	420,000					430,000
Church Open/Dr.	575,000					575,000
New Inventory	9,293,632	873,807	1,300,920	1,631,598	3,150,000	2,347,307
Prior Surplus		1,730,129	1,603,936	1,654,856	2,036,454	3,936,454
Total Available		2,603,936	2,904,856	3,286,454	5,186,454	6,283,761
Less Absorption		(1,000,000)	(1,250,000)	(1,250,000)	(1,250,000)	(1,250,000)
Year-End Surplus		1,603,936	1,654,856	2,036,454	3,936,454	5,033,761
Total Inventory		19,647,012	20,947,932	22,579,530	25,729,530	28,076,837
Year-End Vacancy Rate		8.2%	7.9%	9.0%	15.3%	17.9%

Leasing Summary and Forecast

Total Square Feet Leased as of February 29, 1988:	17,006,475	(33 Buildings)
Total Square Feet Leased as of April 30, 1988:	16,959,044	(33 Buildings)
Total Increase:	(47,431)[a]	Net absorption for this period (2/29/88–4/30/88)
	110,079	Square feet leased this period (2/29/88–4/30/88)
	79,744	Square feet leased in prior period (1/01/88–2/28/88)
	189,823	Total 1988 leased square feet
Total Direct Square Feet Available February 29, 1988:	1,766,730	(33 Buildings)
Total Direct Square Feet Available April 30, 1988:	1,814,161	(33 Buildings)
Total Increase:	47,431	Additional square feet available this period
Total Sublease Square Feet Available February 29, 1988:	505,521	
Total Sublease Square Feet Available April 30, 1988:	600,310	
Total Increase	94,789	Additional square feet available this period
Total 1988 Leased Square Feet:	189,823	(33 Buildings)
Total 1988 Preleased Square Feet:	284,556	(Arco Center and Home Savings Tower)
	474,379	Current total 1988 absorption
	1,000,000	Forecasted 1988 absorption

[a]Net absorption during this period is negative because of additional space that was made available for lease in excess of the 110,079 square feet that was actually leased during this period.

Source: Art Salmonson, Los Angeles.

capture is also an important figure to examine. A common mistake is to assume that a project will capture an unrealistically large share of the entire market.

General Advice on Office Market Research

Alan Kotin, president of Kotin, Regan and Mouchly, Los Angeles, and adjunct professor of planning at USC, emphasizes four points about office market research:[4]

- The larger the tenant, the more difficult it is to determine what the tenant is actually paying in rent after taking into account rent concessions such as free rent, expense caps, free parking, and extra tenant improvements.
- Major markets are stratified by scale as well as by quality, rent, and location. A 10 percent vacancy rate may be very misleading if the largest space available is only 20,000 square feet. The market for 50,000-square-

foot tenants is very different from that for 100,000-square-foot tenants.

- With major buildings, control of a single large tenant is far more important than generic measures of space.
- Despite the sophistication of market analysis, the fact remains that many small- and medium-size firms decide where to rent space on such distinctly unscientific grounds as "where the boss lives."

Site Selection

Site selection for office buildings addresses the same subjects that must be addressed with all product types: location, size and shape, site conditions, and so on. These subjects are discussed in detail in chapters 3 and 4; only those points that are unique to office buildings are discussed here.

Although office buildings may be found in every location and in every size and shape, they are generally located in office clusters such as downtowns, suburban business districts, and office/business parks. In general, office uses can support the highest rents of any land use type and thus are often located on the highest-priced land. Thus, high land prices should not be a deterrent in the search for a site; a high price is usually indicative of the desirability of the location for office uses. Jim Goodell, president of Goodell & Associates, Inc., of Burbank, California, makes the following recommendations regarding office site selection:[5]

- Office buildings should be located in areas with a "sense of place." A synergy exists between office buildings and support activities such as restaurants, shopping, and club facilities. A mixed-use environment generates benefits that translate into higher rents and better leasing.
- Buildings should be located close to freeways or roads that feed into the regional traffic system. Although development opportunities exist for low-end office buildings and professional buildings in suburban shopping areas, such locations offer few, if any, comparative advantages for attracting tenants.
- Traffic loading during peak hours is usually the principal concern with respect to public approvals. Whereas busy streets with high traffic counts are a positive factor for retail buildings, they are a negative factor for office buildings.
- Infill sites in established office locations offer particular opportunities for beginning developers, since amen-

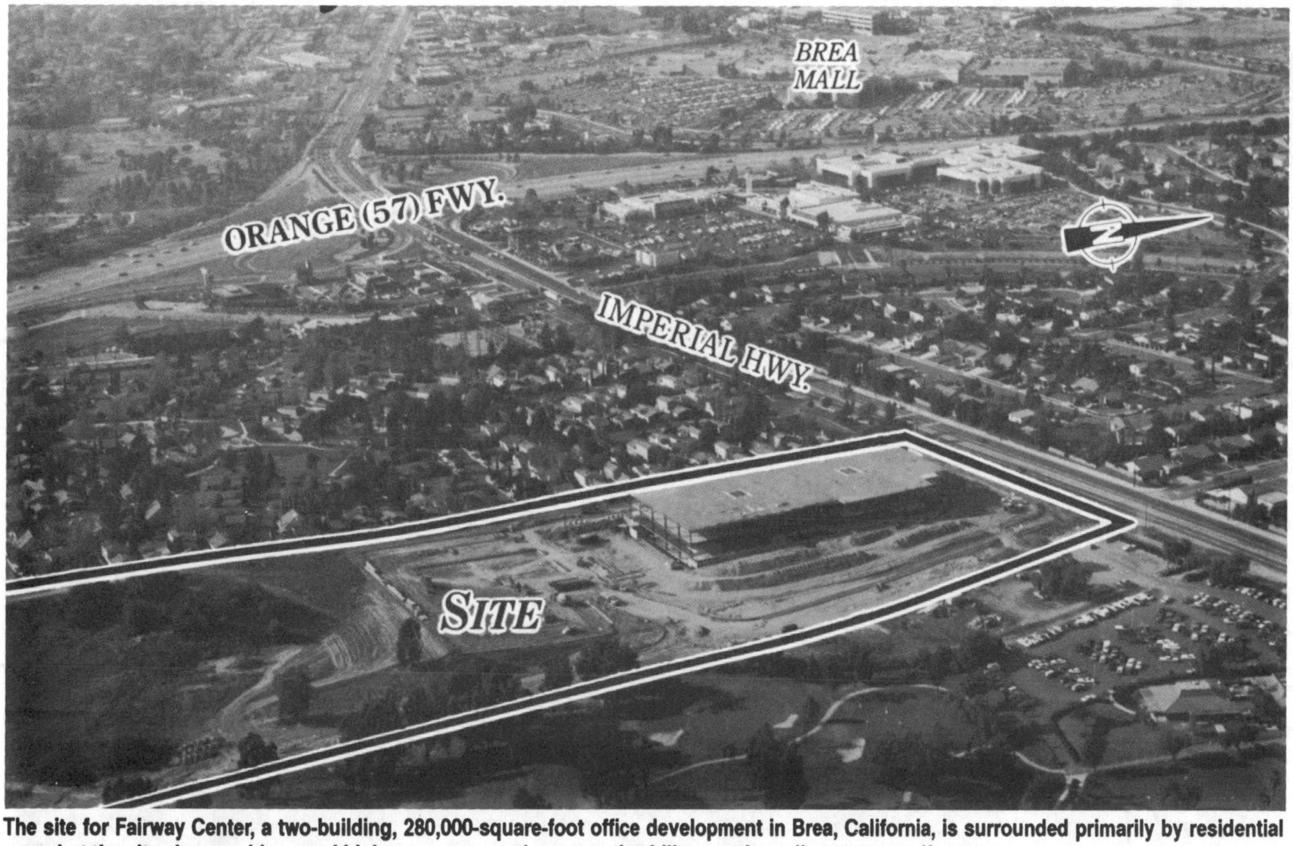

The site for Fairway Center, a two-building, 280,000-square-foot office development in Brea, California, is surrounded primarily by residential uses, but the site also provides good highway access and an attractive hilltop setting adjacent to a golf course.

Tom Guidera

Infill and/or redevelopment sites offer attractive opportunities for beginning developers because infrastructure is already in place. Pictured above is the site for the 1250 24th Street, N.W., office building in Washington, D.C. The project involved the preservation of the facade of this old taxi garage and the construction of a seven-story building behind it.

ities, utilities, and other infrastructure and zoning are already in place.

- The site should be able to accommodate an efficient building design. Office buildings are less flexible in terms of size and shape than are industrial, retail, and residential buildings. Back-office users, such as clerical and data processing operations, prefer floor plates (that is, area per floor) in excess of 20,000 square feet. Small-office users, such as professional firms and smaller companies, prefer buildings with more window area and floor sizes ranging from 16,000 to 20,000 square feet, although smaller floor plates are not uncommon. The most efficient buildings are 100 feet wide and 200 feet long. However, such plain rectangular boxes may lack sufficient design appeal to lease well.
- Structured parking modules with efficient layouts should be either 120 or 180 feet wide and at least 180 feet long.[6] Free-standing parking structures are less expensive to build than structures that are integrated into the office building itself because the structural systems required for parking are different from those required for office buildings. An office building site should, where possible, provide enough room for separate structures.
- Topography can play an important role in site selection. Hilly sites may require extensive grading, which will increase construction costs, but they may also provide excellent opportunities for tuck-under parking that requires less excavation than on a flat site.
- Access to adjacent roads is critical. The location, number, and arrangement of curb cuts into a parking lot can significantly affect the ease of ingress and egress from a site. Parcels located on prime highways may have great visibility but may not be accessible from those highways. Access for buildings on major highways or frontage roads may be limited to side, or even rear, streets. Developers must check with local municipal, county, state, and federal transportation authorities about access concerns.

The terms of site acquisition are essentially the same for office buildings as for the other product types and are discussed in detail in chapters 3 and 4.

Regulatory Issues

Traditionally, office developers were concerned only with local zoning and building codes. How much space they could build was determined primarily by floor/area ratios (FARs), height limitations, building setbacks, and parking requirements.

In the 1980s, developers began to encounter a plethora of new regulations aimed at office buildings. Some of these initiatives were motivated by a local community's need to control negative impacts of office development such as traffic, others were motivated by a community's need to raise tax revenues. As a result, public regulation of office development has been somewhat ambivalent. On the one hand, cities want office development because it is clean, generates jobs, and brings in tax revenues. On the other hand, shrinking local tax revenues from other sources have led many cities to look toward office development as the primary source of funds for subsidizing public projects and even social programs such as low-income housing. The result has been a host of impact fees and new requirements, such as housing linkage programs that require developers to build up to 200 units of low-income housing for every 1 million square feet of office space constructed.

The results have backfired in some cases. San Francisco, for example, experienced an exodus of businesses from the city's core to outlying areas and to Los Angeles when it instituted a combination of very high impact fees, exactions, and housing linkage programs. In another instance, Beverly Hills inherited all of the traffic but none of the tax revenues when it refused to approve a major hotel that was eventually built across the street in the city of Los Angeles.

Certain cities have such unique and attractive locations that they can extract above-average concessions from developers, but even these cities have suffered a slowdown of new business development when the cost of their exactions made development unprofitable. After all, developers pass on the regulatory costs to future tenants in the form of rent. If rents rise too high, present and potential tenants will seek space elsewhere. Furthermore, with the office development slowdown in the early 1990s, many cities that have depended on office development to generate tax revenues will have to look to other sources, most likely, higher property, sales, or income taxes.

Government bodies are also constantly revising local building codes, spurred, in some cases, by litigation, or the threat of litigation, concerning building safety and public health. As more information is gathered about the effects of fire, wind, earthquakes, tornadoes, and hurricanes, local and national building codes are updated. Many government agencies are enacting stringent fire, seismic, and energy codes. This trend toward stricter building codes seems likely to continue.

Zoning and Land Use Controls

In addition to the typical zoning restrictions on building setbacks, height, and site coverage, the regulations that particularly affect office development concern:

- floor/area ratios,
- parking requirements,
- massing, and
- solar shadows.

FARs determine office building densities. Some cities, such as Los Angeles, have passed citizen-sponsored initiatives that dramatically reduce the allowable FARs. Such reductions give cities unusual leverage in negotiating with developers for facilities or services that the city wants.

New York City awards FAR bonuses to developers who provide plazas, subway connections, "pocket parks," theaters, gallerias, and other special features. Trump Tower, for example, originally had an FAR of 15. Because the design of Trump Tower incorporated special features such as a pedestrian arcade, landscaped terracing, and interior retail space, Donald Trump received an FAR bonus of 3. After purchasing additional air rights from an adjacent building, the total allowable FAR reached 21.6 times the buildable lot area.[7]

Parking requirements for office buildings typically stipulate three spaces per 1,000 square feet of net rentable floor area. However, developers who provide only three spaces per 1,000 square feet are usually headed for trouble. Many lenders will only finance suburban office buildings with at least four spaces per 1,000 square feet because the lenders know from experience that parking difficulties will drive away tenants. At the same time, however, some cities are trying to encourage use of mass transit by limiting parking. Some cities have proposed that developers provide mandatory off-site parking for some portion of the parking requirement for buildings in congested downtown areas. In Los Angeles, for example, the Community Redevelopment Agency has proposed that 40 percent of the parking for buildings in the downtown core must be located off site in certain designated areas and that parking is limited to 1 space per 1,000

The original zoning for the site at 1250 24th Street, N.W., in Washington, D.C., stipulated a mix of 50 percent commercial and 50 percent residential or hotel space. The developer had to take the project through the planned unit development process to increase the commercial density and eliminate the residential component. The facade of the existing building on the site also had to be preserved to ensure public and community approval.

square feet of office space. Developers are concerned that such a requirement will cause tenants to search elsewhere for space because employees will not tolerate the additional travel time from the off-site parking to their offices, even if their overall commute is less expensive. On the other hand, developers are finding that lower parking requirements can save them money and that lenders will still provide financing if all developers are subject to the same restrictions.

Building massing and solar restrictions seek to prevent city streets from becoming dark canyons. Most zoning ordinances include provisions that carefully define building envelopes and shapes in order to stop buildings from casting permanent shadows and to prevent the glass on buildings from reflecting excessive heat onto other structures. In addition, some government agencies restrict the types of materials, styles of architecture, location of entries, and various other design aspects of office projects. Developers must recognize and work within these restrictions in order to determine the maximum envelope that their buildings can occupy.

One special regulatory device that has often been used with office development is transferable development rights (TDRs). TDRs allow for the sale of development rights from one owner to another. If one owner wants to retain, say, a two-story building on a site zoned for 10 stories, that owner may sell the right to build the additional square footage to another landowner. Once sold, however, the original owner cannot build any more square footage than that for which zoning rights were retained.

TDRs have not been as widely adopted as planners expected. Markets in TDRs have developed only slowly, not least perhaps because of concern among owners that a developer may legally overbuild a site, causing traffic congestion and dense shadows on neighboring properties. However, TDRs do work well with historic landmark buildings. Property owners often consider historic landmark designations detrimental to property values, even though they confer status. Landmark designation severely complicates, and may even prevent, major changes to the structure and facade of buildings. TDRs allow owners of landmark buildings to receive compensation for their loss of development rights.

Some scholars believe that TDRs and incentive zoning codes are violating the basic purpose of the zoning code, namely, to provide a balance between land use activity and transportation activity. Mel Branch, in his article "Don't Call It City Planning," argues that the incentive mechanisms in various zoning codes are leading to a problem of densification in major U.S. cities. In addition, Branch contends that "zoning is being used as a misplaced form of selective taxation."[8] The future of many of these zoning programs will depend on whether or not the public believes that providing public features and saving historical buildings justifies the increase in traffic that results from urban densification.

Transportation Issues

One of the most politically sensitive areas regarding office development is the impact that such development has on traffic. Congestion was once only a problem for central city areas. Today, many suburbs are experiencing congestion that is as bad as, or worse than, that in the older downtown areas.

Most large office developments and many small ones are now required to provide a traffic impact study during the approval process. Since office development generally contributes large traffic loads during peak hours, traffic mitigation measures are becoming a common requirement for approval. These measures can range from widening the streets in front of a building to adding a traffic signal or widening streets and intersections away from a site. Satisfying off-site infrastructure requirements can be extremely costly and time-consuming, not least because of the need to work with public agencies and other property owners.

An office developer may be required to undertake any of the following actions:

- restripe existing streets,
- add deceleration and acceleration lanes into a project,
- construct a median to control access,
- install signals at intersections or entrances to a project,
- widen streets in front of a project,
- widen streets between a project and major highways or freeways,

The impact of new office development on traffic and the highway system is an issue that projects large and small will have to address.

- build a new street between a project and a major highway, and
- contribute to construction of highway or freeway interchanges.

Instead of requiring certain improvements—exactions—some areas have created impact fee programs to cover traffic improvements. Impact fees are typically assessed on a "per-peak-trip-generated" basis or translated into a square footage fee. Fees can run as high as several thousand dollars per peak trip generated. The number of expected peak trips generated by the project thus becomes a critical factor in the cost of the project.

Several creative solutions have emerged to reduce peak traffic trips, such as adding retail components to a project, providing residential facilities on or adjacent to the site, providing linkages with public transportation systems, or encouraging transportation system management (TSM) programs.

TSM programs have become a popular mechanism for reducing traffic generation in many California cities. A number of cities have passed ordinances requiring developers of projects with a certain number of employees to implement rideshare programs. A TSM plan may also include reduced-price passes for public transit and preferential parking spaces for carpoolers. The developer is normally responsible for ensuring that these programs are implemented.

Financial Feasibility

The financial feasibility process involves gathering market data from the market study, cost data for various alternatives, and financing costs and entering these data into the financial pro forma.

Financial feasibility analysis for office projects uses methods similar to those employed for other income properties, and the general approach is discussed fully in chapter 4. Figure 5-4 provides an example of a financial feasibility analysis for Fairway Center, a 147,319-square-foot office building in southern California.

In estimating operating costs for an office building, one useful source of information is the *BOMA Experience Exchange Report: Income/Expense Analysis for Office Buildings*, an annual study published by BOMA that provides detailed breakdowns of operating costs and revenues for different types and sizes of office buildings in different locations and metropolitan areas.

In light of overbuilt markets in the early 1990s, the key issue in estimating revenues for office projects is to make realistic projections regarding lease-up time, vacancy rates, and achievable rents. Many markets will continue to be overbuilt and/or extremely competitive, making it very difficult for developers to achieve optimistic projections.

Cap-rates and return requirements have risen sharply because of the office glut. Whereas pro-forma cap rates (NOI divided by project cost) for determining project value of 8.5 percent were not uncommon in the mid-1980s, cap rates often exceeded 10 percent in 1991. Developers should consult local mortgage brokers and lenders to determine current appraisal and underwriting criteria before considering a project.

Design and Construction

General Principles

Adaptability must be programmed into initial building design. The design that is decided upon today may be used by tenants for 50 years or more. Furthermore, the office market is an ever-changing market, and a well-designed building will have the flexibility to meet the shifting demands of its tenants. Who could have predicted 50 years ago, for example, that every office in the 1990s would have computers?

The market analysis should provide almost all of the design parameters for the project (some design elements, such as the placement of halls, corridors, and fire walls, and the space requirements for restrooms, corridors, and stairwells, are usually dictated by local building and fire codes). For example, suppose an analysis indicates that the average office tenant leases 4,000 square feet and has a workforce of 16 employees, each of whom occupies an average of 250 square feet. These figures would be the basis for designing the building's size, parking, elevators, building depth, and interior air-circulation requirements.

As a general rule of thumb, total project costs may be broken down into the following percentages:[9]

Building shell and interior	45%
Environmental and service systems	25
Land and site improvements	18
Fees, interest, and contingencies	12
Total	100%

Of course, these numbers differ depending on regional requirements, construction methods, and special fees required by local government bodies.

Among the most important design decisions that must be determined at the outset are those concerning the shape of the building, the design modules, and the bay depths that will be used.

Shape

Although a square shape is the most cost-efficient for a building, it often generates the lowest average revenue per square foot. Rectangular and elongated shapes offer

The three-story 9090 Wilshire Boulevard in Beverly Hills, California, was 100 percent preleased before construction began and was designed specifically for the needs of three tenants. Tenant preferences led to a design that presented a modern interpretation of classic Palladian themes. Local zoning limited the building to three stories.

higher rents per square foot but cost more to build since they frequently provide more perimeter window space and shallower bay depths. Developers prefer rectangular buildings for multitenant speculative space because the interior and perimeter spaces can be more balanced.

The desire for striking architecture produced a strong movement away from the glass boxes of the 1970s and toward the angular buildings of the 1980s. Although nonrectangular shapes may be somewhat less efficient in terms of the ratio of perimeter wall to floor area, they often create more interesting office shapes and more corner offices. In most markets, such offices generate higher rent.

Design Modules and Bay Depths

Office buildings are designed using multiple modules of space, which allow for the repetition of structural and exterior skin materials. Even though the design module affects the outside of the building, the module should evolve from the types of interior spaces planned. Thus, the market study should suggest the type of interior designs (for example, open-plan or executive offices) that the target market segment is demanding.

The most common design module is the structural bay. Defined by the placement of the building's structural columns, the structural bay can be subdivided into modules of three, four, five, or five-and-one-half feet that provide a grid for coordinating interior partitions and

■ 5-4 Financial Feasibility Analysis for Fairway Center

Fairway Center, Phase 1: Project Summary

Land Area (Square Feet)	287,583	Rental Abatement	12 months
Land Cost per Square Foot	$10.28	Construction Period	12 months
Rentable Area (Square Feet)	147,319	Lease-Up Period (from Completion)	12 months
Construction Cost per Rentable Square Foot	$55.74	Vacancy Assumed (Normalized)	5.00%
Land Cost per Building Square Foot	$20.07	Total Costs	$19,404,688
Land per Building (Acres)	3.92	Development Period Receipts	($392,870)
Parking Spaces	598	Total Loan	$20,353,193
Parking Ratio (Spaces per 1,000 Usable Square Feet)	4.40	Average Borrowing Cost	8.76%
Rental Rate per Square Foot per Month (Average)	$1.67	Cap Rate on Sale	9.00%
Tenant Improvement Allowance per Square Foot (Average)	$21.99	Surplus on Sale (January 2000)	$19,299,959
Operating Costs per Square Foot	$0.43	Free and Clear Return	10.74%

Statement of Operations: Normalized First Year		**Statement of Operations: 10th Year (4% Inflation)**	
Gross Rent	$2,960,599	Gross Rent	$4,413,757
Vacancy Allowance	(74,260)	Vacancy Allowance	(220,688)
Operating Expense	(744,846)*	Operating Expense	(744,846)
Net Operating Income	$2,141,492	Net Operating Income	$3,448,223

Major Assumptions:

1. Project is financed with all debt at the predicted prime rate.
2. The first 74,515 square feet are leased one month after completion, 24,268 square feet two months later, an additional 24,268 square feet four months after that, and the final 24,268 square feet four months later (September 1988).
3. Rent abated on the first 74,515 square feet for 20 months after occupancy and the remaining 72,804 square feet for 12 months.
4. Ten-year holding period with sale taking place 10 years after full occupancy.
5. First month of normalized income is September 1989.
6. Rent and operating expenses are increased by an inflation factor of 4 percent each year (1990 to 1999).
7. Outstanding loan of $20,353,193 at the end of the development/lease-up period rolled over as the permanent loan, which is then carried during the six-year holding period at a 9 percent, 30-year amortization.

*See 10-year schedule of normalized operations for breakdown.

■ 5-4 (Continued)

Fairway Center, Phase I: Development Cost Report

Land Purchase	$2,957,217
Construction Costs:	
Building	$ 8,211,353
Tenant Finishes	2,986,074
Total Construction Costs	$11,197,428
Soft Costs:	
Marketing	$ 23,545
Appraisal Fee	18,649
Builders Risk Insurance	59,226
Title Insurance	14,222
Architectural and Engineering	588,965
Miscellaneous Expenses	19,122
Permits and Fees	61,568
Developer's Overhead and Fees	497,841
Financing Fees (Construction)	283,589
Leasing Commissions	768,641
Real Estate Taxes	51,073
Accounting	128,172
Legal Fees—Tenant	26,517
Legal—Other	61,367
City Mitigation Issues	171,278
City Bond Sale	(1,750,000)
Income Credit (Lease-Up)	392,870
Contingency	100,000
Construction Loan Interest	3,626,268
Total Soft Costs	$5,142,914
Lump Sum Fee	$ 500,000
Total Project Cost	$19,797,558

Fairway Center, Phase I: Building Construction Costs*

Development Budget	**Assumptions**	**Total**	**Through 31 Jul. 87**	**Aug. 87**	**Sep. 87**	**Oct. 87**	**Nov. 87**	**Dec. 87**
Interest Rate	Average	Percent		9.25%	9.25%	9.25%	9.25%	8.25%
Construction Costs		per Period:						
Off Sites	$887,990	100.00%	79.48%	20.52%				
Mass Grading	0	0.00%						
Sitework Phase I	0	0.00%						
Parking Structure Phase I	0	0.00%						
Building Shell Phase I	6,006,985	100.00%	77.67%	8.00%	8.00%	6.33%		
HVAC Equip./Dist.	770,751	100.00%	25.95%	74.05%				
Elevator	0	0.00%						
Restrooms	150,000	100.00%			33.00%	33.00%	34.00%	
Electrical/Phone Dist.	101,334	100.00%		34.00%	33.00%			
Sitework Phase II		0.00%						
Parking Structure Phase II		0.00%						
Building Shell Phase II		0.00%						
Tests and Inspection	0.75%	0.00%						
Contractor's Fee		0.00%						
Architectural and Engineering		0.00%						
Tenant Improvements		0.00%						
Permits and Fees		5.00%		5.00%				
Construction Costs:								
Off Sites		$887,990	$705,757	$ 182,233				
Mass Grading								
Sitework Phase I								
Parking Structure Phase I								
Building Shell Phase I		6,006,985	4,665,898	480,603	480,559	379,925		
HVAC Equip./Dist.		770,751	200,000	570,751				
Elevator								
Restrooms		150,000			49,500	49,500	51,000	
Electrical/Switch Gear		101,334		34,454	33,440	33,440		
Sitework Phase II								
Parking Structure Phase II								
Building Shell Phase II								
Tests and Inspection @ .75%		88,814	88,814					
Project Mgmt. Personnel		205,480	205,480	Shift to Developer's Fee				
Total Construction Costs		$8,211,354	$5,865,949	$1,268,041	$563,499	$462,865	$51,000	$0

*Excluding tenant finishes.

■ 5-4 (Continued)

Fairway Center, Phase I: Monthly Cash Flows during Development Period

Development Budget	**Assumptions**		**Total**	**Through 31 Jul. 87**	**Aug. 87**	**Sep. 87**	**Oct. 87**
Interest Rate	8.76% Average			9.25%	9.25%	9.25%	9.25%
Square Feet Leased	147,319		147,319				
Cumulative Square Feet Leased				0	0	0	0
Receipts							
Basic Rent	$1.70	$1.65	$987,683	$0	$0	$0	$0
Vacancy Allowances	5.00%		(30,942)	0	0	0	0
Operating Costs	$0.43	$0.11	(1,349,611)	–	–	(16,205)	(16,205)
Net Rental Receipts			(392,870)	0	0	(16,205)	(16,205)
Disbursements							
Marketing			$23,545	$6,024	$1,500	$1,500	$1,500
Appraisal Fee			18,649	13,000			
Builder Risk Insurance	$0.35	$100	59,226	59,226	0	0	
Title Insurance			14,222	12,855			
Land Purchase	$2,957,217	Sep. 86	2,957,217	2,957,217			
Construction Costs			8,211,353	5,865,949	1,268,040	563,499	462,865
Architectural and Engineering	6.00%	600,000	588,965	588,965	0	0	0
Miscellaneous			19,122	19,122	0	0	0
Tenant Improvements	$22.00	$1.00	2,986,074		0	754,932	754,932
Permits and Fees	$45,000		61,568	52,868	2,250	6,450	0
Developer's Overhead and Fees	5.00%	462,436	497,841	407,841	30,000	30,000	30,000
Construction Financing Fees	1.50%	69,772	283,589	283,589			
Leasing Commissions	4.00%	79,211	768,641	0	0	0	0
Legal Fees—Tenant	$0.18		26,517	0	0	13,413	0
Legal—General	$1,500	20,000	61,367	56,367	500	500	500
Accounting	1.50%	173,414	128,172	110,694	5,826	5,826	5,826
Operating Contingency	4.00%		100,000	3,607	30,000	30,000	30,000
Real Estate Taxes	1.09%		51,073	18,544			
City Mitigation Issues	171,278		171,278	0	171,278		
Loan Interest			3,626,268	350,159	85,925	95,282	110,381
City Bond Sale	1,750,000		(1,750,000)				(1,750,000)
Lump-Sum Fee		500,000	500,000				
Total Disbursements			$19,404,688	$10,806,027	$1,595,319	$1,501,402	$(353,996)
Net Disbursements	10.74%		$19,797,558	$10,806,027	$1,595,319	$1,517,607	$(337,791)
Financed by:	Cap Rate	Reserves					
Sales	9.00%	5.00%	$0				
Sales Costs	2.00%		0				
Loan Interest Draws			3,626,268	$350,159	$85,925	$95,282	$110,381
Loan Draws			16,726,925	10,587,113	1,509,394	1,422,325	0
Loan Repayments			0				
Accounts Payable			0	0			
Equity Contributed			500,000	0	0	0	0
Preferred Return Accrued			3,390				
Preferred Return Paid			0				
Equity Returned			(500,000)		(0)	0	0
Total Financing			$20,356,583	$10,937,272	$1,595,319	$1,517,607	$110,381
Cash on Hand			$559,025	$131,245	$131,245	$131,245	$579,417
Interest Rate	8.76% Average			9.25%	9.25%	9.25%	9.25%
End of Month Balances							
Loan Interest Reserve		$4,500,000	$873,732	$4,149,841	$4,063,916	$3,968,634	$3,858,253
Undisbursed Loan Balance	$21,800,000	17,300,000	573,075	6,712,887	5,203,493	3,781,168	3,781,168
Total Loan Drawn				10,937,272	12,532,591	14,050,198	14,160,579

	Nov. 87	Dec. 87	Jan. 88	Feb. 88	Mar. 88	Apr. 88	May 88	Jun. 88	Jul. 88
	8.25%	8.25%	8.50%	8.50%	8.50%	8.50%	8.50%	8.50%	8.50%
	74,515		24,268				24,268		
	74,515	74,515	98,783	98,783	98,783	98,783	123,051	123,051	123,051
	$0	$0	$0	$0	$0	$0	$0	$0	$0
	0	0	0	0	0	0	0	0	0
	(40,050)	(40,050)	(47,816)	(47,816)	(47,816)	(47,816)	(55,581)	(55,581)	(55,581)
	(40,050)	(40,050)	(47,816)	(47,816)	(47,816)	(47,816)	(55,581)	(55,581)	(55,581)
	$1,500	$1,500	$1,500	$1,500	$1,500	$1,500	$1,500	$1,500	$1,021
	51,000	0	0	0	0	0	0	0	0
	0	0	0	0	0	0	0	0	0
	0	0	0	0	0	0	0	0	0
	246,035	246,035	0	0	246,035	246,035	0	0	246,035
	0	0	0	0	0	0	0	0	0
	0	0	0	0	0	0	0	0	0
	531,009	0	79,211	0	0	0	79,211	0	0
	4,368	0	0	0	4,368	0	0	0	4,368
	500	500	500	500	500	500	500	0	0
	0	0	0	0	0	0	0	0	0
	6,393	0	0	0	0	0	0	0	0
		16,265				16,265			
	96,020	106,066	112,243	106,631	115,114	114,302	121,191	119,084	124,325
	500,000								
	$1,436,825	$370,366	$193,454	$108,631	$367,517	$378,602	$202,402	$120,504	$375,749
	$1,476,875	$410,415	$241,269	$156,446	$415,333	$426,418	$257,983	$176,165	$431,331
	$96,020	$106,066	$112,243	$106,631	$115,114	$114,302	$121,191	$119,084	$124,325
	880,855	304,350	129,026	49,816	300,219	312,115	136,792	57,081	307,006
	500,000	0	0	0	0	0	0	0	0
	0	(500,000)	(0)	0	0	(0)	(0)	(0)	(0)
	$1,476,875	$(89,585)	$241,269	$156,446	$415,333	$426,418	$257,983	$176,165	$431,331
	$579,417	$79,417	$79,417	$79,417	$79,417	$79,417	$79,417	$79,417	$79,417
	8.25%	8.25%	8.50%	8.50%	8.50%	8.50%	8.50%	8.50%	8.50%
	$3,762,233	$3,656,167	$3,543,924	$3,437,293	$3,322,179	$3,207,877	$3,086,686	$2,967,603	$2,843,278
	2,900,313	2,595,964	2,466,937	2,417,122	2,116,903	1,804,787	1,667,995	1,610,914	1,303,908
	15,137,454	15,547,869	15,789,138	15,945,585	16,360,918	16,787,335	17,045,318	17,221,483	17,652,814

■ 5-4 (Continued)

Fairway Center, Phase I: Monthly Cash Flows during Development Period (Continued)

Development Budget	Assumptions		Aug. 88	Sep. 88	Oct. 88	Nov. 88	Dec. 88
Interest Rate	8.76% Average		8.50%	8.50%	8.50%	8.50%	8.50%
Square Feet Leased	147,319			24,268			
Cumulative Square Feet Leased			123,051	147,319	147,319	147,319	147,319
Receipts							
Basic Rent	$1.70	$1.65	$0	$0	$0	$0	$0
Vacancy Allowances	5.00%		0	0	0	0	0
Operating Costs	$0.43	$0.11	(55,581)	(63,347)	(63,347)	(63,347)	(63,347)
Net Rental Receipts			(55,581)	(63,347)	(63,347)	(63,347)	(63,347)
Disbursements			$0	$0	$0	$0	$0
Marketing							
Appraisal Fee							
Builder Risk Insurance	$0.35	$100					
Title Insurance							
Land Purchase	$2,957,217	Sep. 86	0	0	0	0	0
Construction Costs			0	0	0	0	0
Architectural and Engineering	6.00%	600,000	0	0	0	0	0
Miscellaneous			0	0	0	0	0
Tenant Improvements	$22.00	$1.00	246,035	0	0	0	0
Permits and Fees	$45,000		0	0	0	0	0
Developer's Overhead and Fees	5.00%	462,436					
Construction Financing Fees	1.50%	69,772	0	0	0	0	0
Leasing Commissions	4.00%	79,211	0	79,211	0	0	0
Legal Fees—Tenant	$0.18		0	0	0	0	0
Legal—General	$1,500	20,000	0	0	0	0	0
Accounting	1.50%	173,414	0	0	0	0	0
Operating Contingency	4.00%						
Real Estate Taxes	1.09%						
City Mitigation Issues	171,278						
Loan Interest			127,439	126,325	132,477	129,572	135,284
City Bond Sale	1,750,000						
Lump-Sum Fee		500,000					
Total Disbursements			$373,474	$205,536	$132,477	$129,572	$135,284
Net Disbursements	10.74%		$429,055	$268,883	$195,825	$192,919	$198,631
Financed by	Cap Rate	Reserves					
Sales	9.00%	5.00%					
Sales Costs	2.00%						
Loan Interest Draws			$127,439	$126,325	$132,477	$129,572	$135,284
Loan Draws			301,616	142,558	63,347	63,347	63,347
Loan Repayments							
Accounts Payable							
Equity Contributed			0	0	0	0	0
Preferred Return Accrued							
Preferred Return Paid							
Equity Returned			0	0	0	0	0
Total Financing			$429,055	$268,883	$195,825	$192,919	$198,631
Cash on Hand			$79,417	$79,417	$79,417	$79,417	$79,417
Interest Rate	8.76% Average		8.50%	8.50%	8.50%	8.50%	8.50%
End of Month Balances							
Loan Interest Reserve		$4,500,000	$2,715,839	$2,589,514	$2,457,036	$2,327,464	$2,192,180
Undisbursed Loan Balance	$21,800,000	17,300,000	1,002,292	859,734	796,387	733,040	669,692
Total Loan Drawn			18,081,869	18,350,753	18,546,577	18,739,496	18,938,127

Jan. 89	Feb. 89	Mar. 89	Apr. 89	May 89	Jun. 89	Jul. 89	Aug. 89	Sep. 89
9.00%	9.00%	9.00%	9.00%	9.00%	9.00%	9.00%	9.00%	9.00%
147,319	147,319	147,319	147,319	147,319	147,319	147,319	147,319	147,319
$41,256	$41,256	$41,256	$41,256	$82,511	$82,511	$205,461	$205,461	$246,717
(2,063)	(2,063)	(2,063)	(2,063)	(4,126)	(4,126)	(4,126)	(4,126)	(6,188)
(63,347)	(63,347)	(63,347)	(63,347)	(63,347)	(63,347)	(63,347)	(63,347)	(63,347)
(24,154)	(24,154)	(24,154)	(24,154)	15,038	15,038	137,988	137,988	177,181
$0	$0	$0	$0	$0	$0	$0	$0	$0
						5,649		
						1,367		
0	0	0	0	0	0	0	0	0
0	0	0	0	0	0	0	0	0
0	0	0	0	0	0	0	0	0
0	0	0	0	0	0	0	0	0
0	0	0	0	0	0	0	0	0
0	0	0	0	0	0	0	0	0
0	0	0	0	0	0	0	0	0
0	0	0	0	0	0	0	0	0
0	0	0	0	0	0	0	0	0
0	0	0	0	0	0	0	0	0
0	0	0	0	0	0	0	0	0
144,760	131,917	147,244	143,762	149,838	146,113	152,100	153,263	149,452
$144,760	$131,917	$147,244	$143,762	$149,838	$146,113	$159,116	$153,263	$149,452
$168,914	$156,071	$171,398	$167,916	$134,799	$131,074	$21,128	$15,274	$(27,729)
$144,760	$131,917	$147,244	$143,762	$149,838	$146,113	$152,100	$153,263	$149,452
24,154	24,154	24,154	24,154	0	0	0	0	0
0	0	0	0	0	0	0	0	0
								3,390
0	0	0	0	0	0	0	0	0
$168,914	$156,071	$171,398	$167,916	$149,838	$146,113	$152,100	$153,263	$152,843
$79,417	$79,417	$79,417	$79,417	$94,455	$109,493	$240,466	$378,454	$559,025
9.00%	9.00%	9.00%	9.00%	9.00%	9.00%	9.00%	9.00%	9.00%
$2,047,421	$1,915,503	$1,768,259	$1,624,497	$1,474,659	$1,328,547	$1,176,447	$1,023,184	$873,732
645,538	621,384	597,229	573,075	573,075	573,075	573,075	573,075	573,075
19,107,041	19,263,113	19,434,511	19,602,428	19,752,266	19,898,378	20,050,478	20,203,741	20,353,193

■ 5-4 (Continued)

Fairway Center, Phase 1: Schedule of Normalized Operations (1989 through Disposition at January 1, 2000)

Beginning Rent/Month	$1.67				
Rent @ 61st Month	$2.04				
Rent @ 109th Month	$2.50				
Leasable Area	147,319	Oct.–Dec. 1989	1990	1991	1992
Total Gross Rent[a]		$740,150	$2,960,599	$2,960,599	$2,960,599
Vacancy Allowance (5%)		(18,565)	(74,260)	(74,260)	(74,260)
Effective Gross Income		$721,585	$2,886,339	$2,886,339	$2,886,339
Expenses[b]					
Janitorial		$27,596	$110,385	$114,801	$119,393
Electrical/Plumbing Maintenance		1,965	7,859	8,173	8,500
HVAC/Building Engineer		8,853	35,410	36,827	38,300
Elevator		1,629	6,515	6,775	7,047
General Building		2,881	11,526	11,987	12,466
Energy/Utilities		57,932	231,728	240,997	250,637
Grounds Maintenance		5,676	22,703	23,611	24,555
Security		7,081	28,323	29,456	30,634
Administrative		17,612	70,447	73,265	76,196
Taxes		47,711	190,844	198,478	206,417
Insurance		7,277	29,106	30,270	31,481
Bond Amortization		0	0	162,926	162,926
Total Expenses		$186,212	$744,846	$937,566	$968,552
Less Pass Throughs		0	0	(192,720)	(223,705)
Net Expenses		$186,212	744,846	744,846	744,846
Net Operating Income		$535,373	$2,141,492	$2,141,492	$2,141,192
Debt Service (9%, 30 years)		(491,299)	(1,965,197)	(1,965,197)	(1,965,197)
Net Cash Flow		$44,074	$176,295	$176,295	$176,295
Beginning Loan Balance[c]	$20,353,193				
Remaining Loan Balance		$20,319,841	$20,183,430	$20,034,742	$19,872,672

[a]Gross rent is increased in the fifth and tenth years at a compound rate of 4.0 percent per annum.
[b]Operating expenses are increased 4.0 percent per annum.
[c]Beginning loan balance equals loan balance at end of development/lease-up period.
Source: Josephson Properties, Los Angeles, California.
Note: Totals may not add due to rounding.

window panels for the exterior curtain wall. The structural bay determines the spacing of window mullions, which in turn determine the possible locations of the office partitions. The smaller the space between the mullions, the more flexibility in design (see Figure 5-5).

The market analysis should also provide design guidelines for the bay depth, which is defined as the distance from the glass line to the interior core. This distance is calculated by adding up the depths of the exterior offices, hallways, secretarial areas, and the interior offices. Typically, offices are 12 to 14 feet deep, and hallways are five to six feet wide. The width of the hallways plays an important role in setting the tone for the building—wider, more spacious hallways are associated with higher-class buildings.

The bay depth is typically between 36 and 40 feet. However, multitenant buildings with many small professional tenants generally require smaller bay depths, of, say, 32 to 36 feet, to permit a large number of window offices. Institutional users, on the other hand, prefer 40- to 50-foot bay depths, which tend to cost less to rent per square foot. Institutional users are also more likely to use open-space plans and to be less concerned with the number of window offices.

1993	1994	1995	1996	1997	1998	1999	2000
$2,960,599	$3,614,881	$3,614,881	$3,614,881	$3,614,881	$3,614,881	$4,413,757	
(74,260)	(180,744)	(180,744)	(180,744)	(180,744)	(180,744)	(220,688)	
$2,886,339	$3,434,137	$3,434,137	$3,434,137	$3,434,137	$3,434,137	$4,193,069	
$124,169	$129,135	$134,301	$139,673	$145,260	$151,070	$157,113	
8,840	9,193	9,561	9,944	10,341	10,755	11,185	
39,832	41,425	43,082	44,805	46,598	48,462	50,400	
7,328	7,622	7,926	8,243	8,573	8,916	9,273	
12,965	13,484	14,023	14,584	15,167	15,774	16,405	
260,662	271,089	281,933	293,210	304,938	317,136	329,821	Sale of
25,537	26,559	27,621	28,726	29,875	31,070	32,313	Property
31,860	33,134	34,459	35,838	37,271	38,762	40,313	
79,244	82,413	85,710	89,138	92,704	96,412	100,268	
214,674	223,261	232,191	241,479	251,138	261,183	271,631	
32,740	34,050	35,412	36,828	38,302	39,834	41,427	
162,926	162,926	162,926	162,926	162,926	162,926	162,926	
$1,000,777	$1,034,291	$1,069,145	$1,105,394	$1,143,093	$1,182,299	$1,223,074	
(255,930)	(289,444)	(324,299)	(360,548)	(398,246)	(437,453)	(478,228)	
744,846	744,846	744,846	744,846	744,846	744,846	744,846	
$2,141,492	$2,689,290	$2,689,290	$2,689,290	$2,689,290	$2,689,290	$3,448,223	
(1,965,197)	(1,965,197)	(1,965,197)	(1,965,197)	(1,965,197)	(1,965,197)	(1,965,197)	
$176,295	$724,094	$724,094	$724,094	$724,094	$724,094	$1,483,026	
$19,696,015	$19,503,460	$19,293,575	$19,064,800	$18,815,435	$18,543,627	$18,247,357	
						Cap Rate	
					Property Sale	9.00%	$38,313,588
					Sale Cost	2.00%	(766,272)
					Loan Repayment		(18,247,357)
					Cash Surplus on Sale		$19,299,959

Site Planning

The overall design of a building is significantly influenced by the building's location on its site. Generally, a building should enjoy maximum exposure to major local streets and signage should also be visible from these streets. Good site planning will provide a logical progression from the street to the parking lot or structure, and from the parking lot to the entry of the building. The trip from the car to the entry of the building provides visitors and prospective tenants with their first close-up look at the building.

Parking

In theory, an office building in which each employee occupies an average space of 250 square feet would need four spaces per 1,000 square feet of rentable space—assuming that all employees drive. Workers who carpool, ride with their spouses who work elsewhere, or take public transportation reduce the parking requirement. Visitors, on the other hand, raise the parking requirement. For example, consider a doctor who has 1,000 square feet of office space and employs two nurses. If the doctor has, on average, two patients in examining rooms and two patients in the waiting room at any one time, he/she needs seven parking spaces. Of course, doctors are busy at different times, and one doctor's inactivity may ease the parking burden for another doctor's crowded waiting room. Thus, the type of tenants expected in the building and the building's location influence the amount of parking needed.

Lenders prefer that buildings provide at least four spaces per 1,000 square feet of rentable space, even though local zoning may require only three spaces. Medical buildings often require six or seven spaces per 1,000 square feet. Locations served well by public transporta-

■ 5-5 Relationship of Module to Interior Office Size

Module Size	Interior Office Width
3-foot	9, 12, and 15 feet
4-foot	8, 12, and 16 feet
5-foot	10 and 15 feet
5 1/2-foot	11 and 16 1/2 feet

Examples of Structural Bay Modules

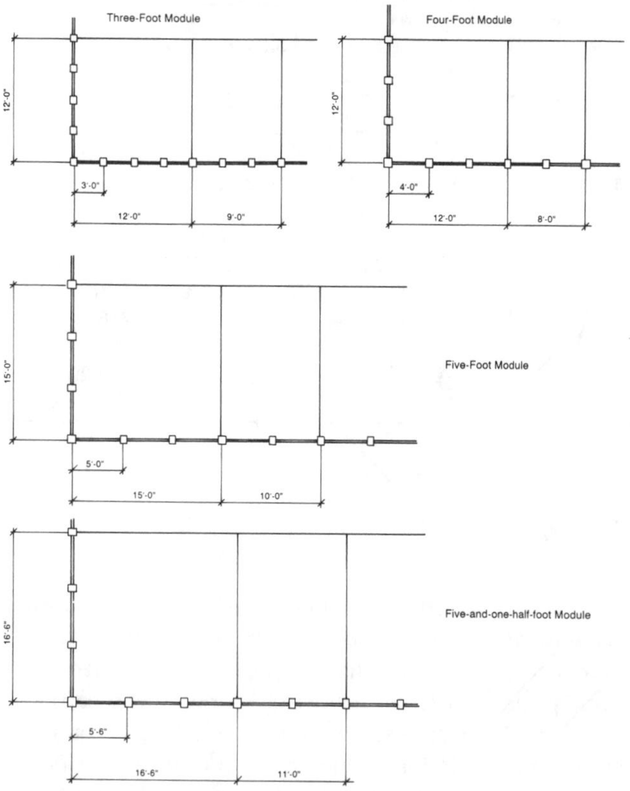

Note: Multiples of the module size determine where interior walls are joined to the exterior window-wall system.

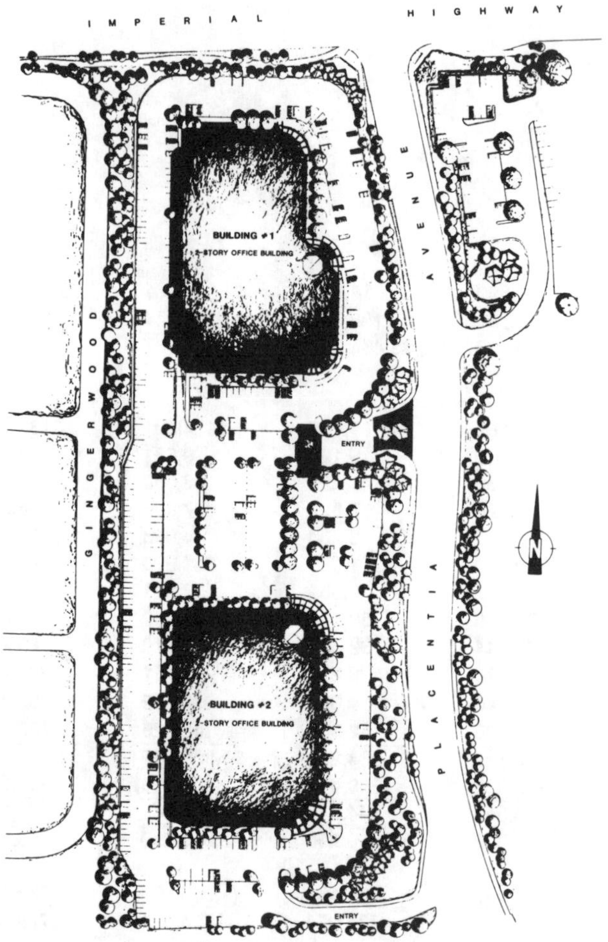

The Fairway Center site plan in Brea, California, includes two two-story buildings, and provides both surface and underground parking.

tion require less parking. However, experienced developers cite inadequate provision of parking as one of the most common flaws of projects undertaken by new developers. Both the availability of parking and its proximity to offices play key roles in developers' ability to attract and hold tenants. If representatives of prospective tenants have trouble finding parking places when they visit a building, the tenants are unlikely to rent there.

Landscaping

The importance of good landscaping to a project's overall appearance cannot be overemphasized. Landscape design can tie diverse buildings together; it can define spaces; it can form walls, canopies, and floors. "Concealing, revealing, modulating, directing, containing, completing are all architectural uses for plants. Trees, shrubs, and ground cover may be used to control soil

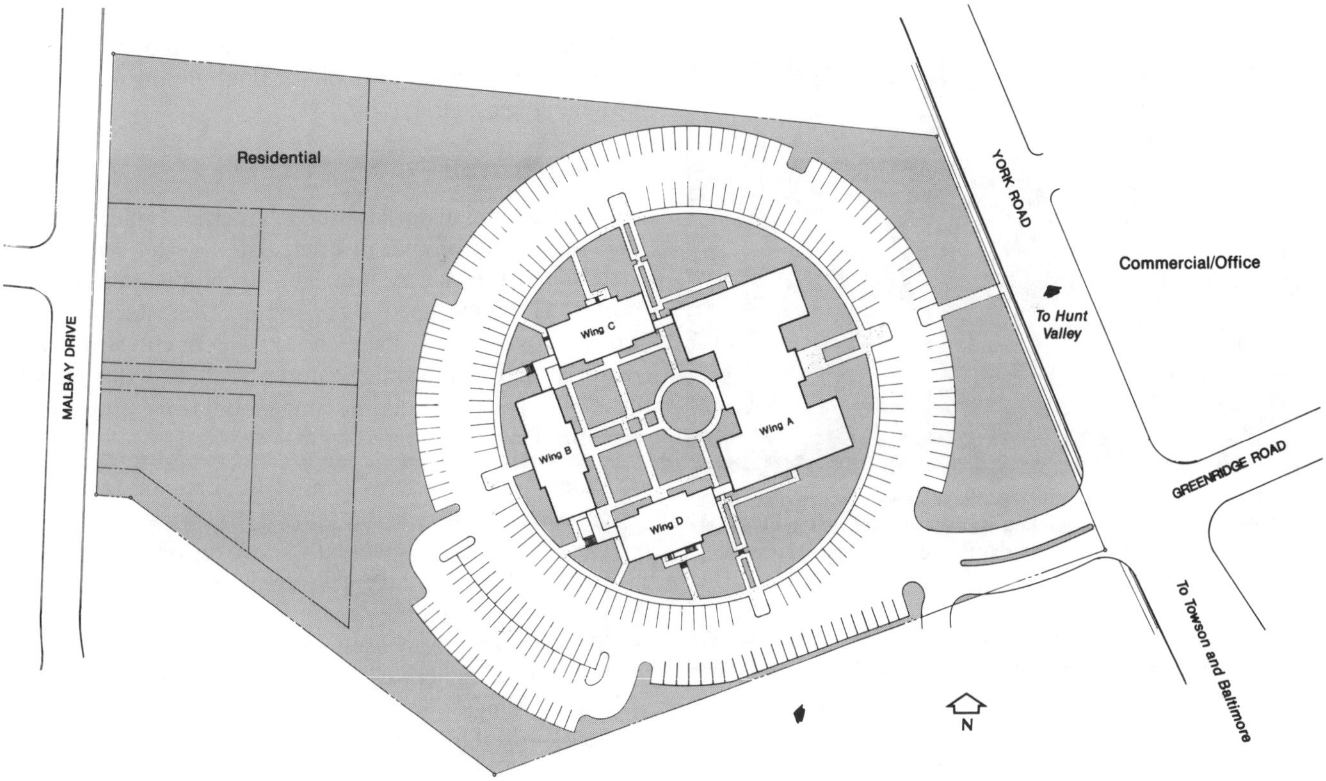

An innovative square within a circle site plan is used at York Green in Lutherville, Maryland. Four low-rise office wings form a square around a central courtyard and are surrounded, in turn, by a circular parking area.

erosion, to mitigate unpleasant sounds, to remove some pollutants from the air, to control glare and reflection, and to slow the effects of erosive winds."[10]

Landscaping elements include not only plants and trees but also rocks, berms, streams, retaining walls, and trellises. Ground cover and low-lying plants provide lush backdrops and help to control foot traffic. Vines, which grow well in shady areas, help to protect steep banks from erosion. A reasonable landscape budget will account for between 1 and 2.5 percent of total project costs.

Trees assist leasing and increase long-term project value. However, if precautions are not taken during construction, mature trees can easily be destroyed. Contractors should build boxes around any trees that developers wish to protect. Soil should be left undisturbed within a 10-foot radius of a tree's trunk. Many trees have survived construction only to die later because their roots were buried too deep in the final grading. Some trees can survive two or three feet of fill dirt, but gravel or stone should be spread to a depth of six to eight inches over their roots to ensure air circulation. Tree wells with at least a two-foot radius should be left around the tree trunk, extending to the original ground level. The services of landscape architects are necessary to help developers save existing trees and design the landscaping.

Plantings and trees should be chosen that will enhance the development both in the near term and the long term. Developers should also bear in mind the size of plantings and trees when they mature. Plants below office windows

Seigel Photographic, Inc.

Fountains, walls, and distinctive trees create an attractive landscape at Western Savings Corporate Center in Phoenix, Arizona.

Visual interest is created by juxtaposing a sleek reflective-glass office building and a lush surrounding landscape treatment, as with this office building in Tampa, Florida, developed by Paragon Development.

should be chosen so as not to obstruct views. Landscape maintenance costs must be assessed with the landscape architect during the initial design of the landscaping. For example, ground cover may be more expensive to install than grass but will not require weekly mowing.

Exterior Design

Exterior design concerns aspects such as exterior building materials, signage, and lighting. Prospective tenants and visitors gain their first impression of a building from its exterior, so the "look" of the building can be an invaluable marketing tool.

Building Materials

The building materials used in an office building generally are part of two distinct systems, the structural system and the skin system. The structural system supports the building, and the skin protects the interior space from the weather. Usually, the skin hides the structural material and is the only material visible to the casual observer. An office building can be built using one of five structural systems:

- Wood frame—generally used for one- or two-story garden offices.
- Concrete tilt-up—generally used on one- to three-story buildings and typically employed in quasi-industrial and garden office settings.
- Masonry—typically used for low-rise buildings.
- Reinforced concrete—used for both low- and high-rise buildings.
- Steel—used for both low- and high-rise buildings.

Each of these systems may be combined with another to produce economical hybrids, such as a lightweight steel frame building with wood truss floors or a masonry building with metal trusses or prestressed concrete floor units. Wood frame construction is used predominantly for residential construction and only infrequently for

Fred George

The cylindrical form at the end of Metro Center in Stamford, Connecticut, provides a memorable visual image for the project. The exterior follows a classic tripartite division of base, shaft, and crown, including the use of columns and pilasters.

A mixture of exterior cladding materials—including glass and granite—is used in this office building at Olen Pointe-Brea in Brea, California.

office development. In some suburban settings, however, a residential "feel" may be appropriate, especially for one- or two-story projects that cater to small businesses.

The exterior of an office building can be covered with the following skins:

- brick;
- glass curtain wall;
- metal panels (such as aluminum);
- granite, marble, limestone, and slate; and
- residential-type materials such as wood, stucco, and stone.

Signage

Signs not only serve the necessary function of identifying a building and some or all of its tenants, but also help create the overall impression that visitors to a building receive. Although tenants will negotiate hard for sign privileges, developers should retain sign approval as a condition in their tenants' leases. "Total acquiescence to a tenant's preconception of its signage needs may damage the environment that attracted the tenant to the development in the first place."[11] Signage restrictions should be specific to a building and should stipulate the size, shape, color, height, materials, content, and location of signs. Typical signage terms include the following:

- No lettering shall be affixed to the building without written approval.
- Signs shall mean any structure, component, fabric, device, or display that bears lettered, pictorial, or sculptured material including forms shaped to resemble any human, animal, or product designed to convey information or images and that is exposed to public view.
- No sign or lettering shall be formed or constructed of paint or similar material applied to the face or other surface of a building within the subdivision.
- No sign shall be constructed or erected upon the roof of any building within the subdivision.
- No sign shall be constructed so that the top of the sign is 15 feet higher than the adjacent finish street grade.
- No sign shall be constructed or erected with more than 72 square feet of surface area per sign facing, and no sign shall consist of more than two such faces.
- No more than one sign shall be constructed upon a building site within the subdivision.[12]

The developer's architect should work with an interior designer and graphic artists to create a signage program for both common areas and individual tenants. A comprehensive signage program will include designs, materials, and color schemes for the following:

5-6 The Costs of Different Structural and Skin Systems

These figures, from 1987, apply only to "average" buildings in Los Angeles. They are, at best, only a rough approximation of building costs. Developers should consult a local contractor for more-accurate cost estimates.

	Cost per Square Foot
Basic Structural Frame Systems:	
Steel, Heavyweight (fireproofed)	$9.71
Reinforced Concrete (fireproofed)	8.92
Lightweight Steel Frame	4.17
Steel Columns, Wood Beams	2.87
Wood, Post, and Beam	2.51
Floor Structures:	
Concrete (flat slab and joists) Floor	$7.23
Concrete Precast Joists and Deck Area	6.25
Steel Joists, Metal Deck, and Concrete	7.39
Steel Joists, Wood Sheathing	5.23
Wood Joists and Sheathing	4.53
Exterior Wall Systems:	
Concrete Block (8")	$11.65
Wall Brick Area	15.64
Reinforced Precast Concrete Panels (4")	10.71
Tilt-Up Concrete Panels (6")	11.42
Precast Concrete and Glass Panels	19.50
Metal and Glass Panels	22.25
Stone or Marble Panels	28.00
Steel Studs and Stucco	11.30
Wood or Steel Stud Walls (brick veneer)	12.45
Wood or Steel Stud Walls (wood siding)	10.10
Wood or Steel Stud Walls (stucco siding)	9.78

Source: Marshall Valuation Service, Marshall & Swift, Los Angeles, California, May 1987.

- exterior signage,
- parking lot signage,
- entry signage,
- directory signage,
- elevator signage,
- directional signage, and
- individual suite/doorplate signage.

Some developers employ a single sign maker to coordinate the signage for an entire project. This policy allows the developer easily to obtain specifications when a sign change is required. The doorplate signage system should allow for easy replacement of old signs when tenants change. The coordination of the installation of the signs should be the responsibility of the on-site building manager.

Exterior Lighting

Exterior lighting can greatly enhance the security of building entries and parking lots, thereby assisting leasing because tenants tend to shy away from buildings that seem "insecure." Inadequately illuminated areas will hurt the image of a building and may pose a liability problem. Lighting can also highlight architectural and landscaping features of a project. The developer should work with an electrical engineer and architect to design exterior lighting that will not only accomplish the desired effects but also be energy efficient. Mercury-vapor, sodium-vapor, quartz, and fluorescent lights may all be used in exterior lighting fixtures and will use only a fraction of the electricity used by incandescent lights. How the lights will be controlled—whether manually or by a timer or photocell—must also be considered.

Lighting standards for parking lots should be placed either around the perimeter of the lot or on the centerline of double rows of car stalls. In order to prevent cars from hitting them, lighting standards should not be placed on the stall line between cars and should, instead, be placed in planter medians. For outdoor parking areas, developers should provide a minimum illumination level of five footcandles. In structured parking, the National Parking Association recommends illumination of 10 footcandles.[13]

Interior Design

Interior design begins with the determination of the building envelope, design modules, and bay depths—discussed earlier in this section—all of which will determine how the various interior elements of the building will be laid out and how the building will function. The interior design must accommodate various systems—such as elevators, plumbing, heating, ventilation, and air conditioning, lighting, wiring, life safety—and the overall design must provide flexibility for the targeted tenant type.

Ways of Measuring Space

Each office market segment will demand that a building contain a certain amount of common area, such as lobbies, to convey the image that segment desires. The cost of this common area is passed on by the developer to the tenants. In order to design an appropriate office building for the market, the developer must understand how to calculate rentable areas. Furthermore, this understanding must be shared by the developer's architect and brokers. Tenants are very sensitive to the percentage of common space that they must pay for. Developers typically charge tenants for their pro-rated share of common space in addition to their usable space. The tenant pays rent at the stated rental rate multiplied by the "rentable square feet." Rentable square feet can be measured in many ways. BOMA has developed standard methods of measuring three distinct types of area: gross construction area, rentable area, and usable area.

Gross construction area is measured from the outside finished surface of the permanent outer walls of a building. It is the sum of all enclosed floors of a building including basements, mechanical equipment floors, and penthouses.

Rentable area is measured from the inside finish of the permanent outer walls of a building or from the inside of the glass line where at least 50 percent of the outer building wall is glass. Rentable area includes all areas within outside walls except vertical penetrations (elevators, stairs, and equipment shafts). According to local definitions, it may also include elevator lobbies, toilet areas, janitorial rooms, and equipment rooms.

Usable area is measured from the inside finish of the outer building walls or glass line to the inside finished surface of the office side of the public corridor. Usable area for full-floor tenants is measured to the building core and includes corridor space. An individual tenant's usable area is measured to the center of partitions that separate the tenant's office from adjoining offices. Usable area excludes public hallways, elevator lobbies, and toilet facilities that open onto public hallways.

The rentable/usable ratio (R/U ratio) is the rentable area divided by the usable area. Tenants normally pay rent on their usable space plus a pro-rated portion of the common space. Their rentable area is derived by multiplying the usable area by the R/U ratio. For example, if a tenant rents 1,000 square feet of usable space in a building with a 1.15 R/U ratio, the tenant will pay rent on 1,150 square feet:

Usable square feet (1,000) x R/U ratio (1.15)
= Rentable square feet (1,150)

Tenants have become very sensitive to the R/U ratio, often referred to as the building "efficiency ratio." The

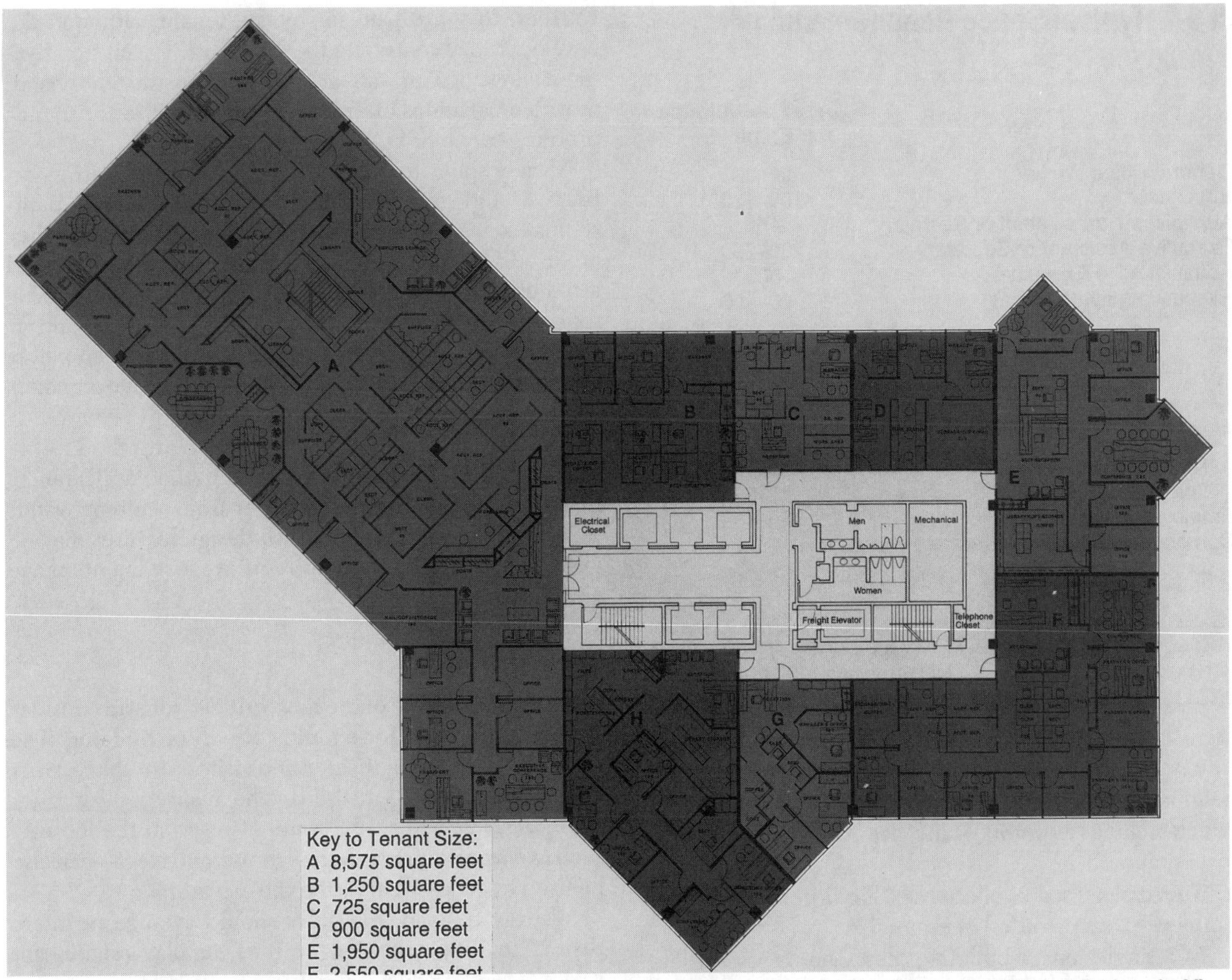

A typical multitenant floor layout at the first building in Minnesota Center, Minneapolis, accommodating eight tenants. The building's typical floor has 21,600 square feet, and the floor plate design is somewhat unique for its market in that there are three major tenant entrances off the core rather than the usual two, and three fire stairwells as opposed to the usual two. The latter feature permits the elimination of a fire corridor for tenants with 8,000 to 12,000 square feet, thereby reducing the common area from 15 percent of the floor area, the market standard, to 8 to 10 percent. The project has captured a disproportionate share of tenants in this size category because of this innovation.

average R/U ratio for high-rise space is about 1.15. Garden-office and low-rise space average around 1.12. Developers with especially inefficient buildings (with R/U ratios greater than 1.2) sometimes arbitrarily reduce the ratio so that their buildings appear more competitive. All developers should be careful to calculate pro-forma project rental income on the actual rentable area and not the construction area.

Despite the BOMA standards, many geographical markets calculate the rentable areas slightly differently depending on local custom and market conditions. Both brokers and architects should be familiar with local measurement customs and should assist developers in designing a building that will meet market standards.

Because they are calculated for each floor, BOMA R/U ratios can be misleading in buildings where a lot of square footage is devoted to common area (for example, lobbies and mail rooms) on the first floor. A building might have a 1.25 factor on the first floor whereas the upper floors have factors of 1.10. These problems can be avoided by calculating a ratio for the entire building.

Space Planning

Effective space planning involves five basic components: the space itself, the people who will use it, their activities, future uses, and energy efficiency.

The amount of space and its functionality are controlled by a building's exterior walls, floors, ceiling

■ 5-7 Typical Space Requirements per Employee

	Square Feet Allotted per Employee
General Office Worker	65–80
Supervisor	100–120
Administrative Assistant or Secretary	150
Executive Assistant or Secretary	200–250
Administrative Executive	300
Executive (private office)	400–500

	Square Feet Allotted per Employee for Common Areas
Conference Space:	
Theater Style	15
Conference Seating	25–30
Employee Lunch Rooms	15
Corridors and Circulation Areas (percent of usable space)	15–20

Source: Duane F. Roberts, *Marketing and Leasing of Office Space* (Chicago: Institute of Real Estate Management, 1979), chapter 10.

heights, column spacing and size, and the building core, which includes elevators, stairs, bathrooms, and mechanical equipment.

The typical space allotments for different types of employees are provided in figure 5-7.

In a single-tenant building, the tenant is responsible for improving the lobby and interior hallways. In a multitenant building, however, the developer improves the lobby, restrooms, and hallways that serve each suite, and the individual tenants are responsible for improvements of hallways and facilities only within their own suites. Developers prefer tenants that occupy entire floors because hallways and elevator lobbies fall within the rentable space of such tenants.

Optimum floor size depends on the type of tenant for which the building is planned. For multistory buildings, optimum floor sizes range from 16,000 to 25,000 square feet. The larger floor plates are better suited for larger users such as institutions and clerical operations; the smaller floor plates are generally used for multitenant and professional uses. Smaller floor plates cost more but provide more offices with windows.

Many modern office layouts use the open-space planning approach, which not only helps to reduce the cost of office design changes, but also costs less than closed offices for initial construction. Partitions in open-space plans are movable and a variety of furniture/wall systems are available that are attractive and use space efficiently. Further, they are paid for by the tenant, although the developer may contribute the "standard" tenant improvement allowance for walls and flooring. On the other hand, movable partitions offer less privacy and inferior soundproofing capabilities.

Money spent to make a building's lobby inviting, attractive, and user-friendly is a wise investment. Bathrooms likewise repay high-quality decoration since they are used by both tenants and visitors. Developers should avoid using fashionable color schemes that will inevitably soon seem outdated. Instead, they should either opt for materials that can be replaced at low cost or employ a neutral color scheme that will blend with whatever colors are used to provide decorating highlights.

Developers should also pay as much attention to the functionality of bathroom fixtures as to their appearance. Countertop areas frequently suffer from standing water; sinks with lips and other modish design features may be fashionable but are likely to require more maintenance and repair.

Elevatoring

Elevators are one of the most critical items to consider in setting the tone for a multistory office building. The initial impressions of tenants and visitors are shaped first by a building's lobby and then by the quality of the interior finish of its elevator cab. Materials used in the lobby—such as carpet, granite, marble, brass, and steel—can also be used to good effect inside the elevator.

Waiting time for elevators should average no more than 20 to 30 seconds; longer waits can play a significant role in a tenant's decision not to renew its lease.

Elevator capacity depends on the kind of tenants that occupy a building. Buildings occupied by larger companies with staff who work regular hours tend to need high-capacity elevators to accommodate peak-hour demand—sufficient capacity to move as many as 30 percent of the employees in a five-minute period. Buildings with a larger percentage of professional staff tend to have lower peak-period demand because more tenants keep irregular hours. On the other hand, professional tenants are more conscious of time lost waiting for elevators.

The following rules of thumb for may be used to gauge elevator capacity.[14]

- Buildings with two floors require one or two elevators depending on the nature of the local market and the size of the floors.
- Buildings with three to five floors require two elevators.
- Ten-story buildings need four elevators.
- Twenty-story buildings need two banks of four elevators.
- Thirty-story buildings need two banks of eight elevators.
- Forty-story buildings need 20 elevators in three banks.

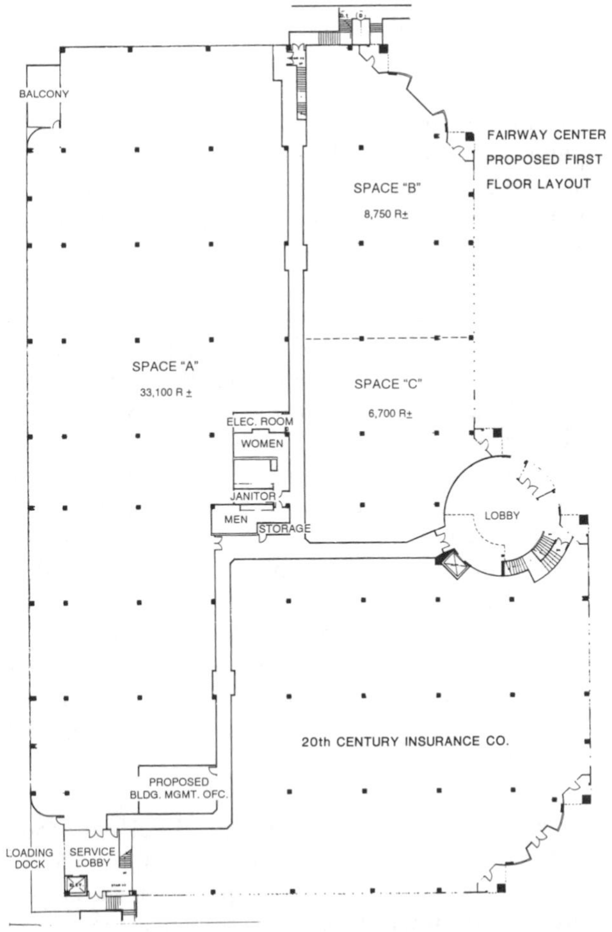

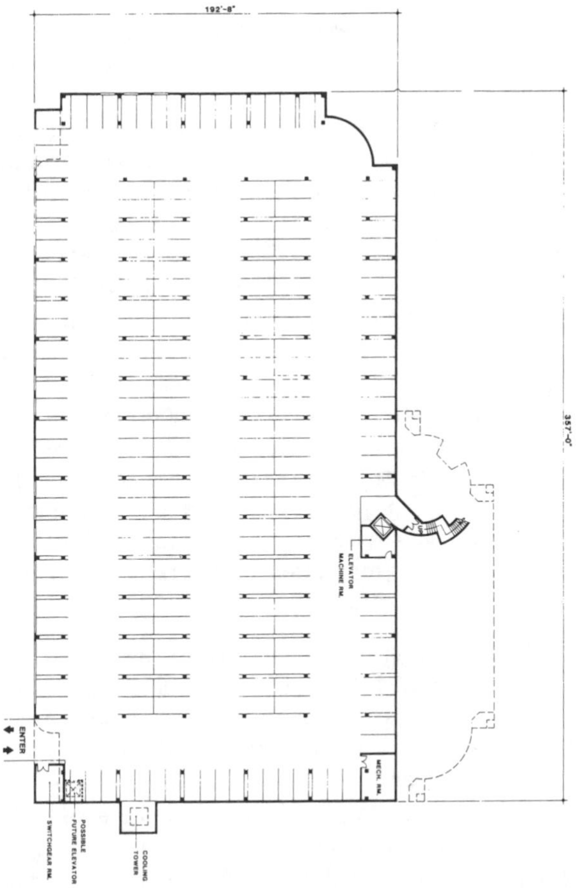

The two-story Fairway Center building number 1 in Brea, California, is a steel-frame structure with metal deck and concrete floors, bay dimensions of 40 feet by 32 feet, a structural ceiling clearance (slab-to-slab) of 15 feet, 73,753 square feet of gross leasable area on the first floor and 73,826 on the second floor, and 194 subterranean parking stalls. A proposed first-floor plan includes four tenant spaces, two of which have separate and prominent exterior entrances. The building includes one elevator and a loading bay that can accommodate 65-foot radius turns.

Lighting

Because it can define spaces, highlight unique features, and create different atmospheres, lighting plays a critical role in how users and visitors perceive office space. The absorptive or reflective qualities of selected colors and fabrics may alter the need for lighting.

Four types of artificial light are available for interior applications:

- *Fluorescent.* Fluorescent fixtures are expensive but have the advantage of long bulb life (18,000 to 20,000 hours).
- *Incandescent.* Less costly than fluorescent fixtures, incandescent fixtures provide superior color-rendering properties but have a short bulb life (750 to 2,000 hours) and are more expensive to operate.
- *High-intensity discharge.* This type of lighting includes mercury-vapor (frequently used outdoors), metal-halide, and high- and low-pressure sodium lamps. Although they are excellent for illuminating outdoor spaces and are very energy efficient, high-intensity discharge lights offer poor color-rendering properties.
- *High-intensity quartz.* Sometimes called "precise lighting," high-intensity quartz lighting is a new trend that is often used in upscale environments. Multifaceted mirrored backs reflect the light onto specific objects or areas, making high-intensity quartz fixtures good for task-oriented lighting.

"Direct lighting is most frequently used in offices. Installed in a grid pattern across a ceiling, this solution offers equal levels of illumination across large spaces when the specific activity to be carried on is unknown. This is most often the case in speculative office buildings."[15] Direct lighting is available in integrated ceiling packages, which can integrate lighting, sprinklers, sound masking, and air distribution. Heat recovery is more efficient when air-distribution outlets are linked to the lighting fixtures because the lighting fixtures contribute heat to the system. Moving fixtures, however, becomes more expensive with integrated systems.

Indirect lighting uses walls, ceilings, and room furnishings to reflect light from other surfaces. The ceiling material plays a critical role in indirect lighting. Acoustical tiles, which are designed to absorb sound, often have poor light-reflecting capabilities. Indirect lighting works best with smooth ceiling textures.

Lighting is measured in footcandles. Acceptable office lighting ranges from 50 to 70 footcandles. Lamp efficiency is measured in lumens per watt, which is the ratio of light output (lumens) to the electrical energy consumed (watts). Another useful measure is the coefficient of utilization (CU)—the ratio of light from the lamp reaching the work surface to the total lamp output. CU indicates the combined effect of fixture efficiency, room shape, and surface reflections on light emitted by lamps.[16]

The electrical engineer, the interior designer, and the architect all play important roles in designing the lighting system.

Heating, Ventilation, and Air Conditioning (HVAC)

A building's heating, ventilation, and air-conditioning system is one of the major line items in its construction budget. Several different types of HVAC systems are available:

- *Package forced-air systems.* These electrical heat pumps, usually located on the roof, heat and cool the air in the package unit, then deliver it through ducts to the appropriate areas of the building. The units are inexpensive to install and work well on one- and two-story buildings.
- *Variable air-volume systems.* In these systems, a large unit on the roof cools the air and delivers it through large supply ducts to the individual floors. Mixing units control the distribution of the air within each zone. This system offers great flexibility, since many mixing units may be installed to create zones as small as one office, but is more expensive to install than forced-air systems. Rooms are heated either by a heating element in the mixing units or by radiant heater panels in the ceiling.
- *Hot- and cold-water systems.* In these systems, a chiller and water heater is centrally located to provide hot and cold water to the various mixing units in the building. The air is heated or cooled in these mixing units and delivered to the local areas.

In choosing an HVAC system, the developer should seek the advice of the architect and mechanical engineer. The developer should also solicit opinions regarding the control mechanisms. These computers, which are an extremely important component of all HVAC systems, can control the timing, level, and operations of the HVAC system and can even bill each tenant separately. Besides heating or cooling the air, the HVAC system provides fresh air from the outside. The American Society of Heating, Refrigerating and Air Conditioning Engineers (ASHRAE) recommends the following minimum standards for flows of outside air to occupied areas: 1.50 cubic feet per minute per square foot for conference rooms; 0.15 cubic feet per minute per square foot for general offices; and 0.10 cubic feet per minute per square foot for computer rooms.

ASHRAE recommends that maximum air velocity be 70 cubic feet per minute. Relative humidity should be between 20 and 60 percent. Air-movement standards for each room depend upon the local climate and the glazing, lighting, and orientation of the building.

The amount of air conditioning likewise depends on such factors as the design of the building, orientation of the building to the sun, the climate, and the types of uses within the building. The output from an air conditioner is measured either in BTUs (British Thermal Units) or in tons (one ton equals 12,000 BTUs). Typical air-conditioning requirements for an office building are shown in figure 5-8.

■ 5-8 Typical Air-Conditioning Requirements for Office Buildings

	BTUS per Square Foot	Square Feet per Ton
High-Rise Building:		
Exterior Office	46	263
Interior Office	37	325
Low-Rise Building:		
Exterior Office	38	320
Interior Office	33	360
Small Suite Office	43	280

Source: Building Construction Cost Data (Kingston, Massachusetts: R.S. Means Company, Inc., 1988).

A well-designed HVAC system divides the building into zones, each of which is controlled by a thermostat. These zones should cover areas with similar characteristics, such as orientation to the sun, types of uses, and intensity of uses. Areas such as conference rooms, waiting rooms, computer rooms, lunch rooms, kitchens, and restrooms have different loads and should, if possible, be in separate air-flow zones from the general office uses. A standard rule of thumb is one thermostat zone per 1,200 square feet. Usually, each zone has one mixing damper that controls temperature by mixing hot and cold air.

Energy Efficiency

The energy efficiency of a building depends on its site orientation, the design of its windows, and the type of mechanical equipment and the energy-control systems it contains. Energy efficiency, which measures all of the components that use energy, can be determined by calculating the energy efficiency ratio (EER). EER is calculated by dividing the amount of energy used by the amount of energy expended.

One of the more popular ways to measure the energy efficiency of different designs is the U-value. U-values measure the rate of heat loss as expressed in BTUs per hour per square foot per degree difference between the interior and exterior temperature. The U-value is the reciprocal of the total resistance of construction multiplied by a temperature or solar factor.

On any building, a film of air exists along the interior and exterior walls. The U-value measures the resistance of the construction to the air and indicates the amount of BTUs gained or lost in the building. All wall and roof construction components—including air space and paint—must be entered into the calculation to determine the U-value. U-values must be recalculated throughout the building whenever changes in materials are involved.

As a general rule of thumb, U-values should be a minimum of 0.1 for insulated exterior walls and 0.8 for insulated roofs. The specific requirements of insulation depend on the local climate. The architect and mechanical engineer can provide recommendations for insulation.

Recessed windows are used at the 4040 East Camelback Office Building to conserve energy in the hot Phoenix climate.

Glass reflection plays an important role in determining energy usage and is measured as the shading coefficient. The shading coefficient equals the amount of solar energy passing through glass divided by the total amount of solar rays hitting the glass. The lower the coefficient is, the larger is the amount of heat reflected away from the building's interior. Lower shading coefficients tend, however, to be more expensive to obtain.

Developers must decide how they wish to trade off construction and operating costs. Higher construction costs can purchase greater energy efficiency and thus lower operating costs. Lower initial installation costs may mean higher operating costs.

Many states and local government agencies have their own energy efficiency requirements. The state of California, for example, has an extensive set of energy regulations called the Title 24 regulations, which provide a trade-off between window areas and heat loss through the windows. They restrict the amount of energy loss allowed in a building and regulate the types and amounts of insulation, glazing, and lighting fixtures.

Life Safety

Life safety is an important consideration in the design and marketing of an office building and involves protecting the building, its contents, and its tenants and visitors. Access into and out of the building can be secured by several methods, including:

- keyed elevators;
- entry-card systems;
- on-site security guards;
- security office with closed-circuit television in lobby; and
- alarm systems.

Access to the building from parking garages should also be controlled. In the case of parking structures that are adjacent to the main building, users find it most convenient if entrances lead from each floor of the garage directly into the building; this arrangement, however, makes access difficult to control. Greater security is obtained if all users of parking are required to enter the building through its main lobby. This method requires installing a separate set of elevators and stairs for the building and the parking structure. Parking garages located below a building should also have separate elevators to maintain security. Staircases should provide access only to the building's lobby.

Security, as well as safety, is enhanced by the inclusion in a building of "life-safety systems." Life-safety systems may include fire sprinklers, alarms, sensors, fire hoses and extinguishers, automatic shut-off systems for the HVAC system, and other monitoring and control systems. The addition of these systems can lower fire insurance rates in some situations.

Fire codes differ from city to city, and developers should check with the local fire authorities to obtain the current codes. Some fire codes require compartmentalization, which involves providing special fire walls[17] between office suites and corridors and exits for tenant suites. This compartmentalization is usually required for suites larger than 3,000 square feet.

Tenant Leasehold Improvements[18]

As a part of the lease for office space, the developer usually provides a set allowance for tenant improvements (TIs) that covers finish-out of the interior space including ceilings, walls, flooring, and electrical and telephone outlets. In the late 1980s, the allowance was typically \$15 to \$20 per square foot of leased space. The allowance provides for only a minimum level of improvements and is usually insufficient to cover all of the costs of TIs. Since leases typically do not require the tenant to pay rent during the improvement phase, it is incumbent on the developer to see that work is done on schedule.

Tenant Improvements Process

Steps in the process of completing TIs in a small office building parallel the steps involved in constructing the building itself: budgeting, preliminary planning, design and construction drawings, approvals and permits, contractor selection and bidding, and construction.

Step 1: Fix the budget. The budget is determined by both the quality desired by the tenant and the resources available. The budget usually exceeds the allowance of the developer. Someone on the developer's staff needs to have a good appreciation of the probable construction cost so that the budget will be realistic and the tenant will understand the level of quality of the improvements. Typically, the tenant is required to pay any costs above the TI allowance, although in some cases the lease rate may be adjusted as an alternative.

Step 2: Prepare a space plan and design for the improvements. The space planner/interior designer may be under contract either to the developer or to the tenant. If the designer is under contract to the developer, the developer maintains greater control but will be liable for the costs if the tenant backs out of the lease.

The design firm is usually selected in one of two ways: either the developer may preselect a design firm and then recommend this firm to all tenants, or the developer may preapprove three or four firms and then allow the tenant to select from these.

The tenant usually has the option of choosing another firm, and larger tenants that lease a large amount of floor space in a building often do so. The developer, who is paying for the work out of the TI allowance, retains the right to approve the designer, however. Only a large developer with a series of ongoing projects would be able to maintain a space planner on staff.

The developer technically owns the TIs and thus has a strong interest in controlling quality and design. However, since the object is to lease space and satisfy the tenant, the developer should hesitate to reject the tenant's proposals.

Step 3: Obtain plan approval. The plans are submitted to the local building department for approval and permits. Whenever improvements require electrical work or partitions, building permits will be required.

Step 4: Select a contractor. The options for selecting a contractor are similar to those for selecting a space planner. Commonly, the developer will select a single contractor—usually not the general contractor for the building—to do all of the TIs in the building, but some developers prefer to preapprove three or four contractors and then submit the drawing to each for bids. Since the continuing happiness of the tenant is of paramount importance to the developer, the developer will usually work with the contractor to see that the bids are within the tenant's budget. If the tenant feels that the bid is too high, the lease usually allows the tenant to secure additional bids, although the developer again retains the right to approve the contractor.

Step 5: Oversee construction. The developer must maintain close contact with the contractor during the construction phase to make certain that the project is proceeding smoothly and that the tenant will be able to move in on time. The developer should carefully monitor any claims for change orders, so that the project remains within the tenant's budget. The tenant may be required to pay its share of the cost at the start of construction, but usually payments are phased. If the project will be completed in less than two months, it is common for the tenant to pay one-half (either to the developer or to the contractor, depending on the agreement) at the start of construction, with the balance due at completion. On longer jobs, a smaller initial payment and regular progressive payments may be made.

Work Letters

Work letters serve as the formal agreements between the developer and the tenant concerning the amount and quality of improvements that the landlord will provide. They specify the work that the landlord will do before the lease commencement date as well as the schedule of costs.

The "Building Standard Installation" is the list of items that are installed in every suite and includes: partitions; doors and hardware; acoustical ceiling tile size and pattern; floor coverings; the size, shape, and location of lighting fixtures; electrical receptacles; switches; telephone outlets; plumbing connections; HVAC; painting; and window coverings or venetian blinds. If the tenant wants items above the building standard, the work letter also specifies these along with their cost and method of payment.

A standard TI work letter is created for improvements throughout the building. This document lays out the minimum improvements that will be constructed in every tenant space. The job is bid to the contractor on a per-unit basis—such as so many dollars for the cost of each light fixture or for each linear square foot of partition space.

Tenant improvements at BDM Columbia Technology Center in Columbia, Maryland, were part of the overall build-to-suit deal. The 115,273-square-foot facility was designed to capture daylight and to facilitate the internal organization of program requirements, including a free-flowing internal design. Special tenant requirements included a 150-seat conference center and a 2,000-square-foot cafeteria.

Level of Tenant Improvements

The quality of the TIs, the TI allowance, and the standard TIs will have a definite bearing on the success of the marketing of the building. The developer is trying to please two parties—the prospective tenants and the brokers—and must be aware of what both the tenants and the brokers perceive as the quality of the standard TIs in relation to the market.

Typical items specified in a TI work letter would include:

- Size and type of ceiling tiles used.
- Number of linear feet of wall for every 100 square feet of rentable space.
- Number and type of doors per 100 square feet of rentable space.

- Type of wall coverings and color of standard paint.
- Quality and type of floor covering—normally, several choices of colors are allowed.
- Number of HVAC registers, mixing units, and thermostats per 100 square feet of rentable space.
- Specifications for the telephone system, including the installation of conduit and boxes and the provision of equipment rooms. (This is a negotiable item, and many businesses will have their own systems and installers.)
- Type and extent of alarm and security systems.
- Type and extent of computer wiring.

A developer should not state the TI allowance in dollars, as this allows tenants to design their own improvements and may result in spaces that are incompatible with each other and that fall below the standard level of quality of the building. Instead, by using a standard TI work letter, the developer can establish the basic quality and style of improvements for every space. Compatible colors and materials will make individual tenant spaces easier to re-lease when tenants move out. With a TI work letter, the tenants have a starting point from which they may pay for extra improvements.

Some of the common upgrades in tenant spaces include:

- Kitchen bar consisting of a microwave, small refrigerator, and sink.
- Full kitchen and lunchroom with a sink, microwave, refrigerator, dishwasher, and stove.
- Executive bar in office with a refrigerator and sink.
- Executive bathroom containing a sink, vanity, toilet, and sometimes a shower.
- Climate-controlled computer room.
- Fireproof safes or fireproof file rooms.
- Built-in fixtures such as shelves, cabinets, worktables, bookshelves, counters, and other cabinetry work.

Pitfalls and Suggestions

- The architect and interior designer may want to carry the exterior finishes and lobby finishes into each tenant's suite. This can provide continuity throughout the building, but it may wed every tenant to the particular color scheme. A better alternative is to create a series of coordinating colors that will harmonize with the materials used in the lobby and common areas, yet allow each tenant to choose a particular color for its own suite.
- Column spacing and mullion spacing can cause many problems in the design of interior spacing. When the mullion spacing and column spacing do not coincide, columns may occur in the middle of a window. Columns can cause leasing problems if they are located in the center of an office. In addition, if the window mullion spacing and the office wall spacing do not coincide and the wall abuts the windows between two window mullions, it can be difficult to create an acceptable junction between the window and the partition wall. The wall cannot be built so that it touches the glass, since the glass must expand and contract as the temperature changes, yet, if a gap exists between the window and the wall, sound can easily filter from one room to another. When a wall must be built between mullions, one alternative is to end the wall six to 12 inches from the window. The wall is turned parallel to the window until it can be fastened to the mullion in a perpendicular joint. This produces odd-shaped spaces, but it does provide a soundproof seal between offices. A flexible scheme of window mullion spacing and column spacing is essential for meeting the particular needs of each tenant.
- Availability of plumbing is also important to the flexibility of the design. Any suite larger than 3,000 square feet should be able to have plumbing for a sink installed at minimal cost.
- When existing spaces are remodeled, such building parts as the light fixtures, ceiling tiles, metal studs, and air-conditioning components can be reused, thereby reducing expense.

Financing

Office buildings have historically been a preferred real estate investment for institutional investors such as life insurance companies and pension funds. As a result, more money was available in the 1980s than either demand or good product warranted—a condition that has contributed to the overbuilt situation that characterizes most office markets in the early 1990s.

Small office buildings are one of the hardest types of real estate to finance. They do not fall into any of the categories traditionally favored by institutional lenders, many of which will not even consider deals smaller than $5 or $10 million. S&Ls were the primary source of financing for smaller projects but they are generally not in the market in the early 1990s.

Wall Street has become a significant source of funding for major office buildings through new instruments such as securitized mortgages and publicly traded master limited partnerships (MLPs).[19] Although investment bankers have been slower to securitize mortgage pools for multiple commercial properties than they have for multiple residential properties, recent attempts to standardize commercial mortgage instruments have increased Wall Street's involvement on the commercial side. In time, mortgage pools for multiple properties promise to make still more money available for office development.

Wall Street, it should be noted, has principally been involved in financing projects that are fully leased, preferably with credit tenants. Nevertheless, Wall Street's involvement increases the supply of money available for new development through its competition with institutional investors for existing projects.

Foreign investors—notably Canadian, German, British, Dutch, and Japanese investors—have also traditionally sought out office projects. Their preferences have leaned toward first-class, high-image, downtown buildings ("trophy buildings" that look good in annual reports) in major cities such as New York City and Los Angeles. Before the extent of overbuilding became apparent, foreign investors were showing increased interest in cities such as Chicago, Boston, Atlanta, Houston, Dallas, and San Francisco and in some suburban markets such as Orange County, California. Beginning developers are unlikely to deal with either foreign buyers or institutional investors. In the environment of the early 1990s, they will need substantial preleasing and equity to be able to find financing.

Construction Loans

Construction financing for office buildings is similar to that for other income properties, except that the lender is more concerned about leasing. Both construction and permanent lenders require some preleasing, typically from 20 to 50 percent of the space in a building. Banks will typically require new, inexperienced developers to have 40 to 50 percent of the building preleased in normal markets and 50 to 70 percent in soft markets. However, these requirements change often, so developers should check with prospective lenders for the latest preleasing requirements.

Judith Hopkinson, president of Berkeley Development Corporation, notes that the typical term for a construction loan on a medium-size office building (50,000 to 75,000 square feet) is 24 months. Points paid upfront vary with the market, but 2 points (2 percent of the loan amount) is common, with 1 additional point to extend the loan for another 12 months.

For beginning developers to obtain financing, they must have land that is free and clear of liens and have executed leases—not merely letters of intent. Richard Zelle, vice chairman of the Center Financial Group of Los Angeles, notes that the major problem encountered by many developers is failing to leave enough cushion for cost overruns and slower leasing.

Robert Kagan, project manager at CalFed in San Francisco, cautions: "Be careful about the lender's ability to change the interest rate on you. It is pretty standard for loan documents to include a clause that lets the lender assess the borrower for increased costs due to higher reserve requirements. But the lender may sell the loan to a small bank in Mississippi with three times their reserve requirement." Kagan tries to negotiate a clause that states that the assessment cannot go up if the lender assigns the loan.

Permanent Loans

With office buildings, as with other types of income property, the permanent mortgage is funded once the building reaches some negotiated level of occupancy—usually, a level sufficient to cover debt service on the mortgage. This normally occurs when the building achieves 70 to 80 percent occupancy at rents stipulated in the loan commitment. Often, the loan commitment provides for funding the mortgage before the building is fully leased. In those cases, the developer must post a letter of credit (LC) for the difference between the amount that the leases will carry and the full loan amount. Alternatively, the permanent lender may fund the mortgage in stages as the building is leased.

"Documentation for the permanent loan can be a nightmare," warns Hopkinson. "There are lots of pitfalls. If you take down the permanent loan before the project is finished, the draws for TIs can take forever to process." She says that it often takes 60 days or more to receive payments.

Lenders are well aware of the tricks that a developer may use to get tenants into a building while showing leases with high *nominal* rents. For example, a developer may give 12 months' free rent and $10 per square foot in additional TIs to a tenant that signs a five-year lease at the market rate, say $30 per square foot. A lender would only see the lease showing $30 per square foot. Similarly, a developer who plans on funding the permanent loan in two years may sign a lease with stepped rent, rising from $20 in the first two years to $30 in the third, fourth, and fifth years. When the lender analyzes the leases two years later, the lease shows $30 per square foot.

Robert Kagan notes, however, that lenders are focusing increasingly on *effective* rents. Because lenders find it difficult to discover what concessions developers have made to attract tenants, they now perform more due diligence than they did a few years ago to determine the effective rents. If the lender has to foreclose on a property, effective rental rates in the marketplace will determine what the space can be leased for. Also, if five-year leases are expected to roll over at a time when effective rents are $1.75 per square foot per month, tenants that have leases with face rental rates of $2.25 will expect either a reduction in rent or new concessions that bring down the face rate to the prevailing effective rate. Kagan advises developers to "expect the lender to underwrite the project on the basis of the effective rental rates." (Calculating effective rents is discussed earlier in this chapter).

Lease Requirements

Developers must execute leases that satisfy the construction and permanent lenders' requirements. Different lenders have different concerns, so knowledge of their requirements is essential if the building is to be financed without the need to renegotiate initial leases. Some of the more common areas of concern among lenders are given below, but developers should work with experienced attorneys before executing any leases and should not rely on standard lease forms.

- Lenders require assignable leases so that they can take assignment of the rents (in other words, receive rent directly) in the event of default. One of their major concerns is not being able to get control of a building's cash flow after default and before foreclosure. Proper maintenance of the building and service of the tenants are essential to protect the interests of lenders.
- Lenders prefer clauses that require tenants to pay rent even if the building burns down or is destroyed by earthquake. Sophisticated tenants, however, will not agree to such clauses, even though insurance is available to cover rent when calamities occur.
- In the event of calamities, lenders want to receive condemnation and insurance awards first and only then pay the developer. Owners, on the other hand, usually want the insurance money to restore the building, especially if they are obliged to make such restoration under the terms of certain leases.
- Lenders do not like rental rates to be offset against increases in pass-through expenses. For example, most leases require tenants to pay increases in operating costs over some base figure. Increased costs are "passed through" to tenants. Lenders dislike exclusions for increases in management fees and similar items because they reduce the ability of owners to cover increased costs.

Mortgage Options

Bullet loans (standard 30-year self-amortizing mortgages with a 10- to 15-year call) are probably now the most common form of permanent financing for office projects. Interest rates usually are lower for short-term mortgages because of the lower interest-rate risk to the lender over time. Occasionally, such as in the early 1980s, when inflation is expected to fall in the future, interest rates were higher for shorter-term mortgages than for longer-term mortgages.

Other common forms of financing are participating mortgages, convertible mortgages, and sale-leasebacks—all of which are forms of joint ventures with lenders. (See chapter 4 for discussion of the various types of mortgages commonly available.)

Standby and Forward Commitments

Although experienced developers can generally obtain open-ended construction financing without a permanent takeout, beginning developers will almost always need a takeout commitment before they can obtain construction financing.

Standby commitments are one alternative. They represent permanent-loan commitments from companies such as credit companies and REITs that are sufficient to secure construction financing but are very expensive if they are actually used. Standby loans, if funded, may run three points or more over prime. Companies typically charge one or two points per year for the commitment while it remains unfunded. Developers use the commitment to start construction and then look for permanent financing once the building is partially leased. Ideally, the standby commitment is never funded because it is replaced by a bullet loan or other standard mortgage.

Standby commitments can be dangerous. Many developers were forced to call on their standby lenders to fund their commitments in the recession of 1973 and 1974. A number of REITs that had expected to fund only a small proportion of their commitments were unable to fund them all. Even those mortgages that were funded had such high interest rates that many projects defaulted.

Another alternative to a permanent mortgage is a presale or forward commitment by an institution to purchase the building. The developer negotiates the sale of the property in advance of construction. The construction loan may be borrowed against the proceeds from sale. The presale price is determined by capitalizing the net operating income (NOI) at a negotiated capitalization (cap) rate. Charles Wurtzebach, formerly vice president of the Prudential Realty Group, Newark, New Jersey and now a partner in JMB Properties, Chicago, says that Prudential almost always requires a lease-up commitment before it will purchase a building, though the company will issue a forward commitment for three to four years in the future. Some of the investor portfolios Prudential represents take leasing risk for up to 50 percent of the total space; most funds, however, require that a building be at least 80 percent leased before Prudential will close on the purchase. Prudential avoids buildings with long-term, flat-rate leases. "Prudential is not in real estate just to get bond-like characteristics," he comments.[20] Although required rates of return change with inflation, in 1991 Prudential was looking for returns of 10 to 11.5 percent on buildings without leasing risk, and 12.5 to 13 percent returns on buildings with leasing risk.[21]

A forward commitment often includes an earn-out provision, whereby the developer is paid part of the purchase price and the balance is paid as the leasing is completed. Suppose, for instance, the negotiated purchase price for a building is determined by capitalizing the gross rent from executed leases on 95 percent of the building's rentable area at 10.467 percent. This would equate approximately to an 8.5 percent cap rate on the NOI. Consider a building with a rentable area of 100,000 square feet, face rents of $28 per square foot, and expenses of $5 per square foot. The purchase price would be calculated as follows (with k representing the overall cap rate):

Gross rent ($28 per square foot × 100,000 square feet)	$2,800,000
Vacancy (5%)	–140,000
Adjusted gross income	$2,660,000
Expenses ($5 per square foot)	–500,000
NOI	$2,160,000

$$\frac{\text{NOI}}{k} = \frac{\$2{,}160{,}000}{0.085} = \$25{,}412{,}000$$

$$\frac{\text{Adjusted gross income}}{k} = \frac{\$2{,}660{,}000}{0.10467} = \$25{,}412{,}000$$

5-9 Earn-Out Provisions in Forward Purchase Contracts: Sample 100,000-Square-Foot Building (Net Rentable Space)

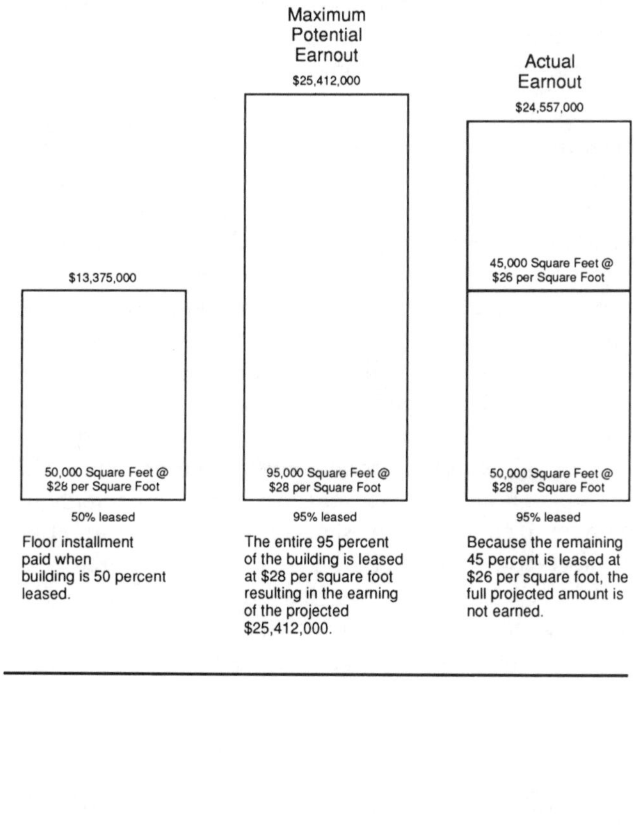

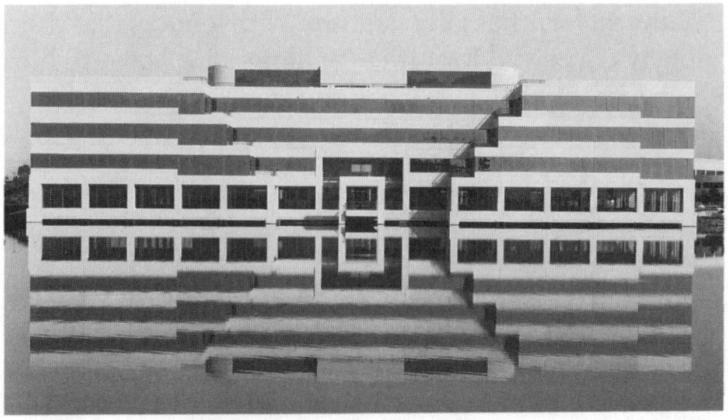

John Sutton Photography

Paragon Point in Redwood Shores, California, is a two-building joint venture project between the Paragon Group and Metropolitan Life Insurance Company. The strategy is to hold the project as a long-term investment; Paragon manages the property.

An earn-out would provide for the purchaser paying the capitalized value on that portion of the building that is leased at the time of closing, say 50 percent, and paying the balance later as leases are signed on the remainder of the building.

For example, if 50 percent of the building is leased at $28 per square foot, the purchaser would pay $13,375,000 ($28 times 50,000 square feet divided by 0.10467) at closing. The balance would be paid as the developer leases the rest of the building. If the remaining 45,000 square feet are leased at $26 per square foot instead of $28, then the developer would receive $11,178,000 for a total of $24,553,000. The developer would have failed to "earn out" the full projected amount of $25,412,000.

Equity

Lenders normally require 20 to 30 percent of the development cost to be funded by equity sources. The amount of equity required depends on the strength of the development team, the difference between the project cost and the value of the project, the strength of the market, and the overall health of the financial lending industry.

Joint ventures with lenders and tenants offer one of the easiest methods for covering a developer's equity requirement. Since the 1980s, major lenders and major tenants have increasingly asked for, and received, a share of the equity ownership. The packaging of their interest takes a variety of forms. Lenders have preferred participating loans, which give them a share of the cash flows during operations and profits from sale while shielding them from liability and downside risk. As major tenants have gained a better understanding of the value of getting a development project off the ground, they too have started to seek a share in the ownership of the building. Developers have obliged as the oversupply of new office space has increased competition for tenants.

Several forms of joint ventures with lenders that were initially conceived for office buildings, are now used for all property types. These are discussed in chapter 4.

Marketing and Leasing

The goal of marketing an office development is to find tenants to pay rent and occupy the building. The crux of the marketing plan for an office building is first to identify the target market segment (a task discussed earlier in this chapter under market analysis) and then to convince that segment of the desirability of the building.

Developers should emphasize the features of their projects that will exercise significant market appeal. Superior features might include:[22]

- design by a well-known architect and/or a spectacular or noteworthy design;
- efficient floor configuration;
- outstanding building services;
- liberal tenant remodelling allowances and a high standard of TIs;
- exceptional location;
- free parking;
- excellent elevatoring;
- competitive rental rates; and
- good access without traffic congestion.

Marketing is also assisted by the presence of such special amenities and features as:

- athletic facilities offering racquetball, squash, swimming, and exercise rooms;
- a running track or jogging path with exercise stations spaced at intervals along the track;
- cafeterias, lounges, executive clubs, and convenience retail such as printing and flower shops;
- conference facilities; and
- packaging and mailing services.

The key to the successful marketing of a project is to select the features attractive to the target market and to emphasize the usefulness of those amenities to the prospective tenants.

Marketing Strategy

Office leasing and marketing in general must focus on canvassing the market, developing attractive brochures, advertising, public relations, merchandising, and working closely with brokers.

In the early 1990s, virtually all financial institutions require substantial preleasing before they will lend money. The preleasing program is thus critical in the office development process and should begin even prior to the completion of the design, especially where a superior location is involved.

In fact, a good location will often attract a build-to-suit tenant. Of course, the developer must be willing to adapt the building to the distinctive requirements of the tenant, which may later pose problems if the building must be leased to another tenant. Nonetheless, the advantages of build-to-suits—especially the advantage of a committed tenant—outweigh their disadvantages.

Advertising

Some developers prefer to coordinate the advertising of their projects themselves; others prefer to hire a professional advertising agency. Robert Comstock, managing partner of Comstock, Crosser, Hickey of Manhattan Beach, California, uses his own staff to perform the following advertising-related tasks:[23]

- Canvass the local area to discover the needs of the market and the weaknesses of competitive buildings, then emphasize how the firm's project fills the market's physical or locational needs.
- Direct mail to every major user and broker in the area and follow up with telephone calls. Comstock's staff increases the intensity of the campaign from 60 days before to 90 days after the completion of construction—that is the key period for leasing, chiefly because prospective tenants can see exactly what is being offered. Direct mail campaigns should be extensive and repetitive.
- Use brokers to advertise (and also to arrange and to negotiate for advertising). Comstock always negotiates which advertising expenses will be borne by the broker, and which by the developer. Brokers often pay for brochures and a stipulated number or amount of advertisements in newspapers and magazines.

Although some developers believe that newspaper advertisements are more likely to enhance public relations than to attract new tenants, advertising in publications can be an effective method of marketing the office building. Advertising in trade journals and magazines can be especially productive if the reading habits of prospective tenants are accurately determined. Periodicals aimed directly at prospective tenants and guides that list office buildings are also effective marketing tools. Newsletters too are an efficient means of keeping brokers and prospective tenants aware of the building and its progress.

Signboards on the project site should announce the amount of available space and give a name and telephone number to contact. If the signs must attract the attention of passersby, they should be perpendicular to the road and the letters should be large enough to read easily. The design of the sign should convey the tone of the building. Regular sign maintenance is necessary.

Public Relations

Public relations firms assist the office developer with news releases, promotional aids, and special ceremonies. Newsworthy items include groundbreaking, land closing, signing of tenant leases, securing public approvals, construction progress, building completion, first move-ins, and human interest stories on individual tenants. Many newspapers will print announcements of lease signings, hirings, and promotions at no charge. These announcements help to keep the name of the firm before the public.

Promotional items typically include free gifts such as pens and paperweights. "For example, the developers of the Daniels and Fisher Tower in Denver encased tall kitchen matches in a brown cardboard replica of the 23-story tower as a giveaway promotional aid for the tower's redevelopment."[24]

Public relations events are designed to obtain press coverage and to generate interest in the project. These events, which include press parties, broker parties, and functions for the community, may be costly, however, and may not be effective in reaching the right group of tenants, especially in the case of small buildings.

Merchandising

Merchandising is just as important for office leasing as it is for house sales, and the developer must address the same questions: How does the landscaping reinforce a good first impression? What do prospects see as they approach the building? What do they see as they walk from the parking lot to the entrance? Does the lobby create the correct atmosphere?

The condition of the site is very important to successful merchandising. Construction traffic should be regulated, trash collected, parking areas policed, and vacant space kept neat. "In successful projects, a quality image is sold; time and money usually have been spent upfront on project landscaping, signage, services, and amenities. Design and protective covenants usually ensure that the quality will be maintained over time."[25]

Ideally, the leasing office should overlook the construction site. At the very least, the leasing office should include an executive office, a staff office, an open secretarial area, and a conference room. In terms of decoration, however, the office should contain only the standard TIs in order to show prospects how attractive their space will be without added expense for extras or upgrades.

Models, pictures, and other graphic aids should be displayed to generate interest and to facilitate movement throughout the sales office. Scale models are not only useful in obtaining financing and gaining public approvals but also help prospective tenants to visualize space. Floor plan handouts serve a similar purpose and also give potential tenants something to look at after they have left the site.

Merchandising at Charleston Place in Mountain View, California, makes use of a prominent sculpture.

Different types of tenants take different approaches in deciding whether or not to lease space. Most users of spaces under 20,000 square feet will stand in the prospective space and analyze the entire area before deciding whether or not to rent it. The decision makers for users of larger spaces will often concentrate on the corner that they envision will serve as their personal offices. They will check the view, how long a walk it is to the restroom, and whether or not they can get to their offices without walking through the reception areas.

Working with Brokers

Outside real estate brokers can be very helpful in the marketing of office buildings. A real estate brokerage firm can bring an in-depth knowledge of such factors as major competitors and major tenants looking for space. These firms frequently have large databases that list key items in recently executed leases, including lease rates, terms, concessions, and TI allowances. Brokers also play an important role in spreading the word about a new development through their contacts with development agencies, local utilities, chambers of commerce, business organizations, and other community groups.

Factors to consider in hiring outside brokers include:

- What is the size and competence of the broker's leasing staff? Often, a broker with a good track record is not supported by a proficient staff.
- How many competitive buildings is the broker managing? Brokers with many clients may not be able to devote sufficient time to a new developer's project. They may also refer prospective tenants to other pro-

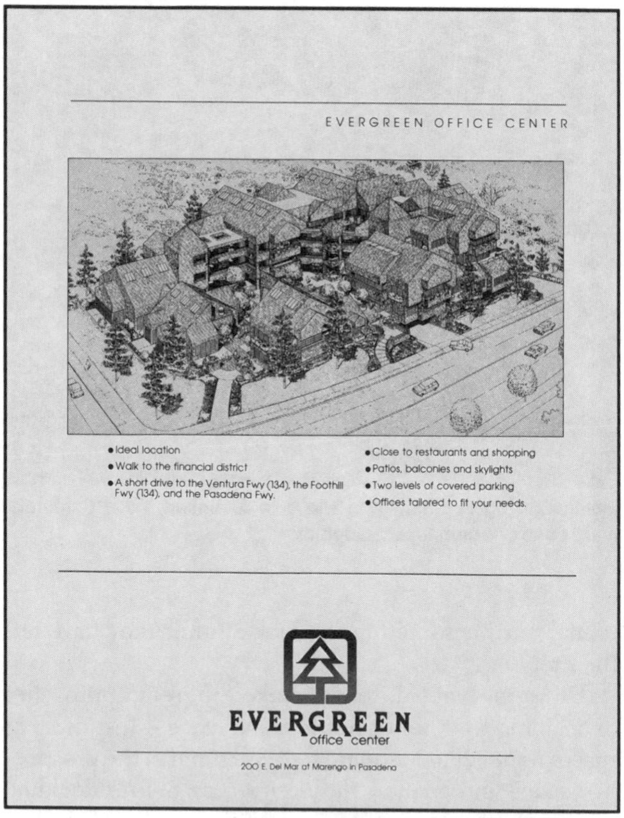

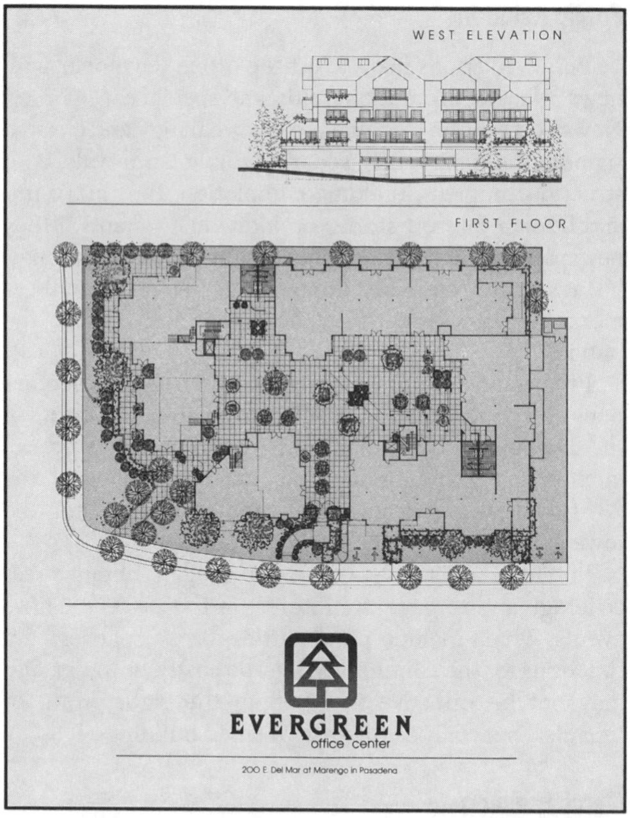

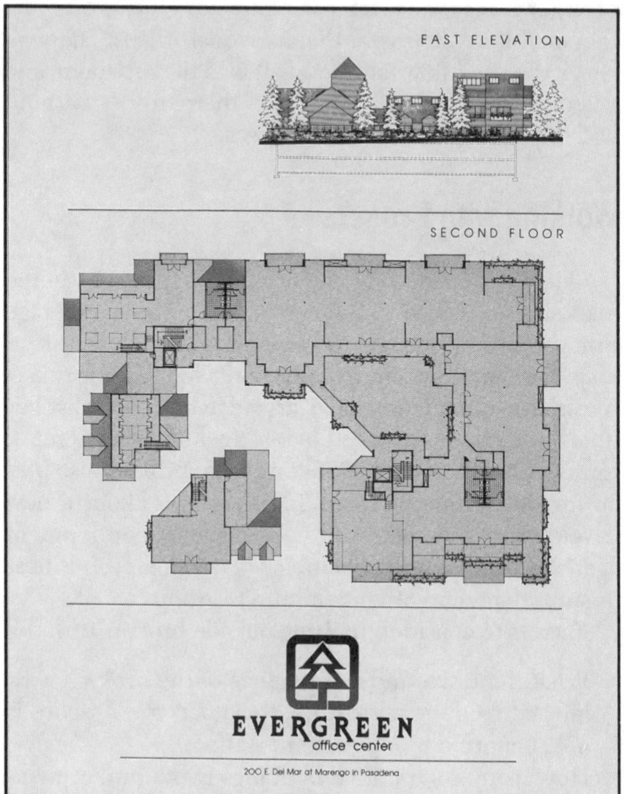

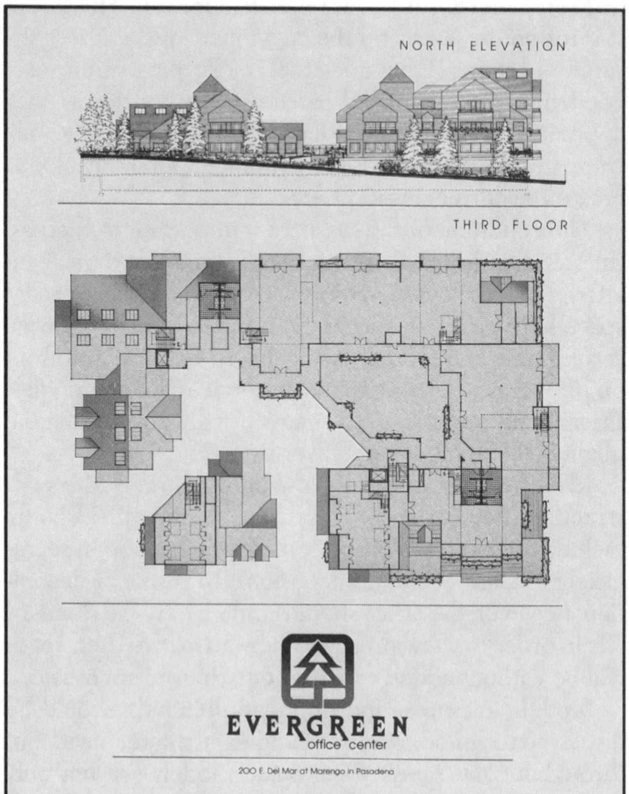

Printed marketing materials for Evergreen Office Center in Pasadena, California, include a rendering, a site plan, floor plans, and elevations to present all aspects of the project concept and design to prospective tenants.

jects that they are handling. A younger agency with fewer clients may offer better service.

Brokers may have a contract with the developer that ensures them the exclusive right to negotiate all deals on the developer's building. Alternatively, the developer may opt for an open listing, which allows any broker to act as the primary broker on a deal. Some developers prefer not to grant an exclusive authorization and right to lease to one broker until the midpoint of construction.

Working with Outside Brokers

Developers should keep outside brokers informed about their projects through presentations, breakfasts, monthly news releases, and recognition banquets. Some developers give as much as 20 to 30 hours of instruction on their products to brokers. The more that members of the brokerage community see of the project, the more likely they are to show it to prospective tenants.

Traditionally, a broker brings a prospective tenant to the developer and assists in negotiating the lease. However, many developers prefer to negotiate the lease themselves.

Commission rates are always negotiable. They depend on the condition of the market, the traditions of the market, and the competitiveness of the market. As a rough guide, however, a beginning developer could expect a broker to request a 6 percent commission rate in the first year of lease, 5 percent in the second, 4 percent in the third, 3.5 percent in the fourth and fifth, and 2.5 percent in the sixth through tenth years.

The payment of brokers' commissions is likewise negotiable, although frequently one-half of the entire commission is paid at the execution of the lease, and the other half is paid at the time of occupancy. In cases in which a substantial period of free rent is offered at the beginning of a lease, it is common for a developer to pay one-third of the commission at the signing of the lease, one-third at the occupancy, and one-third at the commencement of rent.

Using In-House Brokers

An outside broker or consultant should be retained at the beginning of the project to help analyze the type of tenants that might be interested in the building. When it comes to leasing, however, some developers prefer to employ an in-house staff. Such a staff can provide continuity in a marketing program over time. Although costly in terms of salaries, an in-house staff can also substantially reduce the cost of leasing space because in-house brokers receive lower commission rates (typically, 3 to 4 percent of the dollar amount of the lease).[26]

An effective in-house brokerage department will offer its employees many of the same training programs used in outside brokerage firms. For example, some companies have weekly education sessions for sales offices covering self-motivation, product presentation, listening, negotiation techniques, overcoming objections, getting commitments, following up, and closing.

The decision to use in-house brokers or outside brokers depends largely on the market conditions and the size and expertise of a developer's staff. Even development firms that employ in-house brokers recognize the importance of cooperating with outside brokers.

■ 5-10 Typical Breakdown of Gross Rent for Office Space

	Rent per Square Foot
Base Rent	$13.75
Energy	1.63
Cleaning	1.00
Management	.66
Grounds and General	.63
Insurance	.09
Elevators	.09
Alterations	.09
Plumbing	.06
Real Estate Taxes	2.00
Total	$20.00

Types of Leases

Four general types of leases are used in office projects: gross lease, net lease, expense stop, and percentage lease. Each type of lease has advantages and disadvantages to the tenant and landlord.

Gross Lease

Under a gross lease, the landlord pays all operating expenses. Thus, the landlord is absorbing the risk of paying rising expenses. This type of lease is preferred by small tenants that want constant rent payments that do not increase over time. A typical rent breakdown is shown in figure 5-10.

Net Lease

Three variations of net leases are common. "Under a *net lease*, the tenant pays utilities, real estate taxes, and other special assessments associated with the leased property. Under a *net-net* lease, the tenant pays everything in a net lease, plus ordinary repairs and maintenance. Under a *net-net-net* lease (called triple-net lease), the tenant pays all of the above plus capital improvements."[27] According to another definition, under a *triple-*

net lease the tenant pays taxes, insurance, maintenance, and utilities.

Needless to say, developers should ascertain the local definition of the various types of net leases so that there is no confusion in dealing with prospective tenants and brokers.

The net lease has the advantage for the developer of passing through to the tenants several, if not all, of the variable expenses associated with leasing real estate—namely, increasing operating costs, maintenance, and taxes.

Expense Stop Lease

The expense stop lease involves a sharing of expenses between the tenant and the landlord. The landlord pays a stated dollar amount for expenses, and the tenant pays any expenses above that amount. Normally, the expense stop is set at the estimated expenses for the first operating year. Thus, the tenant pays any increases in expenses over the term of the lease.

Percentage Lease

A percentage lease requires the tenant to pay a base rent against a percentage of sales, whichever is higher. These leases are common for retail tenants that can measure sales for a particular location. In office buildings, percentage leases would be appropriate for restaurant, office services, and other types of tenants that have measurable sales associated with their particular space. A 1,000-square-foot tenant might pay, for example, $20 per square foot against 5 percent of sales. The tenant would thus pay $20,000 until its sales exceeded $400,000 ($20,000 divided by 0.05). Above the $400,000 sales level, the percentage clause would determine the rent. If sales were $410,000, the tenant would pay $20,500 in rent. (Additional information on percentage leases is provided in chapter 7.)

The type of lease and term that the developer should offer depends on current market conditions. Historically, tenants prefer fixed increases in the rent rather than variable increases. Tenants usually do not object to increases in the rent due to increases in costs for repairs and maintenance.

Lease Rates and Terms

Tenants pay rent at the stated rental rate multiplied by the "rentable square feet." Developers typically charge tenants for their pro-rated share of public common-area space in addition to their own usable space. Today, many tenants are knowledgeable about building efficiency and its effect on total rent. For this reason, the people who market a building must know and understand a building's R/U ratios when quoting rental rates and lease terms to the prospective tenants.

The lease document sets forth the terms and conditions under which the tenant's rights to use the space are granted. Most office developers have their own standard lease forms that provide the starting point for negotiation with prospective tenants. Many corporate tenants also have their own forms, and negotiation with corporate tenants often begins with determining which form will be used as the starting point.

Lease negotiation usually focuses on four major items: rent, term, TIs, and concessions such as free rent or moving expenses. Rental rates vary with the amount of space a tenant takes and the stage in the project's life that a tenant signs the lease. Lead tenants (the first tenants to lease space in a building) not only receive lower rental rates but also sometimes are given an equity interest in the building.

The lease term for the lead tenant often runs 10 to 15 years, with rent escalations either yearly or every five years. The rest of the tenants usually have three- to five-year leases; the shorter term allows the landlord to renegotiate the terms of the lease to match inflation and also gives tenants greater flexibility.

Because of the long-term nature of leases and the risk involved in long-term leases, several adjustment provisions have been created to allow the rent to be adjusted to better reflect the market value of the leased space.

"Dollar stop" or "full stop" clauses charge the tenant for any increases in operating expenses during the term of the lease. An estimated dollar amount (the dollar stop) for real estate taxes and another amount for operating expenses and insurance is determined at the beginning of the lease. The actual experience for the year is compared to the dollar stop. Any difference between the actual cost and the dollar stop is debited or credited to the tenant on a pro-rata basis.

Under CPI (Consumer Price Index) clauses, rent is adjusted annually based on a specified government price index, usually the CPI or the Wholesale Price Index. Varying percentages (from 20 to 100 percent) of the rent are indexed to the CPI. Tenants initially resisted CPI leases, but they became common during the inflationary period of the late 1970s. Developers tend to prefer CPI leases, especially for buildings under development that tenants will not occupy for another one or two years. Indexing protects developers from the effects of inflation. In softer markets, CPI leases are harder to negotiate.

Buyers of a project will give some value for future rent escalations, but not full value. Because the current market usually does not fully capitalize future escalations in rent, some developers adopt a strategy of holding buildings for sale until the escalations occur. Frequently, de-

■ Marketblock
Toronto, Ontario

Located just to the east of the downtown Toronto Financial District, the Marketblock is an award-winning historic rehabilitation project completed in 1986 by Marketblock Historical Properties, Limited. This 54,000-gross-square-foot office and retail complex capitalized on gaps in the downtown market to deliver a well-received product.

The Marketblock is located at 41-45 Front Street East in the Historical Market district, east of downtown Toronto. Referred to as the Downtown Core-East, this area is the site of the Town of York, the original settlement in the Toronto region, and boasts many historical buildings. Demand for an alternative to the Class A office space found in the central business district led to increased development activity in this area. Rehabilitated historic buildings attract tenants requiring between 3,500 and 6,500 square feet of office space close to the financial core of Toronto.

Background and Site Selection

Marketblock Toronto's president, Andrew Clarke, was originally an architect and turned to development in 1979. Architects, notes Clarke, have a tendency to overextend themselves because they are accustomed to designing large projects to be financed and developed by other people. Clarke resisted this inclination, however, and his first project cost only $400,000. He has since completed 12 rehabilitation projects in the Downtown Core-East, the district in which he likes to concentrate his activities because of his familiarity with its development market. Clarke became interested in the Marketblock building and site in 1981 because of its location and architectural style.

Owned by Continental Salvage, the upper floors and basement were used for warehouse space, and the ground floor was

Marketblock is a 54,000-square-foot historic rehabilitation project developed as an alternative to the Class A office space found in the central business district of Toronto.

■ Marketblock (Continued)

The interior of the building was completely gutted and reconfigured, including the lobby, which now features a chandelier cut into the ceiling.

used for business. Clarke's initial offer of $1 million for the building was rejected. However, after a four-year pursuit, the owners agreed to sell the property for $3.3 million, in March 1985, to close in July of the same year. The closing period gave the developer a four-month lead time to allow the architect, Stark Hicks Spragge Architects, to draw up the plans. One of the main reasons Clarke chooses rehabilitation ("rehab") projects is the opportunity they offer to start physical work on the project immediately.

The Marketblock contains four stories with a basement and is located on an 80-foot by 180-foot rectangular lot. Actually, the Marketblock is made up of two buildings, the Perkins Block and the Dickson Block, both typical commercial warehouses built in the 1870s and 1880s.

Design and Construction

The Marketblock building is constructed of mill and steel on a concrete foundation with brick facing. The north facade of the building was restored to its original appearance. The traditional columns were refurbished, and the cast-iron storefront windows typical of the period were rebuilt. A wrought-iron gate below the windows was also restored.

Because the building was constructed on fill with rafted footings that had sloped three inches, renovation included shoring up the original foundation. Structural work involved underpinning the foundations and driving new piles into the walls. A new roof was installed, as were double-glazed windows.

The interior of the building was completely gutted and reconfigured to suit the anticipated demands of the market. Walls between the Perkins and Dickson Blocks on the upper floors were cut through to provide adequate office space. However, since the two buildings are not exactly level, steps connect their upper floors. The basement was connected to the adjacent building to provide the opportunity to lease storage space to adjacent retailers.

New mechanical systems were installed, including a new main electrical service placed in the basement. A new air-conditioning unit was installed with a 60-ton capacity for the main floor and a 15-ton capacity for the upper office floors. Gas-fired rooftop heating units were provided, and the basement is heated by peripheral units. Each floor was also provided with a men's and women's bathroom finished with ceramic or marble tile and mirrored and painted drywall with decorator lighting.

Ground-floor retail space at 41 and 43 Front Street was provided with hardwood floors and exposed brick walls to impart a distinctive look. At 45 Front Street, the ground floor, which serves as the lobby for the upper-floor office space, features a double-door entrance and is lit by windows and a chandelier that was cut into the ceiling.

After the rehab, the Marketblock now contains 54,000 gross square feet and 44,433 net rentable square feet, of which 23,819 is used for office space and 20,614 for retail. The project earned awards from government and industry for both the developer and the architect.

Marketing and Tenants

During the construction period, the developer preleased the top-floor office space of 6,678 square feet. Clarke prefers to lease space himself, which he advertises simply by hanging a "For Lease" sign outside the building. In this way, he is able to meet directly with potential tenants and use his real estate license to negotiate a deal, thereby eliminating the need to pay broker fees. Additionally, with the six to seven calls he receives per week, Clarke can maintain a contact list that is useful for filling vacancies or finding prospective tenants for future projects.

The retail tenants of the Marketblock are both upscale home-improvement retailers, capitalizing on the nearby active residential rehab market. Aikenhead's occupies two levels, the ground floor and basement at 41 Front Street East, and Space Age Shelving is located on the ground floor at 43 Front Street East. Both of these tenants received six months' free rent but no tenant improvement allowances. All of the space in the basement is leased out as storage space without rental concessions.

The top three floors of the project are occupied by three office tenants, each of which is a professional consulting firm that was looking for a distinctive and smaller alternative to the usual downtown tower office space. Wood Gundy, on the fourth floor, and DMR Associates, on the second and third floor, were given six months' free rent and tenant improvements of $20 per square foot. The other office tenant, Horop Company, leased the remaining vacant space in the building on the second floor in January 1988, 18 months after completion. Horop received a tenant improvement allowance but accepted a cheaper rental rate in lieu of any additional rental concessions. Horop's lease expires at the same time as DMR's, giving Marketblock Historical Properties the option either to offer DMR the opportunity to take over the entire floor or to look for a new tenant willing to lease the floor. All leases are negotiated on a triple-net basis with most of the costs of building upkeep passed on to the tenants.

Wood Gundy's space is finished with trim, baseboards, and a paneled mahogany door. Other improvement items are beveled office partitions, brass hardware throughout, a wood-burning fireplace, a boardroom, a kitchen, and a shower. Skylights on the top floor enhance its appeal. A mahogany staircase connects the fourth floors in the two buildings.

DMR's space on the second and third floor is finished in a contemporary motif with paneled doors and brass hardware. Perhaps the most interesting design feature is the staircase between the two floors that separates the second-floor reception area from the executive offices on the third floor.

Financing

Clarke financed the project with two partners on a cotenancy basis that allowed each to own a portion of the property. Cotenancy allows the investors to treat their liabilities differently for tax purposes. Backed by his partners, Clarke secured a $6 million line of credit at a rate of prime plus 1 point to finance the construction phase of the project. The line of credit was secured on July 3, 1985, and rehabilitation of the Marketblock began the following day.

Construction work was completed 10 months later on May 1, 1986. Rehabilitation of the building cost $2 million, or approximately $30 per square foot. Permanent financing was secured during the construction phase through Prudential Finance for $5.2 million at 11 percent fixed rate, for 10 years, with a 20-year amortization. Marketblock Historical Properties leveraged its current real estate holdings to obtain the line of credit as well as the permanent loan.

Experience Gained

- Clarke believes that developers should act as the management company for all of their projects. Clarke argues that this practice is less expensive than hiring a management company and that it gives developers the opportunity to build up relationships with their tenants. Clarke personally collects each tenant's rent check every month and takes the opportunity to inspect the space and solicit any complaints. In this way, the company is able to monitor the condition of its buildings and to resolve any problems before they get out of hand. Direct contact can also be useful in conducting an informal market survey of what tenants do and do not like about a particular design.
- When trying to lease space in a rehabilitated historic building, it is important to know its history because prospective tenants enjoy hearing stories about the site and may be more inclined to rent space as a consequence.
- A long-term strategy of holding onto projects after their completion allows developers to earn income from the cash flows and benefit from the appreciation in building value. Clarke uses Marketblock Toronto Properties' portfolio as leverage to obtain financing for other projects.

Developer:
Marketblock Historical Properties, Limited
116 Yorkville
Toronto, Ontario
(416) 923-7777

Architect:
Stark Hicks Spragge Architects
5045 Orbitor Drive
Suite 40, Building 12
Mississauga, Ontario L4W 4Y4
(416) 602-6020

■ Marketblock (Continued)

Project Data

Land Use Information:
Site Area: 0.33 acres
Gross Building Area (GBA): 54,000 square feet
Net Rentable Area: 44,433 square feet
Office: 23,819 square feet
Retail: 20,614 square feet

Economic Information:
Site Acquisition Cost: $3,300,000
Construction Costs: $2,000,000

Soft Costs	
Architect	$55,000
Legal	15,000
Loan Fees	60,000
Land Transfer	30,000
Interest	1,500,000
Leasing	200,000
Total Soft Costs	1,860,000

Total Development Costs: $7,160,000
Construction Cost per Square Foot: $30

Tenant Information:
Number of Tenants: 11
Average Size of Tenant Space: 4,035 square feet

Tenant Schedule:

	Rentable Area (Square Feet)	Annual Rent Per Square Foot	Base Net Rent
Basement:			
Aikenhead's (Beaver Lumber Co.)	6,987	$5.00	$34,935
Timbuktu Trading Ltd.	1,034	8.00	8,272
Windy Pine Outfitters	1,400	5.00	7,000
DMR Associates	1,000	5.00	5,000
Horop Company, Ltd.	825	5.00	4,125
First Floor:			
Aikenhead's (Beaver Lumber Co.)	9,127	23.50	214,485
Space Age Shelving (V.F. Marketing Services)	4,500	22.50	101,250
Second Floor:			
DMR Associates	3,529	21.55	76,050
Horop Company, Ltd.	2,641	17.00	44,897
Third Floor:			
DMR Associates	6,678	21.55	143,910
Fourth Floor:			
Wood Gundy Leasing Company	6,678	20.00	133,560
			$773,485
Less 5 Percent Management Fee			38,675
Total Net Rent			$734,810

Note: Steve Webber, PhD candidate, USC, is the author of this case study.

velopers need to find institutional partners to help them carry a building for the first two or three years.

The key to successful lease negotiations is to determine the tenant's needs. For example, does a tenant need free rent, excellent location, low initial rent with later escalations, or above-standard TIs? Everything is negotiable, including the cost of above-standard TIs. Generally, smaller tenants prefer higher TI allowances because they often lack the cash to pay for the improvements in advance. Larger tenants often prefer free rent.

The base rent that can be charged depends on the condition of the office market. If local vacancy rates exceed 15 percent, tenants will enjoy a strong bargaining position, and the base rent may have to be lowered accordingly.

Every lease should specify the following information:

- size and location of the space;
- method of measuring the space;
- options for expansion, if any;

- duration of lease, renewal options, and cancellation privileges;
- rent per square foot;
- services included in the lease;
- interior work to be performed by the developer under the base rent;
- operating hours of the building;
- landlord's obligations for maintenance and services;
- tenant's obligations for maintenance and services;
- escalation provisions within the lease term;
- number of parking spaces, their location, and terms of their use (for example, whether designated or undesignated);
- allowable use of the leased space permitted by local zoning ordinances and building rules;
- date of possession and date that rental payment is due; and
- sublease and assignment privileges, if any.

Operations and Management

The management of the property is the last phase of the office development process. Day-to-day operations are normally managed by the property manager, whose most important function is to keep the tenants satisfied. Larger buildings will have property managers on site, whereas several smaller buildings may share a property manager. Property management is as important to a developer's reputation as is project design or financing.

The agreement between the developer and the property manager should spell out "his/her duties and responsibilities, including the authority to sign leases and other documents, to incur expenses to advertise, and to arrange banking/trust agreements. Also included are provisions on record keeping, insurance, indemnification, employees, and management fees."[28] Management fees typically range from 3 to 5 percent of gross income collected.

With the overbuilt and very competitive office market of the 1990s, the property management function has been upgraded in many development firms to the same level as new development. "Asset management" has become the catchphrase for managing properties to their fullest potential. Although beginning developers may find that hiring outside management for their properties is more convenient or helps their credibility in the search for financing, most developers manage their own buildings, not only for the fees they generate but also to develop and maintain close ties with tenants. Indeed, some developers have strongly promoted their asset management capabilities to institutional owners such as pension funds. Other developers are expanding their property management activities by buying existing properties. Asset management counterbalances a slowdown in new office development while also adding to the developer's base of tenants. Development companies that perform property management well are able to generate much of their new development business from the expansion of existing tenants.

Budgeting and Accounting

The management staff usually provides a range of accounting information, including an annual projection of income and expenditure, updated quarterly. The income side should include rents as though the project were fully occupied, plus garage and parking fees, escalation charges, and miscellaneous income. The gross possible income is adjusted for anticipated losses from vacancy, turnover, and delinquencies. Management staff should also detail expenses, which include electricity, water and sewer, fuel, payroll, employee benefits, cleaning supplies, repairs, decorating, advertising, management fees, administrative costs, taxes, insurance, security, window washing, landscape services, trash removal, and snow removal.

The property manager should prepare a monthly (or quarterly) statement of operations showing the rent roll (that is, all tenant data including income, charges, and lease expirations) and a disbursement statement for all funds expended.

Keeping Tenants Satisfied

The first step towards ensuring the satisfaction of tenants is the coordination of an effective program of TIs. Many developers have their own in-house project manager who undertakes this time-consuming and tedious phase of construction. Thereafter, developers should abide by several policies that will help to create and maintain tenant satisfaction. First, they should demonstrate a concern to uphold the reputation of their company and its projects. Second, they should ensure that any express guarantees or warranties that were offered to the tenants are honored. Third, developers should ensure that the lease agreements and protective covenants spell out each service and maintenance function that each party will provide. And fourth, they should create an organization to attend to maintenance and the provision of services. Four items are key to the successful maintenance of any office building: maintenance and janitorial services, elevator service, HVAC systems, and security. Tenants usually take these items for granted and only notice them when problems occur.

If the lease gives the tenant responsibility for maintenance or landscaping, the developer should retain the right to order the work if the tenant fails to do so. (This

The Oak Lawn Building
Dallas, Texas

The Oak Lawn Building was the first office building/retail renovation project undertaken by the Dallas-based firm of Kenneth H. Hughes Interests. The project involved the construction of a three-floor mixed-use office structure (3311 Oak Lawn) of European-style design (containing 16,012 square feet of leasable space—4,898 in the street-level retail space and 11,114 in the second- and third-floor office spaces) and the renovation of an adjoining one-story retail space (3301 Oak Lawn) with 10,000 square feet.

The building is situated on Oak Lawn Avenue, a thoroughfare connecting upper-income North Dallas to the downtown core. The site itself lies approximately two miles north of downtown Dallas, in an area adjacent to the wealthy inner-city suburb of Highland Park. Although largely considered a transition area at the time the building was developed, Oak Lawn has recently begun to experience rapid improvement as old stores have been torn down to make way for a number of major office and mixed-use projects.

The Oak Lawn Market

The Oak Lawn area has a unique relationship to the rest of Dallas. In many southern cities, the areas immediately surrounding the central business district (CBD) are blighted. Yet, Dallas has the good fortune of having Oak Lawn immediately on the north flank of the CBD. Oak Lawn is an integrated community with strong, viable, single-family and multifamily residential, commercial, and retail space, Class A office space, and good hotel accommodations all within its boundaries. The population is, demographically, a broad mix, and the area has one of the highest per capita incomes in the city of Dallas.

Oak Lawn Avenue is the spine road for the Oak Lawn area and the main thoroughfare that connects the office complexes in the Dallas Market Center and Stemmons areas with Highland Park. Thus, the street has probably the highest amount of daily vehicular traffic in the city. Oak Lawn Avenue is certain to grow in importance as the area develops.

Intense neighborhood interest in the type of local development spawned both the Oak Lawn Committee and the Oak Lawn Forum, two organizations that cooperate with the city and developers concerning plans and concepts for sites in the immediate vicinity. The development team felt that the Oak Lawn building deserved a design that followed the highest and best urban style for office/retail building. Coincidentally, the concept was almost precisely within the guidelines for design that the Oak Lawn Forum had recommended to the city of

The Oak Lawn project includes a new three-story structure consisting of ground-level retail and upper-level office space. The building features a drive-through arch that leads to parking at the rear of the project.

Dallas to be adopted in lieu of current zoning requirements. This building, therefore, was the first to be built in the area under the new guidelines, and thus is an extremely visible, high-profile structure.

Background and Site Selection

Kenneth H. Hughes Interests, which was named for its founder who had previously served as executive vice president and a member of the Henry S. Miller Company's board of directors, was established in July 1983, for the purpose of securing and developing retail, office, and residential properties.

After completing the leasing of the Dallas Galleria project with Gerald Hines in 1983, Hughes announced that he would be leaving the Miller Company in April. He was accompanied by Brian Murphy and Lawrence Attaway, members of a team he had assembled at the Miller Company, which enjoyed a reputation for being its most active transaction group. After an extensive search for appropriate projects, Hughes launched the Oak Lawn project on land in which he owned a quarter interest—the remaining 75 percent belonging to other partners.

A number of factors contributed to the choice of locality, which was an unusual one by most standards. Mainly, the area was heating up in terms of development. Hughes discerned a definite trend toward renovation in the area: the Melrose Hotel, situated nearby and widely regarded as a landmark, had been recently upgraded; and, most significantly, Oak Lawn itself had just undergone an overlay zoning process following negotiations between local homeowners and developers. The district, consequently, established more restrictive building setbacks, heights, exterior materials usage, landscaping, and parking requirements than actually called for by the citywide zoning. Hughes regarded these ostensibly problematic restrictions positively because they lent the area the kind of ambience and environment he deemed suitable for his upscale efforts.

In 1983, the Dallas economy was still booming—virtually anything, it was thought, could be accomplished. Prior to the emergence of the seller's market, Hughes and his partners had bought the bulk of the Oak Lawn site for $28 per square foot. In 1984, nearby developers were paying nearly four times that amount. A year later, Hughes himself picked up the retail renovation portion of the site for $100 per square foot, which, at that time, was considered a reasonable price for the property, given that it included a reusable 10,000-square-foot building. Construction on the project began in 1984 and was completed before the year was out.

Design

The overlay zone code governing construction at Oak Lawn required the building to be close to the street, resulting in considerably less space in front of the building for parking than might have been considered optimal. The new zoning rules, not surprisingly, created potential leasing problems because retail developments had, until that time, almost exclusively maintained parking spaces at the front. Hughes decided, however, to provide parking spaces in the back of the building, and, thus, it became imperative that he find a way to indicate to drivers that the parking lot was situated in the back. He managed this by creating a large drive-through arch, with the appropriate signage, leading out to the parking area.

The office building was designed with large arches patterned after those found in Parisian villas, with carriage courts situated at the center of the building. To achieve a convincing look, Hughes decided to use malleable masonry materials. To convey the proper market image, Hughes instructed his marketing people to avoid the term "stucco" and use instead the word "plaster," which, he believed, connoted European, handcrafted workmanship.

The building is sheathed in high-finish plaster with the base of the building constructed out of cast stone. All storefronts are mullionless glass, and windows on the exterior of the building are solar resistant but nonmirrored in finish. All graphics and signage are controlled by a comprehensive, coordinated program.

The front of the building is landscaped with large trees set in tree gates. To the rear of the building, the landscape features are minimal yet important because this is the building's principal arrival point. Carefully placed trees in large planters with some groundcover highlight the back of the project. The alley, as well as the side properties, were screened from view by masonry and wood fences. The parking spaces total 67, with 28 on the surface and 39 in the covered underground facility connected directly to the office-space elevator.

The interior finishes are consistent with the postmodern approach to the exterior. The building lobby is highly finished, and its principal entrance is through the covered automobile/pedestrian pass.

Because Hughes lacked experience with office building development, he engaged in a detailed study of other such buildings in the area and ultimately researched all extant Class A buildings, finally opting for a nine-and-a-half-foot floor-to-finished-ceiling height. (Floor-to-floor height was between 12 and 14 feet, and the top-floor floor-to-ceiling height was 11 feet.) These were especially luxurious ceiling heights, replete with concealed-spine ceilings.

■ The Oak Lawn Building (Continued)

In addition to new construction, the project involved the renovation of an existing one-story retail structure.

Other upgraded amenities included highly finished bathrooms with granite countertops, incandescent lighting, and brushed stainless steel toilet partitions. Although lavatories in office buildings then possessed ceramic walls, Hughes made good use of wallpaper. Offices were equipped with solid-core oak doors ebonized on the outer layer. These proved to require less maintenance because they could be easily touched up.

Another significant element was security—a concern for most tenants. Hughes equipped his parking garage with an impassable, roll-down metal grill and issued electronic door-openers to tenants, so that they would not have to leave their automobiles upon entering or leaving the building. The garage also was equipped with elevators to provide access to all floors.

A restaurant on the first floor presented another series of challenges to the developer. Grease traps, it was discovered, could only be placed below the building's grade level if back-up pumps were installed. These made it possible to redirect grease some six feet above the grease traps into the sanitary sewer line. Through such foresight, the developer avoided potential future moisture problems.

The adjoining renovation, meanwhile, was a brick veneer structure with large, unsightly signs. Hughes gutted the interior, replaced the roof and the slab, and cleaned up the exterior. Workers found some unexpectedly high-quality stone work under the signs, which they repaired, adding a plaster cornice to the top of the building to match that of the building next door. Expenditures for demolition were $15,000, for roof repairs $22,000, and for storefronts $20,000. Total renovation costs amounted to $101,000.

Financing

A joint venture was entered into by the original four partners who owned the land. These general partners continued their association throughout the construction period.

Although they had anticipated completing the development and selling the building quickly, they had not done so as of this writing. Two of the partners sought to withdraw from the project when the Dallas economy turned sour in 1986. Hughes, seeking to accommodate them, bought them out.

Construction financing was provided by First Republic Bank in the form of a construction miniperm loan—a five-year loan that covered the construction and lease-up period and gave the developer time to find permanent financing after the project reached stabilized occupancy. One year was allotted for completion of construction of the office building and six months for the retail building. As of early 1988, however, Hughes remained under the miniperm.

The original building loan was for $3.2 million, including hard and soft costs. The retail renovation, meanwhile, was financed by another loan of $1.765 million, which was at two-and-a-half points over First Republic's floating cost-of-funds, with a quote rate of approximately 8.5 percent, which was below prime. Hughes had joint liability on the loan.

Because economic conditions in Dallas began to soften in 1986, the bank loaned additional money to cover more lease-up time, and the partners invested some $100,000 to $150,000 of additional equity.

The inability of some tenants, whatever their motivations, to pay their rents forced Hughes to renegotiate his loan with First Republic. The bank declined Hughes' offer of an equity position, forecasting that within two to three years the cash flow would resume to the level that was first anticipated. Hughes remained careful throughout his dealings with First Republic to maintain open, businesslike relations—a strategy that contributed to the success of his endeavor, even during the most trying times.

Sculpture is used to enhance the streetscape.

Marketing and Leasing

Hughes' marketing effort was enhanced by receipt of a design award from the state chapter of the American Institute of Architects, which resulted in a great deal of publicity for Hughes. Publicity was also generated by a Wesselmann sculpture situated at the front of the building—one of the first instances of such decoration in the city's recent history. In addition, a striking building logo was designed by Woody Pirtle, a well-known graphic artist.

These attributes lent the building a preeminence and media presence that was unusual, especially given the project's small size relative to other, far more extensive developments undertaken during the Dallas construction boom.

The leasing experience Hughes had garnered at the Miller Company convinced him that he would have to lease the Oak Lawn Building aggressively. Hughes put together a full-scale leasing plan, replete with maps, brochures, and names of space-planners who were available to show prospective tenants how their space could be designed. Hughes' leasing staff launched the effort early on in the renovation by drawing up a schedule of cold calls to make to residents of every neighborhood believed to have potential commercial tenants and, especially, to members of the brokerage community. Print advertising was also pursued vigorously—an advertisement that Hughes placed in *Adweek* led to the leasing of the top floor to a local advertising agency.

Hughes' lead retail tenant was a New York retailer, Alexander Julian, which leased the 3,518-square-foot retail space on the ground floor. Because high-powered deals were happening nearby—a property across the street had sold for a major development, and a 400,000-square-foot mixed-use project was under construction down the street—Hughes did not feel any great pressure to lease out space hastily. By 1988, however, the boom had become a depression, compelling Hughes to adopt a different strategy.

Because of the downturn in real estate prices, Hughes found himself facing concerted efforts by some of his tenants to renegotiate the terms of their leases. Hughes' readiness to oblige them often depended upon his reading of their sincerity and objective circumstances. For instance, when he leased his top floor to a local advertising agency, rent was established at $29 per square foot, with 22 months of free rent. At the end of that free-rent period, the tenant announced that it could only pay $5 per square foot rather than the agreed-upon rent. Because Hughes valued this tenant's business, he agreed to allow the tenant merely to cover expenses until, after two years, rent gradually rose to $13 per square foot. Hughes was less inclined, however, to accommodate those tenants that appeared to be taking advantage of the market slump by asking for vast and largely unwarranted rate reductions.

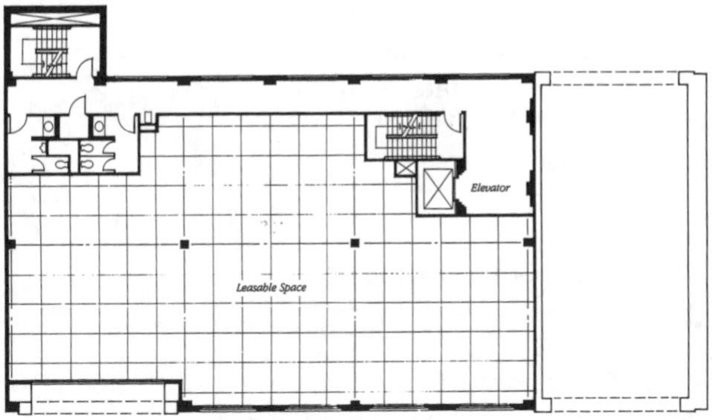

Floor plan for the second floor.

Experience Gained

- Hughes believes that he should not have begun development on the first building without having first obtained ownership of the adjoining structure. He regards his ability to buy the second building late in the game as a stroke of good luck. Had this not proved possible, and had Hughes subsequently been denied access to the side street, the entire project might have proved unrealizable.
- Hughes maintains that developers should never underestimate the value of extensive exposure of projects during the construction period. He warns developers never to enter into "limited notices to proceed" (where construction begins before all plans and contracts are finalized) and advocates that even contractual and design issues should be addressed and resolved before the start of construction. Although change orders are inescapable in any project, developers do well to minimize them when possible. Hughes also advocates allowing a 5 percent contingency for a new building and a 10 percent construction contingency for a renovation.
- Hughes, who had heard all of the cautionary tales of developers who failed to attend to details during the construction phase, vowed never to fall prey to the usual pitfalls. When he began building, for instance, he became aware of pending building regulations in the works and did what he could to determine their nature and to accommodate them, believing that, even though he had a building permit, certificates of occupancy might prove impossible to obtain if his building did not fit the new code perfectly. The only design mistake, in fact, was attributable to the architect's inability to obtain the insurance credits on which Hughes had relied. The architect later paid reparations.

■ The Oak Lawn Building (Continued)

Developer:
Kenneth H. Hughes Company, Inc.
2323 Bryan Street, Suite 2020
Dallas, Texas 75201
(214) 754-7040

Architect:
Philip W. Shepherd, Architects
Dallas, Texas

General Contractor:
Henry Building and Engineering, Inc.
Lancaster, Texas

Landscape Architects:
POD, Inc.
Dallas Texas

Leasing And Management:
Kenneth H. Hughes Interests
Dallas, Texas

Project Data

Land Use Information:
Site Area: 0.72 acres
- Office: 11,114 square feet
- Retail:14,898 square feet
- Net Rentable Area: 26,012 square feet

Parking Spaces: 84
- Surface: 45
- Underground: 39

Economic Information:
Site Acquisition Cost: $1,392,000
Construction Costs: $3,333,080
Other Soft Costs: $335,000
Total Development Costs: $5,060,080
Construction Costs per Square Foot: $183

is necessary because the condition of one building in a multibuilding complex may affect the rentability of other buildings.) Under this type of agreement—called a "condition of premises" clause—the developer must notify the tenant in advance, giving the tenant the opportunity to comply. If the tenant still fails to respond, then the developer can do the work and charge the tenant for the cost.

One of the most important management tools is the lease agreement. Developers should ensure that leases contain clauses stipulating that:

- tenants must not alter the building without the landlord's consent;
- tenants must not do anything that might increase the costs of fire insurance or create noise or nuisance;
- tenants must not use the building for immoral or illegal purposes; and
- if tenants remove floor, wall, or ceiling coverings, they must restore the surfaces to the condition that existed when the tenants took possession.

Despite their responsibilities for enforcing such policies, however, property managers should remember that their most important function is to keep the tenants happy.

Selling the Completed Project

At some point in the life of almost every project, the project will be sold. The decision to sell depends on such factors as the needs of the equity partners, the term of the construction or permanent loan, the market for office building investments, and the developer's analysis of alternative investment opportunities.

Office buildings are commonly sold at one of three points in their development: when stabilized occupancy occurs; after the first full year of occupancy (when the first CPI or fixed adjustments occur); and after the leases are renewed.

The developer's goal is to sell the project at the point when the building will provide the highest return according to the developer's investment objectives. Two common objectives are securing the highest return and holding for long-term investment. Usually, the highest internal rate of return is achieved if the building is sold as soon as it reaches stabilized occupancy. In competitive markets, however, most developers prefer to wait until just after the leases first roll over or the first rent escalations have occurred—at this point, the highest net present value (at a discount rate of 12 to 15 percent) is often reached. On the other hand, long-term investors usually plan to hold buildings for at least seven years. Indeed, some foreign investors claim that they plan to hold their buildings forever.

Developers can take several actions in order to position a building for sale. These include the following:

- hiring a building inspection team to perform a thorough inspection of a building's mechanical and other systems and to prepare a report that can be shown to prospective buyers;
- preparing summaries of a project's income and expenses and ensuring that the accounting records are in order;
- making sure that a building is clean and has a well-landscaped and well-maintained appearance;
- preparing a summary of all of the outstanding leases on a building; and
- creating a marketing brochure that describes a project's unique and noteworthy qualities—its tenants, management, location, and position in the market.

Carol Peerce

In the long run, office development will offer opportunities for developers who can come up with creative solutions to tenant needs. Pictured above is the Evening Star Building in Washington, D.C., which has achieved some of the highest rents in the city due to its excellent location on Pennsylvania Avenue—offering outstanding views of the nation's Capitol—and its attractive blending of old and new architecture.

Conclusion

During the late 1980s and early 1990s, office development became the most overbuilt of the real estate product types in many markets. Consequently, opportunities for developing new office buildings are lower in the 1990s than they were in the 1980s. This situation will not change until the excess supply has been absorbed.

Control of tenants is the most important factor in an overbuilt market. One of the surest ways for beginning developers to obtain financing for a new office building is to secure signed leases for 50 to 70 percent of the space in the building. This is not easily done, of course, especially for beginning developers. Moreover, small office buildings, especially those in suburban locations, are more difficult to finance and harder to sell than larger buildings are.

Despite the difficulties of developing new office space, buildings with seasoned leases remain one of the most preferred investments of institutions, pension funds, and foreign and domestic buyers. Developers who are able to establish working arrangements with financial institutions and other sources of capital that will allow them to bide their time through the early 1990s will be in a strong position to compete once the office development cycle turns around.

In the long run, office development will offer opportunities for developers large and small who can develop and offer creative solutions to the space needs of tenants. Beginning developers can bring new ideas and approaches to this marketplace that can give them an edge.

Notes

1. John Loper, a student in the USC Master of Real Estate Development program, assisted in the preparation of this chapter.

2. See Richard A. Lex, "Marketing Studies of Office Buildings," *Real Estate Review*, vol. 5, no. 2, Summer 1975, p. 103.

3. W. Paul O'Mara, *Office Development Handbook* (Washington, D.C.: ULI–the Urban Land Institute, 1982), p. 39.

4. Taken from an interview with Kotin in 1989.

5. Taken from an interview with Jim Goodell in 1989.

6. Individual parking spaces range from eight-and-one-half feet wide by 16 feet long to 10 feet wide by 16 feet long. A double-loaded parking module requires a 60-foot cross-section for two parking places and an aisle. Two modules (with a combined width of 120 feet) are needed for circulation between floors, with each module floor doubling as a ramp. If spaces are nine feet wide, 20 spaces would require 180 feet, for total parking dimensions of 120 by 180 feet.

7. See Charles F. Floyd, "Shaping the Skyscrapers of Manhattan," *Real Estate Review*, vol. 13, Summer 1983, pp. 48–54.

8. Mel Branch, "Don't Call It City Planning," *International Quarterly on Urban Policy*, vol. 3, no. 4, November 1986, pp. 290–97.

9. O'Mara, *Office Development Handbook*, p. 36.

10. Ibid, p. 59.

11. Ibid, p. 47.

12. These restrictions are taken from the signage program used by Orlando Central Park, Inc., in Orlando, Florida; see ibid.

13. See Parking Consultants Council, *The Dimensions of Parking* (Washington, D.C.: ULI–the Urban Land Institute and the National Parking Association, 1979).

14. See O'Mara, *Office Development Handbook*, p. 72.

15. Ibid., p. 74.

16. See Bernard R. Boylan, *The Lighting Primer* (Ames, Iowa: Iowa State University Press, 1987).

17. Interior fire partitions typically have five-eighths of an inch wallboard and are used where a one-hour fire rating is required.

18. This section was written by Ken Beck, USC MRED student, and is based on interviews with Matthew Kane, assistant project manager with The Robert Mayer Corporation, Newport Beach, California, and Mark Rettig of the Special Projects Office of the President, IDM Corporation, Long Beach, California.

19. MLPs are publicly traded limited partnerships that offer the advantages of public trading and provide the benefits of a limited partnership interest.

20. Taken from an interview with Wurtzebach in April 1989.

21. These returns are calculated before tax (using NOI) on the basis of an all-equity (no mortgage) purchase of the building evaluated over a 10-year holding period. The property is assumed to be sold at the end of the tenth year at a price determined by capitalizing the eleventh year's NOI at the same cap rate used to purchase the building. Prudential looks at complete rollover of leases and assumes 4 to 5 percent inflation on CPI leases.

22. This list taken from O'Mara, *Office Development Handbook*, p. 88.

23. Taken from an interview with Comstock in 1987.

24. O'Mara, *Office Development Handbook*, p. 94.

25. Ibid.

26. Taken from an interview with Joseph A. Jaconi, president, Joseph Jaconi Development, Torrance, California, in 1987.

27. O'Mara, *Office Development Handbook*, p. 96.

28. Ibid., p. 98.

Chapter 6

Industrial Park and Building Development

Introduction

The modern industrial park is the product of an evolutionary process[1] that began in England in 1876 with the development of the first planned industrial estate, Trafford Park Estates. Occupying 1,200 acres along the Manchester Ship Canal, Trafford Park Estates remained the world's largest planned industrial estate until the 1950s. During the intervening years, however, new concepts in the design of industrial parks were pioneered in many places, notably in three projects in Chicago. Chicago's Central Manufacturing District, built in 1902 on 260 acres, had uniform four-story buildings (designed for "gravity flow production," a popular concept at the time), private rail sidings, gridiron streets, landscaping, planting strips, and ornamental street lighting. The Clearing Industrial District, built in 1909 on 530 acres, introduced 40-acre superblocks that eliminated interior grade rail crossings and provided a variety of site sizes and depths.[2] The Pershing Road District, built in 1910 on 91 acres, consisted of buildings with a handsome facade along the freeway and railroad access in the rear.

Industrial development during the 1920s and 1930s was centered around railroad yards and lines, with every site enjoying some form of rail service. Significant industrial developments during the next 30 years included Slough Estates in England (1920); Los Angeles Central Manufacturing District (1922); New England Industrial Center in Needham, Massachusetts (1949); and Stanford Industrial Park in Palo Alto, California (1951).[3]

In the 1950s, the first business parks appeared, designed for office buildings rather than for industrial buildings. By the 1960s, developers introduced research and development (R&D) parks that specialized in laboratory work, prototype development, light manufacturing, assembly, and other technological activities. In the 1970s, a hybrid form of business parks was developed that combined office, industrial, and supporting commercial and recreational uses. The 1980s introduced some residential uses into business parks in order to mitigate traffic congestion and to provide housing close to work. Throughout this evolution, there has been a trend towards greater mixture of uses previously considered incompatible: office buildings located next to manufacturing, and apartments next to office buildings.

Both manufacturing and distribution industries have been decentralizing since the 1950s. Many factors have contributed to the outward migration and suburbanization of industry: interstate highways have improved accessibility to areas outside of major cities; suburban single-family housing has provided laborers with better living conditions; growing firms have required larger quarters; and assembly-line production and distribution compa-

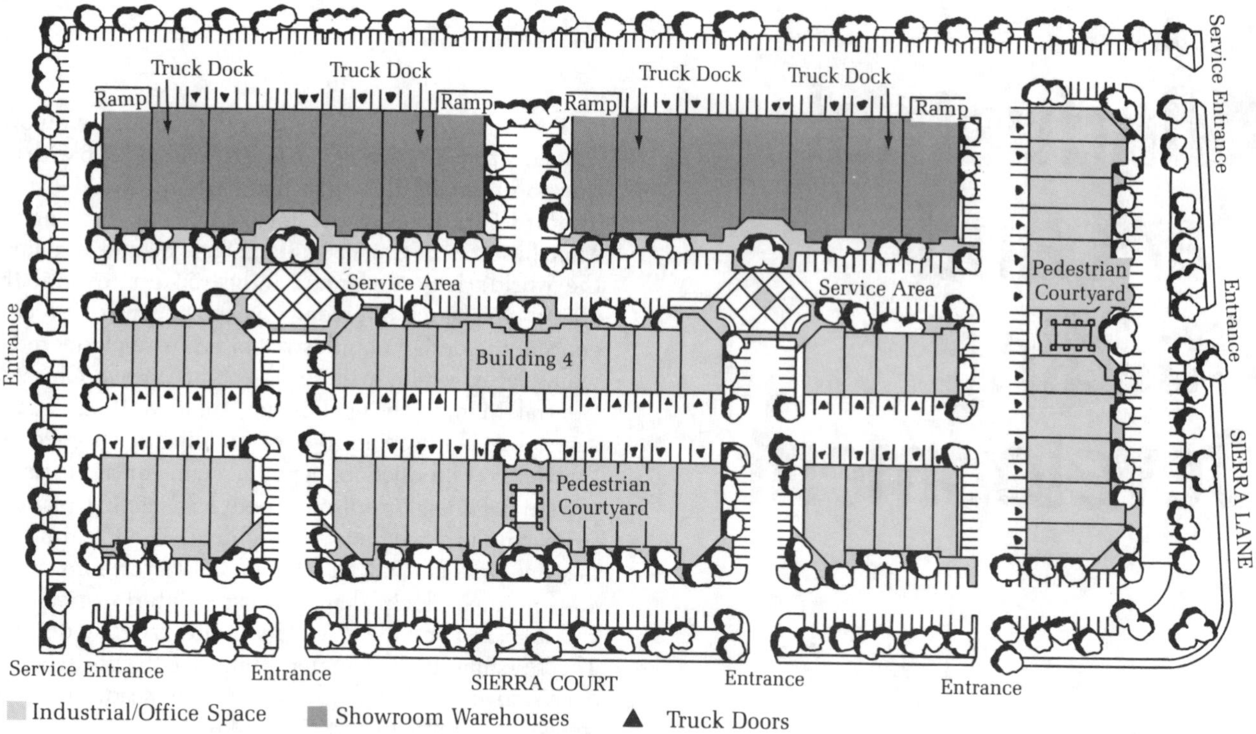

Of all forms of development, industrial park and building development encompasses the broadest range of product types. Pictured is a site plan of Sierra Trinity Park in Dublin, California, a 14-acre industrial/office park designed to provide top-quality, low-cost, leasable space in flexible-use, single-story buildings for R&D, warehouse, showrooms, light manufacturing, and back office uses.

nies have desired large sites for single-floor operations that could not be accommodated in the crowded inner cities. Ironically, certain older inner-city industrial parks with good freeway access, such as the city of Commerce in Los Angeles, are becoming attractive again because land is comparatively inexpensive, and large, obsolete industrial buildings are now available for rehabilitation.

Product Types

Of all forms of development, industrial development encompasses the broadest range of product types. Reflecting this diversity, industrial development can be categorized by three different dimensions: land use, function, and building type. However, no standard typology exists for categorizing industrial real estate. Firms often use the same terms to refer to different types of buildings.

Land Use Categories

ULI's *Business and Industrial Park Development Handbook* identifies three types of industrial land use: industrial areas, industrial parks, and business parks.[4]

Industrial areas. Older industrial areas typically consist of supply yards surrounded by large, freestanding factories and warehouses, characterized by multilevel masonry construction and a high degree of site coverage. In central city areas, efficient operations are often hampered by insufficient parking, crowded streets, and difficult access to highways.

Industrial parks. These are master-planned subdivisions for which control and administration is vested in a single body created by the developer. Restrictive covenants regulate the types of uses that are permitted, and architectural design controls regulate building setbacks, heights, and, often, appearance. The purpose of the restrictions is to create a parklike atmosphere that integrates the industrial areas with surrounding neighborhoods and protects the investment of the developer and tenants.

Business parks. These multiuse parks may include industrial and office uses, as well as retail, hotel, recreational, and other uses, so that a variety of employee needs may be met within their boundaries. Some of the best business parks are found in new communities, such as Irvine, California, and First Colony, Texas, and in large-scale planned unit developments (PUDs).

Functional Categories

A second way to differentiate industrial development types is by their function. Different functions demand different locations, amenities, and so forth, which, in turn, dictate different types of development.

Warehouse and distribution. In the 1980s, most industrial development served the needs of warehouse and distribution functions; in 1986, for example, 61 percent of the industrial absorption that occurred consisted of warehouse and distribution space. Warehouses are land intensive, so they tend to be built in urban fringe areas where land is less expensive. They require large, flat sites with space for trucks or railyards and transshipment areas for bulky goods and containers. Access to transportation facilities is, of course, very important to warehousing and distribution developments. Bulk warehouses have low employee-to-area ratios—typically one or two employees per 1,000 square feet. Some communities oppose the development of bulk warehouses because they bring lower tax benefits than do other types of industry. On the other hand, such buildings generate relatively little traffic and can be attractively designed.

Manufacturing. Manufacturing uses may be found in many industrial park locations. Heavy manufacturing development has slowed considerably in the recent past, and its place has been taken by "clean" light manufactur-

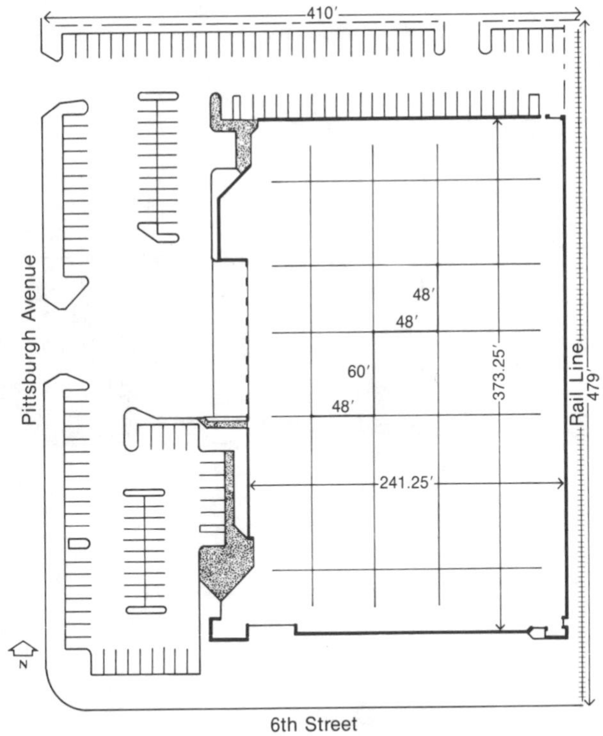

A typical warehouse building at Rancho Cucamonga Distribution Center in Rancho Cucamonga, California. All buildings in the project are one-story, tilt-up concrete buildings with ceilings 22 feet to 24 feet. The project is served by rail.

A pedestrian bridge over a reflecting pool connects the administration building (right) with the production building (left) at the Glaxo Pharmaceutical Manufacturing Facility in Zebulon, North Carolina.

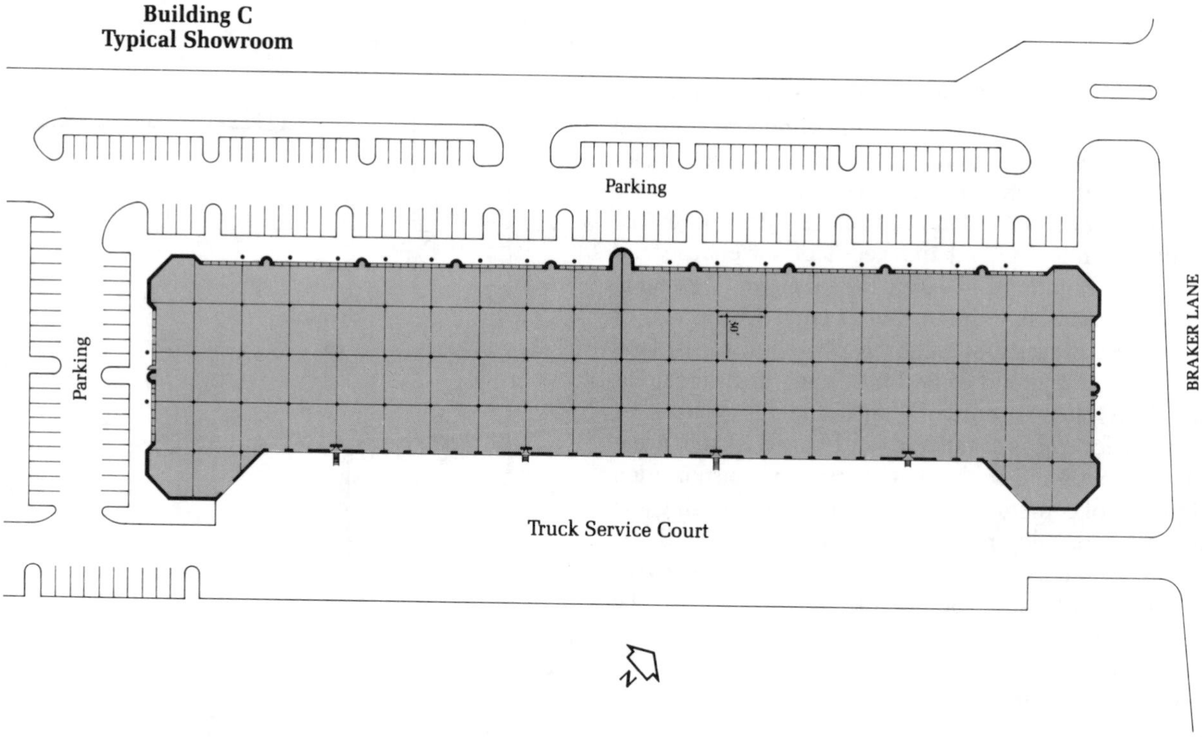

A typical showroom/service center building at Braker Center in Austin, Texas, a 193-acre industrial/office park.

ing industries, which have provided a significant demand for new industrial space. Because they focus on technology-based activities, these industries typically produce fewer of the undesirable side effects that limited the location of the older heavy industries.

R&D and high-technology. These functions utilize over 20 percent of the industrial space in the United States. Many firms are small, startup companies; others are subsidiaries of major corporations. High-technology (high-tech) activities range from the creation and development of new technologies and products to the development, testing, and manufacture of products from existing technology. Related businesses sell, install, or service high-tech products.

The design of tenant improvements is more important for R&D uses than for other industrial space uses and is usually tailored to the needs of specific tenants. The percentage of space allocated to laboratories, research offices, servicing areas, assembly, and storage varies widely. Hard-to-rent space in the center of buildings is well suited for laboratories and computer rooms where environmental control is critical.

Facilities for moderate public contact. These include facilities for wholesale/retail product sales and services, professional offices, auto-related activities, and incubator businesses. Although users desire lower-cost space than office or retail facilities can provide, in designing facilities to attract these users, an upscale image should be conveyed.

Customer-oriented users need showroom space as well as office and storage areas. Smaller users look for 1,000 to 3,000 square feet of space, including a roll-up door in the rear service yard for deliveries and space for parking in front. The modules can be combined to accommodate larger tenants.

Office. These uses in industrial parks range from office/warehouses in which only 10 percent of the space is occupied by office space to corporate office buildings comparable to those found in any urban location. Prime office areas are often segregated into "office subareas" within larger parks, such as the Irvine Ranch office park next to John Wayne Airport in California, or the Park 10 Orchards District in Houston.

Building Categories

The third way to categorize industrial development is by building type. Building types are similar, but not identical, to functional types. For instance, both manufacturing and warehousing functions can be served by the traditional industrial building type. This list of building types roughly parallels the preceding list of functional categories.

Bulk warehouses. These provide storage and handling areas, and only 1 to 5 percent of their space is used for offices. Access to transportation facilities, truck access and parking, and efficient use of space are all important to bulk warehouse users. A small amount of employee parking is needed.

Office/warehouses. Ten to 20 percent of the space in these structures may be allotted to office uses, chiefly to accommodate the purchasing, accounting, and marketing staff of a distribution company. The remaining space is left as warehouse space. Typically, these buildings will have an attractive front elevation with ample windows for the office portion of the building and will provide good truck access to the rear or side of the building. Dock-high and/or drive-in doors should be provided to serve the warehouse functions.

Traditional industrial buildings. These structures are generally large (10,000 square feet or greater) and have few interior improvements. They should have large floor-to-ceiling heights (20 to 24 feet on the average—a height popular for other industrial building categories as well). They usually require low parking ratios—as low as one-and-one-half parking spaces per 1,000 square feet of building area, although the ratio depends on the employee population. Large bay doors with at-grade or dock-high parking for large trucks and ample room in which the trucks may maneuver are usually a necessity. Because of their minimal parking requirements, traditional industrial buildings frequently cover 45 to 50 percent of a site.[5]

R&D buildings. These buildings fall into two distinct categories. One category includes facilities in which research is the primary, or only, activity. Design of the interior spaces of this type of building is frequently unique to the specific research that will be carried out there. The other type of R&D building is intended to serve multiple uses. This type of structure, which may have one or two floors, often has office and administration functions that take place in the front of the building and R&D or other high-tech uses that are housed in the rear.

If the high-tech use involves some form of sales-related support function (for instance, a copier service center), the building is referred to as a service center. Service centers have spaces for public contact in the front and industrial space in the rear.

Multitenant buildings. These industrial buildings cater to smaller tenants that require space in the 800- to 5,000-square-foot range. The buildings are generally one-story, with parking in the front and roll-up doors in the rear for truck loading. They provide parking ratios of two to three spaces per 1,000 square feet and turning radiuses in loading areas that are large enough for small trucks. Lease spaces should be built so that they can be divided into modules as small as 800 square feet. Frequently, 25 to 50 percent of the interior is improved, leaving the balance of the building as manufacturing, assembly, or warehouse space.[6]

Some developers build all of the tenant improvements for a project along with the base building, whereas others initially build just the shell and wait to build the tenant improvements as space is leased. The first method limits flexibility and increases upfront costs. The second method can be expensive if materials for tenant improvements cannot be bought at bulk prices. A middle course to take is to buy materials in bulk at the start of tenant space buildout and then put improvements in place as needed. Methods for building out tenant improvements frequently depend on a project's marketing scheme and anticipated absorption rate.

Office/tech buildings. These buildings are used primarily for office space. They may provide limited truck access and warehouse facilities. Office/tech building users generally look for large volumes of space to house employees and have only limited interest in space for laboratories or computer facilities. Large "paper processors," such as insurance companies and banks, require large office spaces and desire low rental costs for their "back-office" functions; hence, they prefer the cost advantage and efficiency of office/tech industrial buildings. High parking ratios (three-and-one-half to four spaces per 1,000 square feet of net rentable area) are important to office/tech users.

Narod/Pruett

Two-story buildings at Shaw Road Business Park in Sterling, Virginia, provide flexible spaces to accommodate office/R&D/warehouse uses.

Rehabilitation and Adaptive Reuse

Many older industrial areas away from the centers of major cities are being rediscovered. Older industrial areas offer special opportunities to beginning developers, notably, the presence of underutilized buildings suitable for rehabilitation and, sometimes, small infill sites. Many cities have programs to encourage the redevelopment of older industrial areas. Redevelopment agencies and economic development agencies may offer incentives such as tax abatement and financing to developers who build in designated redevelopment areas.

Renovation of older industrial areas offers many opportunities to developers:[7]

- upgrading low-technology (low-tech), light-industrial buildings to keep them competitive with newer facilities;
- redeveloping low-tech, light-industrial buildings for higher-tech R&D and office uses;
- rehabilitating existing older industrial parks;
- rehabilitating obsolete institutional facilities, such as schools and hospitals, into incubator and R&D parks;
- rehabilitating major older plant facilities, such as car plants, into multitenant warehouses and office/warehouses;
- removing heavy industrial facilities and reusing the land for business parks or multiuse developments; and
- adapting obsolete multistory urban warehouses to commercial and office uses.

Upgrading old warehouses or manufacturing buildings may involve many options, such as:

- installing new roofs, insulation, and floors;
- replacing older windows with new, energy-efficient double- and triple-pane glass;
- raising ceilings in entranceways and employing glass and upscale materials to create more dramatic lobbies;
- gutting the interior, since working around existing partitions may be more expensive than removing them and starting from scratch;
- carving out a second floor or mezzanine for new offices, laboratories, and research areas;
- installing skylights for interior lighting;
- renovating or replacing heating, ventilation, and air-conditioning (HVAC) systems;
- replastering, rebricking, and repainting exterior walls;
- removing asbestos, enclosing stairways, providing sprinklers, and making other changes to bring the building up to current fire and safety codes, including bringing unreinforced buildings up to earthquake codes; and
- updating electrical systems.

Deteriorated buildings often are available at very low prices, reflecting their underutilization. Many owners, especially those who have inherited older properties, are nonprofessionals who lack the time, energy, or knowledge to solve a building's problems and are sometimes eager just to rid themselves of a building.

Beginning developers should be mindful of the many potential pitfalls of rehabilitating older buildings, such as cost overruns, title problems, building code problems, poor street and utility infrastructure, and unforeseen construction problems. Also, they should avoid pioneering in older areas that do not have firmly established market demand. Nevertheless, by performing suitable due diligence before buying property, developers can enjoy the benefits of one of the largest pools of bargain prices in real estate.

Project Feasibility

Market Analysis prior to Site Selection

The analysis that precedes site selection for industrial development serves three purposes: to identify the types of users that will be served, to identify the type of product to be built and thus the parameters of the site to be purchased, and to identify where the product should be located. The process is similar to that of office development, insofar as the market group to be analyzed consists of employers engaged in producing goods or services.

Just as with office development, the developer should be familiar with basic data regarding the local economy and its relation to the regional and national picture. Among the items that should be checked are:

- national, regional, and local economic trends;
- socioeconomic characteristics of the metropolitan area, including rates of job creation and employment patterns;
- local growth policies and attitudes toward office and industrial development;
- forecasted demand for various types of office and industrial facilities;
- existing and planned competing projects; and
- absorption trends.

This information is available from a host of sources, including local universities, market analysts, data service firms, chambers of commerce, and major real estate brokerage firms. In addition to evaluating statistics, the developer should consult local brokers, tenants, and other developers to verify the accuracy of the information obtained. A developer who is unfamiliar with the local area should consider hiring a market research firm that specializes in industrial real estate.

Evaluating a Region or a City

An industrial firm looking for a large, single site will address a number of issues:

- availability of land;
- cost of land;
- labor quality and cost;

- tax structure and tax incentives;
- water supply;
- waste disposal;
- comparative transportation rates;
- distribution costs; and
- energy rates.

Although smaller users will address many of the same issues, the scope of their interest will be geographically more restricted. Whereas larger users may evaluate different cities, smaller users are likely to assess different submarkets of a particular city.

Evaluating a Subarea of a City

Market preferences and locations, land costs, labor costs, utility costs, and transportation costs can differ dramatically within the same city or region. Companies with markets outside the city will have different criteria for site selection from those with markets primarily inside the city. The developer's market analysis, prior to site selection, should assess the target market's preferences regarding such factors as access to transportation and location.

Local linkages. Local linkages can be important to many companies. Firms that have frequent contacts with suppliers, distributors, customers, consultants, or government consider the following in choosing a location:[8]

- accessibility to firms with which they do regular business;
- the number of trips to be made to and from their business inside the metropolitan area;
- congestion in and around the site;
- production time lost during travel;
- employee time required for travel in the metropolitan area;

Wm. S. Pearson, Northway Studio

Market preferences can differ significantly within the same metropolitan area, and thus the market analysis must focus on the subarea market as well. Pictured above is the Oakland Ridge Industrial Center and its environs in Columbia, Maryland.

- vehicle cost, including taxes, maintenance, and fuel per mile traveled;
- alternative modes of transportation; and
- air-quality regulations.

Clustering. A number of industries—such as food distribution, garment manufacturing, printing, wholesale flower marts, toy marts, machinery parts and repair, and commercial groceries and kitchen supplies—tend to cluster together. The clustering often relates to time-sensitive products (such as perishable foods) or to the interdependency of firms within a particular industry. In custom printing, for example, typesetters, printers, and binders require swift and easy access to each other.

High-tech firms tend to congregate in research parks near major universities where they can take advantage of resources such as laboratories and libraries, professors and graduate students, and large pools of highly educated and skilled labor. Venture capital is also attracted to universities because of the commercially valuable discoveries they generate.

Airport proximity. Many types of firms value proximity to airports:

- geographically dispersed firms seeking national and regional headquarters offices;
- engineering service companies with a national or international clientele;
- firms that operate warehouse and distribution centers for perishable goods, seasonal merchandise, and lightweight, high-value merchandise; and
- service industries involved in air-freight and airport services.

International trade zones. International trade zones also are often found near major airports. If located in such zones, firms can bring in and assemble parts from abroad and export the finished product without paying customs duties until the goods leave the zone. They also can store goods within the zones and defer duties until the goods leave the trade zone. Many foreign manufacturing firms will transport their products to a warehouse in the trade zone, store the products until they are ordered by a customer or distributor, and pay the import duties when the product leaves the warehouse to be delivered to the customer. Thus, the firms can have a readily available supply of stock without having to pay the associated import fees until the product is actually needed.

Freeway accessibility. In the early 20th century, rail service and waterways were the primary forms of transportation for industry. Rail and waterway patterns determined the location of industrial areas for tenants that needed to import materials for production and to ship finished goods to market. Since the 1950s, however, virtually all industrial users have come to depend on the

The site for Torrance Center (foreground), a 47-acre business park in Torrance, California, is well located in the South Bay area of Los Angeles. Because of a shortage of developable land and a changing market, it was feasible to clear the site of existing heavy industrial uses to make way for a higher-end business park environment, including retail and hotel services, as well as office and high-end industrial space.

interstate highway system. Prime industrial land was redefined in terms of frontage on, or proximity to, freeways. Although rail service availability has remained an important factor for industrial parks, developments oriented to smaller industrial users and high-tech firms are less dependent on rail.

Industrial park developers favor locations near freeway interchanges. Freeway access provides three vital benefits:

- transportation savings—easy access reduces transportation time and costs, and suppliers and workers lose less time in street traffic;
- expanded labor market—more workers can get to the industrial park in less time; and
- expanded market area—companies can reach more customers both in central cities and suburbs.

Although freeway accessibility is critical, freeway visibility for most industrial park tenants is not. The primary consideration is that access from the site is adequate to meet the users' needs.

Site Selection

Evaluating Specific Land Parcels

Because they lack the staying power necessary to survive the many unpredictable delays of the approval process, beginning developers should avoid buying land that is not ready for immediate development.[9] Obtaining zoning changes or variances and conditional use permits, installing major off-site infrastructure improvements, or waiting for the completion of planned transportation improvements tends to require more time and capital than most beginning developers can provide.

In selecting sites for industrial use, it is especially important that water, gas, electricity, telephone, and sewer services be available at competitive rates with appropriate capacities. The site should be flat to accommodate the large pads that are needed for industrial buildings and should have a minimal amount of ledge rock, groundwater, or peat with soft ground.

The presence of oil wells, natural gas, contaminated soils, high water tables, or tanks, pipes, or similar facilities can cause major problems and should be carefully studied to determine present and potential dangers.

When searching for sites for office and high-tech uses, developers should also consider the following criteria:

- interesting and distinct terrain and vegetation, such as a water feature, that can help market the project;
- the standards of development in the surrounding area and the level of commitment among neighbors to maintain high standards;
- proximity to new or restored residential and commercial development appropriate for proposed tenants;
- proximity to recreational and cultural amenities;
- availability of shopping, hotels, restaurants, daycare facilities, and health clubs;
- proximity to mass transit and availability of active transportation management associations and car pools;
- proximity to educational and technical training facilities such as universities, community colleges, or technical schools; and
- visibility from freeways, arterials, or mass transit routes.

Finding and Acquiring the Site

Public agencies, such as local planning departments, redevelopment agencies, and economic development agencies, possess a considerable amount of information useful to developers in the search for potential sites. If the target area lies inside an incorporated city, the municipal planning department, county planning department, or regional planning council will be the relevant authority. Most communities have comprehensive plans or master plans that indicate the areas that city leaders favor for industrial development.

Local brokers are, perhaps, the best source for information on potential sites. Developers should first narrow down their target area and then work with brokers familiar with the local area and able to track down information on sites that may not currently be on the market.

Leftover sites in industrial parks that are approaching buildout as well as superfluous land surrounding existing buildings should also be considered as potential sites. Infill sites offer developers the advantages of readily available streets, sewer, water, and other public services, and of a local workforce. On the downside, neighboring homeowners may resist new traffic, especially trucks. Existing streets may be narrow and congested. Space may be too constricted to allow for the creation of the high standards that tenants now expect of business parks.

Problems with neighbors are less significant in the development of individual infill buildings. As long as the proposed building is consistent with the zoning and neighboring uses, the developer should encounter relatively little opposition to the project. Even with infill projects, however, the developer should consult with local neighborhood groups in order to learn of potential problems in advance.

Site acquisition for industrial property follows the same four steps as for other forms of development: preoffer investigation, offer, due diligence, and closing. (These steps are detailed in chapters 3 and 4.)

During the due diligence phase, developers should pay special attention to hazardous waste, especially in the event that preexisting industrial uses are present nearby. Waste spilled locally may be spread by the water table to an otherwise clean site: a small amount of solvent or gasoline can still show up as hazardous waste two or three years after it was spilled. Appropriately licensed engineers should perform water and soil tests; if necessary, developers should ensure that enough time is allowed to verify that no toxic waste is present by paying for an extension to the option. Sellers typically give buyers 60 days to perform due diligence for soils and toxic waste and 30–60 days for everything else.

Engineering Feasibility

Preliminary engineering investigations should be made in conjunction with the process of preliminary site planning. The civil engineer usually leads the site investigation under the developer's direction. Chapter 3 provides a comprehensive review of the site evaluation process for all types of development. As far as industrial development is concerned, perhaps the two most significant aspects of this process concern utilities and environmental regulations.

Utilities. Because of the low ratio of workers to square feet, the employee-related utility needs of industrial facilities are fewer than those for office or retail uses. However, many manufacturing and some R&D facilities use enormous amounts of water. Since most water is discharged eventually into the sewer system, both water and sewage services are affected by these uses. The capacity to service such customers can be a good draw, especially in areas where water availability is limited.

A developer should meet with the local water company as early as possible to discuss plans. The developer will learn about the utility company's current capabilities and limitations, and the utility company will learn about future expansion needs. The developer's engineer can obtain preliminary information on flow and pressure from the utility company. Fire departments often require that the water system and fire hydrants be installed and activated before construction can start on individual buildings.

Some local agencies require the installation of lines to reclaim water for irrigation and some industrial purposes. Two parallel systems, domestic and reclaimed, must be installed on every lot in areas such as Irvine, California.

The developer should also meet with the sewer company to determine the following information:

- capacity of sewage-treatment facilities;
- capacity of sewer mains;
- whether gravity flow for sewage and drainage is sufficient or if pumps are necessary;
- the party responsible for paying for off-site sewer extension;
- the due date for payments and impact fees;
- quality restrictions on sewage effluent—some sewage-treatment plants impose severe restrictions on the type and quantity of chemicals that firms can discharge into the general sewage system;
- discharge capacity for sewage effluent;
- flow standards; and
- periodic service charges—although the rate structure for service charges does not directly affect the developer, it will influence prospective purchasers of property, especially heavy users such as bottling plants.

Cities that use water consumption as the basis for sewer system service charges may penalize projects that consume a large quantity of water to irrigate landscaping. In such cases, the developer may attempt to negotiate treatment costs based on anticipated discharge rather than on water consumption.

Industrial land developers usually must front the costs for water and sewage lines and for treatment plants. They recover those costs as part of the sales price or rent of sites. They may also be reimbursed by developers of other subdivisions and owners of other properties that tie into the water and sewage mains subsequently. Most cities that provide for reimbursement by subsequent developers, however, do not permit the original developer to recover carrying costs. Also, because of the unpredictable timing of such reimbursements, developers cannot rely on them to help meet cash-flow requirements.

As early as possible, developers should provide the local companies that supply electricity, telephone, and gas with information concerning the type and size of buildings in their plans so that the utility companies can project the estimated demand from the project. The projected demand is used to design the local distribution system as well as the backbone systems that will feed the local systems.

The frequency of power outages and gas curtailments during the winter months should be investigated because this factor may deter potential tenants and buyers. The frequent occurrence of outages also may influence the developer's choice of target market or may change his/her decision to purchase the site altogether.

Environmental regulations. The federal government has many environmental statutes that can affect industrial developments. Some of the more important statutes include the following.

- The National Environmental Policy Act requires that many projects using federal funds must produce an environmental impact statement (EIS) for approval.
- The Clean Air Act requires the provision of information on anticipated traffic flow and indirect vehicle usage.
- The Clean Water Act severely restricts discharge of any pollutant into navigable and certain nonnavigable waters.
- The Occupational Safety and Health Act requires employers to provide safe working conditions for employees.
- The National Flood Insurance Act limits development in flood-prone areas and requires developers who build in flood-prone areas to meet standards concerning height, slope, and water-flow interference. This act

Wetlands preservation was an issue at Tampa Bay Park in Tampa, Florida.

requires that a project does not impede the water-flow speed and volume that exist prior to development in any floodway traversed by the project.
- The Comprehensive Environmental Response, Compensation, and Liability Act, also known as "Superfund," addresses issues concerning toxic waste.

In addition, each state and local municipality may have its own environmental laws that affect industrial development.

Concerns about toxic waste, water supply, sewage-treatment constraints, and sensitive environmental areas are forcing developers to perform very careful site investigation before closing on a tract. Although laws in most states give developers some recourse against prior owners in the chain of title for problems such as toxic waste, such protection is of little use if developers cannot proceed with their plans.

Phil Eschbach

At University Place in Winter Park, Florida, market studies indicated a strong rental market in the area for young, small- to medium-sized growth companies seeking a combination of office space and warehouse distribution space. The project that was built to meet this market includes buildings that contain office/showroom/warehouse space on the first floor and professional office space on the second floor.

Market Analysis after Site Selection

Once the site has been secured with a signed earnest money contract, the second phase of the market analysis begins. The purpose at this stage is to investigate the immediate market area for information on rental rates, occupancy, new supply, and amenities of competing projects. The developer should collect information on competing projects for the following items:[10]

- the year leasing and sales began;
- gross acres added and the years they were added;
- zoning, building characteristics, and site characteristics;
- occupancy levels at the date of the survey (acres sold, total square feet leased for each type of facility, and percentage of space occupied);
- estimated annual land absorption;
- estimated annual space absorption by property type;
- development cost per acre;
- opening price per square foot (land and buildings);
- current price per square foot;
- opening and current building lease rates;
- quality of architectural and landscape design, level of finish, quality of materials, signage, overall park appearance, and maintenance;
- major highway access, rail availability, and utilities;
- lease terms and concessions;
- tenant allowances to finish interior space; and
- amenities such as retail services, restaurants, open space, recreation, daycare, and health and conference facilities.

Allan Kotin, chairman of Kotin, Regan, and Mounchly, Los Angeles, California, observes that market analysis for industrial space has more pitfalls than for other types of development. Industrial zoning is far more permissive with respect to land use than is commercial, office, or residential zoning. Industrial zoning often will allow any of the other uses, except, perhaps, residential, and may lead, therefore, to an overestimation of the size of the market. "There is a blur to important price discrimination," notes Kotin. "Finished industrial space that rents for 85 cents per square foot [per month] cannot be averaged with 10 percent finished space that rents for 45 cents per square foot."[11] Developers must look at the type of use and the degree of finish in order to determine rents accurately.

Industrial development provides a backdoor entry into both office and retail development. Multitenant spaces may be used for low-image retailing, low-cost offices, light manufacturing, and distribution. The distinction between product types can be made primarily by the amount of tenant improvements. Market analysts sometimes mistakenly include absorption figures for office and retail users in their estimates of demand by industrial users; if this is the case, care must be taken to isolate the percentage of nonindustrial users. Office users in industrial buildings are often tempted to move back into higher-image office buildings, especially if office markets are soft.

Another pitfall to be wary of is the incubator approach. Incubator industrial space is a frequently abused concept. Originally, incubator space was intended to house small firms that would grow into large ones. In practice, however, users are often marginal firms. Those firms in incubator space that actually grow and prosper are in the minority, thus both the concept and the potential tenants should be carefully scrutinized.[12]

Other problems with analyzing the market for industrial development arise from the different ways of measuring rents. Some tenants will have full-service leases—the landlord pays all expenses—whereas others will have triple-net leases—the landlord pays no expenses. In addition, some tenants will have "modified industrial gross" (MIG) leases—the tenant pays the direct utility costs, internal janitorial costs, and insurance, but the landlord pays for common-area maintenance. If developers mistakenly interpret MIG leases as full-service gross leases, rent estimates will be too low. If developers interpret MIG leases as triple-net leases, estimates will be too high.[13]

Kotin also emphasizes that the distinction between industrial park land and vacant industrial land is minor in terms of land available for industrial development. Developers often discount land availability outside of industrial parks, forgetting that industrial space does not take long to build whenever vacancy rates become too low. A real market advantage usually will not be obtained simply because an industrial park has improvements in place.

Furthermore, in disadvantaged areas, developers may find that the public sector is a competitor. Cities and redevelopment agencies will offer incentives to industrial tenants that they will not offer to office and retail tenants. If developers are not offered the same benefits as those available to others, they will be at a competitive disadvantage.

Finally, most beginning developers start out with a building that is for lease rather than one that is presold or preleased. Typically, they will purchase a lot and wait for a build-to-suit tenant, or they will proceed with a speculative building. More profit can be made on a speculative building than on a build-to-suit because the negotiations are tougher and competition is greater with build-to-suit tenants.

Gerald Katell of Katell Properties, Incorporated, Los Angeles, California, advises beginning developers to start with a multitenant building so that at least a portion of the building can be rented. "With single-tenant buildings, it is either 100 percent leased or 0 percent. If you have an industrial park project, you can build a variety of building sizes to catch various segments of the market so that single-tenant building risk is reduced."[14]

The market analysis for single-tenant buildings differs considerably from that for multitenant buildings. Multitenant market analysis comes much closer to the office analysis paradigm that focuses on absorption rates over time.[15] "Market research for single-tenant buildings, however, becomes almost moot. The best it can do is describe the envelope of opportunity to determine whether the number of tenants of a certain size is expanding or contracting. The developer's problem is finding the tenant." Next to retail, large-scale industrial development is the most network-dependent type of development and thus requires frequent deal making.[16]

Regulatory Issues

The approval process for industrial parks is similar to that for residential subdivisions (see chapter 3). Although the basic procedures for platting industrial subdivisions depend on the local area, most communities begin with some form of tentative approval, such as a tentative tract map. After appropriate review by the public, the developer is eligible to obtain a final tract map. The final tract map (also called the subdivision plat) indicates the lot lines, setback requirements, allowable floor/area ratios (FARs), and other restrictions that determine the developer's buildable site and density.

The approval process for individual buildings may be as simple as obtaining a building permit or as complicated as the process for a full-scale industrial park. Normally, if the developer is building within the envelope of the existing zoning and subdivision restrictions, the approval process is similar to that for commercial and office buildings. However, if variances or changes in the zoning are sought, the approval process may be lengthy and expensive. Planning commissions and city councils tend to be especially concerned about traffic—traffic through neighborhoods, turning traffic, truck traffic, curb cuts, and so on—as well as noise, fumes, and other negative effects of the planned development. Some communities are eager to attract the employment opportunities that industrial development generates, whereas others are more concerned about the character and quality of the development.

Zoning and Subdivision Restrictions

Several basic types of zoning districts commonly are used for industrial park development. Most common are the "by-right" districts, PUDs (planned unit developments or "floating districts"), and "special" districts.

- By-right districts are the most traditional type of zoning district. Uses permitted by zoning regulations can be built by right without requiring further approvals.
- PUDs are known as floating districts because they can be applied anywhere that the locality approves them. PUDs have flexible land use controls that can increase site coverage and provide for a mixture of uses. They also give the developer flexibility by not requiring precommitments for the exact acreage to be zoned for industrial or commercial purposes and by delaying precise subdivision layout until sales occur.

- Special districts are approved by the local jurisdiction for a specific tract of land. The special district is then adopted as part of the local zoning ordinance. Provisions of the district are site specific and address issues such as land use, design, transportation, and landscaping.

Zoning restrictions determine the size and placement of the structures that can be built on a given site. Typical zoning regulations for industrial buildings include:

- front, side, and rear setbacks;
- height restrictions;
- access requirements;
- parking ratios;
- parking and loading design; and
- landscape requirements and screening regulations.

Most communities have maximum floor/area coverage ratios (FARs) for their industrial zones. In addition, landscape coverage ratios may be predetermined for the entire site or for the parking areas.

Design guidelines or restrictions are becoming increasingly common. Architectural or design review committees may have established rules regarding bulk, height, types of materials, fenestration, and overall aesthetic design of the building. Subdivision restrictions sometimes require facilities for employees such as outdoor lunch areas, recreation areas, and open space.

Public/Private Negotiations

Increasingly, developers are required to negotiate agreements with local municipalities in order to secure approval. These agreements are especially helpful in volatile political climates in which no-growth pressures may cause city councils to change development entitlements unexpectedly. Public/private negotiations are also required when a developer seeks to work with a public agency on publicly owned land or in redevelopment areas.

In California, public/private contracts take the form of "development agreements" that usually take considerable time to negotiate.[17] The agreements protect developers from later changes in zoning or other regulations that affect development entitlements and lend an air of certainty to the regulatory process by delineating most rights, requirements, and procedures in advance. Once adopted, no approval-related surprises should occur. However, most agencies will require something in return, such as special amenities, fees, or exactions.

The use of public/private negotiations to shape the form of industrial and business parks is widespread, albeit not routine. In high-growth areas, public displeasure with the negative impacts of development has led to direct public involvement in negotiations with developers over specific projects. Many municipalities and counties have realized that well-planned industrial parks can provide significant property-tax revenues. Many communities have, therefore, established redevelopment agencies to supervise negotiations with private developers and to represent the community's interests as development proceeds.

Shea Center Baldwin Park in Baldwin Park, California, is an example of a private development on a long-term ground lease of land owned by the county of Los Angeles. To complete the site assembly, a zoning change and general plan amendment were needed from the city.

The public sector's role is expanding, especially on the West Coast and in the Northeast, and its functions can now include:

- sharing risks with the developer through land price writedown and participation in cash flows;
- participating in loan commitments and mortgages;
- sharing operating and capital costs;
- reducing administrative red tape; and
- providing favorable tax treatment.

The role played by private developers is also expanding. Their functions may include paying for major off-site infrastructure and building freeway interchanges.[18]

State and Local Incentives

State and local governments have developed several incentive mechanisms to encourage industrial development:[19]

- Publicly owned business incubator parks are designed to accommodate small startup companies; publicly owned research-oriented parks cater to high-tech companies.
- Enterprise zones, created by many states to encourage new industry in economically depressed urban areas, offer incentives to companies that locate within those zones. These incentives include various combinations of property-tax abatements, industrial development

bonds, income- and sales-tax exemptions, low-interest venture capital, and infrastructure improvements and special public services.
- State and local grants offer revolving commercial loans, loan and development bond guarantees, infrastructure projects that aid particular industries, and even venture capital funds.
- Tax-increment financing is useful in areas that have low tax bases. The difference between new taxes generated by development and the original taxes is reserved for infrastructure improvements for the designated area. Redevelopment agencies frequently use tax-increment financing as a source of revenue for their projects.
- Industrial development bonds (IDBs) were very popular in the late 1970s and early 1980s; however, the 1986 Tax Reform Act severely restricted the types of projects that could qualify for tax-exempt financing. Originally intended to bring manufacturing to depressed areas, cities used the bonds to provide tax-exempt financing for a number of activities, both in industrial and commercial development. Some communities abused IDBs by using them to finance activities such as fast-food restaurants and other businesses in areas in which conventionally financed development was already occurring. Businesses complained that the IDBs gave certain firms an unfair cost advantage and questioned the contention that IDBs actually stimulated much development that would not have otherwise occurred. In spite of these problems, a number of cities have used IDBs effectively to generate development in once-stagnant areas.

Development and Impact Fees

Some stages of the regulatory process require public hearings. Virtually all, however, require some form of fee. The developer should understand the full range and scope of charges before closing on the land. Some of the more common fees that are assessed on industrial development projects include:

- approval and variance fees—either a lump sum or a charge for the actual time spent by government personnel on processing an application;
- plan check fees—generally, a percentage of valuation;
- building permit fees—generally, a percentage of valuation;
- water system fees—can be based on amount of water used, meter size, frontage on water lines, or a combination of these;
- sewer system fees—usually based on expected discharge;
- storm drainage fees—usually based on runoff generated or on acreage;
- transportation fees—based on trips generated or on square footage (some areas have freeway fees, county fees, and local transportation improvement fees);
- school fees—even industrial buildings are charged school fees on a square-footage basis in some areas;
- fire and police fees—usually based on square footage; and
- library, daycare, and various other fees.

The types and amounts of fees vary drastically from one city to another. The developer must learn each city's and each agency's particular system of imposing fees. Since the fees can be imposed by a multitude of agencies, the developer should check with every agency that possibly could set fees. In many jurisdictions, the building department will handle a majority of the fees and can be a good source of preliminary information.

Helpful Hints

Industrial developers offer the following advice for dealing with agencies during the regulatory process:[20]

- In general, industrial development that occurs in areas intended for industrial use is the least regulated of all development types, although many areas prohibit certain industrial uses.
- Check the city's general plan to make sure that the property is intended for industrial uses. Problems are more likely to occur if developers want to change zoning.
- Subdividing a lot and selling it either as raw land or with buildings requires a platting process that will take at least six months.
- Be sensitive to all community activity that may lead a city to restrict or delay development by means of emergency ordinances such as water moratoriums.

Financial Feasibility

As with other product types, financial analysis for industrial development is performed several times during the feasibility period. At the very least, it should be performed before submitting the earnest money contract, approaching lenders, and closing on the land.

At each stage of development, more information is known with greater certainty and accuracy. Data from the market study, design data, and cost estimates are incorporated into the financial pro formas as the information becomes available. However, developers should not wait until these studies are done before performing financial analysis—cruder information based on secondary sources may be used at earlier stages. For example, as soon as an estimate is made of the size of the building to be built, the construction cost can be estimated from average costs per square foot for similar projects. Contractors and other developers usually will share this cost information.

The method of analysis for industrial *park* development is different from that for industrial *building* development. Industrial park development is a form of land development and follows the approach described in chapter 3. The stages of analysis for industrial building development are similar to those described in detail in chapter 4.

For building development, the major decision tool is a five- to 10-year pro forma, showing the property's operations from the completion of construction to sale. This pro forma incorporates rental rates, rent concessions, lease-up time, and expected bumps in rents over the holding period.

Internal rates of return (IRRs) are computed on the before-tax and after-tax cash flows. These IRRs on total project cost should be in the 13 to 15 percent range for the all-equity case in which no mortgage is assumed. IRRs on equity should be in the 20 to 30 percent range for cases in which mortgage financing is assumed.

The developer should use the financial pro formas to investigate a number of questions concerning changes in various assumptions:

- For industrial park development, what effect does lowering land prices in order to sell the land faster have on the IRR?
- What is the effect on the IRR if more money is spent upfront on items such as amenities, roads, utilities, and entrances to permit faster sales or higher prices?
- For industrial building development, what effect do rent concessions or faster leasing schedules have on the IRR?
- How sensitive is the IRR to changes in assumptions with respect to rental rates, construction costs, financing costs, interest rates, release assumptions, and inflation assumptions?

Because in-depth examples of multiperiod cash-flow analyses have been presented in previous chapters, none is included here. Figure 6-1, however, provides an example of an actual construction budget compared to a pro forma cost estimate for an industrial building, as well as a quick-and-dirty return analysis.

■ 6-1 Construction Budget and Return Analysis for an Industrial Building*

Construction Budget

Direct Costs

Site Work			
Rough Grading		$9,300	
Finish Grading		3,100	
Temporary Fence, Trash Bin, and Toilet		1,000	
Yard Fence with Gates	600 lineal feet at $3.50 per lineal foot	3,000	
			$16,400
Concrete			
Building Slab	13,000 square feet at $2.35 per square foot	$30,550	
Loading Dock	4,000 square feet at $2.50 per square foot	10,000	
Curb and Gutter	210 lineal feet at $8.00 per lineal foot	1,680	
Valley Gutter	460 lineal feet at $6.00 per lineal foot	2,760	
A Curbing	360 lineal feet at $7.50 per lineal foot	2,700	
Driveways	720 square feet at $3.00 per square foot	2,160	
			$49,850
Paving			
Asphalt (3")	43,300 square feet at $0.70 per square foot	$30,310	
Aggregate Base (4")	43,300 square feet at $0.20 per square foot	8,660	
Wheel Stops	25 stops at $40.00 per stop	1,000	
Striping		830	
			$40,800
Building			
Shell and Doors (Erected)		$104,834	
Windows	12 windows at $150.00 per window	1,800	
Front Entry		1,000	
Stone Veneer Facade		2,000	
			$109,634

■ 6-1 (Continued)

Plumbing			
Sewer (Lines and Hook-Up)		$5,500	
Water (Lines and Hook-Up)		4,500	
Interceptor for Truck Wash		2,300	
Seepage Pit for Loading Dock		1,800	
Plumbing Hardware and Installation		10,000	
			$24,100
Electrical			
Transformer Vault and Conduit		$ 5,000	
Meter Panel, Wiring, and Outlets		20,000	
Interior Lighting		7,000	
Exterior Lighting		2,000	
			$34,000
HVAC			
Office Heating and Air Conditioning		$15,000	
Warehouse Heating/Gas Line		3,000	
Warehouse Air Conditioning (1 Evaporative Cooler)		3,000	
			$21,000
Tenant Improvements			
Floor	4,000 square feet at $1.50 per square foot	$ 6,000	
Ceiling	3,600 square feet at $1.00 per square foot	3,600	
Framing/Dry Wall	1,100 lineal feet at $14.00 per lineal foot	15,400	
Office Doors	15 doors at $200.00 per door	3,000	
Painting	9,000 square feet at $0.17 per square foot	1,530	
			$29,530
Landscape			
Trees and Shrubs		$2,500	
Fill Dirt, Liner, and Rock		2,000	
Automatic Sprinkler System		2,000	
			$6,500
Miscellaneous			
Telephone Conduit		$1,500	
Fire Alarm System		5,000	
Burglar Alarm System		3,000	
Trash Bin and Enclosure		1,000	
Pipe Guards	16 guards at $30.00 per guard	480	
Warehouse Wall Board	65 boards at $12.00 per board	780	
			$ 11,760
	Total Direct Costs		$343,574
	Per Square Foot	$27.49	

Indirect Costs	
Architecture	$4,500
Environmental Engineering	1,000
Grading Engineering	1,500
Surveying	500
Geotechnical Engineering	2,500
Insurance	1,000
Legal	1,000
Interim Loan Fees (2 points)	8,000
Interim Loan Interest ($400,000 for 4 months at 13.5%)	6,750

Design and Construction

This section deals first with design considerations for industrial parks and second with building design for different industrial building types.

Site Design

Street Design and Traffic

The ideal street layout for an industrial park provides easy access to the nearest major highway or freeway and

■ 6-1 (Continued)

Permits and Fees			
Grading Permit		$ 110	
Building Permit		1,700	
Plan Check		1,100	
Electric Fee		250	
Water Fee		20	
School Fee		3,120	
Sewage Fee		2,500	
Southern California Edison		380	
			$9,180
	Total Indirect Costs		$35,930
	Per Square Foot	$2.87	
Subtotal Direct and Indirect Cost			$379,504
Developer Overhead	5.0% of Subtotal Cost		18,975
Project Contingency	3.0% of Subtotal Cost		11,385
	Total Building Cost		$409,864
	Per Square Foot	$32.79	

Original Budget

(Pro Forma)

Hard Costs	12,000 square feet x $22.00 per square foot =	$264,000
Soft Costs	10% of hard costs =	$ 26,400
Tenant Improvements	4,000 square feet x $20.00 per square foot =	$ 80,000
Subtotal		$370,400
Developer Overhead	5% of subtotal	$18,520
Total		$388,920
Per Square Foot		$32.41

"Quick-and-Dirty" Return Analysis

	Year 1	Year 3	Year 5
Net Operating Income (12,000 square feet at $0.433 per square foot triple net)	$62,400	$68,140	$74,415
Debt Service ($360,000 at 13.25% for 25 years)	$49,537	$49,537	$49,537
Before-Tax Cash Flow	$12,863	$18,603	$24,878
Developer Fee	18,000	0	0
Total Before-Tax Cash Flow	$30,863	$18,603	$24,878
Return on Equity (Equity: land $15,000 + building $40,000 = $55,000)	56.11%	33.82%	45.23%

[a]A 12,000-square-foot building with 4,000 square feet of office space and 8,000 square feet of warehouse space.
Source: Bonanno-Delzer Development, Los Angeles, California.

discourages unrelated traffic. A public highway that runs through the middle of a park reduces the developer's expenditure on internal roads and enhances the value of frontage sites. However, it also tends to divide, rather than unify, the development, brings heavy unrelated traffic through the middle of the park, and increases the possibilities of accidents.

The more points of ingress and egress in a development, the better. For instance, assume that a developer is developing a 160-acre industrial park with an employ-

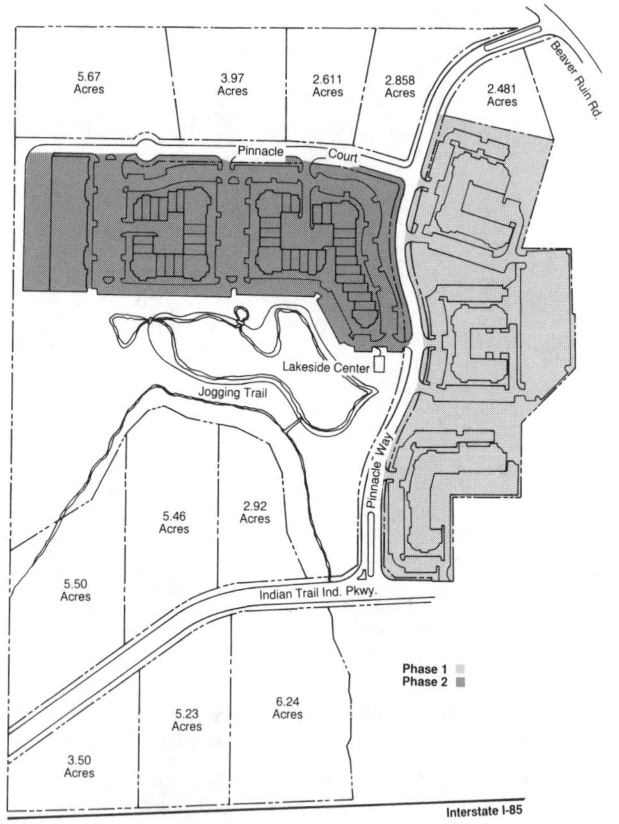

At the 107-acre Pinnacle Center in Norcross, Georgia, roadways are designed to give the best possible depth to all parcels for land utilization. All roadways are three lanes instead of two for ease of access and flow of traffic. The site included 15 acres of floodplain that were reformed into a five-acre lake and recreational area.

ment density of 20 persons per acre. With 3,200 employees at 1.1 per car, approximately 2,900 cars would be in circulation. Three planned access points probably could accommodate that volume in just over an hour. However, if a half-hour traffic jam occurs at the park nightly, and the competing industrial park down the road does not have a traffic jam, this is a marketing problem.

Since traffic is becoming the chief concern of communities, developers should understand the impact that their proposed developments will have on traffic. "Trip generation" refers to the number of vehicle trips that originate from a given source. Figure 6-2 gives some standard figures for trip generation for different types of industry.

One lane of pavement typically will handle 300 to 600 trips per hour, depending on the street layout and traffic control at intersections. For design purposes, developers should estimate the percentage and directional distribution of truck traffic. Overdesigning the traffic system is better than underdesigning it, since the intensity of future uses is unknown.

Design considerations include road thickness, pavement type (concrete or asphalt), road curvatures, and sight distances for stopping, passing, and corners. Standard drawings of the following items are available in most agencies:

- typical street sections;
- commercial entrances and private driveways;
- culs-de-sac and turnarounds;
- intersections, interchanges, and medians;

6-2 Traffic-Generation Rates for Different Industrial Uses

	Sample Projects			Vehicle Trips per Weekday			
		Employee Density					
	Sample Size	Per 1,000 Gross Square Feet	Per Developed Acre	Per Employee Average	Per Employee Range	Per Developed Acre Average	Per 1,000 Square Feet of GFA Average
General Light Industry[a]	18	2.30	17.4	3.0	1.5–4.5	51.8	6.9
General Heavy Industry[b]	4	1.60	7.6	2.0	0.7–11.0	15.6	1.5
Industrial Parks[c]	47	1.89	19.0	3.4	1.2–8.8	62.9	7.0
Manufacturing[d]	60	1.84	20.1	2.1	0.6–6.7	38.9	3.8
Warehousing	15	1.30	14.0	3.9	1.5–15.7	56.0	4.9
Miniwarehouse	11	0.04	0.6	56.3	17–19.4	40.0	2.6
Office Park	5	–	–	3.5	2.9–3.8	195.6	11.4
Research Center[e]	15	2.20	–	2.5	1.0–5.4	66.2	6.1
Business Park[f]	8	–	–	4.6	3.9–6.0	159.8	12.4

[a]Includes facilities engaged in activities such as assembly of data processing equipment, materials testing, and printing.
[b]Facilities engaged in manufacturing large items.
[c]Mix of manufacturing, service, and warehouse facilities.
[d]Facilities engaged in converting raw materials into finished products; also involves office, warehouse, research, and associated functions.
[e]Facilities or groups of facilities primarily devoted to research and development; may contain some offices and light-fabrication areas.
[f]A group of flex-type or incubator buildings of one or two stories.
Source: Institute of Transportation Engineers, *Trip Generation*, 4th edition (Washington, D.C.: author, 1987).

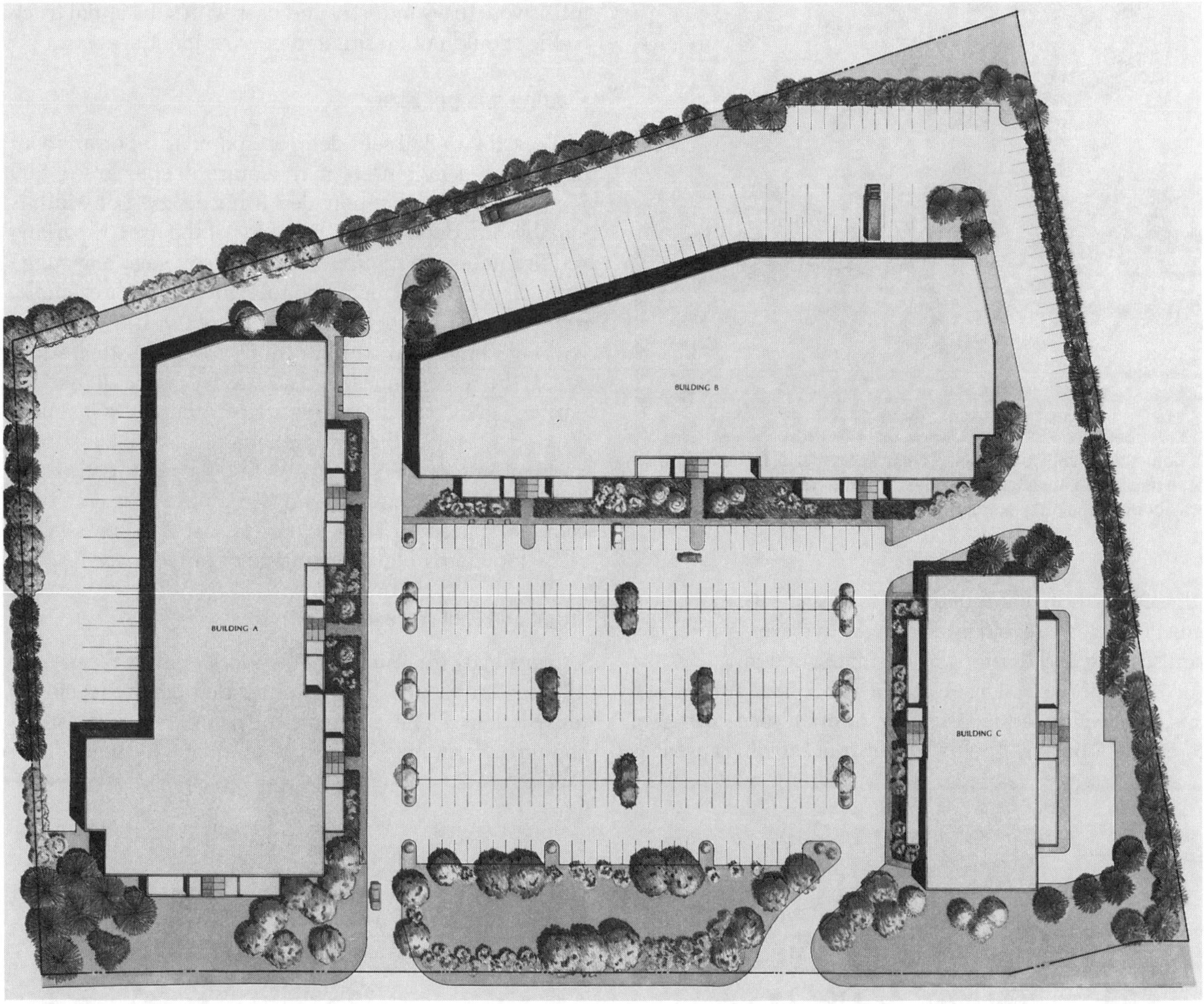

The site plan for Shaw Road Business Park in Loudoun County, Virginia, incorporates three office/warehouse/R&D buildings on 9.62 acres of land surrounding a central parking court.

- guard rails, bridges, and bridge approaches;
- signalization, signage, and lighting;
- drainage, curbs, and gutters;
- erosion-control features;
- sidewalks, paved approaches, and pavement joints;
- safety features; and
- earthwork grading.

Standards are subject to constant revision. The developer usually relies on the civil engineer to ensure that street and utility designs conform to the latest standards.

Culs-de-sac need a paved turnaround of 100 feet in diameter to allow trucks with 45-foot trailers to turn around without backing up. Roadway widths depend on the amount of traffic the roadways handle, median design, and the absence or presence of parking. Some designers prefer that the major roads leading into a project have no parking and that interior access roads allow limited parking. Street parking can be advantageous to some businesses since it can provide space for overflow visitor parking.

Walks and Landscape

Sidewalks in industrial parks are not functional unless retail or recreation areas are nearby. In such cases, a carefully designed pedestrian system can be an attractive selling feature. If the industrial park includes significant open space, then a pathway system (perhaps including a jogging path) through the space, away from heavy traffic, is also an attractive amenity.

In designing aesthetic features such as berms and slopes, developers should be aware that mowing equipment cannot handle slopes steeper than three to one

David Lucas

At Columbia Business Center in Columbia, Maryland, landscaping has been used to create attractive pedestrian courtyards and to buffer the project from unsightly surrounding uses.

(three feet horizontal and one foot vertical). Care also must be taken to avoid interfering with driver visibility by landscaping and berming at road intersections.

Where industrial uses adjoin residential uses, deep lots, berms, fences, landscaping, or open space can help to create a buffer. Low-rise industrial buildings are less intrusive. Heavy industry and uses with substantial truck traffic should not be situated near residential areas.

Platting and Lot Size

Lots 200 to 300 feet deep are popular for a variety of uses. Large single users may require deeper lots of 500 feet, which can be subdivided if necessary. Lot width is variable and depends on the needs of the user. If parking requirements are minimal, building coverage may range from 50 to 70 percent of the total lot area. For example, a 20,000-square-foot building in an area with a 50 percent coverage limitation would occupy a 40,000-square-foot site. If the remaining 20,000 square feet were all used for parking, given that a parking space occupies 350 square feet on average, then approximately 57 spaces, for a parking ratio of 2.9 spaces per 1,000 square feet, would be possible. Parking ratios for warehouse space are typically two spaces per 1,000 square feet, so 2.9 spaces would allow for a fairly high percentage of office space.[21]

Truck and Rail Access

Terminals for trucks with 45-foot trailers often have 129 feet of depth between the door and the closest obstructions.[22] The path from the truck areas to the street should be scrutinized to ensure adequate turning radii for

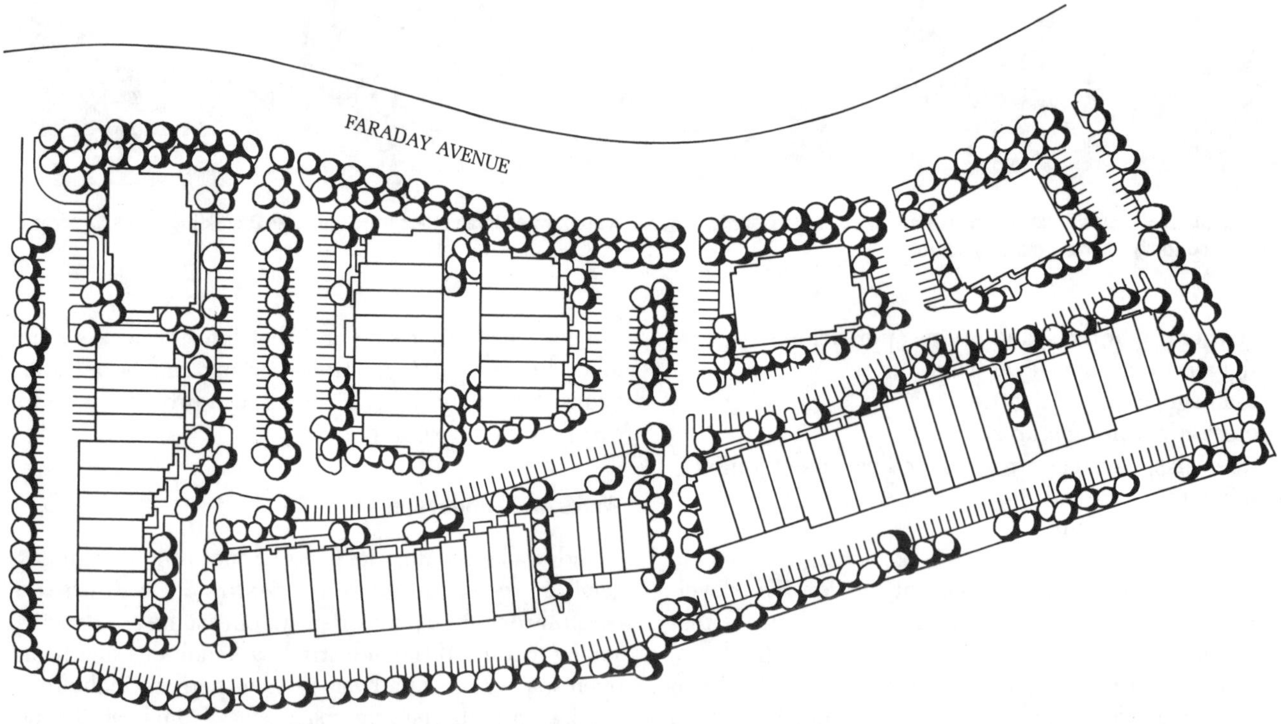

The Koll Commerce Center provides multitenant industrial office space with custom interior improvements in leasable units from about 1,500 square feet. The project is located within the 550-acre Carlsbad Research Center in Carlsbad, California. The overall project was developed under a negotiated specific plan, which stipulates that major streets must have a double row of sycamore trees. Thirty-foot building setbacks are required on major streets, and 20-foot setbacks are required on minor streets.

truck maneuverability. Developers should separate truck loading areas from passenger car areas both to improve safety and to ensure that noise from loading and operating trucks does not interfere with R&D or office tenants.

Most tenants do not require access to rail. However, if the provision of such access is contemplated, railroad officials should be contacted early in the design process to determine design requirements, reciprocal switching limits, frequency of switching service, and general rates. Some industrial park designs allow rail spurs to be installed later if a new tenant desires rail access. Developers must obtain the necessary easements and rights-of-way initially so that no problems will occur later.

Design for Specific Uses

Some of the common design attributes of *R&D space*, a combination of offices and laboratories, include:

- more people per square foot than for typical industrial buildings—indeed, the concentration is almost as intensive as that for office buildings;
- a parking ratio of four spaces per 1,000 square feet, or slightly less;
- site development that provides the greater space and amenities required for multitenant buildings;
- smaller bay depths and lower clear heights (16 feet) than for typical industrial buildings;
- one-story buildings with 15 to 50 percent mezzanine office space, or two-story buildings;
- marketable design features such as the extensive use of glass;
- truck access or optional rail access—rail access, if poorly designed, may lower the value of some R&D space;
- sufficient flexibility of uses; and
- possibly, specialized HVAC or electrical systems.

Bulk warehouse tenants are concerned with the handling of materials. Ease of access, ability to use space efficiently, and location are critical attributes. Some other important attributes are:

- rail access—a plus for larger buildings;
- clear heights of 24 feet—most stacking systems are 21 feet high, and a minimum of three feet is required between the top of stacks and the ceiling for fire sprinklers;
- for large users, specialized stacking systems that can accommodate higher stacks;
- docks that are four feet above ground level;
- dock-high doors that are 10 feet wide and 10 feet high and double doors that are 20 feet wide and 10 feet high, with various spacing between doors—some architects recommend spacing doors 14 feet apart;
- grade-level doors that are 10 feet wide by 14 feet high to allow trucks to drive into the warehouse;
- at least 110 feet of space in front of the door to allow trucks to move in and out—some developers prefer to make this distance 125 to 130 feet to allow room for a double row of parking in the space if the building is later converted into a more intense use;
- trailer storage—an attribute often overlooked;
- careful attention to timing and sequencing of material handling;
- shipping offices that are located near loading ramps;
- carefully designed ramps for at-grade loading and dock ramps that allow trucks to maneuver easily;
- optimally, truck ramps that slope no more than 5 percent;
- floors with a maximum slope of 0.5 percent;
- proper screening requirements for loading docks and truck parking areas; and
- security features such as fencing, gates, and guard facilities.

Manufacturing and assembly users, both single-tenant and multitenant, have the following requirements:

- parking ratios of two to four spaces per 1,000 square feet with an average of about three-and-one-half spaces per 1,000 square feet;
- separate entrances for cars and trucks;
- separate employee and public parking; and
- overhead doors and loading facilities—a mixture of dock-high doors and at-grade doors is usually an advantage.

The following items apply specifically to *multitenant industrial buildings*:

- careful placement of signage—since the turnover rate is potentially high, signs must be designed for easy replacement (one effective method is to hang the sign on spandral glass);
- a mix of unit sizes; and
- flexibility in changing the size of spaces to suit market demand.

Office/tech building requirements are very similar to those for R&D space. Some additional features are:

- generally, two-story buildings;
- truck access without dock-high doors;
- good internal circulation (via hallways and lobbies) within the office space;
- elevators, or at least the option of elevators—developers may want to provide the space for the elevator (the installing pit and the proper structural support) but include the actual installation of the elevator as an optional tenant improvement;

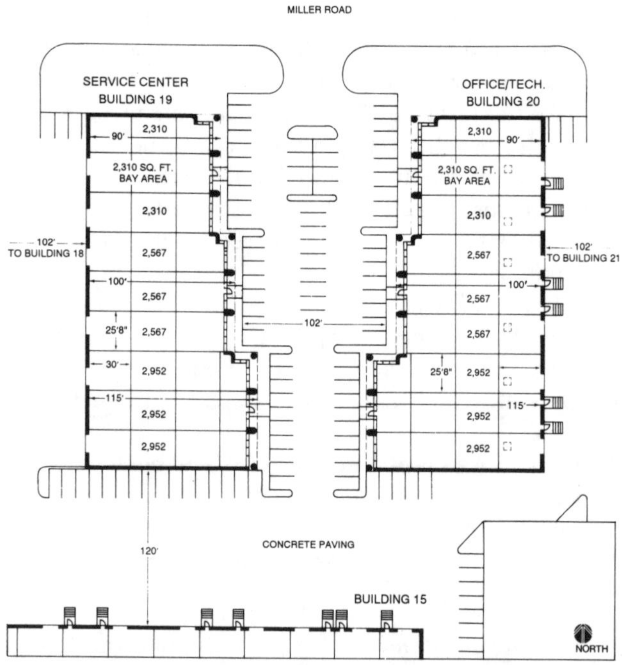

At Northgate Business Park in Dallas, a service center building featuring 16-foot clear heights and generous parking is sited together with an office/tech building with 18-foot clear heights.

- 17-foot floor-to-floor height in the warehouse area that gives 14 feet of clear height to allow for low-pile storage, if needed;
- allowances for pedestrian traffic within the project; and
- adequate parking—generally, a ratio of at least three-and-one-half to four spaces per 1,000 square feet is required.

Service centers are quasi-commercial centers with public spaces in the front and industrial uses in the rear. These buildings require:

- public traffic areas in the front of the center, separate from the service traffic areas in the rear;
- a strong image—the generous use of glass and distinctive architectural features will help lease the space;
- access for pedestrian traffic and ample visitor parking;
- standard office entrance doors in the front of the buildings, preferably with glass or other office-quality materials around the door;
- at least eight-foot doors in the service area so that equipment and supplies can be moved in and out of the building; and
- a comprehensive signage program.

Amenities

In industrial park development, retail services are an important amenity for tenants. For example, the developer of Braker Center, an R&D park in Austin, Texas, placed at the entrance to the main parking lot a kiosk containing automatic teller machines, a Federal Express station, and post office services. Other popular amenities include delicatessens, cafeterias, or full-service restaurants—these amenities, however, require special planning for venting to eliminate cooking odors, siting to maintain the building image, and outdoor seating if possible. Car repair shops and gas stations can also provide useful services to tenants. Larger industrial parks can support small retail centers that cater to their industrial tenants and provide services such as printing, office supplies, computer supplies, and food services. Availability of hotel and restaurant facilities also is important to large-scale industrial parks.

Building Design and Construction

Design elements for industrial buildings are specially tailored to the functional aspects of each particular building type and to economic considerations. Beginning developers should study carefully the design and construction of other buildings that serve the same market. They should speak to tenants to discover which features they prefer and to contractors about ways in which they can save money. Finally, they should choose an architect who specializes in the particular industrial building type that they are planning and talk to contractors and other developers who have previously worked with that architect. An architect who is an expert designer of office/warehouse space is not necessarily also an expert in R&D space. As with other product types, a team approach to design and construction is the most effective, and, ideally, the contractor and the leasing agent should be part of the design team and work with the architect to obtain a design that is both functional and marketable.

A.F. Payne Photographic

Exterior cladding and building curves are used at Building 18 at the Phoenix Tech Center to create a high-tech look.

The design of industrial buildings aims to combine functionality, economy of construction, and easy long-term maintenance. Designers of industrial buildings have pioneered many construction techniques that have been gradually adopted by other product types. Tilt-wall construction, for example, was developed to assist the low-cost construction of large expanses of wall. The technology has been adapted successfully to both retail and office development. The need for open, column-free spaces leads to a structural system largely based on efficient roof construction. Since industrial buildings are typically one story high, the roof is the primary load carried by the columns.

Bay Depths and Ceiling Heights

The bay depths of the building depend on two elements: the stacking plan of the proposed buyer or tenant, and the construction system used. With wood roof systems, the bay depths are based on the four-foot by eight-foot roof system. Thus, the structural system and design of the building should be based on multiples of four feet. Bay depths between columns are commonly 24 feet by 48 feet. Concrete block buildings are designed with the same system, since three 16-inch concrete blocks are equal to four feet. Preengineered metal systems frequently feature multiples of either four or five feet.

When designing any industrial building, the developer must assess its efficiency from the perspective of the buyer or tenant. A minimal number of columns is very important to the tenant. The difference between two and three rows of columns can substantially affect the efficiency of the stacking systems.

The height of the building likewise depends on the prospective tenants. Smaller industrial buildings and small multitenant buildings frequently will have floor-to-ceiling heights of 16, 18, or 20 feet. The floor-to-ceiling height is measured as the minimum distance between the lowest structural member in the roof and the finished floor. Large industrial buildings and warehouse buildings typically have a floor-to-ceiling height of 24 feet. Since the roof must slope to allow rainwater to run off, the ceiling height may range from 24 to 26 feet. A 24-foot ceiling height also readily accommodates a mezzanine (a nine-foot first-floor ceiling height, four feet for floor structure and air-conditioning ducts, a nine-foot ceiling height on the second floor, and two feet for the air-conditioning ducts).

Foundations

Foundation design depends on the dead- and live-loads that go to each part of the building. Various construction methods are used. If tilt-wall construction is used, a concrete beam with steel reinforcement, called a "spread footing" or "continuous beam," is poured along the line of the wall. The beam may be 12 inches to four feet wide, depending on the load, and 12 to 24 inches deep.

In areas with good soil and no earthquakes, "spot footings" may be poured under each point where panels join. Spot footings are typically four-feet square and range in depth from 12 inches in good soil to 18 or more inches.[23]

In areas in which freezing occurs, the beam, or footing, must extend below the frostline because soil tends to expand when frozen. In Michigan, for example, footings are three to four feet deep, and in Alaska they may go down five feet or more, depending on the depth of the frostline. Permafrost areas require special construction.[24]

In areas with poor soils, a grade beam is used rather than a continuous beam to distribute the load over a greater area and to prevent cracking. Steel reinforcement is an integral part of the grade beam design, whereas a continuous beam requires fewer reinforcing bars (rebar) and is tied together only to the extent necessary to prevent movement during the concrete pour. The beams may be formed either with plywood or by the dirt itself.

The slab is poured separately from the foundation beam, leaving a three- to five-foot "pour strip" around the perimeter. The pour strip slab is poured before the walls are formed. In earthquake-prone areas, the pour strip ties the foundation and walls together into a monolithic unit through steel rebar that comes out of the footings, tilt panels, and slab.

Wall Systems

Three basic wall systems are in use today: concrete tilt-up, masonry, and preengineered metal panelized.

Concrete tilt-up buildings are constructed of large concrete panels that are poured on top of the slab, tilted up, and fastened together to create the walls of the building. Each panel is engineered with rebar and various steel fasteners to connect it with the adjacent panels and roof structure. These panels, which can contain windows and doors, are generally six to eight inches thick, 16 to 24 feet wide, and as tall as the building (20 to 40 feet). This type of construction is very economical because the panels act as the structural support system, the interior wall, and the exterior wall. To prepare for tenants, the inside of the wall should be painted, and the outside face of the panels can be painted or patterned, or sandblasted or graveled to provide a textured finish. Concrete tilt-up is one of the fastest methods of construction because the walls are all poured at once, and, as soon as they are dry, they can all be tilted up in one or two days.

The wall subcontractor begins by laying the gravel or finish-stone down inside the form and then pouring the concrete on top of it. The subcontractor should ensure a

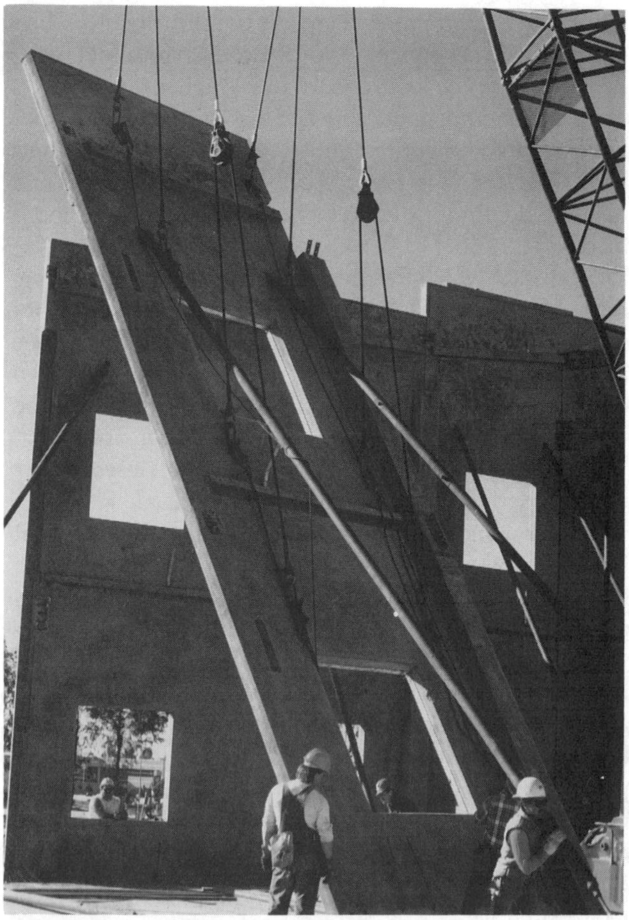

Concrete tilt-up buildings are made of slabs that are tilted up and fastened together; they are very economical and practical for industrial development.

uniform consistency of the concrete aggregate, or the final color or density of the wall will be inconsistent. Samples of concrete are taken during the pour and are broken after seven and 28 days to test the concrete strength. Curing time can be speeded up, if necessary, by adding chemicals to the concrete mix. In seven to 10 days, the concrete panels will be cured, at which time they can be lifted into place on the foundation.

The height of the wall and the kind of exterior aggregate used determine the thickness of the wall. Window and door openings are framed directly into the wall panels. On a 24-foot-wide panel, at least two feet of concrete is needed on each end of a continuous window to prevent cracking. Bottoms of windows on office spaces should be no more than 36 inches from the floor.

After the walls are lifted into place, they may be either welded or bolted (bolting requires considerable accuracy) to small steel plates that are cast into both the wall and the foundation before the concrete is poured. Temporary steel braces are used to support the walls immediately after they are lifted into place and before roof braces are installed.

Panels often break during lifting. James Westling, head of construction, O'Donnell, Armstrong, Brigham, and Partners, Irvine, California, consults a panel hardware engineer who supplies hardware that is cast into the walls to prevent breakage. The panels are sometimes braced with "strongbacks"—steel braces that are applied to the panels while they are being lifted. The strongbacks are later removed.

Masonry is still popular for smaller buildings and in parts of the Northeast, even though tilt-wall construction now dominates industrial building construction in most parts of the country. Bricklayer unions have helped to slow the adoption of tilt-wall construction in the Northeast.

In masonry construction, heavy concrete blocks serve both as walls and as support for the roof. Sometimes a layer of face brick is added on the outside of the concrete block. High-quality blocks with sufficient steel reinforcement should be used to support the ceiling joists and roof. Longer expanses of wall should contain expansion joints to prevent cracking, and weep holes should be provided at regular intervals along the bottom course of bricks to allow the brick cavities to breathe and drain properly.

Generally, a block eight inches deep by 16 inches wide by eight inches high is the basic unit of construction. Rebar can be laid in the hollow cavities of the blocks to provide additional strength. Windows and doors can be constructed using metal or wood headers. Many styles of concrete blocks are available in different textures and colors.

The *preengineered metal panelized system* is fabricated in a factory and shipped to the site to be erected. It consists of a steel post-and-frame structural system and

Raymond Bouley

An aluminum panel curtain wall system is used at Pinnacle Center in Norcross, Georgia, to differentiate the project from the more typical red brick structures found in the area.

Buildings at Narco Elmhurst Centre in Elmhurst, Illinois, feature steel frame construction with precast concrete panels.

a metal, panelized skin that is attached to the structural frame. The panels can be manufactured with a variety of surfaces, ranging from steel or aluminum skin to an aggregate or enamelized paint finish. Panelized systems offer speedy construction and low costs.

Prefabricated metal buildings, which are now more attractive than they used to be and are designed to the developer's specifications, are available from a number of companies that offer delivery directly to the site. Metal panelized systems are less costly than other types of systems in buildings in which the roof beams must support more than just the roof and in which clear-story spans exceed 40 by 80 feet. They are especially popular for traditional manufacturing facilities in which equipment is suspended from the roof.

Roof Systems

The standard industrial roof consists of three layers of tar paper and hot tar topped with a fine aggregate. Special elastic plastics and other materials that provide not only weather-proofing but also often insulation have been created for roofs in recent years. Roofs made of these materials are more expensive but last longer than the five- to seven-year span of a three-ply roof.

Different types of roof systems are popular in different parts of the country. Wood structure systems, for example, dominate industrial construction on the West Coast and throughout much of the Midwest, whereas metal truss systems are more popular in Texas, the South, and on the East Coast. The preferred system is usually the one that is the cheapest in the area.

A *wood structure roof system* consists of laminated wood beams and girders that support the roof, with four- by eight-foot wood and plywood panels. Two- by four-foot (or larger) wood purloins are nailed to four- by eight-foot plywood panels on the site and are lifted into place after the wood beam and girders are in place. This system is fast and economical and requires the least amount of materials.

Metal truss systems may be used to span between the beams and the walls. Either plywood panels or metal panels form the roof deck. This system can provide larger bay spans than the wood structure method.

A *metal panelized system* can span between the steel beams and the girders. The manufactured metal panels are often used with the preengineered wall and structure systems.

James Westling's firm does not use truss systems "because facilities managers from corporations prefer glue-laminated beams. Also, fire sprinkler costs go up because hanging costs are higher from trusses."[25] If a project has enough money, Westling prefers to use four-ply built-up roofs that consist of two plies of 15-pound felt, one ply of 30-pound felt, and a 90-pound cap sheet. Otherwise, he uses a three-ply roof that has one layer of 15-pound felt. A flexible cap sheet is used at all panel joints to allow for movement between panels without breaking the watertight seal.

The connection between the roof and the parapet is also critical. If the parapet (the part of the wall that extends above the roof) is no taller than three feet, the roofing plies should wrap over the top of the parapet to prevent leaks. An alternative (though less recommended) method is to cast a "reglet" into the wall about 18 inches above the roof. The reglet is the female part of a two-part sheet-metal flashing that seals the roof to the building wall.

Skylights are becoming standard features in warehouses. By providing skylights, the developer can save the prospective tenant enormous amounts of money on electricity for lighting. Some electrical companies give rebates or special credits to developers who install not only skylights but also photocells that turn off the electric lights when natural light is adequate to illuminate the facility. In addition to skylights, roof systems must include a roof hatch and ladder to permit roof drains to be cleaned and cleared, air conditioners to be maintained, and the roof to be inspected. Smoke hatches are also required to vent smoke from the building in case of fire.

Building Systems

Fire sprinklers are often required in industrial buildings. The type of construction of the building and the materials stored or manufactured in the building will determine the type of sprinklers that need to be installed. The size of a sprinkler system is normally expressed by the gallons of water it can spray per minute per square foot. The availability and capacity of sprinklers will determine the tenant's fire insurance premiums and thus can be used as a marketing tool. Normally, sprinklers are set off by heat. A small bead in the head of a sprinkler will melt at a prescribed temperature, activating that particular sprinkler. The entire system should be designed so that the activation of any sprinkler will set off an alarm. The alarm company will call the fire department, tenant, and owner of the building to ensure that the water is turned off after the fire is out to avoid further water damage to the contents of the building.

Ideally, each tenant space should have its own air conditioning, electric meter, gas, and water lines. In multitenant buildings, only sewer and telecommunications lines tend to be shared.[26]

In office/warehouses, only the office area is air conditioned, usually by units placed on the roof. Air conditioning for production work and heat-sensitive processes, such as food distribution, requires individual units suspended from the roof beams. Developers can save money on the roof by predetermining the placement of roof equipment and reinforcing only those areas on the roof that will have to bear the load of equipment. Space heaters also are suspended from the roof. Some heating in the warehouse space is always required, even in warmer climates, to prevent freezing of fire sprinkler pipes.

General Advice

A metal building frame can be combined with tilt-wall sides or brick to provide a more traditional facade. To construct these combinations, the prefabricated building is lifted onto the finished slab; anchor bolts in the slab must be located so that the walls can be fastened to the foundation. Roofing systems vary depending on the manufacturer. The better systems, which include insulation, may cost over $1 per square foot and can be designed to drain either into gutters or over the sides of the building.

Interiors of industrial buildings (especially warehouses and flex buildings) are often not finished until the space is leased.

Don Bowers, general partner with Bowers, Perez Associates, Los Angeles, California, has found that a combination steel frame and concrete tilt-up provides an appealing look for R&D buildings. He uses 20-foot-wide concrete panels on the sides of the building to provide shear strength. The front and back of the building have glass skins. Combining steel with tilt-up side walls saves money on steel.[27]

Interior finishes are more important for R&D space than for other types of industrial space. R&D tenants value climate control and comfort; indeed, the developer should treat an R&D building more like office than industrial space. Triple-layer insulating glass may be used to cut down noise near airports or industrial areas.

If the activities in the laboratory or warehouse space generate noise, dust, or toxic fumes, safety features are critical. Air locks may be required to protect the office area from the lab area. James E. Bock of James E. Bock Associates, Houston, Texas, emphasizes that the developer does not, of course, know what type of tenant a building may have in 10 years' time. By having two separate HVAC systems, the developer has the flexibility to seal off the laboratory area should future tenants require it. If toxic materials enter the atmosphere, a shared HVAC system would distribute them throughout the entire building.[28]

The most frequent problems encountered in building industrial buildings concern drainage and roof leaks. "Parking lot slopes must be carefully designed to drain properly. Also, do not skimp on structure. A too-thin wall or undersized column could lead to a roof sag, which, over time, leads to leaks, or worse, roof failure."[29]

Some of the most common mistakes to avoid during construction include the following:[30]

- insufficient slab thickness, causing the slab to be damaged by the crane;
- insufficient wall bracing, causing panels to fall over in high winds;
- failure to preplan the location of utilities under the slab;
- lack of concrete area for truck and trailer storage;
- insufficient electrical service conduit—if a developer does not provide at least one extra conduit for future service needs, the slab and outside pavement may have to be torn up to install it later; and
- an undersized fire sprinkler system—if the system is inadequate, some prospective tenants may not be able to obtain fire insurance at competitive rates.

The market for the industrial space determines the type of construction and the quality of finish—cost-saving construction tips do not save money in the long run if they make a building less appealing to the intended user. Industrial building techniques have been evolving more rapidly than those used for any other types of development. New materials and new systems technology often appear first in industrial structures. Beginning developers should avoid pioneering a new technique alone, but they should be familiar with current alternatives and should not fear innovation as long as experienced contractors and superintendents are working with them.

Financing

The considerations for financing industrial development are essentially the same as those for financing other income property. (These considerations are covered more fully in chapter 4.) Equity—from the developer or from others—is invested and interim construction money is borrowed until the project is completed and leased. At that point (and sometimes earlier), a permanent mortgage can be put into place. For this last step, industrial property may have an advantage over other income property in that some mortgage lenders believe that industrial development is a more stable investment because its market is less volatile than are other markets.

The structure of the financing for a project that involves both land development and building construction is likely to be more complex than that for a project involving building on land that has already been improved. Land development frequently involves more than one interim loan. Separate loans for land acquisition, land development, and building construction may be required. A building project, on the other hand, usually relies solely on a construction loan that also covers land purchase.

Equity is required to pay for the development costs that occur prior to closing on the property, because borrowed funds will not typically be released prior to that event. After closing, equity is still required because loans will rarely cover 100 percent of a project's costs.

Interim financing is usually nonamortizing. Funds are drawn on a monthly basis to cover a percentage of the current project costs, including interest on the current loan balance. A contract period for the loan, which establishes a deadline for repayment of principal, is standard, typically ranging between 12 and 24 months. This repayment usually is made from the proceeds that result from the funding of a permanent mortgage.

For projects combining land development and building, permanent-mortgage funding can occur after sufficient time has elapsed for lenders to evaluate a project's track record. The improved land is appraised, and a loan equal to 65 to 100 percent of the value is given, based on payments that can be supported by existing and projected revenue.

Alternatively, when an industrial park is partially occupied, the developer may use the cash flow from existing tenants to improve the remaining land, thus reducing the need for loans. When a building is sufficiently leased to support the debt service, the permanent lender will fund the long-term mortgage.

Equity Structure

A number of institutional investors look for real estate joint venture opportunities. Although many limit their activities to prime office and retail properties, some may participate in industrial development. In the 1980s, national institutional investors that sought industrial property opportunities included such notable names as Aetna Insurance Company, The Principal Group, Copley Real Estate Advisors, Massachusetts Mutual Insurance Company, and Teachers Insurance and Annuity.

Future tenants can also become partners in a project, an arrangement that provides both equity and financial statement strength as well as preleasing activity. Owners of private companies frequently prefer to own the property in which their company operates. Often, these individuals will become joint venture partners, and their companies will become building tenants. The equity partners enjoy both the benefits of real estate ownership and control over one of the major tenants (their own company). This arrangement also can provide essentially tax-free income to a company owner. The rent paid by an owner's business will be expensed in the same year. The taxable income from the owner's share of that rent usually will be more than offset by the owner's business deduction.

A less common joint venture structure involves an investor that purchases the land, funds the improve-

Tech Center East in Monrovia, California, was developed by Boone Fetter & Associates in partnership with Occidental College, which sought an equity position in the project in an effort to diversify its endowment portfolio with real estate.

ments, and leases the property to the developer for between 40 and 99 years. Profits from the project (from subleasing revenue, sale of the improvements, or refinancing) are typically split 50/50. The developer often has no money in the project.

Construction and Permanent Loans

For industrial land acquisition and land development loans, a pension fund, insurance company, or commercial bank usually takes the first lien position. It may finance up to 75 percent of the land value and 100 percent of the land development costs, depending on the appraisal of the completed improvements and projected sales revenues.

A real estate investment trust (REIT) may possibly take a secondary lien position, providing additional funds at rates typically four or five points above prime. This type of joint participation must be prearranged in a single-financing agreement.

Construction/lease-up financing is arranged for individual buildings just as for other income property. Commercial banks, S&Ls, and insurance companies have been the primary sources for this type of borrowing.

Developers should arrange permanent financing only when they plan to lease a building rather than sell it. If they plan to sell the building to an owner/tenant, permanent financing may hinder the sale if the mortgage has onerous prepayment conditions.

Permanent lenders are concerned with the following items in evaluating loan requests:

- the existing leases on the property, including lease rates, types of lease, and terms and provisions of the leases;
- the financial capabilities and history of the tenants; and
- the general health of the rental market and how the leases compare with others in the market (if they are above market rates, tenants may leave; if they are below market, the property will have to be held a certain amount of time until the leases expire or rise to market levels).

Typically, industrial property must be 75 to 80 percent leased before a permanent mortgage can be obtained.

Mortgages of 75 percent of the value, subject to a debt-service coverage ratio (DCR) of 1.1 to 1.2, are common. Property value is determined by dividing projected stabilized net operating income (NOI) by a cap rate. In the late 1980s, cap rates for single-tenant, triple-net lease industrial buildings ranged from 8.5 to 9.5 percent. The cap rate for multitenant buildings is comparable to that for single-tenant buildings.

Marketing

Industrial developers should start approaching potential tenants as soon as they option a site or consider developing a site already in inventory. A low-key approach that takes advantage of informal contacts often works best. Target firms may range from major national companies to regional firms to local firms, or any combination of the three. The fact that a high-quality company is attracted to the site at the outset helps to launch a park or multitenant building; the initial tenant's prestige sets the tone for the rest of the project. Developers usually begin the marketing campaign by exploiting their existing contacts. Developers also should contact certain key brokers for leads on possible seed tenants. Because the project is still in the conceptual stage, developers will have to "sell" the project themselves and persuade initial tenants that the future building will suit their needs perfectly.

As development progresses, developers proceed with other aspects of the marketing program, including selection of advertising agencies and public relations firms, development of the budget, establishment of broker contacts, and design of the marketing materials. The marketing strategy and the tone set in printed materials must reflect the goals of the developers and target the types of tenants indicated by the detailed market analysis. Care must be taken to avoid excessive and unnecessary costs for advertising and promotion.

Los Angeles developer Gerald Katell says that local brokers tend to be the best source of market information. "They know better than market analysts who specific tenants are likely to be. You want to try to market your project to a specific user type." Prospective tenants—users that need more space or a different type of space—often come from adjacent properties. "You should work outwards from your property in concentric circles," advises Katell. Local chambers of commerce also may provide leads or find potential tenants for a project.[31]

Beginning developers can sometimes turn their lack of experience into an advantage for marketing purposes. Small developers can claim more "hands-on" involvement and can give more personal attention to tenants. Also, their costs tend to be lower because they have lower overheads than do large, established development firms.

Marketing Documents

Two documents are essential to a successful marketing program: a technical services package and a sales brochure. The following discussion applies primarily to full-scale industrial parks, but developers of individual buildings should also have similar information available for prospective tenants.

The Technical Services Package

The technical services package is given by the developer to brokers. It consists of statistical data that describe the project's target market and includes information relating to population growth and other demographic changes, statutory taxes, real estate taxes, sales taxes, interstate commerce trucking zones and rates, and public services. The package should give utility information, such as typical water and sewer dimensions, capacity, static pressure, and design flows, as well as information on fire-protection services and requirements, electrical capacity, and the name and frequency of the railroad carrier, if any. Other items to be addressed in the technical services package are:

- details of protective covenants;
- development constraints, including setbacks, landscaping requirements, and exterior building materials;
- procedures for architectural approvals for tenant-built structures;
- parking and service area locations and requirements;
- the location and design of signage;
- permitted and nonpermitted uses;
- storage requirements; and
- procedures for dealing with objectionable situations, such as noise, odor, vibrations, and smoke.

All procedures should be explained in a positive fashion. It should be clear to prospective tenants that the restrictions will benefit their property and the overall character of the industrial park. The information may be summarized in a small pamphlet that the broker can give to potential clients.

The Sales Brochure

The sales brochure describes the ownership, location, and distinctive features of the project. Usually prepared with the help of a public relations or advertising firm, brochures tend to consist of a nine- by 12-inch fold-out jacket with single-page literature in the jacket pockets. This design allows the contents to be updated without

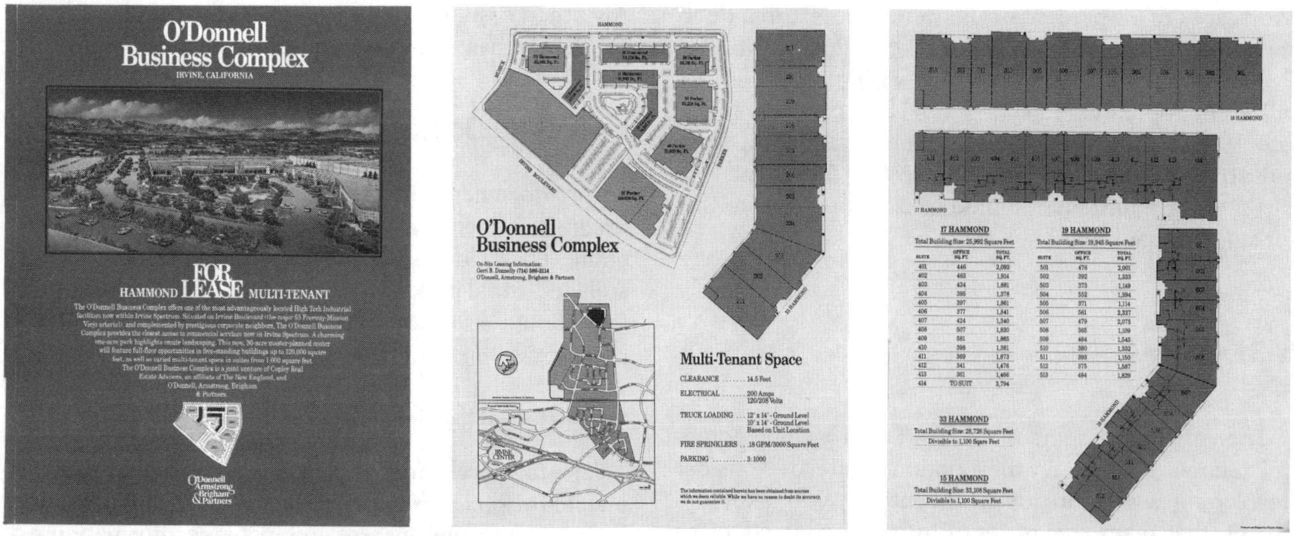

The marketing brochure for O'Donnell Business Complex in Irvine, California, provides key marketing information with a rendering, site plan, location map, building layouts, and important building data.

complete revision and reprinting of the brochure. The sales brochure should include the following information:

- ownership;
- concept of the development;
- a list of seed tenants;
- an overall development plan that identifies the preliminary parcel configuration and proposed road network;
- a location map showing the relationship of the project to the region, immediate community, and road and rail networks;
- a detailed map showing access to the site and the immediate neighborhood;
- data from the technical services package, including truck, rail, air, and port facility information;
- a summary of community characteristics drawn from the market studies; and
- the track record of the ownership group, with photographs of previous developments.

The quality of the brochure that is needed for successful marketing varies from place to place. In Orange County, California, for example, intense competition makes four-color brochures the norm for a 50,000-square-foot building; however, color brochures are not necessary in Los Angeles. Color brochures cost seven to eight times as much as black-and-white brochures.[32] Other marketing programs can also be beneficial. Gerald Katell introduced a "corporate key package" to help reduce the stress of moving for new tenants. The program, which has proven popular with corporate clients, provides relocation planning, moving coordination, and postmove servicing.[33]

Marketing Strategy

The total cost of the marketing program should range from 3 to 5 percent of the total gross projected revenues. Developers who rely on outside brokers to help market their projects should pay full commissions and should be open and accessible, particularly because brokers will inevitably steer their clients toward those projects with cooperative owners.

Whether or not the developer should sign an exclusive arrangement with a single broker depends very much on local practices. In some communities, exclusive arrangements are essential for gaining the necessary attention of any one brokerage firm, especially for smaller projects. In other communities, such arrangements are harmful insofar as they encourage other brokers to steer clients away from the project. Any exclusive arrangement should hold the broker accountable for promotion and sales activities. Client inquiries, direct contacts, sales presentations, and other activities should be monitored monthly.

According to Don Bowers, a 6 percent commission on the first five years of a lease, 3 percent on the second five years, and 2.5 percent for the following five years is the norm. The commission is based on the total rent to be paid over the five-year period. He pays half of the amount when the commission is signed and half when the tenant moves in.[34] Exclusive listings should not require the developer to pay more than a full commission; an outside broker will sometimes try to receive a full commission in addition to the listing broker's 5 percent commission.

Even if developers have broker representation, they also should solicit prospects directly. Brokers will be motivated to make their own contacts when they see that developers are aggressive and capable of making contacts with local and regional industries. Developers should hold regular meetings with, or stage open houses or lunches for, the brokerage community to keep it informed of new developments, pricing modifications, and current sales or leases and should offer regular tours. Also, developers should engage in "missionary work," that is, mailing brochures to clients, industry contacts, and brokers known to them in other communities in the region.

Leads for prospects can come from a number of sources. Developers should maintain close contact with local and state economic development agencies, public departments in the community, utilities and railroads, planning commissions, and redevelopment agencies.

Advertising usually begins with heavy initial exposure in the media and then a steady, consistent marketing program to keep the project in the mind of the public. Spot advertising in trade journals helps to establish an image and maintain visibility.

Sending brochures to prospects seems to be the most effective strategy, especially when the prospects are carefully selected from the market analysis. Peter Reich, associate vice president of Coldwell-Banker, Los Angeles, California, recommends two or three mailings to brokers over a four-month period and emphasizes the importance of repeated contacts.[35]

6-3 Marketing Costs for a Multitenant Incubator Industrial Property

Broker Commissions	$71,500
Advertising	
Newspaper	24,800
Sign, Banner	10,050
Brochure	1,000
Grand Opening Party	3,000
Staff Salaries	120,000
Office Rent	45,800
Total	$276,150

Marketing Cost Ratios:
- $11,500 per month
- $2,125 per unit (includes re-renting of 30 units during 24-month lease-up)
- $2.44 per square-foot building area

Note: These marketing costs are for a 113,000-square-foot industrial building in suburban Southern California. The building was designed for 100 small tenants in spaces ranging from 750 to 1,775 square feet. The building opened in March 1988. It cost $3.5 million and was projected to take 24 months to lease.
Source: Frank J. Piatkowski, A.I.A., Los Angeles, California.

Leasing

Industrial tenants focus on three major concerns: effective rent (not just nominal rent); location; and building design, loading areas, and amenities.

Although developers play a variety of games with the rent to make it seem lower, tenants ultimately focus on the *effective* rent—their costs per square foot after all concessions have been taken into account. (See figure 5-2 on computing effective rent in chapter 5.) In multitenant R&D buildings, tenants also will focus on the costs shared with other tenants (building efficiency).

Leases for single-tenant buildings are typically either triple net or net-net. In the case of triple-net leases, the tenant takes care of everything; with net-net leases, the landlord is responsible for maintaining the structure of the building—the foundations, the walls, and the roof.[36]

In multitenant buildings, the leases typically provide for gross rent. These leases resemble those for office buildings in which the landlord is responsible for building operations.

Individual tenant spaces are separately metered so that each tenant pays its own utilities. In addition, each tenant pays its share of common-area expenses, which are allocated based on square footage. In tight markets, the developer usually can negotiate annual increases in rent based on the Consumer Price Index. Lease terms average two to five years.

Tenant finish-out allowances vary according to the building type. The allowance is usually a small amount, say $10 per square foot, that the tenant can supplement if so desired.

Industrial developers should try to avoid certain lease clauses in their lease agreements. For instance:[37]

- Clauses that require developers to rebuild the building in the event of an uninsured loss are obviously less desirable than those that provide the option to terminate the lease.
- Rights to renew leases should be limited. Every tenant, of course, wants a five-year option to renew on a five-year lease with preset ceilings on rental rate increases.
- Rights to expand into adjacent space should be limited. Such rights may be refused altogether for small tenants. For large tenants, developers may give a right of first refusal when space becomes available.
- Developers never should agree to hold space vacant by giving an unqualified right to expand into new space after a certain number of years (for example, 40,000 square feet now, 20,000 square feet more in five years). If a compromise must be made, developers may agree not to lease a certain space for more than a three- or five-year term. However, if such a constraint on par-

Two buildings totaling 112,000 square feet were available for leasing when the developers of Narco Elmhurst Center in Elmhurst, Illinois, identified a tenant (Household Finance Corporation) that could potentially occupy all of the space. To accommodate the tenant's needs, the developer decided to join the two buildings to create one 123,077-square-foot building. This entailed moving an existing tenant and convincing various entities to vacate their easements between the buildings.

ticular space is agreed upon, finding a tenant for that space may be difficult. For example, if the tenant in the expansion space signs a three-year lease with a two-year option, the space may need to be held vacant for the last two years.
- Short-term leases (say, for only two years) and options to terminate a lease for any reason may make financing difficult, if not impossible. Major tenants often want a right to terminate the lease if a condemnation takes place or if access to the property is impaired.
- In California, smart lessees try to negotiate a tax-increase limitation. If the building is sold, the tenant will not pay the increase in taxes that occurs automatically under Proposition 13. A possible compromise is to limit the number of sales within a 10-year period that can raise the tenant's property taxes.

Property Management

Management of industrial properties involves three stages, and the priorities change during each stage.

Stage 1: Development

During the development phase, the developer's major tasks are to coordinate infrastructure installation and to attract seed tenants. Often, the local community is concerned about environmental issues, and, to sell the project, the developer also must display such concern. Restrictive covenants not only protect the project but help to reassure the community that potential undesirable side effects will not be permitted.

Because of noise, dirt, and increased traffic during the development phase, the developer must foster a "good neighbor" image. Failure to respond to community concerns can result in time-consuming delays in approvals and inspections. On-site management is a necessity. Timely completion of infrastructure is vitally important to the seed tenant—the one that establishes an overall identity for the project. If the seed tenants encounter delays in occupancy because of poor management, they are likely to convey their dissatisfaction to other potential tenants.

Stage 2: Lease-Up

Management during the lease-up stage emphasizes tenant selection, tenant relations, project standard enforcement, and the maintenance of the project's public image. Although the preliminary parcelization of the property is the basis for marketing individual sites, the developer still should maintain flexibility. The principal concerns of the developer during this stage revolve around the compatibility of potential tenants, their locational relationships, and parcelization.

The seed tenant sets the standards for the rest of the tenants. If the first tenant occupies 10,000 square feet of space, subsequent tenants will tend to occupy the same amount of space. If the seed tenant occupies 100,000 square feet, many subsequent tenants will occupy at least 50,000 square feet.

Site planning and the design of individual buildings are critical elements in maintaining the project's marketing appeal. The enforcement of restrictions concerning architecture, outdoor storage, and loading and parking ensure the project's continuing marketability. The developer should enforce the standards on an equal and impartial basis. Close supervision of architectural standards and, especially, exterior yard controls facilitates the financing of the project during its mature stages.

Shell buildings and multitenant spaces within partially occupied buildings can remain empty for months. If such buildings are not properly cared for (for instance, if construction rubble is not removed and landscaping is not maintained), they can become unsightly nuisances that lower the value of neighboring property and give the impression of poor management. Developers who lease or sell land to other builders can avoid the problem of unsightly vacant buildings by requiring builders to post a performance bond to ensure conformity to covenants, conditions, restrictions (CC&Rs) and design controls within a specified period of time. The bond should require that:

- exterior walls are finished and the installation of windows and doors is completed;
- all driveways, walks, parking lots, and truck-loading areas are paved;
- all construction debris is removed;
- the landscaping, including tree and shrub planting in specified locations and installation of sod, is completed and irrigation systems are provided; and
- the landscaped areas and parking areas are well maintained.

Stage 3: Stabilized Operations

The major objective during this stage is to maximize long-run profitability. Revenues, infrastructure costs, and operating expense projections should be updated on a quarterly, or at least annual, basis.

Financial management tasks include cost accounting, pricing, and keeping track of new leasing and sales information, which should include details of prospects, broker contacts, telephone inquiries, the rental rates and space availability of competitive projects, and current tenant status (lease renewal dates).

The mature stage of a project occurs after it has been completely sold out or leased. Management of the completed development and enforcement of restrictive covenants is turned over to an occupants' association, similar to a homeowners' association. If the association is voluntary, it can be created as the developer phases out the project. If it is a mandatory association, it must be established at the beginning of the development so that all tenants and purchasers are bound by its provisions.

Associations can be a source of problems and expense for the developer if they become a means for occupants to press for services or benefits to which they are not entitled. Notwithstanding these concerns, a well-run association benefits not only the tenants and the community but also the developer's reputation by maintaining the standards of the project over time.

The main source of concern for developers during this third stage is the "residuals"—the future proceeds from the sale of buildings developed and any remaining unsold parcels. The developers play the same role in the association as that of other owners: if they own buildings with triple-net leases, they should inspect the property at least semiannually. These inspections are important for determining:

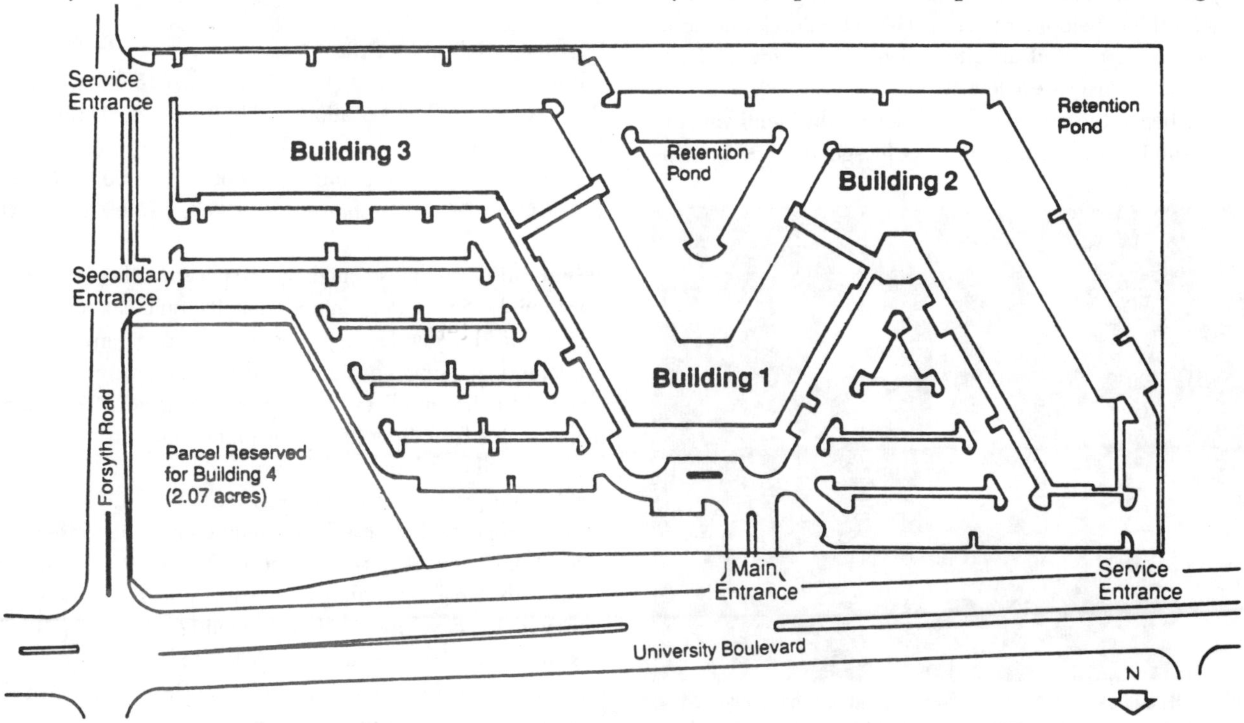

During the development and leasing periods, on-site staff at University Place in Winter Park, Florida, included a property manager, two leasing agents, a secretary, and an in-house construction crew.

■ Addison Business Center[a] Addison, Illinois

Addison Business Center is a 79-acre business park in the Village of Addison in Du Page County, about 45 minutes' drive west of downtown Chicago. The developer is Minneapolis-based Opus North Corporation, a subsidiary of Opus U.S. Corporation. The park was conceived in 1985. The site plan called for 11 low-rise buildings containing approximately 800,000 square feet of office, research, warehouse, and light-assembly space. By autumn 1988, eight of the buildings were completed and all but 13 acres of the site were committed or under construction.

Addison Business Center illustrates how a sound market-driven site selection process can lead to successful development. It also illustrates how a major floodplain problem—two-thirds of the original site lay within the floodplain—can be turned into an asset.

Background and Site Selection

Opus's first major business park in Chicago was Kensington Center, a 300-acre park in Cook County, eight miles north of O'Hare International Airport. Opus discovered one of the pitfalls of 300-acre business parks—the development is so large that it can be adversely affected by business cycles, political cycles, and tax cycles.

By 1985, Opus realized that the market appeal was not as strong for this development as it had been for developments in other cities. It wanted an alternative site outside of Cook County, where taxes were lower.

Opus began the process of site selection by identifying the various submarkets throughout the Chicago area and examining the pluses and minuses of each area. According to James Nygaard of Opus: "We started with the question, 'Where do we want to be?' rather than responding to land as it was presented to us." Most of the sites Opus knew about originally were in western Du Page County. Before the homework was done, Opus's perception was that it should move farther west, where plenty of land was available at lower prices. After looking more closely at the trends of industrial development, however, Opus found that most new developments were in northeast Du Page County, closer to O'Hare International Airport and the city. It was decided that the benefits of a better location were worth the extra cost; results indicate this was a good decision.

Djong Photography

Addison Business Center is a 79-acre business park planned to include 11 buildings and approximately 800,000 square feet of office, research, warehouse, and light-assembly space.

Opus first defined the type of project it wanted to do—the acreage, cost, and target market. Research indicated that the market for new development was moving from office to warehouse space. Starting with the cost of a building that was primarily warehouse with ancillary office space, Opus worked backwards to derive the price it could afford to pay for an improved pad and, in turn, raw land comprising an entire business park.

These calculations indicated the value per square foot (in 1986 dollars) of improved lots:

	Rents (Net Lease)	Improved Land Cost
First-Class Suburban Office Buildings	$18.00	$15.00 (1.10 FAR)
Business Park Office Location	11.50	5.00 (1.00 FAR)
Business Park		
50% Office/50% Warehouse	7.50	4.00 (0.25 FAR)
10% Office/90% Warehouse	3.90	3.00 (0.35 FAR)

For office/warehouse buildings (10 percent office/90 percent warehouse), Opus determined that it could spend $1 per square foot for raw land. In general, the company does not expect to make much profit on land for warehouses. "You can make a little if you sell it in a hurry," says Nygaard. "You mainly make money from building opportunities, adding value to the land through development."

Once the product and economics were defined, Opus searched for the property that best fit its parameters. It identified two pieces and eventually settled on a 79-acre site in Addison because the local community wanted a business park and would work with the developer to alter the zoning as needed. The site was also desirable because it was located near a proposed tollway with two intersections accessing the property. In the long run, if the tollway were built, prospects would be good for marketing more office space.

Opus signed an earnest money contract in June 1985 with a year-end closing. The purchase was subject to rezoning and annexation by the Village of Addison to furnish municipal services.

Land Planning

BRW, a planning firm from Minneapolis with experience in industrial park development, was retained to master-plan the subdivision. The marketing plan placed higher-density buildings along the frontage, higher-end office/warehouses in the middle, and warehouse/distribution uses in the rear of the site.

BRW's traffic planners determined that the site required two entrances to the main road. This was based on a pro forma development plan that included estimates of total square footage to be built, type of user, parking requirements, and traffic generation.

Along with the road plan, the other major concern was the floodplain—a major reason that the property was still available. The Addison Business Center land needed to be elevated an average of three feet, with some portions needing as much as 10 feet of fill—a total of 300,000 cubic yards. "We calculated the cost of doing the work, figured that into the price of the land, and decided it was worth it," said project manager Thomas George. Opus reached an agreement with the adjacent Forest Preserve to obtain dirt from the preserve by digging a seven-acre lake, 38 feet deep. Opus also planned to excavate six retention basins on site, totaling 20 acres. These basins provided additional dirt and served as holding ponds for on-site storage of flood runoff.

Addison's zoning had more stringent setback requirements than the developer desired. Along the south side, where the project backed up to single-family residential property, Opus asked for variable 50- to 100-foot setbacks rather than the standard 100-foot setbacks. For buildings longer than 500 feet, the setback went from 50 to 100 feet. The village agreed to accept the smaller setbacks.

Another important issue concerned the platting of "outlots"—what is left over in a subdivision after other sites are divided. As a rule, developers do not want to establish lot lines in advance unless absolutely necessary because they want the flexibility to tailor sites for individual users. In Du Page County, developers are required only to define roads and water-storage locations. Du Page has an "administrative" subdivision process by which individual lot lines are platted without public hearings.

During the public approval process, Opus agreed to reserve the front portion of the park for buildings with at least 50 percent office buildout. The village wanted the frontage to include buildings with higher-quality finishes to present an office-type image, even though Addison was not considered an office market. Opus agreed to this requirement with the understanding that its flexibility would be retained to respond to future market conditions.

The circulation system features two entrances off Swift Road, one loop road, and one cul-de-sac. The project was developed in a floodplain, requiring substantial fill, and several retention basins were created on site to obtain fill and manage flood runoff.

Financing and Marketing

Opus had the luxury of financing development by a line of credit that is not specific to Addison Business Center. Most developers would have had to take out a land development loan from a commercial bank or other source. Floodplain work can sometimes be financed by a special district (utility, flood control, drainage, or improvement district), although none was used in the present case.

Grubb & Ellis had an exclusive listing to market the developed sites at Addison. For build-to-suit sales, it received a 3 percent commission on the price of the building and 6 percent on the land. For net leases, it received 8 percent on the first year's rent plus 3 percent on the remainder of the term. The park was marketed off site from the broker's suburban office. A trailer was maintained on site for meetings and site visits.

Working with Grubb & Ellis, Opus developed an award-winning single-piece marketing brochure that opened up to show the project's location on the first fold and the site plan on the centerfold.

■ Addison Business Center (Continued)

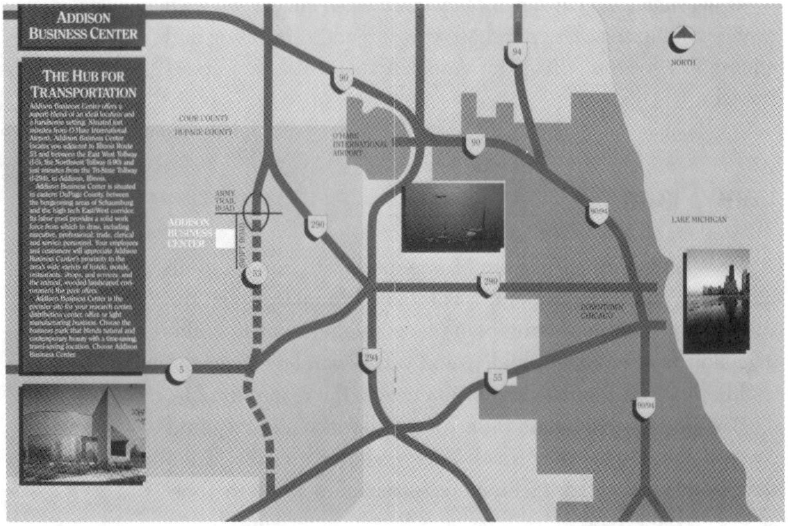

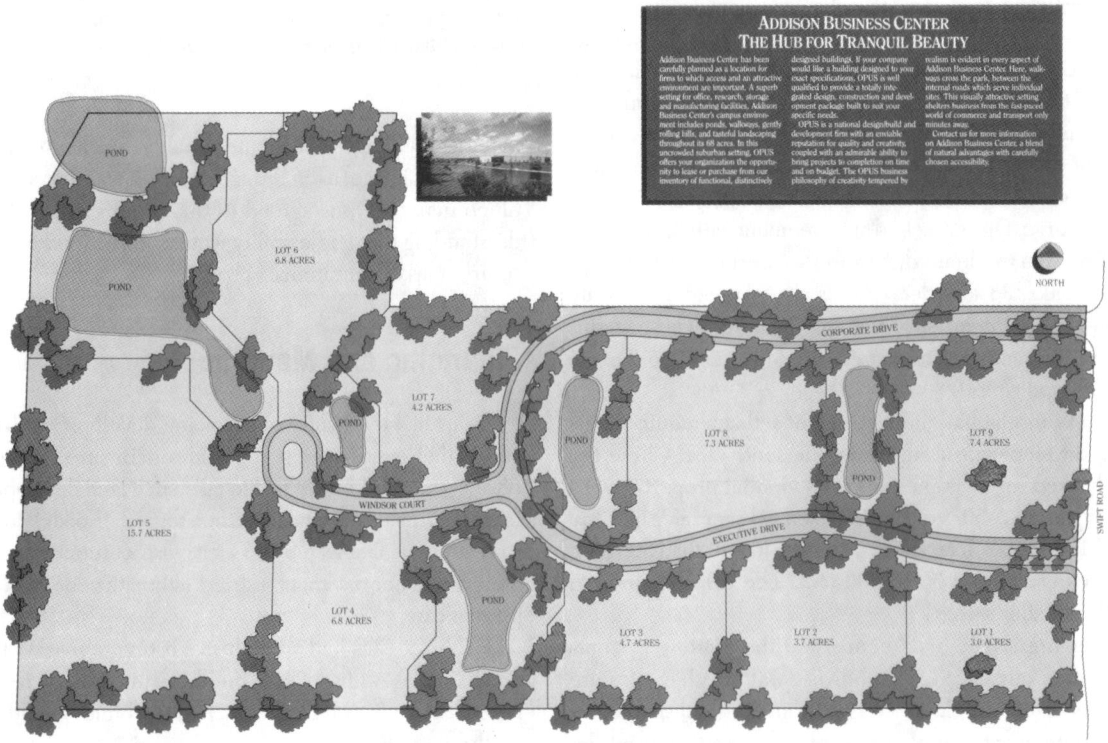

The development brochure opens up to show the project's location on the first fold and the site plan on the second fold.

The easiest parcels to sell first are usually the front parcels. However, Opus prefers to save the best parcels for last so that they realize the value created by prior sales. "Activity breeds activity. You want to start with a spec building on the day you open the subdivision," notes marketing director Richard Wilberg. "Here we started two spec buildings on Day 1 to generate activity." The locations for the spec buildings were determined, in part, by chance. One spec building was located in the rear of the site because the lot was already defined. The other location was selected near the front because the front-to-back dimension, with offices facing the street and docks facing the rear, conveyed a service-center image.

Experience Gained

- Today, more than ever, a developer must cater to the existing marketplace. Creating a market is nearly impossible.
- The land development costs should be carefully assessed upfront. Costs were higher than expected in this case because of the earthmoving necessary to raise the site above the floodplain.
- The relationship that the developer builds and maintains with the municipality is extremely important. The developer must anticipate how the municipality will perform before committing to buy the land.
- A good marketing brochure should be created and distributed as far in advance as possible.
- Keep the master plan flexible. Opus had no idea that most of the buildings in Addison would be build-to-suit.

Developer:
Opus North Corporation
9700 Higgins Road, Suite 900
Rosemont, Illinois 60018
(708) 692-4444

Land Planner:
BRW
700 3rd Street South
Minneapolis, Minnesota 55415
(612) 370-0700

Major Tenants:
Charles Levy Circulating Company, Ingersoll Rand, Raytheon Medical Systems, Global Computer Supplies, Pioneer Standard Electronics, Fujitsu-GTE Business Systems

Project Data

Land Use Information

Total Acreage	78.8
Dedicated Areas	
Interior Roadways	6.4
Swift Right-of-Way	1.6
Net Acreage	70.8
Retention Areas	
Ponds	12.2
Pond Easements	2.5
Buildable Acreage	56.1

Gross Building Area (GBA) at Buildout: 800,000 square feet
Number of Buildings at Buildout: 11 buildings

Economic Information

Site Acquisition Cost	$3,735,000
Planning, Approvals, Legal, and Predevelopment Costs	81,000
On-Site Improvement Costs	4,569,700
Off-Site Development Costs	802,900
Marketing, Administration, and Other Costs	28,550
Interest, Taxes	315,000
Total Land Development Cost	**$9,532,150**

[a]Richard Wilberg and James Nygaard of Opus North Corporation provided generous assistance in assembling material for this case study.

- how well the building is maintained;
- problems of functional obsolescence;
- the existence of restricted activities, such as the storage or manufacturing of items outside buildings;
- the existence of potential toxic-waste problems or liabilities; and
- the health and well-being of the tenants—whether operations are growing, maturing, or reducing.

Various new concerns bedevil the owners of industrial properties. For instance, in earthquake-prone areas, property built before 1934 out of masonry must be rein-

625 Slawin Court
Mount Prospect, Illinois

625 Slawin Court, developed by Opus North Corporation, is located in Kensington Center, a 300-acre business park developed by Opus in Mount Prospect, Illinois. The park is located approximately eight miles north of Chicago's O'Hare International Airport.

Good development projects begin with a marketing concept. 625 Slawin Court is a high-tech industrial building targeted for a very specific market. It illustrates how a good marketing idea, when translated into a good design, increases the developer's chances for success. This speculative building emphasizes single-tenant identity, flexible use with a potential for maximum office space and custom floor plans and finishes, extra parking, and high-quality design.

Background and Site Selection

Opus was started in 1963 by Gerald Rauenhorst, who was a general contractor in Minneapolis. Originally, development was a sideline to the construction business—indeed, Opus's first development project was its own office building that included some extra space for leasing. As his firm grew, Rauenhorst restructured the company with a construction division and a real estate division, each with its own president. Land became the catalyst for the rest of the business. Although Opus develops land, it does not consider itself a land developer; the driving force remains the contracting business.

Some problems result from having construction and development in the same entity because they are two different disciplines with two different kinds of people and levels of compensation. "Good development people do not make good construction people," noted Rauenhorst, in an interview with the *Chicago Tribune* in June 1985, "but construction people do benefit from the real estate side."

As Opus expanded over the years into Milwaukee, Chicago, Phoenix, and Pensacola, the firm became too large to operate centrally. It is now organized geographically so that decisions can be made on the local level as often as possible.

Opus found an underserved market in Chicago for single-tenant high-tech buildings with strong visual identity. Opus called these buildings "signature centers," each bearing the identity, or "signature," of its single occupant. Several features distinguish high-tech from their cousins, office/warehouses, including a higher ratio (25 percent or more) of office-to-warehouse space and higher-quality exterior finish and landscaping. High-tech users are typically fast-growth, high-value, small-bulk service industries such as pharmaceutical, electronic, medical supply, telecommunications, and robotics firms, and their buildings need to be flexible to accommodate a wide range of office/warehouse ratios. Ideally, space for additional parking should be available from an unbuilt adjacent lot so that 100 percent of the building can be used as office if the tenant so desires.

The favored size for signature center spec buildings is 35,000 to 45,000 square feet. Of the 44 single-story nonoffice buildings in Kensington Center, 16 fall within this range—only five are smaller than 20,000 square feet and only five are larger than 100,000 square feet. Floor/area ratios range from 0.25 to 0.45, depending on the amount of office space, with an average of 0.3. The ratios decline as the percentage of office space increases, in order to accommodate the additional parking necessary.

The 625 Slawin Court project is a speculative single-tenant industrial building that features a brick exterior, curved walls, and a semicircular showroom on the prime corner.

Design

625 Slawin Court occupies one of the most prominent corners in Kensington Center. It was clustered with other signature center buildings around a court to accent the views. The building was developed as a spec building with 25 percent office and 75 percent warehouse space. The additional parking necessary for the above-average amount of office space was available because the site layout accommodated a more-efficient double-loaded parking strip and because the lot behind the site was vacant. When a lease was finally signed with the tenant, the existing lot lines accommodated the additional parking, allowing Opus to develop another signature center building on the rear lot.

The floor plan of the building is nearly square, with a semicircular showroom feature on the prime corner, closest to the intersection of Slawin Court and Business Center Drive. The building has two interior loading docks four feet depressed and 65 feet long to allow most semitrailers to be loaded and unloaded while completely inside the building. A drive-in door is at slab-on-grade elevation. The building's roof is a single-ply, rubberized membrane roof (u = 0.07), with a 10-year guarantee.

Surrounding the warehouse area are brick-and-block cavity walls with insulation boards in the cavity. Exterior walls are also brick and block. Half of the exterior walls have windows, and all windows are insulated. Various interior layouts were considered, and the one chosen allows direct light to illuminate 70 percent of the total area.

Ceiling heights were 18 feet clear with stacking racks set, as usual, at five, 10, and 15 feet. If a building is 16 feet clear, the tenant cannot use the top rack. If the clear height is more than 20 feet, the building will require additional fire protection and larger fork-lift trucks.

The Tenant

Opus had a number of offers on the building, but many prospects bid too low because they compared its rents to those of buildings with less distinctive designs; the extra glass and brick gave the building a higher-class image but necessitated extra rent of $1 per square foot. Heidelberg Eastern, Inc., a large distributor of graphic arts equipment and subsidiary of East Asiatic Company from Denmark, signed a 10-year lease shortly after the shell and landscaping were completed.

Development Process Steps for Speculative Building

Identify the client. What does it do? Of what does it consist (number of people and male/female ratio)? What does it require—number of bathrooms, number of conference rooms and private offices, truck access, parking, carpeting, wall coverings?

What are its criteria for making a decision? Does it emphasize office space, showroom, warehouse? What levels of quality for finishes does it anticipate?

Prepare a space plan. The space plan consists of a one-line drawing showing all offices and areas. The client should provide information on the optimum spatial relationships: Should the showroom be next to the front door? Where should offices be in relation to the entrance? Where should the president's office be? What are the relationships between other offices—what types of offices should be next to one another?

Total the construction costs. The tenant has the option to pay for certain tenant improvement costs upfront or to figure the improvement costs with the shell building and land development costs into the rent. Opus's minimum lease has a three-year term, with an average of five to 10 years.

Present the proposal to the client. The proposal includes the one-line drawing, outline specifications (such as wall coverings, HVAC, and electrical), and the lease proposal (including term, rate, time schedule, outline specifications, and proposal drawings).

Negotiate the final lease. To accelerate the process, Opus offers a preconstruction agreement in which the tenant provides a cash deposit that covers design and permit costs. Design drawings are prepared and permits are obtained while lease negotiations are in progress. Construction will not begin until the lease or sale contract is signed without further assurances.

On average, Opus will spend $1,000 to $5,000 before a proposal meeting, depending on the complexity of the deal.

Begin construction. Once the lease is signed and permits are received, construction may begin. Opus markets their skills as a "fast-track" company, able to make changes directly and to accelerate construction. Allowance items (items not spelled out in the contract) include carpeting ($12 to $18 per square yard), wall covering ($1 to $10 per square foot), landscaping, and a lawn sprinkler system. Since the one-line drawing defines each tenant allowance item, extra allowance items are usually unnecessary .

Give the tenant a milepost schedule deadline. This includes a deadline for color selection and outlet location as well as a set date for furniture and telephone ordering. Typical space buildout takes approximately seven to 10 weeks.

■ 625 Slawin Court (Continued)

Heidelberg Eastern was attracted by the distinctive design of the building, which conveyed strength and durability—the same features the company stresses in marketing its printing presses. The building's consistent 18-foot height and curved walls and window lines all fulfilled the showroom needs of the company.

Financing

Construction financing for 625 Slawin Court was provided through Opus's general line of credit. After the building was leased to Heidelberg Eastern, a permanent mortgage was obtained. The interest-only loan was for $1.9 million for five years at 9.5 percent interest.

Experience Gained

- Beware of overdesigning a building. 625 Slawin Court had a wing wall and too many curves and twists that added extra cost. The curved wall cost $20 to $25 per square foot as compared to $15 to $17 for a straight wall. The recessed window wall and amount of glass on the front wall also added to the cost. The market was slow because propects were unwilling to pay for the added cost of certain design features. The same architectural image offered by the building's curved wall probably could have been achieved more efficiently by some other design.
- Design the walls today for the future. Put in lintels and reinforce the block walls in the area of future windows. If a window wall must be added later, $15 per square foot will have to be spent to reinforce the wall just to accommodate the window, whereas the extra cost for reinforcing a masonry or panel wall for future windows is only five cents per square foot.
- Plan ahead for rooftop HVAC equipment. It is advisable to reinforce the structural steel system in certain areas during construction for possible future equipment.

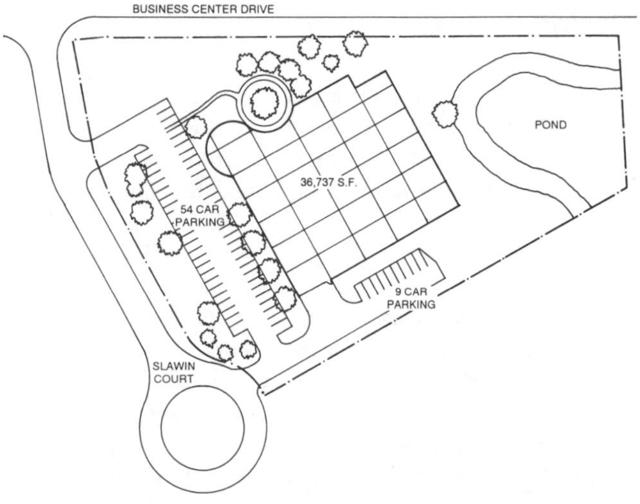

The 36,737-square-foot building—with a floor plan that is almost square—is sited on a cul-de-sac near a pond in the 300-acre Kensington Center business park.

---

forced with steel; dealing with tax reappraisals on existing property and trying to work out mistakes on tax bills can consume enormous amounts of the owner's time; leaking oil tanks on properties several hundred yards away can contaminate groundwater, making it difficult to obtain refinancing on nearby properties; defense contractors insist on four-month escape clauses from leases because they do not know if their contracts with the federal government will be extended. All such concerns demand an increasing amount of attention from developers during the operating phase of the projects.

Selling the Project

Disposition of industrial buildings follows a procedure similar to that for office and retail buildings. A number of features can be emphasized to potential buyers:

- functionality of the building;
- adaptability of the building;
- locational attributes of the site;
- reliability and financial strength of the tenants;
- financial characteristics of the project; and
- future prospects for the project.

Many industrial developers prefer to sell occupied buildings with 10-year leases during their fourth year, just before the rent steps up in the fifth year. Before that time, the rent is often so low that buyers will not pay enough for the building. Generally, buildings start to become profitable only after the first increase in rents.[38]

Although the sales broker will ask for the scheduled commission, commissions are usually negotiable. Typical commissions for properties over $25 million in the Los Angeles area range from 2 to 2.25 percent.[39] For smaller sales above $5 million, the commission usually is higher, 2.25 to 4 percent. Smaller developers probably will have to pay higher commissions in order to obtain the same

- Leave plenty of room for truck maneuvering in loading docks, both inside and outside the building. Local delivery trucks are up to 45 feet long. Trucks with semitrailers for interstate hauling may be up to 70 feet long.
- Make certain that overhead doors will meet the needs of prospective tenants. Overhead doors normally are 14 feet high and 22 feet wide, but some trucks are several inches higher. Depending on the product the client is handling and the slopes of the pavement inside and outside the building, different sizes of doors may be required. Also, outside maneuvering space may be limited, so doors may have to be wider than usual.
- Talk to the tenant about machinery and load requirements before construction. Structural analysis should then be performed to determine the proper thickness of the slab. Adding reinforcement later usually causes problems.

Developer:
Opus North Corporation
9700 Higgins Road, Suite 900
Rosemont, Illinois 60018
(708) 692-4444

Architect:
Opus Architect & Engineers
Rosemont, Illinois

Project Data

Land Use Information:
Site Area: 3.55 acres

Gross Building Area (GBA): 36,737 square feet
Office: 9,184 square feet
Warehouse: 27,553 square feet

Parking Spaces: 63 spaces
Office: 37 spaces (1 per 250 square feet)
Warehouse: 18 spaces (1 per 1,500 square feet)

Ceiling Height: 18 feet
Building Dimensions: 180 feet by 200 feet
Floor/Area Ratio (FAR): 0.24

Economic Information:

Land Costs	$287,000
Site and Shell Construction Costs	$932,975
Tenant Improvement Costs	$605,294
Other Costs	$163,731
Total Development Cost	$1,989,000

Quoted Rent per Square Foot: $5.65 net with 25 percent office finish
Length of Lease: 5 years, with 5-year renewal option and an option to purchase in Year 4

amount of attention from brokers as that given to larger developers who can offer more business.

Mounting concerns over toxic waste and asbestos are making the sale of industrial projects more and more difficult. If the project has any kind of maintenance or fueling facility in which petroleum products or chemicals collect, it probably will have to be cleaned up before a sale can occur. Everyone in the chain of title has liability for cleanup; however, the owner is ultimately responsible. Even though the owner may be able to recover the cleanup costs from the tenant, the cleanup should be done expeditiously.

Conclusion

Successful industrial development depends on three factors: location, tenant control, and cost-effectiveness. The major industrial developers tend to be larger than commercial and office developers because more economies of scale are present in industrial development, especially with regard to tenant control and land control. By controlling major industrial parks, industrial developers can capture a greater percentage of their market than office and commercial developers can.

The emergence of large national firms, such as Trammell Crow Company, will create more competition but will not eliminate the demand for small developers. For small beginning developers, a successful strategy might be to look for markets in which the major developers do not have any special advantage—for example, infill development or smaller, for-sale, single-user buildings. Industrial development has not suffered from as much overbuilding as has office development. Although occupancy rates in most areas have remained 90 percent and above, competition for land has driven prices up to such levels that all-equity yields have fallen below 10 percent in certain tighter markets.

Some possible pitfalls that beginning industrial developers should be wary of are:

- paying too much for land;
- building the wrong product for the market—this mistake can usually be avoided by involving brokers in the development process from the beginning; and
- using an architect who has no experience in the type of product chosen—developers should find someone who can provide a market-oriented, functional design and who knows how to maximize its flexibility.

Industrial development during the 1990s will be influenced by a variety of trends:

- The amount of working capital required will increase.
- Lower current yields will require developers to leave more equity in their projects.
- The entitlement process, which is becoming much more rigorous, will make the cost of improved land much higher—longer approval times will increase carrying costs, and public exactions and development fees will increase service costs.
- After the credit crunch of the early 1990s subsides, finding tenants and suitable land will require more attention than will raising money.
- The use of nonunion contractors will be necessary to hold down costs and maintain competitiveness.
- The need to control tenants will make in-house management increasingly important for incubating future tenants.

The industrial real estate market will continue to reflect strong demand as long as the U.S. manufacturing base continues to revive. Many opportunities for beginning developers to participate will arise; however, they will have to choose their market niches carefully. Major industrial developers arguably have greater competitive advantages over small industrial developers than are found in other product types. They are in a position to respond quickly to market opportunities. Beginning developers will need to know the market well enough to perceive those areas that are inadequately served by their experienced competitors, and they must be ready to pursue those opportunities aggressively.

Notes

1. The process is described in detail in Michael Beyard, *Business and Industrial Park Development Handbook* (Washington, D.C.: ULI–the Urban Land Institute, 1987).

2. See ibid., pp. 16–17.

3. Beyard's *Business and Industrial Park Development Handbook* cites a number of significant industrial parks built in the 1950s in California, New Jersey, Florida, and Illinois. The projects are described in more detail in Robert E. Boley's *Industrial Districts: Principles in Practice*, Technical Bulletin no. 44 (Washington, D.C.: ULI–the Urban Land Institute, 1962).

4. Beyard, *Business and Industrial Park Development Handbook*, pp. 5–11. Other sources for definitions include: National Industrial Zoning Committee, *Planning for Industrial Parks* (Columbus, Ohio: National Industrial Zoning Committee, 1967); Theodore K. Pasma, *Organized Industrial Districts: A Tool for Community Development* (Washington, D.C.: U.S. Department of Commerce, Area Development Division, 1954); and *Proceedings of the National Association of Industrial Parks*, Fourth Annual Seminar and Convention (Arlington, Virginia: National Association of Industrial Parks, 1971).

5. This information taken from an interview with Donald S. Grant, chief executive officer, The O'Donnell Group, Irvine, California, in 1987.

6. Ibid.

7. This list taken from Beyard, *Business and Industrial Park Development Handbook*, chapter 4.

8. Ibid., p. 27.

9. This information taken from an interview with Timothy L. Strader, chairman, The Legacy Companies, Irvine, California, in 1987.

10. This list taken from Beyard, *Business and Industrial Park Development Handbook*, chapter 5, p. 4.

11. From an interview with Allan Kotin in 1988.

12. Ibid.

13. Ibid.

14. This information was taken from an interview with Gerald Katell in 1988.

15. Don Williams, principal, Lestin Dwyer Williams, Houston, Texas, disagrees with the view that office market analysis is driven by the absorption rate. He argues that all development depends on deal making and networking. Overall absorption is less important than cataloging potential tenants by size. For example, in a given city, as many as 50 potential tenants can be identified that have space needs of, say, 40,000 to 50,000 square feet and that have leases that expire within the next two years.

16. Kotin interview, 1988.

17. See Douglas Porter and Lindell Marsh, eds., *Development Agreements* (Washington, D.C.: ULI–the Urban Land Institute, 1989).

18. See Rachelle Levitt and John Kirlin, eds., *Managing Development through Public/Private Negotiations* (Washington, D.C.: ULI–the Urban Land Institute and American Bar Association, 1988).

19. See Beyard, *Business and Industrial Park Development Handbook*, chapter 1.2, pp. 22–24.

20. Much of this advice offered by Donald S. Grant of The O'Donnell Group and Timothy L. Strader of The Legacy Companies.

21. Zoning ordinances usually require three to four spaces per 1,000 square feet of net rentable office area, although most lenders want to see at least four spaces per 1,000 square feet. A simple algebraic equation can be used to calculate the maximum amount of office space if the parking requirement for an office is assumed to be four spaces per 1,000 square feet (one space per 250 square feet) and the parking requirement for warehouse is one space per 500 square feet:

$$\text{Warehouse} + \text{Office} = \text{Total Parking Area}$$

$$\frac{X}{500 \times 350} + \frac{(20{,}000 - X)}{250 \times 230} = 20{,}000 \text{ square feet}$$

X equals the number of square feet of warehouse space, and 20,000 minus *X* equals the number of square feet of office space. Parking spaces consume 350 square feet on average, including drives.

Solving for *X*, calculate *X* equals 11,428 square feet of warehouse, and 20,000 minus *X* equals 8,572 square feet of office. Rounded, a total of 23 parking spaces (11,428 divided by 500) would be needed for the warehouse area and 34 spaces (8,572 divided by 250) for the office area, for a total of 57 spaces.

22. See Beyard, *Business and Industrial Park Development Handbook*, p. 142.

23. This information taken from an interview with Brian W. Courtier, project director, Earl Corporation, Pasadena, California, in 1989.

24. This information taken from interviews with Frank Piatkowski, principal, Frank Piatkowski Real Estate Development, Santa Monica, California, and George Lindbeck, vice president of development, Mat West Company, Van Nuys, California, in 1989.

25. This information was taken from an interview with James Westling in 1988.

26. Courtier interview, 1989.

27. This information taken from an interview with Don Bowers in 1988.

28. This information taken from an interview with James E. Bock in 1988.

29. Ibid.

30. Westling interview, 1989.

31. Katell interview, 1988.

32. This information was taken from an interview with Peter Reich, associate vice president, Coldwell-Banker, Los Angeles, California, in 1988.

33. Katell interview, 1988.

34. Bowers interview, 1988.

35. Reich interview, 1988.

36. Katell interview, 1988.

37. This advice given by Don Bowers in a 1988 interview.

38. This information taken from an interview with Harold Josephson, principal of Josephson Properties, Century City, California, in 1988.

39. Ibid.

Chapter 7

Retail Development

Introduction

Retail development can range from the construction of a single store on a quarter-acre site to the creation of a super regional shopping center covering 100 acres. Typically, beginning developers who work within the retail sector will be involved in the middle range of this spectrum, developing something larger than a single-store building—as such buildings are usually developed and owned by tenants—but smaller than a major regional shopping center.

Shopping centers can be classified in numerous ways—such as size, market served, and shape—but almost all centers fit within the following definition:

> A group of architecturally unified commercial establishments built on a site that is planned, developed, owned, and managed as an operating unit related in its location, size, and type of shops to the trade area that it serves. The unit provides on-site parking in definite relationship to the types and total size of the stores.[1]

A beginning developer usually will be involved in developing a retail project of under 200,000 square feet that serves a convenience, neighborhood, community, or specialty market (as opposed to a regional or super regional market). These small centers are often referred to as "strip centers," as they are often developed in simple linear or L shapes along arterial roads. However, newer centers often involve various shapes and arrangements, and, in fact, because of the increasing competition among small strip centers, standard products and shapes are giving way to more creative concepts, making the development of small centers more challenging and demanding.

Thus, shopping centers are often difficult to categorize. Trade literature often divides centers broadly, into regional malls and strip centers and by size and physical configuration. Considerable variety exists within each of these groups, however, and a more useful way to categorize shopping centers is by the markets that they serve and the types of tenants they contain.

The categories that have become standards in the shopping center industry have evolved over time. The first distinctions drawn were between neighborhood, community, and regional centers. Later additions included convenience centers at the smaller end and super regional centers at the larger end of the spectrum. Each of these has a distinct function, trade area, and tenant mix, as described below.

- Convenience centers are typically 8,000 to 30,000 square feet in size and anchored by a convenience store, usually one that belongs to a national or regional chain. These centers also may include a restaurant, a

Country Club Plaza in Kansas City, Missouri, developed in the 1920s, pioneered many shopping center concepts such as stylized architecture, unified management policies, sign control, and landscaping amenities.

doctor or dentist office, a dry cleaner, a video rental store, and a beauty or barber service.

- Neighborhood centers are typically 30,000 to 100,000 square feet in size and anchored by a supermarket. They usually provide goods for day-to-day living and personal services (such as food, drugs, laundry and drycleaning, hairstyling, and shoe repair).
- Community centers are typically 100,000 to 300,000 square feet and anchored by a discount department store.
- Regional and super regional centers are typically 300,000 to over 1 million square feet and anchored by three or more full-line department stores.
- Specialty centers, in the broadest sense, are those that fail to meet any of the above definitions. For example, tourist-oriented high-end centers such as Ghirardelli Square in San Francisco are a form of specialty center.

The shopping center industry is continually innovating in response to changing markets and the unending desire of developers to identify and serve new niches in the marketplace. New center types, such as power and promotional centers, will continue to stretch existing definitions.

Project Feasibility

Market Analysis

A developer's initial impetus to develop a small shopping center seldom occurs without a basic knowledge of the general market. However, in order to decide whether or not to proceed further and what type of project to build, a more in-depth analysis of the market is required. Unlike industrial or office projects, retail markets are defined by a specific geographic trade area. The trade area for a particular site will depend on demographic characteristics, the street access to the site, and the competition in nearby areas. "A general rule is that the smaller the center, the smaller the market," notes David Nelson of Detroit-based Nelson-Ross Companies.

Market Factors

As with other property types, retail market analysis can be performed in two basic stages: evaluation of the general characteristics of a broad market area to determine its demographic characteristics, the existing retail in the

7-1 Trade Area Analysis for Midtown Promenade

The findings of a customer survey, a customer focus group, previous market analysis completed for Midtown Promenade, and field investigations conducted by Hyett-Palma, Inc., provided data by which to determine both the primary and secondary trade area limits of Midtown Promenade and the demographic characteristics of the trade areas.

Identification of Trade Areas

Primary Trade Area

The primary trade area of Midtown Promenade is bounded by:

- North—Monroe Drive/East Morningside Drive/Johnson Road
- South—Ponce de Leon Avenue/Ponce de Leon Place/MARTA Line
- East—Briarcliff Road/The By Way/East Lake Road
- West—Interstate 75/85 connector

Secondary Trade Area

The secondary trade area of Midtown Promenade is bounded by:

- North—Interstate 85/Lavista Road
- South—Memorial Drive
- East—Clairmont Road/Candler Road
- West—Interstate 75/85 corridor

The secondary trade area includes the area south of Ponce de Leon and the West Dekalb County/Emory/West Decatur areas.

Demographic Characteristics of Trade Areas

Primary Trade Area

Based on the results of the customer survey, approximately 80 percent of the center's customers live within this area.

This area currently is experiencing a significant amount of new commercial and residential development, and a large number of younger, professional people are moving into the area. Based on the results of the CACI [a demographic data service] Siteline report prepared for the primary trade area of the center, the specific characteristics of the customers within this area are as follows:

- The 1987 estimated population of the primary trade area is 32,139, with 19,333 households.
- For 1987, the average family income of those living within the area is $35,510 and is projected to increase to $38,061 by 1992.
- Approximately 60 percent of the households within the area earn over $15,000 per year.
- The median age of those living within the area is 38.7 years, with approximately 62 percent between the ages of 18 and 50.
- Approximately 76 percent of the area residents are white, and 22 percent are black.
- The area contains approximately 53 percent single-person households and 32 percent family households.
- Approximately 86 percent of the area's working residents are employed in white-collar occupations, including executive, professional, technical, sales, clerical, and service jobs.
- Of those residents over the age of 24, approximately 60 percent have attended college, and 37.9 percent hold college degrees.

Secondary Trade Area

The secondary trade area of the center is located primarily to the south and east of the center. This area contains a large amount of older residential and commercial development, but the area is experiencing a significant amount of revitalization, particularly along the west Ponce de Leon corridor and the west North Avenue corridor. The area contains a large number of older households, but younger singles and families are moving into the area at an increasing rate.

Based on the results of the CACI Siteline report prepared for the secondary trade area of the center, the specific characteristics of the customers within this area are as follows:

- The 1987 estimated population of the secondary trade area is 63,430, with 25,007 households.
- For 1987, the average family income of those living within the area is approximately $29,000 and is projected to increase to approximately $32,000 by 1992.
- Approximately 36 percent of the households within the area earn over $15,000 per year.
- The median age of those living within the area is approximately 35 years, with approximately 50 percent between the ages of 18 and 50.
- Approximately 41 percent of the area residents are white, and 57 percent are black.
- The area contains approximately 33 percent single-person households and 54 percent family households.
- Approximately 81 percent of the area's working residents are employed in white-collar occupations, including executive, professional, technical, sales, clerical, and service jobs.
- Of those residents over the age of 24, approximately 34 percent have attended college, and 22 percent hold college degrees.

Source: Hyett-Palma, Inc.

area, any mismatches between supply and demand, and suitable development sites; and evaluation of the specific development potential of a given site. The first stage will produce data and analyses that can be used to identify the most promising market niches and sites; the second stage will scrutinize the actual potential of any identified sites. This second stage involves defining the primary and secondary trade areas, the demographics and buying power of the trade area, and the specific competitors in the trade area.

The boundaries of the trade area are determined by a number of factors, including the type of center, accessibility, physical barriers, location of competing facilities, and the limitations of driving time and distance. The primary trade area for a neighborhood center generally extends around the center about 1.5 miles, or a driving time of five to 10 minutes; for a community center, three to five miles or 10 to 20 minutes is usual.[2] Specialty centers, depending on their size and nature, may be able to draw from a larger trade area.

In defining the trade area, "geographic distance and travel time must be differentiated. The competitive relationships of retail areas largely control the movement of shoppers in an urban area. Distance alone is therefore not a reliable criterion for establishing the extent of the trade area."[3] A map of the area should be used to highlight land uses, population density, competitive facilities and sites, topography, and current and proposed access routes.

After the primary and secondary trade areas have been defined, the following demographic information must be obtained: population breakdowns by age; number of families and households; and per capita, family, and household income. Numerous demographic data services offer detailed breakdowns for specific geographic areas. An illustration of the trade area analysis for Midtown Promenade in Atlanta, Georgia, a neighborhood shopping center with a gross leasable area (GLA) of 110,000 square feet, is presented in feature box 7-1. The project includes an existing center and a proposed Phase II.

The presence of competing retail centers should be mapped and the success or lack of success of the competition closely examined. Maps can be helpful in deciding where new market opportunities may develop. For example, the Fritz Duda Company of Dallas, Texas, has mapped all existing supermarkets in those areas in which it is already operating and in those areas in which it is considering developing supermarket-anchored centers. Some demographic data services also offer a listing of shopping centers for specific trade areas, including anchors and key attributes, although this data should be carefully checked against actual area inspections; a first-hand survey of the competition should always be conducted. In addition to maps, customer surveys are invaluable in determining shopping patterns and potential niches in the marketplace. The assistance of an experienced retail market consultant can be especially helpful in this endeavor. One of the pitfalls that should be guarded against in retail center development is overexpansion in rapidly growing areas. Thus, a survey of the competition should include proposed projects as well as existing ones.

Another example of a market profile, provided in figure 7-2, presents a demographic analysis of the marketplace for a recently completed community shopping center in the Midwest. The data was derived from a demographic trends and income analysis, the local county road commission, and the local township. This project will be used as an example throughout this chapter and will be referred to as Project X.

Market Niches and the Development Concept

The objective of retail market analysis is to find a niche in the market and an appropriate development program to fill that niche.

The market analysis, if positive in its recommendation, should result in the identification of the following kinds of information:

- a superior site for a typical anchored strip center in an emerging area;
- an area that is underserved in terms of the overall amount of retail space or a particular type of center;
- an area in which the competition is weak in terms of the quality of their design, their retail mix, or their marketing and management;
- an anchor tenant that wishes to locate in a particular area; and/or
- a specialty concept appropriate for the area or the site.

The analysis ultimately will suggest the kind of center that would be the most feasible. In addition, "identified market segments may suggest a special character for the proposed center, which would allow it to depart from the traditional neighborhood, community, or regional center tenant mix."[4]

In many cases, the development concept may grow out of a general understanding of the marketplace and actually may precede the formal market analysis. For example, the idea for Market Station—a 50,657-square-foot (GLA) specialty center in Leesburg, Virginia—came about when the developer discovered that the town of Leesburg would be clearing and redeveloping an area containing a turn-of-the-century mill and railroad freight depot. The future partners agreed that new uses and imagination could turn the perceived liabilities into assets. The developers proposed a historic-theme commercial complex, composed of shops, restaurants, and offices, as an extension of the popular downtown historic district

■ 7-2 Project X: Example of Key Demographic Data for a Community Shopping Center[a]

Item	Radius 1-Mile	3-Mile	5-Mile	10-Mile
Population	14,400	72,496	144,519	558,593
Percentage of Population by Age				
0–17 Years	30.9	31.4	29.5	26.3
18–34 Years	31.1	31.1	31.5	30.7
35–64 Years	32.0	31.5	32.1	34.6
65+ Years	6.0	6.0	6.9	8.4
Median Age (Years)	29.4	29.2	29.6	31.1
Families	3,939	19,461	38,090	149,285
Housing Units (Households)	5,008	24,697	48,908	191,281
Per Capita Income ($)	12,720	12,908	12,548	12,024
Average Household Income ($)	36,609	37,836	36,805	34,992
Average Family Income ($)	40,573	41,282	40,155	37,976

Tax Rate for Township: $59.21 per $1,000 of state equalized value (1985)
Main Road Traffic Count: 13,266 cars per day (1982)

[a]All data is for 1984 unless otherwise noted.
Source: A demographic trends and income analysis prepared by Urban Decision Systems, Inc., Los Angeles, California; the Wayne County Road Commission; and the Charter Township of Canton.

of Leesburg. A number of the buildings to be incorporated in the complex were moved to the site from off-site locations.

The developers in this case relied upon their familiarity with the town and the area's market in determining the feasibility of the venture. They sensed that the general area was on the verge of blooming, and developed a creative concept at an appropriate time. Although this approach is not recommended for most cases, it worked here, and the developers agree that the success of the center was a result of both good entrepreneurial insight and luck.

A similar approach was taken at Oakdale Commons, a 12-unit strip center located in Oakdale, New York, on the Mantauk Highway. In this case, however, the project was smaller and more conventional. The project was acquired and the run-down 17,800-square-foot structure was renovated by a group of small retailers looking for new space. The owners formed a general partnership—including seven partners—and bought the center for less than $1 million. The partners then spent about $300,000 to improve the common area and renovate the units.

The biggest problem that the partnership encountered was drawing up the partnership agreement and determining the right tenant mix. The final tenant mix included a realtor's office, a butcher's shop, an attorney's office, and a beauty products/manicure shop, all operated by partners in the project. The remaining tenants included a chain optician, a franchise pizzeria, an auto parts store, a cake and candy shop, and an aerobic fitness center.[5]

These examples prove that although hard market data is critical in determining the feasibility of a project, an intuitive sense of the market and a creative approach are equally important. This fact is especially true of specialty centers, which require a good bit of luck as well as research to achieve success.

An example of how to determine a market niche and development concept is provided in feature box 7-3. The analysis identifies and profiles the primary and secondary customer target group for Midtown Promenade (profiled earlier in feature box 7-1), and presents a concept plan for clustering specific tenant types.

Site Selection

Site locations that may offer attractive market opportunities and niches for small centers include the following:

- newly developing suburban areas;
- jurisdictions in which land use regulations or the political climate have restricted development in recent years, causing the market to become underserved—a developer with special talents or connections may be able to build a project where others could not, but the price may be high;

- older centers that have been undermanaged for years and are in need of updating and renovation—acquisition and renovation could be preferable to new development in this market situation;
- outparcels of existing regional centers;
- close-in suburbs that may be served by centers that are 10 to 20 years old with little new development—such areas may have changed considerably over

■ 7-3 Customer Target Groups for Midtown Promenade

Based on a field investigation by Hyett-Palma, Inc., the findings of a customer survey and focus group, interviews with local real estate and development professionals, the findings of previous market analyses completed for the Ackerman Co., and the results of Acorn Area profile reports prepared by CACI of Fairfax, Virginia, the primary customer target group of Midtown Promenade is described as follows.

Primary Customer Target Group

Midtown Promenade serves a very broad group of customers, best described as an eclectic consumer group. Compared with other portions of the Atlanta metropolitan area, the trade area served by the center contains the greatest diversity of social, racial, ethnic, and income groupings. The trade area is experiencing continuous growth in income, an increasing number of families with children, and a greater number of residents who desire not only the convenience and glamour of an urban lifestyle but also the assortment of goods and services that are found currently only in suburban locations. The consumer within the trade area desires:

- a broad assortment of quality merchandise and services;
- businesses operated with emphasis on customer service and market awareness;
- quality dining and entertainment facilities;
- attractive and aesthetically appealing businesses;
- a broader assortment of artistic and culturally stimulating events and products;
- a cosmopolitan environment;
- facilities to accommodate physical exercise and a health-oriented diet; and
- convenient access via thoroughfares and pedestrian accessways.

The primary target customer group for the center is households that earn over $25,000 per year. (Approximately 40 percent of the households within the primary trade area earn this amount.)

Clustering within Midtown Promenade

The physical arrangements of Midtown Promenade—the separation of the two major portions of the center by the Winn Dixie Store, the change in elevation between the center's existing building space and the new building space, and the visibility of the existing building space to Monroe Drive versus that of the new space—make the creation of both a comparison cluster and a complementary cluster of businesses within Midtown Promenade feasible and desirable.

The complementary cluster should be formed within the existing (Phase I) building space, since this space offers the most exposure to Monroe Drive and will provide more visibility for individual businesses located within the space. Examples of complementary clusters that should be considered for the Phase I space include:

- the clustering of a physical fitness center with sports clothing, casual health-food dining, a dry cleaner, a drugstore, and an upscale grocery store;
- the clustering of a quality sandwich shop, a card and gift shop, a unisex clothing shop, a children's clothing shop, and an athletic equipment/sports clothing shop to encourage browsing; and
- the clustering of an interior design or hardware shop, upscale kitchen or bath shop, bakery, and florist, for a home-oriented focus.

The comparison cluster should be formed within the new (Phase II) building space, since this space will benefit from the customer destination draw of the movie theater, and businesses that appeal to the movie theater's customers can gain potential business through proximity to the theater. Examples of comparison clusters that should be considered for the Phase II space include:

- the clustering of numerous upscale food-related businesses including fine dining, upscale casual dining, champagne/wine bar, upscale cheese delicatessen offering international food items, and upscale specialty retail, such as boutiques offering costume jewelry or fashion-active watches; and
- the clustering of entertainment-related retail services including a specialty bookstore, bicycle shop, athletic clothing, video and electronics shop, and customer-oriented, non-working-hour service businesses such as a travel agency, real estate office, and exercise center.

Source: Hyett-Palma, Inc.

time, and new market opportunities may have been overlooked;
- inner-city areas for which redevelopment funds may be available to help make risky projects acceptable ventures; and
- growing smaller cities in which retail has not yet expanded.

Selecting an appropriate site for a small retail center is critical and will depend on the market analysis described in the previous section and on the developer's objectives and motives. The analysis will initially define the general location and project size necessary to satisfy the desired market and meet the developer's objectives. From this point forward, the site selection process will focus on, and compare, the salient features of various sites.

In terms of marketability, the site should be good enough to preclude any possibility of the development of a similar project in a superior market position. The selected site should not be merely acceptable but the best site available within the market.

The immediate vicinity of the site must be relatively attractive and safe so that shoppers feel secure. On the other hand, if the area is extremely quiet and secure (for instance, if it is adjacent to a residential subdivision), objections may be raised regarding the negative effects of the new shopping center. Walls, solid fences, landscaped berms, or narrow, dense plantings of evergreens can buffer the center's noise and nightlighting, but objections from homeowners may still remain, causing significant problems if the site later needs to be rezoned.

Site Characteristics

Size and shape. Shopping centers can be developed at a range of densities, but the most common configuration for small centers usually involves a one-story building covering 25 percent of the site, or a floor/area ratio (FAR) of 0.25. For this configuration, the site area will need to be approximately four times as large as the gross building area (GBA) of the project. A rule of thumb is to build approximately 10,000 square feet per acre. If the market surrounding the proposed site is expected to grow substantially over succeeding years, the developer may want to acquire a site larger than initially necessary to serve existing market needs and then phase the project or allow for expansion over time. Robert E. Hughes, Jr., of Hughes Real Estate in Greenville, South Carolina, says that some of his firm's most profitable retail developments have come through additions to their existing centers. This also will prevent encroachment from other commercial developments if the project is successful. The downside of this strategy, however, is that the project's initial profitability will be reduced if it is required to cover the carrying cost of a substantial amount of undeveloped land.

The site should be regular and unified in shape and undivided by highways or dedicated streets. Although the term "strip center" connotes a long, narrow site, this is not always the case. A square site with an L-shaped center that wraps around a parking lot is often a preferable shape; if the site is rectangular, its length should usually not exceed more than twice its width. Triangular sites also may be suitable, especially if they are surrounded by major arterials and provide good access from numerous directions.

If a triangular or irregularly shaped site is used, the best solution may be to develop freestanding facilities on the odd portions of the site. For example, Aliso Viejo Plaza in Orange County, California, has been developed on a triangular site surrounded by major arterials on two sides and a freeway on the third (see opposite). The developer chose, in this case, to align the main part of the center with its back to the freeway and then to develop the odd corner as outparcels for fast-food restaurants, convenience facilities, banks, or auto centers.

Accessibility and visibility. These factors are critical in the retail site selection process. Key measures of accessibility are the nature of the roads serving the site and the traffic count on those roads. Any shopping center site should be accessible from numerous directions, and the larger the market to be served, the more important this becomes. Thus, close proximity to major intersections is a major advantage for any site. The volume of traffic that actually passes by the site is also critical, as is the site's orientation to the principal road serving the site.

However, proximity to major roads and a high traffic count alone will not guarantee good access. If a site is not easy to enter and safe to leave, it must have the potential to be made so. Traffic should flow freely as it approaches and enters the site. Cars moving into or out of a center can create bottlenecks at entrances or backups on major traffic routes. Designing or redesigning traffic flow at entrances to centers requires the cooperation both of traffic engineers and of local highway departments. If a road cannot carry the additional traffic and turning movements generated by the center, the cost of necessary improvements and the question of who pays the cost—the highway construction authorities, developers, or both—must be investigated. Developers of large shopping center projects often can afford to cover major road improvement costs, but developers of smaller centers are less likely to be in this favorable financial position.

Good visibility improves a center's accessibility. Shoppers driving at local traffic speeds can easily overshoot the parking area entrance if they cannot see the center from the road. Even though traffic flow attracts retail business, a site that fronts on a highway with many competing

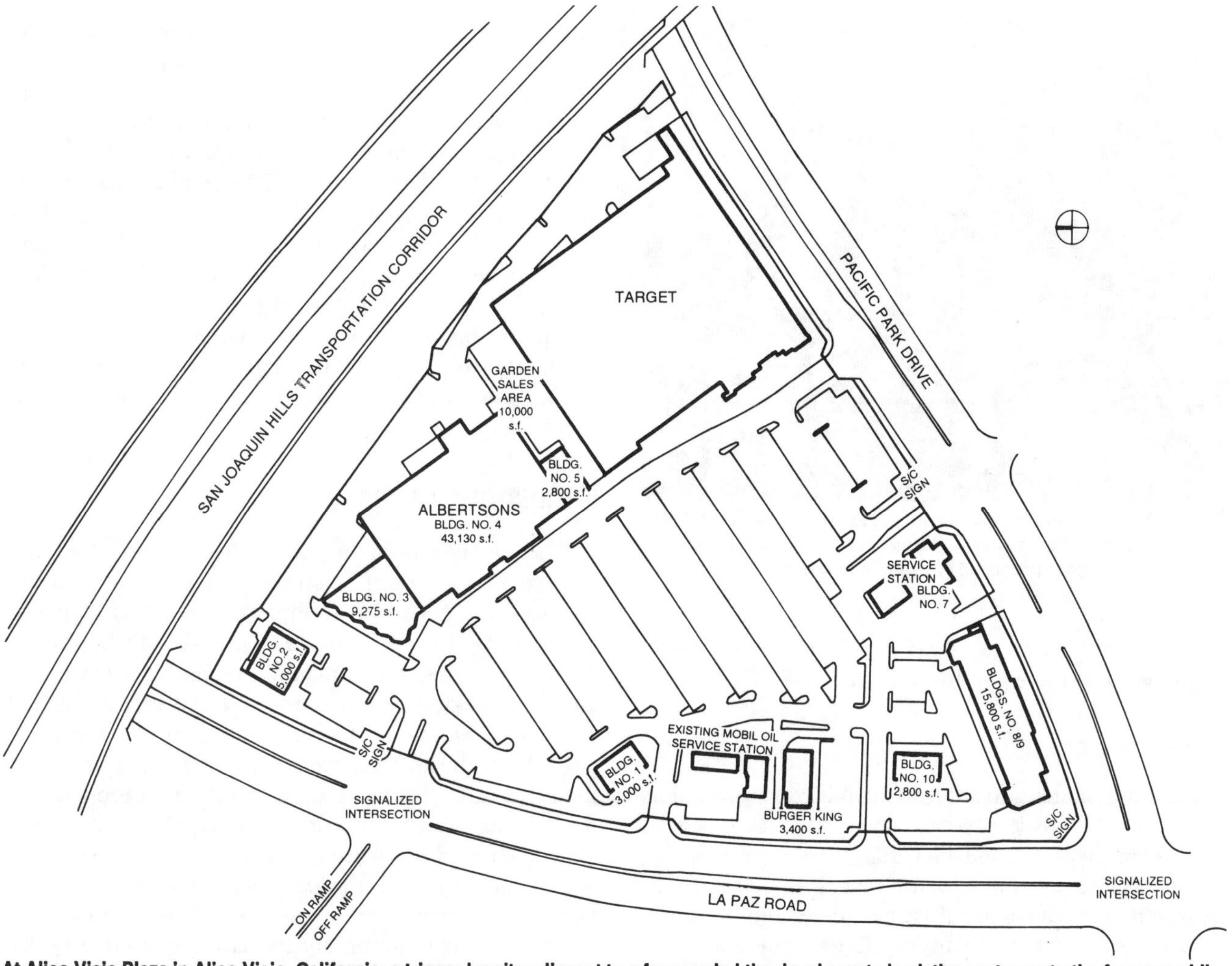

At Aliso Viejo Plaza in Aliso Viejo, California, a triangular site adjacent to a freeway led the developer to back the center up to the freeway while developing the odd corner with freestanding buildings.

distractions (including not only other retail but also signs) can be less accessible and desirable than a site on a less heavily traveled arterial.

Site Conditions

Because shopping centers usually are very horizontal in nature and cover a large footprint, a flat or gently sloping site is preferable. More steeply sloping sites can be adapted for shopping centers, but this may entail higher site improvement costs and lower operational efficiency. For example, the Renaissance Center West in Las Vegas, Nevada, was built on a 16.5-acre site with a 30-foot change in level from one corner to the other. Some 100,000 cubic yards of soil had to be moved to grade the parcel, incurring a cost of nearly $1 million (in 1981 dollars) for grading alone, and making it necessary for the developer to construct a large retaining wall on the western side of the property.

Sites that stand on solid rock or have a high water table should be avoided. "Shifting sand in many layers beneath the surface will also promote problems," notes Mary Alice Hines, author of *Shopping Center Development and Investment*. "In sandy areas, concrete caissons may have to encase foundation materials and retaining walls may have to be constructed to hold back the soft matter until the foundations are completed and the building construction above ground started."[6] The soil's absorptive capacity also should be considered, as this will affect stormwater management later on.

In some cases, topographical and soil problems can be overcome if compensation for the costs incurred is provided in terms of lower land costs or public subsidies. An example is Market Station in Leesburg, Virginia (mentioned earlier), which was built on a floodplain that affected half the site. To resolve this problem, the developers rechanneled the flooding, built the structures higher,

Fashion Square in Tampa, Florida, was developed on a site that was more than 25 percent wetlands. The plan turned this wetland into an asset that included the creation of a geyser fountain.

and added a series of raised wooden decks to connect the buildings and create pedestrian areas.

Site Acquisition

After a desirable site has been identified in terms of its physical characteristics, the developer must follow the steps outlined in chapters 3 and 4 regarding site acquisition.

One site acquisition scenario that is especially pertinent to retail involves acquisition of an existing center in need of renovation or expansion. To determine whether or not to acquire an existing center, its operation must be analyzed. Factors to consider include the center's tenant mix and lease terms, the sales performance of individual tenants, the center's market share, the existing management, the availability of land for expansion, and the appropriateness of the center's current positioning within the market. In acquiring a small center for renovation, the key factors to look for are an outdated appearance, "tired" management that has not kept up with local market changes, or changing local demographics that suggest a new marketing approach. (Because the demographics of surrounding areas can change substantially over the course of years, the existing management may be failing to capture a reasonable market share.)

Opportunities for renovation may even include acquisition of streetfront retail buildings, such as Tanner Market in Pasadena, California (see the case study at the end of this chapter).

Regulatory Issues

The zoning provisions and public approvals required to develop a site must be studied carefully before a site is purchased. According to Phillip R. Hughes of Hughes Real Estate, Inc., Greenville, South Carolina: "Zoning should be verified by the planning commission in writing, and the developer should never rely on wall maps, verbal assurances, etcetera." An early study should explore the attitudes of the local residents, the city's zoning staff, and the approval body toward a shopping center proposal. In many cases, the site proposed for a shopping center is not zoned for commercial use when the development process begins, and, in others, the existing ordinance may have to be modified concerning provisions such as FAR, building height, parking requirements, lot coverage, and setbacks. A developer who is considering a project that is not consistent with the provisions of an ordinance should examine the specific "avenues of relief" that are delineated in the ordinance. Each of these avenues requires an

7-4 Site Selection: Project X Example

Project X occupies an approximately 11-acre site that is located in a mostly single-family detached residential area and stands at the intersection of an arterial (carrying 13,266 cars per day) and a secondary road. Most of the center faces on to the secondary road. The area is situated within a large metropolitan area at the western edge of the metropolitan area's western growth corridor—one of the fastest-growing areas in the state.

Besides being one of the metropolitan area's major bedroom communities, the area has attracted a significant amount of heavy and light manufacturing and has recently become a major warehouse district. The industrial base and the area's easy access to the freeway system have attracted families from all economic strata; the area's average family income exceeds $40,000 per annum, but the area offers a wide range of housing for sale from $85,000 to over $200,000 as well as a variety of rental apartments and townhouses with rents from $450 to over $800 per month.

As part of the site selection process, the developer secured aerial photographs, economic, demographic, and retail surveys, and an arterial road analysis of the area. On the basis of these data, the developer concluded that the site was well suited for a shopping center of the size and quality that the developer wished to build. However, the developer also concluded that the road system in the area needed to be improved to avoid future mobility problems, especially along the secondary road serving the nearest residential areas.

application and approval process. The regulatory process is dealt with in greater detail in chapter 3.

Among the special regulatory concerns in shopping center development are the probable impacts that the project will have— in terms of traffic generation, compatibility with surrounding uses, environmental effects of runoff, and, in some cases, effects on downtown retailing. Historically, developers have found that the specific standards included in the ordinances for commercial zones are difficult to meet and frequently require variances or special exceptions.

In many cities in which strip retail centers are proliferating or are expected to proliferate, strict guidelines are being implemented to control design. For example, in Plano, Texas, the city decided that design guidelines should be established to provide a standardized process for the review of zoning and development requests for strip centers. In 1985, notes Margaret Doyle in *Building, Design & Construction* magazine, the Plano city council approved a retail-corner design guidelines publication and a set of rear-building-facade design guidelines that were subsequently incorporated into the retail-corner guidelines. Previously, design issues were discussed and reviewed with little or no guidance from the zoning ordinance; the guidelines now allow the city to detail explicit objectives. The guidelines encompass 10 design considerations, ranging from "building elements" to "circulation and parking," and include a concise summary of the issues and a list of several planning and design recommendations. These summaries are accompanied by simple illustrations.[7]

If guidelines such as these are not available, developers may want to consult with local planning staff and officials to determine the desired design objectives, especially in jurisdictions in which development proposals are closely scrutinized and often rejected. In many situations, appropriate design requires selecting an architectural style that complements the surroundings; unlike large regional malls, strip centers are considerably more adaptable to their surroundings. Regardless of the situation, good planning and design is always an asset in obtaining project approval, in leasing the center to tenants, and in drawing customers. Because approval times and costs have soared in recent years, developers should be aware that the more effort they expend on good design, the less likely local officials will be to impose excessive demands.

Although local governments are generally seeking to control development, in some cases, the public sector will seek to induce development in order to revitalize blighted neighborhoods. These situations can provide very attractive regulatory environments. For example, Hopkins Development in Southern California has developed nearly 70 convenience and neighborhood centers in association with local redevelopment agencies.[8] Although development under such conditions may be riskier because of the market areas to be served, the cooperation of the public sector can be extremely valuable in enhancing the development's prospects for success.

Financial Feasibility

The actual financial feasibility of a shopping center can be determined only after a specific program has been defined for a specific site, thus allowing the developer to estimate accurately the development costs and operating revenues. (The generic aspects of the financial analysis process are discussed in greater depth in chapter 4.)

The developer should keep in mind that final projections of income must be based on a leasing plan that represents the developer's estimate of the amounts of space to be leased to specific tenant types. Thus, the allocation of space to the various types of tenants is a critical component of the financial feasibility analysis. Preliminary analyses are likely to be less specific, however.

Estimating shopping center revenues is unlike estimating revenues for other income properties. First, the rental rates will vary substantially, depending upon the type of tenant in the space. Second, the revenues will usually be tied to overall sales performance; most shopping center tenant leases include percentage rents, allowing the developer to capture additional rent above the base rent after sales have reached a certain level. (Percentage rents are discussed more fully in a later section in this chapter on marketing and leasing.)

Some developers believe that percentage rents and overages should be excluded from the initial analyses of financial feasibility. Philip E. Klein, in his *Feasibility of Shopping Center Development, Shopping Center Report*, states that:

> While overage income can hardly be discounted, the prudent entrepreneur should first measure the adequacy of the contracted income or economic benefits, in the form of minimum rents, as contrasted to the investment requirements and related risks. Only after the investor is satisfied in this regard should he apply to the figures a positive factor predicated on the likelihood of his tenants achieving "overage" levels of sales in the foreseeable future.[9]

ULI–the Urban Land Institute publishes numerous benchmark publications—providing operating performance figures for shopping centers of various types—that can be helpful in the financial analysis process. For example, figures 7-5 through 7-7 provide operating results for a sampling of convenience centers, neighborhood centers, and community centers for FY 1989. (Note that the sales per square foot, the total operating receipts, the total operating expenses, and the net operating bal-

7-5 U.S. Community Shopping Centers: Base Data, Tenant Data, and Operating Results[a]

Number of centers in sample: 265

	Average	Median	Lower Decile	Upper Decile	Median	Lower Decile	Upper Decile	Number Reporting
Base Data		**Area in Square Feet**						
Center Size (Total Occupancy Area)	186,005	161,162	105,816	275,508				265
Tenant Data		**Area in Square Feet**						
Gross Leasable Area (GLA)	164,723	150,529	93,220	256,102				265
		Dollars per Square Foot of GLA						
Tenant Sales	$176.33	$162.43	$85.59	$278.39				244
Operating Results		**Dollars per Square Foot of GLA**				**Percent of Total Receipts**		
Operating Receipts								
Rental Income—Minimum	$5.66	$4.87	$2.76	$ 9.11	79.35%	61.28%	91.62%	265
Rental Income—Overages	0.59	0.33	0.03	1.28	5.05	0.51	20.66	213
Total Rent	6.14	5.14	3.07	9.74	85.55	70.72	95.45	265
Common Area Charges	0.70	0.39	0.11	1.48	5.93	2.34	14.39	253
Property Taxes	0.51	0.32	0.06	1.02	5.17	1.10	11.65	234
Insurance	0.22	0.06	0.01	0.23	0.80	0.19	2.77	182
Other Escalation Charges	0.19	0.05	0.01	0.53	0.77	0.27	4.54	64
Income from Sale of Utilities	0.29	0.06	0.01	0.66	0.78	0.12	8.75	67
Total Other Charges	0.79	0.44	0.08	1.40	6.80	1.50	15.76	243
Miscellaneous Income	0.13	0.04	0.00	0.28	0.51	0.06	2.89	162
Total Operating Receipts	$7.60	$6.05	$3.52	$12.37				265
Operating Expenses								
Building Maintenance	$0.18	$0.09	$0.01	$0.39	1.51	0.22	5.63	245
Parking Lot, Mall, and Other Common Areas	0.59	0.38	0.13	1.22	6.39	2.37	14.64	259
Central Utility Systems	0.27	0.11	0.02	0.71	1.85	0.46	10.02	83
Office Area Services	0.11	0.05	0.01	0.26	0.74	0.08	3.34	43
Total Maintenance and Housekeeping	0.85	0.57	0.20	1.85	9.28	4.01	20.07	264
Advertising and Promotion	0.15	0.05	0.01	0.32	0.70	0.09	4.12	192
Real Estate Taxes	0.67	0.51	0.21	1.21	8.28	3.82	15.96	264
Insurance	0.16	0.14	0.04	0.32	2.06	0.77	4.33	263
General and Administrative	0.72	0.43	0.17	1.28	6.71	3.04	17.32	258
Management Agent Fees	0.31	0.25	0.12	0.59	4.16	2.27	6.19	212
Leasing Agent Fees	0.15	0.09	0.01	0.38	1.40	0.16	5.97	122
Total Operating Expenses	$2.48	$1.93	$0.91	$4.26	29.89	16.53	52.40	265
Net Operating Balance	$5.12	$4.24	$1.93	$ 8.50	70.11%	47.60%	83.47%	265

[a]Because data are means, medians, and deciles, detail amounts do not add to totals. No median figures are shown if fewer than five values were reported for any income or expense category, and no lower and upper decile amounts are shown if fewer than 10 values were reported.

Source: ULI–the Urban Land Institute, *Dollars & Cents of Shopping Centers: 1990* (Washington, D.C.: ULI–the Urban Land Institute, 1990), p. 121.

ance vary considerably among these three shopping center types.)

One approach to financial feasibility for a shopping center is illustrated in the Project X example. The program called for the following key elements:

- Building area (GBA) of 117,486 square feet (broken down into 42,352 square feet for a supermarket, 12,000 square feet for a hardware store, 10,920 square feet for a drugstore, 49,694 square feet of specialty retail, and 2,520 square feet as a pad site for a bank).
- Landscaped area of 41,243 square feet.
- Drives, walkways, and parking for 630 cars occupying 314,768 square feet.

The development costs for the above, estimated at $8,130,580, are broken down, in feature box 7-8, into construction and nonconstruction costs. This is followed by a revenue and operating income analysis.

Projected revenues yield three key totals: total gross income, gross operating income, and net operating income. The financing assumptions presented here will be

■ 7-6 U.S. Neighborhood Shopping Centers: Base Data, Tenant Data, and Operating Results[a]

Number of centers in sample: 271	Average	Median	Lower Decile	Upper Decile	Median	Lower Decile	Upper Decile	Number Reporting
Base Data		**Area in Square Feet**						
Center Size (Total Occupancy Area)	66,854	67,763	38,117	94,628				271
Tenant Data		**Area in Square Feet**						
Gross Leasable Area (GLA)	64,228	64,760	35,054	94,035				271
		Dollars per Square Foot of GLA						
Tenant Sales	$199.37	$181.07	$69.85	$329.49				210
Operating Results		**Dollars per Square Foot of GLA**				**Percent of Total Receipts**		
Operating Receipts								
Rental Income—Minimum	$ 6.49	$ 5.69	$ 2.67	$10.21	82.13%	64.31%	93.42%	271
Rental Income—Overages	0.71	0.34	0.03	1.69	4.99	0.44	18.03	154
Total Rent	6.89	6.30	2.94	11.09	86.90	71.43	95.06	271
Common Area Charges	0.65	0.41	0.08	1.39	5.36	1.92	12.70	255
Property Taxes	0.64	0.45	0.09	1.24	6.24	1.79	13.67	232
Insurance	0.12	0.08	0.02	0.26	1.08	0.30	3.02	181
Other Escalation Charges	0.28	0.17	0.01	0.67	1.26	0.16	6.82	21
Income from Sale of Utilities	0.20	0.10	0.00	0.33	1.18	0.07	4.78	61
Total Other Charges	0.80	0.58	0.11	1.66	7.81	2.48	16.50	237
Miscellaneous Income	0.15	0.04	0.00	0.29	0.48	0.06	3.19	157
Total Operating Receipts	$8.29	$7.63	$3.36	$13.55				271
Operating Expenses								
Building Maintenance	$0.33	$0.14	$0.02	$0.62	1.94	0.34	8.71	234
Parking Lot, Mall, and Other Common Areas	0.59	0.43	0.11	1.13	5.63	2.02	12.29	257
Central Utility Systems	0.23	0.13	0.02	0.40	1.70	0.37	5.06	78
Office Area Services	0.27	0.08	0.01	0.50	0.81	0.19	5.14	35
Total Maintenance and Housekeeping	0.96	0.66	0.22	1.70	8.41	4.00	20.58	267
Advertising and Promotion	0.19	0.05	0.00	0.24	0.62	0.07	2.70	160
Real Estate Taxes	0.79	0.67	0.18	1.54	8.73	3.99	17.04	260
Insurance	0.19	0.14	0.06	0.36	2.13	0.80	5.21	256
General and Administrative	0.91	0.48	0.15	1.44	6.62	2.30	17.24	258
Management Agent Fees	0.34	0.30	0.13	0.61	4.06	2.18	6.44	196
Leasing Agent Fees	0.20	0.11	0.01	0.51	1.67	0.19	6.33	127
Total Operating Expenses	$2.86	$2.27	$0.79	$4.87	28.10	16.81	53.08	271
Net Operating Balance	$5.43	$ 5.01	$1.61	$ 9.79	72.13%	47.02%	83.53%	271

[a]Because data are means, medians, and deciles, the individual amounts in columns do not add to totals. No median figures are shown if fewer than five values were reported for any income or expense category, and no lower and upper decile amounts are shown if fewer than 10 values were reported.

Source: ULI–the Urban Land Institute, *Dollars & Cents of Shopping Centers: 1990* (Washington, D.C.: ULI–the Urban Land Institute, 1990), p. 171.

discussed at greater length in the financing section of this chapter. (A discussion of cash flow over time has been presented in other chapters of this book.)

Design and Construction

As beginning developers team up with experienced and qualified professionals, they should be aware that no professional will play a more important role in the development process than will the architect. Because of the special requirements of shopping centers, an architect with experience in this area is highly recommended. A typical architect deal for a shopping center, explains Donald J. Howard of the Fritz Duda Company, involves the cost of initial time and materials needed to prepare the elevation study and undertake site plan work, with a price range of between $50 and $100 per hour. When the type of building has been established, payment can be either in the form of a lump sum or in dollars per square foot, say $1 to $1.30 per square foot for a supermarket.

■7-7 U.S. Convenience Shopping Centers: Base Data, Tenant Data, and Operating Results[a]

Number of centers in sample: 66

	Average	Lower Median	Upper Decile	Decile	Lower Median	Upper Decile	Number Decile	Reporting
Base Data		**Area in Square Feet**						
Center Size (Total Occupancy Area)	22,445	18,984	10,195	29,383				66
Tenant Data		**Area in Square Feet**						
Gross Leasable Area (GLA)	18,774	18,556	8,949	28,743				66
		Dollars per Square Foot of GLA						
Tenant Sales	$143.32	$140.24	$52.86	$227.34				27
Operating Results		**Dollars per Square Foot of GLA**				**Percent of Total Receipts**		
Operating Receipts								
Rental Income—Minimum	$10.48	$ 9.25	$4.54	$12.81	87.42%	T72.36%	100.00%	66
Rental Income—Overages	0.38	0.18	0.05	0.86	1.97	0.43	5.95	17
Total Rent	10.58	9.58	4.54	12.81	90.30	73.62	100.00	66
Common Area Charges	0.59	0.41	0.12	1.19	4.22	1.84	10.83	47
Property Taxes	0.86	0.60	0.12	1.67	5.37	1.37	13.16	50
Insurance	0.22	0.12	0.04	0.36	1.24	0.37	3.37	41
Other Escalation Charges	0.37	0.11	0.01	1.48	0.90	0.18	6.03	12
Income from Sale of Utilities	0.21	0.21			1.58			6
Total Other Charges	1.13	0.83	0.11	2.54	7.44	2.45	17.01	51
Miscellaneous Income	1.71	0.09	0.02	3.34	1.54	0.15	12.77	19
Total Operating Receipts	$12.36	$11.29	$4.68	$15.03	n/a	n/a	n/a	66
Operating Expenses								
Building Maintenance	$0.36	$0.17	$0.06	$0.63	1.64	0.50	10.11	55
Parking Lot, Mall, and Other Common Areas	0.77	0.44	0.15	1.33	4.93	1.60	10.32	56
Central Utility Systems	1.78	0.30	0.06	4.57	2.60	0.84	14.81	18
Office Area Services	0.18	0.14			1.81			5
Total Maintenance and Housekeeping	1.55	0.78	0.21	1.83	8.21	1.75	19.88	62
Advertising and Promotion	0.09	0.03	0.01	0.27	0.43	0.06	2.81	25
Real Estate Taxes	1.36	0.96	0.31	2.33	9.72	4.11	18.75	61
Insurance	0.31	0.21	0.11	0.41	2.26	0.98	5.06	60
General and Administrative	0.87	0.57	0.16	1.75	5.39	1.81	15.49	57
Management Agent Fees	0.64	0.50	0.17	0.76	4.74	2.46	8.63	38
Leasing Agent Fees	0.31	0.19	0.05	0.58	2.39	0.48	5.69	22
Total Operating Expenses	$3.78	$2.58	$0.97	$5.73	27.67	12.17	47.01	66
Net Operating Balance	$ 8.58	$ 7.94	$2.95	$12.57	72.33%	52.99%	87.83%	66

[a]Because data are means, medians, and deciles, the individual amounts in columns do not add to totals. No median figures are shown if fewer than five values were reported for any income or expense category, and no lower and upper decile amounts are shown if fewer than 10 values were reported.

Source: ULI–the Urban Land Institute, *Dollars & Cents of Shopping Centers: 1990* (Washington, D.C.: ULI–the Urban Land Institute, 1990), p. 9.

These prices would include project plans and specifications (specs) and the architect's review of the contractor's work to ensure that plans are followed.

The design process will pass through numerous iterations to determine the best layout and configuration, optimal access, and optional financial performance. With experience, a developer can take more control of layout, but a beginning developer should look to an experienced shopping center architect for substantial input on the first project.

Site Plan and Building Configuration

More than for most other project types, site planning and configuration are critical to the success of small shopping centers. Shopping centers are used by more people each day than any other type of real estate project and must be designed to attract and accommodate large volumes of traffic. In most centers, the entire site is put to some functional use (buildings, parking, circulation, deliveries), and the entire site plan must be orchestrated carefully to optimize the attractiveness and accessibility of every store in the center.

Strip Centers

The configuration of traditional strip centers is largely dependent on three factors: the shape of the site, the surrounding roadways, and the anchor tenants. Most strip centers are configured in some variation on one of four general shapes: linear, L-shaped, U-shaped, or Z-shaped. The major reasons for using the L, U, or Z shapes are to restrict the length of the center, create greater visibility for the tenants, and make the center more walkable.

The linear arrangement is best suited for small strip centers and is most commonly applied to the neighborhood center. "The most successful configuration places two major units, usually a supermarket and a drugstore, at the ends of the center. A linear center is generally the least expensive structure to build and is easily adapted to most siteconditions."[10] Linear centers typically range from 500 to 1,000 feet in length, including anchor tenants.

An example of a linear center is presented on page 322. Laguna Niguel Plaza is an 88,239-square-foot neighborhood center in Laguna Niguel, California. The project is located on a rectangular site, and the plan includes a supermarket anchor at one end and a second, smaller anchor dividing a series of small retail shops. Several outparcels are also included.

Hancock Plaza in Phoenix, Arizona, is a good example of an L-shaped center. This 100,000-square-foot neighborhood center is located on a relatively square 11.7-acre site. As is evident from the figure top left of page 323, a linear configuration would not make full use of the site and would provide too much parking. This plan also illustrates a creative use for the space in the corner, which is a standard problem with L-shaped centers. In this case, a preschool and playyard were placed in this space. Daycare centers are also suitable choices.

■ 7-8 Financial Feasibility: Project X Example

Breakdown of Development Costs

Item	Cost per Square Foot of GBA	Total Costs
Construction Costs[a]		
Building		
Supermarket	$40.00	$1,694,080
Hardware	37.00	444,000
Drugstore	37.00	404,040
Specialty Retailers	38.00	1,888,372
Land Development	7.35	845,000
Off-Site Roads	6.00	689,796
Subtotal	$51.86	$5,965,288
Contingency Reserve	1.25	143,708
Total Construction Costs	$53.11	$6,108,996
Nonconstruction Costs[b]		
Land	$3.48	$399,721
Permits and Fees	.69	79,671
General Conditions	2.02	232,500
Other Fees and Expenses		
Closing Costs and Miscellaneous	.20	22,697
Architect and Engineers[c]	1.97	226,890
Appraisal	.05	5,500
Professional Fees	1.03	118,694
Insurance	.23	27,000
Marketing[d]	.84	96,000
Real Estate Taxes	.13	14,800
Construction Loan Fee	1.02	117,000
Interest Reserve	6.05	695,000
Permanent Loan Fee	1.19	136,980
Total Nonconstruction Costs	$19.36	$2,172,453
Total Costs	$72.47	$8,130,580

■ 7-8 (Continued)

Cash-Flow Analysis and Financing

Gross Income[e]		
Supermarket (42,352 @ $7.50 per Square Foot)	$317,640	
Hardware (12,000 @ $7.50 per Square Foot)	90,000	
Drugstore (10,920 @ $8.50 per Square Foot)	92,820	
Specialty Retail (49,694 @ $12.50 per Square Foot)	621,175	
Bank Pad (2,520 @ $13.89 per Square Foot)	35,003	
Total Gross Income (114,705 @ $9.90 per Square Foot)		$1,156,638
Less		
Vacancy (5% of Specialty Retail)	$31,059	
Management Fee (5% of Gross Income)	57,832	
Maintenance Reserve	11,566	
Total Operating Expenses		$100,457
Gross Operating Income		$1,056,181
Proposed Loan Data		
Coverage	1.15	
Mortgage Rate	9.25%	
Amortization Term	30 years	
Permanent Mortgage Term	5/5 years	
Mortgage Constant (Principal Plus Interest Loan)	9.87	
Mortgage Amount (Principal Plus Interest Loan)	$9,305,147	
Mortgage Amount (Interest-Only Loan)	$9,928,846	
Annual Debt Service		$918,418
Net Operating Income		$137,763
Based on the above analysis, the developer is requesting an interest-only loan of:		$9,928,800
If the lender will not grant an interest-only loan, and the loan is based on a repayment of principal and interest, the loan request is:		$9,305,100

[a]Construction costs are based on the GBA of each major and specialty retailer plus the preparation of the bank pad.

Store	Area in Square Feet
Supermarket	42,352
Hardware	12,000
Drugstore	10,920
Specialty Retail	49,694
Pad Site for Bank	2,520
Total	117,486

[b]Land cost per square foot is based on the GBA, including the bank pad.
[c]This category includes fees for the architect, civil engineer, surveyor, soils engineer, and other construction and design consultants.
[d]The marketing expense (calculated at the rate of $1.84 per square foot of leasable area) is based on the 49,694 square feet of specialty retail and the 2,520-square-foot bank pad.
[e]Based on initial base rather than averaged lease rates.

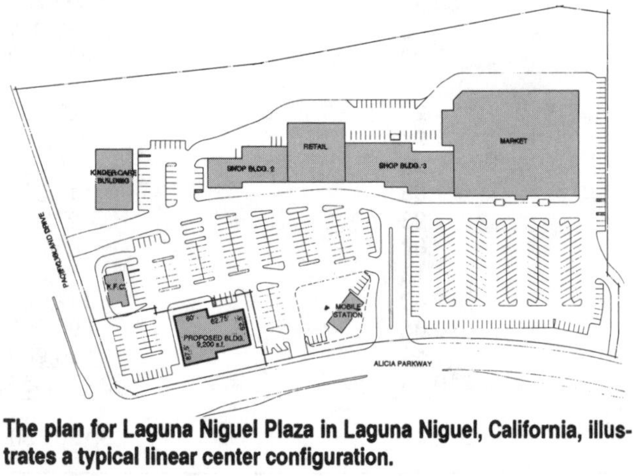

The plan for Laguna Niguel Plaza in Laguna Niguel, California, illustrates a typical linear center configuration.

Mission Viejo Commerce Center in Mission Viejo, California, offers an example of a U-shaped center. The 36,233-square-foot car care service and specialty retail center consists of three buildings of which 13,556 square feet is for service retail and the remainder for car care (see bottom left of facing page).

An example of a Z-shaped site, which allows the center to present three separate facades and often is used on irregularly shaped sites, is Pacific Plaza in Pacific Beach, California, laid out on a 12.75-acre site (see top right of facing page). This community center includes 126,911 square feet of renovated space and 69,489 square feet of new space. The second phase was built on a parcel that was half as deep as the first parcel, creating an irregular shape overall that led to the Z shape. One of the advan-

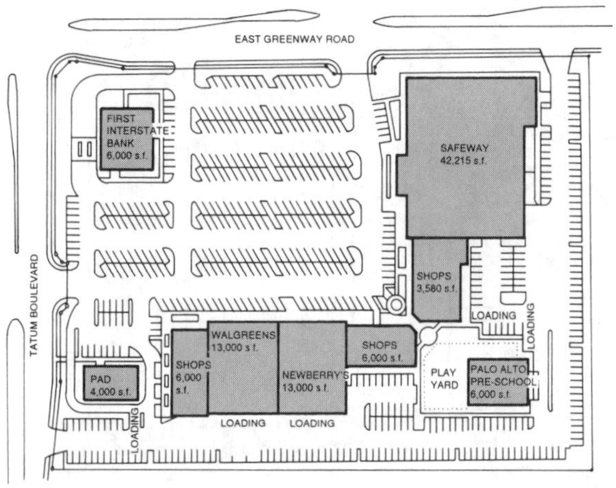

Hancock Plaza in Phoenix, Arizona, exemplifies a typical L-shaped shopping center configuration.

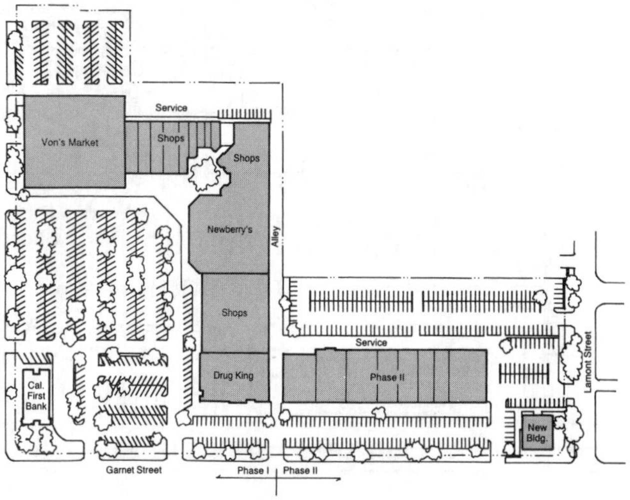

Pacific Plaza site plan shows a Z-shaped center.

tages of this configuration is that it brings some of the storefronts closer to the street and increases the center's overall visibility.

Although parking is usually placed at the front of strip centers to allow for ease of access, some centers use different configurations. For example, Wheatley Plaza in Greenvale, New York, is an L-shaped center, but it deviates from the normal pattern because its parking spaces are on the interior of the lot, and the stores themselves line the adjacent streets (see below). This allows for, and indeed requires, store frontages on both the exterior and the interior. This configuration was used for three reasons. First, it accommodated the city's desire to buffer the center from the surrounding housing—the landscaping and parking serves as the buffer. Second, it prevents parking from becoming a major focus of the suburban streetscape, a problem encountered in many suburban communities. Third, it brought shop windows closer to passing traffic, giving stores better visibility, thereby attracting more business. The drawbacks of this configuration were that the need for a dual facade raised construction costs and that major design challenges were created concerning truck access and delivery. In spite of the challenges, city planners and the architecture profession often favor the placement of buildings along the street rather than set back behind a sea of parking. Especially in contentious urban projects, developers may find support from architects and community groups for designs that enhance the city's streetscape. At the same time, however, they must ensure that tenants will accept parking that is not immediately accessible.

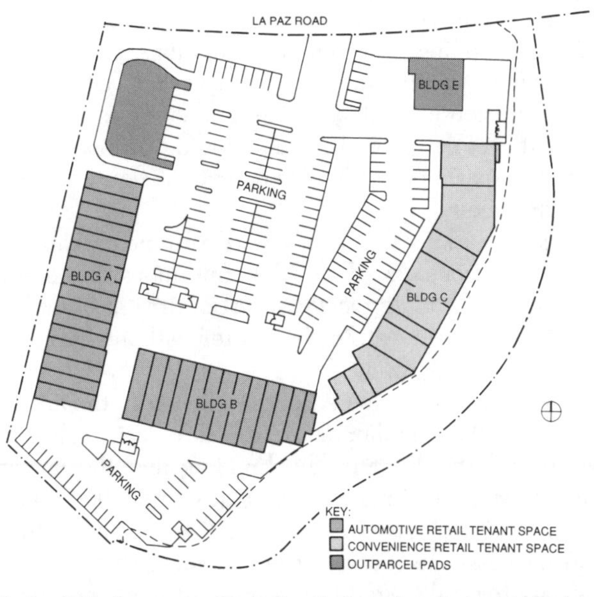

Mission Viejo Commerce Center is a U-shaped center targeted primarily at the car care service market.

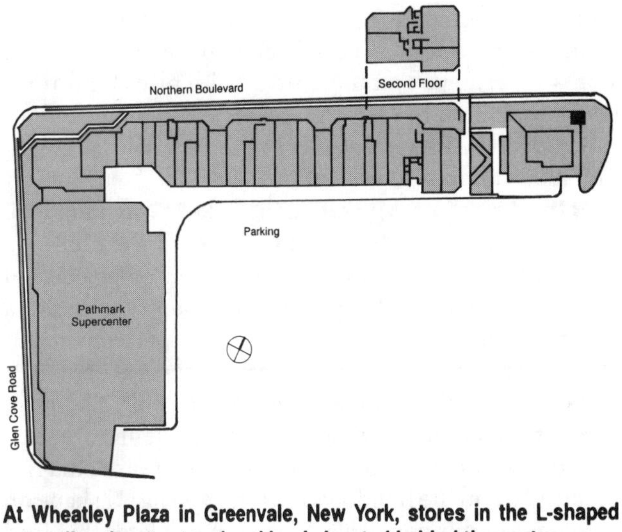

At Wheatley Plaza in Greenvale, New York, stores in the L-shaped center line the street and parking is located behind the center.

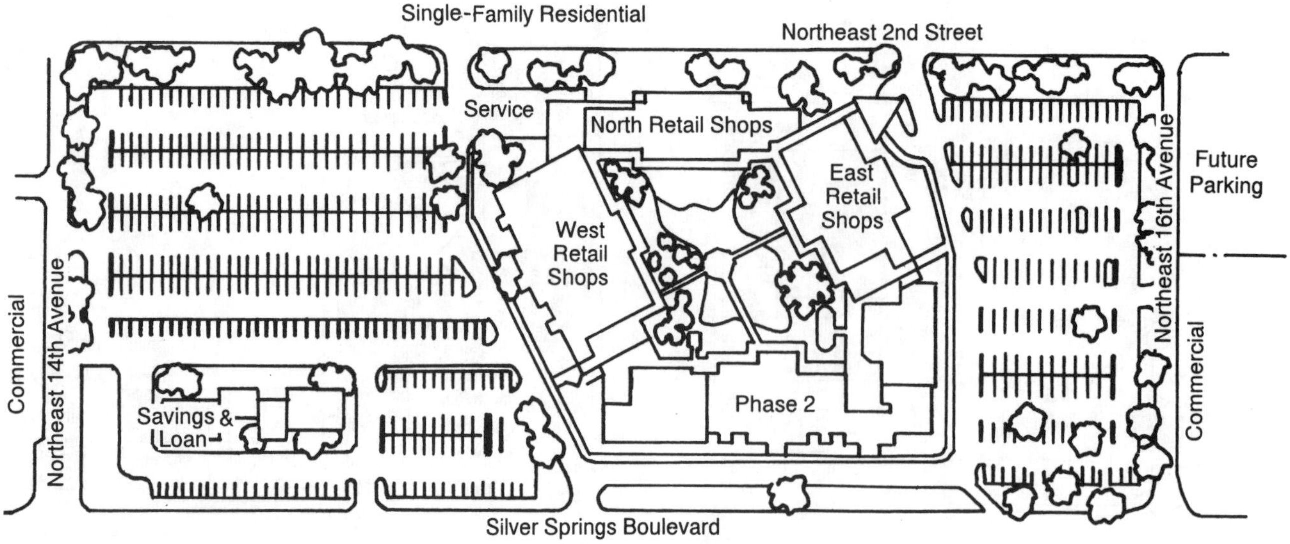

Specialty centers like The Cascades in Ocala, Florida, often use atypical site plans. In this case, a central lagoon is incorporated and parking borders the center on two sides.

Specialty Centers

Although specialty centers may, in fact, be developed as strip centers, they are often configured as something other than a strip. Specialty centers are difficult to describe or categorize; they are usually "special" for a wide variety of reasons, including configuration. They typically do not include traditional anchor tenants, such as supermarkets, and are often more oriented toward pedestrians than toward automobiles. A good example of a specialty center configuration is Tanner Market, a small, downtown retail complex in Pasadena, California (see the case study at the end of this chapter).

A second example of a specialty center is the 79,600-square-foot Cascades in Ocala, Florida. The Cascade's two-level design turned a difficult site condition into an asset, and the center successfully responds to a growing customer preference for leisure shopping in a pleasant, social environment. The site plan (see above) uses a central lagoon and waterfall around which the retail stores are arranged on three sides (with plans for further development on the fourth side). This building configuration divides the rectangular site in two, and parking is provided at opposite ends of the site.

A third example, Market on the Lake in Mission Viejo, California, is a 92,900-square-foot specialty center on a lakefront site. It features a Mediterranean village design theme, extensive landscaping and promenades, plazas, a fountain, outdoor sitting and eating areas, and convenient storefront parking. The primary anchor tenant is a 21,000-square-foot farmers' market. In this site plan, seven freestanding buildings border the lake and are sited to preserve views of the lakefront. The site is actually a peninsula, and the buildings are arranged in a U shape on the edges of this peninsula. Open public plazas that lead to the lakefront were created between the buildings. Unlike most traditional strip centers, a pedestrian focus for the project is provided both on the parking lot side and on the lakefront side of the project.

Parking, Circulation, and Access

Parking should be a positive experience because it will form the customer's first impression of a shopping center. According to a comprehensive study conducted by ULI on parking requirements for shopping centers, a typical shopping center of 25,000 to 400,000 square feet would require four parking spaces per 1,000 square feet of GLA. However, numerous factors can affect the amount required, including government regulations, mass transit availability, walk-in trade, and tenant mix. Other uses within the center, such as offices and cinemas, may also affect the parking needs. Many zoning ordinances require five spaces per 1,000 square feet; the figure will vary by jurisdiction.

Ease of parking should always determine parking layout. Auto circulation should be continuous, preferably one-way, and counterclockwise. Also, drivers should be able to maneuver within the center without having to enter a public highway.

Aisles should be aligned perpendicular to the anchor tenants to allow the shopper to walk directly from his/her car toward the front of the building and the anchor tenants. Major tenants occupying at least 20,000 square feet will want to have parking aisles directed toward their stores. In L-shaped centers, this may mean that the aisles will have to be aligned differently at different ends of the center in order to align perpendicularly with the two sides of the L. For example, at Renaissance Center West in Las Vegas, a 175,000-square-foot neighborhood shopping center anchored by a supermarket, two sections of the lot are directed toward the supermarket and a third toward the tenants at the other end of the center. No aisles are aligned toward the tenants in the middle (see below).

In the case of convenience or neighborhood centers, parking is often best placed along the storefronts. This design accommodates quick visits to the stores and fast turnover of prime spaces.

Two patterns for surface parking layouts may be used: perpendicular and diagonal. Perpendicular (or "90-degree") parking economizes on space and facilitates circulation. It also provides two-way traffic through the aisle, the safety of better sight lines, greater parking capacity, and shorter cruising distances. Diagonal (or "angular") parking spaces, with either 45-degree or 60-degree angles, are easier for drivers to enter.

The question of whether to opt for perpendicular or diagonal parking is best solved by using the pattern that generally prevails in the local community and that can be best adapted to the conditions at the chosen site. Some shopping centers, such as Murrayhill Marketplace, a 153,500-square-foot community center in Beaverton, Oregon, use mixed parking patterns. This mixture may result from anchor tenant requirements that differ from developer preferences. Mixed parking patterns may create some confusion, however, and usually only one pattern should be chosen.

In the case of perpendicular parking, the standard bay for a full-size car is 65 feet deep, comprising two stalls, each 20 feet deep, and a center aisle of 25 feet to allow for two-way circulation. The standard stall has a width of nine feet. Most new centers will probably reduce these measurements to eight-and-one-half to nine feet for stall widths and 17 to 18 feet for stall lengths.[11] A nine-foot stall width is still recommended for the parking area closest to a supermarket; a customer would have difficulty loading groceries into a car parked in a lot with less space.

Employee parking is best placed at the rear of the stores, although security concerns sometimes eliminate this possibility. When rear parking is used, a minimum combined width of 42 feet will be required for the rear service and employee parking area. A width of 60 feet in the rear service area allows for the inclusion of a truck delivery drive and a staging area for unloading without blocking the service drive for other deliveries.

Some experts in the field have suggested that parking stall sizes should diminish in relation to their distance from the center's building—in other words, the spaces closest to the buildings would be the largest, since they are used most often. During peak hours, shoppers value the presence of a vacant space more than its size, thus smaller spaces farther away are acceptable.

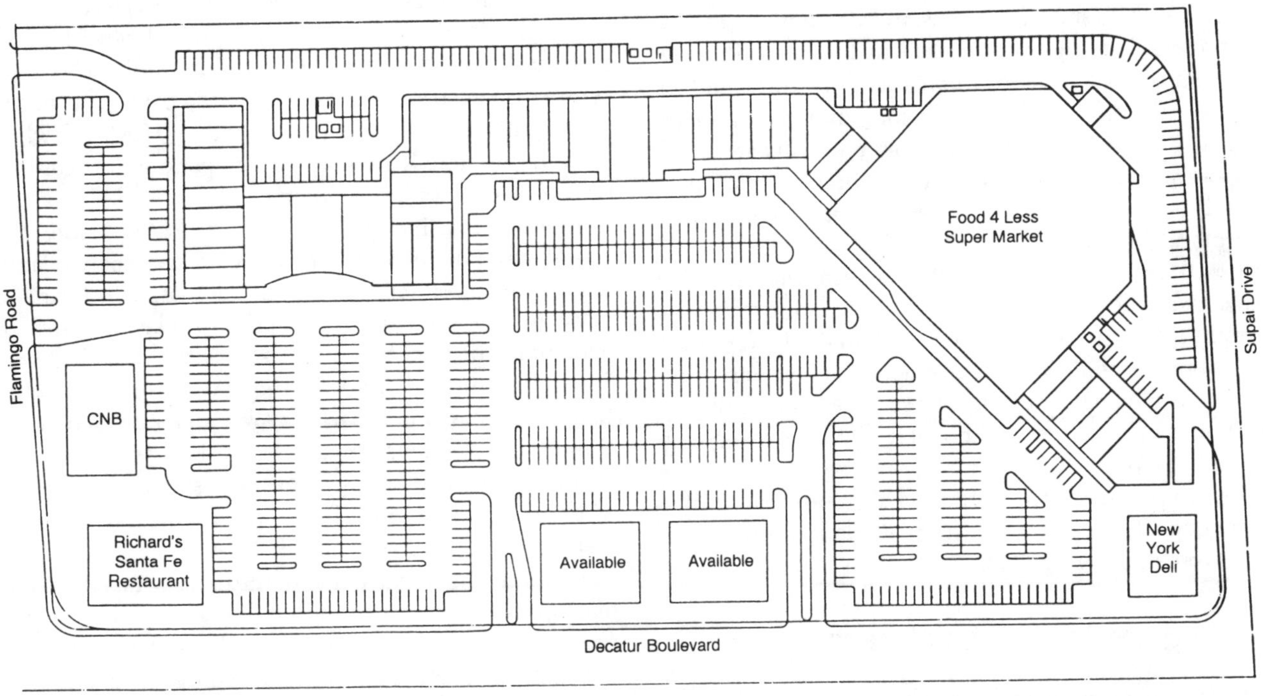

At Renaissance Center West in Las Vegas, Nevada, two sections of the parking lot are directed toward the anchor food store while a third is pointed toward the tenants at the other end of the center.

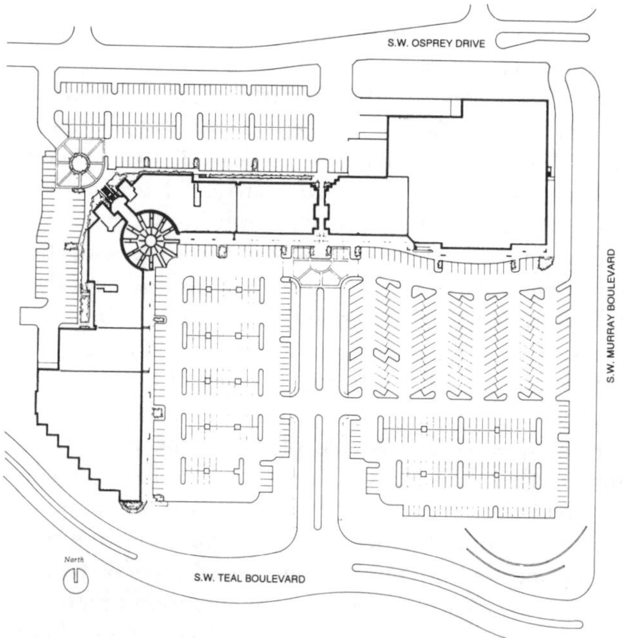

Murrayhill Marketplace in Beaverton, Oregon, uses a mix of both perpendicular and diagonal parking stall patterns.

In addition to parking concerns, a favorable initial impression of the center will also be affected by the proper placement of curb cuts to allow easy ingress and egress and by the design of surrounding roads. The developer should consider all possible turning movements into and out of the site and must work with the local authorities to ensure that necessary road improvements are provided. A significant issue in this regard is the provision of sufficient stop lights to allow turns and to control traffic, thus allowing for more impulse entrances into the center. The ability to obtain curb cuts and road improvements must be addressed during the feasibility period, before the developer's earnest money becomes nonrefundable.

Road improvements are often required not only to make the center more functional, but also to gain approval for the project. Developers should be aware that such improvements may involve significant expense. For example, at Wheatley Plaza in Greenvale, New York, the developer provided an additional traffic lane, extending beyond his property line to the intersection. He also agreed to purchase two traffic signals to assist in traffic regulation. The total cost (in 1980 dollars) for these improvements was $250,000.

Site Engineering and Landscaping

Design requirements for most shopping centers usually dictate that the site must be relatively level. An engineering firm with local experience should be employed to handle site work and assess on-site soils to determine the presence of any special problems. Fortunately, the foundation for most centers usually requires only simple excavations in order to lay column footings and grade beams to support load-bearing walls, thus reducing the likelihood that soil conditions will present major problems.

If the slope of a site corresponds to the grades on surrounding roads, an opportunity may exist for a two-level arrangement of buildings and parking, although the smaller the project, the more difficult this is to achieve. Sensitive use of a site's topography should produce a compatibility between the shopping center and the site's natural characteristics. For example, a sloping site with trees that need to be preserved can skillfully be reshaped to accommodate a stepped, but still single-level, center.

Because large amounts of land are covered by buildings and pavement in a retail project, stormwater runoff is a major issue in shopping center design. Reducing or delaying this runoff may involve significant cost. Most communities have limited storm system capacities and will often require stormwater runoff control methods such as rooftop ponding, temporary detention basins (in portions of the parking lot, for example), detention or retention ponds, or other mechanisms for reducing the runoff rate and total runoff after development. In designing a stormwater management system, the developer should consider safety and visual appearance in addition to the primary function of water storage and should design the system as an integral part of the overall project.

Another critical site planning issue is landscaping. A surface parking lot often takes the bulk of a shopping center's open space, and such a barren expanse exposed to the public's view is usually uninviting. However, when properly designed and landscaped, parking lots can become one of a center's amenities.

In the provisions of site plan approval, under the zoning and building permit clearance documents, landscaping requirements should be discussed in terms of performance standards rather than dollar amounts or percentage of total building costs, as the costs will vary depending on the site and the nature of the center. Landscaping within a parking area generally should be confined to trees and massed plantings in wells or in clearly delineated areas. Plantings should be located where they will not interfere with parking, parking area maintenance, or snow removal.

Landscaping on the edges of the center can effectively mask parking areas and buffer the center from nearby residential areas. Landscaping should not be used excessively, however, or it may hide the center from potential customers. Hardy groundcovers, shrubs, and bushes concentrated at appropriate places within the buffers are sufficient.

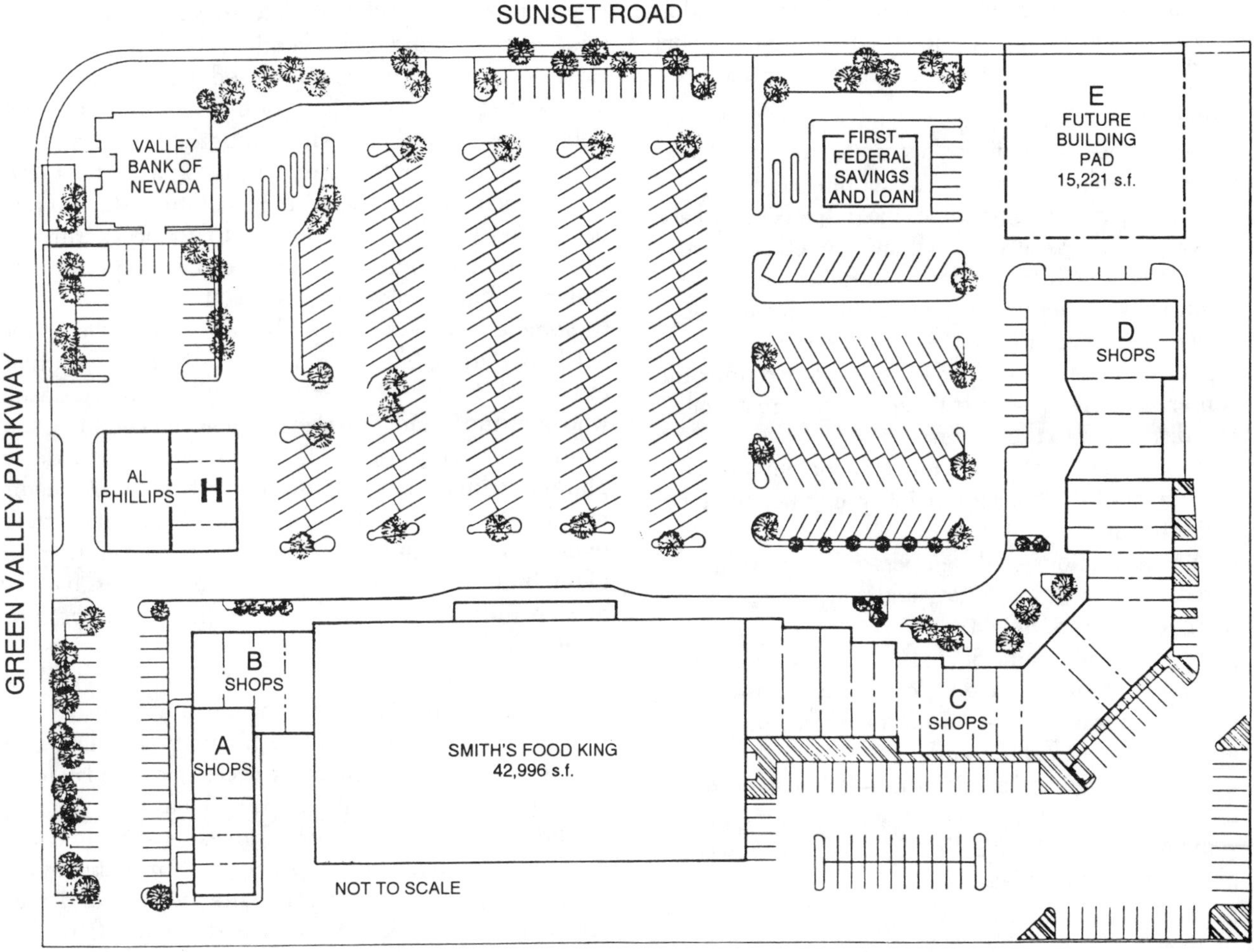

At Green Valley Plaza, a 90,636-square-foot neighborhood center in Henderson, Nevada, four outparcels are used, including one that incorporates several small shops. The design preserves clear views into the center from Sunset Road, emphasizing the visibility of the anchor supermarket.

Landscaping in the area immediately surrounding the center can help to present an attractive environment for the pedestrian. For example, at Renaissance Center West in Las Vegas, fountains, pools, and plants create a cooling atmosphere and offer a series of refreshing vistas to visitors and tenants, 30-foot palm trees give the impression of an oasis, and patio areas offer patrons outdoor dining and resting points.

In addition to landscaping, exterior lighting has become an important design and safety feature because a greater percentage of retail business is now being conducted during the evening. Lighting helps to protect the public and can be used to create an image and character for the center. Lighting in parking areas should usually provide about one-and-one-half footcandles at the pavement surface. Virgil L. Griffin of the Nadel Partnership in Los Angeles prefers three-and-one-half footcandles, however; according to Griffin, more light means more business because it attracts more attention and enhances security.

Lighting in the parking areas should be provided by poles placed in islands at the ends of parking bays. The latest available nonglare and high-intensity lighting should be used to provide adequate illumination, reduce spillover lighting, and avoid excessive electricity costs. An effective lighting system requires consideration of a variety of factors, including mounting height, spacing, light control, and light sources. The latter should be evaluated based on efficiency, durability, color of light, and light output.

Outparcel Development

Outparcels are common and attractive additions to strip centers, but they must be placed and controlled carefully to ensure that they are marketable and do not detract from the center's overall marketability. Developers must be candid with the center tenants about the outparcel development plan so that no one will be surprised by the outcome. The issues that need to be considered in outparcel development, according to an International Council of Shopping Centers (ICSC) study, include:

- ingress and egress—outparcel tenants will be concerned about both direct access to the street and access easements through the shopping center;
- control of parking—sometimes the outparcel may have parking in excess of its need, and sometimes it may need to share parking with the overall center;
- utility lines—whether outparcels will tie into the shopping center lines or have their own lines;
- construction, if the outparcel is developed after the center is opened—construction should create minimal disruption to the center;
- placement and control of dumpsters on outparcels;
- placement of site lines for maintaining the visibility of major tenants;
- height restrictions— developers often restrict outparcel buildings to one story and may further restrict them to a specific height;
- placement and height of signs— signs are critical to outparcel tenants, but developers must ensure that signage does not detract from the overall image and operation of the center; and
- quality of design and architecture—although outparcel tenants will have their own design requirements, developers should reserve the right to review and approve the tenants' plans.

The Building Structure and Shell

Unlike most regional shopping centers, office buildings, and other developments, small shopping centers are usually highly efficient in terms of the ratio between usable/rentable space and GBA. In most instances, the GBA is the same as the GLA. Thus, an effective approach to shopping center design is to think of the building shell as the most efficient and inexpensive bulk space possible, concealed behind an attractively designed canopy and facade.

Unlike many of the strip shopping centers developed in the 1960s and 1970s, attractive architecture and distinctive design are now generally required to achieve a successful center. The structure must be eye-catching as well as functional and should relate to the architecture in the area.

Structure

Small shopping centers usually are constructed of a lightweight steel roof-framing structure and tilt-up concrete walls or concrete masonry units. The design of foundations for shopping center buildings will vary from region to region and from site to site, depending on underlying soils and rock conditions. Generally, however, caissons or spread footings are used to support columns and bearing walls, and a four- or five-inch-thick concrete slab is allowed to "float" within. For the floor slab, tolerances of movement that are set by most major tenants do not exceed three-fourths of an inch. Often, the soil must be treated with lime or cement to reduce shrink and swell; alternatively, on-site soils can be replaced with "select" fill materials of higher quality.

Some developers pour each section of slab as a "tenant-finish" item, but this practice makes quality difficult to control. One developer suggests: "For those owners who pour the foundation slab in the normal building shell construction sequence, allowances must be made for plumbing lines to serve future restrooms. A recommended technique is to place water and sanitary sewer lines parallel to, and three feet away from, the rear wall of the building and delay pouring the rearmost five feet of slab until tenants make decisions about restroom locations."[12]

Any location designated for restaurant use should be constructed without a slab during the initial construction. The heavy utility needs of restaurants and the varied nature of their layouts make it necessary to delay incorporation of the slab until the space is leased.

Shopping center structural frames most often consist of steel tube columns and bar joists. For main support members, joist girders offer lighter weight and more flexibility in duct locations than do "wide flange" or one-inch beams. Efficient structural spans range from 24 to 30 feet for main support beams or girders and 30 to 42 feet for bar joists. Structural bays should not be planned around "typical" store widths, because "typical" conditions simply do not exist.

Shell Components

The center's exterior facing materials contribute to its image and its individual identity. Using more than one material can create an attractive unified exterior and a distinctive image. Materials should be capable of being speedily assembled and erected, should be durable and easily maintained, and, ideally, should be available locally.

The choice of method for enclosing the side and rear walls of a shopping center is driven by cost. Tilt-up concrete wall panels are often favored, primarily because they can be erected by inexpensive laborers. Tilt-up walls designed for a 15- to 20-foot height are only five-and-one-half to seven inches thick and may also serve as load-bearing structural walls. An alternative is to use load-bearing concrete masonry units, eight or 12 inches thick. Both of these wall materials can be painted, plastered, or bricked, if desired.

A regular spacing of rear access and service doors is necessary. Spacing is, generally, calculated by taking the smallest average tenant size expected for the center and dividing this square footage by the lease depth. A good rule of thumb is to provide rear doors 16 to 20 feet apart for a 60- to 80-foot-deep space.

Most of the insulation for the building shell will be a tenant-finish function. However, batt insulation should be installed at perimeter walls and above ceilings.

Roof Systems

Roofs are often one of the most costly and difficult aspects of construction for shopping center developers. One of the most notable products to be developed during the last few years is the single-ply roofing membrane, which is used in overlapping sheets to turn the roof into one continuous liner. The elastomeric properties of the rubber-type membrane allow it to stretch and move with the deck, preventing tears. The membrane is manufactured off site. Although this system has many positive features, it is criticized by some developers who predict that major failures in the membranes will occur within a few years.

The best roof system may well depend on the local climate. Traditional built-up roofing systems—such as those involving layers of tar—remain popular, and many have lasted up to 30 years. These roofs are built up, one ply on top of another, and are often much thicker than single-ply roofs. Other systems include loose-layered ballast systems, clay tile roofing and urethane systems, and single-ply, mop-applied modified bitumen systems. Regardless of the system used, the roof must be well designed, constructed of reliable materials, properly installed, and regularly inspected. A large percentage of lawsuits involving new construction are related to roofing, so careful attention to roof construction is critical.[13]

In general, roofs should slope at least one-quarter-of-an-inch per foot to ensure good drainage. The future installation of rooftop-mounted packaged heating, ventilation, and air-conditioning (HVAC) units should be anticipated in the roof design, with allowances made for their weight and prefabricated roof curbs provided to minimize random penetrations of the roof.

The Front

A considerable portion of the construction budget should be spent on the front of the center, which is obviously the most important side in terms of architectural character and quality and overall image. For the front of the center, four materials are worth considering as facing materials—masonry, metal panels, wood, and tile. Of these, masonry offers the greatest flexibility of treatment and design. Any of these materials may be used to build a colonnaded walk or arcade, the traditional means of sheltering customers and protecting storefronts from weathering. Canopies may be either cantilevered from the building wall or supported by freestanding columns. Their widths and heights will be determined by the chosen architectural style; 10 to 15 feet is an ample width for a walkway.

The image of strip shopping centers has been changing considerably in recent years as developers have sought to create higher-quality centers of greater distinction. One example of a daring design is the shopping center at Fleetwood Square, along Ventura Boulevard in California's San Fernando Valley. The 12,500-square-foot project is shaped like the front end of a pink 1969 Cadillac. The top floor of the two-level center features dual glass-block headlights on either side of a 60-pane plate-glass grille; pink stucco fins—complete with narrow horizontal neon lights—jut out at either end. A hood ornament graces the center of the second story. The project, which was completed in late 1986 by CBS Realcorp, was 100 percent leased four months after leasing began.[14]

The developer of the Fleetwood Square project was looking for a very distinctive design that would give the project identity, and found an architect who could do it. Although this bold approach is not suitable for most projects, a distinctive and attractive design clearly will enhance any project. The immediate surroundings and the general preferences of the region and the market will dictate the appropriate project identity.

Another example of distinctive design is Renaissance Center West in Las Vegas, which was designed by its architect to be an oasis in an arid climate. Heavy walls and small openings along the walkways offer visitors a sense of refuge from the hostile desert environment.

The Market at Westchase in Houston, Texas, is an 84,000-square-foot specialty center that uses an Art Deco design, including ceramic tile pavers and neon lighting.

Renaissance Center West was designed to be an oasis in an arid climate.

Color also plays an important role in establishing the oasis-like setting. The buildings are rose stucco and the walkways are various shades of cool blues. The pedestrian arcade is punctuated by several towers that act as steps and transitions for grade changes. A translucent pyramid, which is illuminated at night, sits atop each tower.

Tenant Signage

Shopping center tenant signage is an important source of color, vitality, and atmosphere for a project and should be an integral part of the building design. The tenant signage options available today are numerous and include the following:

- specially shaped box signs;
- individual letter signs with plexiglass faces, internally illuminated;
- open-face letters with exposed neon;
- reverse-channel letters with "halo effect" lighting;
- bare neon, with or without special backgrounds;
- individual letter signs mounted on a common raceway, with or without a "receiver" channel;
- internally illuminated sign bands; and
- graphics screen-printed on canvas or "Panaflex" awnings.

The optimum height of letters in shopping center tenant signage is a controversial subject. Research on environmental graphics suggests that one inch of letter height is required for every 30 feet between the viewer and the sign. For example, a 24-inch-high sign could be read from a distance of 720 feet. This rule of thumb must be adjusted for the speed at which customer vehicles are traveling, the simplicity of the typeface, and the number of distractions in the immediate environment of the sign.

Although tenants usually pay for their own signs, developers exercise control over what tenants can display by a declaration of permitted and prohibited signage as well as an approval clause in each tenant's lease. Such declarations forbid roof signs and large projecting signs and favor placement at a certain level on, above, or below a canopy, depending on a project's architectural treatment. Insisting on uniformity of scale, size, and placement is a worthwhile practice, but flexibility is important as well; in many centers today, tenants are being given more freedom in designing tasteful, attractive signs that fit into a center's overall image. This flexibility is especially important for chain stores that have specific logos they wish to use.[15]

If signage is not properly addressed early in the development process, problems may occur with tenants that erect inappropriate signs. At Renaissance Center West in Las Vegas, for example, the sign program was not established early enough, and some signs were erected that the developer considers inharmonious with the center's theme or disproportionate to the signs of other tenants.

In sign criteria guidelines established for Thomas Lake Shopping Center in Eagan, Minnesota, the developer chose to use internally illuminated letters with a maximum letter height of 24 inches and a minimum height of 14 inches. The signage document not only dictates the sign specs but also highlights prohibited practices.

Interior Design Features

Tenant Space

The space leased by a tenant typically contains a designated frontage, unfinished party walls separating the space from that of retail neighbors, an unfinished floor, and exposed joists for roof support. Placement of a rear door and utilities usually have been indicated by the architect in plans for the shell.

Most developers use an allowance system for finishing the tenant space. The allowance may include floors and floor coverings, light fixtures, HVAC, and doors, with the tenants paying for other custom fixtures and finishing such as specialty light fixtures, counters, shelves, and painting. In essence, the owner furnishes the bare space. The landlord's responsibilities and the tenant's responsibilities, which are plainly indicated on working drawings and specs, are spelled out in the lease.

To accommodate changing needs, the developer/owner of a shopping center should design for structural flexibility and, if possible, should provide flexible leasing arrangements that allow tenants to be moved to larger or smaller spaces as needed. Except for intervening fire walls, the spacing of which is governed by local fire protection codes, partitions between tenants' spaces should not be used as bearing walls. Tenant partitions should be built of materials and by methods that allow for easy removal—typically, metal studs and gypsum boards. To allow for flexibility in operations, structural elements—such as plumbing and heating stacks, air-conditioning ducts, toilets, and stairways—should be placed on end walls or on the walls least likely to be removed if the store is enlarged or the space redivided.

Each tenant space should be kept to the minimum size necessary, as it is better for the tenant to be a little cramped than to have too much room with insufficient sales to justify the rent. In addition, centers with a variety of smaller tenants seem to be considerably more successful than those with only a few large stores.

Store Size

A standard store width for a particular type of tenant cannot be given. Chain store companies have studied the matter for years and each company has employed experts to ascertain the proper width for its stores. For most modern centers, however, it has been found that the architectural design usually requires structures with wide spans between the structural columns. Stores are fitted into these structural steel frames without regard for column locations, but, with clever layout, columns can be disguised as part of the fixtures and often can be used as part of the store's decorative features.

Providing store depths of between 40 and 120 feet (70 feet is a reasonable standard depth) will often be advantageous in drawing tenants. A key principle in deciding store depth is to create a space that does not include too little or too much store depth. Larry Good of Good, Haas & Fulton Architects in Dallas, Texas, notes that store depths of 50 to 75 feet are ideal but that 40 to 80 feet of depth is quite feasible.[16]

Ceiling Height

The distance from the floor slab to the underside of the bar joists that hold the roof may vary from 10 to 14 feet, depending on the architectural style of the building, the depth of the stores, and the types of tenants. The air space between the finished ceiling and the roof usually contains air-conditioning ducts, electrical wires, plumbing lines, and other utility hardware; such equipment requires two to three feet of space between the finished ceiling and the structure. Although many stores have 11-foot finished ceilings, some small stores may have ceilings as low as nine feet. Certain specialized tenants, such as variety stores and supermarkets, may require finished ceilings as high as 13 feet.

Floors

Tenants usually receive an allowance for the flooring in their spaces, which is installed in accordance with criteria established by the owner and incorporated into the lease. A special floor covering usually is put over the concrete slab in tenant sales areas, although it is often omitted in storage areas. Floor coverings range from various tile materials to carpeting. Wood flooring is not recommended for stores unless required by the decorative scheme.

Utilities

Leases should specify the developer's responsibility for providing vents and drains for tenants such as supermarkets, restaurants, and dry cleaners—those tenants that require large plumbing installations. Installation of the floor slab usually should be deferred until the tenant spaces are leased because the formulation of the tenant's underfloor requirements will extend beyond the developer's construction schedule.

Serious consideration should be given to the use of overhead, rather than underground, water lines. An overhead leak at the back of the store may cause some damage but can be easily located and corrected; an underground leak is difficult to detect, may cause ground heaving, and will be much more damaging and expensive to repair. If overhead water lines are used, however, measures should be taken to ensure that the lines are not exposed to freezing temperatures.

Generally, a primary source of electricity at the rear of the building is provided by the developer. Each tenant is required to provide the secondary electrical service, subject to the landlord's review and approval.

A shopping center can be heated and cooled either by individual units in each store or by a central plant. Tenants are responsible for their own individual units, but the shopping center's management is responsible for a central plant. Hybrid systems, employing large multitenant rooftop units, are also available. Because energy savings are an essential consideration in selecting HVAC systems, the mechanical engineer must evaluate all possible systems and the availability of various fuels.

Construction

Proper management of the construction process is important for maintaining both quality and cost control. Numerous factors dictate the correct time to begin construction, but the developer should make certain that it does not begin prematurely, as this is likely to lead to problems and higher construction costs. For example, at University Mall in Fairfax County, Virginia, construction

■ 7-9 Design for Target Market: Project X Example

The site plan for Project X includes two major access points on one adjacent road and one on the other, as well as service access points. The center is laid out in an L shape, with the principal anchor, the supermarket, facing onto the major arterial and anchoring one end of the center. The other end, nearest the arterial, is anchored by a drugstore; a hardware store is located near the center of the long arm of the L. Notice that the developer has opted not to use the corner of the L, as this space has little visibility, and has used it instead for employee parking. The other parking areas are laid out so that the aisles are generally perpendicular to the anchor tenants. Only one pad site has been used here, thus preserving the visibility of the center.

Based on previous experience in developing shopping centers, the developer designed the smaller tenant spaces of the project so that they are relatively shallow with favorable depth-to-width ratios (three-to-one to four-to-one). Although this design does not maximize the amount of GLA that could be built on the site, it does provide the small tenant spaces that appeal to today's specialty retailers. The developer felt that these stores would lease more quickly and would bring in more money per square foot than would stores that are either deep-narrow (for smaller tenants) or deep-large (for larger tenants). The store sizes and dimensions are provided below:

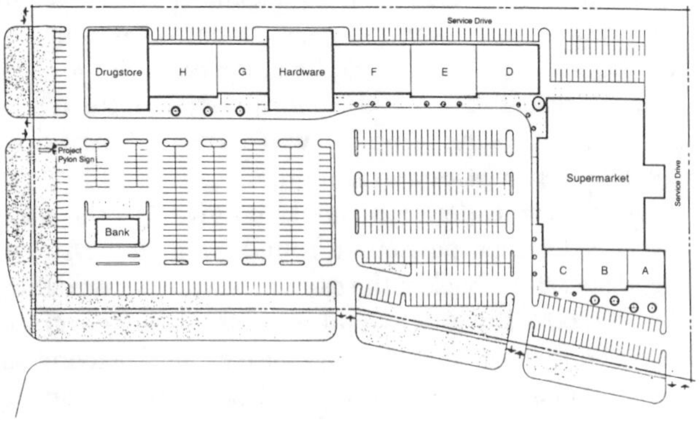

Site plan for Project X.

Store Sizes and Dimensions of Project X

Building	Store Depth (Feet)	Minimum Width (Feet)	Average Store Area (Square Feet)
A and C	55	20.00	1,100
B	60	22.25	1,335
D, F, and G	75	20.00	1,500
E	80	20.00	1,600
H	80	21.00	1,680

was begun before design and contracting decisions were worked out. This early start was an attempt to beat the deadline for a county environmental study program that might have added $15,000 to $20,000 (in 1977 dollars) to the project's cost. However, the problems and delays caused by the premature start eventually cost the developers more than the amount of money they saved.

Shopping center construction, from the developer's point of view, involves two principal areas of concern: construction of the site and shell, and tenant-finish construction. (Contracting arrangements for site and shell construction are discussed thoroughly in chapter 2 and do not differ significantly by property type.)

Tenant-finish construction is an area that presents numerous challenges peculiar to retail development. Most importantly, the developer should establish and maintain close rapport with every tenant. Successful coordination involves:[17]

- a clear understanding of the "deal" and each person's responsibilities;
- agreement on specs, plans, and procedures;
- a follow-through system, enabling both parties to monitor progress; and
- communication so that exigencies are held to a minimum.

The responsibilities of each party and the specs for construction all are included in the tenant-improvement schedule. An example of a standard tenant-improvement schedule, provided in feature box 7-10, was taken from Murrayhill Marketplace, a community center in Beaverton, Oregon. A second example of the breakdown between landlord and tenant improvements is provided in Appendix D.

Tenant-finish construction usually involves variations on two kinds of deals: the shell-and-allowance method and the build-to-suit method. Each method has its own advantages and disadvantages. The simplest approach is the shell-and-allowance method, in which the developer constructs the building shell and allows the tenant a specified sum to complete all other permanent improvements to the store. In the build-to-suit approach, the developer completes the tenant-finish work. This method, although more demanding, allows the developer to control the quality and consistency of construction and also provides a valuable service to small and inexperienced tenants. In some cases, the developer may choose simply to supply the shell and let the tenant construct the interior space with no allowance. This may create problems, however, because the tenant may not be able to raise the capital necessary to do a good job.

In some cases, a combination of methods may be necessary, although this is not recommended. For example, at Wheatley Plaza in Greenvale, New York, the amount of interior finishing provided by the developer varied widely from tenant to tenant. Approximately 50 percent of the tenants leased shell space and were responsible for all interior design, but because many tenants could no longer afford to finish the shells when interest rates rose, the developer gave allowances for finishing work. In fact, tenant allowances can become a negotiating point in the leasing process, especially in soft markets.

Whichever method is chosen, the developer must be sensitive to the needs of the tenant if construction is to proceed smoothly. Supplying pertinent information and guidance will help coordination between the developer and the tenant. By preparing a data book, the developer can provide the retailer and the architect/engineer with answers to the many questions that invariably arise. The data book should contain the following:[18]

Proper developer management of the construction process is important for maintaining both quality and cost control. Pictured is Sunset Corners of Lake Forest, a neighborhood shopping center in Lake Forest, Illinois.

- an index of all of the developer's architectural and engineering plans, specs, and details;

7-10 Murrayhill Marketplace Standard Tenant Improvements

Storefronts. One shopping center standard, painted aluminum storefront, with one standard, double-acting outside door will be provided.

Rear exit. If required by applicable code, one shopping center standard, hollow metal door will be installed.

Floors. Exposed concrete will be smooth-finished, ready for the tenant's floor covering. All floor covering is to be provided at the tenant's expense.

Ceilings. A suspended T-bar acoustical ceiling with two-foot-by-four-foot panels will be installed at a height of approximately 11 feet (in sales and office areas only; storage areas not included).

Demising walls. Interior surfaces of demising walls will be sheetrocked, taped, and finished, ready for paint.

Lighting. Standard two-foot-by-four-foot recessed light fixtures will be provided. At the landlord's option, any stock or warehouse areas in the premises may be lit with eight-foot-long fluorescent fixtures. Lights will be controlled at the electrical panel only.

Electrical. One 100-amp service will be provided to the premises. One 120-volt duplex wall outlet will be furnished for every 20 lineal feet of demising wall.

Heating and air conditioning. Air conditioning and heating will be provided by an energy-efficient heat pump, separately metered. Any extra HVAC required by the tenant's business will be furnished at the tenant's expense.

Sprinklers. Water sprinklers will be installed at ceiling height throughout the premises in accordance with building codes.

Signage. Signage includes directional signs, a band sign above the tenant's location, and a colonnade sign above the walkway. The colonnade sign and the lettering on the band sign are the tenant's responsibility. The design of all signage must be approved in writing by the landlord.

Other improvements. All improvements made to the premises in addition to those listed above must be approved in writing by the landlord prior to beginning construction. The cost, including that for obtaining any additional permits and approvals, will be the tenant's responsibility.

Source: Columbia-Willamette Development Co., Portland, Oregon.

- sections through, and details of, the leased wall construction and of any other elements of construction that may affect the tenant's planning;
- definitions of symbols for all materials, such as walls, partitions, ceilings, doors, various types of electrical outlets and switches, panel boards, riser diagrams, and door and roof finish schedules;
- definitions of standard mechanical symbols and connections;
- definitions of standard HVAC symbols;
- local design factors or criteria available to the tenant's engineer;
- excerpts of unusual building code requirements that will be helpful to the tenant's out-of-town architect/engineer; and
- work rules.

In addition, the developer may provide an outline of the steps and procedures that a tenant should follow to have plans and applications approved by government agencies and to file for a certificate of occupancy. The developer also should inform the tenant about any unusual jurisdictional situations and if union labor is required.

Financing

The various sources and methods of financing for income property are discussed thoroughly in chapter 4. However, several aspects of financing are particular to shopping centers.

Shopping centers are especially attractive to lenders because of the amount of inflation protection they provide. "The shopping center . . . offers inflation protection [via] percentage net leases that are relatively short in duration. As the prices of consumer goods and services rise with inflation, the overage lease payments received by the landlord rise."[19]

Small neighborhood or community centers—often the type of project in which beginning developers are involved—can be particularly stable investments because they are often oriented toward consumer nondurable goods and services that are bought regardless of changes in the economy. Supermarkets and drugstores, generally, can maintain relatively stable sales at all times because they sell products that are needed on a regular basis. Specialty centers, on the other hand, are more subject to fluctuations in the economy and are considered to be more risky investments. Thus, they are inherently more difficult to finance, especially if the developer has no track record.

In some cases, public financing may be available for new shopping centers, especially in inner-city areas or in communities interested in economic development. For example, Windmill Place, a 53,907-square-foot specialty center in Flint, Michigan, was developed by a beginning developer with the benefit of an urban development action grant (UDAG), a Flint Community Development Corporation Loan, and a state Economic Development Administration (EDA) loan. Greenway Plaza, a 70,000-square-foot (GLA) neighborhood center in Yonkers, New York, was developed through a request for proposal (RFP) and with public financial assistance, including a $1,375,000 UDAG, a purchase-money mortgage of $477,000 at 2 percent for 15 years issued by the redevelopment agency, and a $5 million bond package arranged by the Yonkers Industrial Development Authority. The public objective was to create a hub for the community and an anchor for the revitalization of downtown Yonkers. The project is anchored by a 42,000-square-foot Big V supermarket; Big V also served as the developer.

One means of raising equity financing for a shopping center development is to sell parcels to anchor tenants or outparcels to fast-food restaurants, banks, and so forth, after the center plan has taken shape. The value of these outparcels should increase as the certainty of the shopping center being built increases; thus, the developer not only recaptures equity capital previously invested in the land but can also realize a substantial profit. A comparison of typical loans from various financing sources is presented in feature box 7-11.

Marketing

Marketing for a shopping center is more complex and demanding than for any other type of development; it involves creating an effective leasing plan, obtaining commitments from anchor tenants early in the process, leasing the smaller spaces according to the leasing plan, and promoting the center after it is completed.

Leasing Plan

The leasing plan represents the center's investment potential and is fundamental to the planning process. It should be prepared early in the development process and should address the tenant mix, the placement of tenants, rent schedules and the pricing of store spaces, and lease specs.

Tenant Mix

The correct tenant mix for a center cannot be determined by a formula; each market and shopping center is different. After a developer has learned the characteristics of the market to be served, a decision can be made as to the type of anchor tenant and other smaller tenants

■ 7-11 Comparison of Typical Loans on a Retail Project

This table shows the different loan amounts available from different types of lenders for a permanent mortgage on a retail property with a $1 million net operating income. Lenders use a combination of the loan-to-value test and the debt coverage ratio to underwrite the loan amount. The final loan amount is usually the lowest of the two numbers. Rates shown below are suggestive, but not indicative, of prevailing rates at the time the table was prepared.

	Savings & Loan	Bank	Life Company	Pension Fund	Credit Company
Net Operating Income (NOI)	$1,000,000	$1,000,000	$1,000,000	$1,000,000	$1,000,000
Term (Years)	10	5	5	10	5
Note Rate Spread (%)	11th District 300	Treasury Bill plus 200	Fixed	Fixed	Prime plus 1½
Note Rate (%)	8.75 + 300 = 11.75	10.5	9¾	9 plus 50 participation	12
Amortization (Years)	30	30	30	–	–
Constant (%)	10.98	10.98	10.31	9	12
Pay Rate (%)	12.12	10.5	10.31	9	10
Debt Coverage Ratio	1.10	1.15	1.20	1.15	1.10
Maximum Loan Test 1	$7,737,000	$7,912,000	$8,083,000	$9,661,835	$9,091,000
Capitalization Rate (%)	8.75	8.75	9.25	8.75	8.75
Value	$11,428,000	$11,428,000	$10,811,000	$11,428,000	$11,428,000
Loan-to-Value Ratio (%)	75	75	75	100	90
Maximum Loan Test 2	$8,571,000	$8571,000	$8,108,000	$11,428,000	$10,286,000
Maximum Loan	$7,737,000	$7,912,000	$8,083,000	$9,661,835	$9,091,000

The above comparison is for illustrative purposes only. Generally, ranges exist on capitalization rates and debt coverage ratios for equally knowledgeable lenders and appraisers. Some S&Ls will lend 80 percent loan-to-value. Three appaisers may assign a range of capitalization rates from 9 percent to 95 percent, given the same appraisal assignment. This illustrates the sensitivity of loan amounts by nominally varying different underwriting factors.

Source: Steve Bram, Grubb & Ellis Financial in Los Angeles, October, 1989.

that the prospective center will seek to attract. However, a shopping center's composition ultimately will be determined by the developer's search for, and negotiation with, tenants. The mix should be based on the market analysis, but the goals of the initial leasing plan will probably not be met; tenant preferences and resistance will almost inevitably result in a number of compromises.

In recent years, smaller centers have drawn a wider array of tenants, including many that were located previously in regional centers or prime downtown locations. Apparel stores and fashion-oriented retailers, for example, now can be found in specialty centers or even in centers anchored by supermarkets. Anchor tenants in small centers often include off-price apparel stores, home centers, movie theaters, children's stores, and health and racquet clubs.

A balanced tenant mix that meets financial credit requirements should include both strong, credit-rated national firms and good local merchants. Figures 7-12, 7-13, and 7-14 indicate the tenant composition of U.S community, neighborhood, and convenience shopping centers.

In choosing stores for a center in an area experiencing new growth, the developer must secure shops that can render a service to the trade area and that have the financial stamina to weather a pioneering period. The developer should also evaluate each tenant's credit rating, profit and loss experience, advertising policy, type of merchandise, type of customers, housekeeping practices, long-term operational record and merchandising policy, and integrity.

One factor to consider when selecting tenants is that they should be so arranged as to provide the greatest amount of interplay among the stores. The success of a shopping center's tenant mix lies not in including or excluding a specific type of tenant, but rather in selecting and combining a group of mutually reinforcing tenants that will serve the needs of the particular market.

In all types of centers, the developer needs to be flexible in selecting tenants and negotiating with them. Numerous adjustments will be made in interior arrangements and tenant leases as negotiations proceed. Figure 7-15 illustrates a leasing plan for Phase I of Midtown Promenade in Atlanta, Georgia. At least two tenant types have been targeted for each shop to provide flexibility in leasing.

Generally, development of a small shopping center cannot move forward without commitments from anchor tenants; thus, marketing to the chosen tenants must begin very early in the process. In fact, the key tenants—for example, a supermarket, discount store, or drugstore—should be tied in closely with the development team in planning the project. These tenants will influence the developer's decisions on building treatment and architectural style as well as parking, signage, and landscaping.

7-12 U.S. Community Shopping Centers: Composition by Tenant Classification Group

	Percent of Total GLA of Mall Shops	Percent of Total Sales	Ratio: Percent of Sales to Percent of GLA	Percent of Total Charges	Ratio: Percent of Total Charges to Percent of GLA
General Merchandise (Excluding Department Stores)	33.1%	28.5%	0.86%	17.8%	0.54%
Food	15.5	33.5	2.15	13.0	0.83
Food Service	6.1	5.4	0.88	10.3	1.69
Clothing and Accessories	7.5	7.0	0.94	11.3	1.51
Women's Wear	4.2	3.8	0.91	6.4	1.53
Children's Wear	*	*	0.94	*	1.15
Men's Wear	0.5	0.4	0.74	0.9	1.63
Family Wear	0.7	0.8	1.28	1.2	1.77
Shoes	2.1	1.7	0.81	3.0	1.44
Home Furnishings	2.4	1.4	0.56	2.6	1.08
Home Appliances/Music	2.4	3.0	1.27	3.5	1.49
Building Materials/Hardware	3.4	1.6	0.47	2.7	0.81
Automotive	0.9	0.5	0.61	0.8	0.93
Hobby/Special Interest	2.9	2.2	0.77	3.9	1.34
Gifts/Specialty	2.4	1.9	0.79	4.2	1.75
Jewelry	0.6	1.1	1.90	1.5	2.67
Liquor	0.5	0.3	0.70	0.7	1.35
Drugs	5.1	6.8	1.32	4.4	0.86
Other Retail	3.3	1.8	0.54	4.4	1.34
Personal Services	4.6	2.0	0.43	7.0	1.53
Recreation/Community	2.9	0.7	0.24	2.6	0.88
Financial	2.4	0.5	0.22	3.9	1.63
Offices (Other than Financial)	1.9	0.1	*	2.3	1.21
Total	100.0	100.0		100.0	

*Less than 0.1 percent.

Source: ULI–the Urban Land Institute, *Dollars and Cents of Shopping Centers: 1990* (Washington, D.C.: ULI–the Urban Land Institute, 1990), p. 274.

Careful analysis of the kind of anchor tenant to target is one of the first steps necessary. For example, superstore centers can make the search for local tenants difficult because the wide-ranging services of superstores can eliminate as many as 10 types of tenants. Convenience stores are growing in popularity as anchor tenants in small centers and as attractive volume stores for larger strip centers, but these also may cause problems in leasing to other retailers—convenience stores sell a wide variety of goods and may insist upon the exclusive right to sell certain items such as beer, milk, and bread. Other items sold at convenience stores, such as videotapes, liquor, fast food, and ice cream, can also cause clashes with other tenants that sell these items. Supermarkets, drugstores, and even gas stations usually do not want to be located in a center with a convenience store.

In the mid-1980s' market, the expansion plans of anchor tenants often served as the driving force behind center development. For example, the larger discount stores such as Target, Wal-mart, and T.J. Maxx are often cited by developers as promoters of the resurgence of strip centers. However, the presence of a major anchor does not presuppose the attraction of other tenants.

The intermixing of off-price/outlet tenants with more typical strip center tenants is fast becoming a trend. An outlet tenant can benefit from the traffic generated by a supermarket, and the other tenants in the center can, in turn, benefit from the ability of the outlet center to draw customers from greater distances.

Pricing the Store Spaces

Pricing rents will depend on the tenant's size, classification, location in the project, and the amount of tenant allowance. Rent schedules should indicate clearly the tenant's classification, square-footage allocation, minimum rent, and the rate of percentage rent. A standard benchmark used for evaluating tenant pricing is ULI's *Dollars & Cents of Shopping Centers*; related publications focus on off-price centers, superstore centers, fashion malls, and convenience centers.

■ 7-13 U.S. Neighborhood Shopping Centers: Composition by Tenant Classification Group

	Percent of Total GLA of Mall Shops	Percent of Sales	Ratio: Percent of Sales to Percent of GLA	Percent of Total Charges	Ratio: Percent of Total Charges to Percent of GLA
General Merchandise (Excluding Department Stores)	6.8%	4.7%	0.70%	2.8%	0.42%
Food	32.2	62.5	1.94	25.3	0.78
Food Service	8.8	6.0	0.69	13.0	1.49
Clothing and Accessories	4.2	3.1	0.74	5.7	1.38
Women's Wear	2.4	1.8	0.74	3.5	1.44
Children's Wear	*	*	*	*	*
Men's Wear	0.3	0.1	0.51	0.4	1.35
Family Wear	0.4	0.3	0.62	0.6	1.48
Shoes	1.3	0.6	0.51	1.4	1.11
Home Furnishings	3.2	1.1	0.35	2.9	0.91
Home Appliances/Music	2.0	1.9	0.97	2.8	1.39
Building Materials/Hardware	3.2	1.5	0.47	2.4	0.74
Automotive	1.3	0.6	0.46	1.1	0.83
Hobby/Special Interest	2.2	1.3	0.58	2.5	1.13
Gifts/Specialty	2.4	1.4	0.56	3.3	1.37
Jewelry	0.4	0.2	0.52	0.7	1.76
Liquor	1.0	0.7	0.69	1.2	1.22
Drugs	8.9	9.7	1.09	6.7	0.76
Other Retail	4.1	1.9	0.46	4.9	1.21
Personal Services	8.9	2.5	0.28	11.8	1.32
Recreation/Community	1.6	0.2	0.10	1.1	0.66
Financial	3.7	*	*	5.4	1.46
Offices (Other than Financial)	3.8	*	*	4.9	1.27
Total	100.0	100.0		100.0	

*Less than 0.1 percent.

Source: ULI–the Urban Land Institute, *Dollars & Cents of Shopping Centers: 1990* (Washington, D.C.: ULI–the Urban Land Institute, 1990), p. 274.

■ 7-14 U.S. Convenience Shopping Centers: Composition by Tenant Classification Group

	Percent of Total GLA of Mall Shops	Percent of Total Sales	Ratio: Percent of Sales to Percent of GLA	Percent of Total Charges	Ratio: Percent of Total Charges to Percent of GLA
General Merchandise	2.8%	*	*	1.7%	0.61%
Food	12.7	37.1	2.93	10.6	0.84
Food Service	14.8	17.0	1.15	16.0	1.08
Clothing and Accessories	5.9	8.8	1.50	6.2	1.06
Women's Wear	2.6	3.5	1.37	2.1	0.81
Children's Wear	0.4	0.7	1.70	0.5	1.14
Men's Wear	1.3	2.1	1.60	1.6	1.25
Family Wear	0.6	*	*	0.8	1.29
Shoes	1.0	1.1	1.08	1.1	1.10
Home Furnishings	3.7	3.6	0.95	3.9	1.05
Home Appliances/Music	4.6	0.6	0.12	5.4	1.17
Building Materials/Hardware	0.4	*	*	0.6	1.29
Automotive	2.5	0.7	0.27	2.4	0.93
Hobby/Special Interest	3.7	2.0	0.53	4.0	1.06
Gifts/Specialty	2.3	3.4	1.45	2.8	1.22
Jewelry	0.3	2.6	7.65	0.6	1.91
Liquor	2.7	4.7	1.74	3.1	1.15
Drugs	8.5	11.7	1.39	4.9	0.58
Other Retail	5.0	2.4	0.48	5.2	1.02
Personal Services	16.5	4.4	0.27	18.7	1.13
Recreation/Community	0.6	*	*	0.6	0.94
Financial	4.4	*	*	4.5	1.02
Offices (Other than Financial)	7.4	*	*	7.7	1.05
Total	100.0%	100.0%	–	100.0%	

*Less than 0.1 percent.

Source: ULI–the Urban Land Institute, *Dollars & Cents of Convenience Centers: 1990* (Washington, D.C.: ULI–the Urban Land Institute, 1990), p. 22.

■ 7-15 Midtown Promenade—Phase I: Recommended Leasing Plan for Existing Space

Shop Number	Type of Business	Square Feet	Percent of Space
1	Sandwich Shop Sports Shop	1,557	2.5%
2	Card/Gift Shop Photo Shop Hardware/Interior Design/ Garden Shop	1,552	2.5
3	Hair Salon Kitchen Shop/Bath Shop	1,262	2.0
4	Florist Bakery	1,262	2.0
5	Unisex Clothing Photo Shop	1,252	2.0
6	Bakery/Dessert Unisex Clothing	1,257	2.0
7	Pet Supply Children's Clothing	1,155	1.9
8	Sandwich Shop/ Ice Cream Sports Shop	1,129	1.8
9	Children's Clothing Unisex Clothing	1,153	1.8
10	Dry Cleaners/Shoe Repair Shop Physical Fitness	1,155	1.8
11	Physical Fitness Bakery/Cafe	3,356	5.3
12	Physical Fitness Sports Shop	2,143	3.4
13	Drugstore	8,922	14.0
14	Grocery Store (Upscale)	35,922	57.0

Source: Hyett-Palma, Inc.

■ 7-16 Typical Anchors in Strip Centers

In 1987, the ICSC performed a survey of 290 strip centers that opened in 1985 and 1986, and found the following anchor uses:

Type of Anchor	Number	Percent of Total
Supermarket	160	55
Drugstore	121	42
Discount Department Store	41	14
Off-Price Apparel	37	13
Home Center	19	7
Movie Theater	19	7
Children's Store	12	4
Health/Racquet Club	12	4
Catalog Showroom	6	2

Source: John Chapman, "Figures Prove Recent Dominance," *Shopping Centers Today*, June 1987, pp. 16, 18–19.

Figures 7-17, 7-18, and 7-19 provide a breakdown of the median GLA, the median sales per square foot of GLA, and the median total rent per square foot GLA for different tenants in U.S. convenience, community, and neighborhood shopping centers. In the neighborhood center, for example, the median rent ranges from $3.58 per square foot for a supermarket to $12.78 per square foot for a jewelry store. Percentage rents also can vary from as little as 1.25 percent for a large supermarket to 10 percent for a cinema; most percentage rents, however, will cluster between 3 and 6 percent. (See the following section on leases for an explanation of percentage rents.)

Tenant Placement

Tenant placement within the center is an important and complex issue. Tenants may have strong and sometimes apparently arbitrary views about their position

■ 7-17 Tenants Most Frequently Found in U.S. Convenience Shopping Centers

Tenant Classification	Rank	Average Number of Stores	Median GLA	Median Sales Volume per Square Foot GLA	Median Total Rent per Square Foot GLA
Food					
Specialty Food	13	0.1	1,371	$208.52	$14.06
Convenience Market	7	0.2	2,397	186.57	8.71
Food Service					
Restaurant (without Liquor)	17	0.1	2,549	159.87	11.39
Restaurant (with Liquor)	4	0.3	2,400	122.91	8.58
Fast Food/Carryout	2	0.3	1,200	206.10	10.64
Sandwich Shop	14	0.1	1,154	155.05	11.96
Home Appliances/Music					
Radio, Video, Stereo (≤10,000 Square Feet)	9	0.2	1,388	66.07	9.65
Liquor/Wine	8	0.2	2,284	117.28	9.15
Drugs	18	0.1	5,000	159.36	7.93
Other Retail					
Flowers/Plant Stores	10	0.1	1,062	97.16	10.52
Personal Service					
Beauty	1	0.4	1,200	105.71	10.89
Barber	12	0.1	750	–	9.00
Cleaner and Dyer	5	0.3	1,200	95.00	12.18
Laundry	11	0.1	1,354	–	7.47
Health Spa/Figure Salon	20	0.1	1,200	–	9.36
Unisex Hair	15	0.1	1,213	72.14	12.32
Video Tape Rentals	6	0.2	1,453	96.95	11.80
Financial					
Real Estate	16	0.1	2,082	–	8.70
Offices (Other than Financial)					
Medical and Dental	19	0.1	2,088	–	9.58
Legal	3	0.3	1,216	–	12.00

Source: ULI–the Urban Land Institute, *Dollars & Cents of Convenience Centers: 1990* (Washington, D.C.: ULI–the Urban Land Institute, 1990), p. 23.

■ 7-18 Tenants Most Frequently Found in U.S. Neighborhood Shopping Centers

Tenant Classification	Rank	Average Number of Stores	Median GLA	Median Sales Volume per Square Foot GLA	Median Total Rent per Square Foot GLA
Food					
Supermarket	10	0.3	22,413	$278.48	$ 3.58
Superstore	13	0.2	36,953	322.75	5.26
Food Service					
Restaurant (without Liquor)	5	0.4	2,200	152.13	10.00
Restaurant (with Liquor)	2	0.5	3,200	128.71	10.46
Fast Food/Carryout	4	0.5	1,434	127.41	11.00
Clothing and Accessories					
Women's Specialty	9	0.3	1,590	136.52	12.00
Women's Ready-to-Wear	14	0.2	2,100	135.70	9.88
Shoes					
Family Shoes	20	0.2	3,000	103.89	8.29
Home Appliances/Music					
Radio, Video, Stereo (≤10,000 Square Feet)	19	0.2	2,228	131.15	8.71
Gifts/Specialty					
Cards and Gifts	12	0.3	2,050	87.24	10.41
Jewelry	17	0.2	1,000	212.29	12.78
Liquor/Wine	18	0.2	2,400	155.35	9.00
Drugs	6	0.3	7,060	175.40	6.50
Other Retail					
Flowers/Plant Stores	11	0.3	1,320	107.60	10.83
Personal Services					
Beauty	1	0.6	1,200	85.28	10.17
Barber	15	0.2	898	98.25	10.40
Cleaner and Dyer	3	0.5	1,475	99.56	11.50
Video Tape Rentals	7	0.3	1,538	93.93	10.45
Financial					
Banks	16	0.2	2,835	–	11.46
Offices (Other than Financial)					
Legal	8	0.3	1,347	–	11.18

Source: ULI–the Urban Land Institute, *Dollars & Cents of Shopping Centers: 1990* (Washington, D.C.: ULI–the Urban Land Institute, 1990), p. 184.

within a center. A location that is advantageous for one type of business may be entirely wrong for another. Placement also is dependent upon the size and depth of the space desired by the tenant.

In deciding tenant location, developers should consider the following aspects:

- suitability of the tenant for the location, including the tenant's financial resources;
- compatibility and complementary status among adjoining stores;
- compatibility of the tenant's merchandising practices with those of adjoining stores;
- parking needs generated by the tenant; and
- customer convenience.

The Lease

The shopping center lease will, in large measure, determine the center's final atmosphere, customer appeal, and degree of financial success. In the retail field, the percentage lease has become the most popular rental contract for both tenant and landlord. In the simplest form of a percentage lease, the tenant agrees to pay a rent equal to a stipulated percentage of the gross dollar volume of the tenant's sales. In shopping centers, the most common type of percentage lease is one in which the tenant agrees to pay a specified minimum rent plus a percentage of gross sales over a certain amount.

Various types of percentage leases exist, but the typical lease has a natural break point. For example, a 2,000-

■ 7-19 Tenants Most Frequently Found in U.S. Community Shopping Centers

Tenant Classification	Rank	Average Number of Stores	Median GLA	Median Sales Volume per Square Foot GLA	Median Total Rent per Square Foot GLA
General Merchandise					
Junior Department Store	12	0.4	35,390	$110.29	$3.55
Discount Department Store	15	0.4	59,537	133.24	3.38
Food					
Superstore	13	0.4	37,430	346.95	4.48
Food Service					
Restaurant (without Liquor)	8	0.6	2,807	135.12	10.00
Restaurant (with Liquor)	2	0.8	3,537	138.28	10.57
Fast Food/Carryout	3	0.7	1,500	200.00	12.73
Clothing and Accessories					
Women's Specialty	9	0.5	1,600	153.91	12.00
Women's Ready-to-Wear	1	1.2	3,000	124.87	8.75
Shoes					
Family Shoes	5	0.6	3,000	118.88	9.00
Home Appliances/Music					
Radio, Video, Stereo (≤10,000 Square Feet)	14	0.4	2,222	191.86	9.00
Gifts/Specialty					
Cards and Gifts	7	0.6	2,600	101.30	10.00
Books	17	0.3	2,400	144.74	9.70
Jewelry	6	0.6	1,260	265.25	14.20
Drugs					
Superdrug	19	0.3	14,600	172.46	4.88
Drugs	20	0.3	7,532	182.48	6.18
Personal Services					
Beauty	4	0.6	1,300	96.94	10.59
Cleaner and Dyer	11	0.4	1,600	86.42	11.34
Unisex Hair	18	0.3	1,217	125.49	12.00
Video Tape Rentals	16	0.3	2,000	83.51	9.73
Financial					
Banks	10	0.5	2,955	3,356.22	11.80

Source: ULI–the Urban Land Institute, *Dollars & Cents of Shopping Centers: 1990* (Washington, D.C.: ULI–the Urban Land Institute, 1990), p. 134.

square-foot space at $12 per square foot per year, with a percentage lease of 6 percent, would work as follows. The minimum rent would be 2,000 times $12, which equals $24,000 per year. The break point at which the percentage rent would begin is calculated as $24,000 divided by 0.06, which equals $400,000. Thus, the tenant would pay a base rent plus 6 percent of gross sales over $400,000. Gross sales of $500,000 would result in an annual rent of $30,000 ($500,000 times 0.06, or $24,000 base rent plus $6,000 overage or percentage rent). Other percentage leases might have a lower percentage at first and increases at various steps. Some percentage leases can reduce as sales increase.

Because it balances tenant and landlord interests, the percentage lease, with a minimum guarantee, is used for almost all types of tenants in shopping centers. The most common exceptions are financial institutions, service shops, and offices. For these tenants, the developer would be wise to consider short-term leases or leases that escalate based either on a series of specified steps or on the Consumer Price Index (CPI). With long-term fixed leases, the developer is not provided with enough incentive income to promote the center adequately.

The lease also functions as an important management tool. Besides establishing obligations, responsibilities, and leasehold arrangements, the lease incorporates the means of preserving, over a long period of time, the shopping center's character and appearance as a merchandising complex. In effect, it establishes a permanent partnership between the management and the tenant.

Organizing the Leasing Program

Agreements with leasing agents should address such issues as exclusive versus open listing, full commission to outside brokers, participation of inside leasing staff, and incentives for the team leader. The leasing agent should be on the development team from start to finish and should provide guidance in the subtleties of tenant selection. A leasing agent with proven expertise in retail leasing within the specified market area should be chosen.

The developer must be personally involved in all stages, especially in the development of a target list for anchors and minianchors that highlights each tenant's priorities within a particular use category. The leasing process is much more selective in shopping center projects than in office projects; the objective must be not simply to lease space but to lease the right space to the right tenant. Thus, setting priorities for the leasing staff and maintaining these priorities is imperative.

In evaluating tenants for selection, the developer needs to consider numerous factors concerning each tenant, including the following:

- merchandise sold,
- credit rating and references,
- other current locations,
- size needs,
- number of years in business,
- operating success in other stores,
- frontage needs,
- quality of management,
- business plan,
- planned date for store opening,
- compatibility with anchor,
- advertising policies,
- types of customers, and
- housekeeping practices.

Postconstruction Marketing and Promotion

The problem that most small centers encounter in marketing and promotion after opening is a limited budget. Anchor tenants, such as large grocery stores and drugstore chains, often already have their own campaigns and refuse to participate in a centerwide effort. The smaller retailers do not have the cash to spend on promotion. Some developers believe that an owner needs four or five small centers to justify hiring a marketing staff person. Others, however, feel that a center of any size can benefit from an ongoing promotional program.

With a small budget, the marketing program must target a limited market and reach it through a precise means. A good marketing plan extends beyond advertising, sales promotion, and special events and avoids trial-and-error approaches. It must consist of a deliberate series of actions designed to maximize a center's potential volume.

The concept of "positioning" lies at the foundation of a successful marketing plan. Positioning means more than creating a favorable image of a center; it consists of a careful analysis of a center's strengths and weaknesses and a close examination of the competition.

Guidelines for setting up a successful promotional program include the following:[20]

- Financial participation in the center's promotional activities should be mandatory for all tenants, and a clause to this effect should be included in the lease.
- At least six months before the center's opening (or reopening in the case of a renovation/expansion), an aggressive publicity program should be instituted.
- At least three to six months before opening, a merchants' association or a steering committee of merchants structured as a marketing fund, should be operating (see below for more details on these). Of course, this is subject to successful preleasing. When an anchor tenant is in place, joint promotion with the owner and other merchants can stimulate substantial interest in the center.
- The center and its stores should be promoted as a single, cohesive unit. All advertising, including printed materials and radio and television spots, should seek to reinforce this perception.
- The center should be involved in community affairs in order to build goodwill and increase traffic to the center. For example, the center might give financial support to major community endeavors or plan and participate in civic events.
- The center's promotional unit and the merchants should always communicate with each other.

The size of the center will determine the extent to which these activities should be pursued; small centers may find less need for many of these efforts. If a center has a limited individual identity but is well located and attractively designed, little or no marketing may be not only the most cost-effective but also the most successful approach.

As mentioned earlier, either a merchants' association or a marketing fund should be used in the promotional efforts. A merchants' association has traditionally been responsible for the promotion of a shopping center. Such an association "acts as a clearinghouse for suggestions and ideas and is responsible for the programming of promotional events. . . . Most lease agreements stipulate that an association will be formed, that the tenants will pay a specified rate per square foot to the association, and that the developer will pay a certain percentage of the annual costs."[21] The developer/owner must organize and partic-

7-20 Marketing and Management: Project X Example

In Project X, the developer used in-house leasing staff as well as independent real estate brokers. The location of each tenant was carefully considered in the merchandising plan, keeping in play the natural synergy that forms between various types of tenants.

The base lease rates for the specialty retail portion of the Project X development range from $11 to $18 per square foot per year. The tenants are responsible for common-area maintenance and related expenses.

Most of the specialty retail leases are for a five- to seven-year term with no options. The supermarket lease is for a 25-year term with four five-year options. The hardware store lease is for a 15-year term with three five-year options. The drugstore lease is for a 15-year term with two five-year options. The specialty retailers all have annual CPI rent escalators in addition to percentage rent. The leasing plan and an example of a leasing status report prepared during the early stages of the leasing process are presented in figure 7-21.

A marketing/promotion fund provided by the tenants (90 percent) and the developer (10 percent) is used to promote the center.

Common-area maintenance charges were expected to be $1.00 per square foot per year, with additional charges of $0.15 for building and liability insurance and $1.10 for real estate and related taxes, yielding a total of $2.25 per square foot per year.

ipate in the association and will also often be its guide and catalyst.

An alternative to a merchants' association is a marketing fund, a technique begun in the 1970s and now widely used. Tenants are still required to provide funds to promote the center, but the fund is totally controlled and administered by the developer/owner. The key advantage of using a marketing fund is that it allows the marketing director to concentrate on marketing and promotion rather than on association details.

Operations and Management

The effective management of a shopping center must include establishing a management approach and plan, setting up and maintaining effective financial records and accounting procedures, maintaining the property, and establishing good housekeeping practices. The objective on a day-to-day and year-to-year basis is to maximize revenue and minimize operating costs while ensuring the long-term viability of the project.

Perhaps the most important responsibility of the shopping center's management, however, is to stimulate the merchants to create a marketplace that is above the commonplace. One way to achieve this is to work closely with the small tenants to make sure that each has a sound business plan, effective inventory control, and good store layout and merchandising. Educational films and merchant meetings in which retailers can share ideas will provide retailers with useful information. Some developers include a lease clause that requires the retailer to spend time with a consultant at the retailer's expense.

Management Approaches

Depending on the size of the center and the arrangements for operation worked out earlier in the lease negotiations, the shopping center developer/owner provides maintenance and management in one of two ways: either by directly supervising, or by employing a manager to supervise, a maintenance and management force; or by turning the center's operation over to a management firm. By acting directly as manager, the developer/owner maintains control of the property and can influence more immediately the quality of the operation. By using an outside management contractor, however, the developer may derive certain economies of scale and expertise. Centers smaller than 75,000 square feet often use ownership management because the management fees charged for operating small centers are relatively high and because management of small centers is relatively straightforward. Fee-managers generally work on a percentage of rental income, with a range of 2 to 6 percent, depending on the size of the center and the scope of responsibility.[22]

The owner/manager also will need to decide whether or not to employ an on-site manager. For most centers smaller than 400,000 square feet, no on-site manager is needed unless the owner chooses to include offices, usually engaged in other activities, in the project.[23]

Financial Records and Control

In order to ensure success, the owner or the manager obviously must establish acceptable financial accounting and reporting procedures to collect rents, account for

■ 7-21 Leasing Status Report for Project X[a]

	Use	Tenant Space	Store Area (Square Feet)	Lease Rate Year 1	Year 2
Signed Leases, Majors					
	Grocery	M-1	42,352.00	$7.50	$7.50
	Drugstore	M-3	10,920.00	8.50	8.50
	Hardware	M-2	12,000.00	7.50	7.50
Total Leases, Majors	N/A	N/A	62,272.00	N/A	N/A
Year 1 Average Lease Rate	N/A	N/A	N/A	7.67	N/A
Signed Leases, Specialty					
	Video rental	G-1,2,3	4,500.00	11.00	11.00
	Photo finishing	A-3	1,100.00	15.00	15.50
	Bookstore	D-2/3	3,000.00	11.50	12.00
Total Leases, Specialty	N/A	N/A	8,600.00	N/A	N/A
Year 1 Average Lease Rate	N/A	N/A	N/A	11.69	N/A
Letters of Intent					
	Pizzeria	A-1	1,100.00	16.00	16.00
	Bank	Pad	2,520.00	13.89	13.89
	Card and gift	D-4/5	3,000.00	13.07	13.07
	Hair salon	F-2	1,500.00	12.00	12.00
	Coney Island Resort	F-1	1,500.00	13.00	13.00
	Tile store	H-2	2,100.00	11.50	12.00
	Tennis shop	F-5/6	3,000.00	12.50	12.50
	Bakery	G-4	1,500.00	13.00	13.00
	Sporting goods	H-1	2,100.00	13.50	13.50
Total Letters	N/A	N/A	18,320.00	N/A	N/A
Percentage of Letters Out			0.16		
Year 1 Average Rate	N/A	N/A	N/A	13.04	N/A
Total Signed Leases	N/A	N/A	73,872.00	N/A	N/A
Year 1 Average Lease Rate	N/A	N/A	N/A	8.14	N/A
Total Shopping Center Area	N/A	N/A	117,466.00	N/A	N/A
Amount of Center Not Leased	N/A	N/A	43,614.00	N/A	N/A
Percentage Leased	N/A	N/A	0.63	N/A	N/A

[a]These leases are 15- to 25-year leases that call for $.50 to $1.00 per square foot increases every five to 10 years. This program does not allow for proper calculations on leases of this length, thus only the first five years are shown.

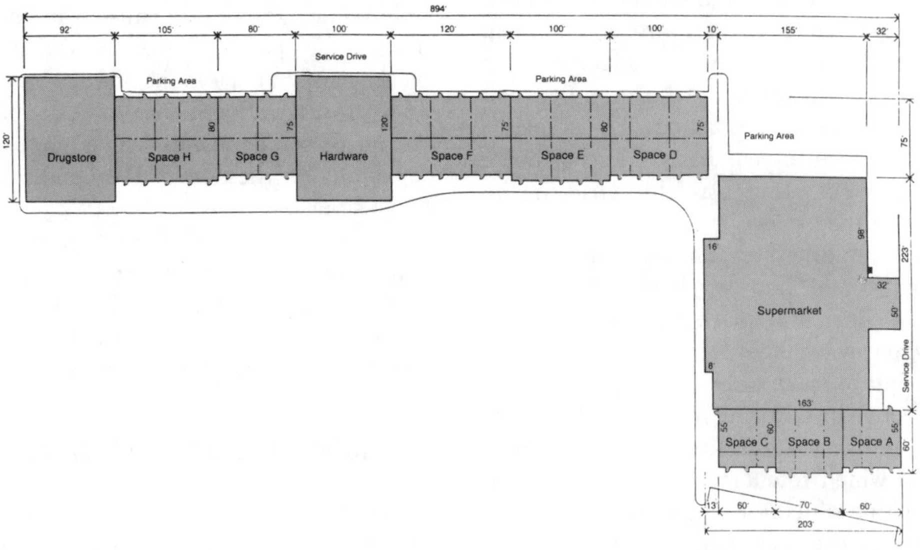

Lease Rate			Balance of	Annual Rent	Annual Rent	Percentage
Year 3	Year 4	Year 5	Lease Term	Year 1	per Square Foot	Rent
$7.50	$7.50	$7.50	N/A	$317,640.00	$9.21	N/A
8.50	8.50	8.50	N/A	92,820.00	10.96	0.03
7.50	7.50	7.50	N/A	90,000.00	8.00	N/A
N/A	N/A	N/A	N/A	500,460.00		N/A
N/A	N/A	N/A	N/A	N/A	N/A	N/A
12.00	13.00	13.00	0.00	49,500.00	12.00	0.04
16.00	16.50	17.00	0.00	16,500.00	16.00	0.06
12.50	13.00	13.50	0.00	34,500.00	12.50	0.05
N/A	N/A	N/A	N/A	100,500.00	N/A	N/A
N/A	N/A	N/A	N/A	N/A	N/A	N/A
16.00	16.00	16.00	16.00	17,600.00	16.00	0.05
13.89	13.89	13.89	N/A	35,002.80	15.48	N/A
13.07	13.07	13.07	0.00	39,210.00	13.07	0.06
13.00	14.00	14.00	0.00	18,000.00	13.00	0.06
13.00	13.00	13.00		19,500.00	13.00	0.06
12.50	13.00	13.50	0.00	24,150.00	12.50	0.06
12.50	12.50	12.50	0.00	37,500.00	12.50	0.06
13.00	13.00	13.00	0.00	19,500.00	13.00	0.06
13.50	13.50	13.50	0.00	28,350.00	13.50	0.05
N/A	N/A	N/A	N/A	238,812.80		N/A
N/A	N/A	N/A	N/A	N/A	N/A	N/A
N/A	N/A	N/A	N/A	600,960.00		N/A
N/A	N/A	N/A	N/A	N/A	N/A	N/A
N/A	N/A	N/A	N/A	N/A	N/A	N/A
N/A	N/A	N/A	N/A	N/A	N/A	N/A
N/A	N/A	N/A	N/A	N/A	N/A	N/A

revenues and expenses, and evaluate performance. A shopping center, once completed, is like any other business in this regard.

Management's most important responsibility is to maintain accurate internal records that provide:

- control and accounting for cash and other physical property,
- production of data useful in policy making and decision making, and
- accurate figures for preparing tax returns.

Data produced in recordkeeping, such as monthly information on sales figures, category performance, and square-footage productivity, is critical in determining percentage rents.[24] Whereas a monthly rent payment (plus expenses, where applicable) is all that is required of the tenant of an office building, in a shopping center the rental calculations are more complicated and require that tenants furnish sales records and financial reports.

In the early days of the shopping center industry, it was the usual practice to call for payment of the percentage overage on an annual basis in accordance with a sales report certified by an outside auditor or a responsible officer of the tenant company. More recent leases have generally provided for overage payments on an uncertified basis quarterly, or sometimes even monthly, with an annual reconciliation on the basis of an audited statement by the tenant. Such an arrangement has the obvious benefit of leveling off the flow of income while keeping a tight rein on less financially responsible tenants.[25]

Maintenance and Housekeeping

The shopping center lease will establish the maintenance responsibilities of the landlord and the tenants. The landlord will typically be responsible for the foundation, walls, roof, parking lot, and exterior open areas. The

Tanner Market
Pasadena, California

Tanner Market, in downtown Pasadena, California, is a 42,000-square-foot gross leasable area (GLA) specialty retail center that was developed by three architect/planners, with additional equity financing from nine limited partner investors and one of the property's original owners. The project involved the adaptive use and rehabilitation of numerous streetfront historic buildings, and it has become an integral part of the retail and pedestrian fabric of downtown Pasadena.

Tanner Market is the second project developed by the three principal developers and was undertaken by them with a minimum of cash investment (only $8,000 each). Although it is a small project, it has been developed in two phases because of limited capital and uncertainty about the market.

The Site

Tanner Market is located in Old Pasadena, a 14-block historic area in the National Register of Historic Places, that was the city's first downtown and shopping district when the town was known as the Indiana Colony in the 1880s. The project serves as the gateway to Old Pasadena, marking the transition from the cultural facilities and luxury car dealers on the west to the heart of Pasadena's regional shopping, governmental, and financial districts to the east. Tanner Market fronts on Colorado Boulevard, route of the Tournament of Roses Parade that starts nearby, and is also located directly adjacent to the Long Beach Freeway and within several miles of the juncture of the Foothill, Ventura, and Long Beach freeways.

The project is part of an entire block that has been master-planned by the architects of Tanner Market. The block includes a public parking garage in the middle of the block facing on its eastern edge; numerous existing low-rise commercial buildings that surround the garage on the north and south; the Cellophane Building, which borders the garage on the east; and Tanner Market, which fills out the eastern end of the block.

The Cellophane Building is a separate 14,000-square-foot retail project, focusing on home furnishings and fashion clothing, that has been functionally integrated with Tanner Market. Tanner Market has an easement through the Cellophane Building to the parking garage, and the Cellophane Building has an easement to the central patio of Tanner Market. In effect, the two projects form a unified complex of nearly 60,000 square feet.

The Tanner Market site was previously occupied by two large livery stable buildings dating to the 1880s, a 1920s office building, and a 1930s Texaco gas station. The gas station, one of Pasadena's first, was a prototype Spanish Revival station. The livery stables were the location for the birth of the touring company Tanner Graylines, known today in most parts of the United States as Grayline Tours. A furniture maker, a florist, and a kitchenware retailer were also located in the buildings when the developer undertook the project.

Tanner Market is a 42,000-square-foot specialty shopping center in downtown Pasadena that involved the adaptive use and rehabilitation of numerous streetfront historic buildings.

Background

The developer of the project—Tanner Market Partnership—was formed by three individuals who were also the principals of the Arroyo Group, an architectural/planning firm in Pasadena that had been integrally involved in planning the redevelopment of downtown Pasadena. The Arroyo Group was formed in the early 1970s, and among its first assignments was the development of a concept plan for the historic district of Old Pasadena. When this was undertaken, the area had been zoned for a high-tech business park. Pasadena Heritage and other civic groups supported the plan, which was eventually adopted as a specific plan with zoning ordinance in 1978 through 1979, including design guidelines.

As the Arroyo Group and its principals continued to be active in the community, they developed a strong base of community contacts, a good understanding of the direction in which the market was moving, and considerable expertise in the design aspects of renovating older buildings, as this was a considerable portion of their practice. Their involvement in the community also included the purchase of a building for their offices in downtown Pasadena. Moreover, one of the firm's principals, James Goodell, served for a time as president of the Pasadena Central Improvement Association, a group of property owners and business people in the area that supported the historic preservation plan. All of this activity contributed greatly to the later success of the project.

The project includes several courtyards with fountains, landscaping, and outdoor seating for its restaurants and other food establishments.

Financing

Having developed such close ties with the area, and with a strong interest in developing a small project that could contribute to the area's revitalization, the Arroyo Group was naturally intrigued when it learned that several properties on the Tanner Market site were for sale, including the gas station and the buildings that wrapped around it. With the notion of developing a small downtown retail project, the three Arroyo Group principals organized a limited partnership, with themselves as general partners and nine local investors as limited partners. The nine limited partners were long-time residents of Pasadena who chose to invest in the deal out of a sense of civic pride as much as for profit. The three principals also convinced the owner of the wraparound building to participate as an equity investor in the deal by putting his existing land and buildings into the project through a subordinated lease.

Through this partnership, six parcels were assembled, including the existing buildings, an alley acquired from the city, and a ground lease of state-owned land across Pasadena Avenue for a small parking lot. All of the parcels were assembled by 1981, and much of the design work was completed by this time as well, but high interest rates delayed further progress. Because the land was owned entirely by the partnership with no outstanding loans, and because the Arroyo Group did all of the design work, this temporary halt did not create a serious problem or carrying burden.

By the spring of 1983, the project began to move forward when the Tanner Market Partnership received a financing commitment from Bank of America, contingent upon the first phase of the project being 100 percent preleased. By this time, the partnership had run out of working capital and had to obtain a $500,000 predevelopment loan from the bank to continue its leasing activities.

Phase I was completed in August 1984; this phase was able to carry the debt but did not throw off any cash to the partners. In developing Phase II, the developer again went to numerous banks before obtaining a development loan. The financing requirements for Phase II included that the project be 60 percent preleased before construction began. The developer achieved this level easily and then stopped leasing space because rents were rising and it could lease the space at higher rates if it waited. Historic tax credits contributed significantly to the feasibility of the project, although the developer was not allowed tax credits on the Ritz Grill because of necessary changes that did not conform to the historic requirements.

Planning and Design

Tanner Market itself consists of approximately 42,000 square feet of GLA in four existing buildings. The project is organized around two open patio areas, one which serves as

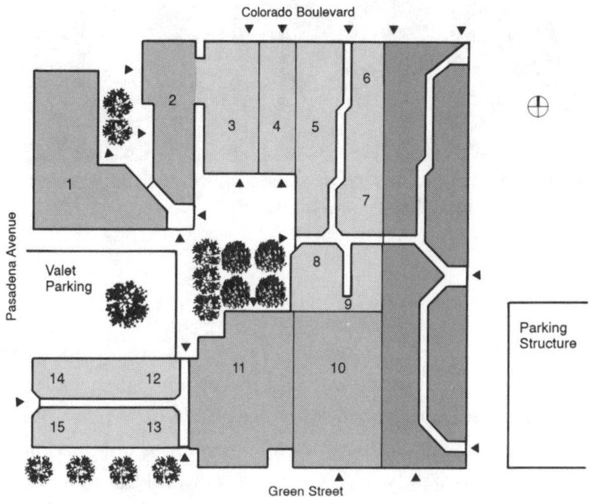

Specialty Shops
Restaurants/Entertainment
The Cellophane Building

1. Ritz Grill
2. Old Town Bakery
3. Areté
4. The Pavilion
5. Bellini
6. A Child's Fancy
7. Roseberry's
8. Jenny Wren
9. Cummings Allen Studio
10. Premiere
11. Pappagallo
12. Willow Springs
13. Optical Oasis
14. Treadle
15. L'Attitude

The project site and tenanting plan (including the adjacent Cellophane Building, which was developed and is owned by a separate entity).

Tanner Market includes several unusual tenants, such as Premiere, a combination banquet facility and nightclub.

both an entrance off Colorado Boulevard and an open-air eating area for the restaurant, and the other that serves as a valet turnaround and central courtyard onto which many of the Phase II shops open. Altogether, the developer obtained and restored approximately 30,000 square feet and built an additional 14,280 square feet, including infill structures and the creation of mezzanine levels within the historic structures.

The old Texaco gas station, now the Ritz Grill, and the Old Pasadena Bakery, together with the commercial building to its west, housing Arete and The Pavilion, make up the first phase of the project. The buildings in which Phase II of the project is located—making up the western and southern borders and surrounding the large central courtyard—were both livery barns and now house a children's toy store, children's furniture and clothing stores, two high-end clothing and jewelry stores, a banquet/nightclub facility, and an Italian restaurant operated by the owner of the Ritz Grill. An open-air walkway off Colorado provides an entrance to this section from the north, and the courtyard provides an entrance on the east.

Providing adequate parking was one of the biggest challenges in planning the project. This was particularly critical in Phase I, as the public parking garage was not yet built. The developer first went to CalTrans, which owned the right-of-way along the Long Beach Freeway just across the street from the project, to obtain a ground lease on a parcel that was subsequently used for valet parking only, in order to maximize the number of cars that could be parked on the small lot (70 spaces). The central court facing on Pasadena Avenue also provided 17 parking spaces during the first phase and was subsequently converted to a valet turnaround and plaza in Phase II. Once the 535-car public parking garage was completed, the developer was required to purchase the rights to 148 spaces as a means of meeting the city parking requirements for the project, although no specific spaces are reserved for use by the patrons of Tanner Market.

The Phase II approach involved continuous construction, starting at the north and moving south and east, thus allowing stores to open as the construction of their space was completed

The contractor who managed the construction was a distinct asset to the project. One of the architects in the Arroyo Group had worked for this contractor as an employee, so a considerable familiarity and trust was present in their relationship. The contractor did a careful job of estimating throughout the process, and the number of change orders was kept to a minimum. The Arroyo Group has designed and managed most of the tenant improvements.

Marketing and Management

The developer's first efforts in leasing involved a large national brokerage firm, but, after six months, the developer determined that this firm was not well suited to specialty retail leasing in a pioneer area, and it began leasing efforts of its own. The leasing plan was not well defined at the outset, although the developer knew the preferred anchor tenant would be a restaurant. Thus, the initial leasing effort involved talking to nearly 20 different restaurant operators and finally identifying an entrepreneur with extensive experience in opening and operating a series of chain restaurants—a man who had also opened two restaurants of his own. This entrepreneur was interested in opening a signature restaurant; he signed the first lease in the project to open the Ritz Grill.

Following this, three additional tenants were lined up to fill out the first phase of the project: Sweet Desires, a chocolate and pastry shop opened by the local planning director (replaced later by the Old Town Bakery); Arete, a beauty salon opened by a friend of a friend of one of the general partners; and The Pavilion, a kitchen gift shop opened by a professional couple who wanted to start a business on the side. All of these tenants were new, and, except for the restaurateur, none had ever opened his or her own shop before.

Leasing for Phase II was easier, as the project was already established, the area had "taken off," and the developer had more experience. One of the first tenants to locate in Phase II was Bellini, a children's furniture store, which had been looking for a location in downtown Pasadena and found Tanner Market to be very suitable. A second tenant selling children's toys—A Child's Fancy—moved in next to Bellini, and Jenny Wren, a maternity and children's clothing store, followed shortly. The developer made no attempt to lease space to national chains, as it believed the key to success was owner- operated quality stores. National chains are, however, now coming into Old Pasadena as it has become established as a major specialty retail and restaurant destination area. Other Phase II tenants include Pappagallo, a 175-seat Italian restaurant, and Premiere, a combination banquet facility and nightclub; both of these are operated by the Ritz Grill operator.

The project offers an attractive, pedestrian-friendly environment.

Little or no formal market analysis was done for this development, although a considerable amount was done for the downtown as a whole as part of the redevelopment effort, and the developer did possess substantial firsthand knowledge of the area. In general, the developer believed that the site was well positioned to draw from the wealthy local market and beyond.

The project opened two weeks before the 1984 Olympics, and performed excellently in its initial month. A 2,000-seat cinema also opened on the block to the immediate west of the project in 1987, and this has provided a big boost for evening business.

Because the operator of the Ritz Grill also operates two other food-service establishments in the project, he is a critical element to the continued success of the project. As a result, the developer has taken out a $1 million life insurance policy on this man.

Rents are all triple net, and a staff person with the Arroyo Group takes care of managing the center. The project's tenants and the partners are very active in the areawide promotional organization, which sponsors group advertising and publishes a quarterly Old Pasadena newspaper.

The project has proven to be a financial success and was appraised at $9.5 million in 1989, well above its $5.9 million development cost. Its value continues to rise as the surrounding area continues to improve. The project's rents range from $24 to $36 per square foot, the highest in Old Pasadena and as high as any in the city.

Experience Gained

- The development of Tanner Market was time-consuming and involved a complicated process for the developer not unlike what might be expected with a considerably larger project. "You've got to start somewhere, sometime," notes general partner James Goodell. "We saw an opportunity in our backyard, and we went for it. No merchant builder would have given the situation a second glance. But lots of hard work has paid off; we paid a big tuition, but we also learned a great deal and survived the experience. We're proud of the project."
- Perhaps the easiest part of the development for the developer was design and construction, as this was the area in which the general partners had the greatest expertise. Even

■ Tanner Market (Continued)

though the general partners had only a short track record in development, their close ties to business leaders in the downtown and surrounding community simplified and smoothed the process of bringing the limitied partner investors together. Obtaining such financial support is often very difficult or impossible for a beginning developer.

- The toughest elements of the project for the developer were the leasing and debt financing. The initial error in using a broker inexperienced in retail leasing cost the developer a six-month delay, and, in general, the leasing process was very time-consuming, especially at the outset. Because the developer was relatively inexperienced, especially in terms of dealing with banks, obtaining debt financing was a difficult process.
- Constantly changing loan terms and loan officers made financing extremely frustrating. Two major financing commitments were canceled within a week of scheduled closings—both because of changes in senior loan officers unfamiliar with the deal. The developer also went through nine loan officers at the Bank of America during the course of the project.
- The key elements in the success of the project were the hard work and commitment to the project displayed by the general partners and the patience of the investors who were willing to hold the property for a relatively long period of time—from 1981, when the land was assembled, to 1988, when it was finally completed.
- Developers engaging in their first retail project often find that developing a small specialty center is easier than developing a neighborhood center because, as novices, it is more difficult to establish relationships with traditional anchor tenants. Moreover, small specialty projects are natural places for developers to start because most major developers are not willing to engage in such high-risk and untested ventures. Such projects are unlikely to provide massive financial returns, but they do provide a good learning opportunity on which to build.

Developer:
Tanner Market Partnership
40 East Colorado Boulevard
Pasadena, California 91105
(818) 795-9771

Architect/Planner:
The Arroyo Group
40 East Colorado Boulevard
Pasadena, California 91105

Management:
Tanner Management
40 East Colorado Boulevard
Pasadena, California 91105

Project Data

Land Use Information:
Site Area: 1.62 acres
Gross Building Area (GBA): 45,000 square feet
Gross Leasable Area (GLA): 42,000 square feet
Parking Spaces: 53 surface
148 structured
Parking Index: 4.47 spaces per 1,000 square feet GLA

Tenant Information:

Classification	Number of Tenants	Area Occupied (Square Feet)
Food Service	4	25,000
Clothing	2	2,400
Shoes	1	1,500
Home Furnishings	1	2,000
Home Applicances/Music	1	1,500
Hobby/Special Interest	1	1,500
Gifts/Specialty	2	1,800
Jewelry and Cosmetics	1	450
Personal Services	1	3,300
Offices (Other than Financial)	1	2,000
Other	2	3,000
Total	17	44,450[a]

Economic Information:
Site Acquisition Cost: $1,200,000
Construction Cost: $3,900,000
Per Gross Square Foot: $87
Total Project Cost: $5,900,000
Rents per Square Foot: $24 to $36.
Length of Lease: 5 years with 5-year option

[a]Includes 2,450 square feet of outdoor dining area.

Ocean Outlets in Rehoboth Beach, Delaware, is a 130,000-square-foot outlet center that is managed by the developer—Gulfstream Properties—which retains one full-time property manager on site. Two full-time maintenance staff are also employed with at least one on site during hours of operation.

tenants will have responsibility for the interior of the premises. The lease serves as the groundwork for the operation of the center, but, beyond this, management expertise must be exercised to make the center a success.

Whether the developer/owner or an outside firm acts as manager, in a small center the maintenance and housekeeping functions usually are handled, at least in part, by independent contractors that specialize in those operations.

The developer should keep in mind that an effective schedule of regular maintenance and operations will prolong a property's life. A planned maintenance program will also help to avoid any crises that may develop as the property ages. The challenge for the developer is to balance the maintenance needs of the project against the costs, which may be substantial.

Proper maintenance will require regular inspections of the property. In general, every shopping center will require three types of inspections: standard, task, and annual.[26] The standard is a general inspection to judge the center's overall appearance. The task inspection is a detailed review of the structure and common grounds. Items in need of regular task inspection include entrances, vestibules, common areas, landscaping, restrooms, corridors, electrical rooms, storage rooms, vacant spaces, occupied stores, surrounding streets, signage, parking lots, lighting, the building exterior, and roofs. The annual inspection is an annual property evaluation involving the review of the condition of the major equipment and structure to determine the rate and degree of property depreciation.

In addition, the property manager should develop a standard operating procedures manual that details all specific policies, procedures, systems, and job functions that relate to the property's operation.[27] The manual should specify and establish a standard for every item requiring periodic attention.

Conclusion

The market for small shopping centers strengthened in the mid-1980s in response to shifting lifestyles and shopping patterns. With the increase in two-career couples, many people now shop at strip centers rather than larger malls in order to save time. In addition, most markets are already saturated with regional malls, whereas opportunities to fill in market gaps and target narrow infill audiences are often available. Small centers also are much easier to develop than are regional centers, requiring fewer tenants, a simpler approval process, and less capital and lead time. Of the 6,000 shopping centers that came on-stream between 1986 and 1988, notes John Chapman of the ICSC, 90 percent were under 100,000 square feet in size.[28]

However, with the numerous opportunities for small center development, competition has increased and many areas are rapidly becoming overbuilt. Other potential problems loom on the horizon. In Southern California, for example, which has been especially strong in strip center development in recent years, nearly 2,000 strip centers were built between 1978 and 1988.[29] Because of the tremendous increase in the number of strip centers, complaints from neighborhood groups about insufficient parking and inadequate buffers between residential and commercial zones led the Los Angeles city council in 1987 to adopt a six-month moratorium against strip center development.

Another potential problem small centers face is a lack of small tenants and a proliferation of superstores that may preclude many other tenants. In many cases, a developer may not be able to find suitable small tenants to fill out a center that has a large anchor tenant. If a superstore insists on the exclusive right to sell certain items, leasing space in the center to other tenants will be especially difficult.

In the difficult markets of the early 1990s, opportunities for small center development are more difficult to find than ever. Moreover, although long-term growth in this area will continue to provide opportunities for developers with limited capital, growth also has served to attract major developers to the field, and, as a result, the level of quality and professionalism has increased, making the situation both more competitive and more difficult for inexperienced developers.

Notes

1. John A. Casazza and Frank H. Spink, Jr., *Shopping Center Development Handbook*, 2nd edition (Washington, D.C.: ULI–the Urban Land Institute, 1985), p. 1.

2. No similar standard guidelines exist for the secondary trade area. As the name suggests, the secondary trade area is a geographic area adjacent to the primary trade area and extending away from the site for a given driving time.

3. Casazza and Spink, *Shopping Center Development Handbook*, p. 23.

4. Ibid., pp. 27–28.

5. See "Where Tenants Are the Landlord," *Shopping Centers Today*, June 1987, p. 14.

6. Mary Alice Hines, *Shopping Center Development and Investment* (New York: John Wiley & Sons, 1983), p. 57.

7. Margaret Doyle, "Strip Centers Shed Shoddy Image," *Building, Design, & Construction*, March 1988, pp. 66–72.

8. See John McCloud, "Strip Centers Are Force of the Future," *Shopping Center World*, April 1987, p. 46.

9. Philip E. Klein, *Feasibility of Shopping Center Development, Shopping Center Report* (New York: International Council of Shopping Centers, 1980), p. 2.

10. Casazza and Spink, *Shopping Center Development Handbook*, p. 61.

11. Ibid., p. 70.

12. Quoted in ULI–the Urban Land Institute, "Shopping Center Design and Operation: Participant's Guide," unpublished manuscript, unpaginated.

13. See John D. Bucholz, "Put the Right Roof over Your Head," *Shopping Center World*, February 1988, pp. 28, 30, 32, 34, 36.

14. See Paula J. Silbey, "This Car Always on the Lot," *Shopping Centers Today*, June 1987, p. 15.

15. See ULI–the Urban Land Institute, "Shopping Centers II Workshop: Participant's Guide,"unpublished guide, prepared in 1988, pp. 36–37.

16. This information was taken from a presentation by Larry Good at "Shopping Center Design and Operation" workshop, organized by ULI–the Urban Land Institute in Los Angeles, California, April 18–19, 1988.

17. This list based on Charles S. Telchin, "How to Improve Developer/Tenant Planning and Construction Coordination," *Shopping Center Report* (New York: International Council of Shopping Centers, 1977), p. 1.

18. Ibid., pp. 3–4.

19. Hines, *Shopping Center Development and Investment*, p. 218.

20. ULI–the Urban Land Institute, "Shopping Centers II Workshop: Participant's Guide," pp. 115–18.

21. Ibid., p. 189.

22. See Robert J. Flynn, ed., *Carpenter's Shopping Center Management: Principles and Practices*, 3rd edition (New York: International Council of Shopping Centers, 1984), p. 29.

23. Ibid., p. 28.

24. Ibid., pp. 36–37.

25. Ibid., p. 56.

26. See Institute of Real Estate Management, *Managing the Shopping Center* (Chicago: Institute of Real Estate Management, 1983), p. 163.

27. Ibid., p. 174.

28. John Chapman, "Small Centers Come of Age," *Stores*, August 1988, pp. 35–38.

29. See Doyle "Strip Centers Shed Shoddy Image," pp. 66–72.

Chapter 8

Trends and Issues

This final chapter focuses on two key topics: the trends and outlook for the development industry, and the social responsibility of developers. The first is critical for beginning developers if they are to identify properly both the opportunities and pitfalls that may lie ahead in the marketplace as they get started in the business. The second is important insofar as both ULI–the Urban Land Institute and this book are concerned about ensuring that all developers live up to their civic responsibilities and create products and developments that make a positive contribution to their communities and the urban environment.

Trends

Changes are occurring at a rapid pace both inside and outside the development industry. Those developers who best understand the ramifications of these changes on their businesses will be the ones who prosper in the 1990s.

Changing Market Factors

To understand where the industry is going, one must understand where it has been. Many developers count their baptism in the industry from their first experience of recession. The industry has changed dramatically from 1936 when ULI was founded, and even from the 1960s when many of today's major developers started their firms. Double-digit inflation of the late 1970s and early 1980s made real estate a preferred investment because it provided one of the best hedges against inflation. Since then, however, several factors have combined to make the early 1990s watershed years in the evolution of the development industry:

- overbuilding of office and commercial space in most markets;
- crisis in the savings and loan industry and a record number of bank failures;
- tax changes in the 1986 Tax Reform Act that have adversely affected real estate;
- increasing government regulation that has increased the time and cost involved in obtaining necessary government approvals;
- an increasingly restrictive lending environment; and
- economic recession traveling from one region of the country to another.

The economy, overbuilding, and lack of credit have combined to cause perhaps the greatest restructuring of the development industry since the Depression of the 1930s. Many firms, especially smaller and mid-size firms without institutional financial backing, are not expected

■ 8-1 Consolidation among Real Estate Firms in 1990

	By Product Type						By Ownership		
	Residential			Commercial					
	Large Firms	Medium/ Small Firms	All Firms	Large Firms	Medium/ Small Firms	All Firms	Public Firms	Private Firms	All Firms
Firms that Downsized in 1990	76%	80%	78%	28%	63%	35%	46%	60%	56%
Percent of Workforce Cut in 1990	13	25	20	9	21	13	13	18	17
Firms that Anticipate Downsizing in 1991	50	31	41	21	50	27	40	32	34

Source: Kibel, Green, Inc., Santa Monica, California.

to survive. Returns in income-producing real estate have been shrinking from the early 1980s; they averaged 12.0 percent for the 10-year period, 1979 to 1988, and 8.3 percent for the five-year period, 1984 to 1988. In 1989, returns were only 6.7 percent.

A consistent characteristic of real estate development over the last 30 years is a marked tendency toward boom-and-bust cycles of activity. The cycles seem to be growing shorter, occurring more often, and affecting different regions of the country at different times. The early 1980s saw prosperity in the oil belt and recession in the Northeast. By the late 1980s, conditions had reversed, with booming economies on the East and West Coasts and depression in the oil states. In the early 1990s, conditions on both coasts are slumping while the oil belt recovers and renews its vigor.

Changing external factors almost always bring opportunities for those who are able to foresee the changes. The influx of women into the labor force in the 1970s and 1980s, for example, helped to fuel the expansion in the service sector that created demand for new office buildings. Changing demographics—notably, the graying of the American population—will create demand for entirely new types of living environments and communities. New modes of communication based on computers and fax machines and other products of technological change will inevitably alter work habits and change the location patterns of offices and commercial buildings. Other major trends are highlighted in the sections that follow.

Industry Restructuring

As a result of the market situation in the early 1990s, the dominant current trend in the real estate development industry as a whole is downsizing the industry. Real Estate Research Corporation (RERC) of Chicago summarized in 1989 the forces causing retrenchment as: "Too much product. Too much money. Too many people. . . . Unforgiving markets and keen competition are winnowing the industry. The amateurs are gone."[1] These forces are still prevailing in 1991.

Many surveys and interviews with industry leaders (appearing in a variety of real estate periodicals) indicate industry restructuring and retrenchment on a broad scale (see figure 8-1). Dramatic shifts in finance and investment philosophy are highlighted by the decline in development activity; the global economy and the U.S. dependence on foreign countries makes the future harder to read; the effects of downsizing the real estate marketplace are difficult to predict.

The development industry is changing fundamentally:

- Real estate finance is undergoing a thorough restructuring with more multiproduct financial providers and a homogenization of services.
- Real estate is becoming more "institutionalized." Investment-quality real estate has earned the status of an asset class comparable to stocks and bonds. Pension funds have introduced unleveraged, free-and-clear ownership on a wide scale.
- Tax reform, which virtually dried up the infusion of money from syndicators, is believed to have helped the industry by restoring the importance of traditional cash-flow criteria. Along with inflation and interest rates, however, the rapid entry and exit of syndicators is "one of the decade's dramatic back-and-forths that fed the uncertainty now overtaking even the stronger and long-term participants."[2]
- Megadeals and the huge debt and equity resources they require have forced many developers to become manufacturers of products rather than long-term owners.

The role of syndicators and S&Ls has declined, and that of foreign investors, pension funds, and commercial banks is expanding. These new capital sources exercise more control over their investments. In fact, many are now investing in land with the idea of finding a developer as a partner, rather than the other way around as in the past.

Large national real estate companies are increasing their market shares. Their influence tends to squeeze out medium-size firms as national companies and specialized, local niche developers dominate; increase the professionalism and standardization of real estate practices; and improve the quality of large-scale construction. Because of the tough marketplace in the early 1990s, many of these large development firms are moving into asset and property management, financing, and brokerage, and away from development.

Small developers are disadvantaged by a variety of current trends in the development industry, most notably the downsizing of the industry as a whole. These trends are unlikely to change in the near future, and beginning developers, especially, should be aware of the long-term impacts that are likely to result from the continued growth of larger firms.

What can small developers do? Phil Walsh, president of Emblem Development Corporation of Montclair, California, sees the progressive demise of the small developer. Walsh observes that when California required cities to have a general plan, personal contacts with members of city councils no longer ensured automatic zoning approval. After the success of Proposition 13, cities began to look for new ways to raise money and turned to impact fees and exactions, which create tremendous front-end cash burdens for builders. "Some cities require as much as $26,000 per unit. Cheap cities are $9,000. The builder has to put up hard cash to get his plat recorded. On one small 62-unit project, I've spent $1 million and 1.5 years without turning any dirt. I still have to pay $480,000 in fees."[3]

Walsh says that small builders and developers are being forced to the sidelines where they are confronted with difficult options:

- they can remain small and pick up what big developers leave behind;
- they can joint venture with larger players or institutions;
- they can build in planned communities where the large profits will be made by the planned community developer; or
- they can move to outlying areas where marketing and holding costs are higher.

Apart from its direct effect on costs, perhaps the most damaging aspect of the sharp increase in regulation is its impact on small developers. As projects and developers both become larger, competition tends to decline. Small developers have historically helped to ensure competition by providing tenants and buyers with alternative products. As small development firms become less viable, the quality of competition will inevitably be reduced.

Paying for Infrastructure

Urban fiscal problems have forced cities to rely increasingly on real estate development to help pay for infrastructure and to balance local budgets. Ten years ago, most municipal services and infrastructure such as roads and utilities were paid for out of general revenues and general obligation bonds. Today, virtually every major city and many small cities have adopted comprehensive systems of impact fees, exactions, and other charges. These charges pay for off-site infrastructure, capital improvements, and sometimes even current operations for public services.

The trend toward greater fees is likely to continue as cities try to maximize revenue without significantly reducing development. Developers are resisting exorbitant charges, primarily in the courts. Recent court decisions have limited the fees that may be charged; fees may be levied to cover the costs imposed by new development on a city, but they may not be used to construct or repair facilities or cover costs that are not directly attributable to new development.

Urban fiscal problems affect developers in several ways. First, higher fees, of course, raise the cost of development. They worsen housing affordability, which already is at crisis levels in certain major cities.[4] Second, these fiscal problems have led to cutbacks in local budgets for maintaining public facilities, causing neighborhoods to deteriorate more quickly and real estate values to fall. Predominantly lower- and middle-income municipalities are unable to maintain public services and facilities as well as upper-income suburbs do, with the result that real estate values do not hold up as well in those communities, reducing the attractiveness of future real estate investment there as well.

The fiscal problems give cities stronger incentives to work with the development community. Some of the best opportunities for beginning developers lie in working with cities on government-owned land or in redevelopment areas. If developers are willing to tolerate red tape and bureaucratic delays, cities and their agencies will help them obtain the necessary public approvals.

Erosion of Development Rights

The erosion of development rights is reflected in the amount of work that developers must do on a site before their right to develop it becomes "vested"—that is, the right cannot be taken away or delayed through city actions such as building moratoriums. One of the greatest risks facing developers today is that they can spend years and millions of dollars on obtaining necessary approvals to develop a site and still lose the right to develop it according to their original plans.[5] Across-the-board density reductions and building moratoriums are becoming increasingly common in cities that are struggling to control or reduce their rate of growth.

One way for developers to hedge against the risk of losing development rights is to buy land subject to obtaining all necessary approvals and permits. Developers must spend more for land under these conditions, but the higher price is worth the reduced risk. Developers of larger projects are dealing with vesting risks by negotiating "development agreements" that require them to build certain facilities in exchange for a city's locking in existing zoning and development rights.[6] The erosion of vested development rights increases development risk significantly, but it is a trend that is not likely to be reversed in the foreseeable future.

The types and amount of regulation on development has been increasing throughout the 20th century. Many types of regulation (zoning, for example) have been supported, and even initiated, by property developers as a means of protecting long-term property values. It is not regulation *per se*, but rather the uncertainty about new regulation and the time and cost of meeting existing regulatory requirements, that imposes the greatest risk on developers. Every decade brings a new set of concerns.

Environmental Concerns

Environmental concerns have been, and will continue to be, of increasing importance to policy makers and the general public. Further regulations to protect the environment will become ever more problematic for developers over the course of the 1990s. Perhaps the most worrisome environmental problem facing developers is toxic-waste liability. When toxic-waste problems are found after a developer has closed on a site, development may be halted for months or even years. Developer liability can be unlimited. Potential lender liability for toxic waste and asbestos has placed lenders in the unusual position of not wanting to foreclose on some loans that are in default.

As always, new problems generate new opportunities. Some development firms are specializing in properties contaminated by toxic waste or asbestos. Because the properties can usually be purchased at very large discounts, careful analysis of the removal costs can generate large profits, although lenders are extremely wary of loans on such properties. Nonetheless, the fact remains that developers who fail to perform adequate due diligence before purchasing new properties will eventually face financial disaster.

In addition, developers will be increasingly affected by programs designed to improve air quality. Special districts in which air quality is rigorously monitored and emissions are tightly restricted are being established in major metropolitan areas. New restrictions not only affect heavy industry but also "clean industry"—indeed, virtually anyone who uses chemicals, sprays, cleaning fluids, fuel, or other substances that generate fumes. Districts such as the Air Quality Control District for Greater Los Angeles are empowered to impose across-the-board taxes based on the levels of air emissions currently generated by building occupants. The restrictions may ultimately force significant portions of industries, such as the furniture industry, to relocate. Developers may even be held liable for their tenants' air emissions.

Communities are also becoming increasingly concerned about the preservation of hillsides, wetlands, canyons, forests, and other environmentally sensitive areas. Developers who address these concerns in planning and designing their buildings will find communities more receptive to their projects. Those who do not will face vocal and increasingly powerful opposition.

Transportation Issues

Transportation has always been one of the major sources of real estate value because of its impact on location, but solving the problem of overburdened roads promises to be one of the development industry's principal concerns in the 1990s. Suburban congestion already has shut down development in some communities and lies behind no-growth movements in many others. Ira Lowry has listed several factors that will play a major role in determining future transportation needs:[7]

- "Within urbanized areas, both residences and workplaces are dispersing from the classical concentric configuration to a sprawling low-density arrangement. . . . Home-to-work travel no longer has much radial orientation; work trips are both short and diffuse as to origin and destination. Nearly all work trips are now, and will continue to be, in private vehicles."[8]
- Work trips, which traditionally have been the main focus of urban transportation planning, now account for less than one-quarter of all local trips and less than one-third of local travel mileage. Most households have as many cars as licensed drivers.
- The most pressing task for local transportation planning over the next 30 years will be to expand capacity and improve traffic management on suburban streets and arterials.

Cities rarely commit resources to build the necessary transportation infrastructure until conditions deteriorate to the point that residents are prepared to vote for bond issues to pay for the improvements. Thus, investment in transportation almost always lags behind the need for improvements. Developers, who will be asked to shoulder much of the burden for improving inadequate transportation in the suburbs, would be well advised to support coordinated, collective efforts to plan transportation in their communities; otherwise, they will be forced to pay a disproportionate share of the cost, and what they do provide will be inadequate to hold congestion constant, let alone reduce it. Traffic congestion will be the major constraint on development in most areas in the 1990s.

Citizen Opposition

The days are gone in which developers could build what they wanted without worrying about the interests or attitudes of the community. Sooner or later, all developers now encounter community groups that are hostile to their projects. This book has sought to stress the need for developers to talk directly, in person, to community groups before becoming irrevocably committed to a project.

Historic and environmental preservation have become two of the most popular weapons used by neighborhood groups to oppose development. Although historic preservation has saved many unique structures and preserved the character of many neighborhoods, it has also been abused by groups who want to stop development at all cost. Likewise, advocates of environmental preservation are sometimes motivated less by their love of flora and fauna than by their hostility to all forms of development. Beginning developers should avoid potential problem properties altogether, unless they are prepared for a long fight.

Developers and planners must satisfy, or at least address, several different constituencies: local residents, local merchants, preservation and arts groups, the homeless, city officials, and public agency officials. Successful developers learn how to operate within their local, inevitably heterogeneous communities.

According to Daniel Rose, community groups can, at their best, provide perspective and insight; at their worst, they can fall prey to the "NIMBY" ("not in my backyard") mentality. "Residents often oppose the construction of a fire station in their neighborhood because they object to the accompanying noise. But the necessary services of an urban system must be located somewhere. Someone will have to work or live near a fire station or a garbage disposal site."[9]

Gerald Hines, owner of Gerald D. Hines Interests, a Houston-based development firm that operates nationally, emphasizes the role that community acceptance plays in marketability. "We look at each city as a different culture, and if we don't know the culture, we're going to have an unsuccessful project. Conferring with community boards and neighborhood associations has become a part of a project's market analysis and its later acceptance by the market."[10]

Paul Goldberger, architectural critic for the *New York Times*, believes that "the impulse to demand more from the urban environment has led to greater conflict between regulatory and private development forces rather than to a conciliatory environment with a shared goal—making cities better."[11]

Social Responsibility

Development touches almost everyone in almost all areas of their lives: at work, at home, at school, at play. Furthermore, what real estate developers build will almost certainly outlast them and may endure for centuries. With this unique position comes unique social responsibilities. These responsibilities are at the very core of ULI's purpose, as stated in its credo: "As responsible citizens/developers, let us leave this land enhanced . . . thereby enriching the lives of all who live on it."

Developers have special responsibilities in part because their activities involve large public commitments to which they become parties. In many communities,

What developers build will almost certainly outlast them and affect the lives of many, and thus developers must ensure that their projects are not only profitable but that they also make a positive contribution to their community. Pictured is Washington Mutual Tower in Seattle.

developers actually build most of the urban infrastructure, including roads, sewer facilities, water-treatment facilities, and drainage channels. In some communities, they provide everything, including schools, hospitals, and police and fire stations.

What do communities have a right to expect from developers? In subdivision development, developers function as the implementing arm of the city. They are the designers as well as the builders, determining land use, parks, and road layouts. The community has a right to expect the highest possible quality of design and implementation. It has a right to expect developers to be sensitive to community concerns, streetscape and landscape, traffic, and other dimensions inherent in development. It has a right to expect developers to be good citizens of the community, concerned to protect its long-term interests. Developers should do what they promise—on time and with appropriate attention to quality.

What do developers have a right to expect from communities? They have a right to expect fairness and consistency and that decisions will be made on the basis of merit rather than politics. They have a right to expect the community to honor its commitments—to build promised infrastructure on time and to maintain public facilities and services properly. They have a right to expect the community to exercise foresight and good planning judgment in setting public policy—to ensure that new regulations are handled efficiently and do not impose unnecessary costs or delays on the development process.

The Developer's Public Image

Developers as a group suffer from a negative public image. That image is often undeserved—as when developers are identified with unwanted change. Sometimes, however, it is deserved—as when developers have built shoddy products, have been insensitive to community needs, or have imposed costs on the community for which they should have taken responsibility.

In expanding communities, where economic growth is desired and the environment is not threatened, developers can overcome the stereotype of greedy hustlers. However, in areas with strong antigrowth sentiments, the suspicion and distrust with which many people view developers in general makes conditions harder for all developers, no matter how good they are.

Beginning developers should understand the sources of the distrust that they will encounter. Many communities and neighborhood groups have relied on promises that were never kept by developers or on predictions that turned out to be inaccurate (such as the new office building that the developer asserted would not cause congestion). Similarly, they have witnessed poorly maintained apartments turn into slums. Even though real estate brokers or property managers may be to blame rather than developers, developers are the standard bearers for the real estate industry as a whole. Public approvals for new development provide the sole opportunity for most people to complain about the full array of urban ills.

The growing difficulty of undertaking development projects in many communities increases the incentives for developers to concentrate on simpler projects. Exactions and fees are so high in many areas that developers cannot afford to provide other amenities that would benefit the community. Nevertheless, developers should recall that many of today's exactions came about because communities felt that developers were giving inadequate consideration to the context and communitywide impacts of their projects. In economic terms, developers were not paying the "full cost," including the indirect costs, of their projects.

All developers suffer from the negative publicity generated by the S&L industry failures and the HUD scandals of the late 1980s. In retrospect, it is apparent that developers should have been more sensitive to conflicts of interest arising from their ownership of, or close alliance to, S&Ls that financed their projects. The HUD scandals raise other ethical concerns. The labyrinth through which developers must navigate to obtain funding under most government programs has long required developers to seek expert, professional consultation. But where does one cross the line between reasonable assistance and scandalous or criminal consultation? In the HUD case, the public was scandalized by the size of fees—as much as $4,000 per hour—collected by prominent political figures to push certain projects.

Beginning developers sooner or later will encounter a situation in which a project in which they have invested considerable time and money will go under unless they receive regulatory or financing approval. The temptation to do whatever is necessary to save the project may be very strong. A strong character is required to withstand such unethical or illegal temptations.

Although developers may be as much sinned against as sinning in such situations, the whole industry suffers guilt by association, making the accomplishment of worthwhile goals that much harder for individual developers.

Successful development—and a good public image—has always meant that developers must work closely with the community. Good developers understand what the community requires and how their projects will enhance the neighborhood and serve the needs of the residents or workers. Recently, however, relations between developers and community groups have become more contentious, and compromise has been harder to reach. Developers should remember that most community groups not only will accept but also will actively support develop-

■ 8-2 Ethical Structures of Five Major Parties to Development Decisions

Planners. Tend to exhibit a utopian perspective, a populist orientation, a suspicion of private interests, and a belief in the irreconcilability of public and private interests.

Developers. Utility maximizers concerned with profits, wealth, and personal distinction. Display a distrust of government typical of the private sector.

Political Figures. Concerned about conserving their political constituencies, maximizing their political power, and increasing their wealth.

Parochial Communities (Neighborhoods, for Example). Concerned with environmental values, property values, amenity values, congestion, intercommunity spillovers, and social values (including the exclusion of "undesirables").

Community at Large. Concerned with economic development values and the quality of the regional environment.

Source: Lowdon Wingo, professor of urban and regional planning at USC.

ment that truly enhances their neighborhoods. Developers must talk directly to local groups, be willing to compromise on points that concern those groups, and, most importantly, be prepared to deliver on promises. Once developers establish credibility with community groups on one project, they will find other groups more sympathetic. Furthermore, if in the future they are confronted by intransigent opponents, they are more likely to receive a sympathetic hearing by planning and public officials because of their reputation for working with the community.

Differing Social Objectives

Every major planning decision involves at least five major parties, each with its own biases and objectives. The five groups include planners, developers, political figures, neighborhood groups, and the community at large. USC professor Lowdon Wingo summarizes the attitudes of the five major parties in feature box 8-2.

Wingo notes that although improved understanding between the groups may sometimes allow consensus to be reached, understanding and empathy can achieve only so much. The various groups seem to possess distinct and incompatible ethical codes. "If I am right," comments Wingo, "the way we actually work out of the paralysis of conflict here is by forming transitory coalitions among the five major elements of the problem."[12]

The community's interest often is at odds with that of individual community groups. For example, a homeowners' group may resist road improvements that benefit the community at large because they bring more traffic through the homeowners' own neighborhood. Similarly, developers may have commitments to investors that limit their ability to provide the extra amenities that neighborhood groups demand.

Although the function of planners is to serve as neutral analysts and advisers to the city in conflicts between developers and neighborhood groups, they naturally have their own private agendas and biases. In their evaluation of projects, they may emphasize different, often contradictory, planning criteria such as:

- efficiency—making the city work better in terms of less congestion, lower-cost utilities, and lower-cost housing;
- equity—avoiding actions that hurt the poor, first-time buyers, renters, or other groups who end up paying for restrictive requirements;
- income redistribution—favoring actions that give the poor more housing, lower rents, or better economic opportunities;
- economic growth—favoring actions that encourage economic activity, industry, and job opportunities;
- environmental protection; and
- neighborhood preservation.

New development and neighborhood revitalization are the best, and sometimes the only, means that communities have available to achieve many of the above objectives. The role of development in stimulating economic growth is obvious, but its role in issues of equity and income redistribution is less so. To the extent that developers build low-income housing and generate fees and taxes to the community that help subsidize other projects, developers provide one of the few sources of revenue to assist lower-income groups. In addition, although developers are often viewed as the destroyers against whom the environment must be protected and neighborhoods preserved, they are in fact more often the instrument by which environmental protection and neighborhood preservation is achieved.

Community leaders should remember that most of their goals for community improvements will be attained only with the participation of developers. Developers are the producers who initiate projects and take the risks necessary to make things happen. Because their actions have far-reaching consequences for the people who live

One of the challenges facing cities and the development community is how to create more exciting spaces. Pictured is Harborplace in Baltimore—developed by the Rouse Company—a model for creating lively and exciting urban spaces; the project is a major tourist attraction and has made a very positive impact on the city of Baltimore and its downtown.

and work near their projects, the community should have a say in the development process. Indeed, this principle has underlain the evolution of land use regulation and community participation throughout this century. The delicate balance between the interests of communities and those of developers must be maintained if communities are to grow.

Sensitivity and Good Urban Design

One of the most common complaints about developers is that they are insensitive: to neighborhood concerns, to community concerns, to design, to the environment, and to the impact of their projects on others. Developers are sometimes justifiably criticized for destroying the fabric of neighborhoods or hastening neighborhood decline by tearing down buildings and not replacing them.[13] All developers should understand the principles of good urban design. Even though developers hire architects to design their buildings, developers must themselves be knowledgeable critics of good design, both from the perspective of what is most marketable and from the community's perspective.

Jonathon Barnett notes that the architectural harmony found in cities such as central Paris is no accident. "It is the result of a series of closely related design guidelines imposed over more than two centuries."[14] Such harmony, whether it be on the grand scale of Paris or the village scale of colonial Williamsburg, is a goal towards which both developers and communities should strive. Large-scale development offers the opportunity for the developer to control urban design more effectively than in most cities where parcels are developed independently. Nevertheless, through careful planning and coordination, independent development projects can achieve a harmony that enhances the city while also increasing property values and tax revenues.

One of the challenges facing both inner-city and suburban communities today is how to create more exciting spaces. Urban designers criticize the building form that results from a preoccupation with the automobile. Shopping centers with huge parking lots in front, for example, deprive suburbs of a sense of enclosure. Urban designers have also found that when the height of buildings is less than one-quarter of the width of the street, the sense of enclosure breaks down.

Why should developers care about streetscapes, urban or suburban?: not just because such concern is part of good citizenship but also because it translates into long-run value. Streets and plazas that are pleasant to drive down and walk through will increase more in value over time than less desirable neighborhoods. The surrounding buildings will likewise command higher rents and sales prices. Developers, however, cannot improve streetscapes by themselves. They are often hamstrung by zoning codes that mandate street widths, setbacks, and building heights, and lender biases that mandate front-door (rather than back-door) parking. On the other hand, early 20th-century planning principles favoring the separation of uses have given way to new trends favoring mixed-use development. Many planning commissions now actively encourage mixed-use development with offices, shopping, and residences on the same or adjacent sites.

Personal Integrity

A developer's reputation for integrity is the foundation of his/her success. The development community is a very small world. Even in the largest cities, news travels very fast and reputations precede every player. Players who lie, cheat, or break the law find that reputable companies and business people will have nothing to do with them.

Years after they occur, little things can come back to haunt developers' affairs: failure to follow through on a promise, slow performance on tenant finish-out, sloppy workmanship, or slow payment on contracts. Many developers will run into some form of cash-flow difficulties at some time during their careers and will consequently have to renegotiate a loan or the terms of a deal. At such times, a past record of honesty and of keeping partners fully informed can make all the difference. No one likes bad news, but everyone likes surprises even less. Projects rarely go bad over night. Symptoms develop over time—declining occupancy, delays in construction, and so forth. When partners and lenders are kept informed of the problems, they are more understanding and more willing to try to work things out. Usually, projects that get into trouble between good partners can be put back on track, or, if one partner must take over, no long-term damage is done to the other partner's reputation. However, if a partner has been dishonest or has failed to tell the whole truth, the consequences for that partner's reputation can be devastating.

Conclusion

Cities are organic in nature. Like living organisms, they experience cycles of birth, growth, and decay. Every section of every city experiences these cycles, no matter how prestigious its origins. Even Athens' Acropolis, Rome's Forum, or New York's Fifth Avenue have gone through periods of economic vitality followed by periods of economic decline. The factors that influence such cycles are very complex. They include transportation, utilities and other infrastructure, the quality, age, and functional obsolescence of the buildings, the quality of design, and the age distribution and incomes of the residents and workers as well as the economic health of the neighborhood, city, region, and country.

Our understanding of how to control development to create better cities and neighborhoods is far from complete. Among the greatest problems facing planners and public policy makers are how and where to invest public funds so that they will do the most to enhance upcoming areas or halt the fall of declining areas. Too often, massive public and private expenditures are made to rejuvenate one section of town, only to pull businesses and homebuyers away from another section of town.

The cyclical nature of urban development extends to the political arena and to the priority that urban issues receive on the national agenda. Government economic support for urban problems declined throughout the 1980s, dropping to less than one-fourth of the level it enjoyed at the end of the 1970s. The elimination of federal revenue sharing forced local communities to cut back on infrastructure improvements and repairs. Cutbacks in many social programs that helped poorer areas hastened neighborhood decline. The problem of homelessness has attracted considerable media attention but as yet no significant federal financial assistance. The time seems ripe for the political cycle to swing round to a renewed concern for urban issues, but the actual timing and pace of increased public support is uncertain.

In general, our performance in developing U.S. cities has been at best mediocre. It is not so much that our cities are drab and ugly as they fall short of their potential. Spaces are poorly planned; boring, repetitive designs are everywhere. Once beautiful neighborhoods are not maintained; the fabric of our urban infrastructure is in an appalling state of disrepair. Developing new areas is easier and cheaper than properly maintaining older areas.

No one individual or group is to blame for this situation, but all are capable of helping to remedy it. The development community must exercise stronger leadership not only in terms of the construction and renovation of U.S. cities but also in correcting the harmful aspects of the present development system. By looking after the interests of the community at large, developers serve their own interests.

Past ULI president Robert Nahas summarizes the attraction of development: "The great developers who I've been privileged to know never worked for money, *per se*. I'm not a psychiatrist, but I think these developers want to leave a footprint in the sand. It's their particular kind of immortality."[15] Successful developers share the same goal: to create better living environments, better places, better cities. All developments must pass the test of serving current market needs or they will fail. But most developments also have a future clientele. Although individual homes and buildings may be replaced, the basic fabric of the community that developers create—street layout, parks, urban design elements—will last for hundreds of years. Indeed, one of development's greatest rewards—and the source of its greatest responsibilities—is its impact on future generations. Development offers a way to extend ourselves beyond our lifetime.

Notes

1. Real Estate Research Corporation, *Emerging Trends in Real Estate: 1989* (New York: Equitable Real Estate Investment Management, 1988), p. 3.

2. Ibid., p. 5.

3. From a speech by Walsh to USC students in November 1988.

4. In June of 1990, 46 percent of all households in the United States could afford a median-priced house. In Los Angeles and San Francisco, only 15 percent and 11 percent of all households, respectively, could afford a median-priced house.

5. In California, for example, development rights become vested after "substantial construction" has been completed. This has been interpreted to mean that a substantial portion of a building's steel or wood frame must be in place.

6. See Rita Fitzgerald and Richard Peiser, "Development (Dis)Agreements at Colorado Place," *Urban Land*, July 1988, pp. 2–5. See also Douglas R. Porter and Lindell L. Marsh, *Development Agreements: Practice, Policy, and Prospects* (Washington, D.C.: ULI–the Urban Land Institute, 1989).

7. Ira S. Lowry, "Planning for Urban Sprawl," *Proceedings of the Conference on Long-Range Trends and Requirements for the Nation's Highway and Public Transit Systems* (Washington, D.C.: Transportation Research Board, National Research Council, 1988).

8. Ibid., p. 276

9. Daniel Rose, chairman of "Design and Politics" conference held in New York City, April 1988. Reported by Maria Brisbane, "Developing in a Politicized Environment," *Urban Land*, July 1988, pp. 6–8.

10. Gerald Hines, quoted in Brisbane, "Developing in a Politicized Environment," p. 7.

11. Quoted in ibid., p. 8.

12. See Richard Peiser, "Who Plans America? Planners or Developers?," *APA Journal*, Autumn 1990, p. 503.

13. It should be noted that developers never tear down buildings without intending to replace them because the purpose of tearing them down is to increase the income generated by the property. When this occurs, a mistake, inability to get financing, or bankruptcy has almost certainly occurred.

14. Jonathon Barnett, "In the Public Interest: Design Guidelines," *Architectural Record*, July 1987, p. 114.

15. Quoted in Ed Micken, "Future Talk: The Next Fifty Years," *Urban Land*, December 1986, p. 16.

Appendices

Appendix A

Contributors and Interviewees

The following people were interviewed for, or otherwise contributed to, this book. The author is indebted to them for their assistance and advice.

Edgar S. Albrecht, Jr.
Assistant Vice President
Corroon & Black
Pasadena, California

David Ball
Vice President
Arnel Development
Costa Mesa, California

Douglas F. Bauer
Vice President
California Real Estate Industries Group
Security Pacific Bank
Irvine, California

Leslie Beckhart
Equitable Life
Irvine, California

Pedro Birba
Partner
The Nadel Partnership, Inc.
Santa Monica, California

Donald Blair
Owner
Blair Development
Houston, Texas

James Bock
President
James Bock & Associates
Houston, Texas

Donald Bonanno
President
Bonanno Land Co.
San Clemente, California

Don Bowers
Principal
Bowers Perez and Associates
Los Angeles, California

Stanley M. Brent, AIA
President
Stanley M. Brent AIA, Inc.
Sherman Oaks, California

Gary A. Brinderson
Chairman of the Board and CEO
Brinderson Corporation
Irvine, California

A. Alexander Bul
Senior Vice President
HSM/Grubb & Ellis Advisors, Inc.
Dallas, Texas

Alan I. Casden
President and CEO, Casden Co.
Chairman, Coast Fed Properties
Beverly Hills, California

Robert Comstock
Managing Partner
Comstock, Crosser, Hickey
Manhattan Beach, California

Michael D. Couch
President
The Couch Company
Palo Alto, California

John Dawson
McDonalds Corporation
Woodland Hills, California

Bernard Delzer
President
Delzer Development
Los Angeles, California

Wendell L. Evans, Jr.
President and Chairman of the Board
Washington Federal Savings
Stillwater, Minnesota

William D. Foote
President
Southwest Diversified, Inc.
Irvine, California

Jerome Frank, Jr.
Jerome Frank, Sr.
Frank Investments
Dallas, Texas

Jim Gallagher
Vice President
Lasalle Partners
Chicago, Illinois

Alex Garvin
Yale University
New Haven, Connecticut

Richard Gleitman
R. J. Investments Associates
Sherman Oaks, California

Robert H. Gluck
Columbia Group, Ltd.
Beverly Hills, California

Jona Goldrich
Chairman of the Board
Goldrich and Kest
Culver City, California

R. Lawrence Good
President
Good Fulton & Farrell Architects
Dallas, Texas

Donald Grant
Chief Operating Partner
O'Donnell, Armstrong, Brighan Partners
Costa Mesa, California

Virgil L. Griffin
Associate of Shopping Center Division
The Nadel Partnership, Inc.
Costa Mesa, California

Alex Haagen
Alexander Haagen Development
Manhattan Beach, California

Peter J. Hall
President
Great American Development Company
San Diego, California

Joseph J. Hemmens
Senior Vice President
Weyerhaeuser Mortgage Company
Woodland Hills, California

Hugh Hilton
Principal
Karson Realty Advisors
Los Angeles, California

Ken Himes
President
Himes, Peters, Mason Architects, Inc.
Costa Mesa, California

Donald J. Howard
Vice President Development
Fritz Duda Company
Orange, California

Haskel Iny
General Partner
Homestead Group Associates
Los Angeles, California

Joseph A. Jaconi
President
Joseph Jaconi Company, Inc.
Torrance, California

Harold Josephson
President
Josephson Properties
Los Angeles, California

Shelby Jean Kaplan
President
Securities Placements, Inc. & Tricap, Inc.
Los Angeles, California

David V. Karney
Owner
Karney Development
Los Angeles, California

Richard Kelly
Vice president
Luma Corp.
Dallas, Texas

Edwin R. Kimsey
Vice President
Niles Bolton Associates, Inc.
Atlanta, Georgia

Allan Kotin
Principal
Kotin, Regan & Mouchly, Inc.
Los Angeles, California

Ronald W. Lee
Senior Vice President/California Real Estate Industry Group
Security Pacific Bank
Los Angeles, California

Lisa M. Lewis
Financial Manager
Trammell Crow Company
San Diego, California

Ralph M. Lewis
Chairman
Lewis Homes
Upland, California

Donald W. Leyman
Senior Vice President
Swinerton and Walberg Company
Los Angeles, California

John D. Lusk
Chairman of the Board
The Lusk Company
Irvine, California

James Maddingly
President
Luma Corp.
Dallas, Texas

Ralph J. Martin
President
Richardson Nagy Martin
Newport Beach, California

Michael L. Matkins
Partner
Allen, Matkins, Leck, Gamble & Mallory
Los Angeles, California

John McMahan
President
McMahan Real Estate Advisors, Inc.
San Francisco, California

Michael Meyer
Senior Partner
Pillsbury, Madison & Sutro
Los Angeles, California

Thomas E. Mitchell, P.E.
Vice President
Barton-Aschman Associates, Inc.
Pasadena, California

C.C. Mow
Chairman and CEO
Century West Development
Santa Monica, California

P. Patrick Murray
President
P. Patrick Murray, Inc.
Los Angeles, California

Herb Nadel
President and Chief Executive Officer
Nadel Partnership
Los Angeles, California

Harry Newman, Jr.
Chairman
Newman Properties
Long Beach, California

Ira Norris
President
Inco Homes
Upland, California

John D. O'Donnell
Managing General Partner
O'Donnell, Armstrong & Partners
Irvine, California

Jack R. Rodman
Managing Partner
Kenneth Leventhal & Company
Los Angeles, California

Thomas B. Rogers
Senior Vice President
Security Pacific National Bank
Irvine, California

John C. Rowlett
Executive Vice president
Club Corporation of America
Dallas, Texas

Paul F. Schultheis
President
Real Estate Property Investment, Inc.
Arcadia, California

Douglas Sjoberg
Vice President Consulting
Grubb & Ellis
Los Angeles, California

Timothy L. Strader
Chairman
The Legacy Companies
Irvine, California

John Tadich
Associate Vice President
Newport Pacific Realty & Investment Corporation
Newport Beach, California

Scott Tanner
Vice President
Metmar Financial, Inc.
Los Angeles, California

Gerald M. Trimble
President
USC Real Estate Development Corporation
Los Angeles, California

Dale R. Walker
Executive Vice President
Wells Fargo Bank
San Francisco, California

James J. Weaver
Associate
Schaefer Dixon Associates
Los Angeles, California

Lewis N. Wolff
Managing Partner
Wolff Sesnon Buttery Development Company
Los Angeles, California

Richard Zelle
Vice Chairman of the Board
Center Financial Group
Los Angeles, California

Appendix B

Sales and Marketing Budget for a 300-Lot Subdivision

The following sales and marketing budget/pro forma is for a 50-acre, 300-lot subdivision. This budget would provide all parties with a thorough and comprehensive program for marketing the subdivision within a 48-month period. It assumes that Builder "A," which acquired the land and installed all of the site improvements, decided to spread its risk by allowing four other builders also to build within the subdivision on 150 lots. An outside sales and marketing company was employed to market the community and sell the finished homes for the five builders.

Assumptions

- 300 finished lots, with water, sewer, and drainage, and filled to grade. All common area improvements and entry features in place. Cost to each builder would be $25,000 per lot.
- Average-size home would be 2,000 square feet.
- Hard construction costs for an average-size home would be $35.00 per square foot, or $70,000 in total.

Pro Forma

Sales Income		
300 homes @ $150,000 per home		$ 45,000,000
Sales Management Expenses		
$1,500 per sale to sales associates	$ 450,000	
$750 per sale to sales manager	225,000	
$750 per sale profit to company	225,000	
$4,500 per sale to cobroker, estimated @ 20% of sales or 60 sales	270,000	
$1,500 per sale to off-site salesperson on all cobroker sales	90,000	
Off-site promotions @ $3,000 per year	12,000	
Travel expenses—$100 per month per person	14,400	
Move-in gifts for buyers	8,475	
Seminars @ $1,000 per person per year	12,000	
Sales training	20,000	
Sales contests @ $3,000 per year	12,000	
	$1,338,875	$1,338,875
Sales Office/Administrative Overhead		
Trailer rental @ $350 per month	$ 16,800	
Furniture rental @ $250 per month	12,000	
Receptionist/secretary @ $15,000 per year	60,000	
Customer administrator @ $22,000 per year	88,000	
Color selection coordinator @ $15,000 per year	60,000	
Weekend hostess @ $5,200 per year	20,800	
Consultants @ $6,000 per year	24,000	
Market research @ $8,000 per year	32,000	
HOW program @ $350 per unit	105,000	
Interior plant rental @ $75 per month	3,600	
Office supplies @ $125 per month	6,000	
Telephone @ $350 per month	16,800	
Maintenance and cleaning @ $125 per month	6,000	
Electric @ $350 per month	16,800	
Water @ $50 per month	2,400	
Alarm system @$50 per month	2,400	
Copier rental @ $350 per month	16,800	
Repairs @ $50 per month	2,400	
Maintenance service contracts @ $150 per month	7,200	
Pest control @ $25 per month	1,200	
Landscape maintenance @ $100 per month	4,800	
Miscellaneous @ $125 per month	6,000	

	$511,000	$511,000

■ (Continued)

Advertising, Production, and Public Relations		
Media advertising @ 0.02% of sales	$ 900,000	
Production charges	90,000	
Brochures and production charges	9,000	
Brochure inserts	2,000	
Newsletters	8,500	
Public relations fee @ $1,000 per month	48,000	
Public relations production	12,000	
Direct mail campaigns	12,000	
On-site promotions	24,000	
	$1,105,500	$1,105,500
Model Merchandising (5 Models)		
Utilities @ $200 per month, per model	$48,000	
Landscape maintenance @ $500 per month	24,000	
Alarms	10,800	
Interior plant rentals @ $375 per month	18,000	
Pest control @ $100 per month	4,800	
Interior maintenance and cleaning @ $625 per month	30,000	
	$135,600	$135,600
Signage and Graphics		
Sales office displays and graphics	$24,000	
On-site directional signage	6,000	
Sales office signage	3,000	
Lot, spec, and model signage	12,000	
Signage and graphic production charges	4,000	
Signage maintenance and repairs	4,775	
	$53,775	$53,775
Deposits and Contingencies		
Trailer deposit @ 2 months' rental—Sales	$700	
Furniture deposit—Sales	500	
Interior plant deposit—Sales	150	
Telephone deposit—Sales	350	
Electric deposit—Sales	350	
Water deposit—Sales	150	
Alarm deposit—Sales	150	
Copier deposit—Sales	700	
Utilities deposit—Models	1,000	
Alarm deposit—Models	450	
Interior plant deposit—Models	750	
Contingency @ 0.0075% of sales	337,500	
	$342,750	$342,750
Total Sales and Marketing Expenses		$ 3,487,500

- A central sales facility operated by a professional sales and marketing company, rather than Builder A's sales team, would market the community. Other builders would likely feel unfairly treated if Builder A's sales team marketed their products at the point-of-sale.
- Each builder would pay the sales and marketing company 7.75 percent on each sale. This would be paid half upon mortgage approval and the final half upon successful closing.
- Projected end prices would be $150,000 per home.
- Projected absorption rates for the development would average 6.25 sales a month over a period of 48 months.
- Each builder would be required to have on site at all times one furnished model, one completed spec home, and one home under construction.
- As part of the agreement, each builder would have to pay an interior designer/merchandiser to merchandise its specific model. The estimated cost would be at least $35,000 per model.

Source: J.R. Math & Company, Inc., Palm Beach Gardens, Florida, 1988.

Appendix C

■ Table of Contents and List of Tables for a Typical Apartment Project Market Analysis

Table of Contents

List of Tables

Source: Kotin, Regan & Mouchly, Inc., and Sunregion Associates, Los Angeles, California.

Appendix D

Description of Landlord's and Tenant's Work

Midtown Promenade, Atlanta, Georgia

	Responsibility	
Description of Work	**Landlord**	**Tenant**
1. Concrete floor slab to accept loads for retail occupancy.	X	
2. Sealed concrete throughout.	X	
3. Storefront: plate glass and aluminum construction plus front door entry.	X	
4. Full-height, one-hour-fire–rated interior demising partitioning, taped and bedded.	X	
5. Exterior walls insulated with 5/8″ drywall taped and bedded.	X	
6. Prime and final coat of paint in retail area only.		X
7. Standard suspended, acoustical, grid ceiling system with 2′ x 4′ lay-in tiles. Ceiling height 10′-00″.	X	
8. Electrical:		
a) 150-amp, three-phase, four-wire 120-208-volt electric service and panel box.	X	
b) Duplex convenience outlets at 15′ o.c. on demising walls.	X	
9. Other utilities:		
a) Rough-in plumbing.	X	
b) Sanitary sewer.	X	
c) Natural gas.	X	
d) Hot-water heater—six-gallon electric.		X
10. Heating, ventilation, and air conditioning:		
a) One ton of HVAC per 400 square feet.	X	
b) Trunk line and distribution.	X	
11. Lighting:		
a) One 2′ x 4′ lay-in fixture per every 100 square feet of floor space.	X	
b) Conduit, wiring, and junction box for tenant-supplied lighted sign.	X	
12. Sprinkler main and distribution.	X	
13. Single handicapped toilet with sink complete with cold-water supply only. Provided with exhaust fan.	X	
14. Rear exit door with hardware.	X	
15. Signs subject to Landlord's approval (size and other criteria to meet applicable city code as well as Landlord's sign criteria).		X
16. Trade fixtures, shelving, and other work necessary for operations.		X
17. Application for separate metering of applicable utilities except for water.	X	
18. All electrical work not stated herein.		X
19. Plans and specifications of construction.		X
20. Telephones:		
a) Outlets and wiring to backboard.		X
b) Wiring from electrical room to 4′ x 4′ backboard.	X	

Tenant Improvement Guidelines

A. The cost of any and all work not specifically delineated as Landlord's work or any increase in costs resulting from subsequent changes shall be the responsibility of, and paid for by, Tenant.

B. Tenant shall prepare, at Tenant's expense, design drawings, working drawings, shop drawings, specifications, and calculations as required. Tenant shall secure Landlord's written approval of all drawings prior to commencement of construction. Tenant shall obtain all licenses and permits necessary to complete Tenant work. Tenant work shall conform to all applicable statutes, ordinances, regulations, and building codes required by regulatory authorities.

C. A minimum of five (5) days prior to construction, Tenant and Tenant's contractor shall meet with Landlord or Landlord's representative, and at such meeting Tenant shall provide the following items:
   1. Copy of building permit.
   2. List of contractors.
   3. Certificate of insurance.

D. Landlord Inspection: The Premises will be inspected periodically by Landlord or Landlord's representative for compliance with requirements as set forth in the Lease and approved drawings. Any unauthorized construction will be corrected by Tenant at Tenant's expense.

E. Punch List: At the completion of the Premises, Tenant and Tenant's contractor will meet with Landlord or Landlord's representative to prepare a punch list that will enumerate any areas of construction that are not in accordance with the Lease or approved drawings. All items appearing on the punch list will be corrected by Tenant, at Tenant's expense, to conform with the Lease or approved drawings.

F. Occupancy Permit: Tenant shall secure its own occupancy permit prior to opening for business and shall provide a copy of the permit to Landlord.

G. Sign Criteria: It is intended that the signage of the Premises be developed in an imaginative and varied manner. Although previous and current signing practices of tenants will be considered, all signs must conform to the criteria set forth in the Lease.

H. All roof penetrations shall be made by Landlord's contractor and shall be billed to Tenant at Landlord's actual cost.

Source: Midtown Promenade, Atlanta, Georgia.

Appendix E

Sign Criteria for Thomas Lake Shopping Center, Eagan, Minnesota

The landlord intends to allow for individual and tasteful signage that distinguishes the tenant's store. Such signage should, however, be consistent with the design standards of the Center. Although previous and current practices of the tenant will be considered, the following criteria must be met:

A. Basic Requirements

1. All tenants are required to have a primary sign on the front of the Center and a sign on the rear door of their space.
2. The primary sign shall be located within the allowable sign area as designated by the Landlord.
3. Signs shall be limited to store name and/or logo.
4. Tenants shall be responsible for the maintenance of their signs and shall keep them clean and in working order.
5. All City permits and fees are the responsibility of the tenant.
6. Tenants vacating the premises shall be responsible for the removal of their sign and repair of the building fascia.
7. Tenants shall have their sign lighted. A sensory eye responding to darkness shall be used, and the sign shall remain lighted through a time agreed upon by the Tenant and the Owner.

B. Permitted Signs

1. All signs shall consist of individual internally illuminated letters. The maximum height of the letters allowed is 24", and the minimum height shall be 14". The letters shall not project more than 6" from the fascia. Logos will be considered and permitted only with the Landlord's approval.
2. The letters shall be internally illuminated. No lamps or exposed neon shall be permitted. The transformers for the letters shall be located in the ceiling within the tenant space.
3. Colors: The edges or returns of the letters shall be duranotic 313 or equal. The face of the letters shall be as listed below or equal. The colors are Rohm & Haas Plexiglas.

2793–red	2016–yellow	2119–orange
7328–white	2648–blue	2050–blue
2215–green	2108–green	

4. The sign shall be positioned so as to be centered top to bottom and left to right within the allowable sign area. No sign shall be closer than 24" to the lease line.
5. The signs shall be constructed as shown on the attached specifications. The tenant shall submit three copies of its sign layout and construction to the Landlord for approval. All signs must be approved by the Landlord.
6. All fastenings and mounting devices shall be rustproof, hidden from view, and attached in a proper workmanlike manner.
7. Rear door signs shall be 18" x 18" and be made of a thin-gauge aluminum painted 313 dark bronze with white vinyl die-cut lettering.
8. The only lighted window sign permitted is the standard OPEN/CLOSED type.

C. Signage Not Allowed

1. Signs employing moving or flashing lights or parts.
2. Exposed raceways or transformer boxes.
3. Box- or cabinet-type signs.
4. Signs in the public areas.
5. Stickers or decals affixed to the sign other than those required by the City.
6. Signs not permitted by City codes.

Procedure for Approval

1. The tenant should submit three copies of shop drawings for review and approval to the Management Department of:

   Towle Real Estate Company
   330 2nd Avenue So.
   Minneapolis, Minnesota 55401

   Telephone: 341-4444

Source: Towle Real Estate Company, Minneapolis, Minnesota.

Appendix F

The Homeowner Association (HOA) Community

An Overview

The legal basis of the HOA community is common law derived from England. Generally, there are no specific state or local laws regulating HOA community developments beyond those contained in state corporation laws and in land use provisions. In an HOA community, the concepts identified above are provided for through the following basic legal documents:

- The **subdivision plat**, which provides the basic legal description of the land to be conveyed.
- The **property deeds** to the individual parcels and the common property, which describe what is owned by whom.
- The **declaration of covenants, conditions, and restrictions**, which contains the basic covenants and conditions that create the common interest and the association that binds the owners together, including various restrictions on the use of the land and the owners' perpetual access to the common area.
- The **articles of incorporation**, which establish the association as a nonprofit corporation under state law and provide the general parameters of the association's structure and financing.
- The **bylaws**, which provide the specific procedures for the administration and operation of the association.
- The **rules and regulations**, which are the operational rules of behavior adopted by the newly created association and are binding upon each owner.

While conceptually the legal documents of the homeowners' association and the condominium association are designed to achieve similar objectives, how these objectives are established depends on the different types of legal documents required. The following section will discuss the basic legal concepts of description, restrictions, administration, financial, and transition and how the legal documents establish these concepts in the HOA community.

Description

The individual lots in an HOA community are described in the subdivision plat and in the deeds to the individual lots, a description that is similar to the description of any other fee simple property in specifying the boundaries of each parcel and the improvements on each. Attached HOA community units, such as row houses or townhouses, require careful delineation of limits and of the responsibility for party walls.

The common area in an HOA community, including grounds, facilities, and improvements to be shared by the individual owners, is described in the subdivision plat and in the deed(s) to the common area. The legal description necessary is the same required for any other fee simple property. The declaration of CC&Rs provides the individual owners with perpetual access to the common area.

Restrictions

The basic fabric of the HOA community is maintained by imposing restrictions on the owners' subsequent use of the land to permit the sharing of common elements and the enhancement of the property values.

In an HOA community, the basic document which binds all future buyers is the declaration of CC&Rs. Once recorded, the CC&Rs become the basis for all deeds (on common property and the individual owner's property), the articles of incorporation, the bylaws, and the rules. The basic purposes of the CC&Rs are:

- To establish that each owner is automatically a member of an association created to maintain the common areas and to enforce the covenants and restrictions.
- To establish that each owner has the right of use of the common property.
- To establish that each owner has a vote in the affairs of the association according to the voting procedure set forth.
- To establish that each owner has a proportionate obligation with all other owners to meet the financial obligations of the association, an obligation that operates as a lien against the owner's property.
- To establish certain protective covenants, standards, and restrictions which are imposed upon the owners in order to assure that during the life of the development a certain comparability of use and appearance is maintained.

The success of the HOA community rests upon these conditions and obligations being imposed on the initial owner and all subsequent owners in order to establish and assure funding of the association and preserve the common elements that are integral to the development. Moreover, these standards provide for continuity of use and appearance.

General Use Restrictions

There are generally two or more levels of use restrictions that are set forth in the declaration of CC&Rs which run with the land. These general use restrictions typically include:

- Provisions absolutely prohibiting uses or actions such as commercial uses, obnoxious uses, television antennas, signs, trailers, or pets.
- Provisions limiting or structuring the process by which the owner may change or alter the construction, design, or appearance of the exterior of his/her unit.

One test of a use restriction is its reasonableness. For example, a prohibition on the use of antennas is not reasonable if television reception is impossible without them, but regulating their location may be more reasonable. A restriction on commercial use is reasonable if the basic character of the community is residential. The developer must take care to protect against future court actions because the use restrictions he/she has imposed are not reasonable in relation to the project.

Reasonableness also affects the enforcement of use restrictions. It is unreasonable to subject an owner to inordinate delays in leasing or selling his/her unit while the association decides on whether to exercise its right of first refusal. Nor is it reasonable to reject architectural changes proposed by an owner without publicizing in advance the standards for such changes. Another important test for the developers to consider is the practical side of enforceability. A prohibition on large pets, for example, leaves to everyone's discretion the issue of what is large.

■ Homeowners' Association Legal Documents

Purpose of Concepts	**Description** to define what is owned by whom. **Restrictions** to establish the interlocking relationships of all owners and establish protective standards. **Administration** to create the association of owners and provide for the operation of the association. **Financial** to provide funding for the association. **Transition** to establish the process by which the developer transfers control of the association to the owners.	
Legal Basis	• English Common law • State corporate law or nonprofit corporate law	
Basic Documents	• Subdivision plat	The **subdivision plat** describes the location of the common elements, and describes the common elements.
	• Property deeds	The **property deeds** are made up of the individual lot deeds and the common property deeds.
	• Declaration of covenants, conditions, and restrictions	The **declaration of CC&Rs** gives perpetual easement to the common elements. It also provides for automatic association membership, voting rights, and certain use restrictions. It also gives power to the association to own and maintain the common property, and to make and enforce the rules.
	• Articles of incorporation	The **articles of incorporation** designate the powers of the association, create the board, and establish the voting procedure.
	• Bylaws	The **bylaws** delineate the meetings process, election procedures, powers and duties, board meetings, committees, insurance requirements, and limited use restrictions.
	• Rules and regulations	The **rules and regulations** include operational provisions or use restrictions adopted by the board upon initiation by the association.

Restricting the color of paint on exterior surfaces to only earthen colors will usually find someone in court to debate the issue. While it may be desirable to impose procedural notice and reporting requirements on an owner who desires to lease or sell his unit, as a practical matter a provision allowing an association the right of first refusal is subject to potential conflict and severe abuse.

Architectural Use Restrictions

Restrictions on architectural changes to the exterior appearance or structure of units is a special circumstance that is an integral feature of the association's basic mission to preserve and protect the character and appearance of the community. Typically, a special committee is established and called upon to develop architectural guidelines against which any proposed change may be reviewed. The use restrictions in the legal documents will provide that any owner who desires to make a change or addition that will affect basic external appearance should first submit his/her proposed change to the committee for review and approval. The issue of reasonableness and standards is very important to successful enforcement of architectural use restrictions. There must be clear standards of allowed changes as well as those not allowed, and these standards must be reasonable and uniformly enforced. Use restrictions are enforceable in court as are any of the restrictions or obligations in the legal documents. The association may seek an injunction or judgment against an owner for failure to comply. The developer should be aware that although most of the restrictions and obligations contained in the documents are operational in nature and it can easily be determined whether or not an individual has complied, in the case of architectural use restrictions the test of reasonableness, enforceability, due process, and proper notice all come into play.

The developer and his/her attorney must consider the implications of ownership in drafting the architectural use restrictions. Ownership will have considerable impact on what type of procedure is established and whether or not that procedure and certain restrictions must be provided for in the declaration of CC&Rs or in the bylaws.

In an HOA community, the purchaser owns his/her lot and home. The exterior of the unit may be maintained by the owner or by the association, but it is owned by the individual. Architectural restrictions control what that individual may do with his unit that might affect the appearance or harmony of the development, a concept that can be difficult to explain to a homeowner who feels that he should be allowed to add a fireplace or a television antenna without previous approval. He can, provided that what he proposes will not detract from the basic value of the development. His protection is that he is assured that no other owner will be permitted to take any action that will adversely affect his own property values.

Because HOA communities usually have no statutory authorization for use restrictions, developers have found it necessary to include the architectural standards and the architectural review process in the declaration of CC&Rs, the superior legal document. Those changes that would adversely affect the project are explicitly prohibited by a covenant that runs with the land and is normally subject to extraordinarily high concurrence by the owners to modify. Other less substantial restrictions are better included in the bylaws, where periodic revisions are more manageable.

Through use restrictions the developer and his/her attorney attempt to mandate certain patterns of use that presumably will preserve and protect the basic design, character, and appearance of the community or development over time. For the most part, this area of legal documentation involves subjective value judgments on the part of the developer rather than any hard business principles or procedures; an obnoxious use to one person may well be a desirable use to another. Therefore, the developer is cautioned to impose only those restrictions that are judged of real benefit to the preservation of the community's character and value. Moreover, the developer should include only the most important restrictions; time-proof use restrictions in the CC&Rs of the HOA community are almost virtually impossible to change. The bylaws or the association rules and regulations that can be more easily modified by the owners as needed should be used for other restrictions. The ability legally to enforce the restrictions, however, is diminished or jeopardized if these bylaws are not recorded with the declaration of CC&Rs and if they are subject to change without a vote of the membership. Today, many developers are separating architectural use restrictions into two categories: 1) new construction, for which the developer retains review authority, and 2) alterations and improvements by existing owners, for which the developer turns over review authority to a homeowners' committee at an early date.

In summary, the developer must be judicious in imposing use restrictions. When restrictions are felt to be necessary, they should be precisely drafted to leave no question as to their intent and scope, and the developer must have clearly established a workable process for compliance with and enforcement of use restrictions.

Administration

The administrative provisions that must be included in the legal documents are those structuring the association's operation. There must be provisions for establishing the association, its officers, committees, voting procedures, elections, and other related administrative activities.

Declaration of Covenants, Conditions, and Restrictions

The homeowners' association is first established in the declaration of CC&Rs, which do the following:

1. Establish the association to which the developer will convey the common property (for which the owner has a perpetual easement).
2. Establish the owners' automatic membership to the association.
3. Establish the owners' voting rights.
4. Establish the owners' obligation to pay a proportionate share of the expenses.
5. Assign the association the responsibility of maintenance, service, and enforcement of the covenants.

Normally, 75 percent or more concurrence of the owners is required to amend the CC&Rs.

1. **Common property and right of enjoyment.** One of the most important features of the HOA community is the conveyance of the common property to the association with every owner being granted the right of enjoyment. This right is generally granted in the CC&Rs subject to the owner complying with the rules of the association and paying his/her assessments.
2. **Automatic membership.** The CC&Rs provide an explicit statement that all owners and their successors shall be members of the association.
3. **Voting and membership classes.** The CC&Rs must set forth the basic membership voting system. In an HOA community, votes are typically assigned to owners on a one unit, one vote basis; all lots of the same type or class of membership have the same number of votes. It is not uncommon, however, to find two or more classes of membership as in the following example:

   Class A. One class of membership is the unit owners, excluding the developer, and each member of this class is entitled to vote according to the procedures and weights established in the documents, usually one vote per lot.

   Class B. The developer is a member of another class of membership and can be assigned more than one vote for each unit he still owns; for instance, the developer-owned units may be assigned three votes each. In this way, the developer retains a majority vote until 75 percent of the units are sold. The class B membership, or as prescribed membership when the total votes outstanding in the class A membership equal the total votes outstanding in the class B membership, or as prescribed by state law or at some date specified in the documents.

   Class C. A third class of membership can be set aside for renters. This special category is usually not assigned votes, but its members have the same rights of participation as the fully assessed owners or class A members.

   The theory of giving participation rights to renters is based on the desire to increase renter involvement in the association and community activities. The alienation of, and the abuse of property by, uninvolved groups such as renters is a concern to the development, and it is felt by granting the right of participation that property values will be protected and communication between renters and the main body of owners will increase.
4. **Assessments.** The CC&Rs contain a covenant that creates a lien on the owners to pay the association's annual and special assessments. This obligation falls to the owner of record at the time of the assessment, and reasonable attorney's fees and other costs of collection should also be authorized as a financial obligation of the owners.

   The developer may choose to impose limits on the level of assessments or the amount of increase in assessments authorized in any given year, but arbitrary limits must be imposed cautiously, if at all. The association may have difficulty raising the necessary operating funds when arbitrary limits are set forth that require an extraordinary vote of the owners to override. (Assessments will be discussed more fully later in this appendix.)
5. **Enforcement.** The association and/or any owner should be authorized to see enforcement of any covenant or restriction contained in the declaration of CC&Rs.

Articles of Incorporation

The articles of incorporation are used to establish the association as a nonprofit corporate entity under state law. The articles repeat several provisions of the declaration of CC&Rs including the legal description of the land encompassed and the membership and voting provisions. The articles also explicitly set forth 1) the powers of the association, and 2) the mechanism for leadership—a board of directors. Amendments to the articles usually require an extraordinary majority vote.

1. The **powers of the association** must be set forth in the articles and the declaration and should include the following functions:

- To perform the duties and obligations contained in the declaration, including enforcement of the CC&Rs.
- To fix and collect assessments.
- To own, maintain, and improve common property.

2. The **board of directors** must be established in the articles, with a list of members generally included. The total number of board members is specified (typically five to nine) and the term of office of each is established. Other details are left to the bylaws.

Bylaws

The bylaws of the homeowners' association provide the basic administrative framework. Typically, the bylaws can be amended by a simple majority vote (51 percent). Drafted along the lines of traditional corporate bylaws (with the exception of their use restrictions), the HOA community bylaws will include:

1. A description of the membership meeting procedure.
2. A description of election procedures.
3. A delineation of the powers and duties of the board and officers.
4. A description of the board meeting procedure.
5. The authorization of, and the procedures for, committees.
6. A provision for insurance.

1. **Membership meetings.** The time and place of the meeting must be specified in the homeowners' association bylaws. Regular membership meetings should be held annually, with the first meeting held within one year of incorporation or following 51 percent of sales, whichever comes first. Quorum and proxy requirements should be specified, but only after careful consideration; an onerous quorum requirement can present problems if the owners are widely dispersed and unable to attend. The developer should require that a quorum be based on a given percentage of each membership class to prevent exclusion of himself or the homeowners. Adequate meeting notice requirements are also necessary.
2. **Board elections.** The business of the association is governed by the board of directors provided for and established in the articles of incorporation. The initial members identified in the articles serve until their replacements are elected, and the first election takes place at the first annual meting of the association. The developer's weighted vote will enable him/her to elect most of the directors during the early phases. Generally, it is felt that staggered two-year terms provide continuity, but if the development period is shorter or if homeowner interest will likely be high, a one-year term will allow for more turnover.
3. **Powers and duties of the board.** In addition to specifying the title and function of each officer, the bylaws should delineate the following general powers and duties of the board of directors:
   - To enforce the provisions of the CC&Rs and the bylaws.
   - To contract for insurance (fire, casualty, liability, and other) for the association, the board, and the common elements.
   - To contract or provide for maintenance and services relating to the common areas, and to employ personnel or services necessary for the operation of the association, including legal or accounting services.
   - To pay taxes and special tax or use assessments that are or would become a lien on the common area or the entire project.
   - To pay for and supervise reconstruction of any portions of the development damaged or destroyed for any cause.
   - To delegate its powers to appropriate committees, agents, or personnel.
   - To maintain and provide security for the common areas and facilities.
   - To prepare the annual operating budget, establish the assessment fee levels, and collect assessments.
   - To maintain necessary ledgers and accounting records to reflect receipts, disbursements, capital reserves, and other financial transactions.
   - To perform other duties and tasks that may be necessary to assure the proper functioning of the association.

   The bylaws should require that all officers and employees of the association who handle or are responsible for funds furnish adequate fidelity bonds. The premiums on such bonds should be paid by the association. Specific language is also needed in the bylaws to ensure that the members of the board are not held liable to any unit owner for any act of omission, mistake of judgment, negligence, or other tort except for deliberate or willful misconduct done in bad faith. The association should also be directed in the bylaws or the CC&Rs to secure liability insurance for the directors and officers to give further protection.
4. **Board meetings.** The bylaws should require that the board of directors meet at least quarterly if not monthly, which is usually the practice, and that the first meeting of the initial board of directors should be convened as soon after the filing of the legal documents establishing the association as practical in order to elect officers, set general policies, and adopt association procedures. At least four regular meetings of the board should be held during the fiscal year

and accurate minutes and records of all meetings should be maintained. Special meetings may be called by the president or a specified percentage of board members with notice to each director. The trend in practice and in some state laws is to have "open" board meetings.

5. **Committees.** A committee structure should be established in the bylaws authorizing the board to create committees for nominations, architectural standards, maintenance, finance, and recreation in order to spread the work load and involve owners. Each committee should consist of a chairman, two or more members, and at least one member of the board of directors.
6. **Insurance.** Insurance requirements for HOA communities present a special administrative problem that must be resolved in the bylaws. The unique common interest character of HOA communities requires that special attention be directed to insurance protection of the common property and the association. The bylaws must direct that appropriate and adequate insurance coverage be obtained on all common elements of the community in order to assure the protection of the individual owners' interests. In addition, the association may be granted the authority to require or even obtain appropriate insurance on individual units and to designate trustees for purposes of allocating insurance proceeds. The association must have the means to assure that any unit or structure that is damaged or destroyed by any cause will be restored to its original condition. The following insurance is considered necessary:
    - The property shall be insured in an amount equal to the maximum replacement value and the policy should provide coverage against loss or damage by fire and other hazards (standard extended coverage endorsement) and such other risks as customarily insured against including vandalism, malicious mischief, windstorm, and water damage.
    - Coverage for general liability and property damage should be required.
    - Workmen's compensation should be provided for in the bylaws when necessary to meet requirements of law.
    - All liability insurance should contain cross liability endorsements to cover liabilities of the owners, the association as a group, and the board of directors.
    - Also needed is directors' and officers' liability coverage.

Financial

The association in an HOA community is charged with the substantial responsibility of delivering services and maintaining the common elements. The legal documents must provide the association with the means to finance these services and the legal documents must obligate the owners to assume this financial responsibility. Provisions must also be made for establishing the assessment level and collecting the assessments.

One significant aspect of the financial concept that is different in these types of developments is the basis for establishing each owner's share of the total expenses of the association. Although discussed in previous sections, a brief review of assessment allocations will enhance a discussion of the financial process.

The declaration of CC&Rs needs to provide that the owner is bound by covenant to pay to the association annual and special assessments used for common area maintenance and repair. These assessments are established as a continuing lien upon the property, and the assessments along with reasonable costs of collection are personal obligation of the owner. The developer in an HOA community may pay less than the usual assessment on his/her unsold units or lots (up to 75 percent less), and this approach should also be specified in the CC&Rs so that there is no question about his/her assessment responsibility. (The FHA permits developer assessments to be as low as 25 percent of the normal level per unit.) The CC&Rs typically contain further provisions regarding collection, penalties for nonpayment, special voting procedures for raising assessments or enacting special assessments, and limits on assessment levels.

Establishing and Budgeting Assessments

One of the responsibilities of the board of directors is the preparation and adoption of an annual budget. The budget becomes the basis for determining the level of annual assessments. The developer must prepare the initial budget and establish fee levels before the first units are sold. Typically, the HOA bylaws require that a budget be prepared annually to include the total estimated costs for the care, maintenance, and improvement of the common elements and the amount that should be set aside for the replacement or repair of major capital improvements and facilities. The budget is then adopted by the board after review or public notice as required by the documents.

The owners' assessments should be established in the declaration or bylaws as an annual obligation that the owner is permitted to meet in periodic monthly, quarterly, or yearly payments. The delinquent owner can then be required to pay the balance of the annual obligation on demand. For most associations, this will be of sufficient concern to the owner to prevent delinquencies, and if they do occur, the total amount due will make it more worthwhile to go to the expense of collecting it.

Limitations on Fee Levels

Typically, developers have attempted to restrict the board's powers to adopt a budget involving a substantial increase in assessment fees, but opinion is mixed regarding a restriction of this type. On the one hand, they protect the owners' mortgage lenders and the developer from excessive association fees, but on the other hand, the results can be disastrous if an inadequately funded association can no longer operate. Various approaches have been tried in order to strike a balance between these concerns. Increases in fee levels can be controlled by prescribing in the legal documents a maximum dollar assessment amount for a fixed period of early development and then permitting the board to increase the assessment in any one year, without a vote, up to a fixed percentage amount or an amount equal to the increase in the cost of living, or a maximum dollar amount set forth in the documents.

The alternative, which prescribes an arbitrary dollar ceiling or a percentage ceiling on increases without a vote, can and does place severe hardships on the association during times of heavy inflation or extraordinary expenses. If more funds are necessary, a vote of the membership is required, and usually an extraordinary affirmative vote is needed such as 75 or even 100 percent. It is difficult, if not impossible, for most associations to obtain such a vote because of the number of absentee owners and the normal resistance to increased financial burden.

In the past, the FHA, VA, and some lenders have imposed restrictions in the superior legal documents of the association (CC&Rs or master deed). Until recently, it was common to find a 5 percent limitation on the amount of yearly increases that could be implemented without a membership vote. More recently, however, in recognition of inflation, a cost-of-living escalator has become an acceptable approach. For example, the developer establishes in the legal documents a maximum assessment amount and the board is authorized to assess up to that amount adjusted by inflation without a membership vote.

If the developer feels that limitations on the discretion of the board to increase fees is necessary, he/she should carefully review the practical effects of the approach he/she selects. The ceiling, whether a fixed dollar amount or a percentage, should be realistic and, it is hoped, will stand the test of time. The provision for a vote of the membership should provide the flexibility needed to achieve such a vote; affirmative votes of 100, 90, 75, or even 66 percent may effectively stop the association from functioning. Finally, the entire procedure is contingent on the developer's original budget and assessment level. If those assessments were set too low, deliberately or otherwise, the association will remain poorly funded for years after the developer has gone. An experienced manager can review this budget for adequacy.

The most workable approach for both the developer and the association appears to be:

- To set a fixed dollar amount ceiling for the first year of operation, but make the ceiling substantially higher than the first year's assessment.
- To permit increases in annual assessments without a vote up to that ceiling as adjusted by the cost of living.
- To provide for automatic adjustment of the ceiling by percentage increase in the cost of living.
- To permit adjustments to the ceiling or permit increases beyond the ceiling on a year-to-year basis by a majority vote of the owners or by a vote of 66 percent of the owners.
- To permit special assessments by majority vote of owners.

The developer must also review the appropriate state laws and the requirements of his/her lending-related organizations. Associations tend to be underfunded rather than overfunded, which should be kept in mind. Typically, the homeowners' association incorporates these assessment level restrictions in the CC&Rs to assure permanence and enforceability.

Transition

One of the major aspects of the association process that must be carefully considered in design and in preparing the legal documents is the transition of control from the developer to the owners. The transition process basically depends on the allocation of votes between the developer and the owners and the control of the seats on the board of directors.

The unsold units are typically assigned a weighted vote that assures the developer a voting majority in the association until such time as he/she has sold off, for example, 75 percent of the units; at that point, transition of majority control has occurred. In the CC&Rs of the homeowners' association, provisions regarding vote allocations and the appointment and election of members to the board determine the transition.

Source: James C. Dowden, *Creating a Community Association: The Developer's Role in Condominium and Homeowner Associations*, Second Revised Edition (Washington, D.C.: ULI–the Urban Land Institute; Alexandria, Virginia: CAI–the Community Associations Institute, 1986), pp. 28–36.

Appendix G

Declaration of Covenants, Conditions, and Restrictions

Koll Business Center–Bothell

Editor's Note: The following CC&Rs represent the type that retain full control in the developer's hands without use of an owners' association. They are presented here solely to illustrate the form and substance of a complete document and are not intended necessarily as models suitable for other research/business parks.

This Declaration, made this ___ day of ________, 19___, by KOLL/INTEREAL SEATTLE, a California general partnership, is made with reference to the following facts:

Recitals

A. Koll/Intereal Seattle is the owner of that certain real property in the City of Bothell, County of King, State of Washington, Described in Exhibit A attached hereto and by this reference incorporated herein, and known as KOLL BUSINESS CENTER–BOTHELL.

B. Koll Business Center–Bothell is being developed as a planned business/industrial park. It is Koll/Intereal Seattle's desire and intention to subject the real property in said business park to certain covenants, conditions, and restrictions for the benefit of the property, Koll/Intereal Seattle, and the purchasers of lots in Koll Business Center–Bothell. It is intended that said covenants, conditions, and restrictions bind and benefit not only said purchasers and Koll/Intereal Seattle but also their respective successors, heirs, and assigns and that all lots in Koll Business Center–Bothell should be held, used, leased, sold, and conveyed subject to the covenants, conditions, and restrictions set forth in this Declaration.

C. It is the intention of Koll/Intereal Seattle to further a plan of subdivision by means of the covenants, conditions, and restrictions set forth in this Declaration. Said covenants, conditions, and restrictions are intended to be common to all of the lots in Koll Business Center–Bothell and to enhance and protect the value, desirability, and attractiveness of all such lots to their mutual benefit.

Article I
Definitions

Unless the context otherwise specifies or requires, the terms defined in this Article I shall, as used in this Declaration, have the meanings herein set forth:

1.1 *Architect.* The term "architect" shall mean a person holding a certificate of registration to practice architecture in the State of Washington under the authority of Title 18, Chapter 18, of the Revised Code of Washington.

1.2 *Beneficiary.* The term "beneficiary" shall mean a mortgagee under a mortgage as well as a beneficiary under a deed of trust.

1.3 *Declarant.* The term "Declarant" shall mean Koll/Intereal Seattle and, to the extent provided in Article VIII of this Declaration, its successors and assigns.

1.4 *Declaration.* The term "Declaration" shall mean this Declaration of Covenants, Conditions, and Restrictions for Koll Business Center–Bothell, as it may from time to time be amended or supplemented.

1.5 *Deed of Trust.* The term "deed of trust" shall mean a mortgage as well as a deed of trust.

1.6 *Koll Business Center–Bothell.* The term "Koll Business Center–Bothell" shall be synonymous with the term "subject property" and shall mean all of the real property now or hereafter made subject to this Declaration.

1.7 *Improvement—Improvements.* The term "improvement" or "improvements" shall include buildings, outbuildings, roads, driveways, parking areas, fences, screening walls and barriers, retaining walls, stairs, decks, water lines, sewers, electrical and gas distribution facilities, hedges, windbreaks, plantings, planted trees and shrubs, poles, signs, loading areas, and all other structures, installations, and landscaping of every type and kind, whether above or below the land surface.

1.8 *Lot.* The term "lot" shall mean a fractional part of the subject property as subdivided on subdivision or parcel maps recorded from time to time in the Office of Records and Elections of the County of King, State of Washington.

1.9 *Mortgage.* The term "mortgage" shall mean a deed of trust as well as a mortgage.

1.10 *Mortgagee.* The term "mortgagee" shall mean a beneficiary under, or holder of, a deed of trust as well as a mortgagee under a mortgage.

1.11 *Occupant.* The term "Occupant" shall mean a lessee or licensee of an Owner, or any other person or entity other than an Owner in lawful possession of a lot with the permission of the Owner.

1.12 *Owner.* The term "Owner" shall mean and refer to any person or entity that is the record Owner of fee simple title to any lot, excluding any entity or person who holds such interest as security for the payment of an obligation, but including contract sellers and any mortgagee or other security holder in actual possession of a lot.

1.13 *Record—Recorded—Recordation.* The terms "record," "recorded," or "recordation" shall mean, with respect to any document, the recordation of said document in the Office of Records and Elections of the County of King, State of Washington.

1.14 *Sign.* The term "sign" shall mean any structure, device, or contrivance, electric or nonelectric, upon or within which any poster, bill, bulletin, printing, lettering, painting, device, or other advertising of any kind whatsoever is used, placed, posted, tacked, nailed, pasted, or otherwise fastened or affixed.

1.15 *Street—Streets.* The term "street" or "streets" shall mean any street, highway, road, or thoroughfare within or adjacent to the subject property and shown on any recorded subdivision or parcel map, or record of survey, whether designated thereon as street, boulevard, place, drive, road, court, terrace, way, lane, circle, or otherwise.

1.16 *Subject Property.* The term "subject property" shall be synonymous with the term "Koll Business Center–Bothell" and shall mean all of the real property now or hereafter made subject to this Declaration.

1.17 *Visible from Neighboring Property.* The term "visible from neighboring property" shall mean, with respect to any given object on a lot, that such object is or would be visible to a person six (6) feet tall, standing on any part of any adjacent lot or other property at an elevation no greater than the elevation of the base of the object being viewed.

Article II
Subject Property

2.1 *General Declaration.* Declarant hereby declares that all of that real property located in the City of Bothell, County of King, State of Washington, and more particularly described in Exhibit A is, and shall be, conveyed, hypothecated, encumbered, leased, occupied, built upon or otherwise used, improved, or transferred in whole or in part, subject to this Declaration. All of the covenants, conditions, and restrictions set forth herein are declared and agreed to be in furtherance of a general plan for the subdivision, improvement, and sale of said real property and every part thereof. All of said covenants, conditions, and restrictions shall run with all of the subject property for all purposes and shall be binding upon and inure to the benefit of Declarant and all Owners, Occupants, and their successors in interest as set forth in this Declaration.

2.2 *Addition of Other Realty.* Declarant may at any time during the pendency of this Declaration add all or a portion of any real property now or hereinafter owned by Declarant to the subject property, and upon recording of a notice of addition of real property containing at least the provisions set forth in Section 2.3, the provisions of this Declaration specified in said notice shall apply to such added real property in the same manner as if it were originally covered by this Declaration. Thereafter, to the extent that this Declaration is made applicable thereto, the rights, powers, and responsibilities of Declarant and the Owners and Occupants of lots within such added real property shall be the same as in the case of the real property described in Exhibit A.

2.3 *Notice of Addition to Land.* The notice of addition of real property referred to in Section 2.2 shall contain at least the following provisions:

(a) A reference to this Declaration stating the date of recording and the book or books of the records of King County, Washington, and the page numbers where this Declaration is recorded;

(b) A statement that the provisions of this Declaration, or some specified part thereof, shall apply to such added real property;

(c) A legal description of such added real property; and

(d) Such other or different covenants, conditions, and restrictions as Declarant shall, in its discretion, specify to regulate and control the use, occupancy, and improvements of such added real property.

Article III
Construction of Improvements

3.1 *Approval of Plans Required.* No improvements shall be erected, placed, altered, maintained, or permitted to remain on any lot by any Owner or Occupant until final plans and specifications shall have been submitted to and approved in writing by Declarant. Such final plans and specifications shall be submitted in duplicate over the authorized signature of the Owner or Occupant or both of the lot or the authorized agent thereof. Such plans and specifications shall be in such form and shall contain such information as may be required by the Declarant but shall in any event include the following:

(a) A site development plan of the lot showing the nature, grading scheme, kind, shape, composition, and location of all structures with respect to the particular lot (including proposed front, rear, and side setback lines), and with respect to structures on adjoining lots, and the number and location of all parking spaces and driveways on the lot;

(b) A landscaping plan for the particular lot;

(c) A plan for the location of signs and lighting; and

(d) A building elevation plan showing dimensions, materials, and exterior color scheme in no less detail than required by the appropriate governmental authority for the issuance of a building permit. Material changes in approved plans must be similarly submitted to and approved by Declarant.

3.2 *Basis for Approval.* Approval shall be based, among other things, upon compliance with the Design Guidelines prepared for the subject property, including adequacy of site dimensions, adequacy of structural design, conformity and harmony of external design with neighboring structures, effect of location and use of proposed improvements upon neighboring lots, proper facing of main elevation with respect to nearby streets, adequacy of screening of mechanical, air-conditioning, or other roof-top installations, and conformity of the plans and specifications to the purpose and general plan and intent of this Declaration. No plans will be approved that do not provide for the underground installation of power, electrical, telephone, and other utility lines from the property line to buildings. Plans that provide for metal-clad buildings will be approved only on the conditions that such buildings are constructed so as not to have the appearance of a preengineered metal building, are designed by an architect, and are specifically approved in writing by Declarant. Declarant shall not arbitrarily or unreasonably withhold its approval of any plans and specifications. Except as otherwise provided in this Declaration, Declarant shall have the right to disapprove any plans and specifications submitted hereunder on any reasonable grounds including, but not limited to, the following:

(a) Failure to comply with any of the restrictions set forth in this Declaration;

(b) Failure to include information in such plans and specifications as may have been reasonably requested by Declarant;

(c) Objection to the exterior design, the appearance of materials, or materials employed in any proposed structure;

(d) Objection on the ground of incompatibility of any proposed structure or use with existing structures or uses upon other lots, or other property in the vicinity of the subject property;

(e) Objection to the location of any proposed structure with reference to other lots, or other property in the vicinity;

(f) Objection to the grading or landscaping plan for any lot;

(g) Objection to the color scheme, finish, proportions, style of architecture, height, bulk, or appropriateness of any structure;

(h) Objection to the number or size of parking spaces, or to the design of the parking area;

(i) Any other matter that, in the judgment of the Declarant, would render the proposed improvements or use inharmonious with the general plan for improvement of the subject property or with improvements located upon other lots or other property in the vicinity.

3.3 *Review Fee.* An architectural review fee shall be paid to Declarant at such time as plans and specifications are submitted to it based upon the following schedule:

(a) When the plans submitted are prepared by an architect, the architectural review fee shall be the sum of One Hundred and no/100ths Dollars ($100.00);

(b) In all other cases, the architectural review fee shall be the sum of Two Hundred Fifty and no/100ths Dollars ($250.00).

3.4 *Result of Inaction.* If Declarant fails either to approve or disapprove plans and specifications submitted to it for approval within forty-five (45) days after the same have been submitted, it shall be conclusively presumed that Declarant has disapproved said plans and specifications; provided, however, that if within the forty-five (45)-day period Declarant gives written notice of the fact that more time is required for the review of such plans and specifications, there shall be no presumption that the same are disapproved until the expiration of such reasonable period of time as is set forth in the notice.

3.5 *Approval.* Declarant may approve plans and specifications as submitted, or as altered or amended, or it may grant its approval to the same subject to specific conditions. Upon approval or conditional approval by Declarant of any plans and specifications submitted, a copy of such plans and specifications, together with any conditions, shall be deposited for permanent record with Declarant, and a copy of such plans and specifications, bearing such approval together with any conditions, shall be returned to the applicant submitting the same.

3.6 *Proceeding with Work.* Upon receipt of approval from Declarant pursuant to Section 3.5, the Owner, or Occupant, or both, to whom the same is given, shall, as soon as practicable, satisfy any and all conditions of such approval and shall diligently proceed with the commencement and completion of all approved excavation, construction, refinishing, and alterations. In all cases, work shall commence within one (1)-year period from the date of approval, and if work is not so commenced, approval shall be deemed revoked unless Declarant, pursuant to written request made and received prior to the expiration of said one (1)-year period, extends the period of time within which work must be commenced.

3.7 *Completion of Work.* Any improvement commenced pursuant hereto shall be completed within two (2) years from the date of Declarant's approval of the plans and specifications therefor, except for so long as such completion is rendered impossible, or unless work upon the proposed improvements would impose a great hardship upon the Owner or Occupant, to whom Declarant's approval is given, due to strike, fire, national emergency, natural disaster, or other supervening force beyond the control of Owner or Occupant. Declarant may, upon written request made and received prior to the expiration of the two (2)-year period, extend the period of time within which work must be completed. Failure to comply with this Section 3.7 shall constitute a breach of this Declaration and subject the party in breach to the enforcement procedures set forth in Article VII.

3.8 *Declarant Not Liable.* Declarant shall not be liable for any damage, loss, or prejudice suffered or claimed by any person on account of:

(a) The approval or disapproval of any plans, drawings, and specifications, whether or not in any way defective;

(b) The construction of any improvement, or performance of any work, whether or not pursuant to approved plans, drawings, and specifications; or

(c) The development of any lot within Koll Business Center–Bothell.

3.9 *Construction without Approval.* If any improvement shall be erected, placed, or maintained upon any lot, or any new use commenced upon any lot, other than in accordance with the approval by the Declarant pursuant to the provisions of this Article III, such alteration, erection, placement, maintenance, or use shall be deemed to have been undertaken in violation of this Declaration, and upon written notice from Declarant, any such improvement so altered, erected, placed, maintained, or used upon any lot in violation of this Declaration shall be removed or altered so as to conform to this Declaration, and any such use shall cease or be amended so as to conform to this Declaration. Should such removal or alteration or cessation or amendment or use not be accomplished within thirty (30) days after receipt of such notice, then the party in breach of this Declaration shall be subject to the enforcement procedures set forth in Article VII.

Article IV
Development Standards

4.1 *Minimum Setback.* No improvements of any kind, and no part thereof, shall be placed closer than permitted by Declarant to an interior property line, except as otherwise provided in Section 4.3. "Interior property line" shall mean the boundary between any lot within the subject property and all other lots bordering upon said lot. No improvements of any kind, and no part thereof, shall be placed closer than twenty-five (25) feet from a property line fronting the following streets: (1) N.E. 195th Street, (2) North Creek Parkway, and (3) 120th Avenue N.E. "Property line" shall mean the boundary of every lot.

4.2 *North Creek Setback.* No improvement of any kind shall be constructed or placed closer than eighteen (18) feet from the property line separating a lot from North Creek and the associated stream corridor if the lot is designated as requiring such a setback on the final plat recorded herewith. This restriction, however, shall not apply to the provision of a public way along North Creek or access thereto.

4.3 *Exceptions to Setback Requirements.* The following improvements, or parts of improvements, are specifically excluded from the setback requirements set forth in Section 4.1:

(a) Roof overhang, subject to approval in writing from Declarant, provided said overhang does not extend more than eighteen (18) inches into the setback area;

(b) Steps and walkways;

(c) Fences, subject to the requirements set forth in Section 4.6;

(d) Landscaping and irrigation systems;

(e) Planters, not to exceed three (3) feet in height, except that planters of greater height may be built within the setback area with the prior written approval of Declarant;

(f) Industrial park identification signs, directional and parking signs, and signs identifying the owner or Occupant of a lot, subject to the prior written approval of Declarant;

(g) Lighting facilities, subject to the prior written approval of Declarant; and

(h) Underground utility facilities and sewers.

4.4 *Landscaping.* Within ninety (90) days following completion of construction, or by the date each improvement is occupied, whichever shall occur first, each lot shall be landscaped in accordance with the plans and specifications. The area of each lot between any street and any minimum setback line as set forth in Section 4.1 shall be landscaped with an attractive combination of trees, shrubs, and other ground cover. All portions of a lot not fronting a street and not used for parking, storage, or buildings shall be landscaped in a complementary and similar manner.

The first fifteen (15) feet of the setback areas along N.E. 195th Street, 120th Avenue N.E., and North Creek Parkway provided for in Section 4.1 shall be landscaped and maintained by an assessment district to be formed by

Declarant. The remaining ten (10) feet of such setback areas shall be landscaped and maintained by the Owner or Occupant of the lot whose property line fronts the street. An underground landscape irrigation system shall be provided and maintained by the Owner or Occupant for all landscaped areas except the first fifteen (15) feet of the setback areas along N.E. 195th Street, 120th Avenue N.E., and North Creek Parkway.

The perimeter of parking areas shall be landscaped with solid screen evergreen plant material so as to screen said areas from view from adjacent streets and freeways. Such screening shall extend at least forty-eight (48) inches above the high point of the finished pavement in said parking area. Landscaped earth berms at least three feet high may substitute for the solid screen planting. In the case of parking areas that abut the setback from property lines adjoining the stream corridor associated with North Creek, as described in Section 4.2, any side of the parking area that faces North Creek shall be screened by landscaped earth berm at least four feet in height above the high point of the finished pavement in said parking area.

If an outdoor parking lot contains fifteen or more parking stalls, not less than 6 percent of the interior of such parking lot shall be landscaped. The use of landscaped earth berms to accomplish such landscaping is encouraged. Strips between parking bays shall also be landscaped with appropriate groundcover and deciduous trees.

After completion, such landscaping as is herein required shall be maintained in a sightly and well-kept condition. If, in Declarant's reasonable opinion, the required landscaping is not maintained in a sightly and well-kept condition, Declarant shall be entitled to the remedies set forth in Article VII.

4.5 *Signs.* No sign shall be permitted on any lot unless approved by Declarant in writing. No sign shall be approved other than business park identification signs, informational and vehicular control signs, signs identifying the building or the business of the Owner or Occupant of a lot, signs offering the lot for sale or lease, and temporary development signs.

4.6 *Fences.* No fences or walls shall be permitted on any lot unless such fence or wall is necessary for security or screening purposes. The Declarant reserves the right to approve the location and design of all fences, and no fence shall be constructed without a letter of approval from the Declarant.

4.7 *Parking Area.* Off-street parking adequate to accommodate the parking needs of the Owner or Occupant and the employees and visitors thereof shall be provided by the Owner or Occupant of each Lot. The intent of this provision is to eliminate the need for any on-street parking; provided, however, that nothing herein shall be deemed to prohibit on-street parking of public transportation vehicles. If parking requirements increase as a result of a change in the use of a lot or in the number of persons employed by the Owner or Occupant, additional off-street parking shall be provided so as to satisfy the intent of this section. All parking areas shall conform to the following standards:

(a) Required off-street parking shall be provided on the lot, on a contiguous lot, or within such distance from the lot as Declarant deems reasonable. Where parking is provided other than upon the lot concerned, Declarant shall be given a certified copy of a recorded instrument, duly executed and acknowledged by the person or persons holding title to the lot or other property upon which the parking area is located, stipulating to the permanent reservation of the use of the lot or other property for such parking area.

(b) Parking areas shall be paved so as to provide dust-free, all-weather surfaces. Each parking space provided shall be designated by lines painted upon the paved surface and shall be adequate in area. All parking areas shall provide, in addition to parking spaces, adequate driveways and space for the movement of vehicles.

4.8 *Storage and Loading Areas.* Storage, maintenance, and loading areas must be constructed, maintained, and used in accordance with the following conditions:

(a) Outside storage of materials, supplies, or equipment, including trucks or other motor vehicles, shall be permitted only if:

(i) The material, equipment, or objects stored outside are incidental to the activities regularly conducted on the premises;

(ii) The area devoted to outside storage does not exceed 5 percent of the gross floor area of the principal structure on the site;

(iii) The area is screened on sides and top and harmonizes with the architecture, design, and appearance of neighboring structures and other surroundings; and

(iv) The area is located upon the rear portions of a lot, unless otherwise approved in writing by Declarant.

(b) Provision shall be made on each site for any necessary vehicle loading, and no on-street vehicle loading shall be permitted.

(c) Loading dock areas shall be set back, recessed, or screened so as not to be visible from neighboring property or streets, and in no event shall a loading dock be closer than seventy-five (75) feet from a property line fronting upon a street unless otherwise approved in writing by Declarant.

Article V
Regulation of Operations and Uses

5.1 *Permitted Uses.* Except as otherwise specifically prohibited herein, any industrial operation and use will be permitted upon a lot, provided that Declarant specifically consents to such use in writing. Such approved use shall be performed or carried out entirely within a building that is so designed and constructed that the enclosed operations and uses do not cause or produce a nuisance to other lots or property, such as, but not limited to, vibration, sound, electromechanical disturbances, electromagnetic disturbances, radiation, air or water pollution, dust, or emission of odorous, toxic, or nontoxic matter (including steam). Certain activities that cannot be carried on within a building may be permitted, provided Declarant specifically consents to such activity in writing and further provided such activity is screened so as not to be visible from neighboring property and streets. All lighting is to be shielded so as not to be visible from neighboring property.

5.2 *Prohibited Uses.* The following operations and uses shall not be permitted on any property subject to this Declaration:

(a) Residential use of any type;

(b) Trailer courts or recreation vehicle campgrounds;

(c) Junk yards, wrecking yards, or recycling facilities;

(d) Mining, drilling for, or removing oil, gas, or other hydrocarbon substances;

(e) Refining of petroleum or of its products;

(f) Commercial excavation of building or construction materials, provided that this prohibition shall not be construed to prohibit any excavation necessary in the course of approved construction pursuant to Article III;

(h) Distillation of bones;

(i) Dumping, disposal, incineration, or reduction of garbage, sewage, offal, dead animals, or other refuse;

(j) Fat rendering;

(k) Stockyard or slaughter or animals;

(l) Smelting of iron, tin, zinc, or any other ore or ores;

(m) Cemeteries;

(n) Jail or honor farms;

(o) Labor or migrant worker camps;

(p) Truck terminals (incidental truck usage is specifically permitted);

(q) Automobile, go-cart, motorcycle, or quarter-midget race tracks and other vehicle endurance or race tracks;

(r) New or used car sales lots; or

(s) Commercial parking lots and structures.

5.3 *Nuisances.* No nuisance shall be permitted to exist or operate upon any lot so as to be offensive or detrimental to any adjacent lot or property or to its occupants. A "nuisance" shall include, but not be limited to, any of the following conditions:

(a) Any use, excluding reasonable construction activity, of the lot that emits dust, sweepings, dirt, or cinders into the atmosphere, or discharges liquid, solid wastes, or other matter into any stream, river, or other waterway that, in the opinion of Declarant, may adversely affect the health, safety, comfort of, or intended use of their property by persons within the area. No waste nor any substance or materials of any kind shall be discharged into any public sewer serving the subject property or any part thereof in violation of any regulation of any public body having jurisdiction over such public sewer;

(b) The escape or discharge of any fumes, odors, gases, vapors, steam, acids, or other substance into the atmosphere, which discharge, in the opinion of Declarant, may be detrimental to the health, safety, or welfare of any person or may interfere wit the comfort of persons within the area or may be harmful to property or vegetation;

(c) The radiation or discharge of intense glare or heat, or atomic, electromagentic, microwave, ultrasonic, laser, or other radiation. Any operation producing intense glare or heat or such other radiation shall be performed only within an enclosed or screened area and then only in such manner that the glare, heat, or radiation emitted will not be discernible from any point exterior to the site or lot upon which the operation is conducted;

(d) *Excessive noise.* At no point outside of any lot plane shall the sound pressure level of any machine, device, or any combination of same, from any individual plant or operation, exceed the decibel levels in the designated preferred octave bands as follows:

Octave Band Center Frequency (Hz)	**Maximum Sound Pressure Levels (dB) at Boundary Plane of Lot**
31.5	78
63	72
125	65
250	59
500	55
1000	52
2000	50
4000	48
8000	47

A-scale levels for monitoring purposes are equivalent to 60 dB(A). The maximum permissible noise levels for the octave bands shown above are equal to an NC-50 Noise Criterion curve when plotted on the preferred frequency scale.

Reasonable noise from motor vehicles and other transportation facilities are exempted, so long as the vehicles or other transportation facilities are not continuously on the subject property.

The operation of signaling devices and other equipment having impulsive or noncontinuous sound characteristics shall have the following corrections applied:

Corrections

Pure Tone Content	– 5 dB
Impulsive Character	– 5 dB
Duration for Noncontinuous Sounds in Daytime Only:	
1 min/hr	+ 5 dB
10 sec/10 min	+10 dB
2 sec/10 min	+15 dB

The reference for the dB values listed above is the pressure of 0.0002 microbar or 0.0002 dyne/cm^2.

(e) Excessive emissions of smoke, steam, or particulate matter. Visible emissions of smoke or steam will not be permitted (outside any building) that exceed Ringlemann No. 1 on the Ringlemann Chart of the United States Bureau of Mines. This requirement shall also be applied to the disposal of trash and waste materials. Wind-borne dust, sprays, and mists originating in plants are not permitted.

(f) Ground vibration. Buildings and other structures shall be constructed and machinery and equipment installed and insulated on each lot so that the ground vibration inherently and recurrently generated is not perceptible without instruments at any point exterior to any lot.

5.4 *North Creek.* The Owner or Occupant of any lot shall at all times conduct its use and activities in a manner that will preserve the integrity of North Creek and the surrounding open space, including the prevention of any degradation of water quality, any reduction or increase in the flow of North Creek, any damage to the streambed or banks of North Creek, or any impairment of the view from North Creek and the associated greenbelt. The Owner or Occupant of any lot shall not conduct or permit the conduct of the following activities:

(a) The discharge of any liquid, solid, or gas into North Creek;

(b) The use of any fertilizers or herbicides in a manner that will result in such fertilizers or herbicides or the residue thereof entering North Creek; or

(c) Any refuse-encouraging activities.

5.5 *Condition of Property.* The Owner or Occupant of any lot shall at all times keep it and the buildings, improvements, and appurtenances thereon in a safe, clean, and wholesome condition and comply, at its own expense, in all respects with all applicable governmental, health, fire and safety ordinances, regulations, requirements, and directives, and the Owner or Occupant shall at regular and frequent intervals remove at its own expense any rubbish of any character whatsoever that may accumulate upon such lot.

5.6 *Maintenance of Grounds.*

(a) Each Owner shall be assessed a charge (the "Maintenance Assessment") for the maintenance of the open space areas, landscape easements, and other common areas located on the subject property. Such charge shall be paid to the Declarant and shall equal an amount that represents that proportion of the total cost of such maintenance as the area of the Lot owned by the Owner is proportionate to the total area of all Lots on the subject property. The Maintenance Assessment shall be assessed on a periodic basis as determined by Declarant.

(b) Each Owner shall be responsible for the maintenance and repair of all parking areas, driveways, walkways, and landscaping on his Lot. Such maintenance and repair shall include, without limitation,

(1) Maintenance of all parking areas, driveways, and walkways in a clean and safe condition, including the paving and repairing or resurfacing of such areas when necessary with the type of material originally installed thereon or such substitute therefor as shall, in all respects, be equal thereto in quality, appearance, and durability; the removal of debris and waste material and the washing and sweeping of paved areas; the painting and repainting of striping markers and directional signals as required;

(2) Cleaning, maintenance, and relamping of any external lighting fixtures, except such fixtures as may be the property of any public utility or government body; and

(3) Performance of all necessary maintenance of all landscaping, including the trimming, watering, and fertilization of all grass, groundcover, shrubs, or trees; the removal of dead or waste materials; the replacement of any dead or diseased grass, groundcover, shrubs, or trees.

(c) Nothing contained herein shall preclude an Owner from recovering from any person liability therefor, damages to which such Owner might be entitled for any act or omission to act requiring an expenditure by the Owner for the maintenance and repair of the parking area, driveway, walkway, and/or landscaping on his Lot.

5.7 *Remedies for Failure to Maintain and Repair.*

(a) *Remedies.* If any Owner shall fail to pay the Maintenance Assessment or to perform the maintenance and repair required by Section 5.6, then Declarant, after fifteen days prior written notice to such delinquent Owner, shall have the right, not the obligation, to pay the Maintenance Assessment or to perform such maintenance and repair and to charge the delinquent Owner with costs of such assessment or such work, together with interest thereon at the rate of twelve percent (12%) per annum from the date of Declarant's advancement of funds for such payment or such work to the date of reimbursement of Declarant by Owner. If the delinquent Owner shall fail to reimburse Declarant for such costs within ten days after demand therefor, Declarant may, at any time within two years after such advance, file for record in the Office of Records and Elections of King County, Washington, a claim of lien signed by Declarant for the amount of such charge together with interest thereon. The lien created by this section shall be effective to establish a lien against the interest of the delinquent Owner in his lot together with interest at twelve percent (12%) per annum on the amount of such advance from the date thereof, in addition to recording fees, cost of title search obtained in connection with such lien or the foreclosure thereof, and court costs and reasonable attorney's fees that may be incurred in the enforcement of such a lien.

(b) *Foreclosure of Lien.* Subject to the provisions of Article XII, such a lien, when so established against the lot described in said claim, shall be prior or superior to any right, title, interest, lien, or claim that may be or may have been acquired in or attached to the real property interests subject to the lien subsequent to the time of filing such claim for record. Such lien shall be for the benefit of Declarant and may be enforced and foreclosed in a like manner as a real estate mortgage is foreclosed in the state of Washington, but without redemption.

(c) *Cure.* If a default for which a notice of claim of lien was filed is cured, Declarant shall file or record a rescission of such notice, upon payment by the defaulting Owner of the cots of preparing and filing or recording such rescission, and other reasonable costs, interest, or fees that have been incurred.

(d) *Nonexclusive remedy.* The foregoing lien and the rights to foreclose thereunder shall be in addition to, and not in substitution for, all other rights and remedies that any party may have hereunder and by law, including any suit to recover a money judgment for unpaid assessments. If any Owner shall fail to perform such maintenance and repair and, notwithstanding such failure, Declarant should fail to exercise its rights and remedies hereunder, then any other Owner, after fifteen (15) days prior written notice to Declarant and such delinquent Owner, shall have the right, but not the obligation, to perform such maintenance and repair and shall have the same rights and remedies with respect thereto as are provided herein to Declarant.

5.8 *Taxes and Assessments.* If an Owner fails to pay taxes or assessments on its lot that become a lien on any portion of the subject property utilized for parking, service, or loading areas, then any other Owner may pay such taxes or assessments, together with any interest, penalties, and costs arising out of or related thereto, except while the validity thereof is being contested by judicial or administrative proceedings, and in such event the defaulting Owner obligated to pay such taxes or assessments shall promptly reimburse the other Owner for all such taxes or assessments, interest, penalties, and costs paid or incurred by such other Owner, and until such reimbursement has been made, the amount of the payment by such other Owner shall constitute a lien on and charge against the lot of the defaulting Owner, subject and subordinate, however, to any mortgage or deed of trust then outstanding and affecting said lot.

5.9 *Refuse Collection Areas.* All outdoor refuse collection areas shall be visually screened so as not to be visible from neighboring property or streets. No refuse collection area shall be permitted between a street and the front of a building.

5.10 *Repair of Buildings.* No building or structure upon any lot shall be permitted to fall into disrepair, and each such building and structure shall at all times be kept in good condition and repair and adequately painted or otherwise finished.

5.11 *Public Utilities.* Declarant reserves the sole right to grant consents for the construction and operation of public utilities, including, but not limited to, street railways, interurban or rapid transit, freight railways, poles or lines for electricity, telephone, or telegraph, above- or below-ground conduits, and gas pipes in and upon any and all streets now existing or hereafter established upon which any portion of the subject property may now or hereafter front or abut. Declarant reserves the exclusive right to grant consents and to petition the proper authorities for any and all street improvements, such as grading, seeding, tree planting, sidewalks, paving, and sewer and water installation, whether it be on the surface or subsurface, which in the opinion of Declarant are necessary on or to the subject property. Notwithstanding the provisions of Section 3.2, Declarant reserves the exclusive right to approve above-ground utility lines across the subject property or any portion thereof on a temporary basis for the purpose of construction, and such lines shall be permitted when required by a government agency. Notwithstanding the provisions of this Section, the construction and operation of public utilities in rights-of-way dedicated to the public must be approved by the appropriate governmental authority.

5.12 *Utility Lines and Antennas.* No sewer, drainage, or utility lines or wires or other devices for the communication or transmission of electric current, power, or signals, including telephone, television, microwave, or radio signals, shall be constructed, placed, or maintained anywhere in or upon any portion of the subject property other than within buildings or structures, unless the same shall be contained in conduits or cables constructed, placed, or maintained underground or concealed in or under buildings or other structures. No antenna for the transmission or reception of telephone, television, microwave, or radio signals shall be placed on any lot within the subject property unless (a) such antenna shall be so located that it cannot be seen from five (5) feet zero (0) inches above the ground or ground-floor level at a distance of two hundred (200) feet in any direction and (b) the consent of Declarant shall first be obtained. Nothing contained herein shall be deemed to forbid the erection or use of temporary power or telephone facilities incidental to the construction or repair of buildings on the subject property.

5.13 *Mechanical Equipment.* All mechanical equipment, utility meters, storage tanks, air-conditioning equipment, and similar items shall be screened with landscaping or attractive architectural features integrated into the structure itself.

5.14 *Mineral Exploration.* No portion of the subject property shall be used in any manner to explore for or to remove any steam, heat, oil or other hydrocarbons, gravel, earth, or any earth substances or other minerals of any kind, provided, however, that this shall not prevent the excavation of earth in connection with the grading or construction of improvements within the subject property. Water may be extracted to the extent permitted by the appropriate governmental agency.

5.15 *Other Operations and Uses.* Operations and uses that are neither specially prohibited nor specifically authorized by this Declaration may be permitted in a specific case if operational plans and specifications are submitted to and approved in writing by Declarant in accordance with the procedures set forth in Article III of this Declaration. Approval or disapproval of such operational plans and specifications shall be based upon the effect of such operations or uses on other property subject to this Declaration or upon the occupants thereof, but shall be in the sole discretion of Declarant.

Article VI
Modification and Repeal

6.1 *Procedure.* Except as otherwise provided in Section 6.2, this Declaration or any provision hereof, or any covenant, condition, or restriction contained herein, may be terminated, extended, modified, or otherwise amended, as to the whole of the subject property or any portion thereof, with the written consent of the Owners of eighty percent (80%) of the subject property, based upon the number of square feet owned as compared to the total number of square feet subject to these covenants, conditions, and restrictions (excluding dedicated streets); provided, however, that so long as Declarant owns at least twenty percent (20%) of the property subject to these covenants, conditions, and restrictions, or for a period of fifteen (15) years from the effective date hereof, whichever period is shorter, no such termination, extension, modification, or other amendment shall be effective without the written approval of Declarant, which approval shall not be unreasonably withheld. Notification of any termination, extension, modification, or amendment shall be provided to the Bothell Department of Community Development, and if the termination, extension, modification, or amendment constitutes a major change to the planned unit development approved for Koll Business Center–Bothell, the termination, extension, modification, or amendment shall not become effective until approved by the Bothell City Council after review and recommendations by the Bothell Planning Commission as provided for in Sections 17.26.230, BMC. No such termination, extension, modification, or other amendment shall be effective if it conflicts with a valid governmental enactment, ordinance, or regulation and until a proper instrument in writing has been executed, acknowledged, and recorded.

6.2 *Modification by Declarant.* For so long as Declarant owns any interest (excepting a leasehold interest) in the subject property, or any part thereof, or for a period of fifteen (15) years from the effective date hereof, whichever period is shorter, Declarant acting alone may modify or amend the provisions of Articles III, IV, and V; provided, however, that (i) any such modification or amendment must be within the spirit and overall intention of the development as set forth herein; (ii) prior to any such modification or amendment Declarant shall obtain the approval of any governmental agency to such modification or amendment where such approval is necessary; and (iii) any modification or amendment shall not provide for any type of improvements or use not presently permitted by this Declaration. No such modification or amendment shall be effective until the Owners have been given thirty (30) days prior written notice of the proposed change and a proper instrument in writing has been executed, acknowledged, and recorded.

6.3 *Governmental Regulation.* All valid governmental enactments, ordinances, and regulations are deemed to be a part of this Declaration, and to the extent that they conflict with any provision, covenant, condition, or restriction hereof, said conflicting governmental enactment, ordinance, and regulation shall control and the provision, covenant, condition, or restriction hereof in conflict therewith shall be deemed (i) amended to the extent necessary to bring it into conformity with said enactment, ordinance, or regulation while still preserving the intent and spirit of the provision, covenant, condition, or restriction; or (ii) stricken herefrom should no amendment conforming to the governmental enactment, ordinance, or regulation be capable of preserving the intent and spirit of said provision, covenant, condition, or restriction.

Article VII
Enforcement

7.1 *Abatement and Suit.* The Owner of each lot shall be primarily liable and the Occupant, if any, secondarily liable for the violation or breach of any covenant, condition, or restriction herein contained. Violation or breach of any covenant, condition, or restriction herein contained shall give to Declarant, following thirty (30) days written notice to the Owner or Occupant in question except in exigent circumstances, the right, privilege, and license to enter upon the lot where said violation or breach exists and to summarily abate and remove, or abate or remove, at the expense of the Owner or Occupant thereof, any improvement, structure, thing, or condition that may be or exist thereon contrary to the intent and meaning of the provisions hereof, or to prosecute a proceeding at law or in equity against the person or persons who have violated or are attempting to violate any of these covenants, conditions, or restrictions to enjoin or prevent them from doing so, to cause said violation to be remedied, or to recover damages for said violation. No such entry by Declarant or its agents shall be deemed a trespass, and neither Declarant nor its agents shall be subject to liability to the Owner or Occupant of said lot for such entry and any action taken to remedy or remove a violation. The cost of any abatement, remedy, or removal hereunder shall be a binding personal obligation on any Owner or Occupant in violation of any provision of this Declaration, as well as a lien (enforceable in the same manner as a mortgage) upon the lot in question. The lien provided for this section shall not be valid as against a bona fide purchaser or mortgagee for value of the lot in question unless a suit to enforce said lien shall have been filed in a court of record in King County, Washington, prior to the recordation of the deed or mortgage conveying or encumbering the lot in question to such purchaser or mortgagee, respectively.

7.2 *Right of Entry.* During reasonable hours and upon reasonable notice and subject to reasonable security requirements, Declarant, or its agents, shall have the right to enter upon and inspect any lot and the improvements thereon covered by this Declaration for the purpose of ascertaining whether or not the provisions of this Declaration have been or are being complied with, and neither Declarant nor its agents shall be deemed to have committed a trespass or other wrongful act by reason of such entry or inspection.

7.3 *Deemed to Constitute a Nuisance.* The result of every act or omission whereby any covenant, condition, or restriction herein contained is violated in whole or in part is hereby declared to be and to constitute a nuisance, and every remedy allowed by law or in equity against an Owner or Occupant either public or private shall be applicable against every such result and may be exercised by Declarant.

7.4 *Attorney's Fees.* In any legal or equitable proceeding for the enforcement of this Declaration or any provision hereof, whether it be an action for damages, declaratory relief, or injunctive relief, or any other action, the losing party or parties shall pay the attorney's fees of the prevailing party or parties, in such reasonable amount as shall be fixed by the court in such proceedings or in a separate action brought for that purpose. The prevailing party shall be entitled to said attorney's fees even though said proceeding is settled prior to judgment. All remedies provided herein or at law or in equity shall be cumulative and not exclusive.

7.5 *Failure to Enforce Is No Waiver.* The failure of Declarant to enforce any requirement, restriction, or standard herein contained shall in no event be deemed to be a waiver of the right to do so thereafter or in other cases nor of the right to enforce any other restriction.

Article VIII Assignment

Any and all of the rights, powers, and reservations of Declarant herein may be assigned to any person, partnership, corporation, or association that will assume the duties of Declarant pertaining to the particular rights, powers, and reservations assigned, and upon any such person, partnership, corporation, or association evidencing its consent in writing to accept such assignment and assume such duties, he or it shall, to the extent of such assignment, have the same rights and powers and be subject to the same obligations and duties as are given to and assumed by Declarant herein. If at any time Declarant ceases to exist and has not made such an assignment, a successor to Declarant may be appointed in the same manner as this Declaration may be modified or amended under Section 6.1. Any assignment or appointment made under this article shall be in reasonable form and shall be recorded.

Article IX Constructive Notice and Acceptance

Every person or entity who now or hereafter owns, occupies, or acquires any right, title, or interest in or to any portion of the subject property is and shall be conclusively deemed to have consented and agreed to every covenant, condition, and restriction contained herein, whether or not any reference to this Declaration is contained in the instrument by which such person acquired an interest in the subject property.

Article X Waiver

Neither Declarant nor its successor or assigns shall be liable to any Owner or Occupant of the subject property by reason of any mistake in judgment, negligence, nonfeasance, action or inaction or for the enforcement or failure to enforce any provision of this Declaration. Every Owner or Occupant of any said property by acquiring its interest therein agrees that it will not bring any action or suit against Declarant to recover any such damages or to seek equitable relief because of same.

Article XI
Runs with Land

All covenants, conditions, restrictions, and agreements herein contained are made for the direct, mutual, and reciprocal benefit of each and every lot of the subject property; shall create mutual equitable servitude upon each lot in favor of every other lot; shall create reciprocal rights and obligations between respective Owners and Occupants of all lots and privity of contract and estate between all grantees of said lots, their heirs, successors, and assigns; and shall, as to the Owner and Occupant of each lot, his heirs, successors, and assigns, operate as covenants running with the land, for the benefit of all other lots, except as provided otherwise herein.

Article XII
Rights of Mortgagees

No breach of any covenant, condition, or restriction herein contained or any enforcement thereof, shall defeat or render invalid the lien of any mortgage or deed of trust now or hereafter executed upon the subject property or a portion thereof, provided, however, that if any portion of said property is sold under a foreclosure of any mortgage or under the provisions of any deed of trust, any purchaser at such sale and its successors and assigns shall hold any and all property so purchased subject to all of the covenants, conditions, and restrictions contained in this Declaration.

Article XIII
Captions

The captions of articles and sections herein are used for convenience only and are not intended to be a part of this Declaration or in any way to define, limit, or describe the scope and intent of the particular article or section to which they refer.

Article XIV
Effect of Invalidation

If any provision of this Declaration is held to be invalid by any court, the invalidity of such provision shall not affect the validity of the remaining provisions hereof.

DECLARANT:
KOLL/INTEREAL SEATTLE
a California general partnership

By:
KOLL ASSOCIATES SEATTLE,
a California General Partnership, general partner of Koll/Intereal Seattle

By:
THE KOLL COMPANY
a California Corporation, general partner of Koll Associates Seattle

By:

____

Rodger E. Fagerholm
Vice President
Northwest Division President

STATE OF____________________ s.s

COUNTY OF____________________

THIS IS TO CERTIFY that on this ___ day of ______________, 19__, before me, the undersigned, a notary public in and for the state of Washington, duly commissioned and sworn, personally appeared ROGER E. FAGERHOLM to me known to be the Vice President of THE KOLL COMPANY, a California corporation, the corporation that executed the within and foregoing instrument as the general partner of Koll Associates Seattle, a California general partnership and general partner of Koll/Intereal Seattle, a California general partnership, and acknowledged the said instrument to be the free and voluntary act and deed of said corporation for the use and purposes therein mentioned, and on oath stated that he was authorized to execute said instrument.

WITNESS my hand and official seal the day and year in this certificate written.

____

Notary public in and for the state of Washington,
residing at ____________________
My Commission Expires ____________________

1714C

Exhibit A
Legal Description of Property

West Half of Northwest Quarter, Section 4; and East Half of Northeast Quarter, Section 5; all in Township 26 North, Range 5 East, W.M., in King County, Washington.

EXCEPT County Roads along Southerly and Westerly Boundaries, and EXCEPT the East 35 feet and the South 30 feet of the West Half of the Northwest Quarter of said Section 4, conveyed to the King County for road by deed recorded under Auditor's file No. 6085498, and EXCEPT that Portion condemned under King County Superior Court Case No. 672709 for Primary State Highway No. 1.

Index